The Viennese Classical Style: Mozart and Haydn (1770-1800)	Nineteenth-Century Music I: Conservative Romantics	Nineteenth-Century Music II: Program, Nationalist, and Hyper-Romantic Composers
(Chapter 4)	(Chapter 5)	(Chapter 6)

Symphony-Sonata Cycle
Mozart: *A Little Night Music* (1787)
Mozart: Symphony No. 40 in G Minor (1788)
Haydn: String Quartet in E-Flat, Op. 33, No. 2 ("The Joke"; 1781)
Haydn: Symphony No. 94 in G Major ("The Surprise"; 1791)

Concerto for Soloist and Orchestra
Mozart: Piano Concerto No. 21 in C Major (1785)

Opera
Gluck: *Orpheus and Euridice* (1762)
Mozart: *Don Giovanni* (1787)
Mozart: *The Magic Flute* (1791)

Beethoven:
"Moonlight" Sonata (1801)
"Eroica" Symphony (1803)
Fifth Symphony (1808)
String Quartet No. 16 in F (1826)

Schubert:
"Morning Greeting" (1823)
"The Ghostly Double" (1828)

Chopin:
Nocturne No. 2 in E-Flat (1833)
Mazurka No. 23 in D (1838)

Mendelssohn:
Scherzo from *A Midsummer Night's Dream* (1843)

Schumann:
Carnaval (1834)

Brahms:
Fourth Symphony (1885)

Berlioz:
"Fantastic" Symphony (1830)

Liszt:
Hungarian Rhapsody No. 6 (ca. 1845-1853)

Wagner:
Prelude to *Tristan and Isolde* (1859)

Tchaikovsky:
Overture-Fantasy, *Romeo and Juliet* (1869-1880)

Mussorgsky:
Pictures at an Exhibition (1874)

Richard Strauss:
Don Juan (1889)

Mahler:
Fifth Symphony (1902)

Music

MUSIC
A LISTENER'S INTRODUCTION

KENNETH LEVY

Princeton University

1817

HARPER & ROW, PUBLISHERS, New York

Cambridge, Philadelphia, San Francisco, London, Mexico City, São Paulo, Sydney

Sponsoring Editor: Phillip Leininger
Development Editor: Robert Ginsberg
Project Editor: Rhonda Roth
Designer: Frances Torbert Tilley
Production Manager: Willie Lane
Compositor: Music-Book Associates, Inc.
Printer and Binder: R. R. Donnelley & Sons Company
Art Studio: J & R Art Services, Inc.
Picture Research: Ann Novotny and Naomi Rush
      of Research Reports & Pictures, Inc., New York
Cover Photograph: Kitharode. A detail from a red-figured Attic vase
      (Greek, 5th-century B.C.), The Metropolitan Museum of Art,
      Fletcher Fund, 1956.
Cover Design: Diane Saxe

Music: A Listener's Introduction

Copyright © 1983 by Kenneth Levy

Library of Congress Cataloging in Publication Data

Levy, Kenneth, 1927-
   Music: a listener's introduction

   Bibliography: p.
   Includes index.
   1. Music—History and criticism. I. Title.
ML160.L592   1983   780'.9   82-9302
ISBN 0-06-043978-5   AACR2

Acknowledgments

We gratefully acknowledge the right to reprint musical excerpts held in copyright by other sources:

P. 306: Igor Stravinsky: *The Rite of Spring.* Copyright © 1921 by Edition Russe de Musique. Copyright assigned 1947 to Boosey & Hawkes, Inc. Reprinted by permission.

P. 318: Alban Berg: "Children's Song" from *Wozzeck.* Copyright © 1931 by Universal Edition A. G., Wien. Copyright renewed. Used by permission of European American Music Distributors Corporation, sole U.S. agent for Universal Edition.

PP. 316-319: Alban Berg: Act 3, Scene 4, and Act 3, Scene 5 from *Wozzeck.* Libretto copyright © 1923 by Universal Edition A. G., Wien. Copyright renewed. Used by permission of European American Music Distributors Corporation, sole U.S. agent for Universal Edition.

P. 323: Charles Ives: *The Unanswered Question.* Trumpet part, measures 16-17. Copyright © 1953 by Southern Music Publishing Co., Inc. Copyright renewed by Peer International Corporation. International copyright secured. All rights reserved including the right of public performance for profit. Used by permission.

P. 334: Igor Stravinsky: *The Soldier's Tale.* "Soldier's March," No. 1, measures 1-5. Copyright © 1918 by J&W Chester Ltd., London. Used by kind permission of J&W Chester/Edition Wilhelm Hansen London Limited.

P. 335: Quotation from backliner notes to "Stravinsky Conducts Favorite Short Works," Columbia Masterworks ML 6048, copyright © 1964 by CBS Inc.

P. 341: Béla Bartók: *Music for String Instruments, Percussion and Celesta.* Copyright © 1937 by Universal Edition; renewed 1964. Copyright and renewal assigned to Boosey & Hawkes, Inc., for USA. Reprinted by permission.

P. 348: Aaron Copland: *Rodeo.* Copyright © 1946 by Aaron Copland, renewed 1973. Reprinted by permission of Aaron Copland, copyright owner, and Boosey & Hawkes, Inc., sole licensees.

P. 348: *If He'd Be a Buckaroo,* collected, adapted, and arranged by John A. Lomax and Alan Lomax. TRO - Copyright © 1941 and renewed 1969 Ludlow Music, Inc., New York, NY. Used by permission.

P. 356: Arnold Schoenberg: *Suite für Klavier, Op. 25.* Copyright © 1925 by Universal Edition. Copyright renewed 1952 by Gertrude Schoenberg. Used by permission of Belmont Music Publishers, Los Angeles, California 90049.

P. 375: Pierre Boulez: *Structures I.* Property of Universal Edition Ltd., London, for all countries of the British Commonwealth, Eire and the USA. Eigentum der Universal Edition A. G., Wien für alle Laender mit Ausnahme der oben erwaehnten.

Illustration credits appear on p. 511.

Contents

In this contents, works to be found in the record program are identified by a Δ symbol.

Chapter 5 **NINETEENTH-CENTURY MUSIC I:
CONSERVATIVE ROMANTICS   190**

Preface

This book is a concise introduction to Western music for readers with little or no musical background. It is the premise of the book that musical works are best introduced to beginning students in the context of the period in which they were created. The level of culture, the historical situation, the sophistication of the audience, and the intellectual atmosphere subtly but inevitably shape the personality of the composer and the music he or she creates. While the past is always irretrievably receding, works of art remain. In changed circumstances, the beginning student's first encounter with the music of the past—the Baroque, for example, or even the Romantic era—can be a bewildering experience. But most students will have some familiarity with nonmusical aspects of earlier periods. Those aspects can be used to introduce and frame the music of the period, and they can be as valuable in helping the student understand and appreciate the music as are the appropriate analyses of technical elements and musical style. In somewhat the same way, the biography of a composer sheds light on the development of an entire body of work as well as on the individual works discussed and analyzed in the text. For these reasons, the cultural matrix out of which the music arose plays an integral part in the musical and stylistic analyses in this text.

Organization of the Book

Music: A Listener's Introduction has ten chapters devoted to musical, cultural, and historical information, three appendixes devoted to technical matters, and a bibliography offering suggestions for further study to readers whose interest has been awakened. To help evoke the spirit of different eras, numerous illustrations have been selected to depict the circumstances in which music making took place in the past. Examples of fine art, as well as interesting contemporary illustrations, have been chosen for their insights into the life of different periods. (Particular care has been taken to show a variety of older musical instruments.) To help beginners orient themselves to each period, each chapter opens with a parallel chronology of major developments in music, the arts, politics, science, and the world of ideas. Several maps are included to show the growth and shift of European musical centers over the years. The chronologies and maps can also be used to review the material of the chapter. Although the book has been aimed at nonmajors, the musico-historical coverage should be thorough enough to provide an overview for undergraduate music education majors and vocal and instrumental majors in conservatories.

Each of the 10 historical chapters is essentially self-contained with regard to subject matter and self-explanatory in its use of musical terms. As a result, readers can begin with virtually any historical chapter without being at a substantial disadvantage for not having covered the previous ones. Many readers will begin with the Baroque (Chapter 3); others will go first to the Romantic period (Chapter 5) or to one of the three discussions devoted to the twentieth century (Chapters 8 through 10). Within each chapter the attempt has been made to introduce necessary technical matters where they naturally come up in the course of the historical sequence. Nevertheless, for those who want a more systematic coverage of musical elements there are ampler explanations in Appendixes A, B, and C.

I have assumed that many readers will be relatively uninformed about musical fundamentals, and I have attempted to make the material accessible to those unfamiliar with musical notation. At the same time, I have tried not to be distrustful of the reader's intelligence. The basic concepts for understanding music in a musician's own terms ought to find a place in a book like this one, and I have made an effort to put them in.

Listening Diagrams

Throughout the book, the emphasis is on the experience of actually hearing music, not on reading scores. The untrained listener may learn to read a score after a fashion, but in the beginner's anxious efforts to keep up—to match the symbols to the sounds while the music goes rushing by—the real sense of the music too often gets lost. The time and effort spent on such "score following" seem to me better spent in listening to the music itself, concentrating on it as the composer expected—with the listening ear.

To help the novice listener along, the book makes use of "listening diagrams." The aim of the diagrams is to supply a rough synopsis of the heard musical events. The diagrams give about the same sense of a music work as can the floor plan of a building. Obviously, we experience little of the effect of Chartres Cathedral by viewing its architectural drawings. Nor do we experience the sophistication and excitement of a Bach fugue by examining the bits of notation, scrawl, and words that make up its listening diagram (see Ex. 3.13). Nevertheless, the drawing lets us see what decisions the architect has made, and the listening diagram gives a corresponding sense of the composer's main choices. The diagram amounts to a summary of the heard sounds, representing what a moderately perceptive listener might take in after three or four attentive hearings. The diagram should not be thought of as "authoritative" or "correct," but only as a provisional guide that can be clarified and improved as the musical sense reveals itself through repeated hearings.

Record Program

In carrying out its overview of Western musical history, the text focuses on a relatively small number of complete works that illustrate the idiom of a composer, the style of an era, or the operation of a compositional technique. Most of the works are acknowledged masterpieces. For the convenience of teachers and students, nearly all the works discussed are contained in the set of six records that is available with the text. This record set comprises an anthology of major works from all ages, a chronologically organized listener's history of music, representing the span of Western styles from plainchant through recent developments in jazz and electronic music. An effort has been made to ensure stylistic accuracy in the recordings, and all the artists are well-known musicians, many of them leading American performers. All the works in the record program are identified by a marginal notation (preceded by a Δ symbol) in the text that gives the composer and title of the work as well as the side and band numbers on the record.

Fundamentals of Music: Notation and Other Elements

Appendix A is an introduction to the basics of musical notation, designed to supply enough information for understanding the bits of notation that appear in the listening diagrams. This introduction provides a conceptual background for the discussions of pitch and rhythm in Chapter 1. After Appendix A is covered, the casual reader can take up the historical chapters without further preliminary. The Glossary (Appendix C) will supply what technical help is necessary. Readers who already have some knowledge of musical notation and fundamentals of theory may skip the discussions of notation and other technical matters and go directly to the historical chapters.

Appendix B, "Musical Fundamentals," expands on the technical coverage found in the main historical chapters. The seven mini-discussions in Appendixes B.1 through B.7 serve to introduce seven principal musical elements: 1) materials of melody, 2) rhythm, 3) texture, 4) harmony, 5) tonality and key relationships, 6) tone color and musical instruments, and 7) tone color and the physics of sound. There are no separate discussions of style, form, or genre because those topics are more appropriately treated where they come up in historical context. Appendix B provides a fund of technical knowledge, arranged in a progressive teaching order and set out in language that I have tried to keep plain and free of jargon. My hope is that the use of Appendix B will make it possible for nonmusicians to converse with musicians on matters of musical substance at a relatively sophisticated level. Appendix B can be ignored without sacrificing the historical-cultural continuity. Or it can be drawn in, either in whole or in part, to supplement the history.

Appendix C is a Glossary in which the technical information that is treated topically earlier is alphabetically ordered and concisely defined, covering among other things the items that are in italics or boldface in the main text.

Course Organization and *Instructor's Manual*

The simplest combination of the history and appendix material would be to use just Appendix A ("Musical Notation") and Appendix B.6 ("Tone Color and Musical Instruments") in conjunction with selected historical chapters. A more comprehensive plan would be to cover all of Appendix B.1 through B.6, which can be done either in an unbroken sequence before beginning the history, or intermixed with the historical readings. The following plan has the advantage of paralleling the early historical sequence with appropriate theoretical topics, reaching Appendix B.5 ("Tonality and Key Relationships") concurrently with Chapter 3.F (the Vivaldi concerto grosso).

Historical Chapters		Appendix B	
Ch. 1.A-B:	Ancient Music and Plainchant	B.1:	Pitch, Scale, and Mode
Ch. 1.C-E:	Medieval Polyphony	B.2:	Rhythm
Ch. 2.B-C:	Dufay, Josquin Des Prez	B.3:	Texture
Ch. 3.B-C:	Monteverdi, Purcell	B.4:	Harmony
Ch. 3.E-F:	Corelli, Vivaldi	B.5:	Tonality and Key Relationships
Ch. 4.C:	The Symphony	B.6:	Tone Color and Musical Instruments

Appendix B.7 ("Tone Color and the Physics of Sound") includes material that may be of interest to readers with a background in science and math but can be omitted by most others. For instructors with a limited number of course hours, and for those who prefer to begin the history with the Baroque or some later chapter, there is a detailed guide to course planning in the 32-page *Instructor's Manual*. This sets out a number of sample plans, accommodating the material to specific allotments of 30 and 45 hours.

Study Guide

The *Study Guide* I have prepared is designed to help students review the material of the text in a series of exercises that closely parallel the readings and listening activities in each chapter. The *Study Guide* contains fill-in questions, matching exercises, and a wide variety of multiple-choice questions. Particular attention has been given to helping students grasp the technical material presented in Appendixes A and B. The pages have been perforated so that they can be used as informal tests. Students who do the exercises and then have them corrected by the instructor will have a valuable study tool for reviewing the material of the course.

Acknowledgments

During the course of production this book has garnered some considerable obligations to some outstanding specialists: to Ann Novotny, whose expertise helped realize the illustration program; to Laura Harth, who with cordial efficiency brought home the record program. Above all, the book and its author have enjoyed the professionalism of a superb editorial group at Harper & Row, where there are four debts of special magnitude to acknowledge: to Frances Torbert Tilley, whose stylish eye lent flair to the visual presentation; to Rhonda Roth, whose skill and resourcefulness overcame obstacles of every description; to Robert Ginsberg, who with rare taste and judgment saw to it that all intellectual and artistic decisions were soundly made; and to Phillip Leininger, whose genial vision and keen sense of language, history, and the arts was the motivating force that gave shape to the whole.

The following reviewers were kind enough to read the manuscript at various stages. Their comments and suggestions were gratefully received: Richard Brooks, Nassau Community College; David Crawford, The University of Michigan School of Music; Robert Falck, University of Toronto; Leila Falk, Reed College; Richard Flusser, Queensborough Community College; Almonte Howell, University of Georgia; Herbert Livingston, The Ohio State University; Ernest May, University of Massachusetts; Anthony Newcomb, University of California, Berkeley; Joyce Newman, The University of Utah; Carl Rath, The University of Oklahoma at Norman; William H. Reynolds, University of California, Riverside; Elaine Sisman, Columbia University; Robert Snow, The University of Texas at Austin; Arthur B. Wenk, Université Laval, Québec; E. Chappell White, Kansas State University; Michael Williams, University of Houston.

Kenneth Levy

Ancient and Medieval Music

The Greek god Hermes in a sculpture by Praxiteles (fourth century B.C.). Later ages would admire the serene beauty of such "classic" models.

The Parthenon at Athens (fifth century B.C.), the most famous temple of Greek antiquity, noted for its perfection of form (shown here in a reconstruction).

The Ancient Mediterranean.

Apollo, the Greek god of music, holding a seven-stringed lyre (ca. 470 B.C.).

An Etruscan player of the double-piped aulos (Italy, fifth century B.C.).

The Ancient World

ANCIENT GREECE

ARTS AND IDEAS	KEY EVENTS
Archaic period (8th-6th century B.C.) Homer, *Iliad* and *Odyssey;* Aesop, *Fables;* Pythagoras, mathematical works *"Classical"-"Hellenic" period (ca. 480-323 B.C.)* Pindar, Odes; Parthenon at Athens; dramas of Aeschylus, Sophocles, Euripides; philosophy of Socrates, Plato, Aristotle; sculpture of Myron, Phidias, Praxiteles *"Hellenistic" period (323 B.C.-2nd century A.D.)* Sculpture: "Dying Gaul"; Winged Victory of Samothrace; Venus de Milo; Laocoön Merger with Roman culture	Trojan War (ca. 1200 B.C.) Greek city-states (from 8th century B.C.) Periclean Athens (5th century B.C.) Peloponnesian War (Sparta defeats Athens) (431-404 B.C.) Death of Alexander the Great (323 B.C.) Romans annex Macedonia, sack Corinth (146 B.C.)

ANCIENT ROME

ARTS AND IDEAS	KEY EVENTS
Etruscan tomb painting and sculpture (ca. 8th-4th century B.C.) Historians, poets: Livy, Vergil, Horace (ca. 25 B.C.) Roman Colosseum, Arch of Titus, and Pantheon (A.D. 70-125) Ptolemy, *Astronomy, Geography,* writings on music (ca. A.D. 150)	Etruscan domination of Italy (ca. 8th-4th century B.C.) "Foundation of Rome" (753 B.C.) Roman Republic (509-27 B.C.) Julius Caesar takes power (60 B.C.); killed (44 B.C.) Roman Empire begun by Augustus (27 B.C.) Julio-Claudian Emperors (1st century A.D.): Augustus, Tiberius, Caligula, Claudius, Nero Destruction of Pompei and Herculaneum (A.D. 79) Emperors Hadrian and Marcus Aurelius (2nd century A.D.)

ANCIENT ISRAEL

ARTS AND IDEAS	KEY EVENTS
Bible: Old Testament (ca. 1100-130 B.C.) "Psalms of David" (7th-2nd century B.C.)	Moses (fl. ca. 1225-1200 B.C.) Canaanite period (ca. 1200-ca. 972 B.C.) King David (ca. 1012-ca. 972 B.C.) King Solomon (ca. 972-ca. 935 B.C.) Kingdoms of Israel and Judah (ca. 935-725 B.C.) Romans annex Palestine (63 B.C.) Romans destroy Jerusalem (A.D. 70)

EARLY CHRISTIAN PERIOD (1st-5th century A.D.)

ARTS AND IDEAS	KEY EVENTS
Bible: New Testament (1st century A.D.) 4th-century theologians: Saints Ambrose, Augustine, Jerome Early plainchants and hymns (4th-5th century) Sta. Maria Maggiore built at Rome (5th century)	Birth of Jesus (ca. 4 B.C.) Christianity becomes Roman state religion (ca. A.D. 325) Constantinople made capital of Eastern Roman Empire (330) Alaric the Goth sacks Rome (410) Attila the Hun's invasion (452) Last Western Roman Emperor deposed (476); barbarian domination

A. ANCIENT GREECE, ROME, THE BIBLE

Music in Greece

The Ancient Greeks had music in every aspect of their public and private lives, yet we know next to nothing of the actual sounds of music they enjoyed. Greek myth launched a cult of Orpheus, the fabled musician of antiquity. Plato and Aristotle gave music a prominent place in molding the character of youths in their ideal city-states. Musicians are shown on vase paintings, frescoes, and mosaics, singing or playing instruments like the harplike *kithara* and oboelike *aulos* (a wind instrument that usually had two pipes), which were the favorites of the time. We know that the tragedies of Aeschylus, Sophocles, and Euripides were declaimed in a musical fashion by the actors and choruses and that they were more like operas than spoken plays. But we have little evidence of the music and dance that helped make those dramas such a powerful medium for the ancients. What we know the most about in Greek music are its **scales**—the raw pitches out of which the melodies and harmonies were formed. Instead of three Western scales—major, minor, and chromatic—that are familiar to us, the Greeks had about two dozen different scales. Many of these had intervals between their pitches that were smaller than our half-steps (such intervals are called **microtones**). On the other hand, there were some intervals larger than our whole steps. Each of these different Greek scales produced a different kind of musical sound, a particular musical character or **mode**. We can define a mode as music with a distinctive character or mood. The Greeks gave names to their modes, Ionian, Phrygian, Dorian, Lydian, etc., which suggests that

Colorplate 1

A circle of dancing Greek maidens includes players of the double-piped aulos and the kithara, the latter a string instrument related to the lyre.

they identified the characters of their musical modes with particular regions of their cultural world. These names are similar to the names given to the capitals on the tops of columns in Greek buildings that are identified as Dorian, Ionian, or Corinthian. We know the pitches that made up the scales of the Greek modes, but these were only the raw materials of the actual melodies, and they scarcely hint at the ways in which the pitches were joined together in the living fabric of the music.

In all likelihood ancient Greek music would have sounded exotic to our ears, perhaps in somewhat the way that present-day Middle Eastern music sounds exotic. The music was essentially melodic, that is, melody alone, without accompanying harmony. At times there was a simple accompaniment; however, it was not like our familiar musical support of chords or independent melodic strands. Plato speaks rather of **heterophony**, meaning that a melody was performed simultaneously by two or more musicians, each of them producing a slightly different personalized version of the same music. The differences reflected the typical qualities of the instruments, voices, and personalities of the individual performers. Heterophony is still a common feature of Middle Eastern music today: A soloist sings the principal song while other singers or instrumental players entwine and cluster their own versions around it.

The Greeks developed rudimentary writing systems for notating their musical pitches and rhythms, using mainly the letters of their

A Greek aulos player

alphabet. But they rarely troubled to write down their music, preferring instead to pass it along from generation to generation by living example. A good deal of the substance of Greek music was left to improvisation anyway. What they wrote down was often put on sheets of flimsy papyrus that have not withstood the abuse of time. Some bits of music were chiseled into durable stone, and those are preserved as the Greeks left them. The earliest such notated inscriptions are two musical hymns found on a wall of the Athenian treasury at Delphi, near the shrine of the famous oracle. They date from the second century B.C., long after the golden age of ancient Greek culture in the fifth century B.C.

Although we lack substantial relics of actual Greek music, there are many stories that tell how much music meant to the Greeks. The essayist Plutarch (first century A.D.) speaks of some Athenian soldiers who were imprisoned in Sicily during the Peloponnesian War (in 413 B.C.). They were set free because they sang some music from the latest plays of Euripides for their Italian captors. The lucky ones returned home to thank Euripides personally. Plato (fifth century B.C.) wanted to ban certain musical modes from his Republic as being too "soft and convivial," an encouragement to laxity in morals. He seems to have viewed these modes as unfriendly critics view pop and rock music today. Many Greeks accepted the idea of the early mathematician Pythagoras (sixth century B.C.) that the motions of the planets produced a celestial "music of the spheres," unhearable by earthlings, which resulted from the orbiting velocities of the heavenly bodies. Pythagoras and his disciples were not musically naive. They discovered, among other things, the number relationships between the lengths of vibrating strings and the basic musical intervals, such as 2:1 for the octave and 3:2 for the fifth. Pythagorean ideas about the music of the spheres were discussed throughout the Middle Ages and the Renaissance, and they still fascinated the great German astronomer Johann Kepler in the seventeenth century.

Music of the Romans

The early Romans regarded music rather less tolerantly than their Greek neighbors. During the Roman Republic (through the first century B.C.), music's qualities of luxury and ostentation were thought to lower moral standards. An early law (mid-fifth century B.C.) prohibited the use of more than ten pipers at a Roman funeral. Cato the Censor, who governed Rome during the second century B.C., ridiculed a political opponent who was known also to be a singer. That sober attitude of the Romans changed during the Empire (after 31 B.C.). Rome's most notorious musician was the Emperor Nero

Etruscan woman with a seven-stringed lyre (ca. 460 B.C.). The invention of the lyre was credited to the god Hermes, who supposedly made it from a tortoise shell.

A Roman four-horse racing chariot, victorious in the arena, is welcomed by its sponsor and a trumpet (lituus) *player.*

(first century A.D.), who preferred showing off as a concert artist to being a thoroughly good ruler. People were obliged to attend his performances. Once they were inside the theater, locks were turned to prevent their leaving. Nero was not a "fiddler," as popular saying has it, but a singer and kithara player, something like a present-day vocalist with guitar. But he may have made music "while Rome burned." The ancient historian Suetonius (not always an impartial witness) tells us that in order to clear part of downtown Rome for a new construction plan, Nero had it set afire. Then, dressed in full stage costume, he sang a long poem about the sack of Troy and exulted in "the beauty of the flames." When Nero was finally compelled to commit suicide in A.D. 69, he complained, "What an artist the world is losing!"

The cultivated Romans created much of their music by imitating Greek styles, but there were other musical infiltrations from Egypt and the Near East as well as some residue from the Etruscans, who Colorplates 2 and 3 fashioned the highest civilization on the Italian peninsula before the rise of Rome. Music had a prominent place in the ceremonies of Roman religion and statecraft. The historian Livy tells us that when the official pipers (the *collegium tibicinum*) went on strike in 311 B.C., the work of government was held up. For the Romans who were constantly at war in winning and defending their Empire, mu-

The Colosseum at Rome (ca. 80 A.D.), the most imposing of preserved ancient Roman buildings, held over 50,000 spectators. It was the scene of gladiatorial combats.

sic filled an indispensable battlefield function. Certain well-known signals of attack, encouragement, and retreat were sounded on powerful wind instruments whose tones penetrated the noise of the action. There were also signals played on less strident winds to mark the posting of new watches of sentries in camp. At times, the wily Roman generals kept their musicians in an empty camp, sounding the usual calls so as to deceive the enemy while the soldiers were being positioned elsewhere.

Music had many roles among the Classical cultures: diverting the spirit, swaying the emotions, forming the character—perhaps in the way that people today feel that patriotic songs and hymns are good influences on social behavior. The ancients knew that music soothed the troubled spirit, and they even thought it could heal the infirm body. A Greek author suggests that the bone-and-muscle miseries of sciatica could be relieved by playing a wind instrument over the afflicted part. Impressed by the majesty of Greco-Roman architecture and by the expressive force of ancient drama, people in later ages of Western civilization were also struck by the stories of ancient music's fabulous effects. In particular, European musicians of the Renaissance strove to achieve similar effects. Although they failed, one fruitful Italian experiment of the late 1500s was an attempt to imitate

A Roman shepherd plays his pi[pe] in this illustration of a poem [by] Vergil.

the musical dramas of the ancient Greeks. This resulted in the first operas around 1600. Different as the operas of Mozart (see Chapter 4) and the music dramas of Wagner (see Chapter 7) are from the sung tragedies of Aeschylus and Euripides, they both descended from that ancient tradition.

Music in the Bible

The Bible is full of song. It is a storehouse of hymn poetry and information about music for worship and in the daily life of the ancient Jews during many centuries of their early history. Among the oldest contents of the Bible are religious lyrics from the Hebrew tribal period (ca. 2000-1200 B.C.), such as the song of Miriam the Prophetess, which was taken up by the exultant throng camped on the shore of the Red Sea:

Sing ye to the Lord
   for he hath triumphed gloriously

The horse and his rider
   hath he thrown into the sea.
          (Exodus 15:21)

Such songs in Biblical times were accompanied by dancing and percussion instruments. This particular lyric was used by Handel in 1738 for the resounding final chorus of the oratorio *Israel in Egypt,* and it is still heard today in all the Christian liturgies. The Bible also contains dirges, such as King David's lament over Jonathan and Saul, with the familiar refrain of

How are the mighty fallen!
      (II Samuel 1:19)

A harpist of Biblical times (ca. 1900 B.C.), painted in a tomb along the Nile.

Roman soldiers removing a seven-branch candlestick and Jewish ceremonial trumpets from the Temple at Jerusalem after sacking the city in 70 A.D.; from the Arch of Titus at Rome.

The chief collection of Biblical lyrics is the Book of Psalms or Psalter, dating from the Canaanite period (ca. 1200-973 B.C.) and later. Its 150 psalms—hymns of praise, petition, and thanksgiving—are the common hymnal of Judaism and Christianity. There are more than 2,500 verse-lines in the Psalter, and among them are many references to music, including the mysterious word *selah,* which may have served as a cue for instrumental interludes. The Psalter's musical imagery is richest in the concluding 150th Psalm, whose six verses contain a recital of ways to praise the Lord in music and dance:

Praise ye the Lord. Praise God in his sanctuary:
Praise him in the firmament of his power.

Praise him for his mighty acts:
Praise him according to his excellent greatness.

Praise him with the sound of the trumpet:
Praise him with the psaltery and harp.

Praise him with the timbrel and dance:
Praise him with stringed instruments and organs.

Praise him upon the loud cymbals:
Praise him upon the high sounding cymbals.

Let every thing that hath breath praise the Lord.
Praise ye the Lord.

Translations of the Psalter, such as this seventeenth-century version from the reign of King James I of England, can scarcely approximate the meanings of the original text since there are no pictures or sculptures of early Palestinian instruments to tell us what they looked like. Among the popular instruments in Biblical times were the *kinnōr,* a kind of harp, perhaps related to the Greek kithara; the *'ugab* or pipe, similar to a vertical flute or recorder; and the *nebel,* a harplike instrument, probably with ten strings. All are mentioned in Psalm 150. The *hālil* was a wind instrument, perhaps like the double-pipe Greek aulos. The ancient *shofar,* a ram's or goat's horn, is a Biblical instrument that is still heard today.

During the era of the Judaic monarchs at Jerusalem, instruments were commonly used in the music of King Solomon's temple (tenth century B.C.), and as in ancient Greece, it is likely that some sort of heterophony or polyphony entered into the accompaniment of the melodies. Later on, instruments were banned in the worship of the synagogues, and the church music became exclusively vocal. When Jesus went to worship at the Temple of Herod, the music he heard was probably just melody alone, without instrumental accompaniment—**monophonic** vocal music. The Judaic exclusion of instruments and accompaniments carried over into the music for worship in the early Christian churches.

*The Roman Emperor
Constantine the Great,
who, ca. 330 A.D.,
established Christianity
as the official religion
of the Empire.
This colossal head
is 8½ feet tall.*

*Christ the Almighty, dome-mosaic
of a Byzantine church
from Sicily (twelfth century).*

*Player of a five-stringed fiddle
or vielle (Spain, twelfth century).*

Medieval centers.

*Piper and juggler
(southern France, ca. 1000).*

The Medieval World (6th-15th century)

MUSIC	ARTS AND IDEAS	KEY EVENTS

EARLY MIDDLE AGES (6th-8th century)

MUSIC	ARTS AND IDEAS	KEY EVENTS
Gregorian chants: Proper of the Mass (6th-9th century)	Churches and mosaics at Ravenna (5th-6th century)	St. Benedict founds monastic order (529) Pope Gregory the Great (590-604) Muslims invade Spain (711) Charles Martel halts Muslims at Poitiers (732)

CAROLINGIAN, OTTONIAN, AND ROMANESQUE ERAS (late 8th-12th century)

MUSIC	ARTS AND IDEAS	KEY EVENTS
Ordinary of the Mass (9th-12th century) Frankish sequences (9th-12th century) Church polyphony at Fleury, Winchester, Limoges, Compostela (11th-12th century) Secular monody: Troubadours and trouvères (11th-13th century)	"Carolingian Renaissance" (late 8th-9th century) "Ottonian art" (10th-early 11th century) *Chanson de Roland* (ca. 1000) "Romanesque" cathedrals at Speyer, Toulouse, Hildesheim, Vezelay (ca. 1030-1150)	Charlemagne crowned "Roman Emperor" (800) Cluniac monastic order founded (910) "Age of Feudalism" (10th-14th century) First Crusade takes Jerusalem (1099)

GOTHIC ERA (13th-early 15th century)

MUSIC	ARTS AND IDEAS	KEY EVENTS
Parisian polyphony: "Notre Dame" organa and motets (12th-13th century); Leonin (ca. 1175); Perotin (ca. 1200) Dies irae; "Sumer is icumen in"; English dances (13th century) French "ars nova" (14th century): Guillaume de Machaut	"Gothic" cathedrals at Chartres, Laon, Paris, Rheims, Salisbury, Milan (mid 12th-15th century) St. Francis of Assisi and St. Thomas Aquinas (13th century) Chaucer, *Canterbury Tales* (ca. 1390)	King John signs Magna Charta (1215) "St. Louis" (Louis IX) reigns in France (1226-1270) Franciscan and Dominican monastic orders founded (13th century)

"PROTO-RENAISSANCE" IN ITALY (14th century)

MUSIC	ARTS AND IDEAS	KEY EVENTS
Italian "ars nova" (14th century): Francesco Landini	Florentine painters and authors: Giotto, Dante, Petrarch, Boccaccio	"Babylonian Captivity": Papacy at Avignon (1309-1378)

B. MEDIEVAL PLAINCHANT

A thousand years of music are our heritage from the Middle Ages —the "medieval" period that extends from the fall of the ancient Roman Empire in Western Europe during the late fifth century A.D. to the flowering of the Italian Renaissance during the fifteenth century. Almost all that has been preserved is music for the Catholic Church. Cathedrals and churches dominated the medieval towns and countryside. Within those edifices there was music throughout the day and often throughout the night, intensifying the quality of religious experience for the pious worshipper and exalting the church's power to bring salvation. The church embraced not only the religious life of the time but also the intellectual and cultural life with a comprehensiveness that is hard to imagine today. It was the focus of communal and artistic activity for a civilization that had abandoned the organized popular diversions of Greco-Roman antiquity. There were no gladiatorial games, no public concerts, no theatrical shows. Such ornaments of pagan society were in disfavor during the medieval "Age of Faith," and it was chiefly the church that provided the stage, the arena, or the concert hall. Most professional musicians made their livelihood by supplying the **sacred music**, an essential factor in Christian worship. Medieval paintings show the nobility enjoying musical diversions in their castles and estates. At popular festivals the streets and fields surely rang with dance tunes and riotous singing of burghers and peasants. But the clerics who mastered the skills of musical notation were concerned mainly with promoting the church's music, and during earlier medieval times they rarely troubled to write down the nonreligious **secular music** that was around. Most nonreligious medieval music has vanished.

Until about the year 800, church music held to an early Christian tradition of being a purely sung, or vocal, music, without instruments and having a style that consisted of melody alone without accompaniment. The monophonic vocal music of the medieval church is called **plainchant**. For centuries, every region of Europe had its own repertory of plainchants. The local collections of church melodies in Rome, Milan, South Italy, Gaul, and Spain numbered in the thousands. Then the Frankish emperor Charlemagne (d. 814) set out to unify Europe musically as well as politically, and he imposed a single repertory of plainchants throughout his realm. The music that was chosen was basically Roman in origin and associated by legend with St. Gregory the Great, the Pope from 590 to 604. It came to be called **Gregorian chant**, yet the name is misleading because Gregory himself was not a musician but a theologian and pastoral administrator. Furthermore, many of the chants were composed well after Gregory's time, during the seventh through ninth centuries, and in Charlemagne's Frankish homeland north of the Alps. The association with Pope

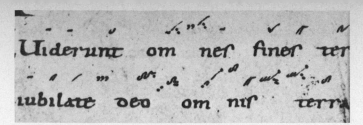

Early German neumes. Beginning of the Christmas Gradual "Viderunt omnes" (see also Ex. 1.2a).

Gregory nevertheless stuck, and, since the ninth century, the plainchants of the Catholic Church have been known as Gregorian chants.

The flourishing of the arts and ideas under Charlemagne, called the Carolingian Renaissance, brought other novelties to church music. Since early Christian times, music for the liturgy had passed from generation to generation through oral example, by having one singer teach another by singing. In the seventh century Saint Isidore of Seville lamented that the sounds of music vanished and there was no way of writing them down. But it was not until Charlemagne began promoting a uniform European plainchant that it was felt that the singers' fragile memories were not adequately conserving the sacred melodies and something was done to fix the plainchants in writing. An elementary musical notation was devised, using little strokes, curves, and dots called **neumes** to produce a rough graph of the ups and downs of the melody. The early neumes did not show specific pitches, thus they could not teach an unknown melody to a singer who had never heard it before. But they could remind a singer who already knew a melody of how it went. By the eleventh century the neumes evolved to a point where they were being carefully graphed or "heighted" so as to indicate specific pitches. The Italian monk Guido d'Arezzo (d. ca. 1050) led the way in advocating a **staff** with horizontally ruled lines on which the pitches were accurately positioned. Guido's musical graph even used colored lines—e.g., the F-lines, red; the C-lines, yellow—to make the pitches easy to spot. By the thirteenth century, musical notation had acquired most of its modern features. The staff consisted of from four to six lines, and the old strokes, curves, and dots of the Carolingian neumes had evolved into notes with square- or diamond-shaped heads. Our familiar round-headed notes appeared in the sixteenth and seventeenth centuries.

Colorplate 4

The introduction of the neume notation after 800 had both good and bad effects for plainchant. On the good side, it meant that an authoritative version of a plainchant melody could be sent and then maintained without deterioration in a foreign land. On the unfavorable side, it meant that the plainchant melodies had in effect become fixed once and for all. During the first eight centuries of Christianity, the musical tradition of plainchant managed to keep alive a certain improvisatory fervor that was also manifest in the spontaneity of prayers and ritual in the early Christian liturgy. Now, with some strokes of a ninth-century pen, the plainchant melodies were caught in a rigid stylization. They became as if embalmed, no longer in essence "early Christian" or even sixth-century Gregorian chants, but rather Carolingian or medieval chants, whose stylistic profiles conformed to ninth-century, and even later, tastes. The plainchants that came into being as "sung prayers" were henceforth crystallized "art objects." Yet once the neume notation was available to church musicians, it was impossible to ignore its capabilities. And soon the notation became a force for artistic experiment, since it gave composers a way to try out new musical ideas, letting them ponder their novelties and circulate them for others to examine and compare.

Medieval worshippers had many occasions to go to church. There were seven musical services spread throughout each day from dawn to dusk, plus one night service, called collectively the **Divine Office**. The most popular of these offices in the public cathedrals and churches of the cities and towns were the early evening services of **Vespers** and **Compline**. In addition to the public churches, however, medieval Europe had hundreds of monasteries where devout souls spent secluded lives, fulfilling vows of spiritual purity. At monastic houses such as Saint Benedict's chief monastery at Monte Cassino in southern Italy (founded in 529), Jarrow in England (where the Venerable Bede labored and eventually died in 735), Saint Gall in Switzerland, or Cluny in Burgundy, the full array of Divine Office services was scrupulously observed, with much of the time spent in singing plainchant. The monastery's inhabitants adhered to a taxing schedule. They arose before dawn for the office called Lauds, followed by Prime (the First Hour) at about 6 A.M. Other brief offices followed at three-hour intervals, called Terce, Sext, and None, con-

Monks singing from a choirbook (late medieval).

taining further prayers, Bible readings, and the singing of psalms and hymns. At the day's end came Vespers and Compline, but the monastic exertions did not end with sundown. The community was awakened after midnight for the most arduous portion of the Divine Office, called Matins, which in early Christian times continued through to the Lauds at dawn and took in the chanting of all 150 psalms of the Psalter. Even in its abbreviated medieval forms, the monastic Matins could last for two hours, with much of that time spent in singing.

The ordinary folk of the town and countryside probably skipped most of the Divine Office, but they were unfailingly drawn toward church each day for the morning celebration of **Mass**. The Mass is the central act of Christian worship, commemorating Christ's Last Supper with the Apostles on the night before the Crucifixion. Its elaborate ritual contains a reenactment of that sacral drama of the First Communion, where thanks are given to God and symbolic bread and wine are shared in the Communion of the congregation. The Mass has Bible readings and prayers, and also spread throughout are many musical numbers. In fact, most of the medieval music that has come down to us is music for the Mass.

Five of the Mass chants form a group that is known as the **Proper of the Mass.** They are "proper" in the sense that their specific texts and music are different from day to day, and are chosen so as to be appropriate, or proper, to the particular saint or holiday being commemorated. The Proper chants of the Mass are:

1. Introit
2. Gradual
3. Alleluia
4. Offertory
5. Communion

They are distributed throughout the service. On solemn and penitential days a "Tract" replaces the joyful Alleluia. The plainchant melodies for the Proper of the Mass generally go back to the sixth through ninth centuries, and over a thousand of them are preserved.

Five other Mass chants form a group known as the **Ordinary of the Mass.** They are "ordinary" in the sense that their texts remain the same for most Masses during the year. The chants of the Ordinary of the Mass are:

1. Kyrie (Lord have mercy)
2. Gloria (Glory to God in the highest)
3. Credo (I believe in one God)
4. Sanctus (Holy, Holy, Holy)
5. Agnus Dei (Lamb of God)

Like the Proper chants, the Ordinary chants are found at different points in the service, and they represent a variety of ritual functions and musical styles. What the Ordinary chants have in common is that they are direct expressions of the congregation's feelings. Originally they were meant to be sung by the whole assemblage of worshippers; thus they are simpler in musical style than many melodies of the Proper, which were meant for professional choirs and soloists. Hundreds of medieval melodies for the Ordinary of the Mass are preserved, dating back to the ninth through eleventh centuries.

Kyrie No. XI of the Vatican Edition of plainchant is one such Ordinary chant. Probably composed in the tenth century, it is one of some 200 medieval melodies for the Kyrie. Like all plainchants, Kyrie XI has the texture of melody alone—it is monophonic vocal music without accompaniment. The music is moderately **melismatic** in style. That is, there tend to be two or more pitches for each syllable of text (Ex. 1.1). Music this complex was probably never meant for the full congregation to sing but rather for a trained choir singing in **unison**, with everyone joining together on a single melody. In the usual practice the choir is split into two halves so that separate unison groups take turns with the melody, alternating phrase by phrase. This kind of delivery with two choirs answering one another is called **antiphonal** singing. The substance of the melody shows the typical rounded contours of plainchant. There are gentle arches that billow upward to occasional peaks; then they settle gracefully downward. Thrusting interval skips, the jagged motions of two skips in a row, are rare in this suave, curvilinear style. Where a skip occurs, the melody tends to fold right back and fill in the vacant space with smooth step motion.

The rhythms of plainchant show the same tendency as the pitches to be gentle and rounded in their flow. In most of the familiar music of recent times—for example, the music of Bach, Mozart, and Tchaikovsky—the rhythms are so-called **metric rhythms**, where musical time is divided into identical **pulses**, or beats, that are parceled out to form **measures**, regular patterns of equal length. A continuous series of symmetrical measures runs through every such piece. Plainchants, however, have **meterless rhythms** that lack any regular pulses or measures. There are no measure lines in plainchant notation. Instead, the music moves in supple rhythmic waves that are free of predictable patterns. Plainchant's meterless rhythms have a flexibility like that of an orator's declamation. For that reason they are sometimes described as "oratorical" rhythms.

Looking deeper into the melody of the plainchant, we find another feature that sets it apart from recent styles of melody. Plainchants are not based on the familiar major and minor scales. Normally they use one of the eight **church modes** whose scales were the

△
Kyrie (Vatican Edition No. XI)
(Side 1, Band 1)

Ex. 1.1. Kyrie (Vatican Edition No. XI)

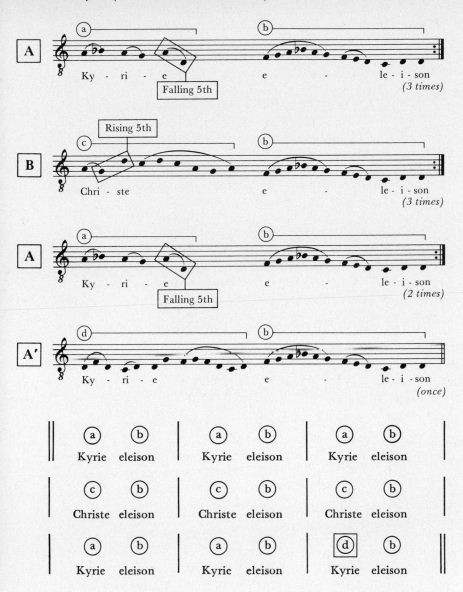

forerunners of the major and minor scales. In practice, medieval composers had more than eight different scales or modes available, each with a distinctive musical character. Those different modal characters were the result of the different orderings of pitches and the special emphases given to certain pitches in each scale. (Some of the early scales are shown in Fig. B.1.12.) Kyrie XI, for example, was built on the scale of the first church mode, whose "home," or "tonic," pitch is D:

C   D   E   F   G   A   B-flat   C   D
      ("tonic")   ("tonic")

This is close to the scale of D minor, but the pitch that occurs just below the "tonic" pitch here is a C-natural, while in the common D-minor scale, it is usually a C-sharp. That is enough to give the first church mode a flavor different from our modern D minor. During the late ninth century, in the backwash of the Carolingian Renaissance, the medieval church modes were given names borrowed from the ancient Greeks. The idea was to associate the fabled musical world of antiquity with some creations of the "modern" West. The first church mode (scale from D to D) was also called the Dorian mode; a scale from E to E was called the Phrygian mode; a scale from F to F was called the Lydian mode; and so forth. The names were misleading because in their ignorance of the old Greek system, the ninth-century musicians connected the wrong Greek scales with their own scales. More to the point, the church modes shared little of real musical substance with the modes of classical Greece. What plainchant and ancient music had in common were the many different modes that were available, each with its own musical flavor.

For all of its suave melodic flow and relaxed meterless rhythm, Kyrie XI is by no means a shapeless creation. Its gentle curves embellish an underlying plan that is as coolly rational as a treatise by

Rounded Romanesque arches. The nave (central corridor) of an early twelfth-century church at Vezelay in Burgundy.

one of Charlemagne's palace theologians, or as the design of a chapel by one of his architects. The plainchant is made up of musical statements, repetitions, and contrasts that have an independent logic of their own. As with any piece of medieval church music, the composer of Kyrie XI was concerned about projecting its sacred text. To understand this music one must know its words. They are a nine-fold prayer for mercy: Kyrie eleison (Lord have mercy), three times; Christe eleison (Christ have mercy), three times; and Kyrie eleison (Lord have mercy), three times. The three petitions to the Lord, the three to Christ, and the three to the Lord make an overall A-B-A verbal form, a kind of symmetrical "arch." In fitting music to these words, one aim of the composer was to mirror such outward symmetries. Only three different words appear, and each has its own musical phrase:

Kyrie—"Lord":   music phrase *a*
eleison—"have mercy": music phrase *b*
Christe—"Christ":   music phrase *c*

The resulting musical design has each Kyrie eleison consisting of phrases *a* and *b,* each Christe eleison of phrases *c* and *b,* and then the Kyrie eleisons again of *a* and *b.* It makes an effective balance between repetition and contrast, between what is familiar and what is fresh. But the composer also had the aim of heightening the emotion and meaning of those prayerful words through more subtle musical means. Thus each Kyrie (phrase *a*) is characterized by the interval of a falling fifth; each Christe (phrase *b*) responds with the interval of a rising fifth; and the eleisons balance those skips with rising and falling motions of their own, now rounded and stepwise as each of the nine invocations to the Lord or to Christ is answered with the same S-shaped curve. The overall symmetry of this plan is broken only at the end, and there in a stroke of high art. For the last Kyrie, the composer introduces the new phrase *d,* which appears only this one time. There at the end it makes an appropriate gesture of musical "contrition," for it has a low profile—it is low in register and without any leaps of a fifth. In music's own language, it adds humility to the ultimate "Lord have mercy."

We have been speaking of the "composer" of Kyrie XI, yet for the musicians who created plainchant, the act of composing meant something a little different from what it does today. It was not just a matter of thinking up fresh and novel sound combinations and putting personal inspiration on display. To be sure, the sacred words were given a musical dress that was calculated to enhance their expression. But this was accomplished largely without injecting the human creative personality. Most plainchant composers were content to practice their craft anonymously in the service of the Church. Their names are unknown, and in their musical techniques a similar impersonality prevails. The plainchants tend to be built out of little twists and turns of melody that everyone had heard and used for generations. The word *composing* actually means putting things together, and that was essentially what the plainchant composers did. They arranged, adjusted, and stylized from a fund of age-old melodic bits and phrases that were active in the communal memory. When a "new" melody was created, it often was not entirely fresh and original. More often it was a refinement of some existing strains. Behind this self-effacement of the composers there lay the ingrained medieval respect for tradition and authority. In this exercise of craft the composers were like the icon painters and artists working with mosaic tiles, who were constantly recreating the same narrow repertory of pictorial subjects while adding relatively modest personalizing touches each time. The music of plainchant helped to solemnize liturgical occasions and lent esthetic substance to the religious sentiments of the worshippers. But the medieval church edifice was not thought of as a concert hall, and the plainchants that were performed there were not merely displayed for the pleasure of the congregation. The church was the *domus Dei,* the House of the Lord, and its music was also the Lord's. This helps to explain why the kind of forthright emotional persuasiveness that is regularly found in the music of later ages is so rarely apparent in earlier medieval music. Even when human ingenuity triumphed and something of admirable beauty was created, the result did not glorify mere mortal creation. It remained a distant mirror of the divine inspiration. Perfect as earthly music might seem, it was an echo of a more perfect music that would be heard in heaven.

C. CHURCH POLYPHONY: THE NOTRE DAME SCHOOL (PARIS, CA. 1200)

The composers of plainchant took the sacred words of the medieval liturgy and clothed them in styles of melody that were naturally suited to the pliancies of the human voice. Plainchant was an art of rounded vocal melody with all its appeals concentrated in a single musical line. The monophonic art of plainchant remained the central outlet for European composers through the ninth century—the Carolingian Era. Then, in the most momentous change that Western music has known, church composers began to turn away from single-stranded monophony and to put their better efforts into polyphony, where two or more melodic strands arc combined. The cultivation of church polyphony spread gradually during the ninth through thirteenth centuries. Its growth was a response to a double need. On the one hand, there was the natural impulse of musicians—irrepressible even in medieval church musicians—to increase the prominence of

Pointed Gothic arches. The nave of Notre Dame, Paris (twelfth-thirteenth century).

their own contributions. On the other hand, there was the fact that by about the year 800, when Charlemagne's emissaries were circulating their official Gregorian plainchants throughout Europe, nearly all the monophonic chants that were needed for the execution of the liturgy had already been composed. Most chants of the Proper of the Mass were in existence by then. During the ninth through eleventh centuries, musicians took care of the rest, concentrating their efforts on the chants of the Ordinary of the Mass. What happened next was that church composers who were intent on finding fresh outlets for their creativity naturally ventured beyond the confines of monophonic styles and explored the textures of polyphony.

Church polyphony arose as an art form during the ninth and tenth centuries when composers began adding new melodic voices as accompaniments to existing plainchants. Their aim was to enhance the effect of the traditional chants. Through the rest of the Middle Ages and into the Renaissance, it remained just that as composers persisted in incorporating some basic line of traditional plainchant melody within each work of church polyphony. The plainchant was right there in the polyphony; the new music was composed over and around the old; and the polyphonic elaboration was substituted for the monophonic original, taking over the plainchant's assigned position in the service. The term **cantus firmus** is used to describe a plainchant melody that is incorporated within a polyphonic work in this way. It means literally a "firm" or pre-existent chant.

The Frankish composers of the ninth century added simple accompaniments to the plainchant melodies, usually by paralleling the

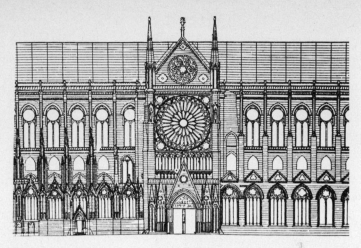

The north side of Notre Dame, Paris. A plan showing the rhythmic repetitions of pointed Gothic windows at three levels.

cantus firmus at the intervals of the octave, the fifth, or the fourth. The result was a style called **organum**, and the name stayed with church polyphony over the next four centuries. An organum is a polyphonic elaboration of a plainchant in a musical style of the ninth through thirteenth centuries. The early organa were so simple in texture and harmony that they scarcely needed to be written down. Generally they were improvised, and they may indeed have been improvised in rudimentary styles long before the first examples in writing. By the year 1000, however, composers were working in more sophisticated styles whose complexity obliged the music to be noted. One center for the artful new organa was Fleury in France; another was Winchester in England; and another was in northern Italy, where Guido d'Arezzo, who contributed to the development of the musical staff in the early eleventh century, also set down rules for organum composition. Guido's newly composed polyphonic voices were no longer bound to the old fashion of running in **parallel motion** to the plainchant cantus firmus. They were imaginatively set off against the plainchant. During the twelfth century there was a center for still more adventurous organum styles at Limoges in southern France, while another center emerged at the popular new pilgrims' shrine of St. James of Compostela in northwest Spain.

The Notre Dame School

Church polyphony reached its first artistic summit at Paris around 1200. At the time Paris was the intellectual capital of Europe, the seat of the brilliant Capetian monarchy—the cultural magnet that drew poets, theologians, artists, and musicians from all over. As in later times, Paris set the styles that others followed. In 1163 the Parisians laid the cornerstone of the Gothic Cathedral of Notre Dame.

The church was not substantially complete until the 1220s, but during the 1180s an altar was consecrated and services began. During the years of the cathedral's slow growth, composers who were working in the orbit of Notre Dame adorned its services with novel styles of organum. The two leading composers of this Notre Dame School were Leonin and Perotin. They are the first "name" polyphonic composers of whom we have substantial artistic remains. Leonin, active around 1175, was the elder of the two. He specialized in a style of organum for two voices called *organum duplum,* where the plainchant melody was situated in the polyphony's lower melodic line, or **voice-part,** and stretched to a slow tempo, with many of its pitches held for a long time as **pedal points.** This lower voice-part, containing the plainchant cantus firmus, was called the **tenor,** a word derived from the Latin, meaning "to hold." The name may have been chosen because the tenor was the seat, or holder, of the plainchant melody, or perhaps because it held the plainchant pitches for so long. Above this slow-moving cantus firmus in the tenor was a second, freshly composed voice-part that indulged in livelier melodic designs. This upper voice-part was called the *duplum,* or second voice, and it gave the name of *organum duplum* to Leonin's two-voice style.

Leonin's chief successor at Notre Dame was Perotin, active around 1200. Perotin's specialties included a more imposing style of organum, called *organum triplum* or *organum quadruplum,* for three or four voices. His polyphony was distinguished from most earlier church polyphony by the use of so many voice-parts. Perotin still incorporated a plainchant in his lowest voice-part, the tenor. But above this slow-moving cantus firmus were two or three lively new voices, engaging at times in almost dancelike motions, in whose animation even the sluggish tenor occasionally joined.

Perotin's four-voice organum "Viderunt omnes" (an *organum quadruplum*) was composed around 1200. It enjoyed a remarkable popularity, being circulated in thirteenth-century copies not only throughout France but as far afield as England, Spain, and Italy. For his cantus firmus Perotin chose the plainchant Gradual "Viderunt omnes fines terrae" ("*All the ends of the earth have seen the salvation of our God . . .*") from the *Mass for Christmas Day.* Christmas was an important observance in every French church, but particularly so at the Cathedral of Notre Dame, which was dedicated to "Our Lady," the Mother of the Lord. Perotin's organum with its festive polyphony was meant to replace the more modest Gregorian plainchant in the liturgy for the day. The underlying plainchant itself consisted of three sections: 1) Viderunt omnes, 2) Notum fecit Dominus, 3) Viderunt omnes (the opening section repeated), as shown in Ex. 1.2a. For his polyphony, Perotin made use of only the openings of the first two plainchant sections. These sections were themselves meant for a soloist, and Perotin's polyphonic elaboration was corres-

△
Perotin: "Viderunt omnes"
(Side 1, Band 2)

Ex. 1.2a. Plainchant Gradual for the *Christmas Mass:*
"Viderunt omnes," with Verse, "Notum fecit Dominus"
(Fifth Church Mode: Final is *F*)

The soloist begins the Gradual:

Vi - de - runt   o -   - mnes

The choir completes the Gradual:

fi - nes ter - rae   sa - lu - ta - re   De -

- i   no - stri: ju - bi - la - te   De -   o

o -   mnis   ter - ra

The soloist begins the Verse:

No - tum   fe - cit   Do -   -   -   -   -

-        -   -   -   -   - mi - nus   sa - lu - ta   - re *etc.*

The choir then concludes the Verse and the whole Gradual is repeated.

Gradual: All the ends of the earth have seen the salvation of our God. Make a
joyful noise unto the Lord, all the earth. *Verse:* The Lord hath made known
his salvation: his righteousness hath he openly shewed in the sight of the
heathen (Psalm 98 [97]: 3-4, 2).

pondingly for solo singers. He left the remainder of the plainchant to
be sung by the choir in its traditional monophony. The entire plainchant "Viderunt omnes" would have taken just a few minutes to
perform. When amplified with Perotin's polyphony the overall length
came to about twelve minutes, and the piece stood out as a high

Ex. 1.2b. Organum Quadruplum: Beginning of "Viderunt omnes" (Perotin) in a Thirteenth-Century Manuscript

point in the *Christmas Mass.* Ex. 1.2b shows the opening section of Perotin's organum as it appears in a Parisian manuscript of the thirteenth century; Ex. 1.2c shows its beginning in modern notation. The entire opening section is based on just the two words of plainchant "Viderunt omnes" ("They all have seen").

The church leaders of Perotin's time thought it essential that the plainchant melodies that were sanctioned by tradition should appear at their designated places in the service. But beyond that, they do not always seem to have cared how distorted the venerable melodies might become in a polyphonic setting, even if they occasionally became unrecognizable. Perotin satisfied the basic requirement by having the pitches of the plainchant "Viderunt omnes" in the tenor

Ex. 1.2c. Organum Quadruplum: Beginning of "Viderunt omnes," Perotin

voice (the lowest voice-part) of his polyphony. They are the only pitches found in that voice-part. But once having incorporated them, he obeyed the dictates of his art in laying out their lengths or rhythms. The first four tenor pitches (on the syllables Vi-, de-, and runt) are all treated as long pedal points, which are held for so long that instruments may have helped in sustaining them. With the pitches on the next syllable (the om- of omnes), the tenor's motion picks up, but then with the final pitches, the slow, pedal-point motion resumes.

Above these elongations and compressions of the underlying plainchant, Perotin composed three upper voices that move in quicker patterns. Their animated designs join together in a texture so tightly woven that at times we may hear only a lively blur rather than distinct pitches. Nevertheless, Perotin took great care in choosing the pitches and shaping the melodic fragments that appear in the upper voices and that are occasionally tossed back and forth among them. In combination the voices produce chords that may sound a bit hollow to present-day ears. This is because they use chiefly the intervals of the fifth and fourth, while we are accustomed to chords that depend chiefly on intervals of a third. Fifths and fourths were the preferred consonances of Perotin's time.

In composing his polyphony, Perotin was no less concerned with effects of rhythm than he was with effects of melody and harmony. The rhythms of earlier styles of church polyphony had been mainly meterless rhythms, like the rhythms of the plainchants on which the polyphony was based. The Notre Dame composers began to exploit new kinds of rhythm. Turning away from the old meterless rhythms, they cultivated styles of rhythm that were more regular and emphatic, so-called metric rhythms, where a succession of evenly spaced pulses and identically shaped "measures" runs throughout an entire work. Perotin's four-voice "Viderunt omnes" has just such a continuous pattern of regular pulses and measures as the basis of its lively upper-voice rhythms. The musical notation of the thirteenth century does not yet show the measure lines and time signatures of our modern notation, but those factors are already present in Perotin's metric rhythms. Most music that we know today has time signatures and equal-length measures. This began in France some eight centuries ago with the trend to strong metric rhythms by Perotin and his colleagues. At first they cultivated only **triple meters**, corresponding to our modern $\frac{3}{8}$ or $\frac{6}{8}$ time signatures. The number three that was the basis of such meters naturally had the approval of contemporary theologians who interpreted the musical threes as reflecting the perfection of the Holy Trinity. Later on in the thirteenth century, composers began employing **duple meters** as well, based on the number two, corresponding to our modern $\frac{2}{4}$ or $\frac{4}{4}$ time signatures. Toward the end of the century, composers produced music that was based on the equivalent of a $\frac{9}{8}$ time signature. With that, the roster of familiar Western meters was essentially complete for centuries to come.

Perotin applied the new metric rhythms in various ways in the texture of his four-voice "Viderunt omnes." The basic level of rhythmic motion is the regular flow of rapid $\frac{3}{8}$ "measures" that continues throughout:

Within many of those identical "measures" there is also a distinctive rhythmic pattern that consists of a "long" followed by a "short": . Then Perotin's rhythmic organization extends beyond such individual measures of long-short rhythm to the joining of several measures together, grouping them into rhythmic phrases that parallel, balance, or otherwise respond to one another. For instance, just after the opening chord on "Vi-," the music consists of seven phrases in a row that are in rhythmic parallel with one another. Each has the rhythmic phrase-pattern "X" (see Ex. 1.2c):

Throughout "Viderunt omnes" Perotin concentrated on the long-short metric pattern. In other works he favored the reverse pattern, or short-long: . In the three-voice organum "Nativitas" he gave an overall breadth of rhythmic shape to the music by alternating sections that feature a short-long pattern with sections featuring a long-short pattern. Those readers who are acquainted with Latin poetry may find that Perotin's two basic rhythmic patterns remind them of the trochaic (long-short) and iambic (short-long) meters of the ancient Romans, who used just such orderings of long and short syllables in constructing their verses. English has no exact equivalents, but here are approximations of the trochaic and iambic meters from the English poets:

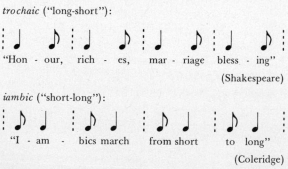

trochaic ("long-short"):

"Hon - our, rich - es, mar - riage bless - ing"

(Shakespeare)

iambic ("short-long"):

"I - am - bics march from short to long"

(Coleridge)

Just why Perotin and his musical contemporaries chose to concentrate on such metric patterns remains something of a mystery. They may have come upon them in the natural course of artistic speculation and adopted them for purely musical reasons. However, there was a lingering interest in ancient Latin meters throughout the Middle Ages, and a widely read patristic work, St. Augustine's *On Music*, a fourth-century manual that was concerned largely with questions of Latin meter, may have set the French composers of the twelfth and thirteenth centuries to exploiting metric rhythms of their own.

Perotin's music is sometimes described as "Gothic" music, the idea being that it represents the same time and place as the great Gothic cathedrals such as Notre Dame, Chartres, and Amiens. Such labels that are shared between the arts sometimes create more misunderstandings than illuminations, but there are two things to be said in favor of this one. The first concerns the preoccupation with the effects of rhythm that we have just observed. What sets Notre Dame polyphony radically apart from earlier polyphony is its metrical rhythm. The shape of Perotin's organum comes primarily from its rhythms, from the way its phrases are blocked out in parallel and answering rhythmic patterns. The use of rhythms is similar in a Gothic cathedral. The repeating patterns of the windows, arches, and buttresses, running the lengths of the structures, create visual effects that are reasonably described by art historians as being rhythmic. The other parallel between the Parisian organa and the Gothic cathedrals involves features that go beyond what is fully seen or heard. The Gothic building is laid out in accordance with a time-honored plan—one that is laden with theological significance. It takes the form of a cross, thus it is a large-scale projection of the most fundamental of Christian symbols. Something similar to this happens in the layout of Perotin's polyphony, for here too there is a theologically related "floor plan": the pitches of Perotin's lowest voice come directly from the authorized repertory of plainchant. And in the polyphonic organum, as in the architectural structure, the treatment of the basic theological material is expansive. The architect's vast cruciform plan is made elaborate with the thrust of arches, buttresses, and windows overhead. In the polyphony, the plainchant tenor, which is swelled to great lengths, serves as a support for the exuberant, many-tiered rhythmic patterns that are active overhead.

In the end, it may not surprise us to discover some esthetic correspondence between the high musical art of the Gothic era—the Parisian organa of Perotin—and the high architectural art of the Gothic structures within which the organa's sound patterns were meant to be heard. Yet whatever kinship we may find, it remains obvious to anyone who experiences the actual works of art that Perotin's music makes a wholly different impression on first hearing than what the beholder senses on first viewing the cathedrals of Notre Dame, Chartres, or Amiens. The churches overwhelm us at once with their radiance and splendor. Perotin's organa may strike us as cold and crude. Still, it is worth remembering that high medieval architecture did not always make the genial effect that it does today. For a long time Gothic art was thought of as cold and crude. It had to be rehabilitated by the nineteenth century and reclaimed from the disdain of the sixteenth through eighteenth centuries, which derided it as "gothic" (referring to the barbarian Goths) because of what struck them as its crudity, its divorce from nature and beauty. The appeals of the Gothic cathedral have gradually won their way, and so too the appeals of the Notre Dame organa are winning theirs. Perotin's organa were the sounds that filled the great shells of vaulted stone and stained glass. Those sounds were widely admired in their own day, and listeners are discovering that they still convey admirable qualities today.

D. THE RISE OF MEDIEVAL SECULAR MUSIC

Polyphony was cultivated on an expanding scale during the ninth through twelfth centuries, but the age-old art of monophony—melody alone—did not simply wither and disappear. It remained an active element in composers' vocabularies and was an impetus to some vital new growths. One was a fresh variety of plainchant called the **sequence**, which was performed as a follow-up to the Alleluia of the Mass on important feast days. Sequences were long poetic-musical sermons, filled with stirring religious imagery, dramatizing the miracles of some popular saint or commenting upon some theological highpoint of the day. The music had a simple melodic style, usually with just a single note of melody for each syllable of text. The topical poetry and emphatic musical delivery of the sequences had an up-to-date appeal for ninth-century listeners, to whom the older styles of plainchant were beginning to seem like venerable relics of the past. The greatest artist of the early sequence was the monk Notker Balbulus ("the Stammerer," d. 912), who served as librarian at the famous Swiss monastery of St. Gall. Notker's forty sequences, which offer vivid commentaries on the principal occasions of the church year, continued to be sung in Germany and Eastern Europe until the sixteenth century. During the late twelfth century, Adam of St. Victor, who took his name from the influential Parisian Abbey of St. Victor where he was a monk, produced sequences in an even more emphatic poetic style than Notker's, adding the enticements of vigorous sing-song rhythms and rhymed endings to his verses. His rhythms were metrical rhythms, similar to the ones that were then about to appear in the polyphony of Notre Dame.

In an era when musical composition was largely an anonymous and all-male affair, there were two women who won renown in sacred monophonic styles like those of Notker and Adam. One was Hildegard of Bingen, the saintly twelfth-century abbess of Ruperts-berg on the Rhine, who wrote spiritual songs that earned her the nickname "The Sibyl of the Rhine." The other was the Byzantine nun Casia (b. ca. 820), who produced Orthodox Church hymns that are still sung in the liturgy today. Casia was one of the outspoken feminists of the Middle Ages. Before entering a monastic retreat, she almost became the Byzantine empress. The historian Gibbon tells how she attracted the Emperor Theophilus when he was looking over candidates for marriage:

With a golden apple in his hand, he slowly walked between two lines of contending beauties; his eye was detained by the charms of Casia, and, in the awkwardness of a first declaration, the prince could only observe that in this world, women had been the cause of much evil. "And surely, sir," she pertly replied, "they have likewise been the occasion of much good." This affectation of unseasonable wit displeased the imperial lover; he turned aside in disgust; Casia concealed her mortification in a convent.

Among the thousands of medieval sequences and hymns, perhaps the most memorable is the "Dies irae" ("Day of wrath": "*dee*-es *ee*-rye"), whose poetic embroideries on the terrors of the Last Judgment have much the same rhythmic verse-style as the sequences of Adam of St. Victor. The possible author of the mournful eight-syllable lines was the thirteenth-century Italian friar Thomas of Celano. The composer of the solemn melody is unknown (Ex. 1.3).

Ex. 1.3. "Dies irae" from Sequence of the Mass for the Dead (Thirteenth Century)

Dies irae, dies illa,	The day of wrath, that dreaded day
Solvet saeclum in favilla:	Shall all the world in ashes lay,
Teste David cum Sibylla.	As David and the Sibyl say.
Quantus tremor est futurus,	What terror will the soul afright
Quando judex est venturus,	When comes that judge with keenest sight
Cuncta stricte discussurus!	To bring all thought and deed to light.
Tuba mirum spargens sonum	The last loud trumpet's wondrous tone
Per sepulcra regionum,	Shall through the realm of tombs be blown,
Coget omnes ante thronum.	To summon all before the throne.
(18 more stanzas)	(etc.)

The "Dies irae" is still chanted in the Mass for the Dead, and the unforgettable opening phrases of its music have often been used by romantic composers, among them Berlioz (see Chapter 6, page 241), Liszt, and Rachmaninoff, for evoking morbid and diabolical effects.

The old texture of monophony found another outlet during the ninth through thirteenth centuries in the rise to prominence of the liturgical dramas—religious plays with monophonic music sung throughout. Such plays were associated at first with the official liturgy; then they became increasingly independent and elaborate in their dramatic pageantry. They were also embellished with instrumental accompaniments. Liturgical dramas, such as the sepulcher plays (eleventh-twelfth centuries), and the *Play of Daniel* and the *Play of Herod* (twelfth-thirteenth centuries), are among the ancestors of Renaissance and modern dramas.

Secular Monophony: Goliards, Troubadours, and Trouvères

During the centuries of polyphony's slow rise and monophony's decline, the essential change was the shift in composers' interest from sacred to secular subjects. What had traditionally passed for art music among medieval composers was sacred, church music. Since the beginnings of musical notation it was chiefly sacred music that the monks took the trouble to write down. But medieval society had its barons as well as bishops, its towns as well as cloisters, and pres-

A medieval knight dresses for combat, with musicians playing an early lute and five-string fiddle, and servants readying his helmet, sword, and spurs.

ently the composers who cultivated learned, sophisticated styles began to turn out music that was destined for secular, wordly entertainment. By the twelfth and thirteenth centuries, musical arts of secular entertainment were flourishing everywhere in Europe. Secular music at first concentrated on songs in monophonic styles. There were songs with Latin texts, for example, those of the goliards, or wandering scholars, a floating population of runaway monks, unfrocked priests, and university dropouts whose bibulous, scandalous verses parodied church Latin and generally pictured a dissolute style of twelfth- and thirteenth-century life. A famous collection of these vagabonds' songs is the *Carmina burana,* so-called because they are found in a manuscript from the old German Abbey of Benediktbeurn (burana).

Colorplates 5 and 6

The emergence of European song took a substantial step forward with the turn from Latin toward the local vernacular languages. By the twelfth and thirteenth centuries, each of the Western nations was cultivating its own styles of secular art song in its own languages. These regional flourishings of secular monophony reflected the widespread prosperity of the feudal courts, whose affluent seigneurs diverted some of their leisure energies from jousting and hunting to cultivation of the arts. Such enterprising nobles would eventually compete with the churches and cathedrals as patrons of outstanding composers and performers. Just as France had led the way in cultivating church polyphony, so it led in secular song. In southern France the *troubadours* used the Provençal language; in northern France the *trouvères* used Old French. The troubadours and trouvères were at once poets and composers, generally setting their own verses to music. Among them were artists of plebian origin, such as the twelfth-century troubadour Marcabru, whose poetry is astonishing for its straight talk and moral urgency. Some of the French bards were nobles. Among them were Guillaume IX, Count of Poitiers (1071-1127), who is called the first troubadour; Thibaut de Champagne, King of Navarre (thirteenth century); and King "Richard the Lion-Hearted" (Richard I of England), whose Old-French song, "Ja nus hons pris ne dira sa raison" ("Unless a prisoner speaks in grief"), bemoaning his captivity while being held for ransom, was composed in 1193-94. There is a legend—charming yet untrue—that Richard's trouvère-friend Blondel de Nesle managed to locate his imprisoned master by caroling through the fortress-courtyards of Europe until finally he heard in return a song they had composed together.

The troubadour and trouvère songs, written down as simple melodies, were so sketchily notated that while we know their pitches we are not often sure of their rhythms. They were probably meant to have instrumental accompaniment since illustrated manuscripts of medieval songs show harps, lutes, fiddles, and percussion. The songs were performed by professional servant-musicians and wandering minstrels, known as *jongleurs*. Some 2,000 troubadour and trouvère melodies are preserved. Among them are historical and topical songs, such as crusaders' songs and laments about imprisonment. Others are more philosophical, debating points of medieval chivalry, the ethic of knightly behavior that struck a needed balance between the licentiousness of a war-ridden society and the constraints of Christian morality. The chief doctrines of chivalry were loyalty to the feudal lord, faithfulness to knightly vows, selfless action in defense of the weak, and worshipful treatment of women.

Like songs of most times and places, medieval French songs are often love songs. There are banal—and quite unchivalrous—flirtations between knights and shepherdesses. There are sophisticated lyrics reflecting the debonair code of upper-class amorous dalliance, known as courtly love, which figures prominently in the English and French literature of the late Middle Ages. Courtly love amounted to a make-believe world of fanciful conventions governing the relationships between the sexes. It was supposed that lordly husbands and their wives often did not get along in those days of arranged marriages. And in an era when the sun never set on fighting, the husbands were often away on some Crusade or knightly errand. There were others around to take their place: indolent knights biding their time at the castle, and even lowly troubadours or trouvères aspiring to a love beyond their station. Such "courtly," or "courteous," lovers were expected to endure long-suffering silences before their passions were declared, followed by long trials of devotion both before and after the secret consummations. The poetic descriptions are often stilted and the situations more literary than real, but the songs describe the amusements of upper-class feudal society. Among all the clever artifices there are touches of genuine emotion.

The Thirteenth-Century Motet

Eventually the rising tide of medieval secularism joined the rising tide of church polyphony. This was the beginning of the development of secular art polyphony. During the ninth through twelfth centuries polyphony remained primarily a technique for religious occasions, but the thirteenth century brought its widespread application to secular entertainment. The chief novelty of thirteenth-century music was a new musical genre called the **motet**, which arose at Paris as an outgrowth of the Notre Dame organa of Leonin and Perotin. Ever since, the word motet has served as a name for vocal church polyphony. That is, an organum is a polyphonic church work of the ninth through thirteenth centuries; a motet is a polyphonic church work of the thirteenth through twentieth centuries. The motet got its start during the early thirteenth century when poets and composers began taking the music of existing organa and adding fresh Latin texts to them. Such added texts were at first limited to pious commentaries on the original, sacred subject matter. But soon the piety and the musical links with the older organum style began to erode, and new motets were composed in lively new styles. Many still had texts in church Latin. But there were others with texts in French, and the subjects they dealt with were wordly as well as religious. Secular and sacred texts were even mixed within a single piece as different voice-parts sang different texts together in incongruous, sometimes blasphemous, mixtures: for example, the worship of the poet's ladylove coupled with the worship of the Virgin; the amours of shepherds and shepherdesses, the dalliance of knights and country wenches, the babble of the Paris streets and markets—all capable of being combined with tenors drawn from Gregorian chant. Hundreds of motets were produced by the thirteenth century. Usually each had some morsel of plainchant—a cantus firmus—laid out in its tenor voice-part as a relic of its churchly origins. But in other respects, many of the motets were not religious at all. They were amusements for the upper stratum of a society that delighted in saucy humor and frivolous pleasures. Inevitably the Church reacted and even the Pope intervened. Pope John XXII issued a scathing denunciation in 1324-25, criticizing the abuses that had become entrenched in church music and demanding stricter decorum. Church music cleansed itself of secular taints during the fourteenth century, but the lively genre of Parisian motets had launched a vogue of secular polyphony that would not be halted. What interested fourteenth-century composers most was not the churchly motet and Mass but a new-found art of polyphonic song.

Fourteenth-Century Music in France, Italy, and England

Three nations were the musical leaders during the fourteenth century. France continued its earlier domination of European styles, but the French supremacy was now challenged by musical styles of Italy and England. French music had the greatest refinement. In the musical works of Philippe de Vitry (1291-1361) and Guillaume de Machaut (ca. 1300-1377) there is a sophistication that surpasses anything else of the time. Machaut was not only the outstanding French musician of his century, but also its outstanding poet. He composed over 100 secular French chansons, finely honed musical settings of his own chiseled lyric verses. He also wrote about two dozen church motets and the first polyphonic setting of the full Ordinary of the Mass by a renowned composer. All of Machaut's music and verse was meticulously copied into manuscripts under his own direction. Later in the fourteenth century, a group of French

A lady playing a portative organ (Italian, fourteenth century).

composers, including Jean Vaillant and Jacques de Senleches, pushed Gallic preciousness to extremes. Their filigree textures are laced with wry harmonies and dainty rhythms that were scarcely matched for subtlety before the twentieth century.

In Italy there was a more robust and earthy music. Italian composers of the fourteenth century put nearly all their efforts into a flowering of secular music. Some 700 Italian compositions have survived from that epoch, the work of over three dozen polyphonic composers who were the contemporaries of Dante (1265-1321), Giotto (1253?-1337), Petrarch (1304-74), and Boccaccio (1313-75). It was no longer the fashion for composers to remain anonymous. These musicians' names and even their portraits are emblazoned in their manuscripts. Francesco Landini (ca. 1325-1397), the most celebrated, served as organist at the cathedral of Florence. Landini's 150 secular compositions for two and three voices have the same direct emotional appeal as the new Italian lyric poetry of the age. The natural gait of his rhythms and the clear, supple textures speak readily to the modern ear. During the early fourteenth century, both French and Italian musicians took occasion to compare their newer musical styles with the older styles of the thirteenth century. They named their own fourteenth-century art a "new art," an *ars nova,* distinguishing it from the stiffer "old art," or *ars antiqua,* of the Parisian organa and early motets. The fourteenth century's secular spirit was captured differently by each of the trend-setting musical nations, but it was Italy, with the greater vigor of its rhythms and its love of robust decoration, that more clearly represented a "new art." In the verve of Landini's "Ecco la primavera" ("Here is spring-time") or the exaltation of his "Gram piant' agli occhi" ("Great grief to the eyes"), there can be sensed something of the momentous change that was beginning as Italy turned from medieval spirituality toward the more human values of the upcoming Renaissance.

Colorplate 7

Late medieval England remained the most tradition-bound of the fourteenth century's three great musical nations. There was no one in the age of Chaucer (ca. 1340-1400) who spoke of English music as representing an *ars nova.* England seems to have been an heir to the lofty traditions of the Notre Dame organa, a bastion of sacred music in the face of the new French and Italian secularism. Still, we are a bit uncertain about the profile of English music in the thirteenth and fourteenth centuries. Reformation zealots destroyed whatever old church manuscripts they could lay hand on during the sixteenth century, so that much of the music and even the names of most early English composers are gone. One thing is clear. Fourteenth-century England was the breeding ground for an appealing musical style that would soon have an important influence on French and Italian music (see Chapter 2, page 52). In particular, the English composers cultivated two techniques. One was the texture of block chords—like the simple chords used in singing church hymns today. The other technique concerned the makeup of those chords, which tended to be full triads of the $\overset{\wedge}{1}$-$\overset{\wedge}{3}$-$\overset{\wedge}{5}$, *do-mi-sol* type that is still familiar in harmonies today. Such chords were based on intervals of a third; they gave a more euphonious sound than the chords favored for chord building in fourteenth-century France and Italy, where intervals of a fourth and a fifth were still emphasized. Both of these fourteenth-century English traits—the texture of block chords and the pleasant-sounding triads—would show up in fifteenth-century continental styles.

Perhaps the most appealing of medieval secular creations, however, comes from an earlier epoch, the thirteenth century in England. "Sumer is icumen in" ("Summer Canon") is a polyphonic song by an unknown English composer who worked in the same century as the creators of the big Notre Dame organa and the first Parisian motets. "Sumer is icumen in" stands apart from the mainstream of medieval music, both in its spirit and in its musical techniques. It is entertainment music with a folklike allure that rarely found its way into manuscript. Its survival is in fact a bit of luck, since it is pre-

Δ
"Sumer is icumen in"
(Side 1, Band 3)

Colorplate 8

served only as a stray entry in a single manuscript (Ex. 1.4). Its words are a celebration of summer's return, not couched in churchly Latin but in an earthy Middle English:

Sumer is icumen in, Lhude sing cuccu,
Groweth sed and bloweth med, And springth the wede nu,
Sing cuccu,
Awe bleteth after lamb, Lhouth after calve cu,
Bulluc sterteth, bucke verteth, Murie sing cuccu,
Cuccu Cuccu,
Wel singes thu cuccu, ne swik thu naver nu. (Ex. 1.5a)

(Summer is a-coming in, Loudly sing, cuckoo! Grows the seed, and blooms the meadow, Springs the wood anew. Sing, cuckoo! Ewe is bleating for the lamb, the cow lows for the calf; the bullock's leaping, buck's cavorting. Merry sing, cuckoo. Cuckoo, cuckoo. Well sings't thou, oh cuckoo. Let's have it ever so.)

**Ex. 1.4. Beginning of "Sumer is icumen in" in the
Thirteenth-Century Manuscript**

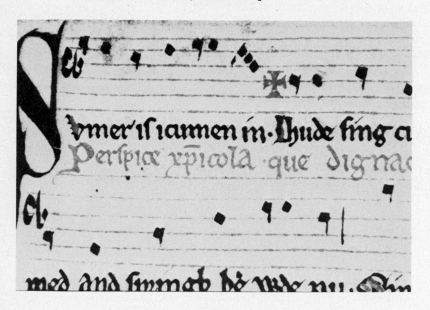

The manuscript also supplies a church-Latin text, *Perspice christi-cola,* that rendered the piece suitable for devotions, but the composer chose to match the lively English words to the lively music. The tune has the same triple meter and indeed more of the same melodic sprightliness found in Perotin. But the astonishing thing about

Ex. 1.5a. Tune of "Sumer is icumen in" (The Summer Canon)

Su - mer is i - cu - men in,___ Lhu - de sing cuc - cu,

Grow - eth sed and blow - eth med, And springth the we - de nu,

Sing cuc - cu,

Aw - e ble - teth af - ter lamb, Lhouth af - ter cal - ve cu,

Bul - luc ster - teth, buc - ke ver - teth, Mu - rie sing cuc - cu,

Cuc - cu Cuc - cu,___

Wel sing - es thu cuc - cu, ne swik thu na - ver nu.

⊕ = entry of a follower voice

"Sumer is icumen in" is how its tune turns out to be the lead voice of a **canon.** That is, the tune is multiplied upon itself so that four individual voices all sing the same melody throughout, all sounding well together even though each voice is at a different point in the music. Everyone nowadays knows pieces called **rounds,** like "Three Blind Mice" and "Frère Jacques." A round is a popular example of the learned musical form that is known as canon. In the technique

Ex. 1.5b, c. "Sumer is icumen in"

b. First four entries

Lead voice — Su - mer is i - cu - men in,_____ Lhu - de sing cuc - cu,

First follower — Su - mer is i - cu - men in,_____

Second follower

Third follower

Grow - eth sed and blow - eth med, And springth the we - de nu, *etc.*

Lhu - de sing cuc - cu, Grow - eth sed and blow - eth med, And *etc.*

Su - mer is i - cu - men in,_____ Lhu - de sing cuc - cu, *etc.*

Su - mer is i - cu - men in,_____ *etc.*

c. The Pes

Sing cuc - cu nu,_____ Sing cuc - cu.

Sing cuc - cu, Sing cuc - cu nu._____

of a round or canon, a "lead" voice sings first, all alone; then before it gets very far a "follower" voice enters and copies exactly what the lead voice has just sung; other voices may enter in turn, each one copying, or imitating, the leader throughout. This musical technique is also known as **strict imitation.** There are usually two or three fol-lower voices that exactly imitate one another within a canon; how-ever, there can be any number of voices, even 12 or more. "Sumer is icumen in" has a lead voice and three followers, all singing the same tune in strict imitation. This seems an extraordinary feat for the thirteenth century, which produced nothing else quite like it (Ex. 1.5b). But there is something more. Even while this canon is unfold-ing in the four upper voice-parts, there are two additional voice-parts that are working out a musical pattern of their own underneath. The manuscript calls them the *pes*—the "foot," or accompaniment. They interchange two short phrases, repeating them constantly, as shown in Ex. 1.5c. Thus there are six voices in all, the four voice-parts of the upper canon plus the two voice-parts of the accompanying *pes*. This is more ambitious than the four-voice organa of Perotin, more than any art-polyphony before this time. "Sumer is icumen in" is a remarkable achievement. Yet what impresses us beyond its inventive musical techniques is how it captures the spirit of nature and spring-time. Its enthusiasms are couched in a musical idiom that not only was fresh years ago but marvelously retains its freshness today.

E. MEDIEVAL INSTRUMENTAL MUSIC

Although musical instruments had a vital role in medieval culture, composers of the Middle Ages distinctly favored vocal music—music that was sung—over instrumental music—music that was played. Today when we think of "serious" or "learned" music, we tend to first think of genres that are purely instrumental, without any ad-mixture of human voices, such as the symphony, sonata, suite, con-certo, quartet, concert overture, tone poem, etc. Yet during the Middle Ages and continuing throughout the Renaissance, the musical emphasis was on genres that gave primacy to the human voice—plain-chant, organum, motet, Mass, and secular song. At the outset plain-chant countenanced no participation of instruments at all. Instru-ments were associated with worship of the pagan gods. In antiquity they accompanied lewd songs and scandalous theatrical spectacles, so for a long time they were banished from medieval churches. But in the end, their effectiveness in enhancing the appeal of church music could not be ignored, and they found increasing use.

The favorite church instrument in medieval times was the pipe organ, the ancestor of our modern pipe and electronic organs. The organ was favored, not because it was considered inherently a sacred instrument, but because for the Middle Ages, it expressed better than any other instrument the notion of imperial pomp. The older organs that were used by the ancient Romans had more or less vanished

Some late medieval instruments.

Hurdy-gurdy. An instrument shaped like a viol; its strings are set in motion by a gummed wheel controlled by a crank at the lower end of the body.

Vielle (Fiddle).

Rebec.

under churchly interdiction. An organ is mentioned by St. Aldhelm of Malmesbury (d. 709). In 757, the Byzantine Emperor Constantine V sent an organ as a gift to his colleague, the Frankish Emperor Pepin. It was an obvious novelty there, as was another such instrument examined half a century later at the court of Pepin's son, Charlemagne. The European vogue of the instrument was launched, and examples were soon to be found everywhere. According to a perhaps exaggerated account by the monk Wulstan (d. 983), there was an enormous organ with 26 bellows from which "seventy strong men drive out the wind with all their strength" at Winchester Cathedral in the tenth century. In front of it sat "two brethren, unified in spirit," playing "sounds so loud that everyone covers their ears with their hands, unable when close by to endure the noise that the various tones give out."

Winchester at that time was a center for the blossoming art of church polyphony. The first large collection of European polyphony is from there, preserved in a famous manuscript of the early eleventh century known as the Winchester Troper. Thus the same era that saw the rise of the organ as a church instrument also saw the rise of polyphony. There was probably a connection, though we are not quite sure what it was. The obvious use for a church organ was to accompany the plainchant. One such accompaniment that was apt for the medieval organ was to supply a sustained chordal background—a bag-

Harp.

Psaltery.

Lute.

pipelike "drone," of the kind still heard in Eastern Orthodox church choirs. Another style of organ accompaniment for plainchant would have been to parallel the chant melodies at intervals such as the fourth, fifth, and octave. This was precisely the style of Carolingian church polyphony, the style of polyphony that was named organum. The name may have been chosen because the polyphony imitated an organ technique, or perhaps because it was accompanied by or doubled by an organ. But the word organum had other connotations, and the relation of the organ to early polyphony remains uncertain.

Even while pipe organs were gaining favor as church instruments, there were other musical instruments in everyday life, providing accompaniments for dances and secular songs. They may have played without voices, developing purely instrumental idioms of their own. Medieval paintings show us the forerunners of many of our modern instruments. There were bowed fiddles, lutes, guitars, oboes, flutes, recorders, trumpets, drums, castanets, and harps. Of course, these instruments were different from modern ones, and they had medieval names, such as *vielle* (fiddle-type), *shawm* (oboe-type), *buisine* (trumpet-type), etc. Some of the medieval instruments—for example, the bagpipe and the hurdy-gurdy—have since become obsolete in art music though they persist in popular music. Other instruments for which we have medieval artistic representations existed only in the artist's fancy. They were imaginary instruments that were made up

Colorplates 5, 6, and 9

to suit a pictorial design, or real instruments whose shapes were modified for the artist's purposes. Certain portrayals of instruments that were carved into stone walls of churches are likely to represent not the current musical practice, but the medieval conceptions of biblical instruments, such as those listed in Psalm 150.

Although painters and sculptors took obvious pleasure in depicting instruments, instrumental music itself was rarely written down. Since it was usually destined for secular entertainment, the monks who copied musical manuscripts did not bother to preserve it. Anyway the bulk of instrumental music was not formally "composed," but was mainly improvised and passed along by example. During the thirteenth and fourteenth centuries, a number of instrumental dances and arrangements of vocal works begin to appear in musical manuscripts. They show a liveliness and informality that are somewhat removed from the high-minded, calculated styles of plainchant and church polyphony. An English dance of the late thirteenth century, Δ "The Oxford 'Major-Mode' Dance" (Side 1, Band 4) which comes from about the same time and place as "Sumer is icumen in," has some of the same jaunty appeal. Its texture is monophonic except for some chords at the end (Ex. 1.6). Medieval music

Ex. 1.6. "The Oxford 'Major-Mode' Dance" (English, Thirteenth Century)

manuscripts do not specify the instruments for such music, but judging from paintings of the time, this piece could be for pipers or fiddlers—or for both—perhaps with percussion reinforcing the brisk duple meter. Like most purely instrumental pieces, this also has an independent musical **form**, a pattern of repetitions and contrasts that give it a sense of shape and logic. This form consists of a series of short phrases, most of which are directly repeated (a a′ b b′ c c′, etc.) while some reappear occasionally later on. No composer is named and there is no title, but since the dance is found in a manuscript at

Oxford it may be called "The Oxford Dance," or perhaps "The Oxford 'Major-Mode' Dance." Why major mode? Because the pitches and intervals on which its merry sounds depend are not really those of any church mode. They are close to the modern major mode. A long time would pass before the late seventeenth century, when the relics of the church modes were shunted aside and the primacy of the major and minor modes was established. Yet here in thirteenth-century England the sound of the major mode can already be heard.

2 Music in the Renaissance (ca. 1420-1600)

Renaissance musical centers.

Verrocchio's David *illustrates the renewed appeal of lithe human figures (Florence, fifteenth century).*

The cathedral of Florence, crowned by the majestic dome of Brunelleschi, greatest of early Renaissance architects (1430s).

Michelangelo. The hand of God reaches out to Adam. Ceiling of the Sistine Chapel (Rome, 1508-1512).

Melozzo da Forli, Angel with Lute *(Italian, fifteenth century).*

The Renaissance *(ca. 1420-1600)*

MUSIC	ARTS AND IDEAS	KEY EVENTS

EARLY RENAISSANCE (ca. 1420-1475)

MUSIC	ARTS AND IDEAS	KEY EVENTS
English composers: Dunstable, Power Franco-Flemish composers: Dufay, Binchois, Ockeghem Musical genres: Mass, motet, chanson Dufay (ca. 1400-1474): "Alma redemptoris mater" (ca. 1430)	Flemish artists: the Van Eycks, Rogier van der Weyden, Memling Rebirth of three-dimensional perspective Donatello and Verrocchio sculptures Masaccio frescos (1426-1428) Brunelleschi, Dome of Florence Cathedral (1430s) Gutenberg's printing press at Mainz (ca. 1440)	Medici domination of Florence Turks take Constantinople (1453)

HIGH RENAISSANCE (ca. 1475-1530)

MUSIC	ARTS AND IDEAS	KEY EVENTS

Franco-Flemish composers: Josquin Des Prez, Obrecht, Isaac, de la Rue
Josquin (ca. 1440-1521):
   Ave maris stella Mass (ca. 1500)
	Leonardo da Vinci, Mona Lisa (ca. 1503)
	Michelangelo, Sistine Chapel ceiling (1508-1512)
	Paintings of Raphael, Bosch, and Grünewald
	Erasmus, *The Praise of Folly* (1509)
	Thomas More, *Utopia* (1516)
	Castiglione, *The Courtier* (1527)
	Machiavelli, *The Prince* (1532)
		Spanish Inquisition begins (1478)
		Columbus discovers San Salvador (1492)
		Savonarola in power at Florence (1494-1498)
		Protestant Reformation:
		   Luther's 95 Theses (1517)
		   Henry VIII establishes Church of England (1533)

LATE RENAISSANCE (ca. 1530-1600)

MUSIC	ARTS AND IDEAS	KEY EVENTS

Musical genres: Mass, motet, chanson, madrigal, canzona
Composers (earlier): Willaert, Jannequin, Rore
Composers (later): Palestrina, Lassus, Victoria, Marenzio, Gesualdo, Monteverdi, G. Gabrieli, Byrd, Weelkes
Palestrina (ca. 1525-1594):
   Pope Marcellus Mass (ca. 1563)
Weelkes (ca. 1575-1623):
   "As Vesta" (1601)
Giovanni Gabrieli (1557-1613):
   Canzona in the Seventh Mode (1597)
	Paintings of Parmigianino and Bronzino
	Rabelais, *Gargantua* (1535)
	St. Ignatius of Loyola, *Spiritual Exercises* (1548)
	Cellini, *Autobiography* (1558-1562)
	Venetian and Roman painting: Titian, Tintoretto, Veronese, Caravaggio
	El Greco, *Burial of the Count of Orgaz* (1586)
	Montaigne, *Essays* (1588)
	Spenser, *The Faerie Queene* (1590s)
	Shakespeare, first plays (ca. 1590)
		Jesuit Order founded (1539)
		Copernicus' theory of solar system (1543)
		Catholic Counter-Reformation:
		   Council of Trent (1545-1563)
		"Elizabethan England" (1558-1603)
		Turks defeated by Spanish and Italians at Lepanto (Greece, 1571)
		Spanish power curbed: the Armada defeated in England (1588)

A. THE RENAISSANCE AND MUSIC

Renaissance means rebirth or revival, a restoration of vitality after a time of decline. Western culture has known various revivals through the ages, sparked by admiration for some attractive civilization of the past. None has been loftier in aspirations or richer in achievements than the Renaissance of the fifteenth and sixteenth centuries, when European artists and intellectuals gradually turned from the austerity of medieval thought to seek models in the ample heritage of classical Greece and Rome. The release of creative energies and the opening up of human values that marked the arts and ideas in the fifteenth century spelled an end of the Middle Ages and an enthusiastic beginning to modern times. At the start the Renaissance was an Italian creation that began to take shape as far back as the 1300s in the Tuscan metropolis of Florence. It reached its first substantial flowering there around 1420, and by the late 1400s the new spirit of the Florentines was spreading across Europe, assuming distinctive national colorings wherever it went. Yet whether in France, Germany, the Netherlands, Spain, or England, the Italianate inspiration would always remain evident.

The World View of the Renaissance

The world view of the declining medieval epoch was summed up in a widely admired manual of fifteenth-century piety, *The Imitation of Christ:* "All that I might desire or imagine for my consolation, I expect, not in this world but in the world of the hereafter." The world view of the burgeoning Renaissance was summed up in the famous statement of Protagoras, the friend of Socrates in ancient Athens, "Mankind is the measure of all things"; and in the words of the Roman playwright Terence (second century B.C.), "I hold nothing that is human foreign to me." For many intervening centuries the dominant philosophy had been one of denying this world and mortifying its flesh. Now the Renaissance began to restore human beings to their own world. It looked for fulfillment in the present; it let individuals be the judges of their knowledge, the shapers of their destiny. To be sure, this did not begin with a blanket rejection of the medieval past. There was a gentle shifting of beliefs, a freeing of sensibilities. God remained the autocratic primal force, but in a manner that was a little less severe, a little more benevolent, granting a greater choice to mortals. The change can be seen in the paintings of Giotto (d. ca. 1337), who portrayed distinctive personalities in three-dimensional flesh rather than in the flat, stylized figures of his predecessors. Another Florentine, the poet Petrarch (d. 1374), wrote sensuous love lyrics that took as their object Madonna Laura, a flesh-and-blood woman, not the older medieval stereotype of the adored woman as a spiritual symbol. Petrarch also expanded the cultural horizons of his time by his intensive study of the Greek and Latin classics. In the fifteenth century there were more Florentines: The painter Masaccio (1401-1428?) showed scenes in a realistic three-dimensional perspective; the sculptor Donatello (ca. 1386-1466) turned to vibrant fleshy nudes after the long medieval tradition of wrapping shapeless bodies in stone or wooden draperies. By the late fifteenth century all Italy was awakened to a new optimism. A philosopher proclaimed that "God endowed humans from birth with the seeds of every possibility." And the optimism readily translated into opportunism. The Medici Pope Leo X reportedly observed on his accession, "Let us enjoy the papacy since God has given it to us."

Genius was all about. The paragon of universal abilities was Leonardo da Vinci (1452-1519), who was not only a supreme artist but also a scientist, philosopher, and musician. There was Michelangelo (1475-1564), a poet as well as sculptor, architect, and painter; and the brawling writer and bronzesmith Benvenuto Cellini (1500-1571). Even less gifted individuals like Castiglione's model *Courtier* (1528) were supposed to be well-rounded in their accomplishments and to use to advantage the talents they had. The exuberance of the age easily churned up into violence, brutality, poisonings, and murder, yet Renaissance culture prized above all the moderation professed by the ancients. It took for its own the Greek motto, "Nothing in excess": it aspired to the Ciceronian "moderation between too much and too little," to the "golden mean" of the Augustan poet Horace. In life and in art, the Renaissance ideals were the noble calm and judicious reserve of the ancient Platonic and Stoic philosophers, whose values seemed even to radiate from the mute stones of ancient temples and statuary.

The Spirit of Humanism

Humanism is a word that often comes up in considering the Renaissance. Humanism is the spirit of the Renaissance. It is an attitude that places human dignity and "humane" values foremost. Today we speak of philosophy, literature, theater, art, and music as being the humanities. These were also the arenas of Renaissance humanistic thought, but, in addition, they included the disciplines of the political, natural, and exact sciences, which since Aristotle were considered as branches of philosophy. Renaissance humanism attempted to link its activities to those of the Greco-Roman past. The humanists probed the aspects of ancient civilization, hoping to profit from such examples. They found that many of their own interests had been taken to very high levels in the past. Most of the classical accomplishments were filtered out by the Middle Ages, whose single-minded purpose for a thousand years had been to perpetuate the Christian faith and

Anonymous, Madonna and Child. *Unemotional figures in a severe, late-medieval style (Italian ca. 1262).*

Giotto, Lamentation over Christ *(1305-1306). Personalized, emotional figures in the new Florentine style.*

to fulfill the promise of salvation. Now the fifteenth-century's humanists hoped to return to the cultural glory of the ancient Mediterranean world during the centuries leading up to the time of Christ. They accommodated themselves to the paganism of antiquity and began rehabilitating the wisdom and cultivating the beauty of Greece and Rome. What the humanists wanted was, in the words of a French poet, "to fly as high as the ancients."

They set to work with energy. Philosopher-scholars such as the Italian Ficino and the Dutch theologian Erasmus began to bypass the standard medieval authorities like St. Augustine (fourth century) and St. Thomas Aquinas (thirteenth century). In their search for knowledge they read Aristotle in the original Greek and rediscovered all of Plato, whom the Middle Ages read only in Latin selections. The humanists mastered the skills of expressing themselves in a flowery classic-style Latin, a more subtle and challenging language than medieval church Latin. Their books and correspondence are couched in elegantly antiquated Latin prose. Literary humanists sifted through the Greek and Latin poets, such as Pindar and Horace. Historians turned to the writings of Herodotus and Livy, some of which had barely survived the indifference of the intervening centuries. The Middle Ages had been content with simple religious dramas. The humanist playwrights now sought out the neglected relics of ancient tragedy and comedy. They revived the masterpieces of Aeschylus, Sophocles, Menander, and Aristophanes; and they went on to imitate them in the modern languages. The philosopher-scientists emulated

Botticelli's "Three Graces" shows the revived interest in sensuous forms (Florence, late fifteenth century).

Pintoricchio's Glorification of San Bernardino *has two Renaissance angels playing a recorder or* shawm *(an early oboe) and a rebec (Italian, ca. 1500).*

the ancient spirit of free inquiry and made startling, sometimes controversial discoveries—changing the world from flat to round, remapping the motions of the planets and stars, revising the medieval hierarchy of heaven, earth, and hell. Renaissance sculptors and architects unearthed models for their work in the rubble of ancient stones, treasures that had lain half-hidden for centuries.

Renaissance musicians too looked back to antiquity, but they could not satisfy their curiosity so easily. There was scarcely any ancient music for them to examine. Instead, the musical humanists had to feed their fancies on the ancient stories of music's compelling effects and on the Greeks' descriptions of their scales and modes. The lack of actual Greek and Roman music had a positive side since it left the composers relatively free to ponder fresh styles of their own. To be sure, certain aspects of ancient music invited imitation. Among these were the literary texts. Some Renaissance composers chose poetry for musical setting that incorporated the long and short syllables of classical verse meters. Composers also emulated the chromatic and enharmonic modes of the Greeks in music that was sprinkled with half-steps—and even smaller intervals. Classical drama was an important stimulus as humanist composers produced music in modern styles to accompany the revivals of ancient stage works. In late sixteenth-century Florence, a group of humanists even devised a musical style they touted as a descendant of the actors' musical

The Tempietto ("Little Temple") by Bramante directed the interest of church builders to Classical architectural designs (Rome, ca. 1500).

recitations in classical dramas. This led to the rise of opera (see Chapter 3). Yet by and large there was too little known about ancient music that could be translated into modern musical styles. Where Renaissance sculptors modeled themselves on supposed works by Phidias or Praxiteles, the Renaissance spirit in music manifested itself ultimately in features that were human and humane rather than classically humanistic. The composers turned to simpler, more readily grasped textures than those of the fourteenth century. They produced gentle, flowing rhythms and newly ingratiating harmonies, and they gave increasing attention to the clear and meaningful projection of literary texts. Some of these changes were already apparent around 1420, when the first phrase of Renaissance musical style began with the importation to the Continent of certain techniques that had been the hallmarks of English style.

B. THE EARLY RENAISSANCE (CA. 1420-1475)

The Northern Composers

As it did in the other arts, the Renaissance style in music began around 1420; but, surprisingly, it was not a creation of Italians. It was a synthesis fashioned by northerners—mainly French, Flemish, and Netherlandish composers—who took something of the newly humane spirit that was emerging in Italy and combined it with musical idioms that were partly nurtured in England to produce a novel style that became the musical representative of the age. A French poet writing around 1440 credited two of his contemporaries, Guillaume Dufay (ca. 1400-1474) and Gilles Binchois (ca. 1400-1460), with having developed "a new manner of making sprightly consonances," and with modeling themselves on the English idiom of John Dunstable (ca. 1385-1453), all of which helped make their music "joyous and notable." Throughout the fourteenth century, English music had kept alive some of the genial appeal of the thirteenth century's "Sumer is icumen in" and "The Oxford 'Major-Mode' Dance." When the pleasant sounding English harmonies reached the Continent in the early fifteenth century they were seized upon by local composers, who found them to be a refreshing alternative to the somewhat drier harmonies of their own inherited styles. The English drew particularly agreeable sounds from progressions of chords of the 1̂-3̂-5̂ type—from **triads** built of thirds. This harmonic idiom was a feature in the music of Dunstable and his English contemporaries Leonel Power (d. 1445) and Walter Frye (d. before 1475). It helped set the style of the Continental generation of the 1430s.

The leading composers of that Continental generation came from a little patch of northern Europe that now comprises northeastern France, Belgium, and Holland, but the style they created soon caught on and spread far beyond its homeland. Franco-Flemish and Netherlandish composers were in great demand throughout France—particularly at the brilliant ducal court of Burgundy—and also among the culture-hungry Italian cities where proud nobles and prosperous merchant families vied with well-endowed churches to snap up the best musical talents that were to be had. Northern singers and composers populated the Renaissance chapels of the Sforzas at Milan, the Estes at Ferrara and Modena, the Papal Chapel at Rome, and churches such as St. Mark's at Venice. The northern singers were prized for the sweetness and agility of their voices, the northern composers for their euphonious harmony and innovative counterpoint. Odd as it seems, fifteenth-century Italy, the fountainhead of the Renaissance, the native land of Fra Angelico, Botticelli, and Leonardo, drew its foremost musicians from abroad.

Guillaume Dufay

The composer who more than any other shaped the musical language of the early Renaissance was Guillaume Dufay. As Dufay's style changed during his long and illustrious career, so did the style of all European music. Dufay's works from the 1430s still show some

Hans Memling's Madonna and Child with Angel-Musicians *(fifteenth century) mirrors the serene world of Flemish piety found also in Dufay's* "Alma Redemptoris Mater."

of the angular melody and intricacy of rhythm found in French and Flemish music of the beginning of the century. By the 1460s, Dufay's style was smoothed out to graceful melodic curves and simple natural rhythms. Dufay was born about 1400, very likely near the town of Cambrai in northeast France where he enrolled as a choirboy in 1409. By about 1420, Dufay was on the east coast of Italy as court composer to the powerful Malatesta family of Rimini and Pesaro. He soon became a celebrity. During the 1420s and 1430s, he was in and out of Bologna, Florence, and the Papal Chapel at Rome. He was repeatedly called upon for music to solemnize important occasions, such as the election of a pope or the signing of a peace treaty. When the architect Brunelleschi's new dome for the cathedral of Florence was dedicated in 1436, it was Dufay who supplied the motet, "Nuper rosarum flores," heard at the ceremony. During the 1450s, Dufay returned to an earlier post with the Count of Savoy in northern Italy. Dufay returned to Cambrai in 1458 and remained there until his death in 1474. The musical leadership then passed to his disciple, the legendary Johannes Ockeghem (d. 1497), and from there to Ockeghem's disciple Josquin Des Prez (d. 1521). Those three great Franco-Flemish masters—Dufay, Ockeghem, and Josquin—led European musical styles through the first century of the Renaissance.

Dufay cultivated every musical genre of his time. He composed Masses for liturgical occasions, Latin motets for ceremonial and devotional occasions, and French and Italian polyphonic songs for the pleasures of his wealthy patrons. Dufay's motet "Alma Redemptoris Mater" was composed around 1430 in the first flush of the musical Renaissance. He took the stately old genre of church motet and gave it a fifteenth-century flair, applying some of the limber style he used in his secular songs or **chansons**. Along with other composers of his generation, Dufay refashioned the austere medieval motet to suit the humane sensibilities of the new times. "Alma Redemptoris Mater," however, retains one constant feature of early church polyphony. It still incorporates a pre-existent plainchant melody, a cantus firmus that runs throughout. For this motet, Dufay chose the particularly beautiful plainchant *Alma Redemptoris Mater,* honoring the Virgin Mary, which was composed in the eleventh century by the German monk Hermannus Contractus (Hermann the Lame). Every fifteenth-century worshipper knew this melody at its regular place in the Compline service; many would have sung it themselves, others would at least recognize its opening melodic arch on the word *Alma* ("Gracious"), which soars upward through a full octave before settling again (Ex. 2.1). Composers of medieval church polyphony normally put such a cantus firmus melody in the lowest voice of the polyphony and transformed its rhythms by slowing down or speeding up, so that a casual listener might no longer

△
Dufay: Motet, "Alma Redemptoris Mater" (Side 1, Band 5)

**Ex. 2.1. Plainchant Antiphon for the Virgin Mary,
Compline Service: "Alma Redemptoris Mater"**

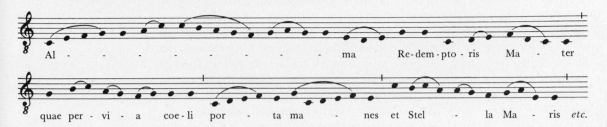

Al - - - - - - - ma Re-dem-pto-ris Ma - ter

quae per - vi - a coe-li por - ta ma - - - nes et Stel - la Ma - ris *etc.*

Alma Redemptoris Mater	Gracious Mother of the Redeemer
quae pervia coeli porta manes	who stayest at the portal of heaven
et Stella Maris	and Star of the Sea
succurre cadenti	take up the faltering
qui curat populo.	thou who watchest o'er the people.
Tu quae genuisti	Thou who didst bear,
natura mirante	to the wonderment of nature,
tuum sanctum Genitorem,	thy holy forbear,
Virgo prius ac posterius,	Thou Virgin first and last,
Gabrielis ab ore	from Gabriel's mouth
sumens illud Ave,	accepting the "Hail!"
peccatorum miserere.	be merciful to sinners.

recognize it. The church polyphony of the Renaissance composers still incorporated a plainchant cantus firmus, but there was less rhythmic distortion, less obscuring in the polyphonic web. In Dufay's motet, the venerable plainchant is in the topmost voice, where

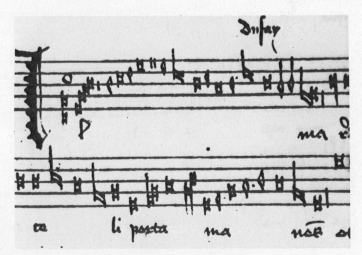

Dufay's "Alma Redemptoris Mater": the beginning of the uppermost part in a fifteenth-century manuscript; Dufay's name is at the top.

it can best be heard. It is not rhythmically distorted but is given a natural, songlike flow. It is directly graspable as melody. Dufay adds a gentle metric pulse to the plainchant's meterless rhythms, and he gives the whole plainchant the suppleness of one of his own chanson melodies by adding filler and embellishing notes that round out the original contours. This practice of subtly reshaping a plainchant to fit "modern" melodic style was adopted by the whole fifteenth century. It is called the **paraphrase technique.**

Dufay builds his whole motet upon the paraphrased version of the plainchant *Alma Redemptoris Mater,* which is heard throughout in the topmost voice. First, the soprano alone sings the distinctive opening melisma ("Alma") in Dufay's stylization (Ex. 2.2). Then,

Ex. 2.2. Motet (3 Voices): "Alma Redemptoris Mater" (Ca. 1430), Dufay

two lower voice-parts appear with an instrumental support where each voice-part develops its own melodic contour—each different in shape from the others. Such a **texture** is called **nonimitative polyphony** (see Fig. B.3.5). This type of polyphonic texture was favored during the late Middle Ages, and it remained a favorite of the composers of Dufay's generation, who from around 1420 to 1475 produced the first flourishing of the musical Renaissance.

Dufay's tranquil rhythms are based on a slow triple meter, with a pulse that, at times, is almost imperceptible. The melody of the paraphrased plainchant sometimes soars yet always is rounded. Together, the three voices are like a three-dimensional projection of the one-dimensional plainchant. Dufay maintains the texture of independent polyphonic strands until just before the motet's end. But there he changes and has the three voice-parts sing together in block chords (Ex. 2.3). Dufay wanted the final supplication to the Virgin ("accepting the 'Hail Mary,' be merciful to sinners") to be clearly understood, so he abandoned the complex texture woven of dissimilar melodic strands for the transparency of block chords.

Something else is notable about Dufay's closing chords. At first hearing they may seem to float aimlessly side by side. But on repeated hearings, one senses that they join together to form short connected phrases. Each phrase consists of a handful of chords (anywhere from two to six), and in each phrase the chords seem to be moving toward a final or "goal" chord. Such directional thrustings of harmonic phrases are only loosely held together in Dufay's style, yet his chordal phrases are mild-mannered forerunners of the more tightly linked, "goal-oriented" chord progressions that are found in the **tonal music** of the eighteenth and nineteenth centuries. In Dufay's "Alma Redemptoris Mater" the effect lacks urgency. The music is relaxed, ethereal; it has something that is similar to the gentle calm that radiates from madonnas by Rogier van der Weyden, the Van Eycks, Memling, and their fellow painters who were Dufay's contemporaries in the Northern Renaissance of the fifteenth century.

Colorplates 10, 11, and 12

Ex. 2.3. Chordal Conclusion of "Alma Redemptoris Mater," Dufay

su - mens   il - lud   A - ve,   pec - ca - to - rum   mi - se - re - re.

C. THE HIGH RENAISSANCE (CA. 1475-1530)

The Dominance of Imitative Polyphony

The hallmarks of early Renaissance musical style, beginning around 1420, were a smoother rhythm, a more transparent texture, and a fresh style of harmony based on consonant triads that were beginning to be linked in emotionally persuasive chord progressions. The musical High Renaissance, beginning around 1475, had as its major novelty a preference for **imitative polyphony**, a texture in which two or more voices copy or "imitate" the same melody that a first voice has sung (see Fig. B.3.4). The techniques of imitative polyphony were known in the Middle Ages (they appear in "Sumer is icumen in"; Chapter 1), but they were used sparingly. It was around 1475 that imitative polyphony became the dominating musical texture—in the works of Josquin Des Prez (ca. 1440-1521) and his major contemporaries, Jacob Obrecht, Pierre de la Rue, Jean Mouton, Heinrich Isaac, and Loyset Compère. The masses, motets, and chansons of those masters, all of whom were Flemings or Netherlanders, established the supremacy of imitative texture, which remained at the crest of musical style from the late 1400s through the time of Bach and Handel in the middle 1700s. During that entire period, the idea of composing music with a serious, high-minded purpose generally meant employing an imitative style.

Something else affected music during the High Renaissance. At Mainz, in about the year 1456, the German printer Johann Gutenberg produced the famous "42-line Bible," which helped launch the art of printing from movable type. That art spread quickly through the rest of Europe. Printing was congenial to the Renaissance spirit of free inquiry and access to information. It made religious, literary, and humanistic texts more readily available than the laboriously handwritten manuscripts of the past had been. Printing also made music available to a growing public, circulating it to aristocrats and burghers who wanted to sing and play the latest novelties for themselves. In 1501 at Venice, the first polyphonic music collection featuring the new process appeared. Issued by the pioneering music printer Ottaviano de' Petrucci, it was a songbook called the *Odhecaton,* or "Hundred Songs." It was the first of many such music books. Josquin and his musical compatriots were well represented among the polyphonic songs of the *Odhecaton.* They were the first composers to reach an international public through the medium of print.

Josquin Des Prez

Josquin Des Prez, the prime figure of the first musical generation of the High Renaissance, was the first "modern" composer in the

Death Takes an Old Woman, Hans Holbein the Younger (149—1543); a familiar theme after the Black Death overran Europe the 1340s. Here Death's companion adds morbid glee by playing a xylophone.

sense that his music speaks readily to us and can be grasped as a direct esthetic experience without any great need to compensate for the distance between two different musical and cultural worlds. Josquin was born around 1440, either in the northeastern French province of Picardy or in the adjacent French-speaking region of Flanders. The same general area bordering on the North Sea produced most of the early Renaissance masters, including Dufay and Binchois, as well as most of their immediate successors, notably Johannes Ockeghem (d. 1497) and Antoine Busnois (d. 1492). During Josquin's youth, as in Dufay's, the path for talented North European musicians still led south to the wealthy Italian cities. The young Josquin was at Milan for twenty years, first as a singer at that city's cathedral from 1459 through 1472. Then, until 1479, Josquin was in the service of the Sforza family. During the late 1480s and 1490s, he served at the Papal Chapel at Rome, where Dufay had been before him. In 1489, Josquin composed music for a Sforza wedding, where he may have known Leonardo da Vinci, who was also involved in the festivities. In 1503-1504 he was at the court of the Estes at Ferrara, and later on he may have frequented the circle of Louis XII at Paris and that of the music-loving Queen Margaret of Austria, who held court in Flanders. During the last fifteen years of his phenomenally successful career, Josquin remained in his native northland.

Personal details about Renaissance composers are very rare, but Josquin was so remarkable a figure that he drew more than casual attention. An emissary of the Duke of Ferrara who was charged with selecting a composer for the ducal chapel reported back in 1502 that Josquin's rival Heinrich Isaac "was better able to get along with his colleagues and composes new pieces more readily, [but] Josquin composes better music. Yet he works only when it suits him, not when asked." Josquin also wanted to be paid 200 ducats while Isaac would have been content with 120, but the Duke had the sense to hire Josquin. The whole age acknowledged his excellence. Martin Luther observed that Josquin alone was "the master of the notes: where other composers do as the notes wish, the notes do as Josquin wishes."

Josquin left about 200 compositions in all. One hundred of them are Latin motets in earnest styles, and there are about 20 settings of the Ordinary of the Mass. Another 75 compositions are lively French and Italian chansons. The basis of Josquin's musical idiom was the flowery polyphonic texture of his Flemish-Netherlandish forebears. But he turned away from the technique of nonimitative polyphony that was preferred by the Dufay generation and cultivated the newly popular technique of imitative polyphony. Josquin also took the chordal declamation (block chords) that was finding favor in Dufay's style and enlivened it with brisk rhythms of the kind found in Italian songs of his own time. Beyond these purely musical factors, Josquin was concerned with the projection of verbal texts. Increasingly in his music the words are emphatically declaimed and made clearly understandable. Josquin, more than any other composer, put all those elements together and created the High Renaissance musical style, illumining his synthesis with the ingenuity that so delighted Luther. Josquin's imagination and musical wit are of an order that Western music had not known before and has only rarely known since.

Josquin's Mass titled *Ave maris stella* maintains the age-old custom of building church polyphony around a cantus firmus—of incorporating a pre-existent melody in the harmony. But instead of using individual plainchant melodies of the Kyrie, Gloria, Credo, Sanctus, and Agnus Dei as the basis for the individual movements of this polyphonic Mass, Josquin imposes an overall musical unity on the entire Ordinary by basing all five movements on the same melodic materials. This practice of musically interrelating the movements of a polyphonic Mass was begun in Dufay's time. Dufay and his contemporaries sometimes even used popular tunes rather than sacred plainchants as the basis for their polyphonic Masses. It was a symptom of the growing secularism of the Renaissance. But Josquin's borrowing in this Mass is sacred. His cantus firmus is a beloved plainchant hymn for the Virgin Mary, *Ave maris stella—Hail, Star of the Sea* (Ex. 2.4). By employing this hymn melody in all five movements, Josquin in effect dedicates the entire Mass to the veneration of the Virgin. The plainchant is paraphrased throughout in the tenor of each movement, much as the plainchant of "Alma Redemptoris Mater" is paraphrased throughout the soprano of Dufay's motet (see page 55). Josquin is no longer content, however, with limiting the paraphrase to just a single line of the polyphonic texture. Instead, he applies the techniques of imitative polyphony and lets the melodic substance of the hymn permeate all four voices of the polyphonic texture. The result is an equal-voice imitative texture—a free imitative polyphony where all the voices share in the same melodic material and have almost equal musical importance.

Ex. 2.4. Plainchant Hymn: "Ave maris stella"

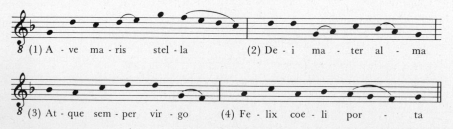

(1) A - ve ma - ris stel - la   (2) De - i ma - ter al - ma

(3) At - que sem - per vir - go   (4) Fe - lix coe - li por - ta

Hail, Star of the Sea, gracious Mother of God, ever virgin, happy gate of heaven.

Josquin divides the text of the Gloria into short phrases:

△
Josquin Des Prez: Gloria
in Excelsis from *Missa Ave
maris stella*
(Side 1, Band 6)

Gloria in excelsis Deo,
   (sung by the Priest)
	Glory to God in the highest,
	   (sung by the Priest)

Et in terra pax hominibus,
   bonae voluntatis.
 Laudamus te,
 Benedicimus te,
 Adoramus te,
 Glorificamus te,
 Gratias agimus tibi
 Propter magnam gloriam tuam.
 Domine Deus, rex coelestis,
 Deus Pater omnipotens.
 Domine, Fili unigenite,
 Jesu Christe:
 Domine Deus,
 Agnus Dei,
 Filius Patris
	And on earth peace to men
	   of good will.
	 We praise thee,
	 We bless thee,
	 We adore thee,
	 We glorify thee,
	 We give thee thanks
	 For thy great glory.
	 O Lord God, heavenly King,
	 God the Father almighty.
	 O Lord, only-begotten Son,
	 Jesus Christ:
	 O Lord Lord,
	 Lamb of God,
	 Son of the Father,

Qui tollis peccata mundi, *Miserere nobis;* *Qui tollis peccata mundi,* *Suscipe deprecationem nostram;* *Qui sedes ad dexteram Patris,* *Miserere nobis.* *Quoniam tu solus Sanctus,* *Tu solus Dominus,* *Tu solus altissimus,* *Jesu Christe.* *Cum sancto Spiritu,* *In gloria Dei Patris.* *Amen.*	Who takest away the sins of the world, Have mercy on us; Who takest away the sins of the world, Receive our prayer; Who sittest at the Father's right hand, Have mercy on us. For thou alone art Holy, Thou alone art Lord, Thou alone art most high, O Jesus Christ. Together with the Holy Spirit, In the Glory of God the Father. Amen.

For each phrase he invents some distinctive musical idea that sharpens the rhythm and enhances the declamation of the words. The opening words, *Gloria in excelsis Deo,* were always reserved for the priest to sing in plainchant, so the polyphony begins at *Et in terra* with a duet that entwines the two upper voices in imitations (Ex. 2.5). When the tenor and bass voices enter at *Gratias agimus tibi,* they still imitate the music of the opening *Et in terra* with its characteristic upward leap of a fifth. Thereafter, Josquin chooses freely among musical styles. At *Propter magnam,* he introduces one of his favorites: duets that answer one another in pairs, alternating between high and low voices. Elsewhere Josquin has the succinct declamation of block chords. About halfway through, at *Qui tollis peccata mundi,* the mood turns solemn, reflecting the emphasis of the text on Jesus as the Redeemer of the world's sins. The music at

Ex. 2.5. Opening Duo of Gloria from *Missa Ave maris stella*, Josquin Des Prez

Ex. 2.6. An Example of a Point of Imitation

that moment offers a classic example of the High Renaissance **point of imitation**, which is a set of imitative entries where each voice in turn presents the same melodic fragment (Ex. 2.6). This is the basic technique employed in free imitative polyphony, thus it is the chief component of High Renaissance musical styles, where whole compositions may be formed as chains of successive points of imitation. This movement of the Mass goes on to other quartets, trios, and duos made up of imitative entries, with each new set of entries built on a new morsel of text. Each is a new point of imitation. Approaching the end, the sounds become richer and the thickening polyphony and intensifying rhythms reach their peak in the final *Amen*. It is a powerful ending, with some of the same fervor that we experience in the music of Bach or Beethoven. Such massive psychological impact was new with Josquin's High Renaissance generation.

Josquin's *Missa Ave maris stella* was published at Venice by Petrucci in 1505. It was probably composed in Italy during the two or three preceding years. The first decade of the sixteenth century saw the publication in Italy of many of the landmark achievements of High Renaissance music, including many of the chief works of Josquin, Obrecht, and Pierre de la Rue. That same decade also saw the flowering of High Renaissance styles in art and architecture. Michelangelo produced the Vatican Pietà in 1501 and the monumental David at Florence in 1504. Leonardo painted the Mona Lisa in 1503. In 1506, the architect Bramante began rebuilding St. Peter's Basilica on a classical plan. Those first-rank artists of the High Renaissance were all Italians. The first-rank composers of the era were all born north of the Alps. Yet Josquin and his musical compatriots came south to enjoy the Italian economic sunshine, and there they basked in the cultural warmth of the humanistic revival. The composers and the artists were different in their media and their nationalities, but they came to share the same esthetic outlook, the same esteem for moderation, naturalness, and grace. Renaissance composers and artists had the technical skills to shape whatever their imaginations proposed. They exercised a long-lost freedom, joining tasteful restraint with human warmth to produce a revival of the classical equilibrium between the intellectual and emotional components of artistic expression. With a rare balance between the mind and the senses, they produced psychological truths having a substance and sharpness that eluded the Middle Ages. Looking back now at the High Renaissance, its achievements may seem to be more compelling in the fine arts than in music—more affecting in the paintings of Leonardo and the sculptures of Michelangelo than in the Masses or chansons of Josquin and Pierre de la Rue. That is deceptive. Performances of Renaissance music that are historically true to their times are becoming more widespread. As they do, the musical language of Josquin and his contemporaries will speak ably for itself.

Colorplates 13 and 14

Josquin's music has the same directness and universality that we find in the greatest visual artists of the Renaissance, and in the greatest composers—Bach, Mozart, Beethoven—of later times.

D. THE LATE RENAISSANCE (CA. 1530-1600)

The innovations of the early Renaissance in music were focused on the emergence of pleasant-sounding consonant triads as the basic harmonies. The High Renaissance added imitative polyphony and a clearer projection of verbal texts. Finally, the late Renaissance turned to the heightening music's expressive capabilities. The composers of the middle and late 1500s strove as never before to impress their listeners with the sensuous beauty and power of musical sounds. Consonant harmonies were made fuller and intermixed with ever more provocative dissonances. Textures were expanded, blown up to five, six, eight, even twelve voices, instead of the standard four voices of the Josquin era or the three of Dufay. Choruses were strengthened with more singers to each part. On occasion brass and wind instruments lent further force and variety, sometimes replacing the singing voices altogether. Two or more choirs would engage in dialogues across the width of a church, adding the elements of competition and physical space to the musical experience. In adopting these techniques, the late Renaissance was not only seeking to enhance the impact of purely musical sounds but also to render more vividly the emotions and meanings of the words.

Martin Luther (1483-1546), in plementing the Protestant Refc mation, translated the Mass in German, as shown here in a pub cation of 1526.

Giovanni Pierluigi da Palestrina

To the modern mind, the composer who typifies late Renaissance music is Giovanni Pierluigi da Palestrina. His surname comes from his birthplace, the small town of Palestrina outside of Rome. His whole career was spent in the orbit of Vatican City. He had a relatively tranquil life. Happily married to a girl from his native town, he was unexpectedly dismissed from the papal choir in 1555 by the incoming Pope Paul IV because his marriage violated the rules of the Sistine Chapel. He was quickly named choirmaster at St. John Lateran; then he held a similar post at Saint Mary Major. Finally, in 1571, he returned to a permanent post at St. Peter's.

Palestrina reached artistic maturity in the 1550s. It was a time when Italy was again producing international-class composers. Since about 1400, Italy had borrowed its chief musicians from the North. The middle and late 1500s were still notable for Flemish and Netherlandish masters who either journeyed to Italy or enjoyed great reputations there—composers such as Gombert, Clemens non Papa, Willaert, Rore, Monte, and Lassus. But, by the middle 1500s, native

Italian composers were asserting leadership in musical styles, just as the Italians had been the leaders in the other arts since the early Renaissance. An Italian domination of European musical styles that began in the late sixteenth century with Palestrina, Marenzio, Vecchi, Ruffo, Porta, Andrea and Giovanni Gabrieli, and Monteverdi continued to be unmatched by any other musical nation until the advent of the Germans Bach and Handel in the eighteenth century.

Palestrina's large output runs to nearly a thousand musical works. They include over one hundred Masses, five hundred motets, and nearly one hundred and fifty secular Italian songs called madrigals (see page 68). Palestrina's *Pope Marcellus Mass* was probably composed during the years 1562-63. This was the time of the Counter-Reformation, when the Church, spurred in part by the inroads made by the Protestant Reformation, was engaged in purging itself, renouncing medieval abuses, and rekindling its spirituality. New guidelines were being promulgated by the reform Council of Trent, which met from 1545-63, and a purer mode of life was being exemplified by some, such as St. Philip Neri (d. 1595) at Rome. The *Pope Marcellus Mass* was composed at just the time when the Council, as a preliminary to winding up its affairs, was addressing the problems of church music. What troubled the bishops gathered in the northern Italian city of Trent was that the music of their time so often distorted and obscured its sacred texts within the folds of thick polyphonic textures. A movement for reform was afoot. Pope Pius IV was ready to propose a ban on church polyphony and a return to simple plainchant. Palestrina, the most eminent of Italian church musicians, evidently responded to this threat by composing the *Pope Marcellus Mass.* Defending his craft and his livelihood, he tried to show that church music could remain dignified and its sacred words intelligible even in an artful, contemporary polyphonic style. The name of Pope Marcellus, invoked in the title of this Mass, referred to an earlier pope, Marcellus II, who during a short reign of three weeks in April 1555 delivered a message to those in the Papal Chapel, Palestrina among them, admonishing that the liturgy's sacred texts must be kept clearly understandable for the listener. Seven years later at the reformers' Council, church composers were no longer admonished. Church polyphony itself was on trial. Supported by the example of Palestrina's *Pope Marcellus Mass* among others, polyphony won out, and the storehouse of Western music has been incalculably richer as a result.

In this Mass Palestrina gave full rein to the late Renaissance desire to be impressive. Defiantly, as if taking up a challenge, he adopted a complex six-voice texture. Yet through all the interweavings of its many melodic strands and the marshallings of choral sonorities, the words of the Ordinary remain more consistently intelligible than in most Masses of the preceding generation. Palestrina departed from

Palestrina presenting a collection of his Mass music to Pope Julius III in 1555.

earlier usage in one other respect. Following rare precedents that go back to the times of Josquin, and even Dufay, there are no segments of borrowed melody woven into this texture. This church polyphony no longer employs a cantus firmus. Palestrina lets the Renaissance spirit speak freely, with everything in the music being his own invention, calculated for direct sensuous effect.

△
Palestrina: Kyrie eleison from *Pope Marcellus Mass* (Side 1, Band 7)

The Kyrie is in three sections, each of which lasts just over a minute: 1) Kyrie eleison I, 2) Christe eleison, 3) Kyrie eleison II. The appeals to the Lord (Kyrie) and to Christ (Christe) for mercy (eleison) can be clearly understood even when all six voices are singing together. The opening Kyrie I is an extended point of imitation. It is built on a melodic fragment that is distinguished by the interval of a rising fourth. Each voice in turn presents its version of this melodic fragment. The tenor enters first (Ex. 2.7). The soprano imitates, adding a descending scale (Ex. 2.8). The bass simplifies. And so on through

Ex. 2.7.

Ex. 2.8.

the remaining voice entries. Palestrina's choirs, like those of his forerunners, made use only of male singers, with boys taking the higher parts. When all six voices are in motion together, the polyphony is too intricately woven for them to be traced individually. Generally the soprano is the easiest to hear because it is the highest. But all six voice-parts maintain the integrity of their individual lines in this equal-voice polyphony, and all contribute to the building of a stately climax at the end of Kyrie I. The Christe eleison offers contrast by avoiding an obvious use of imitative techniques. It obtains an undulating effect from long, smooth polyphonic strands. The closing Kyrie II returns to imitation with a fresh theme (Ex. 2.9), but soon

Ex. 2.9.

the descending scales of the opening Kyrie reappear and tie the entire movement of the Mass together. Everything is serene and mellifluous, like an earthly foretaste of heavenly grace. There were still angular melodic skips and unexpected dissonances in harmony in the musical style of Josquin Des Prez. In Palestrina's honeyed style, such things are all smoothed out. Palestrina's style represents the full bloom of late Renaissance sonority. It is a purely vocal style, which is known also as the **a cappella** style because the music was composed just for the *cappella,* or voices of the choir, without any mixture of instruments. In later ages, people looked back at the Palestrina style, and particularly at the *Pope Marcellus Mass,* in curiosity and awe. They knew that this music helped save church polyphony in its hour of trial during the Counter-Reformation, and they shared the sixteenth century's view of it as representing a pinnacle of musical art. "The style is grave, the harmony pure," observed Charles Burney, an eighteenth-century friend of Samuel Johnson and author of a respected music history. The twentieth-century composer Hans Pfitzner embroidered the legend further in the late-Romantic opera *Palestrina* (1917).

Palestrina's music shares with the music of Dufay and Josquin the quality of musical sound called **modal.** That is, Renaissance music is still *modal* music based on outgrowths of the medieval church modes, rather than *tonal* music based on the major and minor modes that prevailed during the eighteenth and nineteenth centuries. Palestrina's Kyrie begins with a harmonic sound close to G major, yet it is not really G major. For one thing, it lacks the F-sharp—the seventh degree of the G major scale. It has an F-natural as the seventh degree of its scale (a white-key scale from G to G), and the F-natural helps give the music its archaic, modal character. Palestrina's harmonies flow back and forth among a small number of chords, mainly those based on G, F, C, and A. Compared with the tonal harmonies of Bach or Mozart, Palestrina's modal harmonies are less focused on a home or tonic chord. Renaissance composers did not feel obliged to begin and end a piece in the same mode or key, something that tonal composers would always do. Palestrina's Kyrie begins with a focus on the scale of white keys from G to G—the Renaissance's Mixolydian mode (see Fig. B.1.12); thereafter this alternates with a focus on the scale of white keys from C to C—the Renaissance's Ionian mode (see Fig. B.1.12). Kyrie I ends in Ionian; the Christe eleison moves from Ionian to Mixolydian; and Kyrie II again ends in Ionian. Those modal names are Greek, but the sounds of the Renaissance modes have nothing to do with the ancient Greek modes and little to do with the sounds of the medieval church modes. The old names persisted because they were prized by the Renaissance as trappings of antiquity—embellishments of the façade of musical humanism. By the century after Palestrina's time, most vestiges of the old modal harmonies were swept away by the newer sounds of major-minor tonality. The major mode was itself descended from the Renaissance's Ionian mode (the scale from C to C), and the minor mode came chiefly from the Renaissance's Aeolian mode (the scale of white keys from A to A; see Fig. B.1.12). Both the major and minor modes had strong focuses on their **tonic** pitches. The almost inviolable rule of a tonal piece was that it must begin and end in the same key. Thus where Palestrina's modal music moved to sometimes unpredictable harmonic destinations, very large pieces of tonal music would be unified by the organizing control of a single "home" or tonic key.

E. LATE RENAISSANCE ENTERTAINMENT MUSIC: THE MADRIGAL

The Italian Madrigal

During the middle sixteenth century, Italy came forward with a new genre of polyphonic song called the **madrigal**. Madrigals were the vocal chamber music of the late Italian Renaissance. They were social music for solo singers, two or more of whom stood or sat, half-facing one another, and entertained themselves and an assembled company with resourceful, witty pieces that stimulated the spirits and sensibilities. Madrigal poems were usually short lyric verses, packed with delicate sentiments. The novelty of the madrigal music was that it vividly illustrated the meanings and emotions in the poems. The earliest madrigals date from around 1530, and they drew on both the Franco-Flemish style of imitative polyphony found in Josquin's works and the emphatic chordal declamation found in certain Italian songs of the early 1500s called *frottolas*. The first important madrigalists were mainly Northern composers who were active in Italy, such as Jacques Arcadelt, Philippe Verdelot, and Adrian Willaert, though with them was an Italian, Costanzo Festa. By the 1550s madrigals were becoming highly expressive utterances, and their production was firmly in the hands of young Italians such as Palestrina, who published a collection of youthful madrigals in 1555. Later in the sixteenth century, Italian madrigal composers included Luca Marenzio, Andrea Gabrieli, Carlo Gesualdo, and Claudio Monteverdi. They led an already ripe style to unprecedented expression and refinement. The madrigal was by then the great international genre that fascinated everyone. It made a triumphal procession to the Netherlands, Germany, and France. Among the Northerners who cultivated the mature madrigal style were Orlandus Lassus at Munich and Philippe de Monte at Vienna and Prague. The madrigals took root in England, where they were adopted at first in their original Italian—which had become the language of Pan-European culture—and then were translated and imitated in English.

Two Gentlemen of Verona, *one playing a lute (late fifteenth century).*

Madrigals were meant for fairly skilled solo performers—one performer to each voice-part—and for small, sophisticated groups of listeners. With their emphases on elegance and cleverness, they were quite different from the expansive and solemn works of choral polyphony that filled church interiors. If a Mass by Palestrina can be compared to a symphony, then a madrigal is like a string quartet. The essence of any madrigal is in its text. The whole point of the music is to ingeniously reflect the meanings contained in the poetry. Madrigal composers vied with one another in translating the meanings of individual words and poetic phrases into striking musical images. In their quest for novelty and expression, they pushed musical style to new extremes of chromatic harmony and rhythmic variety.

The Madrigal in England

When the madrigal vogue reached England during the later years of Queen Elizabeth's long reign (1558-1603), Italianate things fascinated everyone, as is evident from Shakespeare's plays, which began to appear in the late 1580s. Hundreds of madrigals with English texts were printed during a peak period that lasted from 1588 to about 1616. A contemporary observer described Elizabethan England as "a nest of singing birds." At first, the English composers modeled themselves on celebrated Italian contemporaries such as Marenzio, Croce, Gastoldi, and Alfonso Ferrabosco the Elder. Ferrabosco actually settled in England. But later, there were madrigals in more English styles. Among the best of the native madrigalists were Thomas Morley, Thomas Weelkes, John Wilbye, and William Byrd.

Weelkes's madrigal for six voices, "As Vesta was from Latmos hill descending," appeared in 1601 in an ambitious collection titled *The Triumphs of Oriana.* This anthology contained two dozen madrigals

△
Weelkes: "As Vesta was from Latmos hill descending"
(Side 1, Band 8)

by as many composers, all of them honoring the queen, praising her under the name of "Oriana." Weelkes's poem describes an encounter between the "maiden queen" of England and the goddess Vesta of the ancient Romans, the patron of the Vestal Virgins. When Vesta's attendants come upon Elizabeth/Oriana, they abandon their own mistress to pay homage to the English queen (Ex. 2.10). Compared with other English verse of the time by Shakespeare (b. 1564), Ben Jonson (b. 1572), or John Donne (b. 1572), this poetry is thin. But it needs no excuse. It was chosen not for poetic quality, but as a vehicle for musical display. Thus it is filled with suggestive words and phrases that the madrigal composer can match to illustrative

Ex. 2.10. An Example of Word Painting in an Elizabethan Madrigal: "As Vesta was from Latmos hill descending," Weelkes

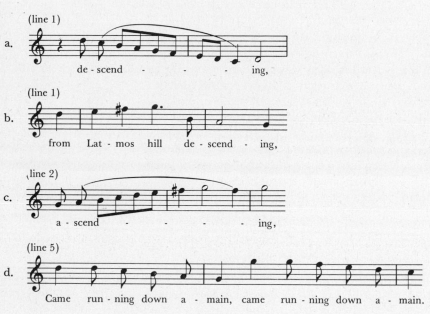

(1) As Vesta was from Latmos hill descending,
(2) She spied a maiden queen the same ascending,
(3) Attended on by all the shepherds swain,
(4) To whom Diana's darlings
(5) Came running down amain.
(6) First two by two,
(7) Then three by three together,
(8) Leaving their goddess all alone, hasted thither,
(9) And mingling with the shepherds of her train
(10) With mirthful tunes her presence entertain.
(11) *Refrain:* Then sang the shepherds and nymphs of Diana,
(12)   Long live fair Oriana!

turns of rhythm, melody, and harmony. Weelkes gives the word "descending" (line 1) a descending scale (Ex. 2.10a); "Latmos hill descending" (line 1) has a hill-shaped melody (Ex. 2.10b); "a maiden queen ascending" (line 2) has ascending scales (Ex. 2.10c); "Came running down amain" (line 5) has a rush of falling notes (Ex. 2.10d). Such musical translations of the text are called **word illustrations**, **word paintings**, or **madrigalisms**. Some of Weelkes's other madrigalisms are more symbolic and less pictorial. "First two by two" (line 6) is sung by precisely two voices; "Then three by three" (line 7), by three voices; at the word "together," all six voices join in. When Diana is left "all alone" (line 8), a lone soprano delivers those words. The madrigal closes with the queen's refrain, "Long live fair Oriana." This is set to serene and mellifluous music that Weelkes keeps repeating in order to suggest the endless serenity of Elizabeth's reign.

Madrigal music tried to fit its words like a glove. Composers wanted music of real substance, but they also wanted to squeeze every drop of suggestion from the poetry. Sometimes the madrigals run to high emotions. The ardors and frustrations of love may be pictured in the musical imagery of suffering and death. At other times, there is gaiety and spoofing. Madrigals were for connoisseurs who relished the clever effects. Often the listeners were performers themselves, cultivated amateurs in the best spirit of the Renaissance, who like Castiglione's *Courtier* were modestly accomplished in music as one side of a many-sided competence. The later Italian madrigals, dating from around 1600, demanded virtuoso professionals who brought the same precision and flair to their performances that we expect today from a string quartet. But the English madrigals of that time—Weelkes's time— remained more in the genteel amateur tradi-

An outdoor concert (middle sixteenth century).

Singers of a four-part madrigal or chanson (middle sixteenth century).

tion. Madrigals nowadays are chiefly a pastime for passive listeners, yet they are listeners who are alert enough to the illustrative possibilities in the poetry to relish the artful twists that composers give them.

The production of madrigals came to an end with the end of the Renaissance, but the word illustrations or madrigalisms, which were the common coins of both the Italian and English madrigals, continued to endear themselves to European tastes for another two centuries. They spread into the madrigals' successors—the cantatas, operas, and oratorios of the early seventeenth century—and were still a prominent factor in the musical languages of Bach and Handel in the early eighteenth century. They continue to turn up as witty touches in the late eighteenth-century styles of Haydn, Mozart, and others.

F. FROM RENAISSANCE TO BAROQUE: THE VENETIAN POLYCHORAL STYLE

The Emergence of Venice as a Leader in Musical Styles

The composers of the late Renaissance did their utmost to grasp their listeners' attention and to stir them with arresting effects. Behind the clever mannerisms of an English madrigal or the animated spirit of a Palestrina Mass lay the common aim of making a strong impression. Nowhere was this more amply realized than in the Venetian music of the late sixteenth century. Renaissance Venice had the sparkle of the Adriatic waters and the assurance of its enormous wealth in everything it did. Set right in the sea and honeycombed with canals instead of streets, its gaudy palaces, colorful piazzas, and gorgeous churches made Venice a showcase of Renaissance splendor, the most beautiful city in Europe. The Venetian light and color were captured by painters such as Gentile and Giovanni Bellini, Giorgione, Titian, and Veronese, who carried the singular qualities of Venetian painting through the sixteenth century, recording the flavor and brilliance of the "Serene Republic," as its self-assured citizenry called their metropolis. Venetian music of the sixteenth century shows a similar vigor. By the close of the Renaissance, Venice had become the leader of European musical styles.

The religious and musical life of the city revolved about the venerable church of San Marco (St. Mark's) and the two spacious outdoor piazzas that front it on the south and west sides. San Marco, a multidomed structure on the plan of an equal-armed Byzantine cross, was begun in the mid-eleventh century. During the high Middle Ages it was adorned with Byzantine mosaics, and by the sixteenth century it was, much as today, a hoary near-Eastern gem in a jewel-like setting

Venice, St. Mark's Church and Square, in an eighteenth-century view by Canaletto.

of pastel-hued Renaissance palaces. During much of the sixteenth century, Flemish composers held the prestigious musical posts at San Marco. The famous Adrian Willaert presided there from 1527 until his death in 1562. He was succeeded by another Fleming, his disciple Cipriano de Rore. Then the Italians took over, chief among them Andrea Gabrieli from 1566 to 1586, and then his nephew Giovanni Gabrieli from 1586 to 1612.

San Marco in Willaert's time was already noted for its organ music and the pealing of instruments that enlivened its outdoor processions. The Venetian taste for splendor also found an outlet in a novel musical texture. Abandoning to some extent the imitative polyphony of the High Renaissance, San Marco's composers of the middle 1500s began to concentrate on a texture of block chords. The chords were given to two separately placed choirs that engaged in spirited dialogues, thrusting their sonorities across the open spaces of the church. This dialoguing, **polychoral** style of the Venetians (*polychoral* means more than one choir) was encouraged by a feature of San Marco's architecture: Facing one another across the apse were two open galleries that served as separate choir and organ lofts. On occasion the number of competing choirs rose to three or four, as composers took advantage of the church's other galleries and network of elevated walkways and placed their musicians so that sounds seemingly issuing from everywhere echoed among the ceiling's gold-encrusted domes.

At first, the Venetians' polychoral, dialogue style was applied to church motets where instruments joined with voices. Then, the participation of voices was sometimes abandoned and the polychoral style was also applied to purely instrumental works called **sonatas** and **canzonas**. A *sonata* was music that was "sounded by instruments" rather than sung by voices. The word came from the Italian

Instrumentalists, ca. 1570

Lute.   *Organ.*   *Bass recorder.*   *Tenor Viol.*

suonare, meaning "to sound." A *canzona* was originally an instrumental genre of the early 1500s that imitated French polyphonic chansons. *Canzona* was the Italian word for chanson. Later the canzonas freed themselves from vocal models and developed their own styles. Their instrumental tone colors stood out well within church interiors, and when wind or brass instruments were used they made a fine impression in the outdoor piazzas. Toward the end of the sixteenth century, the Venetians' instrumental sonatas and canzonas were combined with the polychoral textures of the church motets to produce the first monumental works of Western instrumental music.

The Polychoral Style of Gabrieli

Giovanni Gabrieli's Canzona in the Seventh Mode (No. 2 of his publication of 1597) calls for two instrumental choirs of four voices each—eight instrumental parts in all. The two choirs must be placed far enough apart so that a listener will sense the gap between them. Gabrieli's printed music does not tell which instruments he had in mind, but he probably wanted brass. In other works, he was one of the first composers to prescribe specific instrumentation. Gabrieli's seventh mode in this canzona is the same as the Mixolydian mode used by Palestrina in the *Pope Marcellus Mass.* It has a white-key scale from G to G. The canzona begins with an emphatic musical statement by the first choir in block chords. That same music is sent right back by the second choir (Ex. 2.11). Then the vigorous exchanges continue, shunting the listener's ears back and forth. Medieval plainchant had *antiphonal* performance of this sort, where the music is divided between two choirs, as in the Kyrie eleison discussed in Chapter 1. But earlier polyphony had focused on a single nucleus

△
Giovanni Gabrieli: Canzona in the Seventh Mode (No. 2, 1597)
(Side 2, Band 1)

Ex. 2.11. Beginning of Canzona in the Seventh Mode (No. 2, 1597), Gabrieli

of performers, and such use of choir against choir was a novelty in polyphonic music. Now the polyphonic focus was divided, and it became an essential part of the listening experience to feel the energy of those sonic seesawings. The choirs keep up their dialogue with a succession of textural effects: one choir pitted against the other; one choir alone, then both together; sudden shifts in dynamics between loud and soft. In another instrumental work, the "Sonata pian' e forte" ("Soft and Loud Sonata"), Giovanni Gabrieli was among the first composers to indicate specific changes in dynamics, which until then were usually left to the performers' discretion. Fresh rhythmic ideas appear, and there are crisp exchanges of meter between the opening four-beat measures and later episodes in three-beat measures. There are even some traces of polyphony with separate melodic strands, but above all Gabrieli exploits the texture of block chords. He had good reason for preferring the smack of chords. Without their incisive effect, his music would have been muddled in the cavernous interior of San Marco or lost in the riotous environs of an outdoor piazza. Palestrina's smooth-flowing, separate-stranded polyphony would have dissolved in shapeless reverberations, but Gabrieli's vigorous effects kept their shape. They were attention-getters and attention-holders. Gabrieli needed to engage his audience with a little extra urgency because his instrumental works had no running thread of words and ideas to hold them together. There are no texts to catch the listeners' minds. Vocal music took logic and continuity from its words, which is why Palestrina's Mass or Weelkes's madrigal could move forward from one musical idea to another—from one point of imitation to the next—with rarely a backward glance at music heard earlier. Instrumental music cannot do that, which is why Gabrieli's sonatas and canzonas assail the listener with striking musical effects, with the sharp attacks of block chords and the crisp give-and-take of dialoguing choirs.

Gabrieli's ultimate attention-getter was to provide his instrumental music with an independent musical form. Most of his canzonas are

Brass Players,
*an engraving of 1538
by Heinrich Aldegrever.*

built on simple patterns of statements, repetitions, contrasts, and "backward glances" or returns. Such abstract, organizing forms give each work a musical logic of its own. Gabrieli's overall form in the Canzona in the Seventh Mode amounts to a loose A-B-A′. That is to say, near the end there is a return to the music of the beginning (Ex. 2.11). The return adds an important psychological dimension. It stirs up the listener's memory and gives a satisfying sense of having "come home."

Looking back at a Gabrieli canzona of 1600, it may seem farfetched to discover in it the ancestor of the concertos of Mozart and the symphonies of Brahms. But, in fact, the paths to those later instrumental forms began right here. The Venetian sonatas and canzonas are at a crossroad in Western musical history. Their time, around 1600, is comparable in significance to the years around 1000 when church polyphony first asserted its artistic vigor alongside plainchant. Now, after centuries of taking second place to vocal music in the hierarchy of musical styles, instrumental music came into a significant style of its own. It would continue to solidify that independent status during the decades to come, and during the eighteenth century instrumental music would finally supplant vocal music as the center of musical attention.

There is one other epoch-making aspect of the Venetian sonatas and canzonas. More than any music composed earlier, their purpose was to create strong physical impressions. They operated in architectural space, whipping the listener back and forth within that space. Dressed up in brassy splendor, and exploiting to the full the factors of impact and motion, color and space, the Venetian instrumental works brought musical style to the threshold of the Baroque.

3 Music in the Baroque Era (1600-1750)

Gianlorenzo Bernini, The Ecstasy of St. Teresa,
masterpiece of Baroque emotional sculpture (Rome, 1645-1652).

The Baroque Era (ca. 1600-1750)

MUSIC	ARTS AND IDEAS	POLITICS AND SCIENCE

EARLY BAROQUE (ca. 1600-1650)

MUSIC	ARTS AND IDEAS	POLITICS AND SCIENCE
Monteverdi (1567-1643): *Orfeo* (1607) *Coronation of Poppaea* (1642) Schütz (1585-1672): sacred concerti, passions, oratorio, motets	Painters and sculptors: Caravaggio, El Greco, Bernini, Rubens Cervantes, *Don Quijote*, part I (1605) King James translation of the Bible (1611) Shakespeare dies (1616) Bernini made architect of St. Peter's (1629) Descartes, *Philosophical Principles* (1644)	England under James I (1603) Jamestown: first permanent English settlement in America (1607) Napier's logarithms (1614) Richelieu becomes French Secretary of State (1616) Thirty Years War (1618-1648): erosion of Hapsburg-Spanish "Roman Empire" Pilgrims reach Massachusetts (1620) Scientific discoveries of Descartes and Pascal Galileo's telescope; *Essay on Solar System* (1632)

MIDDLE BAROQUE (ca. 1650-1700)

MUSIC	ARTS AND IDEAS	POLITICS AND SCIENCE
Lully (1632-1687): Tragédies lyriques (1670s and 1680s) Purcell (ca. 1659-1695): Harpsichord Suite in G (ca. 1680) *Dido and Aeneas* (1689) Corelli (1653-1713): Trio Sonata in F, Op. 4, No. 7 (1694)	Molière, *Tartuffe* (1664) Racine, *Andromaque* (1667) Milton, *Paradise Lost* (1667) Spinoza, *Ethics* (1667) Last paintings of Rembrandt (d. 1669) and Poussin (d. 1665) Bunyan, *Pilgrim's Progress* (1678)	"Age of Louis XIV" (France, 1643- 1715) Cromwell, Lord Protector (1653-1658) Great Fire in London (1666) Construction of Versailles (1661-1682) Newton and Leibniz discover the infinitesimal calculus Venetian bombardment damages the Parthenon (1687)

LATE BAROQUE (ca. 1700-1750)

MUSIC	ARTS AND IDEAS	POLITICS AND SCIENCE
Vivaldi (1678-1741): *The Four Seasons:* "Spring" (ca. 1725) J. S. Bach (1685-1750): "Little" Fugue in G Minor (ca. 1708-1717) French Suite No. 5 (ca. 1720) *Brandenburg Concerto* No. 2 (ca. 1720) Cantata No. 140 (1731) Handel (1685-1759): *Messiah* (1742) Pergolesi (1710-1736): *La Serva Padrona* (1733) D. Scarlatti (1685-1757): "Cortège" Sonata (ca. 1750)	Pope, *Rape of the Lock* (1712) Defoe, *Robinson Crusoe* (1719) Paintings by Watteau (d. 1721) Swift, *Gulliver's Travels* (1726) Hogarth, *The Rake's Progress* (1735) Voltaire, *Discours sur l'homme* (1738) Hume, *Treatise of Human Nature* (1740) Fielding, *Tom Jones* (1749)	George I (England, 1714-1727) George II (England, 1727-1760) Louis XV (France, 1723-1774) Frederick the Great (Prussia, 1740-1786) Discovery of Herculaneum (1738)

A. THE BAROQUE

Baroque is the name given to the richly embroidered, emotionally intense music of the seventeenth and early eighteenth centuries. The Baroque was an era of many musical styles that were generally opulent in sound, spacious in design, and lofty in spirit. Composers endeavored as never before to make their music sway the emotions, reaching out to extremes of exaltation and despair. The word *baroque* itself was first used during the late eighteenth century to describe the heightened emotionalism and monumentality that were detectable in the fine arts and architecture beginning around 1600. As a description, it implied creations that were somehow overwrought and misshapen. Gradually the word was expanded to take in the whole cultural epoch, and it acquired the positive sense that it has today.

The Baroque era represented a tough-minded new phase in the evolution of Western thought and institutions. It gave birth to the "new sciences" of Galileo and Newton, to the rational philosophies of Spinoza and Pascal, to the poetic cosmologies of Milton and Corneille. Baroque politics was embodied in the statecraft of Richelieu and Cromwell, the absolutism of Louis XIV and Frederick the Great. Much of Baroque music was conceived on a correspondingly grand scale. It was an exciting, comprehensively organized music that was quite in keeping with the farsighted visions of its princes and the authoritarian efficiency of their reigns. It was the first music in modern Western civilization that set out purposefully to overwhelm its listeners with the logic of its discourse and with its sheer physical splendor.

During the early seventeenth century, all of the arts seemed to be casting off the Renaissance ideal of moderation for a new extravagance and emotionalism. The symmetry and repose that can be sensed in Renaissance palaces and churches was succeeded by the "sculptural" architecture of Bernini and Borromini, who filled vast visual spaces with the tensions of monumental forces in straining motion. The neatly balanced compositional geometries of Renaissance painters such as Raphael, Holbein, and Titian were succeeded by turmoil and exuberance in the canvases of Caravaggio, El Greco, and Rubens. In music, the cooler Renaissance utterances of Josquin Des Prez and Palestrina gave way to the more palpable emotionalism and theatricality of Monteverdi and Purcell. Baroque music and architecture are quite similar in their exploitation of space and motion to generate exciting effects. A chorus by Schütz or Handel sends throbbing sonic images through audible space in somewhat the same way that Gianlorenzo Bernini's colonnade fronting St. Peter's or a Roman Jesuit church interior, such as Sant' Ignazio or the Gesù, Colorplate 15 propels architectural rhythms through visual space. The qualities of vibrant, thrusting rhythmic motion that are shared by Baroque

Bernini's colonnade fronting St. Peter's, Rome (after 1656), fills a vast space with the tensions of monumental shapes in rhythmic motion; shown here in an eighteenth-century engraving by Piranesi.

music and architecture are nowhere closer than in the spectacular seventeenth-century fountains—for example, Le Nôtre's at Versailles or Bernini's at Rome, where water is used like fluid marble, its jets and cascades playing off one another in ever-changing patterns. In their turn, Baroque composers deployed musical figures that are sometimes fragile and shimmering, other times brilliant and powerful, but always in vital, energetic motion.

Baroque music took many forms. Thumping orchestral concertos and majestic festival music for outdoor pageantries matched the wedding cake glitter of Baroque palaces. Elaborate music dramas—the operas—put a wide range of emotions on display, dressed in rich musical styles. The Baroque took religion seriously. Some of its church interiors were like enormous jewelry boxes, decorated in pastel blues and pinks, with golden sunbursts mirroring the heavens. The churches were filled with corresponding musical splendors—sumptuously styled motets and Masses, and the amply dimensioned sacred dramas called **oratorios** and **passions** that were cut out of the same generous fabric as the operas. Alongside all the outward display, however, the Baroque cultivated some less demonstrative music. In churches there were ruminative chorale preludes and studious variations for organ. In aristocratic salons and private living rooms there were gentle suites and sonatas and sober-minded canons and fugues. Bach's *Art of the Fugue* contains music so inner-directed as to seem almost destined for silent contemplation rather than for

The interior of a German Baroque palace (Schloss Bruchsal), elaborately decorated by Balthasar Neumann (1687-1753).

a sounding performance. The deep-seated Baroque urge to overwhelm the listener is still there, but it is sublimated in the intensity of intellectual manipulation.

Leading Composers of the Baroque

Hundreds of composers practiced the art of music at a very high level during the Baroque era, though as always a handful stood out. The last fifty years of the era, from about 1700 to 1750, known as the "High Baroque," or "mature Baroque," produced the best-known masters: Bach and Handel, Vivaldi and Telemann, Rameau and François Couperin "Le Grand." The seventeenth century also had its masters: Monteverdi and Schütz during the "early Baroque," from 1600 to 1650; and Lully, Purcell, and Corelli during the "middle Baroque," from 1650 to 1700. Very often the outstanding composers were Germans—such as Schütz, Bach, Handel, and Telemann. Yet the domination of musical styles by Italian composers that had begun in the late Renaissance with Palestrina and his contemporaries continued into the Baroque, which remained throughout essentially a showcase for a dynasty of innovative Italians—Monteverdi, Cavalli, Cesti, Corelli, Vivaldi, the two Scarlattis (Alessandro and Domenico), and Pergolesi. Indeed, most of Handel's style and much of what is admired in Bach's style have their foundation in Italy.

Baroque Musical Features

No single definition of style can embrace a whole century and a half of European musical production; yet certain features of the music composed between 1600 and 1750 are constant enough to distinguish the Baroque as a coherent style-period and not simply a miscellaneous assortment of works. They can be grouped under four heads: 1) single-mindedness, 2) continuous motion, 3) fugal polyphony, and 4) basso continuo.

1. *Single-mindedness.* In a way, this covers all of the features. The most characteristic aspect of Baroque music is the way each piece seems to be cut from just a single fabric throughout. Once the music starts, it tends to stay in the same track, exploiting the same materials, projecting the same mood—all gay or all melancholy, and not a mixture of contrasting moods. Baroque music typically begins with some distinctive scrap of rhythm, melody, or texture, which then keeps going to the end. It is remarkable how meager the basic material can be and how far the composer stretches it. Like any music, Baroque music needs variety and contrasts, but what contrasts there are generally come from one movement to the next, not within a single movement.

2. *Continuous motion.* Every aspect of musical texture is bound up in the Baroque single-mindedness, but most characteristic is the rhythm. There is an unrelenting thrust to Baroque rhythm that is sometimes described as *continuous motion.* A work begins with some small, emphatic rhythmic idea; then it is kept going to the end, allowing little relaxation along the way. The concentration on a single rhythm that is sometimes machinelike in its regularity carries over into the shape of many Baroque melodies. These typically grow out of small, germinal ideas and evolve into extensive, run-on utterances that are again in continuous motion. It can be a long way from one breath to the next in the twistings of a Baroque melody.

3. *Fugal polyphony.* Along with the persistence of its rhythms and the exuberance of its lengthy melodic contour, the Baroque's single-mindedness is manifest in its predilection for **fugal polyphony**. This is the most complex of the Baroque's musical textures, and it is generally adopted for the era's most austere-minded utterances, such as the fugues of Bach (see pages 116-122) and the fugal choruses of Handel (see pages 141-144). Baroque fugal polyphony was a direct descendent of the Renaissance's imitative polyphony—the texture where various voice-parts imitate the same initial melodic fragment or **subject**. There is this difference: The Renaissance usually builds its polyphony out of a succession of points of imitation, that is, basing the polyphony on different

musical subjects as the piece goes along. The Baroque's fugal polyphony is generally built by imitating a single subject throughout a whole piece. This makes for a tightly integrated effect. When such polyphonic texture is joined with the vigorous forward press of Baroque rhythm, the result is an emphatic thrusting motion that has been described, perhaps overpicturesquely, as "polyphonic motor power."

4. *Basso continuo*. The fourth general feature of Baroque music is the **basso continuo**, or "continuous bass," which is sometimes also called **thorough bass**. The basso continuo is the accompaniment texture of Baroque music that runs through practically every piece. It consists of a bass line plus a filler of improvised chords. It is perhaps the commonest of all Baroque musical features, so common in fact that the whole Baroque era has been called "the era of basso continuo." Generally, two instruments are used to play the continuo. A low-pitched instrument such as a cello, bassoon, or viola da gamba takes the bass line. The other instrument, which may be, among others, an organ, harpsichord, or lute, doubles the bass line and has the capacity to add the filler chords. In essence, the basso continuo is another manifestation of the Baroque's single-mindedness. It is present through the length of nearly every piece. Its contribution may be so unobtrusive as to pass almost unnoticed by the casual listener, yet it would be missed if it were not there. Its thump, crackle, and fuzz somehow make the whole texture stick together. All of the four general characteristics of Baroque music (single-mindedness, continuous motion, fugal polyphony, and basso continuo) may not be present in every piece. However, the basso continuo is the one most regularly found.

B. THE RISE OF OPERA: MONTEVERDI AND THE RECITATIVE STYLE

The Baroque was the first era in Western music history when purely *instrumental music,* that is, music without any admixture of singing voices, took a primary artistic role. This emergence of instrumental music brought with it a host of new musical forms, among them the sonata, suite, and concerto (see pages 95-114). But the first great novelty of the Baroque was a form that combined both voices and instruments. This was the opera, which appeared in Italy just before 1600. An *opera* is a sung drama, a stage work whose actions, conversations, and monologues are delivered by solo singers and choruses accompanied by an orchestra. In Italian the word *opera* simply means "a work." It comes from the fuller description, *opera drammatica in musica,* or "a dramatic work set to music," which was applied to the early musical dramas. Opera had its roots in the 1580s, when a group of humanist intellectuals calling themselves the *Camerata,* or "little club," experimented at finding modern musical counterparts for the ancient Greek and Latin dramas. Gathered at the country house of a certain Count Bardi outside of Florence, the poets and musicians pondered questions of dramatic and musical style. They knew that the dramas of Aeschylus and Sophocles had not merely been declaimed in speech but were sung throughout. Yet they had no real idea of what Greek music was like, and so they entertained no serious notion of returning to the ancient musical styles. They did the next best thing. They came up with a dramatically effective modern style for their own staged entertainments. With this style, they hoped to raise their works to the emotional heights attained by the ancients. The first fruits of these musical endeavors came in the 1580s in the works of Vincenzo Galilei, the father of the great astronomer. The first complete operas, with music by the composers Jacopo Peri and Giulio Caccini, were written in 1597 and 1600. Then, in 1607, Claudio Monteverdi's *Orfeo* (*Orpheus*) gave the fledgling form of opera its first masterpiece.

Claudio Monteverdi

Monteverdi (1567-1643) stands as the last great musician of the Renaissance and the first of the Baroque. He began his career around 1590 at the ducal court of Mantua in northern Italy. In 1613 he succeeded Giovanni Gabrieli as the chief composer at the church of San Marco in Venice, and he remained there for the thirty years until his death. In his youth Monteverdi mastered the Palestrina style of church polyphony and also composed madrigals in the virtuoso styles of the 1580s that he shared with Marenzio, Gesualdo, and Vecchi. Later on, he composed church music for voices and instruments in the Venetian polychoral idiom of Gabrieli, as in the psalms of his Vesper Service of 1610. But Monteverdi's chief contributions were to two more modern styles. He had an important role in transforming the older vocal madrigals of the Renaissance into a congenial new style of Baroque chamber music that mixed vocal and instrumental soloists. And, he was the first master of the new-born opera.

The early Italian operas borrowed their stories from ancient Greece. Yet rather than confront the challenges of tragedy, the poets and musicians around 1600 were content to imitate gentler pastoral subjects that were popular at the time and also had a classical tradition. Monteverdi's *Orfeo,* composed for his patron the Duke of Mantua, deals with the legendary poet-musician of antiquity, Orpheus, whose beloved wife Eurydice has succumbed to a reptile's bite and been transported beyond the river Lethe to the underworld. The desolate Orpheus resolves to use his musical powers—which can charm animals, trees, even rocks to do his bidding—to bring her back to life. In the monologue "Tu sei morta" ("Thou art dead . . .") he laments Eurydice's death. Bidding farewell to the earth, sun, and heavens, he begins his journey to Hades (Ex. 3.1).

Δ
Monteverdi: Orfeo's recitative, "Tu sei morta," from *Orfeo* (Side 2, Band 2)

Ex. 3.1. Orfeo's Recitative, "Tu sei morta," from *Orfeo* (1607), Monteverdi

Tu sei morta, mia vita, ed io respiro,
Thou art dead, love of my life, yet I still breathe,

Tu sei da me partita
Thou hast left me

Per mai più non tornare, ed io rimango.
Never to return, and I remain.

No, che se i versi alcuna cosa ponno
No, for if my music still has powers

N'andrò sicuro a più profondi abissi
I shall surely go to the deepest abyss

E intenerito il cor del Re de l'ombre
And having softened the heart of the King of shadows

Meco trarrotti a riveder le stelle.
Will bring you with me to see again the stars.

O se ciò negherammi empio destino,
Or if proud fate denies it,

Rimarrò teco in compagnia di morte.
I shall remain with you in the company of death.

Addio terra, addio cielo e sole, addio.
Farewell earth, farewell sky and sun, farewell.

The musical style in this monologue is called **recitative** (reh-ci-tah-TEEV) in English, taking over the Italian term *recitativo* (reh-chi-tah-TEE-voh). The recitative was the chief invention of the Camerata, and

An aristocratic theater audience: King Louis XIII of France, Anne of Austria (his queen), and Cardinal Richelieu attend a performance at the Petit Bourbon Palace in 1641.

The ancient gods Zeus and Hera look down on the singer of an aria in a seventeenth-century Venetian opera; set design by Ludovico Burnacini.

it became a mainstay of opera for the next four centuries. A recitative is speech set to music. It is musically heightened speech. The Florentine inventors of opera supposed—probably correctly—that the monologues and dialogues of ancient Greek dramas were declaimed in some half-musical style of recitation, lying between flat, ordinary speech and lyric, tuneful melody. For their operas they proposed a style of recitative that suited the declamation of the Italian language, one that took the natural up-and-down inflections of the spoken language and projected them at the levels of musical pitches. For example, a native speaker of English reciting the line "RecitaTIVE is MUsically HEIGHTened SPEECH" would be likely to emphasize and perhaps lengthen the syllables that are capitalized (-TIVE, MU-, HEIGHT-, SPEECH), while passing matter-of-factly over the others. In a longer sentence, a reciter would also emphasize the more significant words and clauses, perhaps delivering them at a higher pitch while dropping down for the others, and generally dropping the voice at the ends of phrases. What the recitative basically did was to transform those natural inflections of speech into their counterparts of musical pitches, lengths, and accents. A sample version of the line given above is shown in Ex. 3.2. Yet there are countless other ways of translating the spoken inflections of those words into musical pitches and rhythms.

Ex. 3.2. Recitative

Re - ci - ta - tive   is   mu - si - cal - ly height-ened   speech

Operatic recitatives were sung by solo singers—the characters in
the drama. They also had instrumental accompaniments, which in
early operas were supplied by a basso continuo. For this particular
recitative of Orpheus, Monteverdi specifies as the basso continuo
instruments an *organo di legno* (a small organ with wooden pipes)
and a *chitarrone* (a tall, straight-necked relative of the guitar). In addition to their recitatives, the earliest operas had a sprinkling of more
tuneful choruses, dances, and instrumental interludes. But to carry
the basic drama, composers relied mainly on the austere recitative
style. They wanted the drama to remain foremost, so they avoided
catchy tunes that would divert attention and the filigrees of polyphony that would obscure the words. Everything is concentrated in
a solo singer, giving the recitatives a startling directness. The words
go right to the heart of the dramatic situation, the naturally declaimed speech to the essence of the character. Orpheus stammers
with passionate intensity, "Tu sei morta, se morta mia vita, ed io respiro" ("Thou'rt dead, art dead, love of my life, yet I still breathe...").
There is pathos in his last farewells (*addio*) to earth (*terra*), sky
(*cielo*), and sun (*sole*). There still are old-fashioned madrigalesque
touches at the words "più profondi abissi" ("deepest abysses."),
where the vocal line descends, only to rise again at "riveder le stelle"
("to see again the stars"). Near the end, Monteverdi inserts a flowery
melisma on the last farewell (*addio*). But the emphasis remains far
from banal tunefulness. It is on the emotion of the words, heightened
by the recitative dress. Musically restrained as this recitative style is,
we may detect in it a vein of Italian poignance that was still flourishing three centuries later in the operatic melodies of Verdi and Puccini.

In Monteverdi's time orchestras were generally smaller and more
variable in makeup than modern orchestras. *Orfeo,* however, was
conceived as a lavish entertainment for a wealthy nobleman, and its
score calls for as many as forty players, often playing instruments
that have since become obsolete. Monteverdi's strings include two
small "French-style" violins, about ten violins, violas, and cellos,
plus a pair of double bass. The winds and brass include four trombones, two Baroque "cornets" (long wooden pipes with finger holes),
and three usual-size trumpets. None of the early brass instruments
had valves, so their pitches were limited to their tubes' natural series
of harmonics as selected by the players' lips and air pressures. Monteverdi calls for no percussion instruments, but his complement for the

basso continuo was quite rich, including no fewer than two harpsichords, a double harp, two chitarrones, two bass *citterns* (a flat-backed cross between a lute and guitar), three low viols, and three organs—two of them built with wooden pipes and the third with reed pipes.

C. THE SPREAD OF OPERA AND THE RISE OF LYRICISM

The new Italian operas were snapped up by the novelty-hungry Italian cities, and they soon spread to the rest of Europe. The recitative style became established as the standard for musical-dramatic utterances of any sort. Opera itself, undergoing constant change, served as a breeding ground for innovations in musical style throughout the seventeenth and eighteenth centuries. Monteverdi went on to compose other operas after his landmark *Orfeo* of 1607. The changing fashions are obvious in his last opera, *The Coronation of Poppaea,* which was composed for Venice in 1642. Here the subject is no longer an idealized Greek myth played out in a surrounding of nymphs and shepherds. This is a backstairs episode of Roman imperial history—the scheming of Poppaea, mistress of the Emperor Nero, to become his Empress. In 1642, opera had ceased to be a hothouse humanist toy or court pageantry for wealthy princes. It had

Lully's opera Alceste *as performed at Versailles during the reign of Louis XIV. The large orchestra is divided into two groups located at the sides of the stage.*

become a universal entertainment, catering to ordinary citizens who bought tickets to the new public opera houses that were opening everywhere. The advent of populist audiences helped to bring changes in musical style. The earliest operas relied mainly on recitatives, shunning any melodiousness that was thought to be at the expense of the drama. Now, after a generation of the lean musicality of recitatives, that style sometimes seemed tedious. In the operas of the middle seventeenth century, the recitatives still took care of the narrative and dramatic flow, but increasingly their continuity was broken by more melodious **set pieces** or **numbers** (the words are interchangeable), displaying an outright tunefulness that appealed directly to the pleasure-seeking audiences. In any drama there are bound to be some moments devoted to action and decision, and other moments when action stops and the characters reflect on the situation. The recitative continued as the musical style for portraying the dramatic actions. Now the attractive lyric set pieces or numbers—they took the form of solos, duets, choruses, etc.—became the style in places where the story halts and the characters turn reflective. The lyric pieces suited the composers, not only because their musical enticements were winsome and helped assure a flow of money from a satisfied public, but also because they gave ample reign to the musicians' natural desires to express themselves in styles that were musicianly.

What the audiences and composers of the mid-seventeenth century cherished most about the new operas were the tuneful solo numbers called **arias** or **airs**. An *aria* (in Italian) or an *air* (in French and English) is an operatic solo song, a stand-up, stop-the-action musical number where lyricism reigns supreme. Such set pieces were already being inserted judiciously in Monteverdi's last operas, dating from the 1640s. Care was taken so that they did not impede the dramatics of the plot, but in time the balance shifted from the drama-bearing recitatives toward the pure lyric numbers. In Baroque operas of the eighteenth century, the dramatic urgency sometimes diminished to the point where works were a succession of richly musical but dramatically static set pieces, in between which came perfunctory recitatives that were little more than a pretext for bringing on the next set piece.

Early Opera in Germany and France

Opera was transplanted to Germany by Heinrich Schütz (1585-1672), the first of the great German Baroque composers. Schütz owed his decisive musical formation to the Venetian polychoral and madrigal styles of Giovanni Gabrieli, with whom he spent his student years from 1609 to 1612. His single opera, *Dafne* (1627), has not survived, though like Monteverdi's *Orfeo* of 1607 it was a neo-Greek pastoral drama. Many of Schütz's Lutheran church works (*Sacred*

Songs, Sacred Symphonies, Spiritual Concertos) again reflect the innovations of the Italian Baroque. Yet to the splendor and pathos of Italy—the emotional recitatives, lively rhythms, and colorful mixtures of instruments and voices—Schütz adds a Germanic introspection and piety.

Opera was taken into France and reached its first height in the resourceful, Italian-born Jean Baptiste Lully (1632-1687). At the age of twenty-one, Lully was a player in Louis XIV's renowned string ensemble, "The Twenty-four Violins of the King." Beginning in 1664, he composed music for the "comedy ballets" of his great contemporary Molière. Then, in partnership with the playwright Philippe Quinault, he composed over a dozen French operas between 1673 and 1687, calling them "lyrical tragedies" (*tragédies lyriques*) rather than operas, so as to emphasize their distinctive French qualities. Nonetheless, they were full-fledged operas, with dialogues and dramatic actions that were set to continuous music. They dealt with noble subjects, often drawn from Greek myths (Alcestis, Theseus, Psyche, Bellerophon). In their lofty stylizations of plot and character they were worthy counterparts of the poetic tragedies of Corneille and Racine, which were the fruits of the same "grand century."

An opera by Lully begins with a ceremonious **overture**, or opening movement, for orchestra. Lully's type of **French overture** consists of two sections. The first is majestically slow, and distinguished by the motion of stately chords where long and short notes alternate in **dotted rhythms**:

The second section is lively and polyphonic. Toward the end, a trace of the stately opening motion may return. The French overture style became popular everywhere, and it was still being used a half century later in works by Bach and Handel. Lully's recitatives have melodic curvatures suited to the declamation of the French language. His lyric arias, or airs, are simple and tuneful. Further lyric numbers, such as choruses and ballets, play a much larger role than in the contemporary Italian operas. Lully was a clever opportunist in music, seeking effects that would please and earn money; and he was adept at court politics, obtaining from Louis XIV a monopoly for the production of French opera. But he was also a great artist whose unerring taste fashioned an authentically French musical theater out of the operatic initiatives of the Italians. His lyric tragedies, with their dignified address and elegantly formal music, transport us to the milieu of the Sun King for whose pleasure and glorification they were conceived.

Early Opera in England: Henry Purcell

The creator of English opera was Henry Purcell (ca. 1659-1695), who has been called "the greatest English composer." In any event, Purcell is the English composer of most enduring importance before the twentieth century. He was born in London, the son of a court musician. During his short lifetime he rose from choirboy at the Chapel Royal under Charles II to the highest honors under James II and William and Mary. He was endowed with a fanciful imagination and an extraordinary fertility that he applied to many musical genres: stately odes for royalty; large-scale motets and anthems for church use; sacred and secular songs, duets, trios; and miniatures for keyboard instruments. Purcell is best remembered for his stage music. He wrote lyrical numbers for insertion among the spoken dialogues of more than forty plays, including *King Arthur* (1691), *The Fairy Queen* (1692), and *The Tempest* (1695). Purcell's *Dido and Aeneas* (1689) occupies a niche all its own because it has dialogues composed throughout in recitative style. The end-to-end music makes *Dido* a real opera—the first great English opera.

Dido and Aeneas begins with a Lullian, French-style overture: a slow introduction in dotted rhythms, followed by a lively second section. Then the action unfolds in a melodious style of recitative that Purcell molds to the mannerisms of English Restoration speech. Short lyric airs, choruses, and instrumental interludes are interspersed with the recitatives, many of them having the flavor of English dance and folksong. *Dido* is a very short opera. Altogether its three acts take less than an hour. Some of its brevity and simple style are due to its parochial milieu. It was produced "at Mr. Josias Priest's boarding-school at Chelsy by young Gentlewomen . . . to a select audience of their parents and friends." But Purcell and his librettist Nahum Tate create dramatic situations with genuine force and bring a wide range of emotions to life. The plot is drawn from a familiar episode in Vergil's *Aeneid.* Aeneas, the prince of fallen Troy, fleeing from his homeland with the remnants of the defeated Trojan army, finds temporary refuge at Carthage in North Africa. There he falls in love with Dido, the queen, but destiny urges him onward and he departs for Italy and the founding of Rome.

In the opera's final scene the abandoned Dido prepares for suicide. Like most operatic scenes of the later Baroque, this one begins with a recitative, which is followed directly by a concluding aria. Dido first addresses her maid Belinda in the short sorrowful recitative, "Thy hand, Belinda." It is accompanied only by a basso continuo. A look at the music (Ex. 3.3) shows the typical Baroque manner of noting a basso continuo part. This notation is called a **figured bass**. Only the bass line of music is supplied, but along with it are certain numbers and accidentals called *figures.* The figures are a harmonic

Δ
Purcell: Dido's recitative, "Thy hand, Belinda," and lament, "When I am laid in earth," from *Dido and Aeneas* (Side 2, Band 3)

Ex. 3.3. Dido's Recitative, "Thy hand, Belinda," from *Dido and Aeneas,* **Purcell**

shorthand, similar to the guitar chord symbols of today. They give a rough indication of the pitches that are needed for the filler chords, but they leave it up to the individual keyboard player to place those pitches and perhaps add some improvisatory flourishes. The filler chords are not written out—they are improvised from the "figures" of the figured bass.

The vocal recitative unfolds over this skeletal accompaniment by the basso continuo. Dido's recitative music has none of the melodic appeal—none of the inner repetitions and tunefulness—of a real song. Like Orfeo's recitative of 1607, Dido's recitative of 1689 simply mirrors the declamation of its text. It is dramatic speech given a profile of pitches. Where a speaker or declaimer of the words would raise her speaking voice, the music of the recitative tends to do the same. Still, Purcell supplies expressive musical touches, as on the word "darkness," where there is a madrigalesque shudder. And all of the melodic phrases seem to be heading downward, as if mirroring Dido's despair.

Following the musical restraint of the recitative, there comes the lyric expansiveness of the aria or air. Here all is clothed with rich musical substance, as action gives way to contemplation and discourse to an outpouring of personal emotion. Dido's lament, "When I am laid," has been called the most powerful piece of music in the English language. It is an aria, an emotional song. Where a recitative has many words and is a frugal style of music, an aria has few words and is overflowing with melodic and harmonic appeal. Moreover, the full orchestra takes on the accompaniment of this aria. For Dido's lament, Purcell chose one of the Baroque's favorite musical forms, known as **ostinato variations**. It is also known by other names— **ground bass**, **variations on a ground**, **ground**, and **basso ostinato**. They all amount to the same thing. A short musical passage, usually in the bass line, is repeated many times over, end to end. Each repetition brings out some fresh facets of rhythm, melody, harmony, or texture in the other voices (Ex. 3.4). Ostinato variations represent

Ex. 3.4. Ostinato Variations

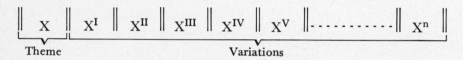

one of the basic principles of music—the principle of variations. The idea is to say something, then say it again with enough change to spur the listener's interest. Ostinato variations take over that principle of variations, spreading it out, crystallizing it in a large-scale form. The word *ostinato* in Italian means "persistent" or "obstinate." The term *ostinato variations* suggests the many end-to-end repetitions that occur in such variation forms.

Purcell's ostinato theme in Dido's lament is a slow, solemn passage of melody in the bass line, just five measures long (Ex. 3.5). Such descending themes were often associated with the idea of death during the Baroque. It is first heard alone, then repeated ten more times—always in the bass, always the same. Above this rigid frame-

Ex. 3.5. Ostinato Bass in "Dido's Lament," from *Dido and Aeneas*, Purcell

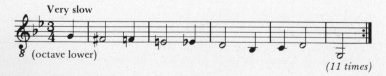

When I am laid in earth
May my wrongs create no trouble in thy breast.
Remember me, but ah! forget my fate.

work of repetitions a supple musical fabric unfolds. Dido's song and the inner strands of her orchestral accompaniment continue through ten presentations of the repeating bass melody. Each time there is a fresh "realization" of the harmonies that are implicit in the bass. The nobly sculptured soprano line and the intensifying inner harmonies produce waves of rising emotion throughout variations 1-8. Then Dido falls silent during variations 9 and 10 while the orchestra muses on her fate. In the final variation (No. 10) the violins trace a slow symbolic descent through the chromatic scale. In listening to this aria, the theme of the ostinato bass should be learned first, but then it can practically be disregarded. Securely planted in the bass, and almost monotonous in its regularity, it serves as a backdrop against which the noble emotions of the vocal part stand out in bold relief.

The coupling of a dramatic recitative with a lyric set piece, as we find it in Dido's recitative and lament, remained the standard procedure in operatic scenes from Purcell's time through the nineteenth century. In this start-and-stop arrangement, each scene begins with a recitative that presents some morsel of story or action, couched in a style that is musically dry and unpretentious. Following this is a set piece—an aria, duet, chorus, etc.—that provides a lyrical commentary on the preceding action. Antidramatic and artificial as such alternations were, the devotees of opera put up with them. They wanted both the storyline of the recitatives and the tuneful displays of the lyric numbers (the set pieces), so they sacrificed some of the dramatic realism in order to have the lyricism. Yet even the lyric numbers do not forsake the drama. They simply go at it a different way. In an aria like Dido's lament, the beauty of the music adds its own matchless excitement to the urgency of the drama.

D. INSTRUMENTAL MUSIC: THE BAROQUE DANCE SUITE

The Baroque, we have said, was the first era in Western music to give primary importance to instrumental music. Instruments often played without voices in earlier times, but what they usually provided was casual entertainment with dances, song arrangements, and improvisations that were less sophisticated than the vocal music of the time. Instrumental music came into its own during the Baroque. Lacking the thread of meaning supplied by a verbal text, instrumental music often relied on abstract designs or forms that had independent logic of their own. Many such forms developed during the Baroque. One favorite was the set of ostinato variations (Ex. 3.4), the same plan as underlies Dido's lament. Another favorite was the **dance suite**, a collection of dance movements with a variety of styles

Colorplates 17 and 18

and moods. Such suites were supposed to be entertaining, but their dances were not for dancing. The rhythms were too intricate and fancy, the textures too learned and stodgy. The composers' aim was to show off musical ingenuity rather than to stimulate bodies and feet. During the Renaissance, the custom arose of joining two or more such stylized dances together. The composer took a familiar tune, went through it in a particular dance rhythm, then repeated it in some other dance rhythm. The resulting *suite,* or succession of two dances, contained movements that were essentially variations of one another. During the early Baroque, such suites often had four movements, all in the same key but no longer necessarily variations of one another. The German composer J. J. Froberger (d. 1667) led the fashion with suites whose four dances were the 1) **Allemande,** 2) **Courante,** 3) **Sarabande,** and 4) **Gigue.** However, composers of suites were free to pick and choose their favorite dances.

The Harpsichord

The **harpsichord,** or "spinet," was the workhorse instrument of Baroque music. It was the everyday instrument for household enter-   Colorplate 16
tainment. In chamber and orchestral groups it supplied the filler harmonies of the basso continuo. Its glittering tone colors and potential for a big sound also made it a display vehicle for concertos. The pinging tone of the harpsichord comes from a mechanism that plucks the strings with quills. The same quill always plucks with the same intensity so that, unlike the modern piano, the force of the player's hand on the key does not affect the force or quality of sound. The harpsichord's sound dies away quickly. To make up for these limitations in dynamics and tone color, harpsichords were fitted with various sets of strings and with quills made of different materials. On large harpsichords there were two different keyboards, called "manuals," and even a set of pedals played by the feet. There were knobs, called "stops," to select particular combinations of quills and strings, and inner mechanisms that coupled two different keyboards or activated two different octave ranges simultaneously. These options gave more than enough variety to the harpsichord. Large Baroque harpsichords can imitate the strum of a guitar, the resonant pluck of a lute, and the pizzicato of a violin. With their tonal resources harnessed together, they approximate the fullness of Baroque orchestral sound.

The Dance Suite of Purcell

△
Purcell: Suite No. 1 in G Major for Harpsichord: Prelude, Allemande, Courante, and Minuet (Side 2, Band 4)

Purcell's Suite No. 1 in G Major calls for only a modest living-room instrument with a single keyboard and no pedals. The music can also be played on the harpsichord's smaller cousin, the **clavichord,** which instead of plucking the strings with a quill sets them in motion by contacting them with a *tangent*. This produces a damped, low-volume sound that scarcely carries across a room. The clavichord, however, offers one effect that is unobtainable on other keyboard instruments. That is the ability to impart a soulful *vibrato* to the tone by the player's wiggling the finger while pressing down the key.

Colorplate 19

Purcell's Suite in G consists of four movements: 1) Prelude, 2) Almand, 3) Corant, and 4) Minuet. The allemande and courante (to give them their common spellings) are regulars of the Baroque dance suite, while the **minuet** is a frequent option. These three dance movements are introduced by another option, an opening **Prelude** (Ex. 3.6). Purcell's four brisk movements were meant as diversions for amateurs, so they are easy to play.

1. *Prelude.* This is based on just a single short motive, , which appears five times during the first five measures, repeated in sequence—in progressively descending repetitions. Then it is turned upside down or **inverted**, and is heard another five times.

Ultimately the whole Prelude is repeated. Even this modest Prelude shows the single-mindedness and continuous motion of the Baroque: The motive with which it begins is present throughout, and there is no letup in the rhythmic motion.

2. *Allemande.* An allemande or "German dance" is the usual first dance of a Baroque suite. Allemandes are in duple meter (time signatures usually of $\frac{2}{4}$ or $\frac{4}{4}$), and they tend to have precise rhythmic motions and intricate ornamental textures that seem studiously "Germanic." Often, as here, they begin with a short upbeat. Purcell's Allemande maintains its opening rhythmic motion throughout each of its two sections, thus representing again the Baroque single-mindedness. The movement serves to introduce one of the most important of Baroque musical forms, the **binary form**. This was widely adopted as a framework for the dances of instrumental suites as well as for other music written in weightier styles. Binary form gets its

Peasants Merrymaking, *by David Teniers, the younger (1610-1690).*

Ex. 3.6. Harpsichord Suite No. 1 in G Major, Purcell

CORANT

MINUET

name from the fact that its outline consists of just two sections (hence "binary"). Each of those sections is supposed to be repeated directly, though the repetitions are sometimes omitted in performances or on recordings as a means of saving time. The general framework of binary form is:

‖: A :‖: A′ :‖

Composers were drawn to such a plan because it provided a point of departure when they set out to shape an instrumental piece. Its outline was simple enough to allow room for imaginative maneuvers and predictable enough to strengthen the sometimes fragile line of communication between composer and listener: It made the music easier to grasp.

Purcell's Allemande illustrates one other important factor in late seventeenth-century music. The Suite in G was composed at just the time when **tonality**, or **major-minor tonality**, was becoming established as the prevailing musical mode in European melody and harmony. Tonality is a decisive factor in the sound and form of Purcell's music. His title informs us that this Suite is in "the key of G Major." That is, it has the sound-character of the major mode, and each of its movements is concentrated on the pitch G as its home or tonic pitch. Each movement starts out with its harmony based on G, and eventually it returns to that same tonic for its close. In between, for the sake of variety, the music may temporarily focus on a pitch other than its home tonic. It may move to some other key—to some substitute, contrasting tonic. The key generally chosen for such excursions is the **dominant key**, which lies at the fifth degree above the tonic on the common scale. Thus in relation to G as the home or tonic pitch, the dominant is D, an interval of a fifth above. Purcell's Allemande makes precisely that tonal journey. It starts out with the key of G as tonic, then moves "up" in pitch and musical tension to the dominant key of D. Musicians use the term **modulation** to describe such passages of travel between tonal keys. A *modulation* is a change of key, a musical passage that leads from one tonal key to another. Modulations are often gradually staged transitions, as in Purcell's suite movements, though we shall see other cases where they shift abruptly from one key to another. A forerunner of Purcell's practice of tonal modulation is found in Palestrina's practice of shifting from one Renaissance mode to another, as from Mixolydian to Ionian (see Chapter 2). But the Renaissance shifts from mode to mode are less purposeful, less clearly directed than the Baroque modulations from key to key. Purcell's Allemande estab-

Woman playing the spinet
(seventeenth century).

lishes the dominant key at the double bar in the middle of the binary form. At this point, the dominant has become a provisional tonic, serving as a home away from home. Right after the double bar, the tonal journey reverses itself and the concluding section has a modulation from the dominant key back to the original tonic. When that tonic is reached, there is a sense of relaxation and "home." Purcell employs this same tonal plan for each of his three dances (Ex. 3.7). It must be acknowledged that most listeners cannot consciously identify these tonal motions. Yet nearly all listeners register them subconsciously. They bypass the intellect and make their mark directly on the nervous system. Tonality is an important factor in what makes pieces like Purcell's seem "right" and satisfying. It is worth knowing about and listening for even if we don't specifically hear it. Our fundamental response to it is very strong. If Purcell had tried ending his piece on some other chord than G, we would know it right away.

All things considered, Purcell's Allemande can be experienced at a number of levels. There is the outer framework of its binary form. There are the inner patterns of melody and the stylized dance rhythms. There is the single-minded Baroque rhetoric that grows from the opening motion and continues uninterrupted until the next double bar. Deeper inside, there is the harmonic framework of tonality and the working of its psychological forces as the music progresses from a state of initial repose in the home or tonic key to the central tension of the dominant key and then to the ultimate relaxation of the tonic.

3. *Courante.* A courante is a lively dance in triple meter with a gently flowing, "coursing" motion. The French word *courant* means "running" or "coursing." Purcell's Corant (like his Almand, an antiquated English spelling) adopts the same formal outline as the allemande. It has a binary form that is shaped by the same inner tonal journey between the tonic and dominant keys (Ex. 3.7). Again it is worth listening for the modulation—for the upward shift from the

Ex. 3.7. Binary Form: Allemande, Courante, and Minuet, Purcell

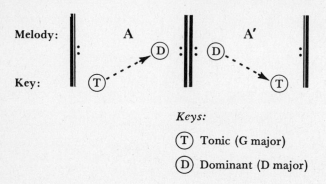

tonic key of G major, which is heard at the start as "home," to the level of the dominant key of D major, which is heard as "away from home." Whether or not we can pick out the details of Purcell's tonal machinery, we register the tension between the two different keys. It is one of the compelling forces that gives logic to the piece and holds it together.

4. *Minuet.* Purcell's Suite in G Major lacks a Baroque suite's usual closing movements, the sarabande and gigue. It ends instead with a minuet, one of a number of optional dances that were inserted, usually just before the gigue. Many such dances have national or regional flavors—for example, the "Germanic" allemande. Among the more popular options are the pavane (Paduan dance), bergamasca (from Bergamo), passamezzo, passepied (from France), gaillard, loure (with bagpipe imitations), gavotte, hornpipe (from England), and two related types of ostinato variations called the **passacaglia** and **chaconne.** The commonest of the Baroque suite's optional dances was the minuet. It originated as a courtly French dance in the seventeenth century, with a stately triple meter that allowed time for the curtsies and bows of aristocratic dancing partners. The minuet retained its airs and graces when it became a stylized instrumental dance in France during the reign of Louis XIV. Purcell's use of it in an instrumental suite reflects a practice that was begun some years earlier by Lully. Like all minuets, Purcell's has a binary form, and

this one is as short as can be. There are just sixteen measures in all. The first eight progress in a single thrust from the tonic key to the dominant key; then eight more measures make the return to the tonic (for the music, see Ex. 3.6; for the form, see Ex. 3.7). Short as this minuet is, it has all the elegance of its upper-class French origins.

E. INSTRUMENTAL MUSIC: THE SONATA

The word **sonata** was used in Venetian music around 1600 to designate music that was played or "sounded" by instruments rather than sung by voices, as had been the preference of the Renaissance (see Chapter 2, page 73). Sonatas were the instrumental chamber music of the Baroque era. They amounted to small-scale music making for intimate music rooms, with only one performer to a part. Actually, two kinds of sonatas were circulating in seventeenth-century Italy. The more serious-minded was the **sonata da chiesa** or church sonata, which generally had four movements in the order slow-fast-slow-fast. The movements were melodically independent, but they hung together in a satisfying succession of moods and ideas, and at least the first and last movements were in the same key. Such sonatas, as their name implies, were suitable for performance in churches. Italian composers also cultivated a lighter-hearted kind of sonata that they called the **sonata da camera** or chamber sonata. This was just another term for the dance suite of Froberger, Lully, or Purcell—a series of stylized dances. The distinction between the serious church sonatas and the frivolous chamber sonatas was not strictly maintained. Many church sonatas conclude with the swinging triple meter of a **jig**. And while chamber sonatas are generally less serious than church sonatas, they, too, have their pensive moods and high-minded polyphonic textures.

The Sonatas of Corelli

The foremost Italian composer of instrumental music around the beginning of the eighteenth century was Arcangelo Corelli (1653-1713), who was born near Ravenna in northeast Italy. Corelli studied at Bologna, then a great center for string music, and as a young artist he made a reputation in Germany. By the age of 30 he was ensconced at Rome under the influential patronage of Cardinal Pietro Ottoboni. The finesse of Corelli's violin playing and the elegance of his musical style spread his fame throughout Europe. His output was almost exclusively for strings. The bulk of it amounts to some five dozen suites and sonatas and a dozen orchestral concertos (see page 109). Among Corelli's concertos is the "Christmas" Concerto, whose

Players of a trio sonata: two violins plus the basso continuo (cello and harpsichord).

elegiac final movement paints a picture of the angels hovering over Bethlehem on the night of the Nativity.

Corelli's sonatas employ one or the other of the two favorite chamber-music textures of the Baroque: the **solo sonata** and **trio sonata**. Neither term accurately describes the number of players involved, because two players are normally used for the support-and-filler of the ever-present basso continuo. A solo sonata uses three players altogether: a single melodic part (flute, oboe, violin) plus the two players of the continuo. A trio sonata uses four players: two melodic parts plus two players of the supporting continuo.

Corelli's Trio Sonata in F Major, Op. 4, No. 7, published at Bologna in 1694, illustrates the standard Baroque "trio" texture. It has two violins in the upper range, competing spiritedly with one another—neither of them really taking the upper hand. They also work together against the lower-range basso continuo. Ex. 3.8 shows the start of the sonata. The violin parts are noted above a basso continuo line that Corelli prescribes as being for a bass viol (*violone*) and an organ. The numerals, sharps, and naturals that are found beneath the basso continuo line are another example of the figured bass notation (cf. Ex. 3.3). The figures tell the organist what chords to supply, but not what ornamental patterns and distribution to give the chords.

The score also fails to show something else that is more significant. There are none of the embellishments that Baroque soloists habitually added to their melodic lines. Baroque music was similar to jazz in the amount of improvisational freedom it allowed to performers. But more than allowing improvisation, it demanded it. Improvisation supplied the ultimate stylistic veneer, the finishing touches that gave the music its refinement and elegance. Solo singers in operas and solo instrumentalists in sonatas and concertos were expected to produce

Δ
Corelli: Trio Sonata in F Major, Op. 4, No. 7: Prelude, Corrente, Grave, Sarabande, and Gigue (Side 2, Band 5)

Ex. 3.8. Prelude, Corrente, Grave, and Sarabande (Beginning) from Trio Sonata in F Major, Op. 4, No. 7, Corelli

PRELUDIO

CORRENTE

SARABANDA

elaborate, on-the-spot embellishments of their melodic lines. Often the musical score they received from the composer was little more than a melodic skeleton that begged for personalizing touches. Corelli's music has need of such improvised embellishments, particularly in its slow movements, where the tranquil pace leaves ample time for display. Much of Corelli's appeal for audiences of his day lay in the quality of his own embellishments. Yet his works, even coming to us as skeletons, have a uniquely flavorful appeal.

1. *Prelude (Largo).* With a majestic tempo and dotted rhythms, this movement is like the slow opening section of a French overture. Toward the end, the violins engage in typical Corellian echo-imitations.

2. *Courante (fast).* Here Corelli adopts the quick motion of the Italian corrente, whose emphatic triple meter races more vigorously than in Purcell's delicate, French-styled courante. Corelli's texture is also more complex than Purcell's. Imitative entries open each section of the binary form. And the form is more expansive (see Ex. 3.9). The second section of this binary form begins with a passage (B), whose chief element of contrast is that it is in a different key. This is followed by a return to the opening (A'). Since the return is coordinated with the harmony's return to the tonic key after the excursion to the dominant, there is the added satisfaction of reaching tonal "home" again.

Ex. 3.9. **Binary Form with Return: Corrente and Giga, Corelli**

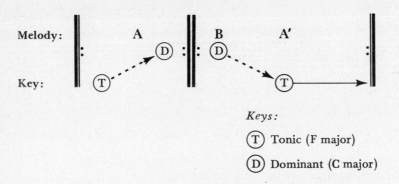

3. *Grave,* and 4. *Sarabande.* The grave is an interlude in a different key, whose slow tempo affords the first violinist a chance to improvise. The sarabande represents the third of the four dances of the standard Baroque suite. When sarabandes first appeared in sixteenth-century Spain, they were lively triple-meter dances. By the late seventeenth century, they had slowed down and adopted a stately tempo, still in triple meter. Here Corelli retains the lively

old tempo. His binary form is of the simple type used by Purcell (see Ex. 3.7), lacking a digression (B) and a return (A'). As if to compensate, Corelli adds a shapely repetition of the final measures.

5. *Giga* or *Jig*. The concluding movement of a standard Baroque suite was a gigue (French), giga (Italian), or jig (English). Musically they are all the same. Corelli's high-spirited Giga has the usual quick triple meter of this popular dance. The rollicking gait was supposed to send the listeners off in a good mood (Ex. 3.10). Corelli's binary form incorporates a digression (B) and a return to A', as in Ex. 3.9.

Ex. 3.10. Giga, Corelli

Corelli's music is a slowly acquired taste for some listeners. It seems bland at first, but the gentle magic generally takes hold. Corelli's style is full of Baroque continuous motion in running sixteenth notes. He likes the struggle of string against string and the chains of resolving dissonances that make their way deliberately up or down the scale. He also likes echo effects. Over all, there is an aura of sound that not only enchanted his contemporaries but still casts its glow across the centuries.

F. ORCHESTRAL MUSIC: THE CONCERTO GROSSO

The most imposing of Baroque instrumental forms was the **concerto grosso**, or "big concerto," which came to maturity just before 1700 in the work of Corelli (d. 1713), Giuseppe Torelli (d. 1709), and Alessandro Scarlatti (d. 1725). The term *concerto* was derived from the Italian *concertare*, which implied a "friendly contention" or coordination of diverse forces. It was used around 1600 for works in the Venetian polychoral style where voices and instruments engaged in vigorous competition. The Venetian concept of deploying bodies of sound against one another remained vital throughout the Baroque. It crystallized in the concerti grossi of the late 1600s; then it flourished in the concerto output of Vivaldi (d. 1741), J. S. Bach (d. 1750), and Handel (d. 1759), for all of whom it was the premier instrumental genre. The main interest in a concerto is a select group of soloists, called the **concertino**, or "little group," who show off

A Baroque player of the bass viol.

Trumpeter.

their virtuosity and the tricks and colors of their instruments both in opposition to one another and to a larger orchestral group. Usually two to six soloists comprise the concertino. They half-blend, half-oppose their musical ideas and colors to those of an orchestra, which is called the **ripieno,** or "fuller group." The solo concertino and orchestral ripieno sometimes play together, in which case they are collectively called the **tutti,** meaning all together. Baroque concertos have these three main features: competition between soloists and orchestra, exploitation of instrumental idioms and tone colors, and virtuoso display by the soloists. On occasion, there is also improvisation by the soloists.

Concerti grossi of the early eighteenth century often consist of three movements that are in the order fast-slow-fast. The musical form most often chosen for the individual movements is called **ritornello form.** This is a musical framework that is organized around the periodic appearances of a **ritornello**—a musical passage that returns. Ritornello form is more complex than the other two Baroque forms we have discussed—binary form and ostinato variations. It usually begins with a vigorous, memorable passage (the ritornello) that is played by the soloists and orchestra together (the tutti). From time to time the ritornello or fragments of it return later on. Ultimately, it closes the movement. Its appearances are like structural pillars sup-

Colorplate 1. An Athenian singer (ca. 490 B.C.) accompanying himself on a seven-string concert kithara. The artist suggests the musical motions by the curves of the figure.

Colorplate 2. An Etruscan fresco of the early fifth century B.C. from Tarquinia in central Italy: a player of double pipes and another of a six-string lyre. The lyre was an ancestor of the kithara. Its original tortoise-shell body is quite apparent here.

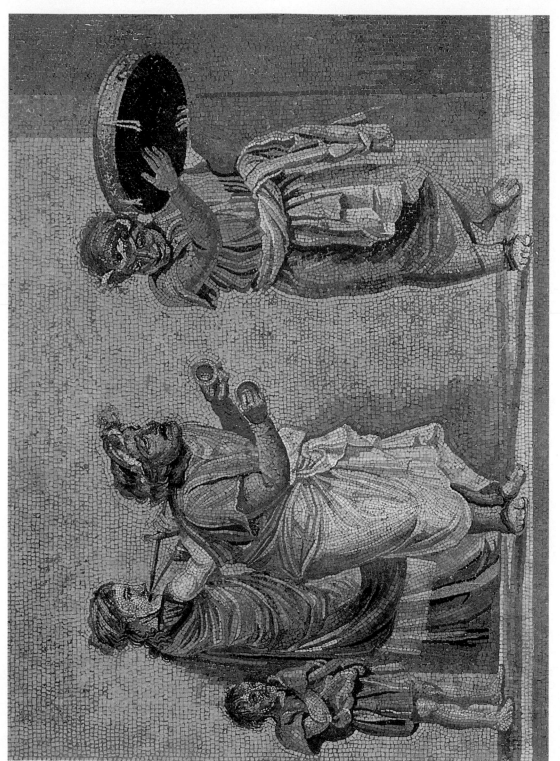

Colorplate 3. Roman street musicians. Pompeii mosaic (ca. 15 B.C. to 60 A.D.). A masked woman playing a double-pipe tibia (aulos) accompanies two male dancers who use Roman hand clappers and a tambourine.

Colorplate 4. Plainchant neumes. An antiphoner from southwestern France, twelfth century.

Colorplate 5. (*Below*) South-Italian instrumentalists (early eleventh century) playing cymbals, a psaltery, and a mandorla (an ancestor of the mandolin).

Colorplate 6. Player of a five-string, bowed vielle (fiddle); northern Spain, twelfth century.

Colorplate 7. Two monks singing from a music manuscript (Florentine, early 1400s). To the right we see the musical notation of a two-voice *ballata* of the Italian *ars nova*.

Colorplate 8. "Sumer is icumen in," as noted in a thirteenth-century English manuscript.

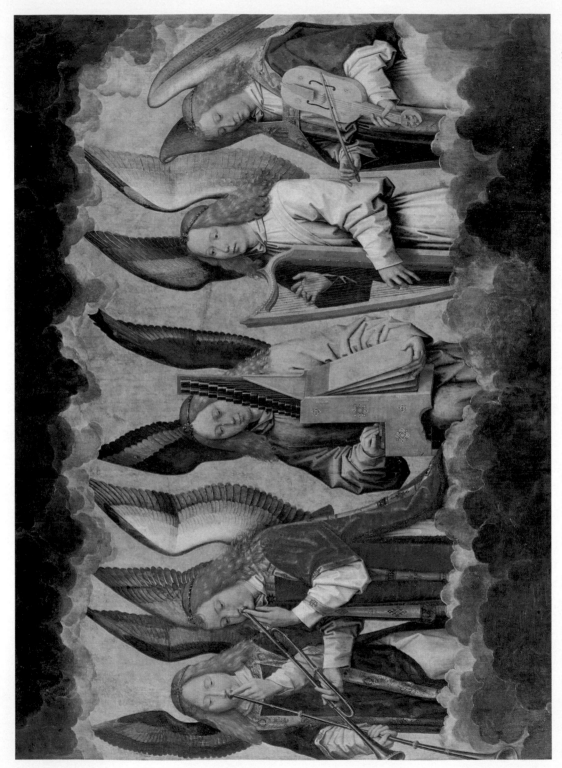

Colorplate 11. Hans Memling (Flemish, ca. 1430–1494). Five *Angel-Musicians* playing a buisine (Renaissance trumpet), another buisine or a sackbut (Renaissance trombone), a portative organ, a harp, and a fiddle.

Colorplate 12. Hans Memling. *Five Angel-Musicians* (second set) playing a psaltery, a tromba marina, a lute, a sackbut (trombone), and a recorder (vertical flute). The tromba marina was a bowed, string instrument that was limited to the playing of harmonics (see App. B.7) and that produced, fanfare-like sounds (hence the name of *tromba,* or trumpet).

Colorplate 13. Melozzo da Forli (Tuscan, 1438–1494), *Angel Playing a Lute*.

Colorplate 14. Bartolomeo Veneto (Venetian, ca. 1520). *Woman Playing a Lute*, showing the angled neck of the Renaissance instrument.

porting the musical architecture. In between the ritornellos there are passages for soloists (the concertino), accompanied by a reduced orchestra (the ripieno) or just by the basso continuo. The soloists' musical ideas tend to be less assertive than the ritornello. They are like arches between the pillars. Sometimes the soloists play commonplace figures such as scales or arpeggios—music that amounts to little in itself yet manages to display the instrument's colors and idioms and the soloists' agility. At other times, the solo sections draw material from fragments of the ritornello or present substantial ideas of their own. A general scheme for ritornello form is shown in Ex. 3.11.

Ex. 3.11. Ritornello Form

Melody:	R♪	s	R♪	s	R♪	s	....	R♪
Instruments:	all ("tutti")	soloists ("concertino")	all	soloists	all	soloists	....	all
"Terraced dynamics":	louder	softer	louder	softer	louder	softer	....	louder

R♪ = "Ritornello": An orchestral refrain played by all the instruments ("tutti").

s = Soloist's passages played by the solo instruments of the "concertino."

It is never a mechanically applied formula. Each musical realization of the form is an imaginative elaboration of different materials.

Rather than gradual shifts of crescendos and diminuendos, Baroque music has a general preference for sudden shifts in dynamic level (as from forte to piano, or piano to mezzo forte). The composers understood how effective a gradual rise or fall of volume could be as a way of raising or lowering psychological tension. They used crescendos and diminuendos in vocal music. But instrumental works tend to feature abrupt changes in dynamics, whose rises and falls are not like gentle slopes or hills, but are more like going from ridge to ridge or terrace to terrace. Such **terraced dynamics** are present already in the polychoral music of Gabrieli, whose antiphonal choirs may change dynamic levels as the action shifts from choir to choir. In a sense, terraced dynamics are built into the Baroque's prime keyboard instrument, the harpsichord, because its sound-producing mechanism cannot yield gradual dynamic changes. They are also built into the texture of the concerto grosso, where one basic concern is to alternate between the fullness of orchestral sound and the thinner sonorities of soloists.

The Concerti Grossi of Antonio Vivaldi

The leading proponent of the mature Baroque concerto grosso was Antonio Vivaldi, who was born in Venice in 1678. Vivaldi was ordained a priest in 1703, and became known as the "red priest" ("il prete rosso") for his flame-colored hair. For years he was the music master at the *Ospedale della pietà,* a Venetian school for orphaned girls that boasted one of the finest orchestras in Italy. The building still stands, a long stone's throw from San Marco. In accumulating a massive output of some 450 concertos, 40 operas, and a great deal of church and chamber music, Vivaldi composed rapidly and sometimes superficially. At his best there is a pungency and radiance that sets him alongside Bach and Handel as a supreme representative of High Baroque style. Indeed, Bach admired some of Vivaldi's early works enough to copy and arrange them. But for all of his fame and productivity, Vivaldi died destitute in 1741 at the age of 63. His best-known works are the four concerti grossi called *The Four Seasons,* which are based on four sonnets describing spring, summer, autumn, and winter. They are forerunners of the descriptive and program music of the nineteenth century. Vivaldi puts the sonnets' words right into the score. The music of the "Winter" Concerto suggests the "horrid wind," the "stamping of feet to keep warm," the "walking gingerly on ice for fear it will crack," and in the slow middle movement, the "comforting warmth of a fire enjoyed indoors while the patter of rain is heard from without."

The traditional concerto grosso used two or more soloists as its concertino group. This fashion was well established by Corelli, who adopted for his concerti grossi the same "trio" of soloists that he used in his trio sonatas: two violins plus basso continuo. Vivaldi ranged farther afield, using solo groups such as flute, oboe, and bassoon; two violins and a lute; two cellos; guitar and viola d'amore; or two mandolins. Vivaldi's major contribution, however, was in developing a vigorous younger branch of the concerto grosso—the *solo concerto,* where just a single soloist plays against the orchestra. Vivaldi wrote solo concertos for flute, cello, trumpet, and guitar, among others. *The Four Seasons* are solo concertos for a single violin with orchestra.

The "Spring" Concerto is cast in the standard mold of three movements (fast-slow-fast); 1) an energetic opening movement, 2) a tranquil central movement, and 3) an impetuous finale. The first movement is a clear example of ritornello form. It begins with a ritornello that is a broad melodious statement, full of Vivaldi's thumping energy (Ex. 3.12). The solo violin enters with its own gentler ideas. Vivaldi's score quotes the sonnet: "the singing of the birds." Then, the orchestral tutti and violin solos alternate. The ritornello appears six times in all while the soloist paints little sound-pictures in between.

△
Vivaldi: "Spring" Concerto from *The Four Seasons,* First Movement (Side 2, Band 6)

Ex. 3.12. "Spring" Concerto from *The Four Seasons,* First Movement, Vivaldi

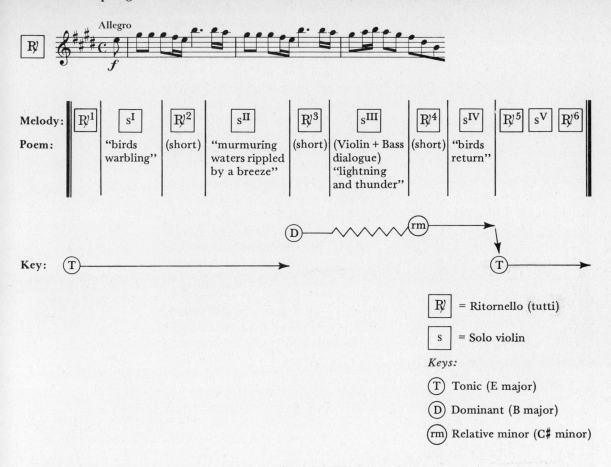

Solo episode II pictures the "murmuring waters"; solo III mimics lightning and thunder in a dialogue between the violin and the low orchestral strings; solo IV returns to the birds. A final round of ritornello-solo-ritornello brings the movement to a close.

Beyond its use of themes, textures, and tone colors, Vivaldi's ritornello form relies on the presence of major-minor tonality for its cogency. Here the relationships between tonal keys support a much larger musical structure than the binary forms of Purcell or Corelli. Ritornello form is the first form in Western musical history to exploit the network of major and minor keys on a panoramic scale. The underlying premise of any large piece of tonal music is that it is seated in a home or tonic key—the key in which it opens and closes, and that in between, the music will journey to other, contrasting keys—in any or all of which it may linger for a while. The keys most often chosen for those tonal excursions are the keys that are most closely related to the tonic in the **circle of fifths**—the space map of the key system. These are the keys that have the readiest tensions and compatibilities with the tonic—for example, the dominant, the subdominant, and the relative major and relative minor keys. Vivaldi begins his "Spring" Concerto by establishing the tonic key of E major. After a while, for the sake of contrast, he modulates to the dominant key of B major; then he goes on to the relative minor key of C-sharp minor; and finally he comes back to E major. Each key that is touched along the way injects some fresh element of tonal tension or relaxation, both in relation to the tonic and to each of the other keys. What binds Vivaldi's whole movement together, perhaps even more than the periodic returns of its ritornello theme, is that even at the remotest point in the journey among different keys, the sense of the home tonic is never wholly erased from our memory. Each new key that appears is heard in relationship to it. And when the tonic is finally reaffirmed near the end, the whole form becomes marvelously tied together. Perhaps only a few listeners can actually trace the details of Vivaldi's journey among the keys. But every listener subconsciously registers something of that network of relationships, above all its message of the tonic as "home."

Vivaldi's ritornello form, like Purcell's and Corelli's binary forms, can be experienced at various levels. There are the stimulations of its vigorous ritornello theme and the delicate figures of the solo violin. There are the alternations of texture between tutti and soloists, and the loud-soft alternations of the terraced dynamics. There are Vivaldi's typical driving rhythms—Baroque "motor power" at its most efficient. There are the descriptive vignettes: the pastoral idyll interrupted by the storm, and the return to nature's calm. There is also the tonal plan, which moves from the tonic through two contrasting keys and then back to the tonic. The high Baroque was the age of discovery for the major-minor key system. In the music of Vivaldi's generation, which was also the generation of Bach and Handel, the organizational powers of tonality found their first large-scale musical realizations. Those architectonic powers would continue to expand and to be refined over the next two centuries.

G. THE FUGUE

The Organ Tradition in the Baroque

The organ is the most versatile of musical instruments. It has the power to fill vast spaces with its hundreds of pipes. More than a harpsichord or piano, it is a self-sufficient instrument, much like an orchestra in the varieties of brass, wind, and stringlike timbres that are activated by the touch of a finger or a toe. The organ also has the aura of a "spiritual" instrument. To hear it played conjures up a churchly mood, above all the religiosity of a Baroque church. The physical appearance of the Baroque organ contributes to this with its sunburst arrays of pipes that confront the listener with gilded splendor. From the isolation of the organ loft, the Baroque organist is like a musical pastor, philosophizing on the familiar hymn tunes and exhorting the congregation to spiritual order through the artistic order of variations and fugues. During the late Renaissance and early Baroque, organ music was a specialty of Italian composers. Its great stylists were the two Gabrielis, Andrea (d. 1586) and Giovanni (d. 1612), along with Claudio Merulo (d. 1604) and Girolamo Frescobaldi (d. 1643). Then came a succession of notable Dutch, Scandinavian, and German composers: Sweelinck (d. 1621), Schein (d. 1630), Scheidt (d. 1654), Pachelbel (d. 1706), and Buxtehude (d. 1707). To hear the aging Buxtehude play at Lübeck the young Johann Sebastian Bach journeyed on foot over 200 kilometers in the year 1705.

Johann Sebastian Bach

The height of the northern organ tradition was reached with Bach, who was born in the central German town of Eisenach in 1685. It was the year that also saw the birth of Handel at Halle, which lay

The Organ, *an engraving by Martin Engelbrecht (1684-1756).*

Bach's musical handwriting; beginning of a fugue for three voices.

150 kilometers to the northeast. Bach's family had been noted throughout the seventeenth century for its composers, singers, and instrumentalists, and three of Bach's own children carried that musical dynasty through the late eighteenth century. Bach held three important posts during his long career. First he was a church organist at the town of Weimar from 1708 to 1717. By all accounts he was the best organist of his day. At Weimar he composed most of his organ music, including the Toccata and Fugue in D Minor and the Passacaglia and Fugue in C Minor. Between 1717 and 1723, he was the director of music for the Prince of Cöthen in north-central Germany. There he composed most of his orchestral and chamber music, including the six *Brandenburg Concertos* and many sonatas and suites. Finally, in 1723, he was named the music director of the Church of St. Thomas in Leipzig, the leading post for a composer in Lutheran north Germany. He remained there until his death in 1750. During those Leipzig years he produced his larger church works, the *St. John Passion,* the *St. Matthew Passion,* and the Mass in B Minor, along with most of his church cantatas. He also taught academic subjects to the choirboys.

Bach was not the first choice of the Leipzig elders for that job. He was a proud, intense person, with a musical style that seemed cold and old-fashioned to many. Other composers with sunnier dispositions and more amiable styles were approached before he was. In a way, the church elders were right. Bach's music was largely ignored by his contemporaries, who preferred the more ingratiating styles of his own sons—Carl Philipp Emanuel Bach in Germany and Johann Christian Bach in Italy and England. But the father's visions have proved the more durable, and Bach now ranks among the most esteemed composers of the West.

The Fugue

Bach's natural mode of expression was imitative polyphony. He thought in fugal polyphony and fugue. A **fugue** is an imitative polyphonic composition where two or more voices or parts state and develop a single melodic fragment called a subject, bringing it many times and in varied combinations. The word *fugue* comes from the Latin *fuga,* meaning "flight." Thus a fugue consists of a number of voices in artful flight and pursuit, literally chasing one another around as they imitate the same melodic fragment. The composers of the Renaissance generally built their works out of successive points of imitation—sets of imitative entries, each based on a different musical subject. Now the fugal polyphony of the Baroque built whole works using a single subject throughout. The result was unified, concentrated—the ultimate example of the Baroque's single-mindedness.

Each fugue has a fixed number of voices or parts, the number often being specified in its title (for example, Fugue for Four Voices). The usual number of such voice-parts is from three to six. Each voice-part maintains its separate melodic identity throughout, whether it is sung by a human voice or played on an instrument. On a keyboard instrument such as the organ or harpsichord, the player's two hands (plus the feet on some organs) may project four, five, or more individual voice-parts. The subject of a fugue can have just about any shape—short or long, slow or fast, angular or smooth. Somehow the subject must be suitable for imitative elaboration. Each fugue starts out with a complete set of subject entries called the **exposition**, or opening exposition. It amounts to the same thing as a Renaissance point of imitation: The subject is presented by each voice in turn, first one alone, then the others in order until all have entered. After a voice makes its entry with the subject, it goes on, adding free melodic material to the polyphonic web. There is no prescribed order of high-, middle-, or low-voice entries. In fact, once past the opening exposition, there are really no "rules" at all in a fugue. The composer just brings in the subject as often and as effectively as possible. More than with the other Baroque forms we have discussed (ostinato variations, binary form, ritornello form), fugues have widely differing shapes and designs.

The presentations of the subject that come after the opening exposition are again called subject entries or expositions, even when the subject appears by itself without an imitative answer. Although fugues begin with one voice alone, they rarely drop back to a single voice after the opening. The later expositions of the subject tend to emerge from the full polyphonic texture. Some fugues incorporate passages of mild contrast called **episodes**. Yet fugal texture is so homogeneous that an episode's "contrast" may amount to little more than the momentary absence of the subject. Many fugues have no episodes at all, just the continued presence of their subject. To the extent that fugues can be said to have a general form, it is a loose alternation between expositions—where the subject is present—and episodes—where it is not:

‖ Exp | Ep | Exp | Ep | Exp | Ep . . . . | Exp ‖

But such diagrams are misleading. Inner demarcations and stopping points are extremely rare in fugues. More than any other form of Baroque music, the fugue epitomizes the ideal of single-minded, continuous motion. Musicians think of fugue as being not a "form," but a "texture" of imitative polyphony where a single subject is exploited through an entire composition.

Bach's "Little" Fugue in G Minor for Organ (BWV 578) was probably composed during his years of service as an organist at Weimar, from 1708 to 1717. It has four voice-parts that are knit together overall by nine presentations of an unusually long fugue subject (Ex. 3.13).

△
J. S. Bach: "Little" Fugue
in G Minor for Organ
(Side 3, Band 1)

Ex. 3.13. "Little" Fugue in G Minor, Bach

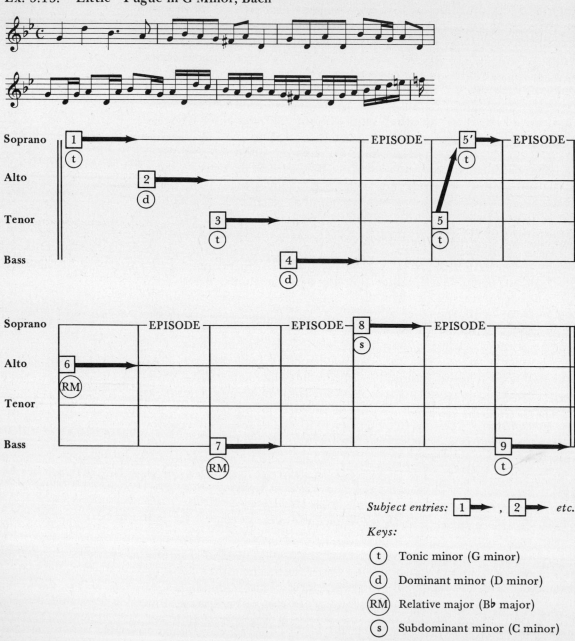

However, the subject's rambling quality masks some careful calculations. There is the gradual increase in rhythmic activity, from the placid quarter notes at the beginning to livelier eighth notes and then flowing sixteenths. There is the fact that the fugue is in the key of G minor, and its subject is contoured so as to highlight the tonic chord in that key: G-B-flat-D. The first three notes of the subject outline the chord, and as the melody unfolds, the same three pitches remain the centers of attention. Bach has an order of voice entries for the opening exposition that runs from the top to the bottom voice, but he could have chosen any order. His nine subject entries follow a tonal plan that gives unity to the entire piece. The opening exposition (entries 1-4) emphasizes the two most important keys of tonality by alternating between the tonic key (G minor) and the dominant key (D minor). Later entries add two further keys (B-flat major and C minor), which make this fugue the same kind of tonal journey as Vivaldi's ritornello form. To end it all, the subject naturally returns in the tonic.

There are four useful steps to take in listening to a fugue:

1. Learn the subject. It is first heard all by itself. It is what the fugue is about. Learn it so you can identify it.
2. Listen to the whole fugue from beginning to end a couple of times to get its overall scope. Pick out some of the subject entries along the way.
3. Listen again, now singling out the voice-parts. How many separate "voices" can you hear? In which register (high, middle, or low) does each subject entry come? Choose some individual voice-part and try to follow it through. But don't be discouraged if you can't. It is often impossible to do just by listening.
4. Listen for the overall form—for the alternations between expositions (where the subject is present) and episodes (where it is not). Remember that many fugues have no episodes.

It takes many hearings to perceive the inner workings of a fugue. Unlike most music, where we expect to hear everything that is going on, this is not possible in a fugue. The ear and mind simply cannot grasp all the ins and outs of many separate voices. Ultimately, we may trust that the composer has set up the inner mechanics, and we abandon ourselves to the fugue's radiant complexity.

In addition to the fugal devices that turn up in Bach's "Little" Fugue in G Minor, there are others worth knowing about as witness to the care that composers lavish on this form. They are options, some of which are more common than others. Some are not even meant to be heard by the listener's ear, but can be perceived only by the score-reader's eye. One of the more hearable options is called **diminution**. This means speeding up a fugue subject so that it is heard twice or even four times faster than before. The opposite of diminution is **augmentation**. Again, this is a generally hearable option. In augmentation the subject is heard twice or four times slower than before. Ex. 3.14 shows the subject of a fugue for piano by Beethoven in its original form (a), in diminution (b), and in augmentation (c). The diminution adds nervous excitement; the augmentation adds breadth. Both are intensifiers, and as such they tend to be saved for the later portions of fugues.

Other fugal options—**inversion**, **retrograde**, and **retrograde inversion**—are more hidden, often passing unnoticed even by the ears of attentive professionals. The composer puts them in for their tidiness and for the private satisfaction of knowing that they are going on inside the music, carrying out their artful polyphonic missions. *Inversion* turns the subject upside down; for instance, what was pre-

Ex. 3.14. Transformation of a Fugue Subject:
  Sonata No. 31 in A-Flat, Op. 110, Beethoven

a) Subject

b) Diminution (altered subject)

c) Augmentation

d) Inversion

e) Retrograde*

f) Retrograde inversion*

*Not used by Beethoven.

viously a rising interval of a fourth becomes a falling interval of a fourth in the inversion (Ex. 3.14d). In *retrograde,* the subject is read backwards, from last note to first. In *retrograde inversion,* the subject is read both backwards and with its melody inverted. These last two techniques are rare, and they are almost never detectable by simply listening. If Beethoven had used them in his piano fugue, they would look like Ex. 3.14e, f.

Two other fugal options are more hearable. They are again intensifiers, tending to find a place toward the end of a fugue. **Stretto** is a shortening or telescoping of the elapsed time between fugal entries. The word *stretto* in Italian means a tight or narrow fit. In an opening exposition, each voice waits for the preceding voice to complete its subject entry. But in a stretto the entries overlap, with the next voice beginning before the last one has finished (Ex. 3.15). Stretto gives a

Ex. 3.15. Normal Imitation versus Stretto Imitation

Normal Imitation

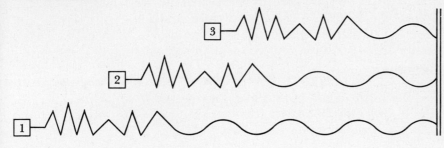

Stretto Imitation

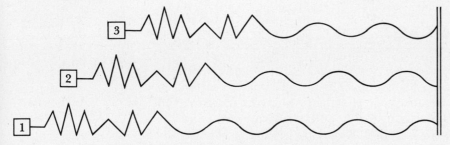

sense of rigor and competition. The listener feels the stimulation of the telescoping entries as they pile on. A final option in fugues is *pedal point.* This consists of a single pitch that is held steadfastly in the bass while the upper voices swirl above it, creating harmonic tensions. On an organ, a pedal point is usually played by the deep-voiced pedals, hence its name. The favorite place for pedal points is near the end of a work, yet they can occur anywhere, and not only in fugues. The style of Notre Dame organum (ca. 1200) already has them (see Chapter 1). In the late nineteenth century, Tchaikovsky put a stirring example near the end of his Fourth Symphony. They remain a common device for increasing tension.

Bach composed many individual fugues for organ and harpsichord, and he included many fugal movements and fugal passages among his chamber and choral works. He collected some fugues in sets. The two-volume anthology of harpsichord fugues called the *Well-Tempered Clavier* contains 48 fugues, each with an introductory prelude. Each volume of the *Well-Tempered Clavier,* which he composed from around 1720 through 1742, has a prelude and a fugue in each of the major and minor keys. Bach's other systematic sets of fugues and related works are the *Musical Offering,* which he sent to Frederick the Great of Prussia in 1747 after a visit to the court at Potsdam, and the *Art of the Fugue,* Bach's last major work, which remained unfinished at his death in 1750. Many of Bach's fugues, for example, those of the *Well-Tempered Clavier,* are prefaced by free, introductory movements, with names like fantasy, toccata, or prelude, that serve as lead-ins to the fugue. They share the same key, but generally have different themes than the fugue. A **fantasy**, or **fantasia**, indicates a work of extraordinary imagination and stylistic freedom. A **toccata** is an improvisatory piece with virtuoso flashes, for example, the Toccata in D Minor, preceding the organ fugue in that key. Among the forty-eight preludes of the *Well-Tempered Clavier,* there are a great many styles and forms. Bach's most elaborate fugal introduction is the Passacaglia in C Minor for Organ. A *passacaglia* is a set of ostinato variations. Bach's spacious work runs to twenty end-on-end variations, prefacing a fugue of correspondingly ample size.

H. THE SUITES OF J. S. BACH

Bach cultivated every Baroque genre except the opera. While much of his music is serious, even austere, he is not always so, not even in his fugues. His suites of dances are the places where he most relaxed and aimed to please. The eighteenth century had various names for its dance collections, including *suite, sonata da camera, partita, divertimento, divertissement, serenade, ordre, cassation,* and even *overture.* All amount to the same thing—a succession of dance movements that are usually in the same key and usually in binary form. Bach produced six English Suites, six French Suites, and six Partitas for harpsichord, all with the basic four-movement format: allemande, courante, sarabande, and gigue. To some he added opening preludes, and there are other dances between the sarabande and concluding gigue. Bach's four orchestral suites were called "overtures" because each one begins with an overture in the French or Lullian style before going on to a set of dances. The Orchestra Suite or Overture No. 3 in D has as its second movement the aria, or air, whose noble melody is familiar in the violin arrangement, "Air for the G String."

Bach's suites for purest entertainment are the six French Suites for harpsichord. The name "French," which may not be his own, reflects the scattering of French-style dances that appear before the final gigues. They include the gavotte, bourrée, loure, etc. The dances are all in binary form, and generally they are used in more expansive ways than the binary forms of Purcell or Corelli. Overall the dances are longer, their ideas are more complex, and their textures are often laced with polyphony. After all, they are by Bach!

The Gigue that concludes Bach's French Suite No. 5 in G Major is one of his sprightliest creations. Its rapid triple meter and vigorous rhythms are likely to put the listener in good spirits. Still, the jig theme serves as the subject of a miniature three-voice fugue. In fact, the Gigue consists of two such fugues, both based on the same subject, one for each section of the binary form (Ex. 3.16). Careful

Δ
J. S. Bach: French Suite No. 5 in G Major: Gigue (Side 3, Band 2)

Ex. 3.16. Gigue from French Suite No. 5 in G, Bach

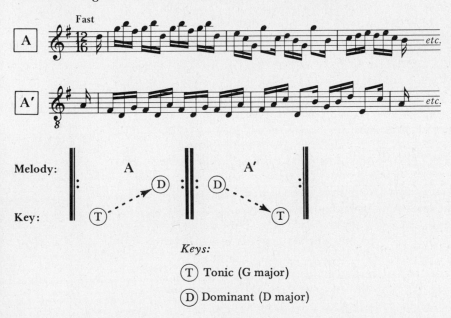

Keys:
Ⓣ Tonic (G major)
Ⓓ Dominant (D major)

listening will reveal that the second fugue—the second section of the binary form—begins with an inversion of the subject used for the first section. But the point of Bach's piece is not in such learned details. Rather it is the infectious enthusiasm of the exhilarations piling on one another. The Gigue should be heard first for its binary-form framework. Then the inner divisions and polyphonic niceties reveal themselves. Some listeners will hear the changes in tonality between the tonic and dominant keys, particularly the abrupt shift where each section begins its repeat. All listeners can hear the single-mindedness of mood and the "polyphonic motor power" that animates the texture. Each section is an unbroken whole—its rhythmic thrust constantly evolving from the little bit of material at the beginning.

I. THE CONCERTOS OF J. S. BACH

Oboist.

Bach's image of the concerto grosso was formed by the concertos of his Italian contemporaries, particularly the three-movement (fast-slow-fast) concertos of Antonio Vivaldi, who was seven years his senior. To the Vivaldian model, Bach added a Germanic sturdiness and intricacy. He thickened the polyphony and illumined everything with a subtle fancy of his own. Some of the concertos that we know today as Bach's were actually his arrangements of early violin concertos by Vivaldi. But the best works are entirely his own—works such as the "Italian" Concerto, which transplants the full apparatus of an orchestral concerto with its solo-orchestra contrasts and terraced dynamics to the hands of a single harpsichordist; or the Concerto for Two Violins in D Minor; or the six *Brandenburg Concertos*.

The *Brandenburg Concertos*

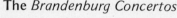

Δ

J. S. Bach: Third Movement of *Brandenburg Concerto* No. 2 in F Major (Side 3, Band 3)

The *Brandenburg Concertos* were composed around 1720 for the pleasure of the Margrave of Brandenburg, a provincial German prince who maintained an orchestra at his palace. Each *Brandenburg Concerto* features a different group of soloists. The *Brandenburg Concerto* No. 2 in F Major has a concertino consisting of a solo flute, oboe, violin, and trumpet, plus a ripieno orchestra of strings and basso continuo. The four soloists capitalize on their distinctive colors, competing among themselves and with the orchestra. Bach's baroque trumpet produced high pitches with an elegant tone. It was difficult to play in its own day, and today's trumpeters, using a modern instrument, tend to negotiate its daringly exposed heights as if they were walking a tightrope. When its silvery peals are well formed, they are enormously gratifying. In the energetic third-movement finale of this concerto, the soloists and orchestra indulge in their usual contrasts. But instead of a ritornello form, this movement is more like a fugue. That is in keeping with Bach's strong inclination toward polyphony. The form is too complex for a listening diagram. It begins with a cocky fugue subject in the solo trumpet, full of skips and

Ex. 3.17. Beginning of Finale from *Brandenburg Concerto No. 2*, Bach

Trumpet, sounding an octave higher

nervous trills (Ex. 3.17). Further subject entries serve to introduce the solo oboe, violin, and flute. A long central section follows, with alternating episodes and subject entries. Finally, the subject returns in the oboe and flute, and then the trumpet mounts the perilous heights for a final time and brings the movement to a close. Like so much of Bach, the music is satisfying both for its majesty and for its detail. It represents "polyphonic motor power" at its most sublime.

J. CANTATA, PASSION, AND MASS

The Church Cantatas of Bach

Bach's purely instrumental music—concertos, suites, sonatas, fugues—is impressive in total bulk, yet he put still greater effort into his church music, where voices join with instruments. During his tenure as music master at St. Thomas's church in Leipzig, beginning in 1723, Bach composed over two hundred church **cantatas.** The genre of *cantata* originated in seventeenth-century Italy as a successor to the madrigal. It was a "sung" ("cantata") chamber work that employed on a smaller scale the same techniques of recitatives and arias that were employed in the Italian operas. *Secular cantatas,* which were the direct outgrowths of the secular madrigals, dealt with allegorical or worldly subjects, such as the amours of shepherds and shepherdesses, and occasionally with moral and philosophical subjects. Almost all of Bach's cantatas were *sacred* or *church cantatas* that were written for church performances. They dealt with high-minded religious subjects to edify and improve the morals of the Lutheran congregation that paid Bach's salary. Each Sunday service in the church had its quota of Bible readings, prayers, and sermons. In addition, there was a cantata, which might take up to half an hour. The cantata was like another sermon. It commented upon and gave dramatic substance to a Bible reading of the day.

In general, Baroque cantatas were chamber music for soloists. Bach's church cantatas, however, were destined for performance in a spacious interior, and they were scored for a chorus and small orchestra, supplementing the vocal and instrumental soloists. Compared to today's orchestras, Bach's orchestra was modest in size and limited in tone colors, but it was already closer to the modern orchestra than to Monteverdi's orchestra for *Orfeo* in 1607. In 1730 at Leipzig, Bach had a basic group of about 24 players: two or three each of first and second violins, four violas, two cellos or violas da gamba, one double bass, two flutes, two or three oboes, one or two bassoons, and three trumpets. Bach himself presided at the harpsichord or organ, supplying the basso continuo's filler chords and coordinating the singers and players. The chorus was correspondingly small—just a handful of singers to each voice-part.

Bach's church cantata, "Wachet auf" ("Sleepers wake, a voice is calling," No. 140 in the complete edition of his works), was composed for a Leipzig Sunday service on November 25, 1731. Like many masters of a craft, Bach produced his works just when they were needed. Thus the cantata "Wachet auf" was copied out in evident haste only a few days before its first performance. The Gospel reading for that day—it was the twenty-seventh Sunday after Trinity—supplied the plot for the cantata's seven movements. It presents the parable of the Wise and Foolish Virgins (Matthew 25: 1-13) who are awakened at midnight to go forth and meet their Bridegroom—the Savior. The wise ones have put enough oil in their lamps, but the imprudent ones have not done so, and it is just the wise ones who find their way to the wedding. Bach's congregation savored the moral: Be prudent and vigilant because you don't know when you'll be called to meet the Lord.

A musical feature in many of Bach's church cantatas that his listeners must have found congenial was the incorporation of one of the well-known Lutheran hymn tunes. Those tunes, known as **Lutheran chorales**, or simply **chorales**, were familiar since childhood to churchgoers in Bach's time. Bach usually wove one of the chorale tunes into two or three movements of a cantata. In the final movement, the chorale was harmonized in simple block chords, which encouraged the worshippers to sing along. A church cantata that incorporates the melody of a Lutheran chorale is called a *chorale cantata.*

Bach used one of the best-loved Lutheran chorales in three of the seven movements of his Cantata No. 140, "Wachet auf." The text of the chorale, and perhaps also its noble music, were composed around 1600 by the Westphalian pastor Philipp Nicolai. The regally simple melody has been called "the king of chorales" (Ex. 3.18). For the other four movements, Bach chose original poetry of his own time dealing with the story of the wise and foolish virgins. He laid out a characteristically symmetrical plan for the seven movements. The outer movements (Nos. 1 and 7) along with the central movement (No. 4) present three stanzas of Nicolai's chorale tune. The movements in between (Nos. 2-3 and 5-6) form two pairs, each one composed, as in a scene from a Baroque opera, of an introductory recitative followed by a lyric set piece (Ex. 3.19).

Δ
J. S. Bach: First Movement of Cantata No. 140, "Sleepers wake"
(Side 3, Band 4)

Ex. 3.18. Chorale: Stanza 1 of "Wachet auf, ruft uns die Stimme" ("Sleepers wake, a voice is calling"), Philipp Nicolai (ca. 1600)

(1) Sleep - ers wake, a voice is call - ing,
(4) Mid - night strikes this ve - ry hour_____

(2) The watch - man high u - pon the tow - er:
(5) They call to us with strong clear voic - es:

(3) Wake up, you, town Je - ru - sa - lem
(6) Where are you, wise young vir - gins, where?

(7) A - rise, your Bride - groom comes,

(8) Rise up and take your lamps,

(9) Al - le - lu - ya!

(10) Your - selves pre - pare, (11) The wed - ding's nigh.

(12) Forth you must go to meet_____ Him.

Ex. 3.19. Overall Plan of Cantata No. 140, "Wachet auf," Bach

MOVEMENT 1	2	3	4	5	6	7
Chorale hymn Stanza 1 Vocal-instrumental fantasy; ritornello form; hymn in soprano	Recitative (Tenor)	Duet (Soprano and bass)	Chorale hymn Stanza 2 Viola and basso continuo; hymn in tenor	Recitative (Bass)	Duet (Soprano and bass)	Chorale hymn Stanza 3 Simple harmony; hymn in soprano

1. First Movement, "The Watchman Awakens the Faithful": Chorale, Stanza 1; Chorale Fantasy (Chorus and Orchestra).

Sleepers wake, a voice is calling, The watchman high upon the tower . . . Midnight strikes . . . Arise, your Bridegroom comes . . . Alleluya . . . Forth you must go to meet Him.

This majestic fantasy for chorus and orchestra is the largest movement in the cantata. It begins with an orchestral ritornello whose dotted rhythms are maintained throughout, giving the music the ceremonial quality of a French overture (Ex. 3.20). The whole move-

Ex. 3.20. Ritornello of First Movement, Cantata No. 140, Bach

ment is framed by the periodic returns of the opening orchestral ritornello. The musical highpoints, however, are the entries of the chorale melody, whose phrases sail in on high, sung slowly and ethereally by the soprano choir. They seem detached from the polyphonic bustle below, with its animation like that of a concerto grosso. Toward the end, the three lower voices spin out an impressive **fugato** on the word "Alleluya" (Ex. 3.21). A *fugato* is an inci-

Ex. 3.21. "Alleluya" of First Movement, Cantata No. 140, Bach

dental use of fugal polyphony within a larger composition whose overall plan is not that of a fugue. The sopranos return with the final phrases of the chorale, and the movement closes with a **da capo** repetition of the opening ritornello. *Da capo* (from the beginning) means that the opening musical section is repeated but the composer does not write it out. The abbreviation D.C. in the score was enough to tell the musicians to go back and do the beginning over again.

2. Second Movement, "Heralding the Bridegroom" (Recitative for Tenor and Basso Continuo).

He comes, he comes . . . Daughters of Zion come forth . . . Wake up and bestir yourselves to receive the Bridegroom . . .

This short tenor recitative serves to prepare the lyric duet that follows.

3. Third Movement, "The Yearning of the Soul and the Savior's Words of Comfort" (Duet for Soprano and Bass, with Solo Violin and Basso Continuo).

When wilt Thou appear, my salvation? I arrive . . . Throw open the hall to the heavenly banquet . . . I open the hall . . . Come, Jesus . . . Come, lovely Soul.

This dialogue between the anxious Soul (soprano) and the beloved Jesus (bass) begins with a flowery violin solo that was intended for a small-size baroque violin called a violino piccolo, though nowadays it is usually playcd on a regular-size instrument. The violinist's melodic embroideries continue through the singers' discourse and eventually bring the movement to a close. Underlying the violin figurations is a very simple melody. Without decorations, it would be inelegant and dull, but Bach never presents it that way (Ex. 3.22). Baroque composers generally left such melodic adornment to the

Ex. 3.22. Third Movement, Cantata No. 140, Bach

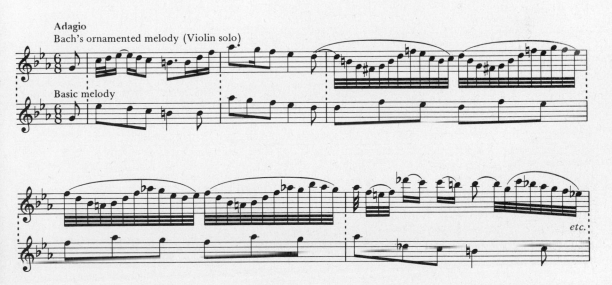

performers, whose taste and skill in improvising ornaments were important factors in their musicianship and audience appeal. But Bach had a mania for imposing his own taste on the details of his work, and he wrote out this ornamentation in full. In its overall form, the duet has a simple plan of A-B-A': that is, its opening A section returns with some change at the end. Such a form is sometimes called a *modified da capo form.*

4. Fourth Movement, "Arrival of the Bridegroom": Chorale, Stanza 2 (Chorus of Tenors, Strings, and Basso Continuo).

Δ
J. S. Bach: Fourth Movement of Cantata No. 140 (Side 3, Band 5)

Zion hears the watchmen singing . . . The friend from heaven comes resplendent . . . Lord Jesus, God's own Son. Hosanna . . .

This central movement of the cantata brings the climax of the drama—the arrival of the Bridegroom. The chorale melody reappears, now treated differently than in the concertolike opening movement: It is simple chamber music in three parts. Just two of the parts—a haunting string melody and a basso continuo accompaniment—are heard at the beginning (Ex. 3.23a). For a while it seems as if there will be only these two parts. And they would be enough: Their music

Ex. 3.23. Fourth Movement, Cantata No. 140, Bach

is complete in itself. But then the chorale flows in, filling up the middle register, and we realize that something was missing all along (Ex. 3.23b). The chorale is sung by the choir of tenors; it is given a lively pulse and human warmth that are lacking in the billowy soprano phrases of the first movement.

The texture offers a striking example of nonimitative polyphony. We usually expect imitative polyphony from Bach. Yet these three voice-parts have different melodic contours, sharing almost nothing with one another. The texture holds together without the usual imitative "glue." The attractive string melody joins with the sturdy continuo to carry the music forward; then the radiant chorale ties all together with its familiar strains. This is the most striking movement in the cantata, indeed one of the most memorable of all Bach's creations. Bach himself liked it well enough to make an arrangement for organ, in which format it became one of the small handful of his works published during his lifetime.

An organ piece that is built upon the phrases of a Lutheran chorale is called a **chorale prelude**. Since the late Renaissance, Lutheran organists had indulged in the custom of prefacing each Sunday's chorale singing with a free organ composition based on the chorale tune of the day. Their instrumental ruminations were sometimes improvised, sometimes carefully composed. In either case, they were "preludes" to the chorale and so became known as chorale preludes. The congregations enjoyed hearing these versions of the familiar hymn phrases. Bach wrote dozens of chorale preludes for organ, elaborating the well-loved tunes.

5. Fifth Movement, "Christ Accepts the Bride (Soul)" (Accompanied Recitative for Bass and Strings).

Come enter with me, my chosen bride. Forget, oh Soul, the anguish and pain you suffered. And on my left shall you rest, and my right shall embrace you.

The part of the Savior is sung by a solemn bass voice whose recitative is supported by a harmony of orchestral strings—as if enveloping Him in a musical halo. The use of full orchestral accompaniment makes this an **accompanied recitative**, as distinct from the "dry" or **secco recitative** in Bach's second movement, where the accompaniment was only the basso continuo. The distinction between *secco* and *accompanied* recitatives was a significant one in the eighteenth century. For ordinary conversations and run-of-the-mill dramatic situations, composers relied on the matter-of-fact secco recitative style, whose accompaniment was the basso continuo. For moments of high drama or emotion they turned to the more expressive melodic declamation of the accompanied recitative style, with its added fullness of orchestral support.

6. Sixth Movement, "The Bliss of Union Between Christ and the Bride (Soul)" (Duet for Soprano and Bass, with Solo Oboe and Basso Continuo).

My friend is mine! And I am Thine! Love shall separate nothing . . . Fullness of joy and rapture shall there be!

Once again, as in an operatic scene, an introductory recitative (No. 5) has a lyric follow-up (No. 6). As in No. 3, it is a duet between Jesus and the Soul, but where the preceding duet dealt with anticipation and yearning, this one deals with contentment and joy. A sprightly tune is introduced by the solo oboe, then is taken up by the vocalists, who bill and coo like lovers in an Italian opera (Ex. 3.24).

Ex. 3.24. Sixth Movement, Cantata No. 140, Bach

The duet's musical form is a broad A-B-A whose opening A is repeated exactly for the closing A. Again, Bach does not trouble to write out the repeat. He simply writes the letters D.C. (da capo) and the whole A section returns unchanged. Arias and duets with A-B-A da capo returns of their opening music were the stock in trade not only of Bach but of his operatic contemporaries—composers such as Porpora, Hasse, Jommelli, and Handel—who habitually filled their stage works with two or three dozen such numbers. These were usually solo arias—so-called **da capo arias**. And each aria or lyric number was prefaced, as in Bach's cantata, by its morsel of introductory recitative.

7. Seventh Movement, "Universal Thanksgiving": Chorale, Stanza 3 (Chorus, Orchestra, Soloists, and Congregation).

△
J. S. Bach: Seventh Movement of Cantata No. 140 (Side 3, Band 6)

Glory be sung to You with human and angelic tongues . . . Of twelve pearls are the gates of Your city . . . No ear has heard such joy. We rejoice forever in sweet jubilation.

The cantata's seventh movement offers the exultant final stanza of Nicolai's chorale. In the first and fourth movements, the chorale was interwoven with complex polyphony. Now in the final movement, the chorale melody is sung as a simple hymn, supported by block chords where everyone can join in the singing. So far, the congregation has been a silent observer. Now the congregation is brought into the musical drama. Raising their voices, they rejoice in its happy conclusion.

The Passions of Bach

Bach composed enough church cantatas during his career to supply more than four years' worth of Leipzig Sunday services. In a cosmopolitan mixture the cantatas combined the pomp of the French overture, the exuberant lyricism and dramatic recitatives of the Italian opera, and the instrumental idioms of the Italian sonata and concerto grosso. To those imported elements, Bach added the serene melodic world of his native Lutheran chorales and an overlay of modern German piety.

Bach took the same varied ingredients found in his church cantatas and elevated them to the pinnacle of sacred musical theater in two epic-length works, the *Passion According to St. John* (1723) and the *Passion According to St. Matthew* (1729). Bach's *Passions* trace the Gospel stories of Jesus' sufferings during the Trial and Crucifixion (the Latin *passio* means suffering). Each work uses the German Bible's own language, with the words of Jesus, Peter, Pilate, and the others sung by solo singers in the style of dramatic recitatives. Interspersed with the age-old Gospel narratives are two layers of contemporary Lutheran spirituality. One consists of musical numbers—arias, duets, and choruses—that like the set pieces in Cantata No. 140 are based on fresh eighteenth-century religious poetry. These musically elaborate numbers give voice to the piety of the eighteenth-century beholder. Their heartfelt expressions of grief and consolation relieve the tense continuity of the Gospel drama. The other spiritual layer is a series of Lutheran chorales that appear throughout in simple harmonizations, just as in the last movement of Cantata No. 140. The chorales are spread among the recitatives and lyric numbers of Bach's *Passions,* and again, they bring the worshipper into the theater of musical action. Everybody sang along.

Bach's Mass in B Minor

Bach's last monumental sacred work was the Mass in B Minor. Practically every leading composer since the fourteenth century had set the Ordinary of the Mass to music, but Bach's setting was by far the longest and the richest. That he undertook to set the Catholic Mass at all was something of an oddity, for in an age when piety was narrowly delimited according to religious sect, Bach in his own church might have used only the Kyrie, Gloria, and Sanctus, and then normally in the German translation by Martin Luther. But he set the entire Latin text. In the hope of obtaining an advantageous appointment, he presented the Kyrie and Gloria to the Catholic Prince of Saxony in 1733. Then he assembled the Credo, Sanctus, and Agnus Dei during the following years. Bach parceled out each of the five main texts into small sections and turned them into arias, duets, or choruses. He employed the same techniques used in his cantatas and passions. But there is one important omission. The Catholic Mass is a sacred ritual, not a dramatic scenario. It offers no occasion for vivid, storytelling recitatives, and Bach's Mass in B Minor consists solely of lyric numbers. With his urge to be expansive and profound, Bach accumulated nearly three hours of music. That is an elephantine length, considering that a priest's spoken Mass may take only a handful of minutes. Bach's music scarcely fits the framework of church usage. For all of its bulk and splendor, it is essentially a private devotion. But by the same token, it is universalized. Everyone of spiritual bent can find edification and renewal in Bach's musical contemplation of the sacred mysteries.

K. HANDEL AND THE ORATORIO

Bach and Handel, the two key figures of the late Baroque, were born in the same year (1685) and in the same small corner of northern Germany. Their careers could scarcely have been more different. Bach came from a family whose offspring for generations had been

Bassoonist.

Timpanist.

musicians. Handel was the son of a well-to-do barber-surgeon who wanted him to become a lawyer. Bach cultivated an ingrown, spiritual art within a narrow circle of German cities, never journeying more than a few hundred kilometers from his birthplace. His reputation scarcely stretched farther than he did. Handel was a cosmopolitan who began by mastering the high-fashion international style of Italian serious opera (*opera seria*). While in his early twenties, he worked in Germany and Italy. Then he went to England, where he established himself in 1712 at the age of twenty-seven. He remained a colorful fixture on the London scene until his death in 1759 at the age of seventy-four. To his native German penchant for elaborateness, Handel added an Italianate sense of drama and an English geniality of sound. In all, he was the Baroque's best-rounded, most satisfying musical personality. Unlike Bach, who married twice and fathered twenty children, Handel remained a bachelor. He was a corpulent giant with crude manners, a hot temper, and a comic German-English accent. He was something of a glutton, which allowed his enemies to caricature him as a pig. Yet he was an intimate of the Hanoverian-English royalty and a shrewd organizer who managed his own opera companies in the London of George I and II. Handel faced financial ruin more than once, but when he died he was serenely wealthy and was honored with burial in Westminster Abbey. Odd as it seems, this Italianate German became the pride of English music. Even more than Purcell, Handel is the "English" composer of modern times who enjoys enduring international stature.

Colorplate 20

Handel produced large quantities of music for keyboard, chamber, and orchestral groups. His popular orchestral music includes the festive *Water Music,* composed in 1715 for a royal celebration that took place in boats on the Thames, and the *Royal Fireworks Music,* written for a similar festivity at a London park in 1749. His main contributions were to the two most monumental of Baroque musical forms, the opera and the oratorio. Between 1705 and 1741, Handel composed over three dozen Italian operas, most of them for the London stage. Their subjects were normally drawn from ancient history, for example, *Julius Caesar* of 1724. By the middle 1730s, however, the Londoners' tastes were turning away from the alien, often stilted operatic dramas, which, marvelous though their music was, were sung in a language that few of the English could understand, and that were extravagantly expensive to stage. An unfriendly wag summed up the feeling, calling Handel and his company "a lousy crew of foreign fiddlers." Handel turned opportunistically to composing concert oratorios in English. An **oratorio** was a sacred opera, a religious or spiritual drama set to music in the style of an opera. It differed from an opera not only in its subject matter, but in not usually being costumed and acted in a theater. Instead, it was performed in concert dress in a church or public hall. Musically, the oratorios relied more heavily on choruses than did the operas. The

Colorplate 21

native English spoke directly to the ticket-buying public, and the high-minded subjects suited the morally regenerate spirit of the times. Between 1732 and 1757 Handel turned out some twenty English oratorios, chiefly on biblical subjects—*Saul, Samson, Joseph and his Brethren, Israel in Egypt, Belshazzar,* and *Solomon.*

Messiah

Handel's greatest success was *Messiah,* produced in 1742. This vast musical panorama of the life of Christ is divided into three parts: 1) the Biblical prophecies and the birth of Jesus, 2) the Crucifixion, and 3) the Resurrection. The texts are all from the Old and New Testaments. Unlike Bach's *St. John Passion* and *St. Matthew Passion* (themselves both representatives of the Baroque oratorio), Handel's *Messiah* does not concern itself directly with dramatic events. Everything unfolds in an atmosphere of philosophical detachment. The opening mood is one of joy in contemplating the Nativity. There is consolation rather than tragedy during the Holy Week sections. Finally, there is the exultant spirit of Easter. Nearly three hours of music make up this epic spiritual biography of Christ, and nearly every one of the musical numbers of *Messiah* has found its way to the public ear. Astonishingly, the whole oratorio was composed in just twenty-three days, but Handel, knowing he had created something superb, continued to improve it for another eleven years.

1. Overture. Like a Baroque opera, *Messiah* begins with an instrumental overture. This one is of the "French" type preferred by Lully, Purcell, and Bach. Majestic dotted rhythms and surging harmonic motions fill the slow opening section. A lively fugal section follows, returning to ponderous chords at the end (Ex. 3.25).

Ex. 3.25. Overture from *Messiah*, Handel

George Frideric Handel.

2. Tenor Recitative: "The voice of him that crieth," and Aria: "Every valley shall be exalted."

Accompanied Recitative: The voice of him that crieth in the wilderness. Prepare ye the way of the Lord, make straight in the desert a highway for our God.

(Isaiah 40:3)

Aria: Every valley shall be exalted, and every mountain and hill made low; the crooked straight and the rough places plain.

(Isaiah 40:4)

Messiah has the same basic elements as an opera. There are mainly recitatives alternating with set pieces, or lyric numbers. The first such set piece in *Messiah* is the tenor aria, "Every valley shall be exalted," and this is introduced by a recitative, "The voice of him that crieth in the wilderness." Baroque composers used different styles of recitative for different sorts of dramatic situations. When dealing with everyday conversations or simple narratives, they chose the secco, or dry, recitative, which clothed the words with an unpretentious dress of musical pitches. In a secco recitative, the reciting vocalist was accompanied only with a basso continuo. It was the commonplace musical-dramatic patter of the eighteenth century. Its forerunner was found in Purcell's "Thy hand, Belinda," from *Dido and Aeneas* (see page 93), but by Handel's time the secco style had thinned down to drab, often mechanical clichés. The second movement of Bach's Cantata No. 140 represents a thoughtful use of the eighteenth century's secco recitative style (see page 129). For dramatic situa-

△
Handel: Recitative, "The voice of him that crieth," and Aria, "Every valley shall be exalted," from *Messiah*
(Side 3, Band 7)

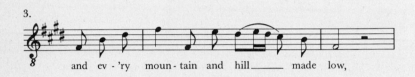

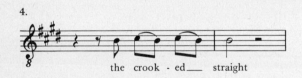

Ex. 3.26b. "Every valley" (Tenor Aria), Handel

Text: (*Isaiah* 40:4): "Every valley shall be exalted, and every mountain and hill made low; the crooked straight and the rough places plain."

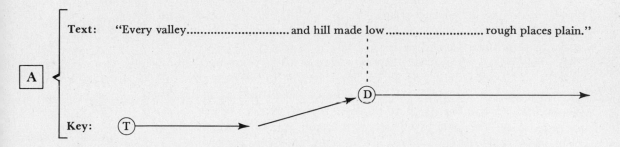

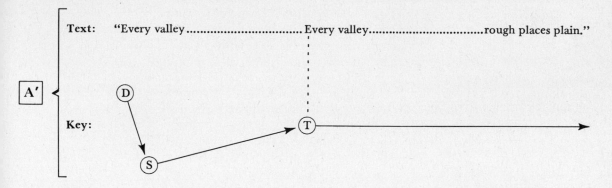

Keys:

Ⓣ Tonic (E major)

Ⓓ Dominant (B major)

Ⓢ Subdominant (A major)

tions that were more highly charged, Handel or Bach chose the musically more emphatic style known as accompanied recitative. Here again the contours of the spoken words were the basis of the melodic recitation, but they were shaped into more expressive musical lines. Their effect was heightened by the use of a full orchestral accompaniment. Bach used an accompanied recitative for the Savior's emotional utterances in the fifth movement of Cantata No. 140. Handel resorts to it for the ecstatic prophecy of "The voice of him that crieth in the wilderness," where the urgent rhetoric of the vocalist is punctuated by forceful orchestral chords.

Handel's enemies found it con-
nient to caricature him as a pig.

The following tenor aria, "Every valley shall be exalted," is in Handel's most luxuriant lyric style. The music is filled with tuneful repetitions that make it a real song. There is a formal plan that is independent of the words, here an overall A A', where the vocalist proceeds twice through essentially the same text and music. The whole vocal part is encased by an opening and closing orchestral ritornello (Ex. 3.26). Several features of this aria are illustrative of Baroque musical taste. Most noticeable is the use of word illustrations, which are direct descendents of the often frivolous madrigalisms found in madrigals of the sixteenth century (Chapter 2). Curious as they seem in a work of such high aspiration, Handel's aria is shot through with word illustrations. He gives the word "exalted" a long ascending musical line that gathers momentum as it climbs through more than an octave (Ex. 3.26a.2). For the words, "and every mountain and hill made low," Handel supplies similarly descriptive vignettes: at "every mountain," the melody skips up and down so as to outline a jagged rock; to picture the "hill," he has the voice roll gently, then fall on "made low" (Ex. 3.26a.3). There is more such amiable mischief at "the crooked [made] straight." "Crooked" is set to a melodic wriggle and "straight" has an unwavering half note (Ex. 3.26a.4). Handel never sacrificed the integrity of a musical line for the sake of a pictorial detail, but when he spied some clever way to illustrate a word, he was obviously happy to use it. Such ingenuities are a curious aspect of Baroque musical taste. They were an obvious delight to the listeners, and a challenge to the composers' craft. Even the austere Bach did not disdain using them.

"Every valley" shows some other aspects of Baroque musical taste: the use of improvised **embellishments**; the display of **virtuosity**; and the ideal of **bel canto** melody. Singers of Handel's day were expected to produce improvised embellishments, adding on-the-spot embroideries to their musical lines. Even the ornate melodic passages that Handel wrote down were not all that he expected to hear in a performance. A lucky circumstance has preserved a passage from "Every valley" as Handel himself supposedly had it embellished. That "improvised" version turns out to be much more florid than the one he actually wrote down. The two versions are compared in the fifth example in Ex. 3.26a. What looks relatively bare in his official score came forth with much richer melodic animation at the performance. An important factor in such vocal embellishment was virtuosity, or strong, exciting performance skills. Faced with the long ascending line at "exalted" (Ex. 3.26a.2), the singer needed great accuracy, a spectacular range, and prodigious breath control. The music had to sparkle, not only for its built-in musical values but for a touch of athleticism in its delivery. The singer was like a gymnast, vaulting through arpeggios and scale passages, warbling provocative trills, sustaining single tones for astonishing lengths. Yet at every instant the quality of sound had to be unforced and appealing. This ideal of effortless loveliness of vocal production is involved in the Italian term *bel canto*. Literally, *bel canto* means "beautiful singing" or "beautiful melody." In practice, it means an effective combination of the two—a beautiful Italianate melody that is beautifully sung, with an impeccable suavity of sound. An essential component of bel canto is the kind of shapely lyric melody that was cultivated in Italian arias and songs of the seventeenth through nineteenth centuries by composers from Alessandro Scarlatti, Handel, and Mozart through Rossini, Verdi, and Puccini (see Chapter 7). The fine-spun lyricism of these composers was an apt vehicle for the flawless vocal production of skilled Italian singers. Thus, not all of the bel canto qualities were written into the score, but the great singers knew how to produce the lofty purified bel canto style that was indispensable in performing a solo aria like Handel's "Every valley."

3. Chorus: "For unto us a child is born."

△
Handel: Chorus, "For unto us a child is born," from *Messiah* (Side 3, Band 8)

Handel's oratorios differ from his Italian operas above all in the greater emphasis that they give to choral numbers. The most striking music of *Messiah* is in its choruses, where the coordinated forces of voices and instruments are massively deployed. Handelian choruses are often built with both fugal and chordal passages, but the big blocklike chords predominate toward the end. Handel was no less skillful a polyphonist than Bach, but he was more pragmatic, worrying less about the hidden voices in a fugue. He shaped his textures, not for the satisfaction of knowing that all the voices were in them, carrying out complex polyphonic missions, but for the simple joys of palpably experienced musical effects. When Handel yokes his chorus and orchestra together, declaiming in great architectonic chords, he is an unmatched musical psychologist.

The chorus "For unto us a child is born" (*Messiah,* No. 12) represents the first great climax of the oratorio. It is where the prophecies of Christ's birth are fulfilled, and Handel uses properly stimulating music for the excitement of the event. He matches three musical materials (A, B, C) to the three lines of text (a, b, c), as shown in Ex. 3.27. Material A is a jaunty fugue subject, declaiming the opening

Ex. 3.27a. "For unto us a child is born," Handel

For un-to us a child is born,

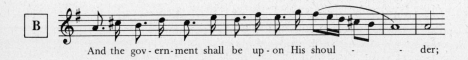

And the gov-ern-ment shall be up-on His shoul - - der;

Won-der-ful, Coun-sel-lor,

Ex. 3.27b. "For unto us a child is born" (Chorus), Handel

a. For unto us a child is born, unto us a son is given:
b. And the government shall be upon His shoulder;
c. And His name shall be called Wonderful, Counsellor, The Mighty God,
   The Everlasting Father, The Prince of Peace.

(Isaiah 9:6)

MUSIC

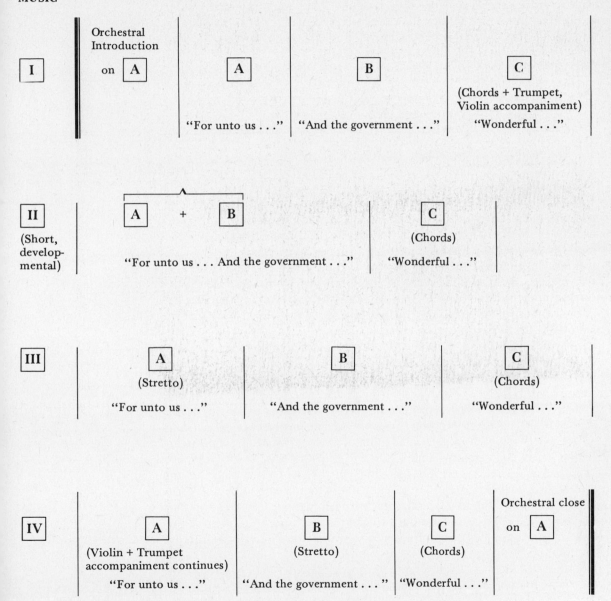

words, "For unto us a child is born." Material B ("And the government shall be upon his shoulder") is a less angular phrase that outlines a laborious raising up to a firm, somewhat rounded "shoulder." At first it is fugal, but then it turns chordal as a transition to material C, which brings the stunning chords on "Wonderful, Counsellor." Handel has shaped this chorus as a set of four variations, going through the A-B-C sequence four times in all. The music thrusts more urgently each time toward the outbursts on "Wonderful, Counsellor," whose crisp choral declamation is highlighted by a resplendent background of brass and strings. The result is powerful without our knowing the words, but it becomes more so when those words and their effect in shaping the music are understood.

L. FROM BAROQUE TO PRE-CLASSICAL STYLE (1730-1750): THE RISE OF COMIC OPERA

The Impetus for Change

Even while Handel in England and Bach in Germany were creating their last profundities in grandiloquent Baroque style, the forces of musical change were stirring elsewhere. Styles in music do not stand still, they always change. Thus during the 1730s and the 1740s, the favorite music of the contemporaries of the aging Bach and Handel was music in a newer, "pre-Classical" style, with a relaxed spirit and transparent texture that were at some remove from the austere, intricate embroideries of the mature Baroque. By the 1730s, musical styles were already turning toward the Classical style of Mozart and Haydn. The impetus for change came mainly from young Italians, chief among them the fertile, facile Neapolitan, Giovanni Battista Pergolesi (1710-1736), who produced a great flood of music during his short lifetime. In Pergolesi's concertos and sonatas the dense Baroque polyphony was thinned down to an easy-going accompanied melody, and much of the old continuity of rhythmic drive was gone. His popular vocal masterpiece, *Stabat Mater,* represents something of the new style. But above all, Pergolesi captivated the European public with the comic opera *La Serva Padrona* (*The Maid who becomes the Mistress*), which appeared in 1733. Unlike the Italian **opera seria** (serious opera) of the 1730s, which dealt with stiff personifications of ancient characters in quasi-historical predicaments, *La Serva Padrona* was an **opera buffa** (comic opera) that took its characters from real life. In reaction to Handel's serious operas, England had already produced its own brand of comic opera. *The Beggar's Opera* of 1728 had an English text by John Gay and music that was partly assembled from popular ballads by the composer

Colorplate 22

Colorplate 23

Three characters of the Italian comic theater, the central one playing a lira, or viola da braccia.

German street musicians in 1756.

Christopher Pepusch. It was a *ballad opera* whose characters included low-life thugs and bawds of the London streets. Its music had the allure of popular tunes, not the brittle elegance of Italian arias. The success of *The Beggar's Opera* helped propel Handel out of the opera house and into composing oratorios. France enjoyed a similar flowering of music-hall comedy, culminating in the works of Charles Simon Favart (1710-1792). But it was Pergolesi who put comic opera on the highroad of European taste with a new musical style that lay between the ornate display of the opera seria and the unaffected simplicity of the ballad operas. From Pergolesi's ingratiating *Serva Padrona* of 1733, the path of opera buffa led to Mozart's sublime comedies of the 1780s, *The Marriage of Figaro* and *Don Giovanni*.

Pergolesi's *La Serva Padrona*

There are just two singing characters in *La Serva Padrona:* Serpina, the beguiling servant girl, and Uberto, the ridiculous, aging bachelor, who employs her as a housekeeper. Serpina has been scheming to marry Uberto, and when the opera ends she gets her way. These were characters to whom the audience could directly relate in sympathy and in ridicule. The opera's closing duet, "Per te ho io nel core" ("For you I have in my heart"), finds Serpina and Uberto celebrating their new-found love in typical opera buffa fashion. There is only scant use of polyphony: The inner polyphonic strands are all but gone. Gone too is the constant forward thrust of baroque melody and rhythm. Instead there is *accompanied melody*—a fresh tunefulness of melody with a simple, transparent accompaniment. The whole idiom is relaxed. There are short phrases and frequent rests. Everything breathes easily, as the phrases balance one another in little statements and counterstatements. Serpina declares her love

Δ
Pergolesi: Closing duet, "Per te ho io nel core," from *La Serva Padrona* (Side 4, Band 1)

(Ex. 3.28a). Uberto echoes her. They banter back and forth, listening to one anothers' heartbeats. Serpina's "tipitipis" are high (Ex. 3.28b), Uberto's pounding "tapatapas" are low. Both are mimicked by the orchestra. Toward the end there are descending half-steps in the melody, full of mock sentiment: Serpina coos, "caro, caro" ("dearest, dearest") and Uberto responds, "gioia, gioia" ("joy, joy") (Ex. 3.28c).

Ex. 3.28. Closing Duet from *La Serva Padrona*, Pergolesi

It is easy to see why this simple style took Europe by storm. After the highminded Baroque, it was a breath of fresh air. Among its admirers was Jean Jacques Rousseau, the philosopher of simplicity and naturalism, who was a part-time composer and author of a musical dictionary. Rousseau's own comic opera *Le Devin du Village* (*The Village Seer*) of 1752 helped transplant Pergolesi's light-opera tradition to France. It remained in the Paris repertory for half a century.

M. PRE-CLASSICAL INSTRUMENTAL MUSIC (1730-1770)

The Sonatas of Domenico Scarlatti

The general "loosening-up" of pre-Classical style is also found in the music of Domenico Scarlatti (1685-1757), who was born in the same year as Bach and Handel, but who, as an Italian, grew up in the

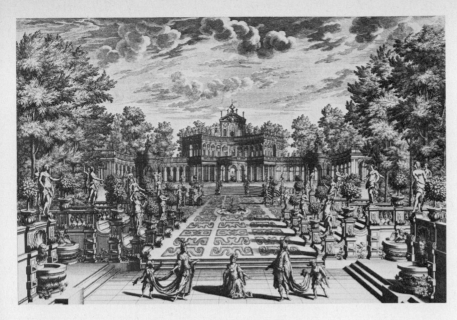

A Baroque formal garden with courtly figures.

vanguard of the new style. He was the son of Alessandro Scarlatti (1660-1725), a very successful composer of concerti grossi and serious operas (opera seria), as well as a precursor of the comic opera of Pergolesi. Domenico Scarlatti began his career as a composer of both operatic and instrumental music, but he ended as a specialist for the harpsichord. About five hundred fifty of his sonatas for solo harpsichord are preserved, mostly creations of his advanced age. Each work consists of a single movement in binary form, the same accommodating form we have seen used by Purcell, Corelli, and Bach. Scarlatti pours a new wealth of musical idiom and texture into that conventional mold. Many of these harpsichord sonatas are radiant with the verve of Italian comic opera, translated to the purely instrumental medium. Many others echo the sounds of Spain and Portugal, in whose royal palaces Scarlatti spent his last thirty-eight years.

Scarlatti's Sonata in E Major, known familiarly as the "Cortège" or "Procession," has some of both qualities. In the ceremonial gesturings of this Spanish-style piece, one can imagine the shake of an aristocratic fan, the rustle of a brocaded silk skirt, the jangle of a guitar. It also has something of the airy comic opera style, where polyphony is thinned down to a texture of transparent accompanied melody that comes out in short, tuneful bursts. The little melodic statements, echoes, and counterstatements afford plenty of places to breathe. "Polyphonic motor power" is almost gone: The propelling

△
Scarlatti: Sonata in E Major
(Side 4, Band 2)

force in this music is the top-voice melody. Gone too is the Baroque's single-mindedness. Within the confines of this binary form, Scarlatti has put some real contrasts of mood, of rhythmic motion, and of melody. The opening melodic material (A) is a tiny gesture—its chiseled profile arches gracefully downward to trills and rests (Ex. 3.29). A strumming figure (B) appears, with a haunting lilt to its

Ex. 3.29. Sonata in E Major ("Cortège"), Domenico Scarlatti

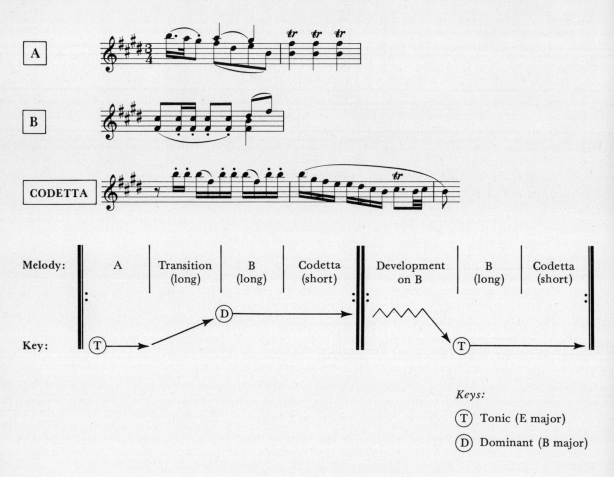

rhythm. Approaching the double bar, there is a sprightly codetta, a miniature closing theme. Thus Scarlatti has put three distinctive materials—A, B, and Codetta—into this first section of the binary form. And he has left breathing places. How different this is from the binary forms of the High Baroque, with their singleness of mood and motion!

Leaders of the Pre-Classical Style

Scarlatti was not alone in this metamorphosis of style. Composers everywhere were airing out and loosening up the old Baroque rhetoric. Even J. S. Bach put contrasting melodies and textures into some of his later works. But it was in the hands of Pergolesi, Scarlatti, and the other pre-Classical composers of the mid-eighteenth century that the Baroque grandeur ended. Its high emotion was watered down, its massiveness eroded, its elaborateness and monumentality flattened out to a simple decorative charm. Among the leaders in the new pre-Classical idioms were two sons of J. S. Bach. Carl Philipp Emanuel Bach (1714-1787) became harpsichordist to Frederick the Great in 1740 and was the chief exponent of the pre-Classical style in Germany. Johann Christian Bach (1735-1782) first went to Italy, then carried the new style to London. There, in 1764, he encountered the eight-year-old Mozart and was an important influence in the formation of that precocious talent.

The varieties of musical style that arose between 1730 and 1770 are generally grouped together under the name of pre-Classical styles because they prefigure Mozart's and Haydn's mature "Classicism" of the later 1770s through 1790s. Those transitional styles also go under other names. Certain French styles of the middle 1700s are called **rococo**, borrowing the name from the fine arts, where it decribes a dainty style of decoration favored in cameos and low reliefs that features elegant curves and ornamental shell motifs (*rocaille* = shell). Another pre-Classical style is the so-called *style galant* ("gallant" or "courtly" style) of certain mid-eighteenth-century German music that emphasizes a breezy flow of accompanied melody. German composers also cultivated a more reflective musical vein that was called the *Empfindsamer Stil,* or "sentimental" style, where they tried to embody true and natural sentiments, as opposed to what they considered the artificial posturings of the Baroque. How willful such judgments were! The early nineteenth century would in its turn reject the late eighteenth century for showing too little of natural sentiment.

Colorplate 24

Different as the local varieties of pre-Classical style are, they represent the same groundswell of change. And attractive as many of them are, they rarely rise above the level of mediocre art. It was bound to be that way. The Baroque of Bach and Handel and the Classical of Mozart and Haydn represent peaks that are at opposite stylistic poles to one another. It took a generation of change, of experiment and marking time, before the new peak could be reached. The virtue of the pre-Classical composers was that they made the transition as attractive and pleasant as they did.

Colorplate 25

4 The Viennese Classical Style (1770-1800): Mozart and Haydn

The charm and frivolity of the age of Louis XVI are displayed in Fragonard's The Swing *(1766).*

Musical centers of the eighteenth century.

The Late Eighteenth Century

MUSIC	ARTS AND IDEAS	POLITICS AND SCIENCE
THE VIENNESE CLASSICAL STYLE	**FROM ROCOCO TO REVOLUTION**	**THE AGE OF REASON: FROM ABSOLUTISM TO THE RIGHTS OF MAN**

Haydn (1732-1809):
    Symphony No. 1 (ca. 1759)
    String Quartet, Op. 33, No. 2 ("Joke") (1781)
    Symphony No. 94 ("Surprise") (1791)
Gluck (1714-1787):
    Orpheus and Euridice (1762)
    Iphigenia in Tauris (1779)
Mozart (1756-1791):
    Symphony No. 1 (1765)
    Piano Concerto No. 21 (1785)
    A Little Night Music (1787)
    Don Giovanni (1787)
    Symphony No. 40 in G Minor (1788)
    The Magic Flute (1791)
	B. Neumann, Church of Vierzehn-heiligen (Bavaria, 1743-1772)
	Diderot's *Encyclopedia* begun (1751)
	The Pantheon begun at Paris (1755)
	Voltaire, *Candide* (1759)
	Rousseau, *The Social Contract* (1762)
	The Petit Trianon at Versailles (1762)
	Winckelmann, *History of Ancient Art* (1764)
	Macpherson's *Ossian* (1765)
	Paintings of Boucher (d. 1770) and Fragonard (d. 1806)
	Fragonard, *The Swing* (1766)
	Sterne, *Tristram Shandy* (1767)
	Goethe, *Sorrows of Young Werther* (1774)
	Sculptures of Houdon (1770s-1780s)
	Kant, *Critique of Pure Reason* (1781)
	Rousseau's *Confessions* (1781)
	David, *Oath of the Horatii* (1784)
	Blake, *Songs of Innocence and Experience* (1789-1794)
	Goethe, *Faust, A Fragment* (1790)
		Maria-Theresa (Hapsburg), Austrian Empress (1740-1780)
		Seven Years' War (1756-1763)
		George III (England, 1760-1820)
		Louis XVI and Marie-Antoinette (France, 1774-1792)
		American Revolution (1776)
		French Revolution (begun 1789)
		Adam Smith, *Wealth of Nations* (1776)
		Discovery of Pompeii (1748)
		Paine, *The Rights of Man; The Age of Reason* (1791-1795)
		Electrical experiments of Franklin, Galvani, Volta, Coulomb
		Chemical discoveries of Dalton, Priestly, Lavoisier
		Jenner develops vaccination
		Watt's steam engine
		Whitney's cotton gin

A. THE VIENNESE CLASSICAL STYLE

The late eighteenth century was the age of the Viennese Classical style. It was an age of coolly elegant music that delighted aristocratic senses and satisfied discriminating spirits. It was the age of Mozart (1756-1791) and Haydn (1732-1809), who uncomplicated the fuss and ennobled the sentimentality of pre-Classical music, fashioning a simple tastefulness that put form above expression and restraint upon emotion. The words *classic* and *classical* are generally applied to works of art, music, and literature that seem models of their kind. Classics have values that are somehow timeless and universal. For over two thousand years the creative arts of ancient Greece and Rome have enjoyed that kind of esteem, and what has elevated them beyond the whim of fashion and has given them such durable appeal continues to fascinate later ages. One apparent quality of ancient art is its calm and reserve. In particular, the temples and statuary of "Hellenic" Greece (fifth century B.C.) seem to have values that are cool and unemotional. Their designs are logical and orderly, not fantastic and turbulent. In looking back at the late eighteenth century, musicians of the nineteenth century thought they could identify similar qualities of restraint and proportion in the music of Mozart and Haydn. They named their style, accordingly, the Classical style. How appropriate that was scarcely matters, for classics represent universally accepted standards of excellence, and Mozart and Haydn became admired models, judged worthy of emulation by later generations of composers. Still, it is a mistake to think of their Classical music as being simply reserved and unemotional. Mozart and Haydn may appear outwardly less demonstrative than Bach and Handel, yet within the narrower context of their understated gestures of the 1780s there is as much emotion and expressive force as in the more flamboyant Baroque gestures of the 1730s.

Reason and Classicism: *The goddess Minerva shows the Temple of Reason to a youth who has been reading the ancient authors (American, 1790s).*

Mozart and Haydn came to artistic maturity during the era of philosophical and political ferment known as the *Age of Enlightenment*. It was the eighteenth-century Enlightenment's quest for truth and social justice that gave birth to the rationalism of Hume (1711-1766), the skepticism of Voltaire (1694-1788), and the sensibility and egalitarianism of Rousseau (1712-1778). It was the Enlightenment's scrutiny of human institutions in the light of reason and natural law that launched the momentous shift of power from the aristocracy to the middle class, leading to the American and French Revolutions of the 1770s and 1780s. Mozart and Haydn were creating music during precisely those dynamic times, yet they remained almost untouched by the intellectual and social groundswells around them. Their music was tailored for the genteel aristocracy that supported them, and naturally it radiates not the firebrand liberalism of the Revolution, but the orderliness of the *ancien régime*. Mozart, to be sure, bridled at the antiquated patronage system on which the livelihood of most eighteenth-century composers depended, and there are traces of libertarian sentiments in his later operas. But Mozart no less than Haydn remained a functionary within the established social system.

In most respects there is a kinship between the music and the fine arts of the time. Eighteenth-century painting and architecture have the same elitist values as the music, and their styles have the same scaling down of the Baroque's expressive showiness toward a Classical reserve and elegance. The facile, ingratiating styles of Italian pre-Classical composers such as Pergolesi, Domenico Scarlatti, Giovanni Platti, Baldassare Galuppi, and Giovanni-Battista Sammartini have their counterparts in the complacent decorative styles of painting by the Tiepolos, Zucarelli, Longhi, and Batoni. In France, the gaiety of the court of Louis XV (1710-1774) found musical expression in delicious harpsichord miniatures by François Couperin (1668-1733) and Jean-Philippe Rameau (1683-1764), and artistic expression in the slender figures of Watteau, who compressed the extremes of Baroque emotion down to the posturings of Rococo sentimentality. With later French painters such as Boucher and Fragonard, there were further turns to airy charm and prettiness. Ornament was cultivated for its own sake in countless shell motifs and curlicues. During the middle 1700s, Rousseau championed a return to nature and to the wholesomeness that is natural in human beings. The spirit of midcentury style is in fact closer to human dimensions than it was in the high-flown Baroque. But the carefree shepherds and milkmaids who populated Marie Antoinette's Petit Trianon (completed in 1768) were not quite the natural creatures that Rousseau had in mind. They were powdered courtiers frolicking in exquisitely manicured gardens.

Colorplate 26

Colorplate 27

Many nations contributed to the shaping of music's Classical style. The strong national flavors of the time were all there—the

Ruins: *The presence of ruins inspired eighteenth-century classicism. The long-forgotten site of Pompeii was rediscovered in 1748, and in 1764 Johann Winckelmann's* History of Ancient Art *launched the modern science of archaeology.*

Italians, French, and Germans. But so too were the English, the Spanish, and the Bohemians. All Europe in the mid-eighteenth century had tired of the ponderous late Baroque. Things came to a head in the later 1770s when the young Mozart and Haydn elevated the breezy commonplaces of the pre-Classical style to the summit of noble economy in the mature Classical style. Mozart and Haydn were Austrians who spent their best creative years in the orbit of the Austrian capital of Vienna. The city was the capital of the Hapsburg empire, and with Mozart and Haydn it became the center of a musical empire. For the century and a half from 1780 to 1930, Vienna remained the chief musical city of Europe, a magnet that drew the best composers of the German-speaking world. Beethoven, Schubert, Brahms, Bruckner, Mahler, and Schoenberg all made their homes there. Because Mozart and Haydn were there, the late eighteenth-century Classical style is known as the Viennese Classical style.

What may strike one first in comparing Classical music with Baroque music is the difference in texture. Baroque music is generally dense and complex. It has the basso continuo filling in all chinks in the façade of sound. Its typical manner of discourse is the busywork of a fugue. Classical music prefers the texture of accompanied melody. It gives prominence to lyric, singable tunes that float over relatively placid harmonies. The thinning out of Baroque density had begun in Italy already in Vivaldi's time. By the late 1770s, the new textures had attained a crystalline transparency that permitted every nuance to show through—delicacies and surprises that would have been lost in the old polyphonic thickets. Bach-like polyphony for a while was shunted aside as an old-fashioned, academic affectation. Yet even as the lucid, aerated Classical texture was reaching its peak during the 1770s, polyphony began to return. Its inherent seriousness and appeal to musicianly craft could not long be ignored. The new polyphony of the 1780s, however, served as just one texture among many. It was rarely carried through a whole movement. Rather, it appeared as an incidental texture within larger movements that offered a variety of textures. Where the Baroque specialized in whole works that were fugues, the Classical preferred **fugatos**—passages that were launched with a fugal exposition but then dissolved into some melodic or chordal texture.

The new importance given to a dominating melodic line brought with it a genial new style of melody. Baroque melodies generally began with small motives that took off on long, unpredictable trajectories. They tended to be breathless and run-on. Classical melodies tend to be shorter-breathed and more symmetrical. They are "tuneful," carrying on musical discourses that often consist of little questions and answers: four measures of "this," followed by four measures of "that." The neat question-and-answer phrases generally balance one another. Their bilateral symmetries are easy to remember and comfortable to sing. The short statements and counterstatements leave plenty of place for relaxing and taking breath. With its clarity of texture and unforced style of melody, Classical music reflects the Enlightenment's ideal of "reason" and Rousseau's ideal of the "natu-

Laureince, The Concert. *Chamber music in a late eighteenth-century salon.*

ral." In their simplicity and naturalness, Classical melodies are often like popular tunes. Some were actually popular tunes. Mozart wrote variations for piano on "Twinkle twinkle little star" (he knew it as "Ah, vous dirais-je maman"). Beethoven wrote variations on "Rule Brittania" and "God Save the King."

The most pervasive feature of Baroque music was the basso continuo, the filler texture that ran unrelentingly through almost every piece. Classical music gradually discarded the old continuo. This left a gap in the middle of the Classical texture—an empty region where the continuo's harmonic filler had been. Classical composers reveled in the new-found transparency, which exposed every tinkle and grace note to the ear. To ensure that clarity, composers were no longer content to let performers improvise their own accompaniment patterns, as with the figured bass. Classical accompaniments are precisely written out, and the composers employ stylized patterns to give a controlled liveliness to the supporting chords. One of the favorites is the *Alberti-bass* pattern, named for a composer who was a minor contemporary of Pergolesi. This pattern spreads out the pitches of the supporting chords, as shown in Mozart's familiar C Major Piano Sonata (Ex. 4.1).

Ex. 4.1. Classical Accompaniment Figure: Alberti Bass

The decline of the basso continuo was coupled with the decline of the harpsichord, the continuo's chief keyboard instrument. The harpsichord was the mainstay of the Baroque. It was gradually supplanted by the nobler-voiced, more genial-sounding *piano,* whose first examples were constructed in Italy around 1710. The full name, *pianoforte,* indicated to the prospective buyer that the instrument could produce not only the dynamic levels of soft and loud but also the levels in between, something that was not possible with the harpsichord's quill-plucked strings. Baroque musicians did not even consider those gradations desirable, preferring the decisive ups and downs of terraced dynamics in their instrumental music. But now a certain flexibility and naturalness were the fashion, and the piano, whose strings were struck with soft hammers, had the ability to respond to different pressures of the player's fingers on the keys with different volumes of sound. The piano could produce the crescendos and diminuendos that came into vogue with the Classical period, and it made it possible to give vent to strong feelings by striking the keys very hard. Some generations would pass before the piano's mechanism and sound chamber produced the brilliance and volume that we know today. But already in Beethoven's time (early nineteenth century), the composers' urges to self-expression were testing the thunderous properties of the instrument.

What distinguishes Baroque from Classical music is above all else a matter of spirit. Baroque music runs to the solemn and high-minded. Its discourses are majestic and emotional. When the Baroque chooses to relax, it descends to the sentimental, stuffy, and intricate, and at times to heavy-handed humor. The Classical spirit takes itself less seriously. It relaxes. It is interested in being natural, in communicating sentiment, and in creating the excitement of fast-paced drama. Classical music on occasion rises to the level of genuine wit. This factor of musical spirit has another side. Whatever mood or spirit a Baroque piece adopts, it tends to hold it throughout its length. The same features of rhythm and melody and the same mood that begin a piece are usually kept going to the end. Thus when a Baroque composer assembles a large-scale work such as a suite, sonata, or cantata, it is done by collecting together some small, single-minded vignettes, each focused on a particular mood. The contrasts in the Baroque come not so much within the boundaries of an individual movement as from movement to movement. The Classical spirit breaks down the old single-mindedness. It prizes diversity, welcomes within a single movement a variety of moods that may offer striking contrasts with one another—the vigorous and relaxed, dramatic and lyric, noble and comic, all molded together in a gripping continuity. Such fluid changes of mood within Classical instrumental movements took their cue from the quick-to-change situations and dramatic paradoxes of the Italian comic operas, where imbroglio and lighthearted turmoil were a matter of course. From the opera buffa this vein of comic-dramatic realism spread to the Italian orchestral sinfonias and keyboard sonatas of Vivaldi, Scarlatti, and their compatriots. Soon it was everywhere. By the mid-eighteenth century, composers throughout Europe were flexing their imaginations in the new freedom of spirit and airiness of texture. Inevitably, the older musical forms of the Baroque could not contain the new utterances. Composers of the mid-eighteenth century were evolving fresh forms of their own to suit the fresh styles. The most significant and versatile of those forms is called *sonata-allegro* or *sonata form*.

B. SONATA-ALLEGRO FORM

The aim of **sonata-allegro form** was to contain within a single instrumental movement an esthetically satisfying mix of the contrasting whims and textures that Classical composers prized. Sonata-allegro was the form adopted for most individual movements of sonatas and symphonies of the late eighteenth and the nineteenth centuries, and it was used particularly in *allegro* or fast movements. That is why it has the name *sonata-allegro*. But the name is often given as just *sonata form,* or *first-movement form,* because of its popularity in quick-paced opening movements.

Sonata form was not wholly new with the Classical period. It was a direct outgrowth of the binary form that was found in Baroque suites and sonatas, particularly the type of binary form whose second section begins with a contrast or digression (B) before returning to the opening material (A'):

‖:   A   :‖:   B   A'   :‖

Composers of the mid-eighteenth century took this framework and filled it with the new Classical textures and spirit. Scarlatti was already doing this in his harpsichord sonatas (see Chapter 3). The old binary form's basic A-B-A' presently evolved into the three conventional sections of sonata-allegro form that are called the **exposition** (A), **development** (B), and **recapitulation** (A'):

‖:   **(A)**   :‖:   **(B)**   **(A')**   :‖
    Exposition   Development   Recapitulation

The whole scope and character of binary form expanded as the Baroque single-mindedness was opened up to admit the livelier Classical give-and-take between different moods and ideas. It was similar to an evolutionary process in which a simpler biological organism develops specialized organs and greater capacities.

(A) The Exposition. The exposition in a sonata-form movement presents the main musical materials of the movement in a loosely predictable order. A first theme group (I), or theme I, offers some opening melodic statements. They are usually vigorous in style. Next comes a restless, transitional passage called the bridge (BR). Then there is often a second theme group (II), or theme II, whose lyricism or relaxation contrasts with the purposeful and volatile materials of theme I and the bridge. Finally, a closing section (CL) returns to the energetic mood of the opening, sometimes even to the opening music itself. The whole exposition is often repeated so that its materials can become familiar. A basic plan for a sonata-allegro exposition is shown in Ex. 4.2. Each element in this plan—I, BR, II, and CL—may

Ex. 4.2. The Exposition Section

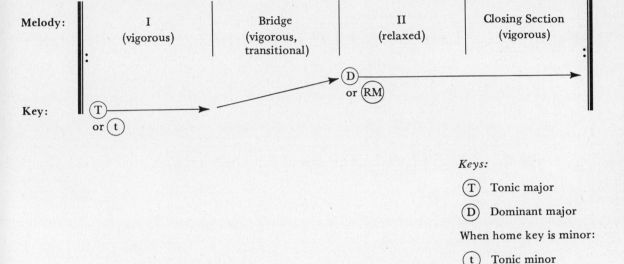

Keys:

(T) Tonic major

(D) Dominant major

When home key is minor:

(t) Tonic minor

(RM) Relative major

consist of just a single theme or motivic fragment, or each may have two or more such materials. This order of themes and typical moods is often followed, but it is not obligatory. The order is a set of "conventions," not of "rules." It has the advantage of giving the composer and listener a common ground for sharing the musical discourse. Yet the composer's aim is not merely to do what is expected but something better, and the listener's pleasure comes from hearing the commonplace conventions transcended.

Sonata-allegro form relies heavily on melodic features—its themes and motives. But it is also grounded in the sound idioms of major-minor tonality and in the network of major and minor keys. Like the Baroque's binary and ritornello forms, the Classical period's sonata-allegro form depends on the relationships between the different tonal keys. Thus, each movement has a home or tonic key that is established at the start and returns before the end. In between, that tonic key is abandoned and a journey is made through contrast-

Ex. 4.3a. Themes from First Movement, *A Little Night Music,* **Mozart**

Ia

Ib

Ic
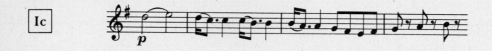

BRIDGE

II

CLa

Ex. 4.3b. Sonata-Allegro Form: First Movement, *A Little Night Music,* **Mozart**

EXPOSITION

Melody:	I a	b	c	c′	Bridge		II	CL a	b	a	b	Extension

Dynamic
level: *f* *f* *p* *p* — *f* *p* *p* *f* *p* *f*

Key:

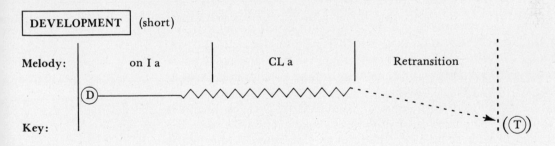

Dynamic levels:
p = *piano* (soft)
f = *forte* (loud)
———— = *crescendo* (growing louder)

DEVELOPMENT (short)

Melody: on I a | CL a | Retransition

Key:

RECAPITULATION

Melody:	I a	b	c	c′	Bridge	II	CL a	b	a	b	Extension	Codetta

Key:

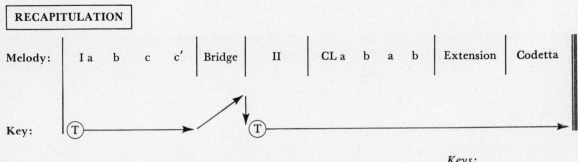

Keys:
(T) Tonic (G major)
(D) Dominant (D major)

ing keys. The most important key is the first contrasting key, which is reached at the end of the bridge and continues through the end of the exposition. The tonal tension that exists between the home key and the first contrasting key (usually the dominant key) is the musical mainspring of the movement. In theatrical terms, it is the central problem of the musical drama, a problem that is ultimately resolved when the recapitulation returns to the home key and provides its affirmations of that key's primacy. Many movements in sonata form lack a melodic contrast between themes I and II, but they never lack the contrast between the tonic key and a first contrasting key.

Mozart's "serenade" (or "night piece") called *Eine kleine Nachtmusik* (*A Little Night Music*), dating from 1787, was written as a lighthearted evening's entertainment. Its first movement illustrates the workings of sonata form in graceful miniature (Ex. 4.3). The movement begins with an energetic first theme (Ia) that leaps up and down through the tonic and dominant chords. Further melodic ideas (Ib, Ic, Ic') prolong the first theme group and establish the sense of the home key. Then the upward thrust of the bridge begins. Its melodic purpose is to lead away from the declarative statements that typified theme group I and to set the stage for the gentle lyricism of theme II. Its tonal purpose is to move away from the home key and prepare the first contrasting key, which is where theme II will appear. Bridge sections are transitions that contain a modulation or change of key. The modulations generally take predictable, readily traceable paths, as Mozart's does. First, the sense of the home key is obscured as the music thrusts upward. Momentarily there is no tonic, only a sense of maneuvering toward the new key. Then the new key is established, hammered in with fanfarelike flourishes. A moment's silence clears the air after the bridge's turbulence. Then the graceful theme II melody appears, its gentle lilt contrasting with the forte energies of the bridge. For the closing section, Mozart does not return at once to a vigorous mood. The CLa prolongs the lyric calm of theme II, and the expected forte arrives only with CLb. The conventions of sonata form are there, but they are conventions meant to be transcended. The composer who does only the expected produces dull music.

(B) Development. Whereas the exposition presents musical ideas in a roughly predictable order, the development has a mandate to be free. Development sections are free in their choice of materials, free in the way they "develop" those materials, and free in their wanderings from key to key (see Ex. 4.4). Some developments are long and theatrical, others are short and unpretentious. The only "rule" is that a development section generally uses material that has made an appearance in the foregoing exposition. The material can be a prominent

Δ
Mozart: First Movement,
A Little Night Music
(Side 4, Band 3)

Ex. 4.4. The Development Section

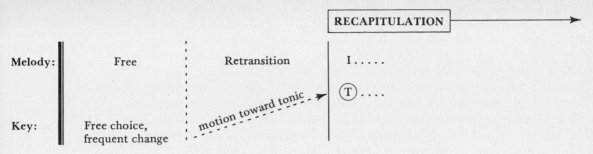

motive or theme from the beginning of the exposition, but it can just as well come from the middle or end. It can be something that barely made an impression on first hearing and now becomes all the more impressive for having passed unnoticed before. Sometimes a composer, feeling that the potential of earlier materials has been depleted, will break the "rule" and introduce something brand new during the development. Yet what first seems like a "new theme" often turns out to be a subtle transformation of material already heard.

Exposition sections tend to be expansive in their discourse, dealing with full-length statements or themes. Development sections favor compression. They generally deal with short segments cut from earlier themes. The idea is to take bits and pieces of the earlier materials and uncover their latent promise. New vistas are opened and emotional temperatures are raised as pithy fragments of rhythm, melody, and harmony are put through the developmental wringer. The common processes of development include end-on-end repetition, sequential repetitions that move up or down the scale, fragmentation into smaller musical bits, and expansion into larger contours. A great favorite is polyphonic elaboration, because saying several things at once adds intensity. The polyphony may be imitative, with a single fragment treated simultaneously in different voices; or it may be nonimitative, with musical fragments that previously led separate lives now combined. Developments are also a place for provocative harmonies and the exploration of distant keys. The exposition stays on the main track between its home key and first contrasting key, but the development can reach out to keys that have only a slight relation to the home key. Yet even at the farthest point in the tonal journey, the organizing force of the home key is felt in the background of our memory. Each key that is visited is linked subconsciously to the reference of the home key.

The chief event in any sonata-allegro form comes as the development ends and the recapitulation begins. At this point the developmental fragmentations and tonal peregrinations are at an end and the opening theme and opening key reappear, coordinated as they were at the beginning of the exposition. The whole expanse of the development has in a way been a preparation for this moment. All the far-flung operations have been calculated to make this homecoming feel more satisfying. Development sections usually close with a passage of preparation or **retransition** that obviously leads up to the point of return. Somewhere along the way a far-out region has been reached, and then a fresh purpose is sensed as the music starts toward home. Many such retransition passages have a steadily intensifying homeward thrust. Yet sometimes, with our expectations focused on a particular point for the return, the composer makes a detour. The recapitulation may seem to be coming as the climax to a long crescendo, but instead it is delayed and appears in a pianissimo. Or it may burst in sooner than expected, with little or no obvious preparation.

Some developments have a different twist appearing relatively early within the section—a so-called "false recapitulation." Here the return actually seems to have taken place, but just as one settles back to chart the recapitulation, the free-wheeling modulations and nervous fragmentations of developmental rhetoric resume. A false recapitulation rings true for a bit, but then it turns out to have been another way of extending the development section.

In Mozart's *A Little Night Music,* the development has none of the trickery or fireworks found elsewhere. In general his aim is to be short and sweet, and in the development he is content to take musical fragments Ia and CLa through some quick changes of key before moving on through a brisk retransition to the recapitulation.

(A′) The Recapitulation (Recap) or Restatement. *Recapitulation* means going back to the beginning. This section of sonata form is sometimes also called a **restatement.** What it promises is a return to the original materials in the original order of the exposition (Ex. 4.5). Yet the recapitulation is never a carbon copy. Quite the con-

Ex. 4.5. The Recapitulation

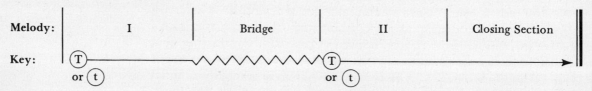

Keys:
(T) Tonic major
(t) Tonic minor

trary, its whole point is to say things over again, but now illumined by the musical experiences that have intervened. The recapitulation is a commentary on everything that has happened, a measure of how far our perceptions have been enlarged. It is a climax of interest and an invitation to be vigilant, for here above all is the place for subtlety. The difference between the recapitulation and the exposition normally concerns the scheme of keys. Instead of moving to the first contrasting key after the bridge, the recapitulation turns right back to the tonic key. The bridge is altered so as to come out where it started. It is a mock excursion that departs from the tonic long enough to turn the tonic's reappearance into a fresh affirmation of the tonal home. Then, from theme II onward, the music remains in the tonic. Other changes that may take place in the recapitulation are less predictable. Theme I is often shortened because it has already been heard at least twice in the repeated exposition. Some of the materials may be given broader play, while others may be condensed or suppressed. Each change reflects the composer's judgment of how familiar the materials have become and what needs to be done to give things a lift.

Mozart's recapitulation in *A Little Night Music* is a close copy of his exposition (see Ex. 4.3). But now the home key is emphasized; theme II and the closing themes stay right in the tonic. A short codetta adds just enough extra weight for a satisfactory close.

Sonata form is not a rigid, scientific "formula." It is a flexible musical form that is alive in thousands of artfully different compositions. No two of those pieces will correspond exactly with one another. No single one will embody all the abstract "rules" or "conventions" of the form. Mozart's little movement comes as close as any to having the main ones.

Slow Introduction and Coda. Sonata form is organically complete in its three main sections: exposition, development, and recapitulation. But two optional additions—a slow introduction and a concluding coda—may come as its beginning and end. They appear only rarely during the infancy of the form, in the 1750s and 1760s. They become commoner and richer in musical substance in the later works of Mozart and Haydn. With Beethoven they are almost the rule. A *slow introduction* is a lyric or dramatic stage-setter for the fast-paced exposition, into which it leads without break. Early examples of a slow introduction rarely share their themes or motives with the rest of the movement, but during the nineteenth century the materials are often the same. A **coda** is a direct outgrowth of the recapitulation, an extension or continuation of the ongoing musical motion, using the movement's main materials. Some codas—for example, Mozart's in *A Little Night Music*—are only small additions, codettas, that amount to just a few closing flourishes. Other codas, including many by Beethoven, are long, restless perorations in which the dramatic spirit of the development reappears. They are again free in their choice of keys and materials, and they revive the storm and stress of earlier motivic and tonal conflicts. Naturally, composers save their best salvos for last.

C. THE SYMPHONY

Every musical age has its showcase vehicles, its large-scale challenges that call forth the composers' best efforts. During the Renaissance, the big formal outlet was the polyphonic Mass. During the Baroque it was the opera or oratorio. During the Classical period it was the orchestral symphony. The rise of the symphony went hand in hand with the rise of the Classical style. In the mid-eighteenth century, the symphony replaced the concerto grosso as the premier genre of orchestral music. It was given a decisive shape by the young Joseph Haydn in the 1760s and 1770s, and it reached a vigorous first maturity in Mozart's and Haydn's symphonies of the 1780s. Then, with remarkable tenacity, it held on to its dominating position through the nineteenth century and into the twentieth.

The symphony is a loosely knit cycle of three or four musical pieces or movements, essentially the same cycle found in the sonatas, string quartets, concertos, etc., of the late eighteenth century. Musicians sometimes speak of "symphony-sonata cycles" to describe such collections of movements. What holds the movements together is not very tangible. They have a conventional order of moods and tempos, and at least the first and last movements are in the same home key. Specific relationships of melodies between the movements are rare in Mozart and Haydn, although they become more common later on.

In its conventional order, the Classical symphony, sonata, or quartet has these three or four movements:

1. *The Opening Allegro.* Vigorous or dramatic in mood, quick in tempo. Form: usually sonata allegro, sometimes prefaced by a slow introduction.
2. *The Slow Movement.* Lyric or philosophical in mood, slow in tempo. Form: sonata allegro, theme and variations (see page 176), rondo (see page 179), or other.
3. *The Minuet and Trio.* Actually two minuets, relics of the Baroque suite, both in binary form; in moderate tempo, triple meter. Sometimes this movement is omitted, giving the Classical symphony the same overall sequence of fast-slow-fast movements as found in the typical concerto by Bach or Vivaldi. The slow movement and the

minuet and trio may be reversed in order, particularly during the nineteenth century.

4. *The Finale, or Closing Movement.* Vigorous, sometimes humorous in mood. Form: sonata allegro, rondo, theme and variations.

Wolfgang Amadeus Mozart

Of all the great Western composers, Wolfgang Amadeus Mozart (1756-1791) had the most extravagant natural gifts. He was already writing music when he was five, and while still a child in body, he turned out symphonies and sonatas that were as polished in style and adventurous in technique as any by his mature contemporaries. During his early youth Mozart basked in an international celebrity. Along with his talented older sister Maria Anna (called Nannerl), he was constantly being shown off, marveled at for his skills on the violin and piano, propped on the knees of royalty. For ten years he was paraded around Europe by a doting, ambitious father, who was himself a well-known authority on the violin. Then young manhood set in and the allure of the child prodigy vanished. Mozart's musical powers continued to increase, but life, from whose realities he had been sheltered as a youth, began to treat him harshly. He was unable to find a job worthy of his talents. Until he was twenty-five he stagnated in a lowly post in his native Salzburg. When he finally left for Vienna in 1781, he had no promise of a regular income. During his remaining ten years, his genius would be so grudgingly acknowledged that in spite of some spectacular successes at Vienna, he never attained financial security. When Mozart died in 1791 at the age of thirty-five he was heavily in debt, partly the result of a passion for gambling and billiards. He was buried along with other paupers in an unmarked common grave. His widow was too ill to be present at the interment, and when she searched later for the grave, no one could tell her where it was.

Louis Carmontelle, Young Mozart (Age 10), his Sister, and Father *(1766).*

This cruel personal fate notwithstanding, Mozart's short life produced well over six hundred works: more than fifty symphonies (a familiar numbering lists 41), including the "Haffner," "Linz," "Prague," "G Minor," and "Jupiter"; over thirty-six concertos; large quantities of chamber and church music (including the great *Requiem*, left unfinished at his death); and a dozen operas, of which the most popular are *The Marriage of Figaro* (1786), *Don Giovanni* (1787), and *The Magic Flute* (1791). A chronological listing of Mozart's works was made long after his death by an admirer named Köchel, whose "K." numbers are now used to identify them.

Mozart had a phenomenal ability to perfect his music in his mind before putting it on paper. The intricate fugal overture to *The Magic Flute* is said to have been written just hours before its first performance, as he carried the whole elegant masterpiece around in his head until he found a convenient time to write it down. Mozart had a legendary fertility, beyond that even of Handel, Schubert, or Rossini. Works of crystalline perfection seemed to flow effortlessly from his pen. When he was plagued with illness and personal frustration during the final years at Vienna, the music sometimes takes on darker colors and a more emotional cast. But this seems to be the presage of an oncoming musical romanticism rather than the expression of his personal suffering. Some of his darkest hours produced some of his most optimistic sounds. Mozart was at his best during that final decade at Vienna from 1781 to 1791: He wrote the last four symphonies (Nos. 38-41), the last string quintets and piano concertos, and the last six of his operas. Nowhere else in the commonwealth of the arts—not even in Shakespeare—are character and emotion more humanely displayed than in these operas. Considering Mozart's work as a whole, it seems safe to say that no one else in the history of Western culture has given so much pleasure to so many people.

Mozart.
A contemporary portrait.

Mozart's Symphony No. 40 in G Minor was composed during the summer of 1788, when he was thirty-two years old. During the space of six weeks he wrote out the scores of his last three symphonies, the mellow No. 39 in E-Flat; No. 41, or "Jupiter," in C Major; and this haunting Symphony in G Minor. Mozart's instrumentation for the symphony shows the already formed core of the modern orchestra. Older instruments that were becoming obsolete in Bach's time, such as the viols, the oboe d'amore, and the oboe da caccia, are gone. Also gone is the basso continuo. Mozart's orchestra has the standard Classical nucleus: the strings of the violin family (violins, violas, cellos) plus double bass; select winds (just two flutes, two oboes, two bassoons); a pair of French horns (no other brass!); and two kettledrums. The total complement of players is small, still a long way from the massive orchestras of Berlioz and Wagner, but the modern orchestral core is formed. Two familiar instruments are missing that were marginal in Mozart's time. The trombones were used chiefly in his operas, never his symphonies. And in the original scoring of the Symphony in G Minor, Mozart ignored the clarinets. Later on he retouched the symphony to include the clarinets' velvet tone.

Δ
Mozart: First Movement,
Symphony No. 40 in
G Minor
(Side 4, Band 4)

The first movement of the Symphony in G Minor represents sonata form at its full Mozartean scale, longer and more dramatic than in *A Little Night Music.* Yet the underlying conventions are the same. There are four principal themes (I, BR, II, and CLa) and two principal motives (x and y) that are parts of the principal themes: Motive x opens theme I; motive y opens theme II (Ex. 4.6). The motives are the germinal cells from which everything in the movement grows. Theme I is a spacious melody that establishes the home key of G minor. Its mournful lilt is cut short by the energetic motion of the bridge, which thrusts purposefully toward a climax. A moment of silence clears the air. Then theme II appears, contrasting with theme I in both its lyric sweetness and melodic direction. Where I swoops upward, II shades gracefully downward. Since the movement is in G minor, a tonic minor key, the first contrasting key is not the dominant but the relative major key (RM), in this case B-flat major. Theme II trails off. There is a short transition where harmonic colors change and orchestral volume rises. Then closing theme "a" (CLa) reinstates the active motion of the bridge with a crisp forte attack. It is the first of three closing materials. Closing theme "b" (CLb) muses on theme I, the reminiscence helping to bind the exposition together. Then resounding fanfares of closing theme "c" (CLc) lead to the double bar.

A curious detail is that Mozart does not wait for the end of the bridge to reach the first contrasting key. He installs B-flat major at the start of the bridge. This deprives the bridge passage of its customary function of changing keys, though it keeps its transitional rhetoric. Along with more obvious appeals for the less informed, good music always has such details to engage the informed listener. Mozart was keenly aware of this. In describing some new concertos in a letter to his father, he observed that "they represent a middle ground between what is too difficult and too simple. They are quite brilliant and pleasing to the ear, though naturally without becoming empty . . . Here and there are things that only someone who really understands music can appreciate. Yet the amateur can still derive satisfaction without knowing why."

The movement's chief subtlety concerns its two chief motives, x and y. At first, they may seem quite dissimilar (see Ex. 4.6a), but they are actually related in the sense that both start out with descending half-steps. These descending half-steps color the whole piece. Much of what happens in point-to-point harmonic motion within the development can be heard as a downward slippage by half-steps. There is also a larger scale effect of half steps. Mozart begins the exposition in G minor; the development is launched with a sur-

Ex. 4.6a. Themes and Motives from First Movement, Symphony No. 40 in G Minor, Mozart

Motive ⓧ  (Beginning of I)

Motive ⓨ  (Beginning of II)

Ex. 4.6b. First Movement, Symphony No. 40 in G Minor, Mozart

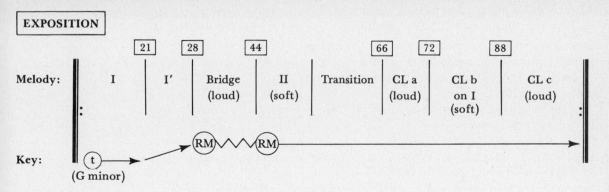

EXPOSITION

| | 21 | 28 | 44 | | 66 | 72 | 88 |

Melody: I   I′   Bridge   II   Transition   CL a   CL b   CL c
                  (loud) (soft)   (loud) on I   (loud)
                                                     (soft)

Key: (t) (G minor)   RM〰〰RM

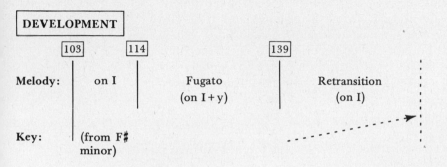

DEVELOPMENT

| 103 | 114 | | 139 |

Melody: on I   Fugato   Retransition
                (on I + y)   (on I)

Key: (from F♯ minor)

RECAPITULATION

| 165 | 184 | 191 | | 227 | | 254 | 260 | 276 | 287 |

Melody: I   I′   Bridge   II   Transition   CL a   CL b   Extension   Codetta
                  (polyphony,
                  longer)

Key: (t)   (SM)   (t)

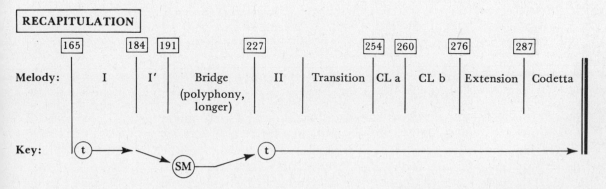

Keys:

(t) Tonic minor (G minor)

(RM) Relative major (B♭ major)

(SM) Submediant major (E♭ major)

prising move to F-sharp minor; then the recapitulation returns to G minor. Some musicians think that in this way Mozart has projected an enormously lengthened shadow of the initial half-step interval across the whole expanse of the movement. Relationships like that are difficult for listeners to consciously grasp. Yet something of this panoramic effect is registered by everyone's inner ear. It contributes another level to the multileveled "meanings" in Mozart's masterpiece. It helps to raise the music above the ordinary conventions of its sonata-allegro framework to the status of a musically convincing form.

D. MINUET AND TRIO FORM

Mozart employed sonata form for the first, second, and fourth movements of the G Minor Symphony, but for the third movement he adopted another conventional form, the minuet and trio. The courtly French minuet, which appeared in many Baroque dance suites, survived beyond the Baroque to become the longest-lived and most influential of the suites' binary-form dances. Minuets serve as the standard third movements of Classical symphonies. Actually they come in pairs, the first minuet specifically called the minuet, the second one called the trio. The trio is followed by an identical, da capo return of the minuet, so that the overall plan comes out to a big A-B-A. That plan is used in all minuet movements of Classical symphonies, sonatas, and string quartets:

△
Mozart: Third Movement,
Symphony No. 40
in G Minor
(Side 4, Band 5)

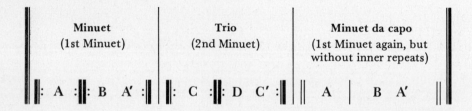

Both the minuet and trio share the stately motion and triple meter of traditional minuets, though on occasion in the later eighteenth century the tempo is livelier. In the trios the orchestration may be thinner, the dynamics less forceful, and the texture less dense than in the minuets. Baroque trios were often reduced in scoring to an actual trio of instruments, and that name persisted even when the performing forces were larger. The Classical minuet and trio, with their vestiges of dance rhythms and their simple binary forms, are the least pretentious of a symphony's four movements. They are meant as pleasant interludes between the profundity of the slow movement and the spirited action of the finale.

Ex. 4.7. Third Movement ("Minuet and Trio"), Symphony No. 40 in G Minor, Mozart

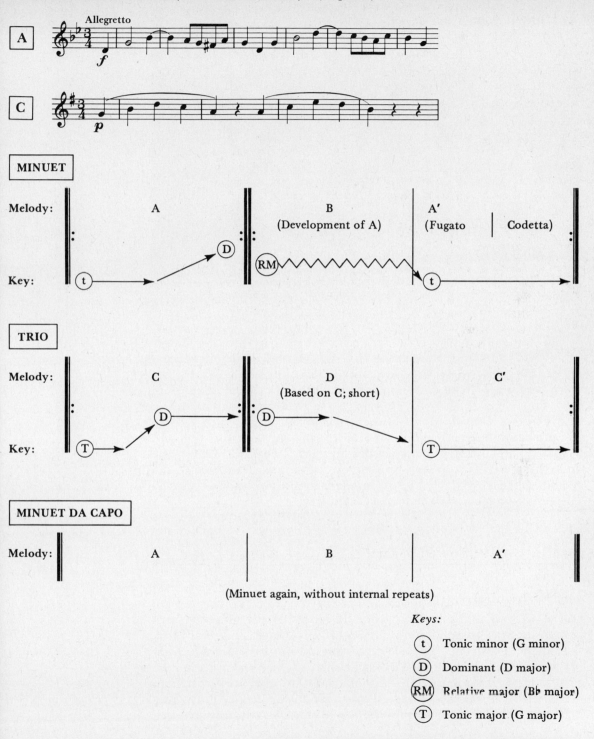

(Minuet again, without internal repeats)

Keys:

(t) Tonic minor (G minor)

(D) Dominant (D major)

(RM) Relative major (B♭ major)

(T) Tonic major (G major)

Giovanni Domenico Tiepolo, A Dance in the Country *(late eighteenth century). Mozart, Haydn, and Beethoven wrote "Country Dances" that were less formal than minuets.*

Yet minuets can also make serious statements, as does the Minuet of Mozart's G Minor Symphony (Ex. 4.7). Its initial theme (A) has an earthy vigor where little remains of the old courtly graces. The B section is a concise development that spins out the material of A with taut energy. Then A' appears, rising boldly through a stretto. The trio is a conversation between strings and winds, shifted from the minuet's somber G minor to a more sanguine G major, and with a sparser orchestration and gentler rhythmic motion. Toward the end, the wind instruments spiral upward in ethereal contrast to the earthbound strings. Finally the minuet returns, rounding out the elemental symmetry of the form.

E. THEME AND VARIATIONS FORM

Franz Joseph Haydn

The wittiest and most intellectually adroit of the great Western composers was Joseph Haydn (1732-1809). Almost single-handedly during the 1760s and 1770s he brought to maturity the airy, dramatic Classical style whose fruition he shared with Mozart during the 1780s. Haydn was born into a poor family in provincial Austria in 1732, eighteen years before the death of Bach, twenty-four years before the birth of Mozart. At the age of eight Haydn was sent as a choirboy to St. Stephen's Cathedral in Vienna, and two decades of precarious existence followed. In 1761, at the age of twenty-nine, he found secure employment with the Austro-Hungarian noble family named Esterhazy, as the composer and conductor for their princely musical establishment. An orchestra and small opera theater were always at his disposal, and he flourished in that fashion for three decades, spending much of each year at the family's Hungarian country estate of Esterhaz and the remainder at the imperial capital of Vienna. Of the years at the Esterhazy court he remarked, "There was no one around to confuse and distract me so I was compelled to become original." Haydn's works of the 1760s through 1780s won international acclaim for their charming and elegant styles. In 1790, when he was nearing sixty, he retired to Vienna where he was lionized by the musical public. Two visits to England in the 1790s were the occasions for the two famous sets of "London" Symphonies, his last twelve symphonies, Nos. 93 through 104. On his first English trip he was made an honorary Doctor of Music at Oxford.

Joseph Haydn.

Haydn had an amiable personality and an admirable benevolence toward younger colleagues. When he first met the young Mozart and heard his music, Haydn spontaneously acknowledged him as the finest composer he knew. After Mozart's premature death in 1791, Haydn lamented, "I was quite beside myself. I could not believe that Providence would call so soon for the presence of this indispensable person." Mozart's mature style shows the influence of Haydn. And Haydn's own music of the 1790s reveals the enriching exposure to Mozart's music of the 1780s. During the early 1790s Haydn also taught the young Beethoven. With the humility of his own greatness, he forecast for Beethoven "a place among the greatest composers in Europe. I shall be proud to be called his teacher."

Haydn composed large quantities of music during half a century of creative endeavor. Best known are his 104 symphonies, which include those with acquired nicknames like the "Farewell" (No. 45), "Maria Theresa" (No. 48), "The Hen" (No. 83), "Oxford" (No. 92), "Surprise" (No. 94), "Miracle" (No. 96), "Military" (No. 100), "Clock" (No. 101), "Drum Roll" (No. 103), and "London" (No. 104). His instrumental output also includes 83 string quartets, 52 piano sonatas, and 31 trios for violin, cello, and piano. There are many operas and Masses. Haydn was so impressed by the oratorios of Handel that he heard in England during the early 1790s that he put special energies into choral music. Between 1796 and 1802 he composed the two great oratorios, *The Creation*, based on Milton's *Paradise Lost*, and *The Seasons*, along with six large settings of the Mass.

Haydn's genial personality and the conversational directness and wit of his musical style made him the most admired composer of the age. In his handling of musical forms, Haydn liked to shape familiar frameworks in original, unexpected ways. In this respect he differed somewhat from Mozart, who was often content to let the "forms" run their expected courses and make his effect through other strokes of imagination. Haydn tried to stimulate the minds of those sophisticated listeners who knew what to expect of the Classical forms and style. In approaching his music the question always to ask is: What clever trick will Haydn play next, how ingeniously will he deal with my expectations? It makes for a rewarding relationship as composer and listener in effect match wits, trying to outsmart one another.

Haydn's Symphony No. 94 in G Major was composed in 1791 for presentation during his first trip to London. Its four movements adopt the same general order of forms, tempos, and moods that are found in Mozart's G Minor Symphony of 1788, though for his second movement Haydn chooses not sonata form but theme and variations:

1. Fast. A slow introduction, then sonata form.
2. Slow. Theme and variation form.
3. Minuet and Trio.
4. Fast. Sonata form.

The slow second movement of this symphony, one of the great favorites in the musical literature, consists of a theme and four variations. Its theme has all the allure of a folksong, but Haydn did not find it in any anthology of well-known tunes. Quite the contrary, he contributed it to the public domain, composing it for this movement. He made it so simple and agreeable that hearing it once is enough to engrave it on the memory. Outwardly, the theme has the shape of a binary form. Because of its slow tempo and the inner repetitions, each variation consumes a fair amount of time, so just four variations and a coda suffice for the complete movement (Ex. 4.8). The theme's binary-form outline is maintained pretty much intact throughout, but each new variation offers some novelties of melody, rhythm, harmony, texture, dynamics, or orchestration. In listening the aim is to trace the original elements of the theme as they reappear, yet also to catch what is fresh each time. Variation 1 adds a graceful countermelody in the violin. Variation 2 shifts from the major to the minor mode, and its B section, abandoning the inner repeat, amounts to a miniature development. Variations 3 and 4 have different music for their inner repeats, alternating staccato and legato, and loud and soft. The codetta returns to the simple opening formulation of the theme, but delicately retouches its harmonies so as to give a sense of closure.

The nickname of Symphony No. 94, "The Surprise," comes from the loud orchestral chord that rattles the unsuspecting listener early in the second movement. The idea occurred to Haydn only after the movement was complete, but it was a provocative one because it

△
Haydn: Second Movement, Symphony No. 94 in G Major ("The Surprise") (Side 5, Band 1)

**Ex. 4.8. Second Movement ("Theme and Variations"),
Symphony No. 94 in G Major ("The Surprise"), Haydn**

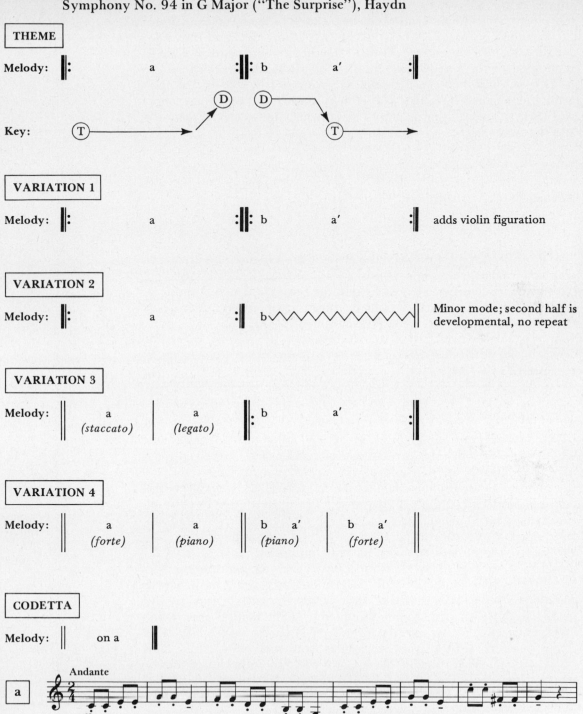

worked in more than one way. Its immediate effect is to startle and amuse. But it has a deeper effect that spreads itself across the whole movement. The single loud orchestral chord in fact triggers a series of soundless echoes, silent surprises. Everything depends on where we suppose the loud chord fits into the theme's binary-form plan: Is it the end of the *a* section of the theme; or is it the beginning of the *b*? If it belongs to the *a*, it should end both *a*s. If it belongs to the *b*, it should begin both *b*s. In fact it does neither. It comes just once, and then at a place that is poised ambiguously between the second *a* and the first *b*:

⊕ = "Surprise" chord

Theme: ‖: A :‖: b a′ :‖

Haydn wanted that ambiguity because for the listener who knew the standard behavior of binary form the "surprise" chord raised its questions, its silent echoes, each time the music returned without it. Where did the chord fit? Would it come again? Of course it never does, but Haydn cleverly keeps one guessing.

F. RONDO FORM

The String Quartet

Haydn's way of provoking and manipulating the listener is nowhere more evident than in the finale of his so-called "Joke" Quartet of 1781. This is an example of the string quartet, which rose to prominence as the leading chamber music genre of the late eighteenth century, replacing the older trio sonata of the Baroque. The rise of the string quartet coincided with the rise of the Classical style itself. It was part of the same vogue of transparency and simplicity that saw the basso continuo disappear and fugal polyphony give way to accompanied melody. The Baroque's favored string instruments had been the slope-shouldered viols, whose ancestry went back to the Middle Ages. The viols gave way during the eighteenth century to the more elegantly shaped, square-shouldered **violin family**—the violin, viola, and cello, which spoke with greater keenness and agility. The string quartet's four instruments are all from the violin family. The "first violin" usually carries the melody while the other three instruments provide the underlying accompaniment, but any of them may on occasion take over the melody. The "second violin" is physically the same instrument as the first violin, though in a typical quartet texture it occupies a lower range. The somewhat larger viola covers an alto or middle range, and the much larger cello takes the lowest part. Gone from the string quartet is the basso continuo and the direct competition between two equal upper-voice instruments, as in the Corellian trio sonata. The quartet fills the empty gap of the harpsichord's improvised chords, partly with the second violin, partly with the viola. But gap-filling is not the point. The quartet texture is altogether more transparent. It is a delicate chamber medium that produces none of an orchestra's robust volume or variety of tone colors. Quartet composers rely on the intrinsic quality of their musical ideas—and that is why quartets often bring forth their very best ideas. Goethe compared a string quartet to a conversation among four intelligent people.

The Rondo Finale in Haydn's "Joke" Quartet

The closing movements, or **finales**, of Classical quartets and symphonies, like the closing movements of Baroque suites and concertos, are often devoted to jolly moods. The finale of Haydn's "Joke" Quartet (the name was not assigned by Haydn) is a notable example. Haydn chose **rondo form** as a framework for this movement, a form with a natural light touch that is less common in the more dramatic sonata form. The rondo form was cultivated throughout the Baroque, but came into its own during the Classical period because its sprightliness was ideal for final movements. The point of a rondo is the return of its opening material, the "rondo refrain" or A section that appears at the beginning, then keeps coming back in the course of the movement, and finally closes the movement. In between the refrains, the composer sandwiches "digressions," or contrasting materials—B sections, C sections, etc. There are three common orderings of the refrains and digressions in a rondo:

△
Haydn: Fourth Movement, String Quartet in E-Flat, Op. 33, No. 2 ("The Joke") (Side 5, Band 2)

1. A B A B A
2. A B A C A
3. A B A C A B A

A string quartet of the late eighteenth century.

There is also a simple tonal plan. In each case the opening refrain or A section establishes the home key, and each time the refrain returns, it is usually in that same key. The contrasting sections (B, C, etc.) are in contrasting keys. Some rondos substitute short development sections for one or more of the inner contrasts. Haydn's finale to the "Joke" Quartet is one of these, taking as its basic form number (1) above (A B A B A), but turning out each of the B sections as a miniature development of the sort that might appear in a small-scale sonata form (Ex. 4.9).

Ex. 4.9. Finale, String Quartet in E-Flat Major, Op. 33, No. 2 ("The Joke"), Haydn

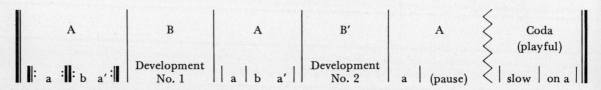

The most important music in any rondo is its opening refrain. Haydn makes this one extraordinarily tuneful and memorable, with a special fuss over the passages that prepare its return, both those leading back to the main A sections and the brief returns to the little *a'* phrases. He toys with each approach, sometimes delaying the return so that it becomes a game to see just how it will arrive.

The best game, and the strokes of Haydnesque wit that have earned this quartet its nickname, "The Joke," come at the end of the movement. They begin at the A section, just before the coda. This starts out like the beginning of the movement, but it is unexpectedly cut short after a single small *a*. Instead of the *b* to follow, there is a pregnant pause. The listener is put on guard. Something is about to happen! What actually does happen is quite simple to understand when we think about it later, but while it is happening we are caught up in delightful suspense. Haydn wants us to guess when the movement has reached its end, but he sets clever traps so that we won't guess correctly. We may commit ourselves in this cat-and-mouse game, basing our guess on the normal behavior of the Classical style. But we will be wrong, for Haydn has done something abnormal. Our reaction is puzzlement, then surprise, then delight at how ingenious he has been.

G. THE CLASSICAL SOLO CONCERTO

The profound changes that turned eighteenth-century music from the Baroque to the Classical style also had their effect on the old concerto grosso. This was not just shunted aside, as was the fate of the old trio sonata, but its status and techniques were altered so that where the concerto had been the chief orchestral genre of the Baroque, it now became a dependency of the symphony, taking its initiatives of form and style from that vigorous, newly risen genre. The basic principle of a concerto remained the same—that of competition between solo and orchestral sonorities. But increasingly in the Classical concerto, a preference was solidified that was already becoming established in Baroque concertos such as *The Four Seasons* of Vivaldi—that of using a single soloist instead of the multiple soloists of the concerto grosso. The Classical solo concerto took over the outer shell of the Baroque's three movements (fast-slow-fast), but it filled those movements with different forms. Shifting away from the Baroque's ritornello form, binary form, and fugue, the new concertos turned to the Classical favorites of sonata form, theme and variations, and rondo.

The first movements of Classical concertos generally employ sonata form with the addition of some special features that suit it to the concerto medium. Most prominent is the so-called "double exposition," meaning that the repeat of the exposition is not identical to the initial exposition. The first, or opening, exposition is for the orchestra alone. Then the soloist, who has been waiting expectantly, finally enters for the second exposition, and a dialogue with the orchestra ensues. That second or "soloist's exposition" becomes a large-scale variation of the first.

Another feature in Classical concerto movements is the **cadenza** or soloist's display piece, which tends to come near the end of fast movements. The orchestra remains silent and the soloist shows off, catering to the increasingly populist audiences of the later eighteenth century, which were beginning to look for virtuoso display and "star" status from their instrumental soloists. In Mozart's time the solo performers still improvised their own cadenzas, perpetuating a custom that went back to Corelli's time. The cadenzas were built on themes drawn from the body of the movement, and the soloists endeavored to impress, with both their manual dexterity and their ingenuity in dealing with the themes. The products of such virtuoso improvisation were sometimes shallow and out of character with the rest of the movement. By Beethoven's time, composers were ensuring the stylistic integrity of their concertos by writing out the cadenzas in full. Beethoven even went so far as to write out some cadenzas for the concertos of Mozart as well as for his own.

Ex. 4.10a. Themes and Motives from Second Movement, Piano Concerto No. 21 in C Major, Mozart

3s (Triplet accompaniment)

a Andante

p (muted Violins)

b

c

d

e

f

g

Ex. 4.10b. Second Movement, Piano Concerto No. 21 in C Major, Mozart

A	(Orchestra)	‖	3s	a	b	c	d	
A	(Add piano solo)			a	b			
B				e		c	d	Transition
C				f		c′		
A″				a′	b′	c	d	b
CODETTA			g + 3s	‖				

Classical concertos, embodying these showy elements, are generally lighter-spirited than Classical symphonies. Often their aim is simply to please rather than to engage the listener's deeper feelings. But the last 16 of Mozart's 27 piano concertos, composed during the 1780s in Vienna, are the equals of his finest symphonies in their range of expression. Mozart's Piano Concerto No. 21 in C Major, dating from 1785, is one of this exalted group. Its first movement is a spacious sonata form with a martial lilt to its themes. The finale is an exhilarating rondo. In between there comes a slow movement, overcast with an aura of sweet melancholy. It is one of Mozart's most exquisite creations. The spell is created at the outset by the pulsing of triplets in the muted strings. This continues throughout as the accompaniment figure (Ex. 4.10). A violin melody floats in. Its fine-spun lyricism consists of four distinct materials that are joined end to end in a continuous melody. Later on they will be separated. Material *a* is elegiac; *b* adds a trace of pathos; *c* is sentimental; *d* is the emotional peak. Examined coolly, *d* amounts to little more than a stately F-major scale, descending to a cadence. But in Mozart's stylization, this commonplace figure is ennobled and becomes a climactic utterance. Finally the solo piano enters, and the ensuing dialogue between piano and orchestra fills the rest of the movement. Mozart builds a form that is wholly original. It is a mosaic design of bits and pieces in which each instant is matched to just the right musical element. No other Classical form is like it, yet everything seems utterly natural, inevitable. Material *d* returns twice with its haunting descending scale. At the end there is a limpid codetta, and Mozart finally drops back to the opening triplets. Original in form, astonishingly romantic in spirit, the movement looks forward to the nineteenth century.

Δ
Mozart: Second Movement,
Piano Concerto No. 21
in C Major, K 467
(Side 5, Band 3)

H. OPERA IN CLASSICAL STYLE

The Operas of Mozart

Mozart's achievements in the symphony, concerto, and chamber music were unmatched by any contemporary except Haydn, yet the full measure of his stature is taken in the opera house, for among the great instrumental composers, only Handel, Tchaikovsky, and Richard Strauss approach him there. Mozart's comic operas in German represent the eighteenth-century style of "sung play" called the **Singspiel**. Its conversations are spoken, not delivered in musical recitative, but interspersed with the spoken dialogues is an array of delightful lyric numbers—songs, duets, and choruses in simple, tuneful styles. Mozart's most impressive Singspielen are *The Abduction from the*

Wilhelm Tischbein, Goethe in the Roman Countryside *(1787). Goethe (1749-1832) was a universal genius whose creativity embraced poetry, the novel, drama, philosophy, science, and fine art. A trip to Italy during 1786 to 1788 helped fire his enthusiasm for classicism and ancient beauty. His novel* Sorrows of Young Werther *(1774) anticipated romanticism, its tragic plot inspiring a wave of suicides by unhappy young lovers.*

Seraglio (1782), which exploits the "Turkish" flavors that were then in European vogue; and *The Magic Flute* (1791), which combines a world of fairy-tale magic with one of Masonic mysticism. Mozart was one of the many personages of his day—Voltaire, Franklin, Washington, Haydn, and Goethe among them—who embraced Freemasonry. Mozart also composed dramatic Italian operas based on intricate semihistorical plots, using the stiff old conventions of the opera seria. The dialogues there are sung in recitatives, which alternate with lyric set pieces that at times are Handelian in their flowery style. The best of Mozart's Italian serious operas are *Idomeneo* (*Idomenaeus, King of Crete,* 1781) and *La Clemenza di Tito* (*The Clemency of Titus,* 1791), where the traditional operatic style is converted to a supple dramatic vehicle. Mozart's most effective operas, however, are his Italian comedies, in particular the three masterpieces, *Le Nozze di Figaro* (1786), *Don Giovanni* (1787), and *Così fan tutte* (*Thus Do All the Ladies,* 1790). They bring the old Pergolesian opera buffa to its artistic summit. The librettist of these three operas was the gifted poet and soldier of fortune, Lorenzo da Ponte, who began life in a north Italian ghetto, then scrambled to the heights as a Viennese court librettist during the 1780s. He ended his career in North America teaching Italian at Columbia University, with a stint thrown in as a gunrunner in New Jersey during the War of 1812. Da Ponte's picaresque *Memoirs* make fascinating reading, filled as they are with vignettes of the high and low life of his times.

The plot of *Don Giovanni* concerns the legendary Spanish nobleman, Don Juan, who cuts a pleasure-loving swath through life and is finally punished for his sins. Molière and Shaw wrote dramas about him, Byron wrote an epic poem, and Richard Strauss composed a tone poem (see Chapter 6). The peerless work is Mozart's. As the opera begins, the dissolute Don Giovanni kills the father of a young noblewoman he has just seduced. As it ends, that grandee returns in the form of a statue—a stone guest at Don Giovanni's dinner party—and drags him, unrepentant, off to hell. Between the tragic beginning and the cautionary ending, the action details Don Giovanni's amorous entanglements with three women, along with his machinations, both desperate and comic, to avoid detection as the seducer-assassin.

The duet "Là ci darem la mano" is the most celebrated number in an opera that is full of memorable set pieces. It comes as the conclusion to a scene of flirtation between Don Giovanni and Zerlina, a pretty country girl who has caught his roving eye. Zerlina's fiancé, the bumpkin Masetto, has just been bullied off stage by Don Giovanni's knavish servant Leporello. This leaves the would-be lovers alone. A dialogue ensues in which the nobleman's blandishments encounter lessening resistance from the not-so-guileless young woman. At the end her head is completely turned and she agrees to go off with him. It affords plenty of opportunity for characterization and for humor.

△
Mozart: Recitative and Duet from Act 1, *Don Giovanni* (Side 5, Band 4)

Like most early operatic scenes, this one is divided into two sections. There is an opening conversation in recitative, followed by a lyric number, the duet "Là ci darem." For the recitative, Mozart adopts the matter-of-fact conversational style of the dry or secco recitative, whose rapid-fire vocal delivery is accompanied only by sparse chords on the harpsichord. The eighteenth-century's secco recitative is often formula-like and mechanical, but in Mozart's hands even the commonplace idioms of recitative come marvelously alive. Da Ponte's libretto is full of comic ironies that Mozart underlines in the musical dialogue, as when Don Giovanni professes disbelief that the lovely Zerlina can be destined to marry the boorish Masetto: "Chi? . . . Colui?" ("Who? . . . Him?"). His suave baritone phrases wax enthusiastic about her dainty features: "quel visetto d'oro, quel viso inzuccherato" ("that precious face, that sweet countenance"). He loftily dismisses Zerlina's observation that a nobleman's promises to a pretty girl are not to be trusted: "Eh, un impostura della gente plebea" ("Oh, that's a falsehood of the common people"). It was just two years before the French Revolution! Finally Giovanni becomes unctuous and points to a house off in the distance: "That house is mine, alone we'll be, and there, my treasure, we will be married" ("ci sposeremo"). On that dubious premise the recitative ends. To enjoy Mozart's subtleties, the Italian text should be followed word for word with the help of the translation:

Mozart's Don Giovanni, *painte by the German romantic M Slevogt.*

DON GIOVANNI

Don Giovanni: *Alfin siam liberati, Zerlinetta gentil, da quel scioccone,*
        At last, my pretty Zerlina, we're rid of that oaf,

       Che ne dite, mio ben? So far pulito?
        What say you, my sweet? Do I know how to handle things?

   Zerlina: *Signore, è mio marito.*
        But sir, he's my fiancé.

Don Giovanni: *Chi? Colui? Vi par che un onest' uomo, un nobil cavalier,*
Who? Him? Do you think a fine fellow like me, a noble cavalier,

qual io mi vanto, possa soffrir che quel visetto d'oro,
as I pride myself, could stand for that precious face of yours,

quel viso inzuccherato da un bifolcaccio vil sia strapazzato?
that sweet countenance, to be abused by that dreadful bumpkin?

Zerlina: *Ma Signor, io gli diedi parola di sposarlo.*
But sir, I've given my word to marry him.

Don Giovanni: *Tal parola non vale un zero.*
Such a promise is not worth anything.

Voi non siete fatta per esser paesana.
You weren't made to be a peasant.

Un' altra sorte vi procuran quegli occhi briconcelli,
A different fortune you'll have with those roguish eyes,

quei labbretti sì belli.
those lovely lips.

Quelle dituccia candide e odorose.
Those white fragrant little fingers.

Parmi toccar giuncata e fiutar rose.
I seem to touch jonquils and scent roses.

Zerlina: *Ah, non vorrei . . .*   Don Giovanni: *Che non vorreste?*
Oh, I shouldn't . . .   What shouldn't you?

Zerlina: *Alfine ingannata restar.*
I shouldn't like to be deceived.

Io so che rado colle donne voi altri cavalieri
I know that rarely with women are you nobles

siete onesti e sinceri.
honest and sincere.

Don Giovanni: *Eh, un impostura della gente plebea!*
Oh, that's a falsehood of the common people.

La nobiltà ha dipinta negli occhi l'onestà.
Nobility has honesty in its eyes.

Orsù, non perdiam tempo;
Come now, let's not waste time;

in questo istante io vi voglio sposar.
at this very instant I want to marry you.

Zerlina: *Voi?*   Don Giovanni: *Certo, io.*
You?   Certainly, I.

Quel casinetto è mio, soli saremo,
That house is mine, alone we'll be,

e là, gioiello mio, ci sposeremo.
and there, my treasure, we will be married.

The duet that comes next is the melodious opposite of the secco recitative. "Là ci darem la mano" is enjoyable as pure music without any words because it has such a wonderful tune (Ex. 4.11). But the duet also covers important dramatic ground. It seals the amorous negotiations between Giovanni and Zerlina. Again the Italian text should be followed to see how Mozart enlivens each twist of argument and character with music. The self-assured Don Giovanni starts

Ex. 4.11. "Là ci darem la mano," Duet, *Don Giovanni,* Mozart

Music:	A	A′	B	A″	B	C
Singer:	Giovanni	Zerlina	Giovanni + Zerlina }	———————————→		Giovanni + Zerlina together
Words: (lines)	1-4	5-8	9-12	1-2, 4-6, 8	9-12	13-15

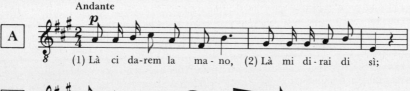

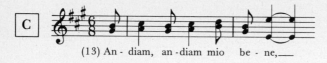

Don Giovanni:
(1) *Là ci darem la mano,*   (1) We'll join our hands together,
(2) *Là mi dirai di sì;*   (2) There to me you'll say "yes";
(3) *Vedi, non è lontano,*   (3) See, it isn't far,
(4) *Partiam, ben mio, da qui.*   (4) Let's go my darling from here.

Zerlina:
(5) *Vorrei, è non vorrei,*   (5) I'd like to . . . and yet I wouldn't,
(6) *Mi trema un poco il cor;*   (6) For my heart trembles a bit;
(7) *Felice, è ver, sarei,*   (7) Happy, 'tis true, I'd be,
(8) *Ma può burlarmi ancor.*   (8) But he might yet deceive me.

Don Giovanni:
(9) *Vieni, mio bel diletto!*   (9) Come, my fair sweetheart!

Zerlina:
(10) *Mi fa pietà Masetto!*   (10) Oh, forgive me, Masetto!

Don Giovanni:
(11) *Io cangierò tua sorte!*   (11) I'll change your lot in life!

Zerlina:
(12) *Presto non son più forte!*   (12) Now I've lost all resistance!

Together:
(13) *Andiam, andiam mio bene,*   (13) Let's go let's go my darling,
(14) *A ristorar le pene,*   (14) To taste the ardent pleasures,
(15) *D'un innocente amor.*   (15) Of an innocent love.

out with four courtly phrases that paint a rosy picture of pleasures to come ("We'll join our hands together," lines 1-4, music A). Zerlina responds by singing essentially the same four phrases, but her doubts and flightiness are reflected in the daintier cut of her vocal line and some frills in the accompaniment ("I'd like to, yet I wouldn't," lines 5-8, music A'). Giovanni resumes his ardent appeal with a lordly sweep of phrase ("Come, my fair sweetheart," line 9, music B). Zerlina responds with music whose mincing half-step intervals tell us that she is already less than firm in her resolve. She manages to stammer that she's engaged ("Oh, forgive me, Masetto . . . ," line 10). On they go, her resistance rapidly fading. At the end they skip off together, hand in hand, while the orchestra mocks their simplistic vision of bliss (music C). The duet is a treat as pure music. But a better treat is to watch the music give a more accurate shape than words alone can muster to the shifting emotional temperatures—to Giovanni's importunings and Zerlina's vacillations.

Mozart's comic operas in Italian represent a fusion of two great operatic traditions of the earlier eighteenth century. There was the opera buffa of Pergolesi. And there was the Baroque opera seria—the "serious," quasi-historical opera of Handel and his contemporaries. Opera seria was reformed during the 1760s and 1770s by Mozart's older Austrian compatriot, Christoph Willibald Gluck (1714-1787). It was Gluck who took over the stiff characters and lofty emotions of the Italian opera and imbued them with a more natural, true-to-life spirit. Gluck's aim, avowed in the preface to his opera *Alceste* (1767), was "to strengthen the emotional expression and impact of dramatic situations." In the "reform operas," *Orpheus and Eurydice* (1762), *Alceste* (1767), *Iphigenia in Aulis* (1774), and his masterpiece, *Iphigenia in Tauris* (1779), Gluck simplified the opera seria's complex plots and cut down on the unnatural segmentation of the dramatic action into recitatives and set pieces. He reduced the profusion of elaborate vocal ornaments and cultivated a simpler, nobler style of melody that was in line with the late-eighteenth-century's emerging ideals of simplicity and freedom from artifice. None of Gluck's reforms were lost on Mozart and Da Ponte. In *The Marriage of Figaro* and *Don Giovanni,* the serious and comic characters all come together, the nobles and commoners sharing as human beings in the same real-life situations, giving vent to the same motivations and feelings. In Mozart's operas the comic characters suffer and the serious characters laugh. There, if anywhere in the realm of Classical music, one finds the counterpart to the naturalism of Rousseau, and the revolutionary materialism of Marat that spread through the Paris streets in the 1780s and 1790s.

5 Nineteenth-Century Music I: Conservative Romantics

Shakespeare's Romeo and Juliet, *performed in the 1820s by Charles Kemble and Harriet Smithson (who soon became the wife of Berlioz). The ecstasy and despair of young lovers were favorite romantic subjects.*

Musical cities of the nineteenth century.

The Nineteenth Century, Part I

MUSIC	*ARTS AND IDEAS*	*POLITICS AND SCIENCE*
CONSERVATIVE ROMANTICS	**ROMANTICISM**	**INDUSTRIAL REVOLUTION**

MUSIC	ARTS AND IDEAS	POLITICS AND SCIENCE

Beethoven (1770-1827):
  "Moonlight" Sonata (1801)
  "Eroica" Symphony (1803)
  Fifth Symphony (1808)
  Quartet No. 16 (1826)
Schubert (1797-1828):
  "Morning Greeting" (1823)
  "The Ghostly Double" (1828)
Chopin (1810-1849):
  Nocturne No. 2 in E-Flat (1833)
  Mazurka No. 23 in D (1838)
Mendelssohn (1809-1847):
  Scherzo from *A Midsummer Night's Dream* (1843)
Schumann (1810-1856):
  "Eusebius" and "Chopin" from *Carnaval* (1834)
Brahms (1833-1897):
  Fourth Symphony (1885)
	Wordsworth, *Lyrical Ballads* (1798)
	Novalis, *Hymns to the Night* (1800)
	David, *Napoleon Crossing the St. Bernard* (1800)
	English poets: Wordsworth, Coleridge, Keats, Byron, Shelley
	Scott, *Lady of the Lake* (1810)
	Goethe, *Faust, Part I* (1811)
	Austen, *Pride and Prejudice* (1813)
	English painters: Fuseli, Blake, Turner, Constable, Martin
	Continental painters: Goya, David, Friedrich, Runge, Ingres, Géricault, Delacroix
	Schopenhauer, *The World as Will and Idea* (1818)
	Poe, *Tamerlane and Other Poems* (1827)
	Hugo, *Hernani* (1830)
	Balzac, *Eugénie Grandet* (1834)
	Dickens, *Pickwick Papers* (1836)
	Stendahl, *The Charterhouse at Parma* (1839)
	Poe, *The Raven* (1845)
	Thackeray, *Vanity Fair* (1848)
		Napoleon, First Consul (1799); Emperor (1804)
		Battle of Waterloo (1815)
		Revolutions of 1830
		Queen Victoria's reign (England, 1837-1901): The "Victorian Age"
		Revolutions of 1848
		Marx and Engels, *Communist Manifesto* (1848)
		Railway steam locomotive (1801)
		Photography: Daguerrotype (1839)
		Morse's telegraph (1844)

A. MUSIC AND ROMANTICISM

The Viennese Classical style was short-lived. Its fertile balance between expressive content and formal design lasted barely longer than a single spectacular generation. Between 1770 and 1800 nearly all the major works of Mozart and Haydn as well as the first works of Beethoven were produced. The designation "Viennese Classical" is still applicable in part to Beethoven (1770-1827), who inherited the artistic scepter at Vienna from his great Austrian predecessors. But as Beethoven's style headed into the nineteenth century there is increasing reason to think of it as becoming romantic rather than remaining classical. Beethoven's "Moonlight" Sonata of 1801, with its freedom of form and bittersweet melancholy (see page 203), bears the symptoms of an awakening musical romanticism. His middle years, from 1803 through 1815, saw the pendulum shift further away from formal and emotional restraint to a greater subjectivity of utterance. During Beethoven's last years, the new romantic esthetic was firmly established in music, if not so obviously in Beethoven himself, then in his younger contemporaries, Weber, Schubert, and Berlioz.

Romanticism was the extravagant emotional temper that held sway over the European creative imagination during the nineteenth century. It was ushered in by Beethoven, Schubert, and Berlioz in music, by Turner and Géricault in painting, by Wordsworth and Goethe in literature. Certain techniques of musical romanticism were by their nature peculiar to music, but the romantic point of view itself was shared broadly by all the arts. Romanticism began when the

Jean Auguste Dominique Ingres, A Composer (Cherubini) and the Muse of Lyric Poetry. *Creative artists strained for "inspiration." "Muse, come and kiss me" was the plea of the poet Alfred de Musset.*

late eighteenth century's revolutionary turmoil released artistic energies that could no longer be held in check within the lucid Classical forms. "Freedom" was the rallying cry of the middle class that broke the grip of the ancient French monarchy, and it became the watchword of a new generation of creators who released themselves from the constricting molds of classicism and sought fresh realizations of the human condition in their work. The romantics' chief aim was to express human feeling. Thus music, whose essence is so uniquely emotional, became in the words of Beethoven's contemporary E. T. A. Hoffmann "the most romantic of all the arts." Still, musical romanticism arose not in acts of revolutionary defiance but in a gradual counterreaction to the tight emotional range and tidy formal outlines of the late eighteenth century. Within the Classical style it was nurtured in works such as the slow movement of Mozart's Piano Concerto No. 21, dating from 1785 (see Chapter 4), where the esthetic balance can already be seen shifting from formal constraint toward expressive freedom. With Beethoven, the artist's options in the choice and treatment of materials were notably expanded, and with Schubert, who reached maturity around 1816 as Beethoven's heir apparent at Vienna, the romantic temper was well entrenched. When Berlioz came forward at Paris in 1830 with his "Fantastic" Symphony, he encountered resistance from a conservative French public but was welcomed by the younger Germans who long since had embraced the expressiveness and flamboyance of the new esthetic.

The word *romantic* has to do with love and emotion. It comes from the French literature of the Middle Ages, where a *roman* was a poetic novel of amorous romance and chivalrous adventure. In the French and German languages today, a *roman* is still a novel or imaginative story. Around 1800, writers and artists throughout Europe were turning spontaneously from rational, everyday realities to subjective, exotic fantasies. They abandoned the fashion of truer-than-life satires such as Voltaire's *Candide,* Swift's *Gulliver's Travels,* or Hogarth's *Rake's Progress,* and dealt in make-believe worlds that were alive with fantasy and passion. For a while, people would believe in fairy tales. Around 1800 the German critic Schlegel applied the word *romantic* to the newly emotional literature of his turn-of-the-century generation. And, precisely in 1800, William Wordsworth issued his memorable description of poetry as "the spontaneous overflow of powerful feelings." The "romantic century" was launched.

Colorplate 28

Romanticism's first priority was to convey emotion. Its preferred subjects were the ecstasy and despair of young lovers. Shakespeare became an idol because he created the tenderest heroines—Juliet, Ophelia, Desdemona—and subjected them to the grisliest fates. The romantic imagination fed on adventure and horror, on the terrifying and the poignant. Artists and writers dealt with extremes of behavior: madness, violence, and the bizarre. They took up Rousseau's cult of unspoiled nature and made a fetish of forest reveries, musings by peaceable waters, solitary contemplations on mountaintops while sounds of thunder or shepherds' pipes wafted in from afar.

The romantics were attracted by far-off places. Their jaded European sensibilities were fired by visions of the Orient, of Araby, of the noble savages of the Americas. The passion for the esoteric led to visions of the distant past, above all the medieval past, whose remoteness gave it fresh appeal. Nostalgia for the Middle Ages was nurtured by the ruins of crumbling abbeys and the ravaged castles that were everywhere suggestively at hand. Romantic artists and writers called forth Arthur's Round Table, the age of Charlemagne, the Crusades. Tales about captive maidens in distant towers and armored knights endeavoring to free them were the stuff of popular adventure romances, for example, Walter Scott's *Ivanhoe*. Transcending other appeals of the Middle Ages, there was the solace of its authoritarian Christian faith. The sacred truths became pure again in their medieval environment, cleansed of the skepticism and doubt that tarnished the religious attitudes of the Renaissance and the Enlightenment. Romanticism ushered in a new age of faith where the Church's consoling mysteries were accepted emotionally, unquestioningly.

Popular adventure novels we filled with gallant knights and f maidens. Typical is this illustr tion for Sir Walter Scott's Quent Durward.

The romantic preference for what was novel and stirring fell in line with the nationalist and libertarian movements of the nineteenth century. Romantic creators tended to liberalism in politics as they were free spirits in art. Beethoven spurned the "Emperor" Napoleon (see page 205). An idealistic Lord Byron helped win the independence of Greece. The young Wagner was a political militant during the upheavals of 1848. Expression was found in the romantic arts for the national spirit of established nations such as France and Russia, and the spread of musical nationalism served to fuel the movements for unity and liberation of divided and oppressed nations such as Italy and Poland (see page 222).

All of these varied romantic stimuli had their effects on music, but most obviously in the flowering of "descriptive" or **program music**. A literary critic of Victorian England observed that "all art aspires toward the condition of music," yet the romantic composers more than returned this compliment by aspiring toward the conditions of painting and literature. Many musical works were conceived with the help of ideas borrowed from poetry, drama, history, painting, or philosophy. Basing music on associations from outside of music—on "extramusical" associations—could claim a long history that went back to Vivaldi's *The Four Seasons* (see Chapter 3) or the word illustrations of sixteenth-century madrigals (see Chapter 2) and certain medieval songs that incorporated street cries and bird calls or evoked vivid hunting scenes. None of the earlier essays in musical description compared with the nineteenth century's program music. This found a point of departure in Beethoven's "Eroica" Symphony of

1803, where he dealt roundly with such concepts as the "heroic" and "funereal" (see page 205). Beethoven was more specific in the "Coriolanus" Overture of 1808, which is the character study of a Roman general disintegrating psychologically under the pressure of circumstances. In the Sixth, or "Pastorale," Symphony of 1808, Beethoven had the birds twittering, peasants merrymaking, and a smashing thunderstorm. The nineteenth century's more daring practitioners of program music, led by Berlioz, Liszt, and Richard Strauss, went on from Beethoven's modest descriptive tableaux and matched plots that were ever more detailed with musical imagery that was ever more specific.

While romantic composers were expanding their programmatic efforts and exploiting a broad spectrum of sources from outside of music, they were also turning their artistic focus more intensively than ever inward. The romantics were above all subjective. Their primary interest was in their own personal emotion, and the art of music was an ideal medium for projecting their inner dramas. The furthest reaching of musical romanticism's journeys were not to the outer confines of exotic worlds but to the spiritual gropings within the composers' selves, such as the autobiographical reveries of Berlioz (see pages 238-245) or the barings of soul by Tchaikovsky (see pages 255-258) and Mahler (see pages 269-272).

As the programmatic descriptions became more elaborate and the self-revelations more confessional, it was inevitable that musical forms would grow in scale to accommodate them. In the 1760s a complete symphony by Haydn or Mozart might come to only seven or eight minutes worth of music. Now just the finale of Beethoven's Ninth Symphony in 1824 took almost half an hour, and at the end of the romantic era a single movement of Mahler's Eighth Symphony took almost an hour. As if to compensate for the swelling dimensions, composers began to cultivate the opposite. There was a flowering of miniature forms, some having their full say in a scant minute or two of music. The most popular of the new miniatures was the **character piece** for solo piano, whose aim was often simply to evoke a mood or capture a fleeting impression. Everyone from Beethoven through Brahms and Tchaikovsky produced flavorful morsels with fanciful names such as Bagatelle (trifle), Intermezzo (between the acts), Impromptu (casually made up), Moment Musical (musical moment), Capriccio (caprice), Novelette (little novelty), Fantasy Piece, Arabesque, Mood Picture, and Album Leaf. The piano was an ideal romantic instrument because of its variety of tone colors, and because it focused the audiences' attention on the evocations of a single interpreter. Another miniature genre was the **art song**, which coupled the piano with a solo singer. This was much cultivated in Germany, where an art song is called a **lied** (pronounced *leed*). The lieder of Schubert, Schumann, Brahms, and Hugo Wolf are some of music's

Gustave Doré shows the romantic liking for the mysterious in this illustration for Poe's The Raven.

most expressive creations, joining the riches of German romantic poetry with the wealths of pianistic timbre and the emotionality of the human voice.

Once the early romantics had opened the floodgates of imagination, the quest for greater novelty and more compelling effects would not stop. Listeners who were charmed by one romantic effusion naturally wanted greater charm from the next one. Composers urged their imaginations on, sought out bizarre, erotic, pathetic subject matter, explored the fringes of behavior, strained for the unattainable. There are two aspects to this phenomenon of romantic originality, which separates the nineteenth-century viewpoint from the eighteenth. One is a factor of pure art—of a changed esthetic spirit. The other is a factor of sociology—of a change in the composers' economic status. Romantic composers, in their own pure world of "art for art's sake," cherished freedom of fancy, wanted imagination to roam, wanted to put their personal stamp on each new work. Eighteenth-century composers, by comparison, seem less concerned with freedom, originality, distinctiveness. When we hear an unfamiliar work by Haydn or Mozart, we may recognize it as a Classical work, but we are less than likely to guess who wrote it, so similar are their styles (or so similar do they appear from our distant perspective). When we hear an unfamiliar work by Brahms or Tchaikovsky, however, we can often identify it right away, not just as a romantic work but as the work of its particular creator, because the stylistic profile is so obvious. For the romantics, who were obsessed with originality, each new composition could represent a massive challenge. More so than earlier composers, romantic composers seem to have pressed and pampered their imaginations, waited and hoped for inspiration. "Muse, come and give me a kiss" was the plea of Chopin's friend Alfred de Musset, a poet who epitomized the ro-

A familiar nineteenth-century figure: the "romantic solitary" contemplating the grandeurs of nature.

European tastes were stimulated by visions of far-off places such as "Araby."

mantic outlook. For the eighteenth century, invention may have come more easily. It was not that Bach or Mozart stamped out music with machinelike ease, yet when they set to work it was more matter-of-factly, relying confidently on the bedrock of habits and technical skills acquired in their youth. The romantics' turn from craft toward inspiration meant that they produced more originally but they produced less music. Beethoven's nine symphonies and Brahms's four amount to a smaller overall bulk of music than the 104 symphonies of Haydn and the 41 of Mozart.

In cultivating their distinctive styles, the romantics were obeying an inner urge to be original. They were pleasing themselves. But they were also responding to changes in the economic system that obliged them to personalize their styles so they could compete in the new musical marketplace. The nineteenth-century composer had a different place in society. Aristocratic patronage was no longer so common as in the eighteenth century, when provincial nobles and bishops often imitated their monarchs and popes with musical establishments in their own palaces and churches. Most eighteenth-century composers found regular employment in such establishments, where they were treated like white-collar employees—in a way even blue-collar, since they generally ate at the servants' table. Bach and Mozart were essentially workers in a craft, producing much of their music to order, tailoring it to the tastes of a benefactor or the requirements of an occasion. Haydn composed dozens of pieces for an antiquated string instrument called the *baryton* (it had strings that were plucked or left to vibrate freely as well as strings that were fingered and bowed) because that was the favorite of his patron, Prince Nicolas Esterhazy. With Mozart there were signs of change. Unhappy with the patronage opportunities under the archbishop of his native Salzburg, Mozart went to Vienna and tried subsisting without regular support, but he died before his efforts could assure a steady income. Beethoven managed to exist as an independent artist, but had to accept help discreetly offered by his wealthy friends. Schubert maintained himself after a fashion on his own commercial power, by giving lessons and by selling copies of his music and tickets to his rare concerts. That was the wave of the future. There were no radios or recordings, so the way to hear music was to go to a concert or to buy a copy and play it oneself. Still, quantities of Schubert's finest music, including the "Unfinished" Symphony, lay ignored for decades after his death. Old-style patronage was not quite gone or Wagner's *Ring of the Nibelung* might never have been completed. Yet romantic composers were generally free-lance artists without regular jobs, and there is some truth to the image of the romantic genius starving in a garret. The greatest material rewards were enjoyed by composers of opera, such as Rossini, Meyerbeer, and Verdi, and by those who were virtuoso performers, such as the violinist Paganini and the pianist Liszt. Paganini could afford to order a viola concerto from Berlioz, but instead the willful, romantic Berlioz, unwilling to be simply "patronized," wrote *Harold in Italy,* a program symphony with a soloist's part that was scarcely what Paganini had in mind. The composers who could not attract a fickle and often lowbrow public with their technical wizardry or their musical styles fell back on teaching, or like Berlioz and the young Wagner, on writing music criticism.

The combination of the romantic cult of originality with the use of that originality in promoting economic survival resulted in a great variety of musical styles, seemingly a greater variety than in past ages. There were as many styles as there were outstanding composers, indeed more, since the best composers could give each work something of an individual style. Still, there are certain features of romantic music that serve to distinguish it from the music of the Classical period. Three of the main ones are: 1) **melodic contour,** 2) **chromaticism,** and 3) **instrumentation**.

1. Melodic Contour. Romantic melodies often seem vocal in conception. Even when they are composed for instruments, they seem to want to be sung. They may vocally sigh and wail, as in Beethoven's "Moonlight" Sonata (see page 203), or billow and soar, as in a nocturne by Chopin or an opera aria by Bellini. Baroque and Classical melodies more often seem instrumental in conception. They are likelier to contain scales and the angular hops of arpeggios, which are better suited to the manual techniques of a piano keyboard or the bow and fingerwork of a violin than to the human vocal chords. Romantic melodies are back to the natural pliancies of the voice, and in this they are generally closer to the essence of pure vocalism than any styles of melody since Palestrina. A related point concerns the layout of melodic phrases. In Classical melody, phrases tend to have symmetrical lengths, and their symmetries tend to project a kind of logical order. Their clear rhetoric, where one phrase asks a little question and then another supplies an appropriate answer, represents the rational world of the eighteenth century engaging in a musical discourse that is itself rational. In romantic melody, the lengths and combinations of phrases tend to be less regular and orderly. Some phrases are lengthy statements, others are shorter; and there is a flexibility and naturalness to the spinning out of melodic contours that makes romantic melody seem more capable of mirroring the flexibility and irrationality of human emotion.

2. Chromaticism. The nineteenth century was the last great epoch of major-minor tonality. Composers continued to produce tonal music based on the major and minor scales, but increasingly the "extra" five pitches of the full chromatic scale were mixed in with the seven pitches of the tonal scales. The resulting effects of chromaticism gave romantic music much of its flavor and emotionality. The great stylist of early romantic chromaticism was Chopin, in whose melody and harmony chromatic mannerisms are the essence. Chopin's Nocturne in E-Flat of 1833 begins with a melody made up of typically romantic swoops and sighs (Ex. 5.1, A). Behind its elegant curves, we can discern a basic melodic shape that is so simple and bland, so devoid of poetic grace, that Chopin never lets us hear it unadorned (Ex. 5.1, A°). At its first presentation, this shape has already acquired redeeming touches of chromaticism and rhythmic variety (Ex. 5.1, A). At a later presentation, Chopin supplies a still richer chromatic overlay, with accidentals filling in many of the intervals between the basic tonal pitches (Ex. 5.1, A'). The "extra" chromatic pitches are what give the melody its subtlety and flair. Without them it lacks character.

Ex. 5.1. **Romantic Melody (Embellishment of a Melodic Line):**
Nocturne No. 2 in E-Flat, Chopin

The resources of chromaticism were applied no less generously to romantic harmony than to melody. Composers still relied on the seven tonal triads for their basic chords, but chromatic enrichments in the melody were compounded in the accompanying chords. There were chromatic filler pitches and intervening chromatic chords. Each chromatic addition to melody or harmony represented an extra bit of dissonance, and, in the hands of skilled composers, each dissonance was a nuance of musical tension that translated into a pleasurable subtlety. The great master of late romantic chromaticism was Richard Wagner. In his *Tristan and Isolde* of 1859, the sensation-hungry audiences found the era's most persuasive emotional chemistry. Wagner's melodies and chords were honeycombed with chromaticism, and his chord progressions moved freely among distant keys that were connected by sometimes cunning, sometimes startling chromatic modulations. With Wagner's successors, musical styles became so saturated with chromatic pitches that the seven tonal pitches began losing their primacy. The chromatically supercharged idioms turned overwrought and decadent. By the end of the century, the influx of chromaticism brought the system of major-minor tonality close to a point of dissolution, and it carried with it much of what remained of the aging romantic esthetic.

3. **Instrumentation.** The nineteenth-century's quest for novelty resulted in a fuller exploitation of available tone colors and an abundance of new ones. Orchestras expanded in bulk and diversity. Haydn's London orchestra of the 1790s had only about fifty players. In 1828, the year after Beethoven's death, an orchestra at Paris had eighty-five, while in 1837 the mammoth *Requiem* of Berlioz called for a hundred and forty. Some now-familiar instrumental colors joined the standard orchestra in the early nineteenth century. Clarinets began to appear regularly in the early symphonies of Beethoven; the trombone's first important symphonic use was in the Finale of Beethoven's Fifth Symphony in 1808. The romantic's fascination with tone color brought two harps and an English horn (a low-pitched oboe) into the Berlioz "Fantastic" Symphony of 1830, and Wagner massively enriched his brass sections in the 1860s and 1870s. Bizet, the composer of *Carmen,* wrote a solo for the newly invented saxophone in 1872. Percussion effects became more varied. Instruments themselves underwent considerable technological change during the nineteenth century. The piano was altered, progressing from the late eighteenth century's modest salon instrument to become a vehicle for poetic, emotion-filled utterances and a virtuoso showhorse of the concert hall. The piano's spongy hammers, which rebounded as soon as they struck the strings, had originally yielded shallow tinklings that suited the transparency of Mozart or Haydn's brisk scales and arpeggios. Now the nineteenth-century builders enlarged the piano case for greater resonance and stiffened its frame so as to support thicker and longer strings. The result was greater variety and volume—thunderous basses and an upper register of piercing brilliance. Pianos were fitted with a "sustaining" pedal that let the strings continue to vibrate after the key that activated them was released. Several strings sounding together in that way produced a harmonic blur, a suggestive mingling of consonance and dissonance that cast up the kind of romantic haze found in Beethoven's "Moonlight" Sonata or Chopin's nocturnes. When the romantic piano's capacities were all displayed it rivaled a symphony orchestra in fullness of sound. The piano found use everywhere, but its most effective utterances were in the two miniature genres that established themselves as the quintessential media of romantic expression, the character piece for solo piano (see page 221) and the art song, or lied, for solo voice and piano (see page 215). The beginnings of both those developments, as of so much else in nineteenth-century music, are found already in Beethoven.

B. BEETHOVEN: THE EARLY YEARS (1790-1802)

Beethoven died in 1827, but his persuasive musical idiom and defiant personal image still capture the popular imagination. He was born in 1770, the son of a court musician in the provincial Rhineland town of Bonn. When he was thirteen he had to take charge of his family because of his father's alcoholism, so he found a job in the local orchestra. Mozart singled him out when he was sixteen as "a young man who will leave his mark on the world." In 1792, at the age of twenty-one, Beethoven went to Vienna, where for a while he studied with the aging Haydn. He remained in Vienna for the rest of his life. His first success came during the 1790s when he exhibited a powerful brand of pianism and a resourceful improvisatory imagination in the salons of the Viennese aristocracy. By 1800 he was also known for an exceptionally bold creative gift, and, at times, a rebellious personality. Unlike other composers, he disdained accepting regular employment in some noble household or well-endowed church. He once haughtily declined to join with the great Goethe in tipping his hat in the presence of nobility. Beethoven had resolved to remain a free artist, writing only what pleased him and living off the earnings of his compositions. That he survived in this unorthodox manner was the result of his overwhelming musical gifts, but it was also a tribute to the quiet tolerance of some admiring Viennese nobles who banded together to support him without restraining his personal and artistic freedom.

Young Beethoven.
A contemporary engraving.

Beginning around 1800, the thirty-year-old Beethoven's professional and emotional outlook was clouded by the specter of oncoming deafness. Eventually this put an end to his career as a public performer. In the summer of 1802 it almost brought him to suicide. Fortunately, he resisted and emerged from the emotional crucible with a greatly strengthened personal and artistic force. By 1815 he was almost totally deaf, so much so that after a performance of the Ninth Symphony in the 1820s the soprano soloist had to turn him around to see that the audience was still applauding. The loss of physical hearing had scant effect on his composition, which was done in his mind's "inner ear." But it took a devastating human toll, shutting a personality that was by nature brusque and imperious almost entirely within itself. Beethoven became ever more a loner, intoxicated with a sense of his high artistic mission. He never married. Short, pockmarked, and personally untidy, he was unable to inspire lasting affection in any of the women he found desirable. In old age he was an embittered semirecluse whose friends communicated with him by writing down what they had to say in little notebooks—his "conversation books."

Beethoven's early works, composed through the year 1802, include the first two of his nine symphonies, the first three of his five piano concertos, the so-called "Pathétique" and "Moonlight" Sonatas for Piano, and the "Kreutzer" Sonata for Violin and Piano. All still bear the imprint of the Classical style. Yet there are plentiful signs of a growing expressiveness and formal breadth. Beginning with the Third Symphony, the "Eroica," or "Heroic," Symphony of 1803, the personal stamp that the world identifies as Beethovenian is clear. Between 1803 and 1815 he produced most of the brilliant, dramatic, outgoing compositions for which he is best known: the Fifth through Eighth Symphonies, the Fourth and Fifth ("Emperor") Piano Concertos, the Violin Concerto, the "Rasumowsky" and "Harp" String Quartets, the "Archduke" Trio, and the "Waldstein" and "Appassionata" Piano Sonatas. Then in his last works, composed between 1817 and 1826, Beethoven became musically withdrawn and wary of facile display or overt effect. The works of this period are highly personal. They include the last five of his 32 piano sonatas and the last five of his 16 string quartets. On occasion the impulse to overwhelm was stronger than ever, as in the *Missa Solemnis* and the massive Ninth ("Choral") Symphony.

Beethoven's career and personality are exceptionally well documented. He was the object of much curiosity and awe during his lifetime; therefore many friends and acquaintances preserved souvenirs of their encounters with him. Because of his deafness, the notebooks in which the conversations of his last years were partially written down add a remarkable window on the everyday aspects of his existence. Yet the most singular records of Beethoven's life are those of his creative process. We know an extraordinary amount about how he went about composing, because he had the practice of working out his musical ideas on paper through several stages of conception and realization. This was rather different from Mozart's regular practice of setting down a composition just once after he had worked it out in his mind. Providentially, Beethoven held on to the scribbled traces of those intermediate stages in the process, and many of his sketchbooks are still preserved. It is one of intellectual history's most fascinating spectacles to witness Beethoven's changing conceptions of a work as it approaches the inevitability of its final shape.

Beethoven's Viennese works of the middle 1790s scarcely departed from the prevailing Classical idioms. Compared with Mozart and Haydn in the 1780s and 1790s, Beethoven was still lacking in refinement and verve. He partly made up for this with daring touches of color, stronger impulses of rhythm, and a new spaciousness of form. Haydn was sufficiently impressed to consider taking Beethoven to London as his assistant in 1794, but he decided against it because of the young man's rough-shod personality. Still, Haydn admired the piano trios that Beethoven published as his Opus 1 in 1795. If Haydn counseled against printing the third of those trios (the Piano Trio in

C Minor), it was because he judged the music too far ahead of prevailing taste to win friends for Beethoven just then.

During the later 1790s there are increasing signs of the unique imagination that we identify as Beethovenian. By the time of the "Moonlight" Sonata of 1801, the distinctive artistic profile was formed. Beethoven did not attach the popular nickname of "Moonlight" to this fourteenth of his piano sonatas, but he indicated there was something special about it by describing it on the title page as a "fantasylike" sonata (*sonata quasi una fantasia*). Compared with the standard three- or four-movement sonatas of the time, it has some unusual features. It is in the out-of-the-way key of C-sharp minor, which was rarely used by the Classical composers. It contains only three of the four movements of a standard sonata (or symphony); but instead of omitting the minuet and trio, as Mozart might have done, Beethoven chose extraordinarily to omit the dramatic opening allegro. Thus the "Moonlight" Sonata begins with a slow movement, traditionally the second movement, and that movement is one with an unprecedented aura of melancholy. Beethoven dedicated the sonata to the seventeen-year-old countess Giulietta Guicciardi, a piano pupil at the time, who had evidently caught his fancy. The ineffable sadness of the opening may mirror his infatuation. In any event, its sombre, suggestive quality proclaims the coming of the romantic esthetic to music.

Much of the vague, atmospheric effect that Beethoven creates is due to the absence of any graspable strains of melody. The music is built of short melodic fragments that seem suspended in a haze of harmonies. All is purposely blurred by the use of the sustaining pedal. The large plan is very simple:

Δ
Beethoven: First Movement, Piano Sonata No. 14 in C-Sharp Minor (Side 5, Band 5)

‖ Introduction ⁝ A ⁝ B ⁝ A′ ⁝ Codetta ‖

The internal divisions are kept in soft focus, subordinated to the continuity of atmosphere. The short introduction establishes the mood by presenting the two materials of the accompaniment: material w—the ponderous bass octaves moving in half notes and quarter notes; material x—the undulating triplet arpeggios in eighth notes (Ex. 5.2). Section A introduces the first fragments of melody: material y (a "lament"), followed by material z (a "wail"). Beethoven adds to the sense of romantic abandon by moving from the tonic key of C-sharp minor to the subdominant key of F-sharp minor, producing an effect of tonal relaxation. Section B is built first on y (the "lament"), then on the more animated "sighs" of material z′. Finally, the music heads toward home with wandering triplet arpeggios (x′) that stabilize on the tonic as the A′ section appears. Beethoven's

Ex. 5.2. First Movement, Sonata No. 14 ("Moonlight"), Beethoven

(w) Slow bass octaves

(x) Flowing triplet accompaniment

(x′) Wandering triplet arpeggios

(y) Adagio ... *pp* ... "lament"

(z) ... *pp* ... "wail"

(z′) ... *p* ... "sigh"

	Introduction	A	B	A′	Codetta
Melody:	———	y z	y z′ x′	y z	x′
Accompaniment:	$\frac{x}{w}$ ———————————————→		w $\frac{x}{w}$ ————→		$\frac{y}{w}$ ————→
Key:	(t) ————————→		(s) ————→	(t) ————————→	

Keys:

(t) Tonic minor (C♯ minor)

(s) Subdominant minor (F♯ minor)

form is Classical in its clarity of outline, but the animating details are wholly romantic. There is no tuneful melody, nothing one can whistle, as one can the theme of a slow movement by Mozart or Haydn. In this atmospheric compound of tuneless melodic fragments, provocative chromatic harmonies, and suggestive, mystic moods, Beethoven caught the spirit of the new age. His German romantic contemporary Jean-Paul Richter may not yet have heard Beethoven's Sonata in C-Sharp Minor when he wrote in 1803 that "Music is the moonlight in the gloomy mist of life."

C. BEETHOVEN: THE MIDDLE YEARS (1803-1815)

The artists and musicians of the late eighteenth century ignored social ills and saw the aristocratic institutions that supported them crumble in revolution. As the new century dawned, the fragments of European society were pieced together in a promising new order by the Corsican adventurer Napoleon Buonaparte, first as general, then as consul, then as emperor of the French and master of Europe. Napoleon took pains to create a heroic legend for himself. The vision of the man on horseback coming from nowhere to fulfill an historic destiny enthralled Beethoven no less than it did the rest of liberty-minded Europe, and Beethoven's musical response was the Third Symphony, the "Eroica" or "Heroic" of 1803, a symphony of vaster proportions and more potent effects than any composed earlier. Originally the "Eroica" was titled "Buonaparte," but Beethoven angrily crossed out that designation when he learned that Napoleon had abandoned all democratic pretense and crowned himself emperor in May 1804. Still, Beethoven remarked after Napoleon's death in 1821 that he had composed music for the occasion eighteen years earlier. He had in mind the slow second movement of the "Eroica," an imposing threnody with the title "Funeral March."

The Scherzo and Trio Form

For the third movement of the "Eroica," Beethoven chose the form called **scherzo and trio**, which was an outgrowth and successor of the old minuet and trio. It had the same outer shell: two binary

△
Beethoven: Third Movement (Scherzo and Trio), Symphony No. 3 ("Eroica") (Side 6, Band 1)

The ancien régime ends.
Marie-Antoinette on the guillotine (October, 1793).

The Napoleonic image: Jacques-Louis David,
Napoleon Crossing the Alps, May 20, 1800.

forms plus a da capo repeat of the first one. It even had the old triple meter. But the relaxed charm and gentle pace of the minuet were gone. In Italian *scherzo* means caprice or jest, and Beethoven's scherzo and its complementary trio (a second scherzo) are filled with rough whims and powerful energies moving at breakneck speed (Ex. 5.3). Haydn had composed scherzos in the 1780s, and Beetho-

Ex. 5.3. Third Movement, "Eroica" Symphony, Beethoven

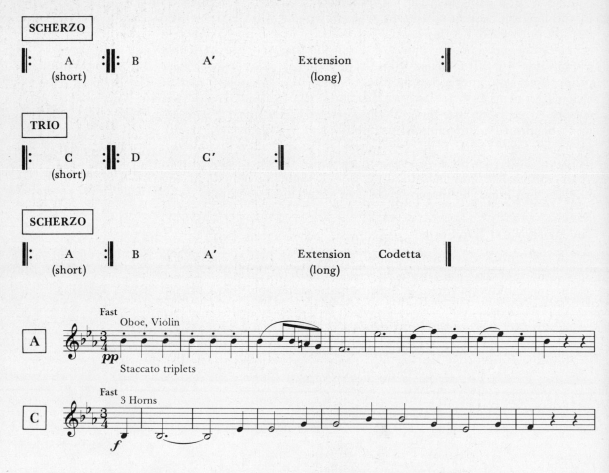

ven's "Moonlight" Sonata of 1801 contains an amiable scherzo, not yet rough in mood. But none of the earlier scherzos have the force and drama of the Third Symphony's. Suiting the Napoleonic inspiration, there is a martial spirit throughout. The opening scherzo, the bigger of the two sections, is welded into a taut unit by the unrelenting pressure of rapid triple meter and an unbroken flow of melody. Rhythm and melody are cut of a single cloth; the B section is no more than a variant of the A section. Beethoven's urge to be ex-

Colorplate 18. Jan Steen (Dutch, 1626–1679), *The Dancing Couple* (1663). Steen's painting
reflects the vibrant life of the rising Dutch middle class in the seventeenth century. In a tavern
courtyard two youthful players of a violin and flute accompany a young couple in a spon-

Colorplate 19. (*Above*) Jan van Hemessen, *Girl Playing a Clavichord* (Dutch, 1534). The painter suggests the delicacy of clavichord sound by the caressing attitude of the player's fingers on the keys.

Colorplate 20. (*Right*) Thomas Rowlandson (1756-1827), *Vauxhall, 1732.* An outdoor concert at Vauxhall (*vawks*-hall), London's fashionable pleasure garden, where Handel's music was often heard.

Colorplate 21. (*Above*) Giovanni Pannini (1692–1765). An opera performance at Rome in 1740. The splendor of the Baroque style is apparent not only in the sets and costumes of the performers on stage, but in the elaborately decorated hall and extravagantly dressed audience as well.

Colorplate 22. (*Right*) Antoine Watteau (1684–1721), *Le Mezzetin*. Mezzetino was a stock character of Italian popular comedies, a self-assured lackey who liked to serenade his sweethearts on the guitar. Watteau's paintings, notable for their nostalgic, sensuous qualities as well as for their tinge of melancholy, often feature musical subjects.

Colorplate 23. (*Above*) Marco Marcola, *A Commedia dell'Arte in the Arena at Verona, 1722.* A genre of Italian popular comedy related to *opera buffa.*

Colorplate 24. (*Right*) Balthasar Neumann (1687–1753). The interior of the church of Vierzehnheiligen in Bavaria, the most celebrated architectural monument of the German rococo, is a sumptuous ensemble of lofty arches and graceful decorations, radiant with light and pastel colors.

Colorplate 25. (*Above*) Giuseppe Zocchi (1711–1767), *La Musica* (Florentine, ca. 1750). One of four allegorical panels executed for the Grand Duke Francis of Tuscany, representing the four branches of the fine arts: painting, sculpture, architecture, and music. The refinement of the scene and the graceful bearing of the aristocratic musicians seem worlds removed from the vigorous energies of the Baroque, pointing instead toward the coming classical style.

Colorplate 26. (*Right*) Jean Honoré Fragonard (1732–1806), *The Lover Crowned*. A scene of lighthearted rococo gallantry with a hint of musical background.

Colorplate 29. Eugène Delacroix (1798–1863), *Portrait of Frédéric Chopin*. France's leading romantic painter captures the sensitivity and quiet ardor of his musician friend.

Colorplate 30. Pierre Auguste Renoir (1841–1919), *Young Spanish Woman with Guitar*. An Impressionist treatment of a musical subject, with softened focus of outline and detail.

Colorplate 31. Edouard Vuillard (1868–1940), *Girl at the Piano* (ca. 1897). The painting's strong decorative patterns represent a step beyond Impressionism toward abstraction. Pianos were familiar household instruments in the era before the vogue of the phonograph. Well-to-do families had grand pianos like this one in a Parisian salon of the 1890s.

Colorplate 33. John Singer Sargent (1856–1925), *El Jaleo: Spanish Dancer with Guitarists* (1882). A vigorous work by a famous American expatriate painter.

Colorplate 32. (*Left*) Arnold Schoenberg (1874–1951), *The Red Gaze* (1910). An Expressionist painting by Schoenberg, produced two years before the composition of *Pierrot lunaire*.

Colorplate 34. Henry O. Tanner, *The Banjo Lesson*. The American banjo had its origin in long-necked lutes brought by slaves from West Africa. It became an important factor in folk music, country music, and jazz.

pansive is never more evident than in the long extension that fleshes out the return at A', which in itself amounts to a full-scale development. The motion of the scherzo flows without break into the trio, where Beethoven employs three French horns to emulate the brassy excitement of an outdoor encounter. The high-geared rhythms slip back just as smoothly to the scherzo, but Beethoven is not content with a simple da capo repeat. He rewrites all the music, recalculating each psychological moment, subtly modifying what went before. Energy and excitement are the watchwords of Beethoven's scherzos. The mild, genial minuets were obsolete. For a while composers would concentrate on scherzos.

The powers that were spread so lavishly through the pages of the "Eroica" Symphony of 1803 were distilled with a more mature economy just five years later in Beethoven's Fifth Symphony. The work was completed in 1808, but its gestation, as so often in Beethoven's major works, went back over a period of years. The first movement of the Fifth Symphony, with its explosive "motto" opening is perhaps the best-known piece of Western music. For its outer shell Beethoven chose sonata form (Ex. 5.4). A tight-knit exposition unfolds from the striking initial "motto" (x). Theme I, dark and dramatic, moves without break into the nervous dynamism of the bridge. Theme II supplies a token of relaxation with its flowing violin melody, but this quickly heads into the closing section, where the energies of the opening are revived. Closing theme b (CL b), which rounds off the exposition, returns to the materials of theme I. The action so far described takes place at the level of the melody or the themes. Yet in the mature Beethoven, the more significant actions take place at the level of the motives. In this movement, everything grows from the opening motive x—the famous three shorts and a long. Theme I and the bridge are compounded of end to end repetitions of x. Even the lyric theme II has the mutterings of x going on as its accompaniment. Clearly, Beethoven is unwilling to give up intensity even at this relaxed point in the sonata-form design. The movement's extraordinary concentration comes from the unrelenting pressure of x. Yet x by itself is too much. Some needed relief is supplied by motive y, which appears in a fortissimo blast of French horns, between the end of the bridge and the entry of lyric theme II. Even y turns out to be a factor in the overall unity: It is an expansion of x, beginning with the three shorts and a long, ⌣⌣⌣ _ , then adding two further longs: ⌣⌣⌣ _ _ _.

The development is launched with fragments of I taken through a number of different keys. The motions build toward climactic orchestral chords, whose vigor goes beyond the purely musical. The listener is shaken physically by a use of force that is one of Beethoven's trademarks. Classical composers never employed dynamics as a bludgeon. But romantic composers welcomed this license of Beetho-

△
Beethoven: First Movement, Symphony No. 5 in C Minor
(Side 6, Band 2)

Ex. 5.4a. Motives and Themes from First Movement, Symphony No. 5, Beethoven

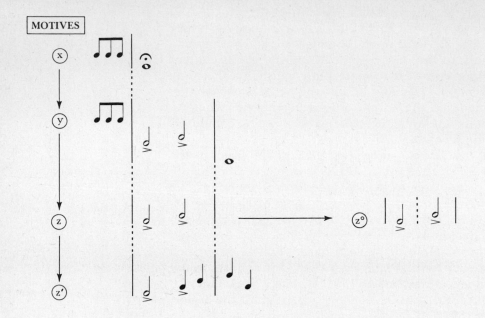

Ex. 5.4b. Sonata-Allegro Form: First Movement, Symphony No. 5, Beethoven

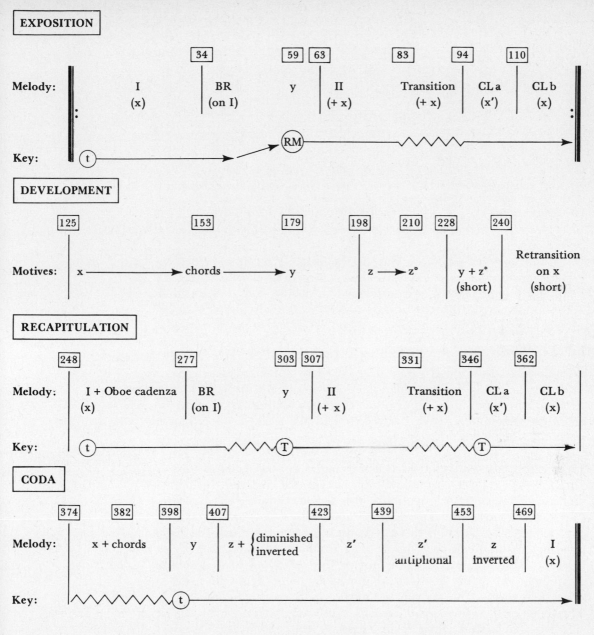

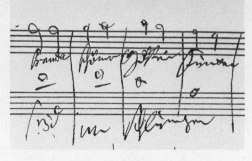

The aging Beethoven, drawn in 1823 when he was completing the Ninth Symphony.

A sketch by Beethoven for the choral finale of the Ninth Symphony, showing the beginning of the famous hymn theme and Schiller's German words.

ven's and enlarged upon it. Out of the turmoil of those audience-rattling chords, motive y returns, heard forcefully twice. At a third hearing y is unexpectedly transformed into motive z. Earlier, Beethoven derived y from x by adding two notes. Now he derives z from y by slicing away y's beginning and end. That leaves the two middle notes, moving stepwise upward: 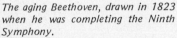 . The remainder of the development—the most intense of all developmental passages—is built on the two-note motive z. The two notes echo back and forth between the winds and strings. Then there is a further fragmentation, an astonishing one: motive z is reduced to just a single note. This is motive z°, , which continues to resound back and forth in single string and wind chords. It is the last link in the chain of motive derivations (x→y→z→z°) that has carried the listener from the stormy energies of the opening to this far-out point in the development. All of the sound and fury have come down to this single sound. No less remarkably, all of this has happened while the music has been growing softer. Beethoven knew how to thunder, but this peak of musical excitement is reached not in the pounding of a dramatic fortissimo but in the hush of an almost inaudible pianissimo. For a miraculous instant Beethoven has all the angels on the head of a pin. Then the spell is broken: y returns brusquely, followed by x. The crescendo of a short retransition passage leads to the fortissimo of the recapitulation. The whole development takes only moments to play, but there is an extreme of power in its extreme of economy.

The recapitulation gives way almost at once to a melodious digression—a short solo for the oboe, whose mellow timbre adds soulfulness to the unrelieved storm and stress. The excitement of the development is revived in the long coda, where a further derivative of z—the marchlike z'—appears. Beethoven resumes his developmental processes here, at times presenting z and z' at double speed and turning them upside down (inverting them). At the end he ties all together by restating the music of the "motto" opening.

D. BEETHOVEN: THE LAST YEARS (1816-1827)

Beethoven's middle years between 1803 and 1815 were filled with powerful, outgoing works like the Third and the Fifth Symphonies, where rhythmic vigor, harmonic boldness, and forceful dramatic rhetoric assured an immediate popular appeal. During the years 1815 through 1817 Beethoven was mired in a web of personal crises that precluded any major musical undertaking. When he resumed serious work in the autumn of 1817 with the "Hammerklavier" Sonata for Piano, Op. 106, his style and outlook had taken on a new refinement and introspection. Beethoven's late works, completed between 1818 and 1826, are a unique wing in music's museum. They are the creations of an aging, emotionally alienated genius whose friends could communicate with him only by writing down what they had to say. Hopelessly deaf, he could hear his music and that of others only by reading the score. Small wonder that some of his conceptions at first seem odd. They are curiously polarized in scale. Some are exceptionally long and complex, for example, the mammoth fugal Finale of the "Hammerklavier" Sonata, the hour-long "Diabelli" Variations for Piano, the thirty-minute "Great Fugue" for String Quartet. The final years produced two large-scale compositions for voices and orchestra, both with strong spiritual commitments. The *Missa Solemnis* (1823) was Beethoven's giant setting of the Ordinary of the Mass. The Ninth Symphony (1824) took for its subject matter the sister- and brotherhood of all humankind, as given utterance in the *Ode to Joy* of the romantic poet Friedrich Schiller. Yet alongside these expansive creations, there are the very short, astonishingly facile movements of some of the last string quartets and the delightful transparencies of the last piano Bagatelles. During his final years, Beethoven's best thoughts tended toward chamber-music media such as the sonata and string quartet, where show and pretension are at a minimum. Even in the monumental late works for orchestra, the crowd-pleasing gestures of the middle years are rare. Virtuosity, rhythmic juggernauts, groundswell crescendos, and great marshalings of tonal color have become almost alien to him. Running obsessively through his mind are the sounds of trills and the texture of fugue. Time and again, trills are sustained for extraordinary lengths in the late works. Beethoven still relies on conventional forms (sonata and rondo), but they are transformed to suit his personal visions. He treats sonata

Ex. 5.5. Theme and Variations: Third Movement,
String Quartet No. 16 in F Major, Beethoven

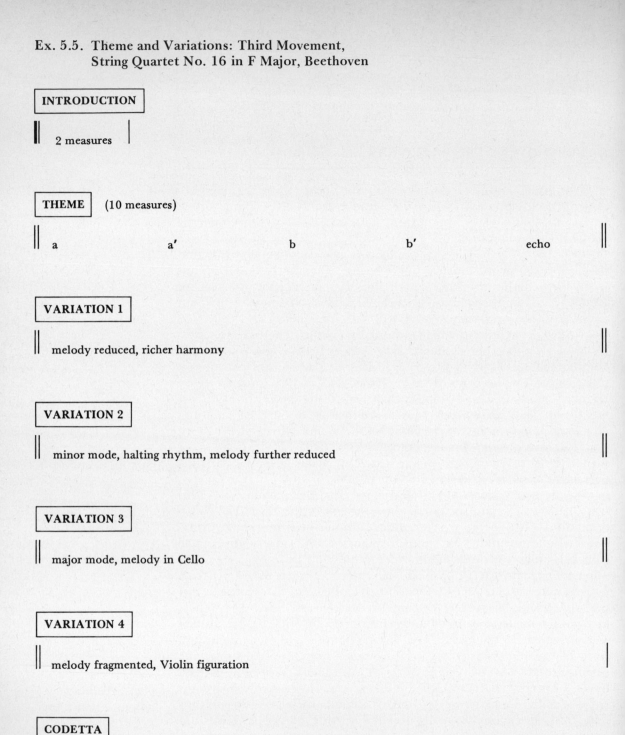

INTRODUCTION

2 measures

THEME   (10 measures)

a   a'   b   b'   echo

VARIATION 1

melody reduced, richer harmony

VARIATION 2

minor mode, halting rhythm, melody further reduced

VARIATION 3

major mode, melody in Cello

VARIATION 4

melody fragmented, Violin figuration

CODETTA

2 measures

Ex. 5.5. *(Continued)*

form willfully. Instead of well-oiled transitions, there are brusque, impatient ones, and sometimes there are no transitions at all: just one idea and then the next. The forms that fascinate him most are those pure challenges of a composer's ingenuity—variation and fugue. But what marks the late works above all is not so much technical as personal. There is an almost confessional outpouring of private feeling. Again and again Beethoven seems to lay his soul bare, so that what he gives up in outer display he makes up in the profundity of inner search.

Beethoven's final string quartet, No. 16 in F Major, was composed in the summer of 1826, during the year before his death. The slow movements of his last quartets, Nos. 12 through 16, are, by and large, his most personal statements. That is surely true of the slow movement (Lento assai) of this quartet, even though its emotion is held in check almost throughout by the tight vise of variation form. The treatment of the form could scarcely be simpler. A short lyric theme is stated, then restated through four variations (Ex. 5.5). The theme consists of five phrases: five noble curves of melody, played by the violin, each just two measures long. In most variation sets there is an increase in animation and significant detail as the end approaches. But Beethoven's method here is almost the opposite. He seems always to be reducing, disembodying the material as he goes along. The theme returns clearly in the cello in variation 3, but otherwise it is almost lost from view. Beethoven shuns overt gestures.

Everything is understated, most remarkably in the climactic final variation (variation 4), where he shapes tiny fragments of the theme in a graceful violin figuration. Somehow those broken bits, their delicate sweeps and sighs, touch a layer of deep feeling. They have as much force and meaning as are conveyed by the swagger and passion of his earlier works.

E. THE GERMAN ART SONG (LIED)

Franz Peter Schubert

Franz Schubert (1797-1828) was the first native Viennese in the galaxy of Germanic composers who made the Austrian capital their home. He was born on the city's outskirts, the son of a schoolteacher. Despite an obvious musical talent he seemed destined to be a teacher himself. But for the last nine years of a short life that ended prematurely at the age of thirty-one, Schubert had a middling existence as a free artist, supporting himself by giving music lessons and by the occasional sale of a piece of music to a publisher. He earned a fair amount but squandered it, living to the full the romantic notion that a life is well spent for love and for art. Unknown to the larger public, he was nevertheless the favorite of an animated group of young artists and dilettantes who called themselves "The Schubertians" in his honor. He inspired lively evenings of music, dance, and drink in their company, presiding at the piano and playing his latest waltzes and songs. Personally, Schubert was a modest spirit. He admired Beethoven from a respectful distance and perhaps only once summoned up the courage to introduce himself to the older master. When Beethoven died in 1827, the Viennese closed the schools and tens of thousands turned out to witness the funeral

Schubert drinking with two friends, drawn by Moritz von Schwind.

procession. Schubert himself was a pallbearer. A year later Schubert was dead, mourned only by a devoted circle of intimates. Though he was barely over thirty, he had nevertheless outlived some of his romantic contemporaries such as Shelley (1792-1822) and Keats (1795-1821) whose mercurial geniuses are comparable to his own.

Schubert had perhaps the richest melodic gift of the nineteenth century. To that he added a fertility like Mozart's. The masterpieces began to appear while he was in his teens, and they continued to come as if effortlessly. Legend has it that he composed six art songs in one day. During the single year of 1815, he turned out nearly one hundred and fifty songs. Schubert rarely chose to thunder like Beethoven. He was a more complacent bourgeois, preferring the lyrical and sentimental. In large-scale works he generally clung to the formal restraints of Mozart's and Haydn's time. Yet his harmonies, particularly in later works such as the String Quartet in G Major, Op. 161, and the String Quintet in C Major, Op. 163, have the bolder flavorings of the new century. His moods are romantically atmospheric and evocative. Born a generation after Beethoven, Schubert had both feet planted in the nineteenth century.

Schubert's most perfect creations are his art songs, or lieder, for solo voice and piano. There are over six hundred in all, among them the fiery "Erl King" ("Erlkönig"), composed before he was eighteen to a celebrated poem by Goethe, and the haunting "Serenade." Many of Schubert's chamber works share the lyricism of his songs. They include the Piano Trios in B-Flat (Op. 99) and E-Flat (Op. 100), the "Death and the Maiden" String Quartet, and the "Trout" Quintet. In the last two works he used melodies from his well-known songs. Among Schubert's eight symphonies, only the "Unfinished" in B Minor (No. 8) and the "Great" Symphony in C Major (No. 9) of 1825 really stand comparison with Beethoven. The "Unfinished" was composed in 1822, just before Beethoven's Ninth. It was rediscovered decades after Schubert's death, a torso consisting of two highly original opening movements and the incomplete draft of a scherzo, which is poorer in quality. Schubert may have abandoned the symphony because he felt the rest would not equal the first two movements.

Schubert's lieder represent an ideal union between the human voice and the piano, the two most expressive romantic instruments. With its manifold tone colors, the piano contributes no less than the singer to the moods and descriptive effects. When the resources of voice and piano are joined with the sentiments and sensibilities of romantic poetry, the result is the most romantic of art forms. Schubert drew texts from the best German poets, including Goethe, Schiller, and Heine, but he also drew on translations from Shakespeare (*Hark hark the lark*), from the proto-romantic *Ossian* of James Macpherson, and from the English romantic Walter Scott, whose *Lady of the Lake* supplied the words for the immortal "Ave Maria." Each song of Schubert offers a complete emotional experience. Each poem receives just the right musical dress. When the poetry tells a story or projects a series of changing moods, Schubert supplies changeable

Ex. 5.6. "Der Doppelgänger" ("The Ghostly Double"), Schubert

(1) *Still ist die Nacht, es ruhen die Gassen.*
    Still is the night, and quiet the streets.

(2) *In diese Hause wohnte mein Schatz;*
    In this house lived my love;

(3) *Sie hat schon längst die Stadt verlassen,*
    She has long since the city deserted,

(4) *Doch steht noch das Haus auf demselben Platz.*
    Yet there stands the house at the same place.

(5) *Da steht auch ein Mensch und starrt in die Höhe,*
    There too stands a man who stares bleakly upward,

(6) *Und ringt die Hände vor Schmerzensgewalt;*
    And wrings his hands in sorrow's anguish;

(7) *Mir graust es, wenn ich sein Antlitz sehe . . .*
    I shudder when his face I behold . . .

(8) *Der Mond zeigt mir meine eigne Gestalt.*
    The moon shows me my own face.

(9) *Du Doppelgänger! du bleicher Geselle!*
    Thou ghostly double! thou pale companion!

(10) *Was äffst du nach mein Liebesleid,*
    Why apest thou my lover's pain,

(11) *Das mich gequält auf dieser Stelle*
    That tortured me upon this spot

(12) *So manche Nacht in alter Zeit?*
    So many nights in times gone by?

music that reflects the poetic details. Such songs, with their music tailored to different moods and events, even specific phrases and words, are called **through-composed songs**. Then there are other songs where the poetry is less descriptive, more blandly consistent in its overall mood. For such poems, Schubert provides music only for the first stanza. As in a hymn or folksong, the remaining stanzas are sung to the same music. Such songs are called **strophic songs**.

Schubert's more powerful lieder are generally the ones that are through-composed. An example is "The Ghostly Double" ("Der Doppelgänger"). Based on a poem by Heinrich Heine (1797-1856), Schubert wrote it just before his death in 1828. It portrays the emotions of a rejected lover who has come to gaze again at the house where his beloved once lived. He is frightened by a spectral vision of his formal self—a "ghostly double." Schubert wrings every drop of anguish from the poem: the distraught lover, the shadowy figure he spies, the flash of revelatory moonlight, the agonized cry from within. The text should be followed in Heine's German, using the translation (Ex. 5.6). The music is built of two main components, one pianistic, the other vocal. Four ominous piano chords are heard at the start. They set the sombre mood, and they give shape to the whole song as they reappear throughout in the accompaniment. Ultimately they provide the grim epilogue. Their "hollow" sound represents the gloomy state of the lover, grappling with memory and hallucination. The quality of sound results in part from the harmony's use of parallel octaves. When the voice enters, it is not with a shapely melody. The lover declaims only in broken, recitativelike utterances that rise fitfully from a depressive monotone to a first bitter peak at "Schmerzensgewalt" ("sorrow's anguish") in line 6, and eventually to the tremendous moment of recognition at "eigne Gestalt" ("my own face") in line 8, before dropping back to muttered fragments. With a scene this dramatic, a vapid, commonplace tune would have been useless. Only a naturalistic rendering does it justice. The phrases of Schubert's melody, by turns passionate and pathetic, track the ebb and flow of emotional tensions.

Quite another sort of song is represented in Schubert's strophic song, "Morning Greeting" ("Morgengruss"). This has all the tunefulness of a folksong. The subject of the poetry is a pretty miller's daughter who is viewed from afar by a miller's apprentice who hopes to win her love. Four poetic stanzas are filled with the boy's naive sentimentalizing (Ex. 5.7). The mood is so consistent overall that Schubert supplies music only for the first stanza. The other stanzas fit this music perfectly. Like most art songs, "Morning Greeting" begins with a piano introduction. Then the young miller's declarations are set out in a tune that has three sections. Section A, in the major mode, ends with a lilting piano echo. Section B has cloudy,

△
Schubert: "The Ghostly Double" ("Der Doppelgänger") from *Schwanengesang* (Side 6, Band 3)

△
Schubert: "Morning Greeting" ("Morgengruss") from *Die schöne Müllerin* (Side 6, Band 4)

Ex. 5.7. "Morgengruss" ("Morning Greeting"), Schubert

Piano Introduction

Melody A

Gu-ten Mor-gen, schö-ne Mül-le-rin! Wo steckst du gleich das Köpf-chen hin, Als wär' dir was ge-sche-hen?

Melody B

Ver - driesst dich denn mein Gruss so schwer? Ver - stört dich denn mein Blick so sehr?

Melody C

So muss ich wie-der ge-hen, So muss ich wie-der ge-hen, wie-der ge-hen.

Piano Epilogue

"MORGENGRUSS" ("MORNING GREETING")

Stanza 1

A *Guten Morgen, schöne Müllerin! Wo steckst du gleich das Köpfchen hin,*
 Good morning, pretty miller-maid! Why do you turn your face away,

 Als wär' dir was geschehen?
  As if something had happened?

 B *Verdriesst dich denn mein Gruss so schwer?*
  Does my greeting displease you so?

  Verstört dich denn mein Blick so sehr?
  Does my glance trouble you so?

  C *So muss ich wieder gehen.*
   Then I must leave you.

Stanza 2

A *O lass mich nur von ferne steh'n, Nach deinem lieben Fenster seh'n,*
 Oh, let me but stand in the distance, And gaze toward your window,

 Von ferne, ganz von ferne.
  From far away, quite far away.

 B *Du blondes Köpfchen, komm hervor, Hervor aus eurem runden Thor,*
  Thou fair face, come forth, Forth from your rounded arch,

  C *Ihr blauen Morgensterne.*
   You blue morning stars.

Stanza 3

A *Ihr schlummertrunknen Äugelein, Ihr taubetrübten Blümelein,*
 You slumber-laden little eyes, You little blossoms tipped with dew,

 Was scheuet ihr die Sonne?
  Why shy now from the sun?

 B *Hat es die Nacht so gutgemeint,*
  Has night then passed so blissfully

 Dass ihr euch schliesst und bückt und weint
  That, eyes still closed, you droop and weep

  C *Nach ihrer stillen Wonne?*
   In purely selfish rapture?

Stanza 4

A *Nun schüttelt ab der Träume Flor, Und hebt euch frisch und frei empor,*
 Shake off the veil of dreams, And rise up fresh and free,

 In Gottes hellen Morgen.
  In God's bright morning.

 B *Die Lerche wirbelt in der Luft, Und aus dem tiefen Herzen ruft*
  The lark is singing on the breeze, And from the depths of his heart

  C *Der Liebe Leid und Sorgen.*
   Tells love's suffering and sorrow.

minor-mode tints. Section C returns to the major mode, its lyric flow enriched by smooth triplets in the accompaniment. The marvel of a great strophic song like this is that the same melody can return so many times without wearing out its welcome. Schubert's "Ghostly Double," intense and through-composed, leaves us emotionally drained after a single hearing. His humble strophic "Morning Greeting" refreshes the spirit with each stanza, leaves us wanting more. Of course, neither type can be judged the finer. They represent two different sides of art and life.

Schubert's Song Cycles

"Morning Greeting" is the eighth in a series of 20 lieder that Schubert composed as a group in 1823, forming the song cycle *The Fair Miller-Maid* (*Die schöne Müllerin*). That sequence of songs is the saga of the miller boy, who starts out as a wanderer, finds work at a mill, falls in love with the miller's daughter, discovers that his love is returned, but then is rejected for a huntsman. In the end, after some romantic sentimentalizing, he drowns himself in a brook whose lullaby provides nature's funeral oration. The twenty songs in *Die schöne Müllerin* are not related in their musical substance. Each song has a different melody. But Schubert gives the cycle an overall musical unity by carefully choosing the order of keys from song to song and by a varied sequence of moods, textures, and forms. Some of the songs are strophic, others are through-composed. Some fall in an in-between category. They are *strophic variations,* all of whose stanzas receive essentially the same music, but the music is a little different each time, reflecting subtle differences in the poetry. In 1827, the year before his death, Schubert composed the second of his two great song cycles, *The Winter's Journey* (*Winterreise*). It is the more powerful of the cycles, recounting again an unhappy love story. *Winterreise* lacks the grisly ending of *Die schöne Müllerin,* but even before it begins, the love affair is over. It is an unrelieved series of bleak reflections, opening and closing in quiet despair.

F. THE CHARACTER PIECE FOR PIANO

Frédéric Chopin

Frédéric Chopin (1810-1849) brought the full bloom of romanticism to the piano. He was a miniaturist at heart. His specialty was the character piece for piano. Each such piece strikes some romantic mood or poetic stance—picturesque, emotional, dramatic. Chopin was the offspring of a Polish mother and a French father, which in itself set him apart from the other leading musical romantics, most of whom were German and Austrian. He was educated at his father's school for sons of the Polish nobility at Warsaw, where he picked up a taste for good living and aristocratic company that lasted through his short life. After winning early acclaim as a piano prodigy in Poland, Chopin toured Europe, and, in 1831, when he was twenty-one he settled in Paris. He was quickly taken into an elite circle of artists, including the poet Musset, the painter Delacroix, and the pianist-composer Liszt. Chopin could have become a crowd-pleasing virtuoso like Liszt, but he chose a less visible career, devoting himself chiefly to composition and to the exercise of his personal charm and neurasthenia. He never married, but from 1838 through 1847 he carried on a stormy and personally draining relationship with the feminist author Aurore Dudevant, who was famous for her cigar smoking and her flamboyant, emotion-filled novels that appeared under her pen name, George Sand. Chopin died of tuberculosis two years after the breakup of their liaison. He was only thirty-nine.

Colorplate 29

Unlike Schubert and Beethoven, who cultivated every musical genre, large and small, Chopin chiefly wrote miniatures for the piano. A handful of his works (two piano concertos and four sonatas) represent traditional, multimovement forms. Some of his longer one-movement works, such as the scherzos, polonaises, and ballades, strike heroic poses that establish him as a romantic heir to Beethoven. But, by and large, he produced short works—etudes, preludes, waltzes, impromptus, mazurkas—in whose perfumed atmospheres the young romantic movement found its quintessential stylist. Chopin uncovered vast new realms of pianistic color. His manner is rich in chromatically decorated melodies and opulent twists of harmony. Often there is an overlay of colors from his native Poland. But above all else there is a sybaritic delicacy. Chopin has been called "the poet of the piano," and at times he seems to be translating Shelley's romantic posturing, "I die, I faint, I fail" to the keyboard. Yet it is a mistake to think of him as having what a jealous English rival called "a sick-chamber mentality." A more accurate judgment was that of Robert Schumann, who praised Chopin in 1839 as "the boldest and proudest poetic spirit of our time."

The Preludes of Chopin

Chopin's twenty-four preludes were completed during the frigid winter of 1838-39 that he spent on the island of Mallorca with George Sand. Unlike Bach's preludes to the fugues of *The Well-Tempered Clavier,* these are preludes to nothing at all. They introduce no other pieces, and in some cases they are remarkably free of dependence on traditional forms. For Chopin it was sometimes enough to strike some provocative attitude, to utter a few sighs. The shortest of his preludes last only a matter of seconds. The Prelude

△
Chopin: Prelude No. 1 in
C Major
(Side 6, Band 7)

No. 1 in C Major amounts to a single, gently curving line that rises in graceful surges toward a peak and then quickly subsides, taking scarcely more than half a minute. The Prelude No. 18 in F Minor is a series of rhetorical gestures, in the manner of a recitative. Its impetuous sixteenth-note motion hurtles forward, creating its own highly original form as it goes. The piece lasts a mere fifty seconds.

Δ
Chopin: Prelude No. 18
in F Minor
(Side 6, Band 8)

The Mazurkas of Chopin

Chopin's fifty-six mazurkas reveal him again as a miniaturist, but now relying on more conventional formal plans and drawing inspiration from the distinctive idioms of the popular Polish dance called the **mazurka**. The nineteenth century's political nationalism left its mark on music, particularly in the music of the smaller, oppressed nations. In Chopin's time Poland was partly under Russian domination, and Chopin found an outlet for his nationalist spirit in two genres of the character piece that featured strong Polish dance rhythms: the epic-scale **polonaises** and short, gentle mazurkas. The mazurkas were close to his heart. He wrote more of them than of any other kind of piece, and their output spanned his whole career. A mazurka is similar to a waltz in its moderate-to-lively triple meter. It also has a characteristic rhythm:

whose "dotted" beat 1 and touch of prolongation, or emphasis, on beat 2 helps distinguish it from a waltz. In addition to those rhythmic features, mazurkas have twists of melody and harmony with the flavors of Poland. Robert Schumann wrote, "If the mighty Czar of Russia knew how dangerous an adversary lurked in Chopin, in the simple melodies of the mazurkas, he would ban that music. Chopin's works are guns hidden in flowers."

Chopin's Mazurka No. 23 in D Major has a simple overall plan that is reminiscent of a minuet and trio (Ex. 5.8). Its most prominent musical feature is the constant repetition of the opening phrase a, which appears no less than 24 times. The up-and-down gyrations of the music mirror the dancers' energetic whirlings. A middle section is more relaxed, with touches of chromaticism and the typical mazurka rhythm (phrase b). The opening returns. Then a codetta sustains a pedal point while subtle melodic twists at first gently accelerate, then slow to a close. Dynamics play an important role in giving shape to this piece. The constant repetitions of short phrases are differentiated from one another by abrupt contrasts between forte and pianissimo, which adds an excitement to the dance's intoxicating roll.

Δ
Chopin: Mazurka No. 23
in D Major
(Side 6, Band 5)
(The pianist, Horowitz,
does not strictly observe
Chopin's dynamics.)

Ex. 5.8. Mazurka No. 23 in D Major, Chopin

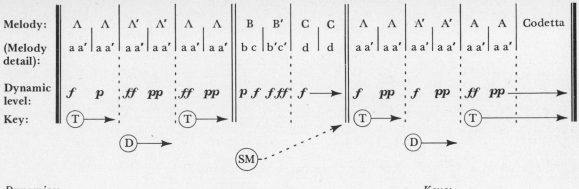

Melody:	Λ	Λ	Λ′	Λ′	Λ	Λ	B	B′	C	C	Λ	Λ	Λ′	Λ′	Λ	Λ	Codetta
(Melody detail):	a a′	a a′	a a′	a a′	a a′	a a′	b c	b′ c′	d	d	a a′	a a′	a a′	a a′	a a′	a a′	
Dynamic level:	*f*	*p*	*ff*	*pp*	*ff*	*pp*	*p f*	*f ff*	*f* →		*f*	*pp*	*f*	*pp*	*ff*	*pp* →	→
Key:	T →			T →						SM	T →		D →		T →		

Dynamics:

f forte
p piano
ff fortissimo
pp pianissimo

Keys:

Ⓣ Tonic (D major)
Ⓓ Dominant (A major)
ⓈⓂ Submediant (B♭ major)

The Nocturnes of Chopin

Chopin's twenty nocturnes are his most unrestrainedly lyrical creations. The name **nocturne** (night piece) suggests tender moonlit reveries. The slow, contemplative music of these character pieces has bittersweet melodies braced with harplike accompaniments. The sweeping melodies of the nocturnes are in a melancholy emotional style that Chopin shares with his Italian operatic contemporaries Vincenzo Bellini and Gaetano Donizetti. Chopin's Nocturne No. 2 in E-Flat begins with a long, elastic line of melody over a sustained accompaniment of slow triplets (Ex. 5.9). Like the triplets in the atmospheric accompaniment of Beethoven's "Moonlight" Sonata,

△
Chopin: Nocturne No. 2
in E-Flat
(Side 6, Band 6)

Ex. 5.9. Nocturne No. 2 in E-Flat, Chopin

Chopin's triplets continue throughout. His manner of enriching this melody has already been seen in Ex. 5.1. Each time the melody returns, the chromatic nuances are more exquisite, the mannerisms bolder. Toward the end, virtuoso excitement fuses for a moment with passionate emotionalism. Then it all dissolves in a chromatic cadenza that settles to an elegiac close. The famous line of T. S. Eliot about having been to hear "the latest Pole transmit the preludes through his hair and finger tips" is supposedly about Chopin's preludes, but it applies no less aptly to the magical weavings of spells in the nocturnes.

G. CONSERVATIVE ROMANTICISM: MENDELSSOHN

Of all the leading romantics, Felix Mendelssohn (1809-1847) had the life least clouded by financial hardship or personal torment. He was born into a cultured, wealthy family (his grandfather was a famous philosopher, his father a successful banker), and he was encouraged to pursue his precocious musical talent. Unlike Beethoven, Schubert, and Chopin, who remained bachelors, Mendelssohn had a happy marriage. His Overture to Shakespeare's *A Midsummer Night's Dream* was composed when he was only seventeen, but it was already a mature work, showing all the sprightly refinement of his best style. The years that followed brought unbroken success as a conductor and composer. Mendelssohn became an international figure, particularly admired in England, where the oratorio *Elijah* (1846) established him in musical affections as the successor to Handel. His cheerful personality won the friendship of the young Queen Victoria and her German consort Prince Albert, who would turn away from cares of state to spend hours with their musical crony. Mendelssohn was also an important advocate of earlier music. His production of Bach's *St. Matthew Passion* at Leipzig in 1829, a century after its original performance, did much to spark the ensuing revival of Bach's music.

Mendelssohn died at the age of thirty-eight, far from having exhausted his capacities. His works include five mature symphonies (among them the "Scottish," "Italian," and "Reformation"), a sparkling Violin Concerto, the romantically evocative concert-overtures to *Fingal's Cave* and *Ruy Blas,* and quantities of fine chamber music, songs, oratorios, and keyboard works, among which the most familiar are his character pieces, the *Songs Without Words* for piano solo. Mendelssohn was a conservative at heart, a classicist among the musical romantics of his time. He was content, by and large, to follow complacently in the footsteps of Mozart or Beethoven, sometimes even those of Bach, rather than strike out in bold ventures of his own. Yet if he was not remarkably original in his use of forms and style, the quality of his taste and inspiration were high. Mendelssohn has his own artistic profile, with an urbane grace and elegance that only rarely descend to the level of facile charm.

Seventeen years after Mendelssohn completed his youthful Overture to *A Midsummer Night's Dream,* he composed the twelve little pieces that comprise the "incidental music" for a performance of that Shakespeare play at Potsdam in 1843. Among them are the popular Wedding March, Nocturne, and Scherzo. They all share in the play's light-fantastic spirit. The Scherzo shows the purest Mendelssohn—precise and effervescent, with delicate romantic tints that fuse perfectly with Shakespeare's elfin drollery. As the second act opens, Puck cries, "How now, spirit, Whither wander you?" to which the Fairy replies, "Over hill, over dale, through bush, through briar . . . I do wander everywhere swifter than the moon's sphere." Mendelssohn's Scherzo traces those wanderings. It is a scherzo, not in form but in its airy whims. The form itself is a very compact sonata allegro whose two chief themes (I and II) barely contrast with one another and share the same incessant motion of rapid sixteenth notes (Ex. 5.10). The bridge adds touches of a "braying" sound, a reminder of the clown wearing a donkey's head with whom the drugged Queen Titania imagines herself in love. The texture is gossamer thinnest in the coda, which trails off in a rhythmic tour de force for a solo flute. The English critic Tovey compared this to "pronouncing two hundred and forty intelligible syllables at the uniform rate of nine to a second without taking breath."

△
Mendelssohn: Scherzo
from *A Midsummer Night's Dream*
(Side 7, Band 1)

Ex. 5.10. Scherzo from _A Midsummer Night's Dream_, Mendelssohn

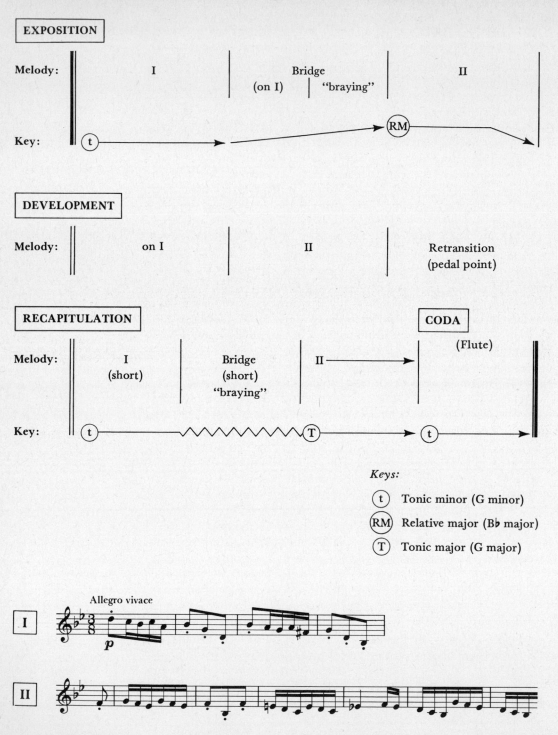

H. CONSERVATIVE ROMANTICISM: SCHUMANN

Robert Schumann (1810-1856) was the intellectual leader among the German musical romantics of the 1830s and 1840s. He was a north German, a Rhinelander, the son of a writer and bookseller whose literary example did much to shape his youthful interests. For a while Schumann studied law, which he then abandoned for music, being just twenty when he left Leipzig University in 1830. For two years he labored at the piano, hoping to become a virtuoso performer. Then an injury to his right hand, caused by a device that he had invented to improve his finger technique, put an end to visions of a concert career. Schumann turned to musical journalism and founded an influential review in 1834, the *New Journal for Music* (*Neue Zeitschrift für Musik*). During the next two decades he produced a stream of critical articles that served as the guardian angels of music's romantic movement. Schumann acclaimed genius when he saw it, and he also chastised the departures of lesser talents from serious taste and high ideals. Always a generous spirit and filled with the extravagant enthusiasm of the times, Schumann was among the first to hail the young Berlioz and Chopin during the 1830s. He was a devoted admirer of Mendelssohn, and in one of his last articles, written in 1853, he was the first to herald the young Brahms. Schumann signed many of his articles with fanciful pen names. Actually he divided himself into three distinct critical personalities: a genial, lyrical spirit whom he called "Eusebius"; an impetuous, headstrong "Florestan"; and the reasonable, judicious "Master Raro." His writings were also peopled with an imaginary coterie of friends that he called the "League of David" (*"Davidsbündler"*), who were the upholders of good musical taste (they were mainly Germans) against the debased "Philistine" composers of salon and operatic music (mainly Italians).

The youthful Schumann at about the time he composed Carnaval *(1834-1835).*

Far outweighing his influence as a critic, Schumann's lasting contribution was where he hoped it would be—as a composer. His music of the 1830s is mainly for solo piano. Like Chopin, he specialized in romantic character pieces. In 1840, Schumann married the young Clara Wieck, who was to become one of the foremost piano virtuosi of her time. With this change in his personal life, Schumann turned romantically to love songs, composing some ten dozen German lieder within that single year. They include the two song cycles, *A Woman's Love and Life* (*Frauenliebe und Leben*) and *A Poet's Love* (*Dichterliebe*). The latter can be compared to *The Winter's Journey* of Schubert. Schumann finally turned to works for orchestra, producing in 1841 his First Symphony ("Spring") and the first movement of his fantasylike Piano Concerto in A Minor. Three other symphonies followed during the decade of the 1840s, along with a good deal of chamber music, some of it self-consciously modeled on Beethoven. Then tragedy struck. Beginning about 1843 Schumann showed signs of an emotional and intellectual disintegration that worsened with the years. Finally, during the carnival festivities at Düsseldorf in 1854, tormented by hallucinations, he threw himself into the Rhine. He was hauled up by a passing boat and taken to an asylum near Beethoven's birthplace at nearby Bonn. He died there two years later, hopelessly insane.

Schumann's most perfect creations are the romantic miniatures of his early years—the character pieces for piano and the art songs. The piano pieces are usually grouped in collections whose titles reveal the kind of romantic kaleidoscope that he delighted in: *Scenes from Childhood, Album Leaves, Colored Leaves, Arabesque, Forest Scenes, Fantasy Pieces, Carnival Pranks at Vienna,* and *Carnaval.* Some of the piano collections are similar to song cycles in having a unifying thread or idea. *Carnaval* is one of these. Composed during Schumann's twenty-fifth year, it is filled with a graceful brand of pianism and with a youthful ebullience that is lit up by touches of humor and irony. The title proclaims a gallery of piquant moods and ribald types. They are the masked, costumed characters one encounters at a Mardi Gras ball on the last riotous night of partying before the Lenten penitence begins. Among Schumann's twenty-one musical vignettes there are stock figures of the French-Italian pantomime theater: Pierrot (No. 2) is the familiar buffoon in a large tunic with a white-painted face; Harlequin (No. 3) is a nimble, witty rogue; Pantalon (No. 15) is a grotesque old lecher, along with Colombine, the not-so-dumb beauty who is usually the object of Harlequin's affections. Then there are Schumann's other selves: Eusebius (No. 5) and Florestan (No. 6). There are characterizations of his two loves: Chiarina or Clara (No. 11), whom he eventually married, and Estrella (No. 13), a girl named Ernestine, with whom he fancied himself in love at the time. Concluding it all is March of the "League of David" (the *"Davidsbündler"*) Against the Philistines.*

Carnaval bears the subtitle, "Picturesque Scenes Based on Four Pitches." Each piece makes some clever use of the four pitches:

*In Schumann's order the titles are: 1. Preamble, 2. Pierrot, 3. Harlequin, 4. Valse Noble, 5. Eusebius, 6. Florestan, 7. Coquette, 8. Response, 9. Butterflies, 10. Dancing Letters: A-E-flat-C-B and E-flat-C-B-A, 11. Chiarina (Clara), 12. Chopin, 13. Estrella (Ernestine), 14. Recognition, 15. Pantalon and Colombine, 16. German Waltz, 17. Paganini, plus German Waltz, da capo, 18. Avowal, 19. Promenade, 20. Pause, 21. March of the "League of David" Against the Philistines.

or a related selection of three pitches:

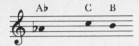

They are worked into the fabric throughout, making *Carnaval* into a very loose set of variations. It is fun to discover those pitches among the torrents of notes. But the real fun lies in Schumann's sketches of the different personalities—the pantomime figures, the self-portraits, the two young women, and the witty parodies of his musical contemporaries: Paganini (No. 16), the great virtuoso of the violin, and Chopin (No. 12). Schumann claimed that the names were added later, but so apt are some of the portraits that it is hard to take him at his word. "Eusebius" (No. 5) represents Schumann as he himself most wanted to be, wearing a mantle of youthful good will and generosity (Ex. 5.11a). The four pitches A-E-flat-C-B can be heard poking their heads up here and there. Number 12 is his admiring tribute to Chopin, who at the time—like Schumann himself—was just twenty-four years old (Ex. 5.11b). Schumann may already have known Chopin's supple "Andante Spianato," composed in 1831-32, which so resembles this. His "Chopin" has a trace of caricature, but above all it is an act of homage. The four pitches appear at the middle and end of the melody line, more subtly disguised than elsewhere.

Schumann's bloom as a songwriter came in 1840, at just the time that he found his short-lived happiness with Clara Wieck. His lieder combine the color and emotionalism of his short piano works with the deeper sentiment and human compassion that are best expressed by the human voice. Schumann was the finest composer of German art songs after Schubert, but with his turn from song to orchestral writing during the 1840s, his style became stodgier, and a troublesome intellctuality begins to show through. The four symphonies completed between 1841 and 1851 are often Olympian, but they are also at times simply labored. Schumann was all too aware of the shadow of Beethoven. When he turned to the orchestra—Beethoven's prime instrument—his own inspiration stiffened and showed fatigue. It was one thing to toss off an emotional love song. It was quite another for a high-minded Rhinelander like Schumann to undertake a symphony while that other Rhenish symphonist had been gone barely two decades. Perhaps Schumann's best orchestral work is the Piano Concerto in A Minor, composed in 1841-45, a full-blooded romantic creation that displays his favorite instrument, the piano.

Δ
Schumann: "Eusebius" and "Chopin" from *Carnaval* (Side 7, Band 2)

Ex. 5.11. Two movements from *Carnaval*, Schumann

a. No. 5, "Eusebius"

b. No. 12, "Chopin"

*2ª volta **pp**

I. CONSERVATIVE ROMANTICISM: BRAHMS

Johannes Brahms (1833-1897) was the son of a double-bass player in the north German coast city of Hamburg. As a boy he mastered the piano and for a while supported himself by playing in sailors' taverns. In 1853, when he was twenty, he showed his first sonatas to Robert Schumann, who at once proclaimed him as the hope of the new generation. Schumann's flowery prose speaks of "a musician who is destined to voice ideally the spirit of his times, who reveals his mastery, not in a gradual unfolding, but like Athena springing full-armed from the head of Zeus . . . a young man over whose cradle the Graces and Heroes have stood their watch. His name is Johannes Brahms . . ." Brahms remained a close friend of Clara Schumann's after her husband's tragic death in 1856. When Brahms was thirty he followed in the hallowed steps of Mozart, Haydn, Beethoven, and Schubert by settling in Vienna, and he remained there for his last three decades, acknowledged as the great Viennese master of his day. Musically, Brahms was a conservative—a classicist, a formalist, an absolutist, in the tradition of Beethoven, Schubert, Mendelssohn, and Schumann. In an era when storytelling and theatrical rhetoric were being exploited with increasing freedom in the music of Liszt and Wagner, Brahms remained the staunchest defender of the abstract, emotionally reserved esthetic. But he held his views without militancy and readily acknowledged what was admirable in others. Brahms wrote neither operas nor program music, though a lighter side shows up in his Viennese waltzes and gypsy-flavored Hungarian dances. His finest music combines the austcrity of his north German homeland with the sensuous grace of his adopted Vienna.

Young Brahms.

Brahms's major works are his four symphonies and four concertos for solo instruments and orchestra (two for piano, one for violin, one for violin and cello soloists). There are also some large chamber and choral works, piano miniatures, and German songs. More than any other nineteenth-century master—more even than Schumann—Brahms was self-consciously aware of the artistic shadow of Beethoven. This so constrained him that he delayed in producing a symphony until he was forty years old. In his heart Brahms yearned to write "Beethoven's Tenth," and when his First Symphony appeared it was greeted by a well-disposed critic as the worthiest successor to Beethoven's Ninth. Like Mendelssohn, Brahms had a keen interest in older music. He helped to edit the keyboard works of François Couperin, a French contemporary of Bach's, and his admiration for Bach lead to an arrangement of Bach's famous Chaconne for Unaccompanied Violin as a work for a pianist's left hand. It was a gift for Schumann's widow at a time when her right hand was ailing. Brahms paid other homages to the past. Two of his finest works are the Variations on a Theme by Handel for Piano and the Variations on a Theme by Haydn for Orchestra.

Brahms cast the finale of his Fourth Symphony (1885) as a set of ostinato variations. They are indebted in technique and in spirit to two great ostinato sets by Bach—the Chaconne for Unaccompanied Violin and the Passacaglia in C Minor for Organ. For his ostinato theme Brahms composed an austere eight-measure passage in the minor mode. It is sounded at the start by the winds and brass, without any warmth of strings. The theme's essence lies in its chords rather than its melody, but its journey through the variations can be traced by following just its upper melodic profile (Ex. 5.12). There

Δ
Brahms: Final Movement,
Symphony No. 4
in E Minor
(Side 7, Band 3)

Ex. 5.12. Theme and Variations from Finale, Symphony No. 4, Brahms

Var.	Meas.	
1	9	drum roll, pizzicato
2	17	winds, countermelody
3	25	loud, staccato
4	33	loud, flowing strings
5	41	flowing strings
6	49	flowing strings
7	57	loud, dotted rhythm
8	65	sixteenth-note motion
9	73	sixteenth-note motion
10	81	slow, echoes
11	89	airy triplets
12	97	slow, flute solo
13	105	slow, major mode, clarinet and oboe
14	113	slow, major mode, trombones
15	121	slow, major mode, winds
16	129	fast, minor mode, return of theme (see Ex. 5.13)
17	137	soft, tremolo
18	145	loud, horns
19	153	loud, eighth notes, arpeggios
20	161	loud, triplets

Ex. 5.12. *(Continued)*

21	169	very loud, rising scales, trombones
22	177	soft, triplets
23	185	loud, brass, triplets
24	193	loud, brass vs. string triplets
25	201	loud, strings vs. brass triplets
26	209	soft, legato
27	217	soft, flowing strings
28	225	half-loud, winds vs. strings
29	233	soft, rising winds, falling strings
30	241	loud, rising winds, falling strings, plus extension (meas. 249-252)
Coda	253-311	free, on theme

are thirty consecutive variations, each eight measures long, each turning up a fresh face of the basic pattern. The variations become more active in rhythm and richer in chromatic harmony as the final climax is approached. But the overall form has some other careful calculations. There is a big A-B-A of tempos, changing from fast to slow to fast, with the slow middle section (variations 12 through 15) surrounded by more vigorous motion on either side (variations 1-11 and 16-30). Brahms also has a plan in the use of tonalities. He opens in E minor, then shifts to E major in variation 13, and then back to E minor from variation 16. There are some deeper calculations built into the plan, symmetries so large in scope that they are not graspable at the hearing level. Brahms has divided the thirty variations into three groups of ten: Variation 10 ends the first group with a retrospective echo; variation 11 picks up with an airy freshness; variation 21 begins the third group with a fortissimo surge of rising glissandos that launch the thrust toward the close. Brahms has also divided the thirty variations into two equal halves of fifteen: the first half ends with the mellow philosophizing of variation 15; the second half begins with variation 16 bringing back the music of the opening theme in the winds and brass, restored to its original minor mode and brisk opening tempo. But in that sixteenth variation, instead of maintaining the theme just as before, there is an electrifying stroke halfway through. A vigorous descending scale in the strings unexpectedly answers the slowly rising scale of the theme in the winds (Ex. 5.13). The emotional effect is powerful, but there is also a compelling logic. Those first four notes of the strings' purposeful descent are a retrograde, inversion, and diminution of the first four notes of the theme's rising scale. It is one of many touches of craft that make this the most skillful set of variations since Beethoven.

An elderly Brahms making way to "The Red Hedgehog," Viennese artists' café that patronized daily.

Ex. 5.13. Variation 16 from Finale, Symphony No. 4, Brahms

After the thirtieth variation has run its course, Brahms breaks out of the vise of recurring eight-measure sections with a tempestuous expansion that carries the music to its close. Here he is free of the rigid segmentations, but the melodic materials still come from the original theme, which continues to dominate grimly until the end. The movement shows Brahms at his best, with his imagination typically yoked to a tight, demanding form, yet operating with the full array of nineteenth-century chromatic resources in melody and harmony and with a richly varied spectrum of orchestral effects. Brahms meets technical challenges with the ease and ingenuity of a great Baroque contrapuntist. Along with this exercise of the composer's craft, there is the unfettered emotional quality of Brahms's own age, an age rich in feeling, whose touches of drama, passion, and elegy mark this movement as a work of the "romantic century."

6 Nineteenth-Century Music II: Program, Nationalist, and Hyper-Romantic Composers

Francisco Goya, Kronos, God of Time, Devouring One of His Children *(ca. 1818); gruesome events and lunatic frenzy provided artists with subject matter.*

The Nineteenth Century, Part II

MUSIC	*ARTS AND IDEAS*	*POLITICS AND SCIENCE*
PROGRAM, NATIONALIST, AND HYPER-ROMANTIC COMPOSERS	**FROM ROMANTICISM TO SYMBOLISM AND IMPRESSIONISM**	**INDUSTRIAL AND SOCIAL REVOLUTION**

Berlioz (1803-1869): "Fantastic" Symphony (1830)	Flaubert, *Madame Bovary* (1857)	Italian unification movement ("Risorgimento," 1848-1861)
Liszt (1811-1886): Hungarian Rhapsody No. 6 (ca. 1845-1853)	Baudelaire, *Les Fleurs du Mal* (1857)	Lincoln's Emancipation Proclamation (1863)
Wagner (1813-1883): *Tristan and Isolde* (1859)	Darwin, *Origin of Species* (1859)	Ludwig II ("Mad Ludwig") reigns in Bavaria (1864-1886)
Tchaikovsky (1840-1893): Overture-Fantasy, *Romeo and Juliet* (1869-1880)	Romantic-realist painters: Courbet, Daumier (1850s-1860s)	Bismarck, Premier of Prussia (1862-1890)
Mussorgsky (1839-1881): *Pictures at an Exhibition* (1874)	Tolstoy, *War and Peace* (1865-1869)	Franco-Prussian War (1870)
Richard Strauss (1864-1949): *Don Juan* (1889)	Dostoevski, *Crime and Punishment* (1866)	Queen Victoria's Golden Jubilee (1887)
Mahler (1860-1911): Fifth Symphony (1902)	Eliot, *Middlemarch* (1871)	Transatlantic telegraph cable (1866)
	Mallarmé, early symbolist poetry (1870s)	Bell's telephone (1876)
	Early "Impressionist" paintings by Monet, Cézanne, Degas, Renoir, Whistler (1872-1876)	Liquid-fuel internal combustion engine (1860-1885)
	Nietzsche, *Thus Spake Zarathustra* (1883)	Edison's microphone, phonograph, electric lighting, motion-picture projection (1870s-1880s)
	Rodin, *The Burghers of Calais* (1884)	Kodak camera (Eastman) uses celluloid film (1889)

A. THE PROGRAM SYMPHONY

The colossal image of Beethoven cast two lengthy shadows across the remainder of the nineteenth century. Under one shadow was the line of conservative romantics, including Schubert, Mendelssohn, Schumann, and Brahms, whose main interests were in cultivating abstract or **absolute music**, much as Beethoven had done in his Fifth, Seventh, and Eighth Symphonies. Their doctrine was that music's "meaning" lay only in itself, in the shape and thrust of its sound patterns. Under the other shadow was the line of more progressive composers, including Berlioz, Liszt, Wagner, and Richard Strauss, whose emotional, storytelling, and nationalist works brought more personal expression into the realm of musical utterance. They often took inspiration from "extramusical" ideas, drawn from outside the realm of music. They looked back to Beethoven's "Eroica" Symphony of 1803, where symphonic substance was given to the popular visions of Napoleonic grandeur. Even more, they took cues from Beethoven's programmatic "Pastorale" Symphony of 1808 and from the "Choral" Symphony of 1824, where voices and poetry were added to the symphonic complement. Beethoven insisted that his musical descriptions in the "Pastorale" Symphony were "more an expression of feeling than of tone painting." Nevertheless, he supplied each movement with a literary vignette, or program. "Cheerful feelings on coming into the country," "Scene by the brook," "Peasants' merrymaking," and "Thunderstorm" are some of the tags. His realism was most vivid at the end of the slow movement, where he imitated the sounds of a nightingale, quail, and cuckoo, and named the birds in the score. Inevitably, Beethoven's departures from the esthetic of absolute music would be carried farther.

Hector Berlioz

The standard-bearer of the new program music was Hector Berlioz (1803-1869), and his manifesto was the "Fantastic" Symphony of 1830. Young Berlioz was a colorful personality with a fiery temper and untamable ego. Heinrich Heine described him as having a "monstrous, antediluvian head of hair that bristled upon his brow like a forest upon a craggy cliff." Bursting with novel reveries and passions, Berlioz was the voice of music in the Parisian romantic revolution of the 1830s. The leaders in art and literature were Delacroix and Victor Hugo, Vigny and Balzac. Berlioz, like Chopin, was unusual among the leading romantic composers in being neither German nor Austrian. Precisely because he came from outside the Germanic tradition, he seemed freer to stir up gusts of romantic air.

Berlioz was the son of a provincial doctor in southeast France who sent him to study medicine in Paris, only to have him spend his time at the opera house and the music conservatory. He never became an accomplished performer. His best instrument seems to have been the guitar. What he cared most about was composing. His first substantial work was the "Fantastic" Symphony, produced when he was twenty-seven. It was the first of the nineteenth-century's grandly theatrical symphonies. The bizarre plot was autobiographical—a mirror of Berlioz's infatuation with an Irish Shakespearean actress named Harriet Smithson, who later became his first wife. Berlioz was respected enough by his conservatory teachers at this time to win a Prix de Rome. But the Parisian public never learned to care much for his music, so during most of his career he supported himself as a librarian and music critic. His musical visions were too expansive, too full of surprises for the timid local tastes. Foreigners took to his exhibitionism more readily. He was admired by Liszt and Wagner, and even extravagantly praised by the conservative Schumann for his bold harmonies, novel instrumentation, and pathbreaking forays into program music. Berlioz wrote two other program symphonies, *Harold in Italy* (1834), based on Byron's romantic antihero, Childe Harold, and *Romeo and Juliet* (1839), a "dramatic symphony" based on Shakespeare's play, using voices as in Beethoven's Ninth. Berlioz also composed operas (*The Trojans, Beatrice and Benedict*), concert overtures, songs, and sacred music (the *Requiem Mass* and *The Childhood of Christ*). His ideas are sometimes banal, but more often sublime. He is always vivid and appealing. His *Memoirs,* personal recollections written late in life, offer glimpses of the romantic scene through the eyes of a gifted, eccentric insider.

Harriet Smithson as Ophelia.

The "Fantastic" Symphony appeared only six years after Beethoven's Ninth Symphony and four years after the "Great" C Major Symphony of Schubert, but its pictorial imagery and astonishing musical effects seem worlds removed from the milieu of those orderly Viennese. Berlioz's program, or story, is highly specific. Its subject matter is unprecedentedly personal. In Berlioz's words:

Berlioz.
An engraving of the 1850s
after Gustave Courbet.

A *Young Musician* of morbid temperament and ardent imagination has poisoned himself with opium in a fit of lovesick despair. The narcotic dose is too weak to kill him, but it plunges him into a heavy sleep accompanied by strange visions, during which his feelings and memories are transformed by his sick brain into musical thoughts and imagery. His *Beloved Woman* has become for him an obsessive melody, a *fixed musical idea* (*idée fixe*) or *Beloved-melody,* that he finds and hears everywhere.

This is unashamedly autobiographical. Berlioz went along with the current fashion in experimenting with drugs. (De Quincey's *Confessions of an Opium-Eater* was published in 1821.) He had met with little success in courting Harriet Smithson. He was penniless; she spoke no French and he no English. But his enthusiastic visions of her are given musical substance in an ethereal "Beloved" melody that soars, gasps, and sighs with romantic abandon. That melody, particularly its opening bars, represents Harriet through all five movements of the symphony (Ex. 6.1).

Ex. 6.1. Beginning of Idée fixe ("Beloved" Melody): "Fantastic" Symphony, Berlioz

The first movement paints "the soul-sickness, the surges of passion, melancholies, and aimless joys that the Young Musician felt before he first saw his Beloved. Then the volcanic love that she immediately inspired, its delirious anguish, fits of jealousy, returns to tenderness, and consolations of religion." Berlioz touches most points of the romantic compass here, yet the movement has shreds of traditional sonata form. In the second movement he "encounters his Beloved at a ball in the tumult of a brilliant assemblage." The movement is a waltz, in effect a replacement for the old symphonic minuet and trio. It starts out graphically, depicting the arrival at the ball; then the swirling dance takes over. Instead of a trio, there is a glimpse of the Beloved as fragments of her melody float through the orchestra. The slow third movement is a romantic staple, a pastoral elegy where the Young Musician seeks consolation in nature. Alone in the country on a summer evening, he is lost in thought. Two shepherds play their pipes. He thinks of the Beloved and is troubled. Sounds of distant thunder and feelings of loneliness bring the revery to a close. The fourth movement, "March to the Scaffold," is a garish fantasy where Berlioz moves onto novel emotional ground. The Young Musician dreams that he has killed his Beloved and is about to be executed. This goes well beyond Schubert's "Doppelgänger" in the macabre and grotesque. The tumbrel's procession to the scaffold winds through the streets to the strains of a march "that is at moments sombre and fierce, at others brilliant and solemn, and in which the muffled sound of heavy footsteps is followed suddenly by bursts of jarring brilliance. At the end the "Beloved" melody re-

Bizarre and macabre effects were prized: a scene by Doré.

turns for an instant, like a last thought of love, interrupted by the guillotine."

After the fourth movement's gruesome tableau of public execution (still on everyone's mind a generation after the French Revolution's "reign of terror"), Berlioz turns to another psychopathic vision. He calls his final movement "Dream of a Witches' Sabbath," and once referred to it as "the dream of a cut-off head." What is striking about the movement is not so much the outlandish subject as the musical form. In each of the first four movements Berlioz has held to some basis in conventional form. Here there is none. An outright storytelling takes over as the unifying thread. The Young Musician finds himself:

△
Berlioz: Fifth Movement ("Dream of a Witches' Sabbath"), "Fantastic" Symphony (Side 7, Band 4)

in the midst of a frightful troop of ghosts, sorcerers, and monsters of every sort who are there for his funeral. There are strange sounds, groans, bursts of laughter, distant cries that others seem to answer. The Beloved-melody appears, but has lost its nobility and reserve; it has become a cheap dance-tune, trivial and grotesque. It is the Beloved herself who has come to this witches' sabbath. A roar of joy greets her arrival and she joins in the devilish orgy. Funeral bells peal. The Dies irae is parodied. The witches dance their Round-Dance. The Round-Dance combines with the Dies irae.

What actually holds the music together is the use of three melodies (Ex. 6.2). They are: 1) the "Beloved" melody, or idée fixe, carried over from the earlier movements; 2) the Dies irae (*dee*-es *ee*-rye), the familiar medieval plainchant (see Chapter 1, Ex. 1.3); and 3) the

Ex. 6.2a. Themes from Fifth Movement, "Fantastic" Symphony, Berlioz

Idée fixe ("Beloved" melody)

Fifth movement parody

Very lively

Clarinet

ppp staccato

First movement original

Moderate

Violin

p legato

Dies irae

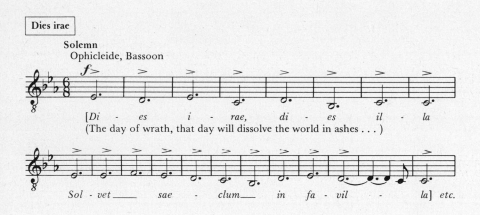

Solemn

Ophicleide, Bassoon

f

[*Di - es i - rae, di - es il - la*
(The day of wrath, that day will dissolve the world in ashes . . .)

Sol - vet___ sae - clum___ in fa - vil - - la] *etc.*

Round Dance

Lively

Viola, Cello

ff

etc.

**Ex. 6.2b. Fifth Movement ("Dream of a Witches' Sabbath"),
        "Fantastic" Symphony, Berlioz**

1. Introduction: "Strange sounds, groans, bursts of laughter"

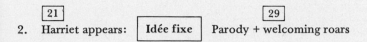

2. Harriet appears: |21| **Idée fixe** |29| Parody + welcoming roars

3. Harriet dances: |40| **Idée fixe** Parody

4. Transition |83|

5. Bells + Hints of Witches' |102| |107| **Round Dance**

6. |127| **Dies irae** Parody + Bells; Mocking diminutions
    (Ophicleide + Bassoon)

7. Transition to |221| **Round Dance**

8. |241| **Round Dance** (Pseudo-Fugue); Diminuendo to: { Traces of **Dies irae**
    (long) |347| +
                                                        Traces of **Round Dance** }

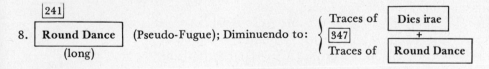

9. Transition to Finale: Crescendo on |363| **Round Dance**

10. Finale: "Diabolical Orgy" on |407| { **Round Dance**
                                           +
                                           Dies irae }

"Round Dance of the Witches," which Berlioz composed just for this movement.

1. The "Beloved" melody still represents Harriet, but it is no longer suavely played by the violins. It is mimicked grotesquely by a clarinet. The deformations of its melody and rhythm represent the Young Musician's distorted view of the Beloved, whom he spies hopping around on a witch's broomstick. That notion of transforming a musical theme in order to illustrate an altered psychological perception or a changed dramatic situation had already occurred to Beethoven. For instance, the heroic first theme of Beethoven's "Coriolanus" Overture dissolves in pitiful stammers as the hero dies at the end. Berlioz takes such theme transformation further. In earlier movements of the "Fantastic" Symphony, the "Beloved" melody has already been fragmented and altered. Now the final movement carries this to an extreme.

2. The Dies irae was the age-old dirge of the Roman Catholic funeral service. It was known to everyone. Berlioz was the first to shift this sacred melody into other than sacred surroundings. His use of it shows the appeal of medieval religiosity to the romantic imagination, but his treatment is anything but pious. He again calls on theme transformation and parodies the venerable melody. It first appears at a low pitch, in a slow, solemn tempo, as if sung by a monks' chorus. The phrase then reappears, played twice as fast, and then four times as fast, each time by higher-pitched instruments. The last high-spirited "diminutions" are like witches cackling. But even the lugubrious, slow phrases in the bass are not entirely serious. Berlioz scores them incongruously for the bassoon and the ophicleide (a large, keyed bugle that is shaped something like a bassoon), which had rarely been used in a symphony orchestra before. It lent a vulgar rasp to the sound.

3. "Round Dance of the Witches" is a raucous jig, brimming with evil glee. Berlioz instructs the violinists at one point to strike their strings with the wood of the bow, producing a sound that may remind us of broomsticks. The whole symphony was a showplace of captivating orchestral effects. In addition to the ophicleide, there are four harps, an English horn, snare drum, cymbals, sponge-headed drum sticks, and bells.

   All the noisiest sounds are thrown into the melée of this last movement, which follows Berlioz's "plot" quite exactly. Ten exciting minutes are wrung from the story. The great novelty of the movement is the way it is held together, not by the conventions of a traditional musical form but by its literary "program." Musically it is also held together by the use of the three memorable melodies and the succession of stunning harmonic and orchestral effects. Berlioz sees to it that there is plenty to occupy us even without knowing the story.

The "Fantastic" Symphony was a pioneering work that brought into sharp focus three principles that would be embraced by a whole line of future "program music" composers:

1. *The literary program.* Berlioz supplies a storyline so explicit that the symphony in effect has become a novel, each movement a chapter.
2. *Theme identification.* Berlioz attaches a specific theme (the "Beloved" melody) to a specific character (the Beloved). Others, such as Liszt and Wagner, would significantly expand this process, supplying many different musical themes to represent diverse characters, ideas, objects, and events in their musical tableaux.
3. *Theme transformation.* Berlioz went a step beyond simply representing the Beloved with a single melody. He saw fit to alter the melody, transforming the music to illustrate transformations in the Beloved's character, in the circumstances in which she is found, in the view of her that filters through the consciousness of the Young Musician. That idea of transforming musical themes so as to show changes in plot proved irresistible to the rest of the century. It became the standard practice of program composers.

B. NATIONALISM AND VIRTUOSITY

Franz Liszt

Franz Liszt (1811-1886) was born in Hungary during the same decade that produced so many other first-rank romantic composers. Berlioz, Chopin, Mendelssohn, Schumann, Wagner, and Verdi were all born between 1803 and 1813. Liszt outlived them all, except Verdi. He was the model of the romantic virtuoso whose aim was to achieve the impossible with steely fingers, while making it all seem easy. He had a charmed life, wielding a benign influence and living long enough to become a patriarchal figure among musicians. By the late 1820s, his magnetic presence was already a fixture on the concert stages of Europe. A handsome youth, he exuded personal charm. George Sand tells how for a thrill she and Chopin sat under the piano while Liszt played. Liszt never married, but an early romantic union with Countess Marie d'Agoult, who wrote novels under the pen name Daniel Stern, produced three daughters. One of them, Cosima, became the wife of Richard Wagner. Liszt's later consort was the Princess Carolyn of Sayn-Wittgenstein, who turned him from his dazzling virtuoso career toward more serious activity as a composer. Late in life Liszt took holy orders, and under the genial Pope Pius IX he was domiciled for a while at the Vatican. He must have been an odd sight. A Roman contemporary described him in 1865 as "Mephisto-

Liszt beatific; Liszt transcendent; Liszt receiving plaudits.

pheles disguised as an abbé." As a Hungarian, Liszt was a citizen of the world, equally at home in Berlin, Vienna, Paris, and Rome. Wherever he went in later life, he was surrounded by adoring retinues of younger composers and fledgling virtuosos. He was more blessed than most composers. Life granted him the chief pleasures it can bestow.

Behind Liszt's fascinating public image and sensational pianistic abilities there lay a shrewd intellect and a spacious musical imagination. His compositions rarely match the best inspirations of the nineteenth century, but they helped to fuel some of those inspirations. It was not the choleric, frustrated Berlioz who emerged as the leader among the composers of program music. It was the genial Liszt, whose theatrical gestures and daring harmonies converted audiences to the new esthetic. Taking a cue from Berlioz, he produced two large program symphonies with substantial literary associations. The "Faust" Symphony draws on Goethe's masterpiece; its three movements are titled "Faust," "Gretchen," and "Mephistopheles." The "Dante" Symphony draws on the Divine Comedy; its first two movements are titled "Inferno" and "Purgatory." But even Liszt's audacity shrank from the Paradiso as a finale. He took Wagner's advice and was content with a setting of the Catholic Magnificat.

Progressing beyond the multimovement program symphony, Liszt cultivated a new genre of program music that he called the **symphonic poem,** where everything takes place within a single continuous movement. The term *symphonic poem* puts the emphasis on the poetic, or extramusical, inspiration as much as on the musical or symphonic. Liszt's 12 symphonic poems have the most varied sources—literary, philosophical, historical, pictorial. *Orpheus* and *Prometheus* draw on the ancient Greek myths. *The Ideal* (Schiller), *Tasso* (Byron), *Mazeppa* (Victor Hugo), and *What Was Heard Upon the Mountain* (Hugo) are based on narrative and philosophical poetry by Liszt's romantic contemporaries. *Hamlet* draws on Shakespeare. *Hungaria* is nationalist. *The Battle of the Huns* evokes a romantic canvas by the painter Wilhelm von Kaulbach, showing the Christian victory over Attila the Hun in the fifth century. In that work, following Berlioz's lead with the Dies irae, Liszt introduced the melody of the medieval hymn "Crux fidelis," on the subject of Christ's cross. Liszt's program symphonies and symphonic poems also took over from Berlioz the twin principles of *theme identification* (associating musical themes with specific personages, concepts, and events) and *theme transformation* (altering those musical materials to reflect changes in the plot). Where Berlioz did this modestly, Liszt does it on a grand scale. His best-known symphonic poem, *The Preludes,* carries theme transformation to an extreme: practically the entire seventeen-minute work is built of transformed versions of its opening theme. *The Preludes* also shows how insubstantial the link between "program music" and its "program" can be. The work was supposedly inspired by the high-flown *Nouvelle Méditation No. 15* of Alphonse de Lamartine, titled *Les Préludes.* Actually the music was composed in connection with verses by a lesser-known poet named Autran, on a completely different subject. Later, on the initiative of Liszt's friend Princess Carolyn, it was linked to the more charismatic Lamartine.

Liszt's character pieces for piano include the local-color miniatures in his *Années de Pèlerinage* (*Pilgrimage Years: Italy and Switzerland*); the pictorial *Two Legends* (*St. Francis of Assisi Preaching to the Birds* and *St. Francis de Paul Walking on the Waters*); and *Funérailles,* an emotion-charged memorial to the dead Chopin, filled with virtuoso heroics and bathos. Liszt often treats the piano as if it were a whole orchestra, exploiting every scrap of variety in its range of tone colors. On occasion he instructs the pianist to sound like a horn or an oboe. He exploits particularly the high and low registers. Among all of Liszt's works, the Hungarian Rhapsodies for Piano have perhaps the least pretense to artistic merit. However, their flashy mixtures of nationalist veneer and virtuoso display come close to the popular taste of the time; they are revealing cultural documents. The name **rhapsody** suggests impassioned utterances in high-flown style, spilling out ecstatically without much regard for form. Liszt's rhapsodies are full of breathtaking fingerwork, clusters of sound in sparkling motion, and prodigious storms of octaves where the pianist's hands can be seen moving only as a rapid blur across the keys. The virtuoso fireworks sold concert tickets. The rhapsodies have the further appeal of their gypsy idioms and tone colors. Liszt imitates the jangle and shake of the *cimbalom,* the big Hungarian zither whose strings are played with drumsticks. He mimics the mannerisms of gypsy fiddlers—the soulful improvisatory style, the bite of the bow on the low strings, the impassioned declamations and capricious changes of tempo.

Liszt's Hungarian Rhapsody No. 6 has the usual potpourri of Hungarian moods. Its nationalism is more vulgar than Chopin's in the mazurkas and polonaises, and its pianistic displays are more sensational. It consists of four connected sections, making it similar to a brief four-movement sonata (Ex. 6.3). The opening A section is

△
Liszt: Hungarian Rhapsody No. 6
(Side 8, Band 1)

Ex. 6.3. Hungarian Rhapsody No. 6, Liszt

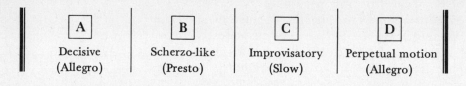

A	B	C	D
Decisive (Allegro)	Scherzo-like (Presto)	Improvisatory (Slow)	Perpetual motion (Allegro)

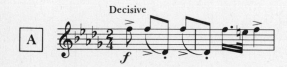

grand and assertive, puffed up with pounding chords. The short B section has the breathless activity of a scherzo. The C section is slow and rhetorical. It evokes the gypsy fiddler with cimbalom accompaniment, then dissolves in a flashy cadenza where one can imagine Liszt tossing his mane of hair and eyeing the ladies soulfully while his fingers work magic on the keys. The concluding D section is obviously designed to bring the house down. It begins innocently with a naive melody over a simple, thumping bass. The melody repeats, doubled in octaves, and then it launches on a set of variations whose perpetual motion never relents. Rhythmic intensity and virtuosity increase. The left hand pounds out octaves against fiery right-hand arpeggios. At the end, both hands unleash jarring dissonant harmonies in fortissimo octaves. The effect is electrifying, the circus atmosphere so engaging that we perhaps ignore the thinness of the material on which it is based. Much is trite, but in one respect Liszt shows prophetic originality. The formal unity in tonal music always depends on beginning and ending in the same key. Liszt's rhapsodies are still tonal, but sometimes they ignore that overarching tonal unity. Hungarian Rhapsody No. 6 begins in D-flat major, but ends in the unexpected, somewhat distant key of B-flat major.

C. CHROMATICISM AND EMOTIONALISM

Richard Wagner

"Darwin, Marx, and Wagner . . ." is how a recent author summed up the intellectual power elite of the late nineteenth century. Oddly enough, Richard Wagner, the musician, was the most significant of the three in shaping the European thought of his time. He became a cult figure with an influence that extended well beyond music into art, politics, and life. Wagner (1813-1883) was born at Leipzig in northern Germany, the same general region that produced Bach, Handel, Beethoven, Mendelssohn, Schumann, and Brahms. Wagner's whole career was a passionate struggle to create a distinctively German style of opera. As a musician he was partly self-taught, absorbing as much from his own study of Beethoven's works as from formal training. He was not a child prodigy, and, like Berlioz, he never became an accomplished instrumentalist. His chief interest was in literature; his idol was Shakespeare. The intellectual leanings deepened as he set about molding the vast theatrical, political, and religious cosmos that is found in his mature music dramas. Wagner's first employment was as a conductor in small-town German opera houses and as a journeyman music critic. His first great operas came in the 1840s when he was barely thirty: *The Flying Dutchman,* *Tannhäuser,* and *Lohengrin.* The subjects were ringed with medieval Germanic gloom. Wagner's radical leanings in politics during the revolutions of 1848-49 obliged him to abandon an influential conductorship at Dresden and take refuge in Switzerland. There he spent the first years of a long and frustrated exile by writing essays on politics, esthetics, and musical dramaturgy. He reached a low point in finances and personal morale during the early 1860s when his

Wagner.

visionary new breed of music dramas (*The Rhinegold, The Valkyrie,* and *Tristan and Isolde*) proved too expensive to stage. Then, in 1864, he was providentially rescued by an ardent, unstable nineteen-year-old admirer who had just mounted the throne of Bavaria as King Ludwig II. "Mad Ludwig," as he soon became known to his exasperated subjects, saw to it that Wagner was ensconced at Munich and given whatever he needed to see his complete works produced. Thus Wagner, having always been an imperialist in his art, became a monarchist in politics. He witnessed the construction of his personal opera theater at Bayreuth near Munich, at vast expense to the Bavarian state treasury. This Festival Playhouse (Festspielhaus) was built to his own specifications, and none but his own creations were destined to be performed there. In 1868 he completed the magnificent comedy, *The Mastersingers of Nuremberg.* And in 1870 he took Liszt's daughter Cosima as his second wife, legitimizing a long-standing relationship during which he borrowed her from her husband, the conductor Hans von Bülow. He also completed the four-opera cycle *The Ring of the Nibelung,* by adding the music for *Siegfried* (1871) and *The Twilight of the Gods* (1874) to *The Rhinegold* and *The Valkyrie,* which were completed during the 1850s. The crowning point in Wagner's career came in 1876 when his operatic shrine, the Festspielhaus, was opened at Bayreuth with the first complete performance of *The Ring.* His last great work, *Parsifal* (1882), was completed during the year before his death in Venice at the age of seventy.

Among all of history's leading composers, Wagner was perhaps the least admirable as a person. He was an egotist and a liar, a deadbeat who borrowed large sums that were rarely repaid, a voluptuary with shameless cravings for luxury in his personal surroundings and uninhibited lusts for the wives of his friends and benefactors. Such things no longer matter. What does matter is that Wagner was the stormy center of artistic life during the entire late nineteenth century. His ten great music dramas—as he preferred to call his operas—stand with the most durable and compelling creations of Western music. Seated in the Wagnerian opera house, one experiences the world of late romanticism with a directness that nothing else conveys.

Wagner had the matchless ability to create a fresh world of sound with each new dramatic subject that he undertook. *Tristan and Isolde* was the most compelling art work of the late nineteenth century because it offered sensation-hungry romantic audiences the most vivid musical counterparts to physical voluptuousness and passion. It richly satisfied the romantic view of art as a fulfillment of life. The story, drawn from medieval romance, tells of the doomed love of the Cornish knight Tristan for the Irish girl Isolde, the wife of his king. Wagner composed this monument to eroticism and despair in part to memorialize his own love affair with Mathilde von Wesendonck, the talented wife of a wealthy Swiss patron. His emphasis on frustrated passion drew heavily on the philosophy of Arthur Schopenhauer, whose *The World as Will and Idea* (1818) set the mode of pessimism for the nineteenth century. Schopenhauer's doctrine of the irrational Will—the passions and inner drives—as the blind force that lies behind human behavior appealed to Wagner, as did his concept of life's inability to satisfy the Will so that humans ultimately must live in pain. Wagner found inspiration also in the hyper-romantic effusions called *Hymns to Night* (1800), by the German poet Novalis. In his verse imagery the youthful Novalis equated sexual ecstasy with an intoxicated sense of the "blessed infinity" of death. In *Tristan and Isolde,* Wagner combined these philosophical threads with a dramatic plot that is constructed with the utmost symmetry. The music drama is in three acts, and the central scene of the second act (Act II, Scene 2) takes place in Novalis's world of Night, Schopenhauer's world of the Will. It is an impassioned "Liebesnacht" or "Love Night" in which Wagner's lovers are united for fleeting moments. All the rest takes place in the depressed, unhappy world of Day, Schopenhauer's world of "appearances," morality, and duty, where the lovers are kept apart by the circumstances of their lives.

The Prelude to *Tristan* foreshadows the overall Day-Night-Day outline of the three-act drama. Wagner called it a prelude because he disdained the trivial style of many of the Italian operas and opera overtures of the time. The music begins in a bleak atmosphere of foreboding and yearning. A long central section is given over to rising waves of passion. Then at the moment where emotions peak, the musical-erotic fulfillment is thwarted by the return of the pessimistic opening material, and the Prelude ends more gloomily than it began. The broad shape of the Prelude is similar to a conventional A-B-A', but Wagner's eleven resourceful minutes of music can scarcely be reduced to so simple a formula (Ex. 6.4). The substance of the Prelude grows out of the combination of two typical Wagnerian techniques: the use of motives and chromaticism. Wagner took up the initiatives of Berlioz and Liszt and built his musical continuity from a handful of motives that are manipulated through a maze of chromatic harmonies. The Prelude uses three principal motives. They will be called x, y, and z, though they are sometimes known by fanciful names that were not sanctioned by Wagner. Motive x, with its initial upward skip of a minor sixth, has been called the motive of "Yearning"; motive y, with its slow, steely chromatic ascent, the motive of "Fate"; motive z, luxuriant and rounded, the motive of "Passion." Names aside, motives x and y are both essentially chromatic, and motive z becomes chromatic in its chief transformations (z^2, z^3, and z^4). Motive z^2 is in fact almost a replica of motive y. Wagner's basic procedure is to repeat, alter, and combine the three motives, constantly giving them new faces as they move in a dense flux of

Δ
Wagner: Prelude to
Tristan and Isolde
(Side 8, Band 2)

Peter Behrens' morbid, decorative The Kiss *(1896) is one of many examples of the profound influence that Wagner's* Tristan and Isolde *had on European writers and artists.*

Ex. 6.4a. Motives from Prelude to *Tristan and Isolde*, Wagner

"Yearning"

"Fate"

"Passion"

(compare (y))

Ex. 6.4b. Prelude to *Tristan and Isolde,* **Wagner**

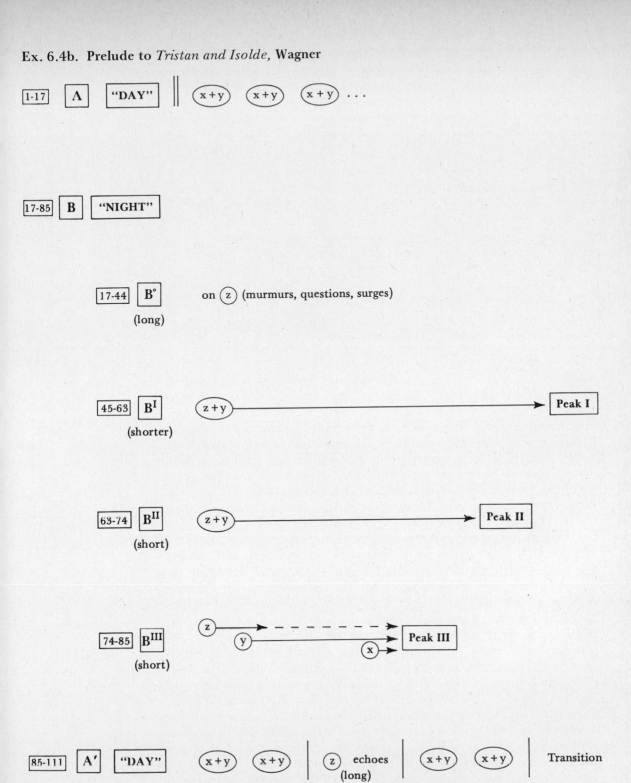

chromatic harmony and slip elastically from key to key. Often the tonic changes from measure to measure as Wagner weaves a tissue of modulations whose nuances and destinations keep taking us by surprise.

Motives x and y appear in direct succession at the start. At the point where they intersect, Wagner introduces a venomous, tugging chord whose four pitches are F, B, D-sharp, and G-sharp (Ex. 6.5).

Ex. 6.5. The "Tristan Chord"

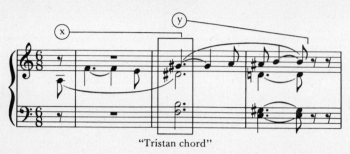

"Tristan chord"

This first chord in the opera is the famous "Tristan chord." Its dour, provicative sound seems to portend all the fatal emotional entanglements to come. The chord belongs to no clear key; it is precisely this absence of a tonic that produces its unique vagueness and psychological unrest. Wagner repeats the succession of x and y two more times, each time at a higher pitch and with heightened emotional intensity, each time with an insinuating chord coming in between. Then the long middle section begins. This section (Night) of the Prelude is given over to a churning of elemental passions. Wagner evokes the nocturnal world of Novalis with mounting flushes of emotion that remain wrapped in morbid gloom. He sustains the continuity by avoiding any interruption to the maze of intertwining motives. There are no musical stopping points. He shuns the clarity of tonic cadences, preferring the murkiness of deceptive cadences. This central section is built mainly of repetitions and transformations of motive z. The sensuous gyrations are worked up to a series of emotional peaks, each more convulsive than the last. As the final peak is approached, the euphoria is soured by reminders of motive y, and then motive x returns fortissimo in a stentorian grimace. The ardent emotions cool through echoes of z. Finally, harsh Day prevails, and motives x and y lead without a break to the curtain's rise on the scene of a ship bearing the unhappy Isolde as a bride to Cornwall.

Tristan and Isolde was the single most influential work of musical romanticism. It was a Pandora's box of chromatic devices. Once Wagner demonstrated the potency of this emotionally supercharged style in 1859, there was no turning back in the quest for heightened effects. Wagner's successors took his chromatic idiom and strove to obtain ever more powerful alchemies from it. For a generation music remained within the confines of the traditional major-minor system, but in the end it broke away. All the free-wheeling chromatic modulations loosened the grip of the tonic key and exhausted the emotional capacities of the tonal system. The chromaticism of *Tristan* lit a flame that by the end of the century threatened to consume the whole edifice of tonal style.

D. RUSSIAN ROMANTICISM

Peter Ilyich Tchaikovsky

For the broad public, Peter Ilyich Tchaikovsky (1840-1893) is the most appealing of the Russian romantics, perhaps the most appealing of all the romantic composers. He was the son of a well-to-do mining engineer and was raised in comfortable circumstances in St. Petersburg, which is now Leningrad. Nervous and sensitive as a child, he grew up to a troubled later existence. He began a career as a lawyer in the czarist Ministry of Justice, but soon broke from the bureaucratic routine to devote himself to music. His style was rooted in the culture of his homeland, particularly in the brilliant life of St. Petersburg. He used Russian folksongs in his music, and even more so than Chopin, his imagination had a Slavic, East European cast. Still, his nationalist zeal never matched that of his more striking contemporaries, such as Mussorgsky (see page 259). For all of his Russian qualities of melody and harmony, his techniques remained close to the Germanic idioms of Beethoven and Schumann. In most respects Tchaikovsky was a conservative romantic, yet he went well beyond composers such as Schumann or Brahms in sheer expressiveness. To an unprecedented degree his music plumbs emotional depths and produces what at times seem like personal revelations. Tchaikovsky was a homosexual, always in fear of exposure to a hostile society. Under the Czarist criminal code, the punishment was a lashing with birch rods, loss of civil rights, and deportation to Siberia. The confessional frankness and melancholy that mark some of his finest movements may reflect this vulnerability. He contracted a short disastrous marriage in 1877 when he was thirty-seven. Afterwards he lived alone, yet already in 1876 he entered into one of the most curious personal relationships in the history of music. Nadezhda von Meck was a wealthy widow in her middle forties, an admirer of his music. She arranged to provide Tchaikovsky with a regular income, and they corresponded intimately for fourteen years, sometimes every day. During all that time, however, she insisted that they never meet; and in 1890 she abruptly terminated the arrangement without a word of genuine explanation. Tchaikovsky was deeply hurt. Friends persuaded him to travel, and in 1891 he toured the United States.

Ex. 6.6a. Themes and Motives from *Romeo and Juliet*, Tchaikovsky

Ex. 6.6b. Sonata-Allegro Form: *Romeo and Juliet,* **Tchaikovsky**

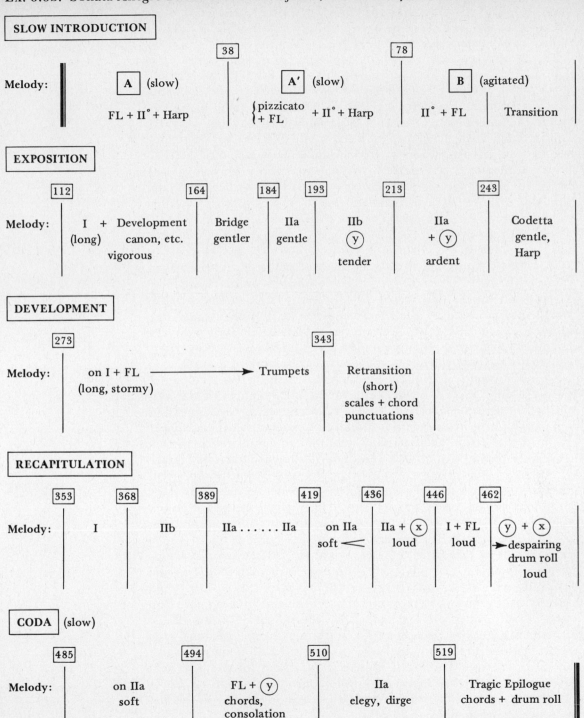

SLOW INTRODUCTION

| 38 | | 78 |

Melody: **A** (slow) **A′** (slow) **B** (agitated)

FL + II° + Harp { pizzicato + FL } + II° + Harp II° + FL | Transition

EXPOSITION

| 112 | | 164 | 184 | 193 | | 213 | | 243 |

Melody: I + Development Bridge IIa IIb IIa Codetta
(long) canon, etc. gentler gentle (y) + (y) gentle,
vigorous tender ardent Harp

DEVELOPMENT

| 273 | | 343 |

Melody: on I + FL ⎯⎯⎯⎯→ Trumpets Retransition
(long, stormy) (short)
scales + chord
punctuations

RECAPITULATION

| 353 | 368 | 389 | 419 | 436 | 446 | 462 |

Melody: I IIb IIa . . . . . . IIa on IIa IIa + (x) I + FL (y) + (x)
soft ⟨ loud loud →despairing
drum roll
loud

CODA (slow)

| 485 | 494 | 510 | 519 |

Melody: on IIa FL + (y) IIa Tragic Epilogue
soft chords, elegy, dirge chords + drum roll
consolation

Shortly later he was back in St. Petersburg, where he died in 1893. There is a story that he poisoned himself. Another, that death came after he thoughtlessly or perhaps willfully drank unboiled water while a cholera epidemic was raging.

Tchaikovsky's major works include some of the most durable in the orchestral repertoire: the Fourth, Fifth, and Sixth ("Pathétique") Symphonies, the program symphony titled "Manfred," and the "Fantasy after Dante, Francesca da Rimini," the First Piano Concerto, and a brilliant Violin Concerto. His best works may be the three ballets, *Swan Lake, The Sleeping Beauty,* and *The Nutcracker,* which are the least flawed by sentimentality. Like many romantics, Tchaikovsky turned to Shakespeare for inspiration, and in three works he projected the situations and moods of *Hamlet, The Tempest,* and *Romeo and Juliet.* None of them adheres to Shakespeare's plot. They are orchestral dramas, musically self-sufficient. Thus the "fantasy overture" *Romeo and Juliet* has a dramatic program that is worked out symphonically, not through realistic illustration. Tchaikovsky even tailors the program to fit a framework of sonata form by associating the three main factors in Shakespeare's drama with three main themes in his music. Theme I, full of pessimism and nervous energy, represents the bloody feud between the Montagues and Capulets. Theme IIa reflects the lyric passion of the young lovers. A solemn philosophical theme (FL) represents Friar Lawrence, whose plan to unite the lovers goes so tragically awry (Ex. 6.6).

The sombre introduction begins with the theme of Friar Lawrence (FL). Its slow, hollow harmonies and the cool timbres of clarinets and bassoons create an atmosphere of monastic calm. The strings and a plaintive horn intrude with a brooding foretaste of the passionate lovers' theme (II°). Then tensions mount in a transition to the exposition, which bursts in with the angry rhythms of the feud (theme I). When the lovers' theme appears (IIa), it is wreathed in sweet innocence. But when it returns after a tender interlude of wry harmonies in the muted strings (IIb), it has taken on the gentle undulations of IIb and uses them as a passionate, throbbing accompaniment. Throughout a stormy development the families feud (I), disregarding the entreaties of Friar Lawrence (FL). Their conflict whips up to a frenzy that spills over into the return of theme I in the recapitulation. Tchaikovsky moves quickly from I to IIb, then extracts every drop of emotion from the lovers' theme (IIa). The upward pressures of IIa are broken by the return of I and FL. A heated exchange between motives x (strife) and y (passion) ends with a fatal drum roll. The coda offers consolation in an elegiac funeral procession. The lovers' theme (IIa) returns for the last time, now gently transformed, and with the balm of soothing harp arpeggios. But Tchaikovsky ends it all with agitated, biting chords—a final reminder of the tragedy.

E. RUSSIAN NATIONALISM

Modest Mussorgsky

Modest Mussorgsky (1839-1881) was the most original of the nineteenth-century Russian nationalists. He was the key figure in the "Russian Five" or "mighty handful," as a sympathetic critic described them in 1867. The others in this group were Balakirev, Cui, Borodin, and Rimsky-Korsakov, the composer of *Scheherezade*. Mussorgsky was born to a family of the Czarist lesser nobility. Like other youths of his class with obvious musical talents, he was matter-of-factly destined for a nonmusical career. He resigned his army commission at age twenty to devote himself to music, but he was still doomed to spend most of his remaining twenty-two years in uncongenial toil as a government clerk in St. Petersburg because the abolition of serfdom in 1861 wiped out his family's fortune. When he died in 1881 at the age of forty-two, it was after a long, losing struggle with poverty, alcohol, and nervous depression.

Mussorgsky's circle of enthusiastic Russian nationalists ridiculed Tchaikovsky for what they regarded as his stodgy German affectations, his failure to fully exploit native folk idioms. Mussorgsky's own formal training was weak in harmony and orchestration, but that lack of standard tradition was turned to an advantage because it

Mussorgsky.
An oil by Ilya Repin.

Onion-shaped church domes
in the Old Russian style.

freed his imagination for exploration. Beyond their marked Slavic colorings, his works have a sure instinct for the vivid and poignant. He left some powerful songs along with a handful of larger works such as the symphonic poem *A Night on the Bald Mountain* (1866), which is an orgiastic fantasy that renews the fireworks of Berlioz's "Witches' Sabbath" with a strong Slavic twist. There are the operas *Boris Godunov* (1874) and *Khovantchina* (unfinished at his death). *Boris Godunov,* based on Pushkin's tragedy, is a melodious tapestry of sixteenth-century Russian history, written in an authentic Russian musical style and free of Italian operatic conventions.

Mussorgsky's *Pictures at an Exhibition* is a cycle of piano miniatures in the manner of Schumann's *Carnaval,* but again with strong Russian flavors and with more graphic descriptions. He was inspired by the paintings of an artist friend, Victor Hartmann, whose death in 1873 had occasioned a memorial exhibition of his work. Based on the impressions gained there, Mussorgsky composed ten sound pictures. He had the idea of tying the musical pictures together by using a recurring melody that he calls the "Promenade," which represents the viewer's outlook on the way from one picture to the next. Each time the "Promenade" theme returns it is transformed to reflect the musings and psychological states occasioned by Hartmann's works. *Pictures at an Exhibition* was originally composed for piano, but its implied richness of colors led other musicians to attempt its orchestration. Most often heard is the version by Maurice Ravel (1921), a brilliant composer in his own right, whose transparent, sometimes brittle sonorities of a half-century later are not quite true to Mussorgsky's original conception, yet they do have their independent value as a work of art.

Promenade A. The opening walk through the gallery has the musical form A-B-A'. Its rambling quality comes in part from an unusual alternation of measures having five beats and six beats (Ex. 6.7). The "Promenade's" pungent modal flavor—Mussorgsky describes it as being "in Russian style"—comes from the use of a **pentatonic scale** whose five pitches are B-flat-C-D-F-G. When the "Promenade" re-

△
Mussorgsky: "Promenade" from *Pictures at an Exhibition* (Side 8, Band 3)

Ex. 6.7. **"Promenade" from** *Pictures at an Exhibition,* **Mussorgsky**

appears later in different shapes, its harmonizations and melodic twists continue to be Russian-sounding.

Picture 1: Gnome. Hartmann drew a nutcracker in the shape of an ungainly old man, and Mussorgsky's music describes that gnome's clumsy springs and hops on distorted legs (Ex. 6.8). He lurches and crawls irregularly, with awkward skips, especially the leap of a diminished fourth between D-natural and G-flat in the opening motive.

Ex. 6.8. "Picture 1, Gnome," Mussorgsky

Promenade B. Sobered by the sight of Hartmann's gnome, Mussorgsky moves thoughtfully onward.

Picture 2: The Ruined Castle. A medieval castle with a troubadour singing outside to an undulating rhythm and pedal point that run throughout. Ravel gives the desolate opening tune to a bassoon, then the expressive one that follows to an alto saxophone (Ex. 6.9).

Ex. 6.9. "Picture 2, The Ruined Castle," Mussorgsky

Promenade C. A shortened version, intensified by strong contrapuntal lines.

Picture 3: The Tuileries Gardens at Paris with Children Quarreling. This is a brisk A B A′ form, whose middle section describes the children being coaxed and admonished by their nannies.

Picture 4: The Polish Ox-Cart. A clumsy cart with giant wheels lumbers up, then disappears down the muddy, rutted road. Ravel has a ponderous bass tuba carry the melody, along with a grinding, square-wheeled accompaniment (Ex. 6.10).

Ex. 6.10. "Picture 4, The Polish Ox-Cart," Mussorgsky

Promenade D. As if shaking off the crude image of the oxen, this "Promenade" shifts suddenly from the Polish cart's G-sharp minor to a distant D minor.

Picture 5: Ballet of the Baby Chicks in Their Shells. Hartmann designed egg-shell costumes for a picturesque ballet produced in 1871. Mussorgsky's gossamer "scherzo"-trio-scherzo in $\frac{2}{4}$ meter is as delicate as if composed for a music box.

Picture 6: Samuel Goldenberg and Schmule. Two Polish Jews, drawn with little compassion. Goldenberg, well-to-do and pompous, opens the conversation with broad sweeps of orientalizing rhetoric Ex. 6.11). In Ravel's orchestration, poor, wheedling Schmule responds with nagging repeated squeaks of a muted trumpet. They converse a bit, then with an imperious wave Goldenberg dismisses his importunate friend.

Ex. 6.11. "Picture 6, Samuel Goldenberg," Mussorgsky

Promenade E. Mussorgsky returns to the original "Promenade" music. Ravel does not reorchestrate it.

Picture 7: The Market at Limoges. The chatter of vendors and fishwives in the open-air market at Limoges in southern France. It is a perpetual motion of gossip and bustle.

Picture 8: The Roman Catacombs. The dank underground passageways where the early Christians hid themselves and were buried. This mood picture is filled with solemn harmonies, sudden flashes of bright sound, and ominous echoes. Hartmann put himself into his own illustration, examining the interior of a catacomb by lantern light.

Promenade F. Mussorgsky remains obsessed with the lugubrious mood of the catacombs. The "Promenade" theme appears in the minor mode beneath an eerie tremolo. It is the spirit of the dead Hartmann leading him to a viewing of skulls that are softly illumined by an interior light.

Picture 9: The Hut of the Witch, Baba Yaga. Hartmann drew a fantastic clock tower shaped like a hut on chicken's legs—the abode of the sorceress Baba Yaga. Mussorgsky fills the music with angry, spooky intervals, and mimics the witch's grotesque flight. There is a simple form:

‖ A-B-C | D (compare A) | A-B-C ‖

Its bright, mocking B theme sticks in the memory (Ex. 6.12). Without break, the witch's flight swoops to the final picture.

Ex. 6.12. "Picture 9, The Hut of the Witch, Baba Yaga," Mussorgsky

Picture 10: The Great Gate at Kiev. Kiev was the capital of medieval Russia. Hartmann's fanciful design for a splendid city gate was conceived in the massive old-Russian style, with rounded Romanesque arches, onion-shaped domes, and three giant bells visible in the watchtower. This grandiose musical picture is Mussorgsky's jubilant climax to the cycle. Clangorous sonorities and pealing church bells suggest the Russian Easter. There is a sacred hymn, as if chanted by a monkish procession. Eventually the "Promenade" appears, wreathed in the full splendor of the Slavic ceremonial. Mussorgsky adopts the broad plan of a rondo for this movement, with a very striking A material (Ex. 6.13). Yet almost as important as the themes themselves are the

△
Mussorgsky: Transition, then "The Great Gate at Kiev" from *Pictures at an Exhibition*
(Side 8, Band 4)

alternations of dynamic levels between loud and soft. In the end everything works up to a glorious fortissimo.

Ex. 6.13. "Picture 10, The Great Gate at Kiev," Mussorgsky

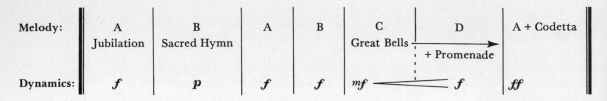

Pictures at an Exhibition still captures our imagination with its striking themes, pungent harmonies, and vivid tone painting. Yet Mussorgsky knew that such things were not enough. "Beautiful sounds are always appealing," he wrote in 1873, "and they may so fascinate us that we are drenched with tears . . . But something more concrete is needed. Art must embody more than beauty alone. A building is good only when, in addition to a beautiful façade, it is well planned and solid, when one can sense the aim of the construction and see the artist's spirit." Mussorgsky's *Pictures* are based on such well-ordered plans. Even when his musical language is at its most pictorial, there are the underlying formal logics of the As, Bs, and Cs, and their patterns of inner repetitions. Like all good "descriptive" music, this music succeeds fundamentally because it is good "abstract" music.

F. THE TONE POEM

Richard Wagner had three spiritual heirs, Bruckner, Strauss, and Mahler. Anton Bruckner (1824-1896) was the first and least original. Richard Strauss (1864-1949) was the last and most facile. Gustav Mahler (1860-1911) was the most significant. Bruckner was hailed by the legion of Wagner's admirers during the 1870s as their own symphonist, as the concert-hall representative of Wagnerian style, a paragon to match against the conservative model of Brahms. Bruckner wrote nine ponderous symphonies in which he swallowed the whole apparatus of Wagner's chromaticism and orchestration. To purely instrumental concert music he adapted the bulkiness and structural technique of the Wagner operas, which were woven from the repetitions and transformations of short musical motives. Yet Bruckner was no craven imitator. His symphonies sustain their Wagnerian lengths with noble simplicity and passages of genuine grandeur.

Richard Strauss

Richard Strauss came from a Munich family that was not related to the Austrian dynasty of musical Strausses who specialized in Viennese waltzes. His father was the reigning French horn virtuoso of the day. While in his teens, Richard composed skillful sonatas and symphonies in a conservative Mendelssohn-Brahms vein. Then he was won over to the ideas of program music, and his avowed ideal became "to cultivate the expressive, poetic elements in music." He embraced the lush chromatic idiom of Wagner, whose last years were spent in young Strauss's Bavarian homeland. During the 1880s he earned a reputation as a virtuoso conductor, but at the same time he was composing an important series of orchestral works in an effusive romantic style. Going beyond Liszt's single-movement symphonic poems, Strauss dropped the word "symphonic" altogether and substituted the new term **tone poem,** so as to emphasize the poetic and dramatic elements in his music. Among Strauss's tone poems of the 1880s are *Don Juan, Death and Transfiguration, Till Eulenspiegel's Merry Pranks, Thus Spake Zarathustra* (based on Nietzsche), and *Don Quixote* (after Cervantes). After 1900 Strauss turned to opera, electrifying everyone with two jarring character studies, *Salome* (1905), to a text by Oscar Wilde, and *Electra* (1909), to a text by Hugo von Hofmannsthal. The musical idiom in those works at times crosses the borderline from tonal to post-tonal (see Chapter 8). But then Strauss recoiled and settled back to a cream-puff tonal romanticism. In *Der Rosenkavalier* (*Cavalier of the Rose,* 1911), a masterpiece of sentimentality, Strauss showed that he too could turn out a memorable Viennese waltz. A string of operas in a ripe romantic style followed, including *Ariadne* (1912), *Woman Without a Shadow* (1919), and *Capriccio* (1942). Strauss survived World War II and lived to be eighty-five. He still cultivated the old tonal chromaticism in a glowing final work, the *Four Last Songs,* completed in the year before his death in 1949.

Of all the great program composers, Strauss was the most literal in his musical descriptions, yet he never sacrificed a musical point to make a descriptive one. *Don Juan,* completed in 1889 when he was only twenty-five, has as its protagonist the same noble Spanish libertine as Mozart's *Don Giovanni.* Strauss's Don, however, was a creation of the Hungarian poet Nicholas Lenau (1802-1850), who began his work in 1843, then went insane and left it unfinished at his death. Lenau's fragment appealed to Strauss because along with

Ex. 6.14a. Themes from *Don Juan*, Richard Strauss

Ex. 6.14b. *Don Juan*, Richard Strauss

EXPOSITION ①

Melody: ‖ H^1 | F^1 | L^1 |

EXPOSITION ②

Melody: | H^1 | F^2 | L^2 |

DEVELOPMENT AND OUTCOME

| Development | | Recapitulation | Memories |

Melody: | H^2 H^{1+2} ⋀⋀⋀⋀ | Retransition H^{1+2} L^{1+2+1}
$(+L^2)$ ↓   ↓
(short)   Sword thrust   Death

CODA

| Glorification | Void |

Melody: | H^{1+2+1} | ‖

the surface machismo there was the psychological portrait of a deeply troubled personality. Strauss's score is prefaced with three excerpts from the poem. The first has the tone of empty bravado:

Oh, that I might run the magic circle . . . of beautiful women's charms,
to die with a kiss at the mouth of the last one . . .

In the end, Lenau's Don Juan dies in a duel with the avenger of one of the women he has wronged. Actually, disillusioned with life, he has allowed himself to be run through. Strauss's musical plot is simple enough. The Don swaggers through two love affairs. Then, on the prowl for a third, he encounters the avenger and dies. An extensive coda glorifies his romantic legend, but all ends on a note of despair. Strauss's last excerpt from Lenau reads:

Beautiful was the storm that drove me on; its rage is spent,
and silence now remains . . . the fuel is gone, the hearth is cold and dark.

The bare bones of this plot are given very graphic musical flesh in Strauss's tone poem. It was all very well for Oscar Wilde to insist at about this time that "art never expresses anything but itself." Wilde had not seen Strauss's score. An opening theme (H^1) that represents Don Juan as flamboyant hero surges upward (Ex. 6.14). An ensuing flirtation (F^1) is filled with prancings and cajolings. This leads to the first love scene (L^1), where Strauss rekindles the kind of musical-erotic flame first lit in *Tristan and Isolde*. Shaking off this amorous entanglement, Don Juan returns, a free spirit (H^1), yet more complex and worldly-wise than before. A second flirtation (F^2) leads to a new love (L^2), personified by a gentle oboe rather than the impassioned violins of L^1. The affair ends less bitterly, but again the Don breaks away. A new fortissimo theme in the French horn introduces a nobler side of his character (H^2), and those two sides (H^1 and H^2) are developed. All the cocky antics lead to the fatal sword thrust. Before Don Juan dies, garbled memories of the two loves (L^1 and L^2) flash through his mind. He is glorified in a passage that wrings the last drops of excitement from the two H themes. But at its height the euphoria is interrupted, and a hushed ending draws a cool judgment on his dissolute existence.

Strauss has made all this quite explicit, but he has also taken care to give his musical work an independent coherence. It has a musical shape drawn from sonata form, where even the normal key relationships are observed. The opening exposition's vigorous first theme (H^1) modulates from its home key through a bridge (F^1) on the way to a lyrical second theme (L^1) that is in the dominant key. The second exposition begins with the opening theme (H^1) again in the home key. Now there is a new second theme (L^2) in a different key, and for a while the "plot" takes charge of the musical continuity.

But at the end Strauss ties the whole form together by musical means: his coda returns to the home key where it all started.

G. THE TWILIGHT OF ROMANTICISM

Gustav Mahler

Gustav Mahler (1860-1911) was the last great romantic to remain within the boundaries of major-minor tonality. Mahler was born in Bohemia and made his way to Vienna, where for a while he studied with Bruckner. While still young he was launched on an important conducting career. He was director of the Budapest Opera when he was only twenty-eight and of the prestigious Vienna Opera at thirty-seven. Shortly before his death at fifty-one he headed the Philharmonic in New York and conducted at the Metropolitan Opera. In middle age Mahler married the much younger Alma Schindler, an amateur artist and composer, who was the most fascinating beauty in Viennese intellectual circles of the time. She outlived him by many years, compiling a list of infatuations, conquests, and husbands that reads like a "cultural Who's Who of Central Europe." Besides Mahler, there were the artists Klimt and Kokoschka, the architect Gropius, the conductor Bruno Walter, the novelist Franz Werfel. Alma Mahler's *Memoirs* contain vivid glimpses of the triumphs and miseries of the composer's last years.

Mahler in 1909.
By Auguste Rodin.

Mahler's ten massive symphonies (the last one incomplete) and three song collections with orchestra (*Songs of a Wayfarer, Songs on the Death of a Child,* and the *Song of the Earth*) constitute a farewell to romanticism. Even before he died, younger composers of the Viennese avant-garde were taking the first hesitant steps beyond tonal romanticism. Mahler, however, stayed with the cumbersome musical idiom he inherited from Wagner and Bruckner, and to this he added a ponderousness and stridency of his own. He used more dissonant chromatic harmonies and more complex profilings of melodic strands within crowded contrapuntal textures. Mahler had a musical personality that reeked of world-weariness and inner trouble. Even more than the exhibitionistic Berlioz or the self-indulgent Tchaikovsky, Mahler was confessional in his utterance. His music seems filled with inner agonies and self-doubts. He was not unique in this. The spirit of the times—the Central European "Zeitgeist"—was right there with him. Freud was at large in Vienna, unfolding the inner creases of the psyche. Freud was even consulted about Mahler, but he declined to tamper with a creative personality that he thought might be upset through his doctoring. In the realm of drama, Ibsen and Strindberg were giving up the tailored conventions of the "well-made" plays and substituting a dramatic reality that was less smugly ordered, truer to life. Mahler accomplished something similar. In effect, he gave up the concept of "well-made" music. Composers since the beginnings of Western music history had implicitly believed that what music had to express must be communicated through effects that were compellingly "beautiful." Now, with a fanatic energy and blunt honesty, Mahler seemed to be letting all sorts of other things come out. For the seamy, ugly shapes he found within himself, he offered musical correlatives that might actually sound seamy and ugly. This willingness to expose himself in artful misshapenness went beyond what his predecessors had dared. It turned many of his contemporaries away, and it still turns some audiences away today. But Mahler's perverse honesty and the boldness of his musical imagination appealed to many. Thomas Mann addressed him in 1910 as "the most serious, the most saintly artistic determination of our time." His music was a revelation to a circle of younger Viennese, such as Schoenberg, Webern, and Berg, who were just beginning to compose. And the future lay with them.

Effective as Mahler can be in his confessional vein, he is also capable of being cool and Olympian. The Adagietto of his Fifth Symphony (1902) represents both those poles of his paradox-ridden personality. This is a luminous slow movement in the grand tradition of romantic slow movements that runs from Beethoven's Ninth through the adagios of Brahms and Bruckner. Mahler adopts a simple overall plan of A-B-A'. In the opening and closing A sections an emotional calm prevails, while in the central B section there is some of his eloquent hand wringing. At the back of his mind in shaping this movement there may be the model of Wagner's Prelude to *Tristan* (see page 251). But instead of Wagner's initial gloom, Mahler begins in a mood of elegiac exaltation. In the central section, where Wagner turns to incandescent passion, Mahler does something comparable, but with an end-of-an-era disillusionment he backs away from mounting a grandly romantic emotional line and produces only a febrile eroticism.

Δ
Mahler: Fourth Movement, Adagietto, Symphony No. 5 in C-Sharp Minor (Side 9, Band 1)

The ten minutes of the Adagietto are almost unprecedentedly slow. They represent an ultimate stage in the tendency of romantic composers to push musical tempos to extremes and stretch utterances to monumental lengths. The opening A section contains a theme and two variations (Ex. 6.15). The theme (a^1) rises, glacial and serene, out of a mist of romantic harmonies that are punctuated by random pluckings of a harp. There are other romantic beginnings like this one, yet none so gorgeous and unfathomable. Rhythmic motion is held to a minimum. A regular pattern is avoided so that the music seems pulseless. The long seamless line of melody (a^1) winds upward, then curves back to where it came. That same melody starts again more emotionally (a^2) and moves into a chromatic byway. It starts up a third time (a^3), now growing in lyric warmth to a fortis-

Ex. 6.15. Adagietto from Symphony No. 5, Mahler

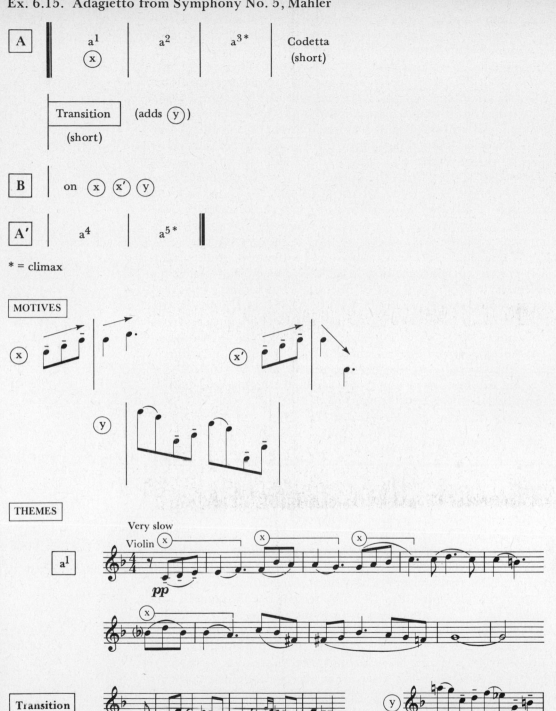

simo climax. Then a transition whose motion is more animated introduces the sinuous motive y. Mahler's central section, the B section, is formed as a *Tristan*-like web of motives (x, x', y). But Mahler's music, rather than scaling progressive peaks on the way to a convincing climax, wallows in disorganized surges and gasps. Mahler knew quite well how to shape a conventionally satisfying emotional line. But times had changed since *Tristan,* and he chose a less idealized, less romantic solution than Wagner's. It was a solution truer to the Viennese cultural ferment at the turn of the century. The intertwined musical motives are taken through a maze of chromatic modulations in the B section. They find release in a last, mystical modulation that slips back to the opening key and reestablishes the initial elegiac mood. Two final variations (a^4 and a^5) round out the design in the concluding A' section. The best stroke comes at the end. There, in a single noble curve, the melody drops rapidly from the climax of a^5 to the close, taking no time to sentimentalize.

Mahler's ten minutes of nearly suspended animation require extraordinary efforts of concentration from the listener. For some, his bittersweet style produces states of liberation and supreme bliss that are like the consciousness-expanding exercises of Eastern mysticism. Yet whether or not one shares in such musical experiences or views his achievement with sympathy, Mahler's idiom, with its juxtapositions of the emotional and monumental, the frenetic and sublime, was representative of an end-of-an-era quality that had taken hold of the aging esthetic of romanticism. The roseate glow was fading, and urgent new truths were waiting to be heard.

H. LATE CONSERVATIVE ROMANTICISM

Edward Elgar

Although the more progressive European composers would turn their backs on tonal romanticism during the decades before World War I (see Chapter 8), an important stream of composers lagged conservatively behind the trendsetters and clung to the idioms of Wagner and Brahms. The standard of tonal romanticism was upheld in central Germany even through the 1940s by Richard Strauss, and it was widely represented by composers in outlying nations, such as Elgar in England and Sibelius in Finland. Edward Elgar (1857-1934) was the "musician laureate" of late Victorian and Edwardian England. He is known for the Pomp and Circumstance March No. 1; its tune "Land of Hope and Glory" has served as ceremonial music for British royalty since the coronation of Edward VII in 1902. Yet to relegate Elgar to an official and insular niche is unfair. He had the rare gift of melody. Such a tune as "Land of Hope and Glory" comes once in a generation. Rarer still was his combination of a distinctive personal imagination and a strong national flavor with a polished craft in the tools of harmony, counterpoint, and orchestration. Elgar had to struggle for success, which came only during his middle years. He was nearing forty when his reputation was established by the "Enigma" Variations (1899), the oratorio *The Dream of Gerontius* (1900), based on a text by Cardinal Newman, and the "Cockaigne" Overture (1901), subtitled "In London Town." Over the next two decades he produced a series of memorable works, among them two symphonies (1908 and 1910), the concertos for violin (1910) and cello (1919), the tone poem *Falstaff* (1913), and three large chamber pieces, a violin sonata, a string quartet, and a piano quintet (1918-19).

Elgar admired Brahms and Richard Strauss. He thought that Debussy "lacked guts" (see Chapter 8, page 299), yet his path during the first decades of this century was not unlike Debussy's. Elgar responded cautiously to the dismantling of tonality that was taking place on the Continent. Though his later works show a growing acceptance of new harmonies and irregular rhythms, his "Enigma" Variations for Orchestra are from the beginning of this period (1899), when he was very much under the German romantic spell, and the work shows him at his best. It consists of a theme and fourteen variations. On the first page Elgar wrote the word "Enigma," but there are actually three different enigmas or puzzles associated with the music. One concerns the spacious theme on which the variations

Picasso, The Old Guitarist *(1903). Picasso soon turned to cubist abstractions (see Chapter 8); but in 1903, aged 21, he was a representational artist responding to romantic sentiments.*

are based. Its music was rumored to be the accompaniment of some well-known tune, but that tune never surfaces in Elgar's version and musicians have vainly sought it ever since. A second enigma lies in the fact that each of the fourteen variations was conceived as the character sketch of some person: Elgar's wife (var. 1); Elgar himself (var. 14); and a dozen of the well-mannered, sometimes eccentric people in the Elgars' circle of friends (vars. 2-13). Their identities are masked behind initials and nicknames. The third enigma is that Elgar let it be known that there was some "dark saying," or hidden meaning—probably with religious overtones—behind the conception of the work. He never bothered to explain.

Enigmas aside, these orchestral variations rank with the best late-romantic creations. Variation 8 ("W.N.") is Elgar's portrait of a lady named Winifred Norbury, who with her sister occupied an eighteenth-century house near his own. She had a "trilly laugh" that Elgar works into the middle of the variation. The music begins in the manner of a Brahms intermezzo (Brahms died the year before Elgar sketched the variations), but then the sturdy British imagination asserts itself. The music of "W.N." flows into one of the grandest of romantic slow movements, variation 9, the famous "Nimrod" variation. This is a philosophical revery describing Elgar's close friend August Jaeger, whose German name means "hunter," hence the title of "Nimrod." It was Jaeger, who at a time of earlier despair, turned Elgar back to composing. The deeply expressive music, with its echoes of the central Adagio of Beethoven's "Pathétique" Sonata, pours out the musician's affection and gratitude. Elgar told his friend that it represented "the good, lovable, honest soul in the middle of you."

George Bernard Shaw said of Elgar that his music was that of "a perfect gentleman." Coming from Shaw, that may have been more of a barb than a compliment. Yet behind Elgar's aura of Victorian self-assurance, there is an uncommonly subtle mind. Elgar's best music can hold its own with that of Mahler, Strauss, and Debussy. He was the first British-born composer in ages to produce durable, exportable music, and his example lit the way for the important generations of British composers who would follow during the twentieth century. Elgar himself lived until 1934, but his last fifteen years were relatively barren. He was oppressed by the death of his wife in 1920, and he was perhaps unable to reconcile himself to the newer styles that were issuing from the Continent. He remained in creative silence while well-deserved honors continued to rain.

Jean Sibelius

The Finnish composer Jean Sibelius (1865-1957) was the last great romantic nationalist in the line of Chopin, Liszt, Mussorgsky, Dvořák

(Czech), Smetana (Czech), and Grieg (Norwegian). During the first three decades of this century, Sibelius turned out sumptuous tonal works whose epic breadths and gorgeous climaxes are suffused with the musical colors of his Baltic homeland. Sibelius was born in 1865, the year after Richard Strauss. He was a student at Berlin and Vienna in 1889-91, when the sensational tone poems of the young Strauss were much in evidence. Returning home, Sibelius was caught up in the Finnish movement of national liberation, seeking autonomy from the Russians, and he drew subjects for a number of tone poems from the Kalevala, the Finnish national epic. His first great success, *The Swan of Tuonela* (1893), was based on a Kalevala legend. Tuonela is the Finnish Hades, a mythological underworld that is surrounded by a body of black water upon which floats a majestic swan, singing a mournful song that strikes those who hear it with the desire for death. Sibelius assigns this slow, rhapsodic swan song to a solo English horn, supported by a luminous accompaniment of strings. The full orchestra takes over in a passionate middle section. Then the soulful wail of the English horn returns. *The Swan of Tuonela*, in its simple overall form of A-B-A′, is reminiscent of Wagner's Prelude to *Tristan,* but Sibelius's mystic modal harmonies represent a stage beyond Wagnerian tonal chromaticism.

The work that brought world renown to Sibelius was *Finlandia* (1900), a vivid eight-minute tone poem that seemed to sum up the heroic and lyric qualities of the Finnish national spirit. Finnish audiences found it so stirring that its performance was banned by the Czarist authorities. In another popular success, the "Valse Triste" (1903), Sibelius took the sometimes hackneyed idiom of the Viennese waltz and gave it a brooding Finnish overlay, slowing it down and turning it philosophical. Sibelius's most important compositions were in larger forms. His Violin Concerto in D Minor (1905) is the last of the epic romantic display pieces for violin and orchestra, a successor to the concertos of Beethoven, Mendelssohn, Brahms, and Tchaikovsky. His seven symphonies, composed during the first quarter of this century, show a gradual evolution from the popularly persuasive tonal style of his First and Second Symphonies (1899-1901) to a cautious exploitation of post-tonal idioms in the Sixth and Seventh Symphonies (1923-24). Sibelius never abandoned tonality. He responded to the newer stylistic currents that circulated during the years around World War I by holding more doggedly to romantic tradition, as in the jubilant finale of his Fifth Symphony (1915). During the late 1920s Sibelius gave up composing altogether. He may have felt that his ideas had run dry, or that the new times were leaving him behind—that further accommodation was impossible between his own essentially romantic imagination and the "modernist" techniques of the reigning avant-garde (see Chapter 8). Like Elgar, Sibelius lived out his last decades in barrenness.

7 | Romantic Opera

Siegfried's Funeral March, *from the first staging of Wagner's*
Twilight of the Gods *(1876)*.

Romantic Opera

MUSIC

Rossini (1792-1868):
Barber of Seville (1816)
William Tell (1829)
Bellini (1801-1835):
Norma (1831)
Donizetti (1797-1848):
Lucia di Lammermoor (1835)
Verdi (1813-1901):
Rigoletto (1851)
La Traviata (1853)
Aïda (1871)
Otello (1887)
Falstaff (1893)
Wagner (1813-1883):
Lohengrin (1848)
The Ring of the Nibelung
   (4 music dramas, 1852-1874)
Tristan and Isolde (1859)
Parsifal (1882)
Gounod (1818-1893):
Faust (1859)
Bizet (1838-1875):
Carmen (1875)
Puccini (1858-1924):
La Bohème (1896)
Tosca (1900)

An opera performance at Dresden in 1842.

A. ITALIAN OPERA

Romantic opera had something for everyone. There were the thrills of the plot, the stage effects, the costumes, the ballet, the flowery verse, the catchy tunes, the glory of the voices, the glitter of the social occasions. Opera was the universal entertainment of European society in the age before the motion pictures. It began around 1600 as an Italian specialty, and it remained essentially Italian in spirit throughout the seventeenth and eighteenth centuries. Even the greatest of the eighteenth-century Germans—Handel, Haydn, and Mozart—wrote operas mainly to Italian texts. During the nineteenth century, a galaxy of resourceful Italians, including Rossini, Bellini, Donizetti, Verdi, and Puccini, assured the continued vigor of their national tradition.

Giuseppe Verdi

Italy's greatest romantic composer was Giuseppe Verdi (1813-1901), who ranks with Mozart and Wagner as a supreme creator of opera. Verdi was born near Parma in northern Italy in the same year as Wagner. His early musical training was so inadequate that he could not gain admission to the Milan Conservatory. But his natural talent surfaced, and he won a first success at Milan's opera house, La Scala, when he was just twenty-six. In 1842 his opera *Nabucco,* based on the biblical story of Nebuchadnezzar, established Verdi at the age of twenty-nine in musical theaters throughout Europe. He has been there ever since, by far the most beloved of all opera composers. During a long and productive career, Verdi composed two dozen operas and little else—a string quartet, some sacred choruses, and a *Requiem,* whose style is as stagy as his operas. The cornerstone of his enduring reputation was laid with three operas of the early 1850s: *Rigoletto,* based on Victor Hugo's *Le Roi s'amuse; Il Trovatore (The Troubadour),* a blood-and-thunder story of gypsies, adapted from a Spanish drama; and *La Traviata,* scenes of the contemporary Parisian *demimonde,* drawn from Alexander Dumas the Younger's play, *The Lady of the Camelias.* Verdi's successes of the later 1850s and 1860s included *A Masked Ball, The Force of Destiny,* and *Don Carlo* (based on a play by Schiller). In 1871, for the Turkish viceroy of Egypt, he produced the most popular of all romantic operas, *Aïda,* to help celebrate the opening of the Suez Canal. In his old age Verdi turned to Shakespeare. He had written a youthful opera based on *Macbeth* in the 1840s. Now in 1887, collaborating with the librettist Arrigo Boito, Verdi reached a pinnacle of romantic realism in the tragedy of *Otello.* He again used a Boito libretto drawn from Shakespeare in 1892 (his eightieth year) for the comic masterpiece *Falstaff,* based on *The Merry Wives of Windsor.* Verdi had long since become a na-

Verdi conducting.

tional hero. His early operas rang with libertarian sentiments that helped fan the flames of the *Risorgimento,* the Italian movement for national unity of the 1850s and 1860s. After freedom from Austria was won, Verdi became an honorary member of the Italian parliament. His old age was filled with veneration, and when he died in 1901 at the age of eighty-eight the whole nation mourned.

Verdi liked to portray powerful emotions in exciting situations. His plots are filled with strong egos that are caught up in stressful relationships and provoked to violent actions. *Rigoletto* (1851), Verdi's first great success, is a grisly shocker set against a colorful background of the Italian Renaissance. It crosses threads of innocence and fatherly love with brutal passion and murderous revenge. Rigoletto is the hunchbacked jester at the court of the handsome, libertine Duke of Mantua. In the courtier's eyes Rigoletto is a misshapen buffoon. In private he is the fiercely protective father of an only daughter named Gilda, whom he has shielded through young womanhood from the vices of the court. The philandering Duke has discovered Gilda and managed to seduce her. Now Rigoletto, his happiness shattered, plots the Duke's murder. The Duke is lured to a country inn outside of Mantua by the flirtatious Maddalena, sister of Rigoletto's hired assassin. Rigoletto brings Gilda there to witness the Duke's perfidy, and so, he hopes, to rid her of her infatuation. The stage is set for the celebrated Quartet. This kind of operatic number is called an **ensemble**. In an ensemble, two or more characters give vent to their individual feelings, expressing themselves in a single, coordinated outpouring of music, yet coming through vividly and personally because each character's musical line is shaped to his or her emotions and point of view. Ensembles are the most dramatic numbers in operas, for unlike solo arias, where the action generally halts in favor of pure lyricism, in the course of an ensemble the sentiments keep changing and the theatrical situation continues to evolve. Mozart was the first great master of operatic ensembles. He created ensemble scenes of matchless realism for as many as six different characters. His duet "Là ci darem la mano" (Chapter 4) is an ensemble for two, with its distinctively tailored music for Don Giovanni and Zerlina, and the unfolding of their relationship as the music proceeds. Verdi's Quartet from *Rigoletto* is a more complex ensemble, taking in four different points of view. The lovesick Gilda (soprano) and her father Rigoletto (bass) are spying from outside the inn upon the Duke (tenor) and Maddalena (alto), who are inside. The Duke begins with a flowery address to Maddalena: "Bella figlia dell'Amore" ("Fair daughter of Venus, I am a slave to your charms"). Verdi clothes the Duke's declarations with a melody of great sensuous beauty. All of the Duke's suave, vibrant personality is embodied in his melodic line (Ex. 7.1). This is another example of the Italian bel canto tradition, the tradition of vocal lyricism that was already present in Handel's tenor aria, "Every valley" (Chapter 3). *Bel canto* implies beautiful song, beautifully delivered. The Duke's song has a supple melodic loveliness that needs to be fulfilled in an effortless elegance of vocal delivery. When Maddalena finally answers, it is with a chuckling staccato: "Oh, you really make me laugh. How little such flattery means" (Ex. 7.2). Verdi has found just the right musical profile for her woman-of-the-world banter. The distressed Gilda overhears all this and responds with anguished swoops and flutters: "Oh, to speak thus of love, the same I heard myself" (Ex. 7.3). Rigoletto hushes her: "Quiet! To wail now is useless" (Ex. 7.4). Once they are all singing together the words are often indistinguishable, but we know their individual sentiments because they are carved into the distinctive shapes of the musical lines. People sometimes reproach Italian opera for being artificial in treating the drama, yet there is little else in the realm of theater that matches the realism of such an ensemble. Here are four different points of view issuing forth as spontaneously as they would be in the heat of a living situation. Verdi took pains to make his quartet as musically appealing as possible. He gave it a tunefulness and an independent musical form that would attract those listeners who cared more for melody and singing than for character and situation (Ex. 7.5). But the marvel is that the music also amplifies the personalities and intensifies the drama. Things that are too complex to be said can sometimes be sung. When the song is gorgeous, something special is added to the spoken meaning. And when the song is also wonderfully delivered,

△
Verdi: Quartet, "Bella figlia dell'Amore" from Act 4, *Rigoletto* (Side 9, Band 2)

Ex. 7.1. The Duke (Tenor)

Andante *p*

Bel - la fi - glia dell' a - mo - - re,
Fair daughter of Venus . . .

Ex. 7.2. Maddalena (Alto)

Ah! Ah! ri - do ben di co - re, chè tai ba - ie cos - tan po - co
Oh, you really make me laugh . . .

Ex. 7.3. Gilda (Soprano)

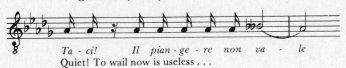

Ah!_____ co - sì___ par - lar___ d'a - mo - re
Oh, to speak thus of love . . .

Ex. 7.4. Rigoletto (Bass)

Ta - ci! Il pian - ge - re non va - le
Quiet! To wail now is useless . . .

Ex. 7.5. Quartet from *Rigoletto,* Verdi

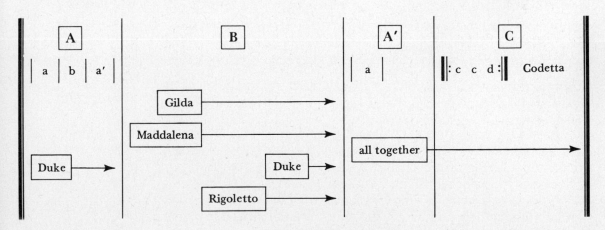

a transcendent quality attaches to the dramatic experience. That is why people stand for long hours on ticket lines and spend immoderate amounts of money to hear live opera performances. Prodigious singing by great vocal artists who send forth magnificent tones and take acrobatic risks with perilous high notes and exhausting runs adds a unique dimension of musical excitement to the fireworks of the drama.

Verdi was never one to brag, but he had no modesty about the *Rigoletto* Quartet: "It will remain one of the finest creations that our theater can boast." As for poor Gilda, the story ends sadly. Unable to be rid of her infatuation, she manages to be stabbed by Rigoletto's assassin, sacrificing herself in place of the Duke. Her body is given to her father, tied up in a sack. He gloats for an instant, thinking he has the Duke's body. But as he is about to throw it into the river the Duke's own tenor voice floats in from the distance, warm from the tryst with Maddalena. It is an electrifying moment. Rigoletto, dumbfounded, opens the sack and finds his Gilda dying.

Verdi's *Rigoletto* of 1851 was still an old-fashioned **number opera**, filled with lyric set pieces that alternated with orchestrally accompanied recitatives. Like the operas of Verdi's romantic forbears, Vincenzo Bellini (1801-1835) and Gaetano Donizetti (1797-1848), it was packed with thrills and tunes and with the thumping accompaniments that assured the primacy of the solo singers by treating the orchestra like a "big guitar." As Verdi moved toward the mature styles of *Aïda, Otello,* and *Falstaff,* he developed a more flexible manner, with less segmenting of the dramatic continuity into recitatives and lyric numbers. But he never wholly abandoned the old lyric show stoppers, and neither did his chief successors, Puccini, Giordano, Ponchielli, Mascagni, and Leoncavallo. Those wily Italian masters found plenty of emotional juice in the old-style tunes. There was the matchless drama that results when a beautiful melody is beautifully sung.

B. WAGNER'S MUSIC DRAMAS

Before the nineteenth century, Germany was an operatic tributary of Italy. Operas by German composers were usually written in the Italian language—for example, Handel's *Julius Caesar* and Mozart's *Don Giovanni.* Mozart chose a more native path in *The Abduction from the Seraglio* (1782) and *The Magic Flute* (1791). Both were examples—exalted examples—of the popular genre of German musical comedy called the Singspiel (song-play). This differed from Italian opera in having German texts that were delivered in spoken dialogue rather than sung recitative and in the simple folklike style of the musical numbers that were liberally interspersed among the dialogues. *Fidelio* (1805-14), Beethoven's only opera, was in the German language and in his most serious musical-dramatic style, owing nothing to the comic Singspiel tradition. It was a Revolutionary-epoch tale of an imprisoned patriot who is rescued in the nick of time through the perseverence of his zealous wife. Still, the dialogues in *Fidelio* were spoken, not sung. Carl Maria von Weber (1786-1826) gave German opera a fresh romantic stance in *Der Freischütz* (*The Magic Bullet,* 1820), an imaginative work that helped separate the German musical theater from its long Italian dependency. *Der Freischütz* has spectacular effects in the "Wolf's Glen" scene, where the young hero Max is joined by the Devil in casting magic silver bullets while ghostly nightbirds flap their wings and phantom chariots ride through the stormy skies. Weber established a new tone for German opera with his provocative harmonies, colorful instrumentation, and evocation of the German forest. Yet, like Beethoven, he remained faithful to the conventions of the old number opera. *Der Freischütz* was still laid out as a chain of set pieces, and its connecting dialogues were again spoken, not sung.

It was with Richard Wagner's three great dramatic works of the 1840s that a genuinely Germanic musical theater, using a continuous flow of music, appeared. Wagner was drawn to old legends where Christian piety triumphs over dark supernatural powers. *The Flying Dutchman* (1841) is about a phantom ship, which is doomed to perpetually sail the fog-shrouded northern seas while its master seeks redemption through the love of a devoted woman. *Tannhäuser* (1845) is a medieval knightly tale of sacred and profane love. *Lohengrin* (1848) is another mirror of medieval chivalry, played out against the spiritual background of the Holy Grail, the chalice used by Jesus at the Last Supper. In *The Flying Dutchman* Wagner employed a style of German musical declamation that still owed something to the formulas of Italian recitative. But increasingly in *Tannhäuser* and *Lohengrin* his recitative gained in musical flexibility and was idiomatically shaped to the German language. Wagner gave those works a more natural dramatic flow, reducing the divisions that set off recitatives from lyric numbers. Those three operas of the 1840s were the first in a succession of ten masterpieces that revolutionized the realm of opera and transformed the whole outlook of nineteenth-century music. The other seven were:

The Ring of the Nibelung (1852-74):
   The Rhinegold (1852-54)
   The Valkyrie (1854-56)
   Siegfried (1856-71)
   The Twilight of the Gods (*Die Götterdämmerung,* 1873-74)
Tristan and Isolde (1859)
The Mastersingers of Nuremberg (1867)
Parsifal (1882)

Two views of the Bayreuth Festspielhaus (Festival Playhouse) in 1876, the year of its inauguration.

From the outset Wagner's purpose was to create an authentically German musical theater. He disdained the Italian term *opera* as being too burdened with trivial and artificial associations. He substituted a personal term, a personal ideal, that he called **music drama**, meaning an integrated dramatic work where all the theatrical elements—music, poetry, action, dance, costume, and stage design—were equal partners in the musical-dramatic fabric, where none took unnatural precedence over the others. Wagner also had a name for the totality of this conception, calling it the "unified" or "total work of art" (*Gesamtkunstwerk*). Earlier composers had been content to take over someone else's poetic drama and set it to music, and then hand it on to others to stage. But not Wagner. He chose his own subject, laid out the plot, wrote the poetic drama, composed the music, even penned a manual telling how it was all to be staged. Whenever possible he supervised the actual production. During his final years, after the Festival Playhouse at Bayreuth was built to his architectural and acoustical specifications (1876), Wagner even tried to prevent his new works from being performed anywhere else but there. All of this represented an enormous power of will. For it to succeed required an enormous creative imagination. Wagner also had that—in superabundance.

As a German nationalist he derived his plots from old Germanic myths and legends. Instead of writing out his dramatic poetry in conventional verses with final syllables that rhyme, Wagner revived a medieval style of *alliterative verse* where the chief words in a phrase or line tend to begin with the same consonant sounds, for example, "Fearless Frederick rode into the fray," or "Wailing in the winter wind." To some extent the words in alliterative poetry also sound like what they mean, as in "Love gives pleasure to life," which is full of "liquid" *l*s and *r*s. To replace the stiff stylizations of Italian recitative, Wagner cultivated a supple style of musical declamation that mirrored the contours of German speech and was dramatically pliable, shifting between narrative and lyric manners, being at one moment a mere communication in musically expressive speech, at another taking on an animated lyric sweep. Wagner detested the interruption of the dramatic continuity by audience applause, something that happened traditionally at the end of every aria or set piece in an Italianate number opera. He wanted a sequence of moods and a sweep of action that was psychologically and dramatically true, moving forward without unnatural interruptions. At some moments the substance would obviously be more thoughtful or lyrical, at others more active or conversational. But throughout there was to be a seamless musical flow, an "endless melody," reflecting faithfully the dramatic nuance of each instant, and never locked into the rigid old compartments of recitative and set piece. Wagner discarded the Italianate overture, an independent instrumental number that bore little relation to the ensuing drama. Overtures were followed by a pause, allowing latecomers to be seated. Instead, Wagner wrote preludes to his music dramas (see the Prelude to *Tristan,* Chapter 6). Wagner's preludes set the mood and introduced some of the musical materials that would appear in the drama. They flowed without break into the opening scene. Ticket holders who lingered over a meal and missed the opening downbeat received no mercy. There was no break between the prelude and the first act, and in Wagner's opera house they waited until the second act to be seated. In the case of *Twilight of the Gods* or *Parsifal,* that meant waiting almost two hours (the lengths of the first acts). In the case of *The Rhinegold,* it meant missing the entire work because there was only a single, uninterruptable musical action, two and a half hours long.

Wagner gave his orchestra a larger share of such action than earlier composers. There were many more players than in a Mozart, Beethoven, or Weber orchestra. Strings were multiplied and new winds and brass appeared, such as the bass clarinets and tubas. The essential change was that the orchestra was treated as an equal partner with the voices. Gone was its use as mainly a subordinate accompaniment. Now the orchestra shared fully in the musical interest and was an important bearer of the dramatic message. Wagner's musical continuity was based on short musical motives and themes that constantly reappeared in fresh combinations and transformations. The Prelude to *Tristan* is one such web, its few motives compounded into a long orchestral tissue.

Musical motives had a further role to play in Wagner's music dramas. From Berlioz, Liszt, and Weber, he took over the idea of using specific musical motives to represent specific persons, places, objects, and ideas in his plot. He expanded the use of motives beyond anything done before. The plot-related motives in Wagnerian terminology are called **leitmotifs**, or identification motives. His fertile imagination discovered just the right leitmotif for each character and situation. To represent a sword that is the young hero Siegfried's sole legacy from his unknown hero-father, Wagner uses a C-major trumpet call that has all the sheen and sharpness of the steel (Ex. 7.6). To represent the shiny gold submerged beneath the waters of the Rhine, Wagner has another pithy motive, sounded with the mellow gleam of a French horn (Ex. 7.7). The Gods' abode, Valhalla, to which the goddesses on horseback, called Valkyries, bear the souls of warriors heroically slain, is represented by solemn, lustrous chords (Ex. 7.8). As in the "Fantastic" Symphony of Berlioz, Wagner's identification motives can be transformed to show changes in circumstance and character. Thus a spirited solo horn characterizes the ebullient young Siegfried (Ex. 7.9), but when the same Siegfried has grown to maturity, that motive is fleshed with resonant

The Ride of the Valkyries. *A famous scene from* The Valkyrie *in a production of the 1870s.*

The leitmotif for The Ride of the Valkyries *in Wagner's hand.*

Ex. 7.6. The Sword

Ex. 7.7. The Gold

Ex. 7.8. Valhalla

Ex. 7.9. Young Siegfried

Ex. 7.10. Mature Siegfried

chords and a ponderous orchestration (Ex. 7.10). There are dozens of leitmotifs in each of Wagner's later operas, and each time a motive is heard, it conveys its parcel of message. This has enormous potential for the unfolding of the drama. It means that the drama operates on two simultaneous tracks. As in any spoken drama, there are the words and actions of the characters on stage. But now in the throats of the singers and even in the instruments of the orchestra, there are also the musical leitmotifs, spinning their web of associations and commentary that runs parallel to, but to some extent independent of, the discourse and actions of the characters. The leitmotifs penetrate deeper than words into the essence of the drama. They utter prophecies. They reveal the subtlety of complex situations. They enter the characters' minds and disclose thoughts that are never uttered and that the characters themselves are not aware of.

The showcase of Wagner's mature style was the cycle of four music dramas called *The Ring of the Nibelung,* consisting of *The Rhinegold, The Valkyrie, Siegfried,* and *The Twilight of the Gods* (*Götterdämmerung*). They were meant to be performed on four successive days. Altogether there are dozens of characters and almost two hundred leitmotifs strewn throughout the nineteen hours of music. The scope of this musical-dramatic creation was so large and its success so convincing that no one has attempted anything similar. The origins of Wagner's *Ring* go back to the year 1848 when he wrote a poetic drama called *Siegfried's Death,* based on legends from the Scandinavian *Edda* and the medieval German epic called the *Song of the Nibelung* (*Nibelungenlied*). The subject gradually expanded in his mind so that he eventually had three additional poetic dramas leading up to Siegfried's death. By 1852 there was enough text for four full evenings of musical theater, and Wagner set about composing the music. After completing a little over half the work during the 1850s, however, he despaired of ever getting such a monumental creation staged, and he interrupted his labors. They were not completed until 1874, twenty-two years after he began. Wagner is the one musician in history to carry out so vast and unified a design over so long a period.

The Ring of the Nibelung is a panorama of the medieval mythic world, so universal in its allegory and strong in its human qualities that it retains much of its original communicative power today. The story spans the whole of heaven and earth, which Wagner divides into four interrelated realms. First, there is the realm of nature and primordial innocence, represented by the river Rhine and the water nymphs (Rhine maidens) who frolic in its depths. They are the custodians of the pure shining gold of the Rhine. Second, there is a satanic underworld inhabited by gnomes called Nibelungs who labor feverishly in subterranean caverns. Third, there is the realm of fragile mortals who inhabit the face of the earth. Fourth, there is the realm of the undying gods, whose heavenly abode is the great hall of Valhalla. Those four realms are fatally linked in Wagner's cosmology by a craving for the Rhine's golden hoard. The gold is first wrested from the Rhine maidens by the Nibelung Alberich, who makes a ring from it, a ring that confers limitless power on its bearer. Next the ring and the hoard are stolen from Alberich by Loki, the wily god of fire. Loki's trickery is employed on behalf of Wotan, the king of the gods, who has need of the ring's power to carry out his own lofty designs. But Wotan is obliged to turn it over as payment of a debt to some hostile giants, who fortunately are too stupid to exploit it. As *The Rhinegold* ends, the giant Fafner has turned himself into an enormous, slumbering dragon who sluggishly guards his treasure. During the remaining three dramas, the fate of the ring and the golden hoard are traced through generations yet unborn, as the god Wotan and the Nibelung Alberich struggle to regain the gold's power by manipulating the actions of their children and grandchildren. In the end, all their desperate craft is wasted. Wotan's daughter Brunhilde and his grandson Siegfried are creatures of good and pure instinct. They are themselves destroyed, but through their selfless actions the gold returns to the Rhine. The gods, like the Nibelung dwarfs, are rendered powerless, and Valhalla goes up in flames.

There have been many interpretations of Wagner's elephantine creation. The German philosopher Nietzsche saw in it a denial of the Christian doctrine that the meek and the pure inherit the earth. Nietzsche also found in the stolid valor of Wagnerian heroes such as Siegfried and his father Siegmund the qualities of his own superman. George Bernard Shaw, the Irish playwright and wit, who was also an ardent socialist, saw Wagner's *Ring* as an allegory of the struggle between socialism and capitalism. Its lesson was that the lust for gold leads to the downfall of the money-grubbing classes. Wagner himself was something of a socialist militant during the revolutionary years of 1848-49, at just the time when he was plotting the *Ring*. In the twentieth century Hitler saw the cycle as prophetic of victory by his master race: Wagner's Siegfried was doomed through treachery in the *Ring*, but such Germanic heroes would gain world domination through the Third Reich. Wagner's conception is actually so vast and intellectually muddled that many theories can be supported. They scarcely matter. Transcending all theories, the *Ring* remains as compelling an artistic experience today as when it was first performed at Bayreuth over a century ago.

The closing scene of the second drama, *The Valkyrie,* is a long baritone monologue known as Wotan's Farewell. Wotan, a complex brooding personage, has fathered two sets of children in the course of his godly meanderings. By the goddess Erda he has the warrior-maiden Valkyries, led by his favorite, Brunhilde. By a mortal woman he has the twin Volsungs, a girl and a boy named Sieglinde and Siegmund, who are now grown to maturity. Just before Wotan's Farewell begins, Brunhilde has disobeyed her father and violated a treaty that he must observe. She has shielded Siegmund from death in battle, and Wotan now must punish her. Brunhilde is to be deprived of her godhood and left slumbering on an exposed mountaintop where she will become the wife of the first mortal who discovers her. Horrified, she pleads for a surrounding curtain of fire as assurance that only someone of exceptional valor will win her. Wotan grants this request, knowing that the hero will be his own Volsung-grandson Siegfried, son of Siegmund, who at the moment is still in his mother's womb. As the music of Wotan's Farewell begins, Wotan's anger has somewhat diminished. He gazes lovingly at Brunhilde for a last time, and the anguish of his situation cuts home. What moves us here is not the battery of Wagnerian dramatic theories but the very human expression that he gives to the love of a father for his daughter. Still, the theory is present, contributing to the dramatic effect. The leitmotifs are heard, both in the orchestra and in Wotan's own music, coveying what is on his mind no less eloquently than the heartfelt words he utters. Ten leitmotifs are woven into the fabric of Wotan's Farewell. They illuminate every step of the words and actions, sustaining the line of the drama on their own purely musical track.

Wotan first sings to Brunhilde in fond memory of their past happiness as motive No. 1, Sleep, winds through the orchestra. Its music is an arch of just five notes, whose slow hypnotic repetitions mirror the solemn obsession of Wotan's mind (Ex. 7.11):

Ex. 7.11. No. 1, Sleep

Leb' wohl, du kühnes, herrliches Kind!
  Farewell, thou valiant, glorious child!

  Du meines Herzens heiligster Stolz.
    Thou once the holiest pride of my heart.

    Leb' wohl! Leb' wohl! Leb' wohl!
      Farewell! Farewell! Farewell!

Muss ich dich meiden, und darf nicht minnig mein Gruss dich mehr grüssen,
  Must I forsake thee, and may my welcome of love no more greet thee,

Sollst du nun nicht mehr neben mir reiten, noch Meth beim Mahl mir reichen,
  May'st thou now ne'er more ride as my comrade, nor bear me mead at banquet,

Muss ich verlieren dich, die ich liebe, du lachende Lust meines Auges?
  Must I abandon thee whom I loved so, thou laughing delight of my eyes?

When he speaks of the curtain of fire that will protect Brunhilde, motive No. 2, Fire, wells up in the orchestra, a bright crackle of harps and high woodwinds (Ex. 7.12):

Ex. 7.12. No. 2, Fire

Ein bräutliches Feuer soll dir nun brennen, wie nie einer Braut es gebrannt!
   Such a bridal fire for thee shall be kindled as ne'er yet has burned for a bride!

Flammende Gluth umglühe den Fels,
   Threatening flames shall flare round the crag,

Mit zehrenden Schrecken scheuch' es den Zagen,
   Let withering terrors daunt the craven,

Der Feige fliehe Brünnhilde's Fels!
   Let cowards fly from Brunhilde's rock!

Wotan sings of the "one alone" who will win Brunhilde as bride. The hero is not named, but motive No. 3, Siegfried as Hero, is heard (Ex. 7.13):

Ex. 7.13. No. 3, Siegfried as Hero

Denn Einer nur freie die Braut, der freier als ich der Gott!
   For one alone winneth the bride, one freer than I the God!

All ten of Wagner's leitmotifs have a significant role in the music of this scene, yet a listener can understand his method by recognizing just Nos. 1, 2, and 3 as they occur: Sleep, Fire, and Siegfried as Hero.
   The echoes of No. 3 fade into an orchestral interlude that begins with No. 4, Wotan's Love for the Volsungs (Ex. 7.14):

Ex. 7.14. No. 4, Wotan's Love for the Volsungs

Brunhilde has sunk upon Wotan's breast. But his earthly children are also on Wotan's mind: Siegmund, who has met death in combat, and Sieglinde, who will soon give birth to Siegfried. The sweeping phrases of No. 4 are worked to a climax whose energies pour over into No. 1, Sleep, returning with gentle insistence. Wotan gazes rapturously at Brunhilde, and to the melody of No. 5, Fond Memories, he sings of her childhood while Sleep winds through the orchestra (Ex. 7.15):

Ex. 7.15. No. 5, Fond Memories

Der   *Au - gen*   *leuch - ten - des*   *Paar*
Thy   bright - ly   glit - ter - ing   eyes

Der Augen leuchtendes Paar, das oft ich lächelnd gekos't,
    Thy brightly glittering eyes, that smiling oft I caressed,

Wenn Kampfeslust ein Kuss dir lohnte,
    When valour was rewarded with a kiss,

Wenn kindisch lallend der Helden Lob von holden Lippen dir floss.
    When childish lispings of heroes' praise from sweetest lips flowed forth.

Dieser Augen strahlendes Paar das oft im Sturm mir geglänzt,
    Those gleaming radiant eyes that oft in storms on me shone,

Wenn Hoffnungssehnen das Herz mir sengte,
    When hopeless yearning my heart had wasted,

Nach Weltenwonne mein Wunsch verlangte, aus wild webendem Bangen.
    When world's delights all my wishes wakened, through wild-weaving heartache.

Sleep is in the orchestral background as he gives her a Last Embrace (No. 6, Ex. 7.16):

Ex. 7.16. No. 6, Last Embrace

Zum   *letz - ten Mal*   *letz' ich mich heut' mit des*   *Le - be - woh - les*   *letz - tem Kuss!*
For   one last time,   lured by their light, my⎯   lips shall give them love's last kiss!

Zum letzten Mal, letz' es mich heut',
    For one last time, lured by their light,

Mit des Lebewohles letztem Kuss!
    My lips shall give them love's last kiss!

Dem glücklicher'n Manne glänze sein Stern,
On mortal more blessed once more may they shine,

Dem unseligen Ew'gen muss es scheidend sich schliessen.
On me, hapless immortal, must they now forever close.

Then motive No. 7, Fate, appears, solemnly played by four trombones and a contrabass tuba. It takes only two chords to establish the ominous mood. Later it comes twice with a pregnant twist of harmony (Ex. 7.17):

Ex. 7.17. No. 7, Fate (two times)

Wotan clasps Brunhilde to him while an English horn sounds the doleful No. 8, Renunciation of Love. On its last notes the melancholy father utters the dire words: ". . . so kisses thy godhood from thee" (Ex. 7.18):

Ex. 7.18. No. 8, Renunciation of Love

Denn so kehrt der Gott sich dir ab,
For so turns the god now from thee,

So küsst er die Gottheit von dir!
So kisses thy godhood from thee!

That kiss transforms Brunhilde from a goddess to a mortal woman, and with it first the woodwinds, then the strings, flood in with the mystic chromatic harmonies of No. 9, Magic Sleep (Ex. 7.19):

Ex. 7.19. No. 9, Magic Sleep

Wotan bears the unconscious Brunhilde gently to a mossy mound while the orchestra ruminates on No. 1, Sleep, and No. 5, Fond Memories. He closes her helmet for a last time and covers her slumbering form with the great shield of the Valkyrie. Fate, No. 7, is heard again softly in the orchestra. Wotan breaks his revery, striding with solemn decision toward a large rock. As he moves, the trombones and tuba blast forth an energetic descending scale. This is motive No. 10, The Treaty, representing the laws and obligations under which Wotan governs (Ex. 7.20):

Ex. 7.20. No. 10, The Treaty

Loge hör'! Lausche hieher!
  Loki, hear! Listen here!

Wie zuerst ich dich fand, als feurige Gluth,
  As first I found thee, a glimmering flame,

Wie dann einst du mir schwandest, als schweifende Lohe,
  As from me thou didst vanish in wandering fire,

Wie ich dich band, bann' ich dich heut'!
  As once I bound thee, bound be thou now!

Herauf, wabernde Lohe, umlod're mir feurig den Fels!
  Appear, wavering fire, and wind thee in flames round the crag!

  Loge! Loge! Hieher!
    Loki! Loki! Appear!

He calls upon Loki, the god of fire, and in anticipation of Loki's appearance the strings surge upward. Wotan strikes the rock three times with his spear, and a column of fire is seen, growing steadily brighter.

Motive No. 2, Fire, reappears, with its crackle of harp and winds. As the flames lick out from the rock and encircle the sleeping Brunhilde, the music of No. 9, Magic Sleep, merges with No. 3, Fire, in the orchestra. To end, Wotan voices a solemn warning to cowards to shun the rock and its wondrous prize:

Wer meines Speeres Spitze fürchtet
  He who my spearpoint's sharpness fears

Durchschreite das Feuer nie!
  Shall ne'er cross this flaming fire!

As he sings, the orchestral background is interwoven of Nos. 1, Sleep, and 2, Fire, but Wotan's own words are sung prophetically to No. 3, Siegfried as Hero—a Siegfried still unnamed, still unborn. Wotan remains frozen and dejected, silently gripping his spear while the orchestra echoes No. 3, Siegfried as Hero, then projects a tapestry of Fire, Sleep, and Last Embrace, and finally, Fate, Fire, and Sleep.

Wagner was a disagreeable autocrat with occasionally shoddy morals and a mania for dominating whatever he touched—women, his friends, his environment, his art. Little eluded his absolute control, not even his audiences, to whom he allowed no lateness, no breaks for applause, scarcely a license to move or breathe. Still Wagner finds passionate admirers today. That he does so is in part the result of his tyranny. For there are unique satisfactions in abandoning oneself to the embrace of such an imagination, to an artistic totalitarianism that found something to fascinate everyone: the mythic stories, unforgettable characters, lofty poetic address, compelling vocalism, innovative harmonies, rich orchestral colors. Not least are the leitmotifs, so apt in their musical portraiture that they mark our minds even when we don't know they are doing so. Wagner's music dramas sway the emotions and dazzle the imagination like nothing else in the nineteenth century. To be sure, they have long arid patches. His audiences put up with over five hours in the theater, some of it spent fighting tedium during long narratives and conversations. But then the rewards flood in, the rich emotional persuaders such as Wotan's Farewell, to which even the duller stretches have contributed by rendering the lyricism more welcome. When Wagner turns up the high voltage of his imagination for those rapturous moments, the effects he achieves are among the finest in romantic art.

8 From Romantic to Modern (1890-1920)

Cubism. *Pablo Picasso,* Nude ► *(1910). Visual realism is broken down, the three-dimensional figure flattened almost to a single plane, its fleshy details reduced to curves, angles, "cubes."*

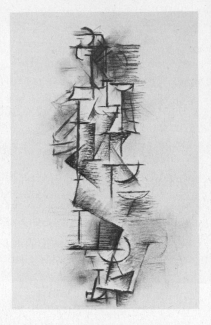

Impressionism. *Auguste Renoir,* By the Seashore *(1883). The precise outlines of objects (rocks, sea, the human figure) are softened, their details blurred in short brush strokes and gentle pastel colors.*

◄ *Edvard Munch,* The Scream *(1893). The Norwegian artist externalizes the terror of a nightmare shriek in this death's head figure. The swirls and long lines of sky and shore spread the echoes of the scream so that every corner of the picture seems to vibrate with the sound.*

Nonobjective Expressionism. *Wassily Kandinsky,* Improvisation 28 (?) *(1912). German Expressionist painters turned to nonobjective, nonrepresentational subjects around 1910-1912, at about the same time that Parisian painters were embracing cubism.*

From Romantic to Modern *(1890-1920)*

MUSIC	ARTS AND IDEAS	POLITICS AND SCIENCE
THE DISSOLUTION OF TONALITY	**SYMBOLISM, IMPRESSION-ISM, ART NOUVEAU, EXPRESSIONISM, FUTURISM, DADAISM**	**END OF THE OLD ORDER**

Debussy (1862-1918):
    Prelude to the Afternoon of a Faun (1894)
Stravinsky (1882-1971):
    The Rite of Spring (1913)
Schoenberg (1874-1951):
    Pierrot lunaire (1912)
Berg (1885-1935):
    Wozzeck (1914-1921)
Ives (1874-1954):
    The Unanswered Question (1908)
Elgar (1857-1934):
    "Enigma" Variations (1899)
Sibelius (1865-1957)
    The Swan of Tuonela (1893)
Ragtime, blues, and jazz (1890s through 1920s)
	Symbolist poetry by Mallarmé, Verlaine, and Rimbaud (1870s-1890s)
	Mallarmé, *The Afternoon of a Faun* (1876)
	Impressionist paintings by Monet Cézanne, Degas, Renoir, Pissarro, Whistler (1870s-1890s)
	Dramas by Ibsen and Strindberg (1860s-1890s)
	Van Gogh, *Self-Portrait with Severed Ear* (1889)
	Wilde, *Picture of Dorian Gray* (1891)
	Beardsley, black-and-white illustrations (1880s-1890s)
	Yeats, *Poems* (first collection, 1895)
	Bergson, *Matter and Memory* (1896); *Creative Evolution* (1907)
	Rilke, *The Book of Pictures* (1902-1906)
	"Die Brücke": Expressionist painters in Dresden (1905-1913: Kirchner, Heckel, Nolde, etc.)
	Cubist paintings by Picasso, Braque, Duchamp, etc. (from 1905)
	Marinetti, *Futurist Manifesto* (1909)
	German Expressionist abstractions by Kandinsky, Marc, Klee, Macke, Kokoschka, etc. (from 1911)
	Proust, *A la recherche du temps perdu* (from 1913)
	Kafka, *The Judgment; The Metamorphosis* (1913-1915)
	Dadaism (1916-1923): Arp and Duchamp
		Eiffel Tower (1889)
		Discovery of x-rays and radium (1895-1898)
		Marconi's wireless telegraphy (1896)
		Edward VII succeeds Queen Victoria (1901)
		First powered air flight (Wright brothers) (1903)
		Freud, *Psychopathology of Everyday Life* (1904)
		Einstein, *Special Theory of Relativity* (1905)
		World War I (1914-1918)
		Bolsheviks control Russia (1917)

When Wagner died in 1883, much of the vigor went out of romanticism. The long domination of music by that emotion-ridden esthetic had almost run its course. The even longer primacy of major-minor tonality, which began before 1700, was also rapidly approaching an end in classical art music. Wagner's final music drama, *Parsifal,* completed in 1882, was still decked out in full romantic and tonal regalia. But at some points in its buildup of chromaticism, the forces that were linking the melody and harmony to an overall governing tonic seemed to be losing their hold. There are passages in the Prelude to Act 3 of *Parsifal* where the chords move in a loose harmonic flux, from one chromatic chord to another, with little sense of being subordinated to a central tonic. Wagner arrived at this mature point in his musical language as a result of artistic necessity. The tonal idiom had exhausted much of its ability to say fresh and moving things, and with the same sure judgment that made him the pathfinder in the realm of tonal chromaticism, Wagner now groped for a new harmonic idiom to replenish the arsenal of musical effects. He himself never took the ultimate step of going beyond tonality, but during the generation that followed his death, avant-garde composers in Europe and America worked their way free of the old tonal constraints and began to cultivate new **post-tonal** idioms that were no longer linked to an organizing key or tonal center. Tonality had always been a selective, restrictive musical language. It imposed quite narrow limits on what was said and how it was said. Whole worlds of musical effects were unobtainable because they were foreign to the tonal style. Many chords were unusable because they were too dissonant; that is, their unorthodox combinations of pitches lessened and threatened the authority of the tonic. Yet tonality and its circumscribed roster of tolerable chords and progressions had no manifest basis in the physics of sound. It had no human basis either, no psychological or cultural mandate. Outside the Western world, tonality was viewed as an exotic system, an import whose expressive powers rarely seemed superior to the local musical system. Within Western culture itself, other systems of organizing pitches had come before tonality. Now other systems would follow.

As the nineteenth century turned into the twentieth, composers began reaching beyond the boundaries of tonality. Lead by Debussy and Stravinsky in France, by Schoenberg, Webern, and Berg in Austria and Germany, and by Ives in America, during the decades from 1890 to 1920 music entered a new phase of its history, one that in a broad sense carries over to today. Composers began to produce music that was based on selections and organizations of pitches other than the tonal ones. Many new idioms arose during those three decades of ferment and experimentation, and they do not easily boil down to a single description. Perhaps the term that best suits the musical era as a whole is *post-tonal.* That is to say, tonality's exclusive grasp on musical styles was broken, yet it remained a potent factor on the musical scene. The bulk of the past's acknowledged masterpieces were tonal pieces. The powers of emotional persuasion that resided in tonality still seemed formidable. Tonality shifted to the background during the post-tonal decades of the early twentieth century; however, by no means was it the distant background. Composers were constantly faced with its blandishments. Many composers simply kept working in traditional tonal idioms. Others reacted militantly, doing everything possible to fend off the old tradition and to avoid slipping back into tonal idioms. Most composers compromised in one way or another, mixing the old and the new as they endeavored to find some clearly personal style to represent the new times.

A. THE DISSOLUTION OF TONALITY IN FRANCE: "MUSICAL IMPRESSIONISM"

Claude Debussy

The transition from tonal to post-tonal idioms began sooner in France than in Germany and Austria. This was because French composers were less under the spell of Wagner. As a youth in Austria, Schoenberg was enthralled by Wagnerian tonal chromaticism and broke from it to produce an avowedly post-tonal or atonal work only in 1908 (see page 311). Debussy's *Prelude to the Afternoon of a Faun* opened the breach with tonality in France already in 1894. Debussy accomplished this with a suave, easy-to-take musical style, so deftly reshaping the old tonal romantic idiom that he aroused none of the antagonism that met the pioneering work of Schoenberg and Stravinsky (see page 305) later on. Claude Debussy (1862-1918) was a Parisian who was trained at the Paris Conservatory and stayed in Paris for his entire career. When he was eighteen he traveled briefly to Russia, where he worked as a household pianist for Tchaikovsky's aloof patroness, Mme. von Meck. While there he became acquainted with the music of Mussorgsky. At the age of twenty he was awarded the Prix de Rome. In 1888-89 he visited Wagner's artistic shrine at Bayreuth, where he was attracted, yet even more strongly repelled, by the heavily Teutonic atmosphere of the music dramas. Like all the French, Debussy still simmered after the defeat by the Germans in the war of 1870. His earlier music did not escape Wagnerian influence, but his ultimate judgment of Wagner was cool and correct: "a beautiful sunset that has been mistaken for a sunrise."

Many of Debussy's influences were found at home, and not all of them were in the realm of music. One strong influence was the literary movement of symbolism, whose poetic tissues were compounded of delicate imageries and subtle meanings. The symbolist poets, led by Stéphane Mallarmé (1842-1898) and Paul Verlaine (1844-1896), considered themselves heirs to the tradition of poetic fantasies of Edgar Allan Poe (1809-1849) and Charles Baudelaire (1821-1867). Their goal was not to make outright statements and objective descriptions but to be suggestive. "Suggestion . . . that's the ideal," Mallarmé observed. Debussy may also have found stimulation in the French painters' movement of **impressionism**, which aimed to put on canvas the fleeting effects of visual impressions, often captured in the evanescent light of out-of-doors. Claude Monet (1840-1926) and Pierre-Auguste Renoir (1841-1919) composed paintings out of Colorplate 30 touches of color that shimmer and coalesce when viewed from a distance. They preferred small brush strokes that deposited dabs of paint to broad slabs of solid color. Their techniques were not unlike those of the symbolist poets—again suggestion rather than statement.

An important influence on Debussy came from abroad. Some musicians from Southeast Asia demonstrated an exotic musical style at the Paris International Exposition of 1889. It was based on a scale of five pitches, a pentatonic scale that divided the octave into five nearly equal intervals. The novel Asian musical sounds prompted Debussy to try a comparable scale of his own. One that was obtainable on Western instruments—which the Asian scale was not—was a scale of six pitches, dividing the octave into six equal intervals. There are two such scales on Western keyboards, each making use of six of the twelve pitches. They are called **whole-tone scales** because their pitches are whole tones or whole steps apart (Ex. 8.1). The resulting

Ex. 8.1. The Whole-Tone Scales

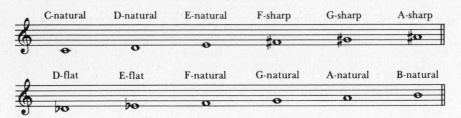

musical sounds, while different from the Asians', were nonetheless exotic and provocative. Debussy's whole-tone scale was no longer tonal, yet he did not simply abandon tonality. He mixed the new whole-tone melodies and harmonies with aspects of tonal chromaticism. Out of that mixture he fashioned the first significant departures from major-minor tonality. Debussy's involvement with exotic scales came at roughly the same time that the impressionist painters were fascinated with Japanese graphics and Paul Gauguin was filling canvases with Tahitian subjects.

The whole-tone scale has a further parallel with impressionist painting and symbolist poetry. The six pitches of the whole-tone scale have no tonic. That is, the six whole-step intervals are all the same size, and their equal-size intervals rule out any built-in focus upon one of the pitches, any preference that would distinguish one among them as a tonic. The toniceless nature of the whole-tone scale gives the resulting music an unfocused quality; its tonal vagueness is not unlike the gentle suggestiveness of the poems and the hazy irridescence of the paintings.

Debussy's *Prelude to the Afternoon of a Faun* (1894) is the first important example of "musical impressionism." It represents in sound something of the quality of impressionist paintings. But its immediate inspiration is literary. Stéphane Mallarmé's pastoral fantasy, *The Afternoon of a Faun* (1876), is the chief poetic monument of the symbolist movement. It is the revery of a faun of classical myth, a lustful meadow sprite with the body of a human male but the extremities (horns, ears, tail, and legs) of a goat. In ancient poetry fauns chased nymphs, and Mallarmé's faun has been doing just that. Or perhaps—and Mallarmé purposely leaves this vague—with his mind dulled by wine on a drowsy Sicilian summer afternoon, this faun has only dreamed of chasing nymphs. The poem's celebrated beginning runs, "Ces nymphes, je les veux perpétuer" ("These nymphs, how I'd love them always by me . . . their fleshy lightness so bright that it lingers in this air, heavy with stuffy dozings . . ."). The faun's erotic rhapsodizing goes on to thoughts of wine and of playing on the

△
Debussy: *Prelude to the Afternoon of a Faun* (Side 9, Band 3)

Ker Xavier Roussel, Faun and Nymphs *(1890s). French impressionist painters produced nature scenes inspired by Mallarmé's and Debussy's* Afternoon of a Faun, *using the technique of small dabs of color that coalesce when viewed from a distance.*

pipes, then back to the nymphs. It is a potpourri of sensations and fantasies, floating between dream and reality. Debussy's music was not intended to be a precise rendering of the nebulous litarary content of the poem but as a free evocation of the poetic atmosphere. To match the delicate vapors of Mallarmé, Debussy creates a loose fabric made up of tiny fragments of melody, clusters of piquant harmony, and dabs of orchestral color. Debussy rejected the standard tonal technique of stating themes and then purposefully developing them. He thought of it as being too heavy-handed and Germanic. His rhetoric is one of little gasps, not of rounded sentences. Over a dozen musical fragments dart in and out of the texture: melodic motives consisting of just a few notes, splashes of instrumental timbre. Pregnant ambiguities drift in, then trail away without leaving a solid residue. It is like the impressionists' brushes depositing their touches of light and color, and it results in something like the same luminescent shimmer.

The opening flute solo represents the faun's pipes. Playing in its velvety middle register, the flute glides downward through a segment of the whole-tone scale (C-sharp-B-A-G) that is filled with passing half-steps (Ex. 8.2). Then a splash of harp glissando and a touch of French horn cast a voluptuous spell (Ex. 8.3). The relaxed rhythms

Ex. 8.2. *Afternoon of a Faun,* **Measures 1-4, Debussy**

Ex. 8.3.

move across the bar lines in a pulseless float that suggests the dreamy afternoon. Motives appear and are quickly liquidated. There is a vagueness that comes from having no clear tonal center. The dynamics remain subdued, rarely rising above a mezzo forte. Debussy scores the *Prelude* for a large orchestra, but his use of instruments is sparing, focused on individual timbres, not on massive doublings. Ponderous and brassy effects are gone. The orchestra has no tuba or kettledrums, not even trumpets or trombones. The opening flute solo keeps returning, each time a bit differently. In measures 32-33 the clarinet and flute play an undiluted whole-tone scale (Ex. 8.4). Then an oboe introduces an animated new material (Ex. 8.5).

Ex. 8.4.

Ex. 8.5.

At length the big central section begins. Debussy's *Prelude* has an overall form of A-B-A′; that is, it has a form like the *Tristan* Prelude. When the sustained lyric thrust takes over in Debussy's central section, it is clear that Wagner's spirit is still exercising its claim (Ex. 8.6).

Ex. 8.6.

Wagner was ostensibly his bête noire, yet the debt is never clearer than in this noble passage where Debussy luxuriates for some moments in the grand manner of late romantic melody, indulging in a majestic line that throbs upward to an incandescent climax, then subsides with Wagnerian breadth. If we think about it, there is something else Wagnerian. Even the fabric of small motives out of which Debussy's opening section is built has its forerunner in the Wagnerian continuity of leitmotifs.

At last the opening flute solo returns (A′) and is put through subtle transformations. A long epilogue is punctuated by almost inaudible touches of winds, strings, and cymbals. In the end, everything dissolves into thin air—like the faun's revery. When Mallarmé heard the work he expressed approval: "The music extends the emotion of my poem . . . evokes the scene more vividly than a painter's colors." Debussy, to be sure, did not follow the poem in a literal way. But in one hidden gesture he paid a pointed homage to the poem. Mallarmé's work consists of 110 precisely chiseled alexandrine (12-syllable) verses. To these Debussy matched a tone poem of 110 finely crafted measures.

Debussy continued to cultivate this liquid, suggestive style in three additional tone poems, the Nocturnes for Orchestra (*Clouds, Festivals,* and *Sirens,* 1899); in the opera *Pelléas et Mélisande* (1902); in the long orchestral tone poem *La Mer* (*The Sea,* 1905); and in the two series of piano miniatures that he called Préludes and Etudes. Colorplate 31 Over the years his style turned drier, losing some of its "impressionist" haze and becoming less reliant on the vestiges of tonal harmony. In the ballet *Jeux* (*Games*) of 1912, and in passages of his three late sonatas of 1915-17, Debussy's musical style attained a crispness that is a musical counterpart to the French painters' movement of postimpressionism, which made an appearance in works by Cézanne, Matisse, and others exhibited during 1910-12. Debussy remained influential throughout his career, not only as a composer but also as an occasionally acid-penned music critic. His distaste for Germanic music extended beyond Wagner to a lack of enthusiasm even for Beethoven and Bach. Always a fierce nationalist, he styled himself in later years "Claude Debussy, French Musician." He loved France—the walks along the Parisian boulevards, the stimulations of the artists' cafés. Sadly, when he died in 1918, the German artillery still rumbled outside his favorite city.

B. POST-TONALITY IN PARIS

During the first two decades of this century, French music was under the twin stars of the aging Debussy and the rising Stravinsky (1882-1971). Debussy's gentle erosion of the edifice of tonality, which began in the 1890s, became a frontal assault with Igor Stravinsky, a pre-World War I émigré from czarist Russia, whose *The Rite of Spring* (*Le Sacre du Printemps*) proclaimed its vigorous new posttonal idiom at Paris in 1913. Stravinsky was the son of a bass singer at the Imperial Opera in St. Petersburg. He seemed headed for a safe career as a government lawyer. But in 1902 he showed some early compositions to the aging master Rimsky-Korsakov and was presently taken on as a student. Stravinsky's first successes were two ballets based on colorful Russian fairy-tale subjects. *The Firebird* (1910) and *Petrushka* (1911) were composed for the Russian Ballet Company (Ballet Russe de Paris) of the famous impresario Sergei Diaghilev. They were romantic creations, still in the picturesque, nationalist vein of Mussorgsky's *Pictures at an Exposition* or Rimsky-Korsakov's own popular *Scheherezade.* They also owed something to the harmonic innovations of Debussy. But certain aspects of Stravinsky's uninhibited rhythms, post-tonal harmony, and exotic Russianism were distinctly his own. The decisive rupture with the tonal past came with his next ballet, *The Rite of Spring,* which was also composed for Diaghilev. Its first performance in May 1913 set off a minor riot as members of the Parisian audience, jarred from their complacency by the violence of Stravinsky's willful rhythms and unexpected dissonances, reacted violently. The comfortable assurances of tonality were gone. Also gone was the traditional regularity of meter. In its place was a new rhythmic idiom that capitalized on irregular meters and unpredictable, nervously alive accentual patterns. Stravinsky's *The Rite of Spring* proclaimed rhythm as a vitally enriched factor in twentieth-century music.

The Rite of Spring is about the fertility rites of a primitive tribe in pagan Russia. Part I of its hodgepodge of cultural anthropology represents the gathering of the tribe to welcome the new spring; part II describes the ritual of human sacrifice:

Part I: The Fertility of the Earth

a. Introduction
b. Dance of the Adolescents
c. Ritual of Abduction
d. Round Dances of Spring
e. Games of the Rival Tribes
f. Procession of the Sage
g. Adoration of the Earth: Dance of the Earth

Part II: The Sacrifice

a. Introduction
b. Mysterious Circles of the Adolescents
c. Glorification of the Chosen Maiden
d. Evocation of the Ancestors
e. Ritual Activity of the Ancestors
f. Sacrificial Dance of the Chosen Maiden

Ia. Introduction (3 minutes). The work begins with a famous bassoon solo that is reminiscent of the opening flute solo in Debussy's *Afternoon of a Faun.* But instead of Debussy's instant voluptu-

Δ
Stravinsky: "Introduction," "Dance of the Adolescents," and "Ritual of Abduction" from *The Rite of Spring* (Side 10, Band 1)

ousness, Stravinsky's awkward melodic line and the uncanny sound of his bassoon, which is forced well above its normal register, produce an effect that is instantly grotesque (Ex. 8.7). Other melodic

Ex. 8.7. Opening Bassoon Solo from *The Rite of Spring*, Stravinsky

lines appear—the French horn, clarinet, and English horn—with their eccentric melodic contours joining to form a texture that is completely without a tonal center. Stravinsky gives no "program" for this Introduction, but its fizzles, pops, and gurgles seem to describe the awakening of nature as the frozen mud melts and the sap bubbles up. Stravinsky's musical fabric is not unlike Debussy's in its loose weave of disconnected fragments of melody, rhythm, and tone color. But the glow of Debussy's silken harmony is gone. More instruments are added to the pulsating mass. Then for a shrill instant the naked bassoon reappears. It is Stravinsky's only gesture of formal "return." A soft pizzicato in the violins introduces the rhythmic motive that will dominate the next section (Ex. 8.8).

Ex. 8.8. Opening Rhythmic Motive (Violin Pizzicato) of "Dance of the Adolescents" from *The Rite of Spring*, Stravinsky

Ib. Dance of the Adolescents (3 minutes, 10 seconds). Here Stravinsky unleashes the full force of his savage irregular rhythms. The dance opens with a passage of startling vigor: thirty-two loud, fast chords in a row, identical in harmony, enough to fill eight measures of $\frac{2}{4}$ time with four chords apiece. But Stravinsky divides those chords irregularly, always contradicting the regular meter. On the old 4 + 4 + 4 + 4, etc., he imposes a pattern of irregular accents so powerful that each irregular accent seems to begin a new measure of its own. The result is a flow of surprises, where no two measures in a row have the same number of beats:

>	>	>	>	>	>	>	>
1 2 3 4	1 2 3 4 5	1 2	1 2 3 4 5 6	1 2 3	1 2 3 4	1 2 3 4 5	1 2 3

The excitement is compounded if the listener tries to anticipate where the next accent will come. Stravinsky stayed with this idiom of rhythmic surprise throughout his later years, even when his style in other respects had changed. Something else is remarkable about his thirty-two loud, fast chords. They sound, not like the chords of some lucid harmony, but rather like opaque, chordal grunts. That is because they are a combination of two quite different and incompatible tonal chords: an E major chord in the low strings, against an E-flat major chord in the upper strings (Ex. 8.9). Their tonal clash

Ex. 8.9. Polytonal Chord (32 Times) from *The Rite of Spring,* **Stravinsky**

Upper chord:
E-flat major

Eb
Db
Bb
G

Lower chord:
E major

E
B
G#
E

produces a jarring seven-pitch result, unthinkably dissonant by nineteenth-century tonal standards but a respectable and provocative effect for the post-tonal twentieth century. Such combinations of two tonal keys are called bitonal. **Bitonality** and **polytonality**, simultaneously using harmonic materials from two or more of the old tonal keys, would remain prominent among the resources of post-tonal harmony. Stravinsky's "Dance of the Adolescents" is peppered with such harmonic touches along with unpredictable accents and repetitions of its opening rhythmic cell (Ex. 8.8). Snappy bits of folk melody keep appearing. They are generally tonal, and add a mellow patina to the otherwise starkly modern sound.

Ic. Ritual of Abduction (1½ minutes). This is the first big climax in *The Rite of Spring.* The tempo shifts to presto and the music takes off in rhythmic fireworks and splashes of vaulting color. Where the "Introduction" (Ia) displays the century's new freedom of melody and harmony, and the "Dance of the Adolescents" (Ib) the new rhythmic freedom, the "Ritual of Abduction" (Ic) puts those novelties together with supercharged effect.

Other Prewar Innovators

Original as *The Rite of Spring* was, it did not come out of a vacuum. Most of its elements were in the air in prewar Paris. Its large orchestra was a holdover from romanticism. Its nervous rhythms and post-tonal harmonies were anticipated to some extent in Stravinsky's own *Firebird* and *Petrushka* of 1909-1911, even in Mussorgsky's works of the 1870s. Debussy's turn from tonal to post-tonal harmony, which began in *Afternoon of a Faun* (1894), was continued in the ballet *Jeux,* which was given its premiere by Diaghilev's Ballet Russe in 1912, just months before Stravinsky's *The Rite of Spring.* By that time, even Debussy's harmonies had discarded much of their tonal basis, though he remained less aggressive in his modernism and never sought Stravinsky's shocking effects. Jean Cocteau summed up the difference: "After the silk brush came the axe." *The Rite of Spring* distressed the complacent admirers of the tonal past, but its vitality changed the public's way of thinking. Eventually those who came to scoff stayed to worship.

Other young composers were moving in Stravinsky's direction. In Hungary, Béla Bartók (1881-1945) produced his intense, percussive Allegro Barbaro for Piano in 1911, two years before *The Rite of Spring.* The Russian Sergei Prokofiev (1891-1953) cultivated a similar "primitivist" vein in his *Scythian Suite* of 1914, drawing inspiration again from pagan Russia. The English composer Gustav Holst (1874-1934) produced "Mars," the spectacular opening movement of his suite, *The Planets* (1914-16). Alexander Scriabin (1872-1915), a Russian émigré who spent most of his career in the Parisian orbit, wrote visionary works that were stylistic outgrowths of Liszt and Mussorgsky and relied increasingly on esoteric post-tonal harmonies. Scriabin's last orchestral works are marked by a personal brand of pantheistic mysticism. They include *The Divine Poem* (1905), *Poem of Ecstasy* (1908), and *Prometheus: The Poem of Fire* (1910). Scriabin based *Prometheus* on a post-tonal "mystic chord" that contains the eighth through fourteenth pitches of the harmonic series (Ex. 8.10). (On the harmonic series, see Appendix B.7.) The work also

Marcel Duchamp, Nude Descending a Staircase, No. 2 *(1912). [A] famous cubist painting, remarkable for representing continuous motion through a succession [of] overlapping figures.*

Ex. 8.10. The "Mystic Chord" (Intervals of a Fourth) from *Prometheus,* Scriabin

Pitch:	C	F♯	B♭	E	A	D	(G)
Harmonic series (based on C):	8	11	14	10	13	9	(12)

calls for a "color keyboard" that projects colors on a screen while the music is played. Scriabin matched the colors of the visible spectrum to the pitches of the circle of fifths: C - red, G - orange, D - yellow, A - green, E - light blue, etc. Other pitches are assigned hues such as purple, gray, and brown.

Giacomo Balla, Dynamism of a Dog on a Leash *(1912). An Italian Futurist work, showing speed and motion. It was painted in the same year as Duchamp's* Nude Descending a Staircase, *a year before Stravinsky's* The Rite of Spring.

The new expressive freedom and the expansion of post-tonal idioms in music were part of a groundswell movement in all the European arts that saw earlier conventions being overthrown and new techniques tried out. In 1905 the painters Braque and Picasso began fragmenting visible reality into small geometrical shapes, breaking down the images of life into "cubes." The movement of *cubism* arose in France at the same time as the Brücke school of the painters Kirchner and Nolde in Germany turned from depicting recognizable images of life toward the representation of inner emotional states (see page 314). By 1911, when Kandinsky and the "Blue Rider" group in Germany were cultivating their new, "nonobjective" ideal of graphic expression, the cubists' own transformations had become so abstract that traces of the representational world were practically gone. In 1909 some energetic Italians, Marinetti, Carrá, and Boccioni, launched the **futurist** movement in art. Belligerently rejecting sentiment and romanticism, they exalted the beauty of modern efficiency, speed, aggressiveness, and the dynamism of "the machine."

The most anarchistic of the avant-garde cultural ideologies was **dadaism**, the invention of a group that in 1916 clustered about the eccentric Rumanian-French poet Tristan Tzara. The dadaists felt that traditional values in art and morality were rendered inoperative by the monstrosity of the Great War. They responded with a brand of artistic nihilism for which they chose the name *dada*, supposedly by picking it at random from a dictionary. It was a French babytalk word for a hobbyhorse. The group, including the important artist Jean Arp, lived in Switzerland during the war and produced antiwar protests that featured chance effects and nonsense. It was a dadaist idea for Marcel Duchamp to "improve" on Leonardo da Vinci's *Mona Lisa* by adding a mustache and goatee to a copy of the painting. The dadaist gatherings also featured novel sorts of "noise-music" and the recitation of poems composed of meaningless syllables or spoken simultaneously in several languages.

Dada had an important musical forerunner in the eccentric French composer Eric Satie (1866-1925). Satie was a gifted maverick who in the 1890s began producing piano miniatures with ironic, mystifying titles. They are filled with dry, sometimes perversely antitonal harmonies. His "Vexations" is a thorny patch of melody and harmony that takes less than a minute to play, but he suggests that he really wants it played 840 times in a row. It has been played that way, taking exhausted pianists anywhere from twelve to nineteen hours. Some of Satie's early pieces have hints of Eastern mysticism. Among *Gymnopédies* (1888, for instance, No. 3), *Gnossiennes* (1890), *Cold Pieces* (1907), and *Three Pieces in the Shape of a Pear* (1903), there are works with a cool, almost motionless detachment. Satie provided literary texts to be read with certain works, for example, his *Dessicated Embryos* (1913). His passion for clarity and disdain for stuffiness impressed Debussy, who orchestrated some of his early works. Satie also influenced composers after World War I, including Ravel, Milhaud, and Poulenc. Dada and its offshoots went on until about 1923, by which time the immediate emotional debris of the Great War was cleared away and composers were looking for more positive ideologies. Yet dada would find echoes in the chance, or "indeterminate," music that followed in the aftermath of World War II.

C. THE DISSOLUTION OF TONALITY IN GERMANY

Wagner's immediate heirs were Bruckner, Mahler, and Richard Strauss, none of whom came out sufficiently from under the enormous Wagnerian shadow to break radically with the tonal past. Bruckner, born in 1824, was too old. Mahler, dying prematurely in 1911, never quite propelled his fantasies beyond the tonal realm. Strauss tested the post-tonal waters briefly with *Salome* (1905) and *Electra* (1909), then retreated to firmer shores with *Der Rosenkavalier* (1911). The decisive changes were bound to come from younger composers. In Germany they came from Schoenberg, Webern, and Berg, all of whom reached artistic maturity during the first decade of the twentieth century.

Arnold Schoenberg

Arnold Schoenberg (1874-1951) grew up in Vienna at a time when that city's musical life was dominated by the eminences of Brahms and Mahler. Schoenberg was practically self-taught but, possessed of an extraordinary personal force and a keen musical intelligence, he began his professional career by turning himself into the last great technician of the German romantic style. His early tone poem *Trans-*

figured Night (1899) and portions of his *Gurre-Lieder* (begun in 1900) are convincing late-tonal effusions, still drenched in Wagnerian chromaticism. In 1901 Schoenberg became a teacher of music theory at Berlin, and in 1911 he published an authoritative textbook on tonal harmony. But during that same decade, he and a handful of disciples were gravitating toward a new musical idiom and a new musical esthetic to replace the outworn formulas of tonal romanticism. Schoenberg's path led with astonishing directness from the lush tonal language of 1900 to a crisp post-tonal, or atonal, language in 1908, and then on to a wholly novel manner of composing with pitches in 1912. The term *atonal* is used to describe the post-tonal music of Schoenberg and his Austrian disciples during the first quarter of this century. *Atonality* is Schoenberg's dialect of post-tonality. The Austrians, even more than their French and Russian contemporaries, were militant in their rejection of tonality. Many of the old harmonic trappings were already gone in Schoenberg's Chamber Symphony, Op. 9, of 1906. Then, in the last movement of his Second String Quartet (1908), he abandoned all pretense of having a key signature and produced a first avowedly atonal work.

The first masterpiece in the new style was Schoenberg's *Pierrot lunaire* (*Moon-Crazed Peter*) of 1912. This was a setting for solo voice and chamber instruments of twenty-one poems by the Belgian, Albert Giraud, a follower of the symbolist poet Mallarmé. Giraud's provocative verses might easily have attracted Debussy or Ravel. They are a series of "moon-crazed" ("lunatic") fantasies, centered on the familiar Pierrot of the comic pantomimes and puppet shows— the broken-hearted clown, caught between tears and laughter. That clown-figure, reflecting the decadent world view of the turn of the century, was perpetuated for recent times by the mimic eloquence of Charlie Chaplin. A few of Giraud's titles convey the atmosphere of his poetry: "Moondrunk" (No. 1), "Columbine" (No. 2), "Chopin Waltz" (No. 5), "The Ailing Moon" (No. 7), "Gallows Song" (No. 12), "Beheading" (No. 13), "Olden Fragrance" (No. 21). It is a bit like Schumann's *Carnaval* gone awry. Schoenberg set to music a German adaptation of Giraud's French verse. But later he sanctioned a performance in French, and an English translation is sometimes heard. Each poem becomes a chamber-music miniature, lasting only a minute or two. For Schoenberg, abandoning the romantic esthetic also meant abandoning the opulence of Wagner's or Mahler's orchestration and the vastness of late-romantic formal conceptions. Like most works of this first Viennese "atonal" decade, the pieces in *Pierrot lunaire* are short, frugal transparencies where every pitch can be heard and every nuance of tone color makes its effect. Schoenberg uses the soprano voice and piano for each poem but changes the other instruments from poem to poem. He ensures clarity by never

Pierrot lunaire. *An illustration (1893) for the German poetic translation on which Schoenberg's music was based.*

having more than four additional instruments, chosen from among a piccolo, flute, clarinet, bass clarinet, violin, viola, and cello. The soprano intones Giraud's verse in a special kind of recitative devised by Schoenberg, which he calls **Sprechstimme**, or speech music. It is an exaggerated, rhetorical delivery of the text, something like traditional recitative but with the fullness of the musical pitches pressed out. The score shows the soprano's pitches with little Xs through their tails, informing the singer that they are basically to be recited, not sung. Instead of stable, rounded tones, there are scoops, whines, sweeps, and an array of vocal colors that are by turns soft, hard-edged, or raspy. Schoenberg remarked, "It must not be reminiscent of song."

"Moondrunk" (No. 1) is scored for vocal soloist and piano plus a solo flute, violin, and cello. It portrays the distracted Pierrot gazing anxiously at the moon. After the music is heard a few times the

Δ
Schoenberg: "Moondrunk" (No. 1) from *Pierrot lunaire* (Side 10, Band 2)

"MOONDRUNK" (NO. 1, PIERROT LUNAIRE)

(1) The wine that one drinks through the eyes
 Den Wein, den man mit Augen trinkt

(2) Pours nightly from the moon in waves,
 Giesst nachts der Mond in Wogen nieder,

(3) A springlike gush that overflows
 Und eine Springflut überschwemmt

(4) The still horizon.
 Den stillen Horizont.

(5) Desires, tremulous and sweet,
 Gelüste, schauerlich und süss,

(6) Swim, numberless, through the deluge
 Durchschwimmen ohne Zahl die Fluten

(7) Of wine that one drinks through the eyes
 Den Wein, den man mit Augen trinkt,

(8) Poured nightly from the moon in waves.
 Giesst nachts der Mond in Wogen nieder.

(9) The poet, driv'n by awesome visions,
 Der Dichter, den die Andacht treibt,

(10) Enraptured by the sacred draught,
 Berauscht sich an dem heil'gen Tranke,

(11) Ecstatically toward heaven turns
 Den Himmel wendet er verzückt

(12) His head, and giddily sucks and slurps
 Das Haupt, und taumelnd saugt und schlürft er

(13) The wine that one drinks through the eyes.
 Den Wein, den man mit Augen trinkt.

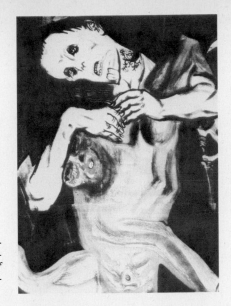

A poster of 1909 by the Viennese expressionist artist Oskar Kokoschka. Expressionists cultivated distortions of visual reality before turning to non-objective subjects ca. 1910.

novelty of the *Sprechstimme* delivery wears off and Schoenberg's web of sounds can be assessed on its own terms. All the intensity of Mahler is here, but the sentimentality is gone, leaving the emotions more stark. Something else is gone. Within the lucid fabric of chamber sonorities, there is no favored pitch, no tonic, no organizing key. No single pitch asserts itself over the others. The old focus on the tonic as home is replaced by a harmonic flux where all twelve chromatic pitches contribute more or less equally. Schoenberg has slipped from the tonal chromaticism of the late romantics, with its tenuous focus on one pitch among the twelve, to an atonal chromaticism where those same twelve pitches are used, but with the focus so distributed and diffused that none of them emerges as the organizing tonic.

Schoenberg's dissolution of tonality and his espousal of atonality during the first years of this century opened the way for vast new resources of harmony. In the idioms of tonality, the allowable dissonance of chords was held within narrow limits. Now the old conception of consonance and dissonance was overthrown. Dissonance was "emancipated" (in Schoenberg's word) from the obligation to resolve in an approaching tonal consonance. A whole new vocabulary of chords appeared, made up of pitches that were not previously combinable. And with the new resources of harmony came new wealths of musical and psychological effects. Looking back at this turn toward Germanic atonality, one can see Wagner headed that way in 1880. By the first decade of the twentieth century, tonality had used up so much of its remaining effectiveness that Schoenberg's path was a logical next step for a progressive musician to take.

The same decade that saw the dissolution of tonality by Schoenberg witnessed similar changes in the other Germanic arts. The movement called **expressionism** was born of certain painters' desire to give visual substance to inner emotional states. Artists shifted from realistic representations of the external world to new sorts of representation, based on subject matter they discovered within themselves. Impelled by "inner force" and "inner necessity," they drew their materials from the deepest layers of personal experience. They plumbed the subconscious and the unconscious and treated what they found with unprecedented frankness. The expressionist movement had its beginnings in 1905 at Dresden and Berlin with a group calling itself "The Bridge" (*"Die Brücke"*). They took inspiration from the last powerful canvases of Vincent van Gogh, which were painted during his final months of demented activity before his death in 1890. Among its members were Ernst Ludwig Kirchner and Emil Nolde. Expressionism entered a new phase in 1911 with the Munich group calling itself "The Blue Rider" (*"Blaue Reiter"*), led by Wassily Kandinsky (1866-1944) and Franz Marc (1880-1916). Schoenberg himself was a member of this group, contributing essays   Colorplate 32
to its journal and paintings to its exhibitions. Kandinsky observed that Schoenberg could have been a success as an artist as well as in music. The world just then seemed primed for breakthroughs. Einstein and Freud were shattering the faith in physical and psychological "reality." The rumblings of international conflict were threatening the durability of the social order. The response of the German artists was more drastic than that of their French and Italian colleagues (see page 309). They gave up depicting the external, visible world and focused instead on their inner spiritual visions. They no longer dealt in portraits of people, in recognizable objects, in landscapes drawn true to nature. Now their images were intuitively conceived, their subject matter was inner-derived and expressionistic, abstract and nonobjective. The titles of paintings became abstract; for example, "Composition" and "Improvisation"—names the artists borrowed from the realm of music. Kandinsky's "abstract expressionism" evolved between 1910 and 1914. Its turn from representational subjects to the evocation of inner emotional states corresponds remarkably with Schoenberg's rejection of conventional tonality and adoption of the new atonal idiom.

D. GERMAN ATONAL OPERA

Alban Berg

Two gifted disciples followed Schoenberg into the uncharted realm of atonality. Anton von Webern (1883-1945) was a specialist in chamber miniatures, for example, his pithy Five Movements for String Quartet of 1909. Along with Schoenberg, Webern showed that brief pieces of atonal music lasting only a minute or two could match the intensity and varied expression of tonal works lasting much longer. Alban Berg (1885-1935) became Schoenberg's pupil in 1904. He produced the most tangible success of German musical expressionism with his atonal opera *Wozzeck,* composed between 1914 and 1921. In *Wozzeck,* Berg brought the ugly underside of life to the musical stage with a force that still shocks us today. Based on a drama by the early romantic playwright Georg Büchner (1813-1837), the opera portrays a miserable common soldier, Wozzeck, who has been hopelessly depraved by the oppressive social order and is ultimately destroyed. The three acts trace his decline from depressive incoherence to violence—to the murder of his mistress and his suicide. Büchner's *Wozzeck* was an ideal vehicle for an expressionist composer seeking to give artistic shape to the horrors of contemporary experience. Berg's indictment of social injustice and probing of psychological trauma held up a mirror to the torment of World War I and the aftermath of the German defeat.

Berg's music is uncompromisingly atonal. No tuneful arias, no choruses with old-style lyricism soften the impact of the grisly drama. Some traces of tonality appear, but with a sure instinct, Berg turns the old order upside down, relegating tonality to unreal, mocking situations. It is used for the distorted barroom waltzes and polkas that filter through Wozzeck's half-crazed mind. It is used for the make-believe world of children's play and for the parody of middle-class values. When the impoverished Wozzeck turns over his meager pay to his mistress Marie for the support of their two-year-old son,

George Grosz, "Fit for Active Service" (1916-1917). A World War I cartoon with a current-events background to Berg's Woz-zeck. There was undisguised hatred within Germany for the arrogant Prussian officers and cynical doctors who fed their military machines with human fodder. "K.V." stands for Kriegsverwendungfähig, or "fit for war service."

the orchestra sustains a pure C major chord for eight pianissimo measures. Berg's sarcastic explanation was that this most commonplace of tonal chords symbolized better than anything else the commonplace nature of money.

In the end, Wozzeck is driven wild by Marie's infidelities and he cuts her throat. Act 3, Scene 4 finds him returning at night to the pond where he left her body, in search of the knife. Finding it, he throws it farther, but still not far enough. Desperately he wades deeper to throw it out again and wash off the blood that has spattered him. A blood-red moon rises and the water itself seems to turn to blood as he continues on and drowns. Two gentlemanly characters come strolling by. They are the sadistic Captain of Wozzeck's troop, whose persecutions have helped reduce Wozzeck to this strait, and the psychopathic Doctor whom Wozzeck has served as a guinea pig, subsisting on a diet of beans while the Doctor fantasized about a glorious reputation to be gained from such medical experiments. They overhear the agonies of drowning. "Come away, Doctor," the Captain advises, "that is not good to hear." Berg constructed all the music for this scene from a selection of six pitches that he carefully chose so there would not be any lingering reminders of tonality (Ex. 8.11). The six pitches are B-flat, C-sharp, E-natural, G-sharp, E-flat, and F-natural. They are combined into atonal melodies and harmonies, given constantly different rhythmic shapes, and transposed to different pitch levels. They are even sounded in inversion—upside down.

Ex. 8.11. The "Six Pitches" from Act 3, Scene 4, *Wozzeck,* **Berg**

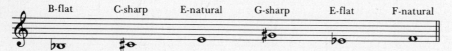

Following the death of Wozzeck, a long orchestral interlude fills the change of scene. At this single point in the opera Berg reverts to an emotionally committed use of tonality. This "invention on a tonality," as he calls it, is cast in the rich chromatic idiom of Mahler. It is a deeply felt commentary on the tragedy, communicating an overwhelming compassion, a balm for the tragic bruises.

WOZZECK, ACT 3, SCENE 4

Wozzeck: Das Messer? Wo ist das Messer?
    The knife! Where's the knife?

    Ich hab's dagelassen. Näher, noch näher.
    I left it somewhere. Where? Where?

Mir graut's da regt sich was. Still! Alles still und tot.
Oh ghastly, something moved there. Still! All still and dead.

Mörder! Mörder! Ha! Da ruft's. Nein, ich selbst.
Murder! Murder! Ha! They're calling. No, it was me.

Marie! Marie! Was hast Du fur eine rote Schnur um den Hals?
Marie! Marie! What's the red ribbon around your neck?

Hast Dir das rote Halsband verdient,
Did you get that red necklace,.

wie die Ohrringlein, mit Deiner Sünde!
like the earrings, by whoring?

Was hängen Dir die schwarzen Haare so wild?
Why does your black hair hang so wild?

Mörder! Mörder! Sie werden nach mir suchen.
Murder! Murder! They'll be looking for me.

Das Messer verrät mich!
The knife will give me away!

Da, da ist's. So! Da hinunter.
There, there it is. There, underneath.

Es taucht ins dunkle Wasser wie ein Stein.
It sinks through the dark water like a stone.

Aber der Mond verrat mich, der Mond ist blutig.
Now the moon betrays me, the moon is bloody.

Will denn die ganze Welt es ausplaudern?
Is the whole world watching?

Das Messer, es liegt zu weit vorn,
The knife, it's in too close.

sie finden's beim Baden oder wenn sie nach Muscheln tauchen.
They'll find it when they're swimming or musseling.

Ich find's nicht. Aber ich muss mich waschen.
I've lost it. I've got to wash off.

Ich bin blutig. Da ein Fleck und noch einer.
There's a stain, here's another.

Weh! Weh! Ich wasche mich mit Blut,
Oh! Oh! I'm washing with blood.

das Wasser ist Blut . . . Blut . . . [Drowns]
The water is blood . . . blood . . .

Captain: *Halt!*
Hold on!

Doctor: *Hören Sie? Dort!*
D'ya hear there?

Captain: *Jesus! Das war ein Ton.*
Jesus, what a sound.

Doctor: *Ja, dort!*
Yes, there.

Captain: *Es ist das Wasser im Teich. Das Wasser ruft.*
It's the water in the pond. It's the water calling.

Es ist schon lange Niemand ertrunken.
It's long since anyone drowned.

Kommen Sie, Doktor! Es ist nicht gut zu hören.
Come away, Doctor. That is not good to hear.

Doctor:	*Das stöhnt als stürbe ein Mensch. Da ertrinkt Jemand!*
	It's a groan, like a man dying. Someone's drowning!
Captain:	*Unheimlich! Der Mond rot, und die Nebel grau.*
	Awful! The moon red, the fog gray.
	Hören Sie? Jetzt wieder das Ächzen.
	Do you hear? There's the groaning again.
Doctor:	*Stiller, jetzt ganz still.*
	Quieter. Now all still.
Captain:	*Kommen Sie! Kommen Sie schnell!*
	Come away, come away quickly.

Orchestral Interlude

The final scene of Wozzeck (Act 3, Scene 5) may be the most poignant in any opera. The setting is outside Marie's house the next morning. Wozzeck's child rides his hobbyhorse. The other children romp in the sun, singing Berg's wry version of "Ring around a rosy" (Ex. 8.12). Others come in with the news: "Hey you! Your mother's

Ex. 8.12. "Children's Song" from Act 3, Scene 5, *Wozzeck,* Berg*

Rin - gel, Rin - gel Ro - sen - kranz, Rin — gel Reih'n . . .
Ring around a rosy, all fall down . . .

dead!" Wozzeck's child rides on, uncomprehending. The children rush off to see the body. He hesitates for an instant, then follows, still uncomprehending. Berg calls this scene an "invention on a regular pulse." Steady eighth notes are heard throughout. They mirror the hop-hop motion of the hobbyhorse and the placid lifebeat of the child-victim. After all the cataclysmic emotions the depth of tragedy lingers on, and this pulsing understatement cuts to the heart.

WOZZECK, ACT 3, SCENE 5

Children:	*Ringel, Ringel, Rosenkranz, Ringel Reih'n!*
	Ring around a rosy. All fall down.
	Ringel, Ringel, Rosenkranz, Rin . . .
	Ring around a rosy. All . . .
First Child:	*Du, Käthie! Marie . . .*
	Hey, Kathy, Marie . . .
Second Child:	*Was ist?*
	What is it?

First Child:	*Weisst' es nit? Sie sind schon Alle 'naus.*
	Don't you know? They're all out there.
Third Child:	*Du! Dein Mutter ist tot!*
	Hey you! Your mother's dead!
Wozzeck's Child:	*Hopp, hopp! Hopp, hopp! Hopp, hopp!*
	Hop, hop. Hop, hop. Hop, hop.
Second Child:	*Wo ist sie denn?*
	Where is she, then?
First Child:	*Drauss' liegt sie, am Weg, neben dem Teich.*
	She's out there on the path by the pond.
Third Child:	*Kommt anschau'n!*
	Let's go and see!
Wozzeck's Child:	*Hopp, hopp! Hopp, hopp! Hopp, hopp!*
	Hop, hop. Hop, hop. Hop, hop.

[Left alone, he hesitates, then goes after the others.] END OF OPERA

E. POST-TONALITY IN AMERICA

Pre-Twentieth Century American Music

European music came to America with the first waves of settlers. The Jamestown colonists and Pilgrim fathers brought English music with them. It was mainly stern religious music, yet even in the *Ainsworth Psalter* that accompanied the Pilgrims to New England in 1620 the psalms were sung in animated, stirring rhythms. The *Bay Psalm Book* was the first music book printed in the New World, published in Massachusetts in 1640. Eighteenth-century America saw a departure from English origins and a growth of native-style popular music. Fiddle tunes and ballads reflected the vigor of the young country and the diversity of its regions. The blacks who came as slaves brought their own music from Africa, and a similar transformation took place with the separation from their old life and beginning of the new (see p. 324). But the emphasis in colonial times remained on devotional music. Local "singing societies" that specialized in psalms, hymns, and anthems arose. Their weekly meetings, enlivening the cultural life of the communities, were often led by traveling professionals who went from town to town, peddling the latest music books and directing the rehearsals and concerts. A notable American composer of the Revolutionary period was William Billings of Boston (1746-1800). He was a self-taught musician, an American "primitive" who lacked some of the European technical skills but didn't care. Billings made up for the shortage of Old World finesse with the fervor and originality of his hymns and *fuguing tunes*. The latter (probably pronounced "fudging" tunes) closed with vigorous sections of fuguelike polyphony. Billings's hymn-melody "Chester"

("Let tyrants shake their iron rod") served the Continental Army as a marching song. A contemporary of Billings was Francis Hopkinson of Philadelphia (1737-1791). He was an aristocratic amateur who was proud to bill himself as an "American" composer and claimed in 1788 to be "the first native of the [new] United States who has produced a musical composition." Hopkinson is remembered for the song "My days have been so wondrous free."

Both Benjamin Franklin and Thomas Jefferson had musical interests. Franklin (1706-1790), in his Age of Enlightenment versatility, may have been something of a composer. Around 1761 he also perfected a form of *glass harmonica*, an instrument with eerie, silvery sounds that are produced by rubbing moistened fingers along the outsides of thin glass bowls. Mozart wrote music for such an instrument. Jefferson (1743-1826) was an accomplished violinist who enjoyed playing in weekly string-quartet sessions. Among the skillful American composers of the Federal period was Daniel Read of Massachusetts (1757-1836), who promoted the cause of "American masters" in the monthly *American Musical Magazine,* which he began publishing in 1786. Another was Oliver Shaw (1777-1848), whose attractive instrumental suite *For the Gentlemen* was published in 1807.

Billings, Read, and Shaw were American-trained and American-inspired. But the American composers who succeeded them during the nineteenth century often looked to Europe for their formative influences, and their originality suffered. The musical styles of John Knowles Paine (1839-1906), Horatio Parker (1863-1919), and George Whitefield Chadwick (1854-1931) tend to reflect the prevailing German idioms of the time. More original were Edward MacDowell (1860-1908), who used melodies of the North American Indians, and Charles Tomlinson Griffes (1884-1920), New York-born and Berlin-trained, who produced works in a variety of American, Amerindic, German, and French styles. Notable among the latter is his impressionist tone poem *The White Peacock* (1917).

On balance, nineteenth-century America produced no "serious" composers with the originality and high artistry of Poe and Melville in literature, or Whistler and Ryder in painting. America's richest musical imaginations belonged to composers who worked in genial lyric styles—to Foster, Gottschalk, Sousa, and Joplin. A convincing vein of Americana flourished in Stephen Foster (1826-1864), whose expressive songs caught the moods and flavors of the nation during the decades before the Civil War. Foster's masterpiece may be "Jeannie with the Light Brown Hair" (1854), but there are plenty of others: "Oh Susanna," "Camptown Races," "Old Folks at Home," "My Old Kentucky Home," "Beautiful Dreamer." Louis Moreau Gottschalk (1829-1869) was an American counterpart of Liszt, a virtuoso pianist with a magnetic stage presence. He was the composer

Colorplate 33

of enchanting salon morsels, such as "The Banjo" and "Le Bananier," whose exotic colorings reflect Gottschalk's partly New Orleans Creole ancestry. John Philip Sousa (1854-1932) was the longtime leader of the Marine Corps Band and America's "March King." He earned an international reputation, spreading a genial vision of United States vigor and élan with his stirring marches, of which the most celebrated is "The Stars and Stripes Forever." Scott Joplin (1868-1917) helped to originate and perfect the ragtime style that rose to prominence at the turn of the twentieth century. Of all the nineteenth-century American accomplishments in popular styles, Joplin's was the most significant and long-lived (see page 327).

Charles Ives

Finally an American composer of substantial originality in learned, noncommercial styles arrived in Charles Ives (1874-1954). Ives was the son of a bandmaster at Danbury, Connecticut, and was educated in music at nearby Yale. He viewed things unconventionally from the start. His works bristled with odd harmonies and maverick ideas. In his New England isolation, Ives knew almost nothing of what was going on in Paris, Vienna, and Berlin. His acquaintance with European music stopped with Tchaikovsky and Brahms (1890s). But during the first two decades of the twentieth century, just when Schoenberg and Stravinsky were turning the European scene around, Ives in America was moving in the same direction, from tonal to post-tonal idioms. The times were unfavorable for American composers with eccentric leanings, and Ives had to limit his composing to weekends while he pursued a successful career in the insurance business in New York. After a while he gave up composing altogether. Most of his works were written before 1920, and he made little effort to promote them. Following his quirky, mystic Yankee bent, he produced, more or less for his private satisfaction, an impressive number of symphonies, chamber works, and songs that were filled with American flavors. Ives liked to weave in quotations of his favorite melodies—bits of hymns, patriotic tunes, and ragtime—along with themes from Beethoven, Tchaikovsky, and Brahms. But more than with nostalgic bits, he filled his works with original melodic ideas, complex rhythms, polytonal harmonies (combinations of different keys, such as Stravinsky's simultaneous E major and E-flat major chords in *The Rite of Spring*), and other post-tonal effects. He experimented with quarter tones—intervals half as large as those on the piano. The adventurous spirit of the new age spoke as clearly through Ives in Connecticut as through his contemporaries in Paris, Vienna, and Berlin. Some of his experiments were earlier than the European ones. But for most of his life, Ives was a prophet without honor.

Anonymous, Meditation by the Sea *(ca. 1850-1860). An "unanswered question" by a New England predecessor of Charles Ives.*

Ives's important orchestral works include the Symphony No. 2 (1902), Symphony No. 3 ("The Camp Meeting: 1901-12"), and Symphony No. 4 (1916); the orchestral tone poem *Three Places in New England* (1914); and the "Holidays" Symphony (1904-13), whose movements are Washington's Birthday, Decoration Day, The Fourth of July, and Thanksgiving. His chamber works include the "Concord" Sonata for Piano, composed in 1915. Its full title is "Concord, Massachusetts: 1840-60," and its four movements— Emerson, Hawthorne, The Alcotts, and Thoreau—were meant to evoke the great age of New England transcendentalism. The pianist must use an elbow as well as fingers to play it, and at one point Ives says that a chord has to be played "using a strip of board 14 and 3/4 inches long, and heavy enough to press the keys down without striking."

Ives's chamber work *The Unanswered Question* was composed in the same year (1908) that saw Schoenberg venture into outright atonality. Ives takes something of the same path in this six-minute work, which is scored for three distinct tone colors: 1) a choir of strings, 2) a solo trumpet, and 3) a quartet of flutes. They produce three quite different kinds of music, which do not fit together in a unified shape of harmony and rhythm. Instead they coexist like strangers in a room. The choir of strings maintains an almost motion-less pianissimo of pure tonal harmonies. Ives describes it as "The Silence of the Druids—Who Know, See, and Hear Nothing." Their hymnlike revery is interrupted six times by the solo trumpet, playing a jagged nontonal phrase that Ives describes as "The Perennial Question of Existence . . . stated in the same tone of voice each time" (Ex. 8.13). To each of these nontonal "questions" by the trumpet,

Ex. 8.13. The Trumpet's "Question" from *The Unanswered Question*, Ives

a response is given by the quartet of flutes. Ives says they represent "human beings" in "a hunt for the Invisible Answer." The first of the flutes' "answers" is nontonal and disputatious in style. The succeeding answers become louder and even more agitated. By the sixth answer those "humans" (the flutes) are shouting heatedly—"mocking the Question," Ives says. Then they vanish, leaving only the serene tonal harmonies of the strings. The trumpet asks the nontonal Question for a seventh time, and this time it remains Unanswered. Ives's homespun metaphysics and his numerology are less significant than his purely musical techniques. The flute quartet plays music that is not tonal. He hedges that radicalism with the backdrop of tonal harmony in the strings. But he has the further novelty of combining unrelated planes of rhythmic motion in the flute and strings. They do not share the same bar lines. Then there is a remarkable improvisatory freedom. Ives says that the flutes "need not be played in the exact position indicated [but] in somewhat of an impromptu way." The strings are told to "continue their last chord for two measures or so after the trumpet stops." Ives anticipates in this some of the "work-in-progress" and "chance" techniques that have flourished in music since World War II.

Opinions about Ives's place in musical history remain divided. It may take another generation before the staying power of his music can be judged. For the moment, many musicians consider him a major figure, and his blend of musical visionary and American individualist assure him an attentive audience.

F. AFRO-AMERICAN MUSIC: RAGTIME, BLUES, AND JAZZ

Of all the music composed in North America, it is jazz that has captured the world's imagination. The word **jazz** has a wealth of associations. It is an Afro-American musical idiom with a strong steady beat, flexible inner rhythms, and an infectious lilt. That covers a lot of music. From the ragtimes of the 1890s through the modern sounds of the 1980s, jazz has been a living art that continues to grow. Its inspiration is black. Its essence is improvisation. Jazz musicians are usually composing as they perform. Real jazz is too full of

An African Barrel-Drummer. *Drums represented power and tribal spirit in the Western sub-Saharan regions, where most Africans who came to the Americas had their roots. Traditional rhythms, fascinating in their complexity, were carefully passed down from generation to generation.*

spontaneous nuance ever to be frozen on paper in musical notation. It lives essentially in live performance, created fresh each time. The origins of jazz go far back in the historical meeting of the African and North American cultures. The black slaves who came to America in the seventeenth through nineteenth centuries brought their native traditions with them—songs and dances, hollers and cries, occult languages of African drumming, work songs whose pace and patterns were mated to the physical motions of the laborers. Some of the black music seemed menacing to the whites, who tried to suppress it. Some of it survived by adapting to white customs. Black religiosity joined with white devotional song styles to produce the noble tradition of Negro spirituals, such as "Roll Jordan, Roll." Emancipation came in the 1860s, bringing hollow tokens of freedom. For blacks there was greater viability in the professions of comics and musical entertainers. Optimistic song-and-dance routines were aimed partly at pleasing white society. Emancipation also released deeper personal Colorplate 34 feelings that had been bottled up before. There were new Gospel songs and spirituals. Above all, the inner suffering of the black American life experience found musical expression in the haunting folk art of the blues.

Blues

For untold years the blues laments circulated as an oral art, sung by blacks to blacks. Then, during the first decades of the twentieth century, the blues came into history. They were written down in sheet music, punched onto player-piano rolls, sculpted in the wax and shellac of phonograph records. Blues are slow, serious meditations on the melancholy of black life. Born of poverty, loneliness, and troubled spirit, they are Western civilization's most heartfelt expression of human misery, yet they glow with a consoling warmth that comes from an awareness of their unique beauty. The typical blues stanza has three lines of text. A first line is sung; it is repeated; then another line provides the close. Bessie Smith's classic "Lost Your Head Blues" has that basic plan in its first stanza (see Ex. 8.14). Further stanzas follow, spinning out the all-too-human story. The blues have strong, unforgettable tunes, yet the essence of blues

△
Bessie Smith
"Lost Your Head Blues"
(Side 10, Band 3)

Ex. 8.14. First Stanza (Music Repeats for Other Stanzas) of "Lost Your Head Blues," Bessie Smith

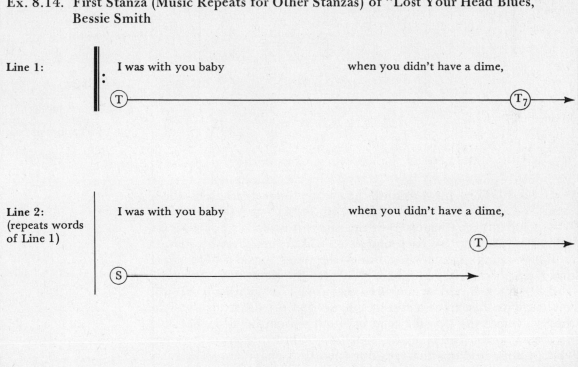

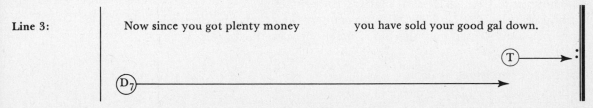

T_7 and D_7 are "7th-chords" based on the tonic T and dominant D triads. S = subdominant triad.

music is not melodic but harmonic. The typical chord plan of the blues is that of the so-called 12-bar blues, where each of the three lines of text gets four bars of music. The simple, basic harmonies are always the same. They are a framework of chords that is in the blood of every blues performer (Ex. 8.15). Musicians don't have to think

Ex. 8.15. Chord Outline of the Blues Stanza

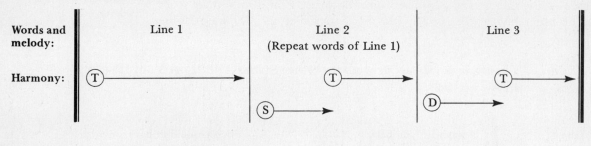

about those chord progressions, they just produce variations above them. The blues are a variation form, an ostinato variation form like Dido's Lament (see Chapter 3) or the finale of Brahms's Fourth Symphony (see Chapter 5). Each blues stanza is an improvised variation on the opening stanza. What brings the blues music to life is the subtle magic of the performers' touches: the delicately "bent" or "glided" pitches of the melody, the slowly undulating beat, the **syncopations** that come a stylish split second off the beat; the little rasps of voice, the "passing chords" that enrich the space between the basic chords. The blues are tonal music, but their scale has some extra options—pitches that are not found on any piano. These are the **blue notes**, which are alternatives for pitches $\hat{3}$, $\hat{5}$, and $\hat{7}$ of the common scale. They are slightly lower than the regular pitches, and their off-sounds help give the blues their poignant flavor (Ex. 8.16).

Ex. 8.16. The Blues Scale

$\bullet$ = "blue note"

Bessie Smith.
"Empress of the Blues."

Originally all blues were sung, but then they made their way to the solo piano and to the small "band" of instrumentalists. Jelly Roll Morton (1885-1938) was the first great blues stylist on the piano. Among other prime blues soloists were the legendary vocalist Bessie Smith (1895-1937) and the trumpeter Louis "Satchmo" Armstrong (1900-1971). To hear Bessie Smith sing the blues is to know the mother lode of black emotion and creativity. The early generations of blues performers are gone, but fortunately their art is preserved in recordings. And the centuries-old blues sorrows, rooted in the deepest layers of human experience, are still being re-created today.

Ragtime

Other sounds besides the blues welled up from the southern black genius. **Ragtime** was making the rounds of the saloons and minstrel shows around 1900. The rags were piano music with a catchy melody and a thumping accompaniment. Unlike the personal, inner-directed blues, ragtime was extroverted entertainment music with a lilt that intoxicated blacks and white alike. Ragtime was not just improvised by the artists. It was written down, published, and sold for the pleasure of amateurs playing at home. Ragtime's patriarchs were Ben Harney, who printed a *Ragtime Instructor* in 1897, and Scott

Joplin, whose "Maple Leaf Rag" in 1899 launched the wordwide craze. Its main features were a booming bass, usually in $\frac{2}{4}$ time; an appealing thrust of melody, filled with piano tinkle, mincing syncopations, and echoings at higher and lower octaves; and some sweet chromaticisms in the harmony. It had tight formal and tonal structures, modeled on white music such as the Strauss watzes. The "scintillating syncopations" of the rags caught on, reaching Europe during the War. Stravinsky copied them, and even the dainty epicure Debussy took them up for the prancing step of his "Golliwog's Cake-Walk."

Jazz

Then alongside the rags and the blues came jazz. What we know as **New Orleans** or **Dixieland jazz** was born around 1900 in the saloons and bawdy houses of Storyville, the red-light district of New Orleans. No one knows where the name came from, but it was applied to a ragged, "razzing" mixture of styles that combined the bright optimism of the black popular shows, the tinkle of the ragtime piano, and more than a touch of the melancholy blues. It had the flavorful bounce of Louisiana Creole banjo music, the brassy thump of a Sousa band, and the fake elegance of ensembles playing midst the potted palms of old-South Victorian hotels. All were there in a magical mixture, stirred with a dash of genius.

Jazz was a way of "playing a melody with a beat." Its essence, like that of the blues, was improvisation. It was created live and new each time. Sometimes the musicians went marching, jollying up the blues on military instruments left over from the Civil War. But the first great jazz—New Orleans jazz—was basically sit-down chamber music. Small bands of black musicians who were not traditionally trained but playing intuitively on raw talent improvised variations on familiar tunes. Their results were racy and alive, not for a concert hall but for some earthy house of pleasure. The band divided in two groups. The front line did the main melodic improvising: a trumpet or cornet usually took the lead (a cornet is a smaller, gentler-voiced trumpet); a clarinet played solos and added "licks" around the main melody; a trombone played occasional solos in simpler style than the rest. Then there was the "rhythm section": a guitar or banjo for the chords, a double bass or tuba for the low thumps, sometimes a piano to affirm the harmony, and percussion instruments for the never-too-distant memories of African drumming. With its brassy façade and alert rhythms, New Orleans jazz created a provocative atmosphere. The leader "stomped out" the beat. Then each soloist took a turn at the basic tune, which could be a blues song, a rag tune, or a sentimental ballad. They played around with it, jollied it up, mourned over it. As each soloist finished a stanza, the others might close in with lively fill-ins called "riffs." For the last stanza they all improvised together, producing masterpieces of spontaneous counterpoint. Jazz style had a looseness, a free-and-easy swagger that was uniquely American. But above all it was black American. The original "kings" of New Orleans jazz were the pianist Jelly Roll Morton and the cornettist Joe "King" Oliver (1858-1938). Compared with the sophistication of later northern jazz, the hard-driving, high-spirited New Orleans jazz idiom seems naive, even crude. But it had the vitality of being close to its racy, popular origins. It went on to enchant the world.

9 Between the World Wars

Picasso, Three Musicians *(1921). The neoclassic movement in music had counterparts in art, as in this painting in which Picasso turned from cubism to more conventional subject matter.*

Between the World Wars

MUSIC	ARTS AND IDEAS	POLITICS AND SCIENCE
## POST-TONALITY AND NEOCLASSICISM	## MODERN TIMES	## THE MASSES, THE MEDIA, THE MENACE OF FASCISM

Stravinsky (1882-1971):	Brancusi, *Bird in Space* (1919-1927)	Women's suffrage in the United
The Soldier's Tale (1918)	Geometrical, mechanistic paintings	States (1920)
Pulcinella (1920)	by Leger and Mondrian (1920-1921)	Disastrous inflation in postwar
Apollo (1928)	Picasso, *Three Musicians* (1921)	Germany (1920s)
Ravel (1875-1937):	T. S. Eliot, *The Waste Land* (1922)	Mussolini's march on Rome (1922)
La Valse (1920)	Joyce, *Ulysses* (1922)	Growth of commercial radio and films
Bolero (1928)	Breton, *Surrealist Manifesto* (1924)	(1920s)
Hindemith (1895-1963):	Pound, *Cantos* (from 1925)	First demonstration of television
Symphony, *Mathis der Maler* (1934)	Hemingway, *The Sun Also Rises* (1926)	(1926)
Walton (b. 1902):	Yeats, *The Tower* (1928)	Discovery of penicillin (1928)
Façade (1922)	Illusionistic surrealism: Dali,	Great Depression (from 1929)
Copland (b. 1900):	Tanguy, Magritte (1930s)	Growth of "talking pictures" and
Rodeo (1938)	Mobiles of Calder (from 1932)	color film (1930s)
Schoenberg (1874-1951):	Picasso, *Guernica* (1937)	Roosevelt and Hitler come to power
Suite for Piano, Op. 25 (1924)		(1933)
Webern (1883-1945):		Keynes, *General Theory of Employ-*
String Quartet, Op. 28 (1928)		*ment, Interest, and Money* (1936)
Prokofiev (1891-1953):		Spanish Civil War (1936-1939)
Violin Concerto No. 2 (1935)		World War II (1939-1945)
Shostakovich (1906-1974):		
Symphony No. 5 (1937)		
Varèse (1883-1965):		
Ionisation (1931)		
Gershwin (1898-1937):		
Rhapsody in Blue (1924)		
Porgy and Bess (1935)		
Harris (1898-1979):		
Third Symphony (1938)		
Louis Armstrong (1900-1971)		

A. NEOCLASSICISM IN FRANCE

Igor Stravinsky

Before World War I composers had searched for new musical techniques to replace those of major-minor tonality and for a new expressive rhetoric to replace the old romanticism. Their endeavors reached fruition on the eve of the war in Schoenberg's *Pierrot lunaire* (1912) and Stravinsky's *The Rite of Spring* (1913). Schoenberg and Stravinsky brought a welcome freshness into the musical arena with their post-tonal ventures, but as creators they gave up something essential. When a creative imagination is operating at white heat, pure inspiration may suffice to give results of lasting value. But artists cannot often produce that way. Generally they depend on familiar, time-tested techniques to get them started and keep them going in a productive track. Composers of the nineteenth century had relied on the melodic and harmonic idioms of tonality, the regularity of metric rhythms, the conventional forms such as rondo, fugue, and sonata form. Twentieth-century composers were giving up those supports. They were making up works from scratch, each with a fresh content and form, each exploring a novel expressive "language." For a while it seemed that everyone was speaking a different language. That unsettled situation posed difficulties, and it could not last. Composers inevitably groped for new conventions and a new common language to help in shaping their musical ideas and understanding the ideas of others. Even before the war's end the musical pendulum was swinging toward new methods of giving order to post-tonal sound structures and a new esthetic to replace romanticism.

The new esthetic appeared first. It is generally known as **neoclassicism** because it brought back into twentieth-century music some of the ideals and techniques of the eighteenth-century "classics"— both those of the Viennese masters like Mozart and Haydn and those of the mature Baroque masters like Bach and Handel. *Neoclassicism,* meaning literally a new classicism, revived the composers' commitment to musical sounds for their own sake, and reasserted the primacy of absolute or abstract music over the use of music for picture painting, storytelling, and emotional self-revelation. The romantics' heart-on-sleeve effusions were supplanted by less demonstrative utterances. Composers gave up suggestive titles. They again wrote pieces with simple musical titles, such as sonata, suite, and concerto. Gone too were the overweight orchestrations of late romanticism. They were replaced by lean chamber sonorities that assigned just one player to each musical part, allowing every wisp of sound and color to show through. What neoclassicism represented above all was a return to the common-sense view of the eighteenth century, which saw the art of music as an exercise in craft and a

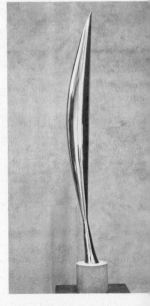

Constantin Brancusi, Bird in S (1919-1925). The cool, clean of Brancusi's sculpture reflec other aspect of the neocl movement.

vehicle for instruction and diversion, not as an outlet for the personal catharsis of composers and—vicariously—of their listeners. The twentieth century's "new classic" music, however, no longer took shape within the boundaries of the eighteenth century's tonal language. It had new resources of pitch, rhythm, and forms to draw on as it gave expression to the optimism and energy of the postwar era.

Stirrings of a nascent neoclassicism can be found even in the archromantic Tchaikovsky. He described a new Serenade for Strings to Mme. von Meck in the 1880s as "my homage to Mozart . . . intended to be an imitation of his style. I should be delighted if I felt I had in any way approached my model." The first essays in post-tonal music by Schoenberg, Webern, and Berg from the years 1905-12 already show a preference for a lean, epigrammatic style of discourse and Mozartean chamber-music dimensions. The works are often called just "movements" or "pieces," and one finds in them a return to favor of such traditional forms as variations and canon.

At Paris, Debussy's Three Sonatas (1915-17) show the same "abstract" attitude, and Prokofiev, whose "Scythian" Suite (1914) rang with the primitivist clangor of Stravinsky's *The Rite of Spring* (1913), produced in 1917 a "Classical" Symphony where verve, transparency, and traditional forms are on a Mozartean scale. The leading figure of Franco-Russian neoclassicism, however, was Stravinsky. Just five years after *The Rite of Spring,* Stravinsky moved onto neoclassic ground with *The Soldier's Tale* of 1918.

The Rite of Spring still gave its audience the kind of colorful display found in Mussorgsky and Rimsky-Korsakov. *The Soldier's Tale* has none of the old romantic splash. It is a miniature theatrical, based on a Russian folk tale about a poor soldier returning from the war. He carries a violin that he stops to play along the way. He encounters a stranger (the Devil) who offers to trade for his violin (which is the soldier's soul) a miraculous book that assures wealth and happiness. The deal is struck, but then the unhappy soldier trails the Devil for three years, trying to get the fiddle back. He returns home, finds that his sweetheart has married, and knows that the Devil has won. *The Soldier's Tale* is staged, danced, and recited. At one side of the stage is a narrator, telling the story. At center stage there are actors or puppets doing a pantomime. On the other side there is a group of chamber players that is rather like a 1916 New Orleans jazz band: clarinet, bassoon, cornet, trombone, violin, double bass, and drums. Stravinsky's friends, in fact, had brought back recordings of the new ragtime and jazz from wartime America. The musical movements are brisk, like those of an eighteenth-century suite. There are stylized dances (a tango and a waltz), ragtime, the parody of a Lutheran chorale, and the Devil's triumphal march. The rhetoric is terse and unemotional, the texture transparent, the harmony wryly post tonal. The music has an ironic glint, born of the

Marc Chagall, Green Violinist *(1918). Chagall, like Stravinsky, was Russian-born and eventually became a resident of France (1910). This painting, still Russian in inspiration, dates from the time of Stravinsky's* The Soldier's Tale.

war years. There are the same jaunty rhythms as in *The Rite of Spring* but no longer pounded with the same brute force. The opening "Soldier's March" (2 minutes) represents the soldier's homeward trudge. It begins with a jazzy outburst by the cornet and trombone. A double bass takes over with a slogging accompaniment and continues while other instruments add counterpoints (Ex. 9.1). The effervescent, tongue-in-cheek style is as close to the tidy Mozart as to the effusive *The Rite of Spring*. The harmonies are modern, at times bitonal (using two keys at once) as in 1913. This music moves forward with barely a backward glance. The forms are free of the old repetition schemes. The weight of interest is on the rhythm, a lively, unpredictable rhythm where prickly irregularities have supplanted the regularity of metrical rhythm. Rhythm has been upgraded. Where nineteenth-century music emphasized melody and harmony, the new music emphasizes rhythmic sparkle and surprise. Rhythm has come forward to fill the gap left by the departure of tonality.

△
Stravinsky: "Soldier's March" from *The Soldier's Tale* (Side 10, Band 4)

Ex. 9.1. "Soldier's March," No. 1, from *The Soldier's Tale,* Stravinsky

Stravinsky persisted in this urbane, energetic style well into the 1950s. He often hovered on the fringes of tonality, but he never quite came back to embrace tonality in the old way. In the ballet *Pulcinella* (1920) he added another factor that is distinctively neoclassic. There he took some eighteenth-century music by Pergolesi, the composer of *La Serva Padrona* (see Chapter 3), and recomposed it, giving it an overlay of his own bright twentieth-century rhythms and colors. In the ballet *The Fairy's Kiss* (1928), again he reused music of the past, taking fragments from Tchaikovsky. The ballet *Card Game* (1936) features a scene in a gambling salon, with nostalgic color taken from bits of Rossini, Tchaikovsky, Ravel, and Johann Strauss. Stravinsky's "Dumbarton Oaks" Concerto (1938) contains

Picasso, Four Dancers *(1925). The lithe motions of ballet dancers are recreated by flowing, economical lines.*

substantial hints of Bach's *Brandenburg Concerto* No. 3. He gave a characteristically arch explanation:

I played Bach very regularly during the composition of the Concerto, and was greatly attracted to the *Brandenburg Concertos.* Whether or not the first theme of my first movement is a conscious borrowing from the Third *Brandenburg,* I do not know. What I can say is that Bach would most certainly have been delighted to have loaned it to me.

Such borrowings were not pointless affectations. They represented an acknowledgment of past marvels and an artful reinterpretation of them in the context of the present. Stravinsky's ballets, symphonies, and concertos after 1920, even when they were not involved with specific references to earlier music, still referred back to the ambiance of the eighteenth-century classics in their elegant textures and economical rhetoric. Stravinsky's last opera, *The Rake's Progress* (1951), was inspired by the eighteenth-century engravings of Hogarth, and though it uses no actual music of Mozart, the forms and spirit are distinctly Mozartean.

Stravinsky represented another aspect of "classicism" in some other works that show a predilection for ancient Greece. The opera-oratorio *Oedipus the King* (1927, text by Cocteau), the melodrama *Persephone* (1934, text by Gide), and the ballets *Apollo* (1928), *Orpheus* (1947), and *Agon* (1957) are all on Grecian subjects. Stravinsky remained in the forefront of musical developments throughout his long life. He was much like Picasso (his senior by a year) in the protean ability to change his style and exert a wide influence with each change. Stravinsky brought a sense of liberation to other composers who were struggling with post-tonal idioms. He seemed able to take any material and make music out of it. Throughout his middle years, Stravinsky held fast to the neoclassic esthetic and to the mixture of post-tonal and tonal idioms that he first cultivated in 1918 in *The Soldier's Tale*. After World War II, however, at the age of seventy, he surprised the musical world. In an astonishing show of creative vitality he turned to a rather different style during the early 1950s, embracing idioms and techniques that came from the mature work of Schoenberg and Webern. It was music for which he had earlier found little sympathy.

Maurice Ravel

If there is a third major figure beside Debussy and Stravinsky in French music of the early twentieth century, it is Maurice Ravel. Ravel (1875-1937) was born in the decade after Debussy, the decade before Stravinsky. He studied at the Paris Conservatory and began under Debussy's stylistic shadow, but soon took a distinctive path. His first success was the *Pavane for a Dead Princess* (1899), a salon piece with a sombre modal quality that seems coated with artificial sweetener. It proved so popular that Ravel never had to worry about money, yet everything he composed thereafter was calculated to please and rewarded with huge success. The only blot of failure came while he was still a student, when he did not receive a coveted Prix de Rome. That was the result of political machinations, however, not doubt about his talent. Ravel later redressed the snub by French officialdom. Basking in popularity, he refused the proffered Legion of Honor, which prompted the catty remark of Satie, that while Ravel personally declined the honor, every note of his music courted it. Ravel dealt more generously with Satie. He acknowledged him as a powerful force, an "indispensable" composer, from whom he learned the value of simple expression in his later works. Ravel was also generous with Schoenberg, advocating his right to be heard in France during World War I, even though Schoenberg was in the hostile Austrian army while Ravel was in the Allied ambulance corps.

Ravel never adopted Debussy's whole-tone scale. He tried it only once in a forgotten overture named "Scheherezade." Yet he began as a musical "impressionist." His early *Jeux d'Eaux (Fountains,* 1901) has tinkling droplets and splashing jets of piano sound, enveloped in an impressionistic haze. Ravel there was indebted to Debussy, but the debt soon ran the other way. Some of the pianistic effects in Debussy's Préludes (1910-13) are prefigured in Ravel's exploitations of keyboard colors. Some of Ravel's use of Spanish colors also rubbed off on Debussy. The Hispanic link was natural since Ravel was born in the Pyrenees of a Basque mother. There are Spanish idioms in *Alborada del Gracioso (Serenade of a Clown,* 1905), in

Rhapsodie Espagnole (1907), in the amusing one-act opera *L'Heure Espagnol* (*The Spanish Hour,* 1907), and again in the *Bolero* (1928). He had a liking for distant places and exotic colors, thus the gypsy idioms in *Tzigane,* a rhapsody for violin and orchestra (1924), the Judaic material in "Two Hebrew Melodies" (1914), and the imitation of a Javanese gamelan in the movement from his *Mother Goose Suite* called "The Empress of the Pagodas" (1908). Beyond impressionism and the exotic, throughout Ravel's work there is a taste for opulent sounds and lush effects. This is nowhere more apparent than in the ballet *Daphnis and Chloe* (1912), based on an ancient Greek pastoral romance, from which two popular orchestral suites are drawn. Suite No. 1 consists of a "Nocturne," "Interlude," and "War Dance"; Suite No. 2 consists of "Daybreak," "Pantomime," and "General Dance."

For all of the pleasurable qualities that fill Ravel's music, he was himself a notably prim personality. He never married and seems never to have been touched by a deep romantic attachment. A certain Proustian delicacy shows up in his music. There is a taste for the urbane and epigrammatic that becomes more precise and austere with time. Ravel never lost his eagerness to please, his habit of luxuriating in the physical qualities of sounds. But even before the neoclassical tendency can be discerned in Debussy or Stravinsky, Ravel began edging toward a more abstract, more classically restrained style. His "Menuet antique" (1895) and *Pavane for a Dead Princess* (1899) are based on old-time dances. His *Valses nobles et sentimentales* (1911) takes a sentimental look at the waltzes of Schubert and the Paris salons of the 1820s. His Piano Trio (1915) is in a markedly drier style. Ravel's *Le Tombeau de Couperin* (1917) is a piano suite evocative of the spirit of François Couperin (1688-1733), the greatest of the early French harpsichord masters. A *tombeau* in French is a memorial tribute. Ravel admired Couperin as embodying traditional French grace and refinement. The six short pieces of *Tombeau* were also a memorial for some of his fallen wartime comrades. Written at a time of personal depression, they typically understate his grief, which is couched in quaint harpsichordlike textures and precise Couperinesque forms: a Prelude, Fugue, Forlane, Rigaudon, Minuet, and Toccata. Ravel revisited the realm of Viennese waltzes in 1920, producing *La Valse,* a "choreographic poem" for orchestra, which goes beyond the naive nostalgia of his *Valses nobles* of 1911. Ravel begins *La Valse* by conjuring up a festive ballroom scene in a Hapsburg palace of the 1850s. The whirling sounds of the dance presently become edged with irony, and the vortex of waltz rhythms and dissonant harmonies reaches a frenzied climax. The pomp of Imperial Austria seems to be coming down, engulfed in a sarcastic cacophony. *La Valse* was Ravel's bitter musical parable, engendered by the hatreds of the Great War.

Toward the end of his life Ravel singled out his Sonata for Violin and Cello (1922) as marking "a turning-point in my evolution, [where] reduction to essentials is carried to extremes." Some other works in a mature, economical style are his Violin Sonata (1927) and the two Piano Concertos (1931). Drier in substance and more abstract in conception than his earlier music, they represent in full flower the vogue of neoclassicism that was appearing everywhere in the 1920s. Into some of these works Ravel also put touches of the American blues and the fox trot. He admired Gershwin and even visited America in 1928. He liked the country, but his fine French palate was repelled by the food. "I was dying of hunger," he told a friend.

Ravel's *Bolero* (1928) is from this final period, and in its way is a "neoclassic" essay. It uses a traditional dance idiom and is occupied with abstract problems of rhythm, tonality, and orchestration. Notwithstanding its sensuous, gaudy surface, *Bolero* represents the same esthetic impulse that animates Ravel's late sonata and concertos. The piece was composed in a hurry, and Ravel claimed that he didn't think much of it. "*Bolero* contains no music . . . [only] orchestral tissue without music . . . one long crescendo." Actually he went to great pains to fill it with sure-fire effects, and it is hard to take him at his belittling words. The music begins with a jangle of the Spanish bolero rhythm that Beethoven and Chopin also found attractive:

A flute enters almost inaudibly with a stately curve of melody whose intricate twists take nearly two minutes to unfold. The melody appears nine times in all during the course of the work, done up in ever richer colors and fuller orchestration. Everything is obviously headed toward a massive climax. Along with the slow, steady growth in sonority and rhythmic intensity, there is an astonishing tonal effect. Throughout the seventeen-minute work, the music remains stubbornly in the opening key of C, longer than any other masterwork holds to a single key, testing the listener's powers of tonal endurance to the limit. Just fifteen measures from the end, the tonal dam breaks with the pressure of the monotonously overexposed C, and the music is wrenched to an unexpected E major. The anthropologist Lévi-Strauss drew a characteristic metaphor to describe it: "the happy solution to . . . impotence." But then Ravel closes right back in C. *Bolero* is a tour de force in the manipulation of rhythm, color, and key, but above all it impresses in its psychological dimension. With its obsessive repetitions, it is a forerunner of the minimalist music, psychedelic rock, and hallucinatory styles of recent decades (see Chapter 10). It has been remarkably durable. Composed more than half a century ago, it still fascinates today.

B. SONATA FORM IN THE TWENTIETH CENTURY

Béla Bartók

Nearly every major composer of the 1920s and 1930s had some stake in the neoclassic movement. For the Hungarian Béla Bartók (1881-1945), neoclassicism was bound up with the folk idioms of his native land. Bartók was a European modernist, as Stravinsky was, but he was also one of the great musical nationalists. Educated at the Musical Academy in Budapest, he showed extraordinary promise before he was ten. He had an uncommon breadth of musical interests, becoming a composer of high seriousness and originality and excelling as a concert pianist. He was an ingenious piano pedagogue; his collection of pieces called *Mikrokosmos* is still used by students today. He was also an outstanding scholar of Balkan and Near Eastern folk music. Beginning in 1905, Bartók's research took him on field trips throughout Hungary and Rumania, and also into Turkey and North Africa. What interested him most were the angular melodies and bristling rhythms of Hungarian Magyar music. It was a body of national song quite different from the sometimes cloying "Hungarian gypsy" idiom that Liszt and even Brahms so slickly exploited. Bartók rarely put actual Magyar folksongs into his compositions, but the idiom permeated his musical thought and gave flavor to his style.

From the start he was a composer with a distinctive voice, never an imitator of Stravinsky, to whom his style comes closest. Bartók's *Allegro Barbaro* (1911) projects the same dynamism as Stravinsky's *The Rite of Spring*, but it was composed two years earlier. Ever his

Joan Miró, Painting *(1933). Miró specializes in simple, sometimes amoeba-like shapes, with patches of strong color.*

own master, he then turned to purer neoclassic abstractions—clear forms, taut emotions, unromantic titles. Bartók was intrigued by the craft of composition as practiced by a great contrapuntist such as Bach. He exploited the links between music and numbers, even laying out the lengths of musical sections in certain of his works in conformity with mathematical proportions. Bartók's six String Quartets, composed between 1908 and 1940, are as intimate in address and lofty in ambition as the last quartets of Beethoven. His main orchestral works of the 1920s through 1940s are a series of concertos in showier styles: the Second and Third Piano Concertos, the Violin Concerto, the Viola Concerto, and a Concerto for Orchestra. For all of his commitment to modernism, Bartók was never ashamed to be personal and emotional in his music. Among the leaders of the neoclassic generation, he was spiritually the least alienated from a natural, even romantic expressiveness. After the outbreak of World War II, Bartók was persuaded to seek safety in the United States. Relatively unknown, eventually dying of leukemia, he was barely able to support himself in New York on meager fellowships granted for his musicological studies of folk music. Recognition and lasting international success came just after he died in 1945.

Two of Bartók's finest creations are half-chamber, half-symphonic works that reveal their neoclassic attitude in their noncommital titles: Sonata for Two Pianos and Percussion (1938) and Music for Strings, Percussion, and Celeste (1936). The latter is scored for two small string orchestras, a rhythm section that includes drums and cymbals, and four instruments that command a great spread of pitches and colors—the xylophone, celeste, harp, and piano. Bartók was interested here in the old concerto ideal, in the competition between instrumental groups and the display of distinctive tone colors. The music is full of novel effects, notably the glissandos for strings and for the tympani. The second movement of Music for Strings, Percussion, and Celeste is a spacious allegro where Bartók adopts the old framework of sonata-allegro form. There are tonal reminiscences throughout, as well as "Hungarian" scales and modes. He even preserves something of the old tonal key relationship between the first and second themes. But he never really lapses back into tonality. As with Stravinsky in the same epoch, everything is given a smart, post-tonal veneer.

An energetic first theme (Ex. 9.2) leads by way of tympani strokes to a gentler bridge theme that Bartók labels "scherzando," or "joking" (Ex. 9.3). There is a rise to a climax that is followed, as in an eighteenth-century symphony, by an air-clearing silence. Theme II is light in spirit, punctuated with grace notes (Ex. 9.4). Closing theme *a* (CLa) appears in a crescendo, bringing strong, undulating trills with growing dissonance and rhythmic pressure (Ex. 9.5). The short closing theme *b* (CLb) begins with an angular idea in the piano

Δ

Bartók: Second Movement, Music for Strings, Percussion, and Celeste (Side 10, Band 5)

Ex. 9.2. Theme I of Second Movement, Music for Strings, Percussion, and Celeste, Bartók

Ex. 9.3. Bridge Theme

Ex. 9.4. Theme II

Ex. 9.5. Closing Theme *a*

Ex. 9.6. Closing Theme *b*

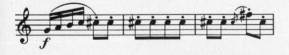

(Ex. 9.6). Closing theme *c* (CLc) consists of glissandos moving up and down, with touches of the celeste, then decisive chords and the tympani fading away. In the development, theme I is embellished with tingling piano sounds and pizzicato strings. The strings play scale fragments in a slower middle section. The retransition is a long crescendo of murky trills and nervous fragments of theme I. After the climax at the recapitulation, everything is compressed, moving in a rush through the coda. Bartók's use of sonata form in this movement has the same economy and dramatic urgency as an eighteenth-century sonata movement. The old framework is certainly here, but other things have changed. The question is, how vital does the sonata framework remain in this modern, post-tonal idiom, where it is deprived of its original basis in tonality?

C. NEOCLASSICISM IN GERMANY, ENGLAND, AND AMERICA

Paul Hindemith

Paul Hindemith (1895-1963) was the most highly regarded composer in Germany after World War I and the chief exponent of German neoclassicism. Hindemith was an all-round musician and musical intellectual. At the age of twenty he was a skilled conductor and, as a violin virtuoso, the concertmaster of the Frankfurt opera. He also cultivated the viola, playing in a renowned string quartet, and mastered most of the other orchestra instruments. He was a musicologist with an abiding curiosity about medieval and renaissance music and an educational innovator with his own system for teaching musical fundamentals and nurturing young talents. He was an important theorist and critic of modern music. During the 1940s Hindemith was doctrinaire enough to recompose his long, early song cycle, *Das Marienleben* (*The Life of Mary*, 1924), so that it would conform to

George Grosz, Political Automa-tons *(1920). Grosz satirizes the politics of Germany's Weimar Republic: Vacant-headed, war-mutilated automatons are on their way to cast futile votes. The economic inflation caused by World War I helped undermine the Republic and led to the Nazi dictatorship in 1933.*

his later notions about how music should go. Throughout his life he was a student of philosophy, pondering the function of music among the ancient Greeks and the Church fathers. Hindemith felt that music was not destined simply for entertainment. Along with Plato, Aristotle, and St. Augustine, he held the conviction that music should serve as "an agent of moral elevation." Always concerning himself with how society could be made better with the aid of music, Hindemith was a musical philosopher and a "politician" in the best sense of that maligned word.

Hindemith came to artistic maturity in the early 1920s, during the time of the Weimar Republic, and he was affected by the social and economic problems that plagued Germany after the wartime defeat. During the 1920s he concentrated on a series of neoclassic chamber works, written for practically every familiar instrument. An example is the short, witty "Kleine Kammermusik" ("Little Chamber Music") for Winds, Op. 24, No. 2, composed in 1922. Such works have non-committal titles, for example, chamber music, sonata, trio, etc. Their musical ideas are abstract, their forms compact, their expression terse. One reason for Hindemith's emphasis on chamber music was economic. It was difficult to make ends meet in the nightmare German inflation of the early 1920s, where large fortunes were wiped out overnight. Hindemith half-joked that he gave up writing orchestral music because the paper for large scores was too expensive. Few copies of orchestral music were sold and performances were difficult to obtain. There was also a social-political reason for the chamber music. Just then German artists were coming out of romantic isolation. Pure creation in an ivory tower no longer seemed enough in those politically volatile times. Artists and composers felt the need to reach large audiences. One of Hindemith's aims was to produce music in a style that was relatively accessible and uncomplicated, one that he himself found easy to turn out and that others would find easy to grasp as audiences and even to play in their homes. Hindemith's name for such chamber music was "practical music" or "music to be used" ("Gebrauchsmusik"). He was not exactly addressing it to the ordinary person in the street; it was for the musically cultured bourgeoisie. Still, there is a parallel to the playwright Berthold Brecht's doctrine of the same time, that works of art should communicate directly to an unsophisticated—in Brecht's view, proletarian—audience.

Hindemith's accessible chamber music had yet another reason. It was conceived as a reproach to the "difficult" music of Schoenberg and his disciples, to that other important school of German music in the early 1920s, whose creations could be performed only by virtuosos and whose appeals seemed limited to small, elite audiences. Hindemith remained an ideological adversary of Schoenberg throughout their long parallel careers. He felt a need to counteract what he called "the dangers of an esoteric isolationism in music." His cantata *Frau Musica* (*Lady of Music*), composed in 1944, still advocated his "accessible" vein by including a part to be sung by the audience.

In his musical style, Hindemith maintained strong links with the German past, particularly the venerable polyphonic craft of Bach and Handel. He was a believer in the old-fashioned virtues of canons and fugues, not only for teaching compositional skills to apprentices but in his own new music. His style is muscled with counterpoint, and there is a rhythmic aggressiveness reminiscent of the German Baroque. He also clung to tonality, particularly as he turned mellower during the late 1920s and the 1930s. Instead of abandoning tonality like Schoenberg or Stravinsky, he stretched it, made it more varied by the use of unusual melodic intervals and dissonant harmonies. But again and again his music seeks out simple tonal chords as its resting places. He is always reassuring the audience with that conventionality.

Hindemith was very prolific, perhaps overly so, and his music has occasionally worn thin. It seems as if, instead of waiting for inspiration, he cut lengths of musical fabric from long, drab-colored bolts. But his best works are masterpieces. The opera *Mathis der Maler* (*Matthias the Painter,* completed in 1935) is one of these. It is based on the life of the Northern Renaissance master Mathias Grünewald (ca. 1480-1530), whose stunning Isenheim Altarpiece is today at Colmar in eastern France. Hindemith's largely fictional plot casts Grünewald as a Church artist who abandons his successful career and throws in his lot with a revolt of peasants seeking the abolition of serfdom. Three orchestral pieces that Hindemith extracted from this opera in 1934 are an attractive three-movement symphony. They represent three of the panel paintings of Grünewald's Altarpiece: I. The "Concert of Angels" gently serenading the Virgin and Child, in whose music Hindemith incorporates a medieval religious folksong, "There sang three angels"; II. "The Entombment," a slow lament, reflecting the morbid scene that appears on the pradella, just below the scene of the Crucifixion; and III. "The Temptation of St. Anthony," a vigorous finale inspired by Grünewald's depiction of the saint being tormented by grotesque animals.

Hindemith was of pure Aryan blood, but there was little about his music or his personality that pleased the Nazi regime. The president of the Third Reich's musicians' guild from 1933 to 1935 was Richard Strauss, who once told Hindemith, "You don't have to write music like that. You have talent . . ." Hindemith never took the hint. He was eventually accused of "spiritual non-Aryanism" and his music was banned. Deeply German, yet no less deeply a concerned citizen of the world, Hindemith left his homeland and accepted an invitation from the Turkish government to reform the system of musical education in that newly Westernizing nation. After 1937 he found a home in the United States, teaching at Yale. In 1953 he returned to Europe but to Switzerland, not Germany. Three of Hindemith's "American" works illustrate the range and quality of his mature style. *The Four Temperaments* (1940) consists of a theme and four variations for piano and strings. The variations represent the ancient fourfold classification of the aspects of human character as Melancholic, Sanguine (cheerful), Phlegmatic (placid), and Choleric (given to anger). Hindemith's *Ludus Tonalis* (*Games with Pitches*) of 1942, for piano, revives the spirit of Bach's *Well-Tempered Clavier* and *Art of the Fugue*. It consists of twelve fugues and eleven interludes that explore a variety of contrapuntal devices and offer some challenging technical difficulties to the soloist. The *Ludus Tonalis* is framed by a Prelude and a Postlude, the latter an upside-down musical version of the former. In 1943, still in a neoclassic vein, Hindemith combined some themes borrowed from a German romantic forbear with his own genial inspiration to produce the attractive *Symphonic Metamorphoses on Themes of Carl Maria von Weber.*

William Walton

William Walton (b. 1902) was the leading modernist in Britain's musical galaxy of the 1920s and 1930s. He added a British lustre and impish wit to the neoclassic tendencies then flourishing on the Continent. Walton was sixteen when he was admitted to Oxford, where he fell in with the fabulous Sitwells—Edith, Osbert, and Sacheverell—a family of aristocratic esthetes whose tastes did much to shape the English arts and letters of their time. They saw to it that young Walton's education was not blighted by stodgy musical academicism. He was soon exposed to Stravinsky and the newer styles of the Continent. At age twenty he established his musical reputation in a collaboration with Edith Sitwell, producing the famous poetical-musical "entertainment" called *Façade*. Edith, a picturesque lady

Wyndham Lewis, Portrait of Edith Sitwell *(begun 1923). The artist conveys some of the quirky cool of his aristocratic sitter.*

who was fourteen years his senior, provided flamboyant poetry for Walton's musical setting. *Façade* was an artistic venture of a novel kind. Sitwell's suavely melodic verse was not designed for silent reading but rather to be heard aloud as an "accented and rhythmic reading to a foreground of music" (said Sacheverell). It was declaimed through a megaphone to the accompaniment of six chamber instruments. Both speaker and musicians were hidden behind a colorfully painted screen through which a hole was cut for the megaphone's horn. The idea was to eliminate the performers' personalities and concentrate on the poetic and musical imageries. It would surface again in concerts of electronic music after World War II.

The poetry of *Façade* rings with the cleverness and optimism of the London smart set of the 1920s, though the number of twenty-one poems in Walton's final musical version may be an intentional echo of the thrice seven poems in Schoenberg's *Pierrot lunaire*. Sitwell's verse is a collage of stagy affections, snobbish attitudes, odd bits of information, and references to the seaside world where the Sitwell children spent their summers. It is filled with plays on the sound of pure words and echoes of the nonsense style of Edward Lear's *The Owl and the Pussycat*. *Façade*'s opening number is titled "Hornpipe," a traditional tune of British sailors. It begins:

Sailors come / to the drum / Out of Babylon; /

Hobby-horses / Foam, the dumb / Sky rhinoceros-glum /

Watched the courses of the breaker's rocking-horses . . .*

Much of the poetry is declaimed at breakneck speed, like a Gilbert and Sullivan patter song. Walton's chamber music transparencies caress every nuance of the surreal imagery and odd combinations of word sounds, "matching, underlining, exhibiting the words," said Osbert Sitwell. Naturally, Walton weaves in the familiar hornpipe:

Façade caught some of the irony of Satie, the verve of Stravinsky's *Soldier's Tale*, the intensity of Schoenberg's *Pierrot*. It delighted the more fashionable Britishers, just recovering from the dreariness of the war, and caused a sensation at its first performances during the early 1920s. The reception was not always favorable. Musical tastes in Britain were still mainly romantic, Elgarian. A clarinetist at a rehearsal was offended by the music he was playing. He asked Walton, "Excuse me sir, has a clarinet player ever done you an in-

*Copyright 1954 by Edith Sitwell. Reprinted by permission.

jury?" Walton's vision won out. *Façade* established him as a composer of large and progressive talent. When its verses are delivered in the patrician singsong of Edith Sitwell (who recorded it more than once), *Façade* makes a strong impression and uncannily evokes its bygone age.

Walton's later works represent a solidified English neoclassicism. Among them are a Viola Concerto (1929), the oratorio *Belshazzar's Feast* (1931), and the Violin Concerto (1939). All are distinguished by stimulating uses of rhythm, persuasive climactic effects, and an impressive lyric flow. Walton's style gradually took on a more romantic bias, as in the film scores for *Henry V* (1944) and *Richard III* (1954). He ultimately enjoyed the same official recognition as Elgar before him—a knighthood in 1951 and the cachet of composing coronation music. He kept pace in the conservative mainstream of the sixties with his Second Symphony (1961) and Variations for Orchestra on a Theme of Hindemith (1963), the latter a memorial tribute to his fellow master in the neoclassic pantheon of the 1920s.

Aaron Copland

The leading American composer of the 1920s and 1930s was Aaron Copland (b. 1900), who grew up in Brooklyn but was most influenced by a stay in Paris from 1921 to 1924—just the time when Stravinsky's neoclassic idiom was taking hold. Copland joined a wave of notably creative Americans in postwar Europe, including the composers Roger Sessions, Walter Piston, and Virgil Thomson, as well as the authors Hemingway, Pound, and Fitzgerald. When Copland returned to the United States in the mid-1920s he was determined to write music with a distinctly American character. To help accomplish that he drew on the rich idioms of American folk music, blues, and jazz. Some of his works, such as *Music for the Theater* (1925) and the Concerto for Piano and Orchestra (1927), joined American rhythmic and harmonic features with the neoclassic manner of Stravinsky. Copland also cultivated a more learned style, stripped of outright Americanism, as in his Piano Variations (1930). But the Great Depression of the 1930s convinced him that he needed an accessible style. Feeling that it was "worth the effort to see if I couldn't say what I had to say in the simplest possible terms," he veered away from severely abstract music. His later works, the Piano Sonata (1941), Violin Sonata (1946), and Third Symphony (1950) reflect this desire to communicate.

Copland, like Stravinsky, often turned to ballet, and three of his ballet scores are built around American folklore. *Rodeo* (1938) and *Billy the Kid* (1942) make use of Western tunes. *Appalachian Spring* (1944) features a set of variations on the Shaker tune, "A gift to be simple." The idea for the ballet *Rodeo* came from its choreographer,

Ex. 9.7. "Buckaroo Holiday" from *Rodeo*, Copland

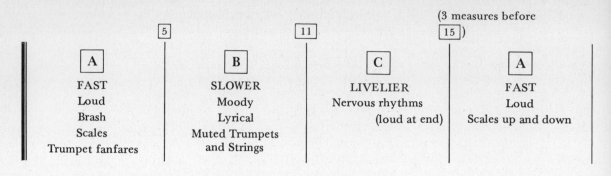

(3 measures before [15])

[A]	[5] [B]	[11] [C]	[15] [A]
FAST	SLOWER	LIVELIER	FAST
Loud	Moody	Nervous rhythms	Loud
Brash	Lyrical	(loud at end)	Scales up and down
Scales	Muted Trumpets		
Trumpet fanfares	and Strings		

Allegro con spirito

[A]

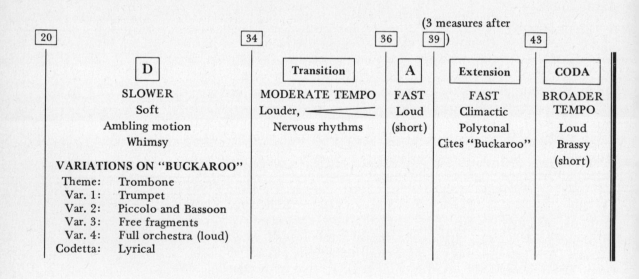

(3 measures after [39])

[20] [D]	[34] Transition	[36] [A]	[39] Extension	[43] CODA
SLOWER	MODERATE TEMPO	FAST	FAST	BROADER TEMPO
Soft	Louder,	Loud	Climactic	Loud
Ambling motion	Nervous rhythms	(short)	Polytonal	Brassy
Whimsy			Cites "Buckaroo"	(short)

VARIATIONS ON "BUCKAROO"
Theme: Trombone
Var. 1:   Trumpet
Var. 2:   Piccolo and Bassoon
Var. 3:   Free fragments
Var. 4:   Full orchestra (loud)
Codetta: Lyrical

IF HE'D BE A BUCKAROO (Cowboy Tune)

Lively

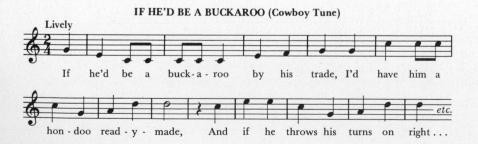

If   he'd   be   a   buck-a-roo   by   his   trade,   I'd   have   him   a

hon-doo read-y-made,   And   if   he   throws   his   turns   on   right . . .   *etc.*

Dance-House. *A cowboy saloon in the American Southwest in 1874.*

"DANCE-HOUSE."

Agnes de Mille: "Throughout the American Southwest, the Saturday afternoon rodeo is a tradition. On remote ranches, as well as in the trading centers and the towns, the 'hands' get together to show off their skill in roping, riding, branding, and throwing . . ." The dance episode from *Rodeo,* titled "Buckaroo Holiday" (7½ minutes), captures this free-and-easy spirit. It incorporates two authentic cowboy songs, "Sis Joe" and "If He'd Be a Buckaroo." Not content with just quoting them, Copland dresses them up with his own brand of rhythm, melody, and harmony. "Buckaroo Holiday" has the loose form of a rondo (Ex. 9.7). The brash opening refrain (A) starts with a scale that careens downward in syncopated rhythm. Other jazzy rhythms appear. Fragments of cowboy tunes bob in and out, mainly the horsy "If He'd Be a Buckaroo." This spawns a set of variations in the middle of the movement, given first to the trombone, then the trumpet, then the piccolo plus bassoon, etc. The variations are full of good-humored surprises. Finally the A material returns, leading to a short, rhythmically intense coda. The whole movement has a free-and-easy western spirit. There are echoes of Stravinsky's jazz-influenced syncopated rhythms and polytonal harmonies. But Copland's Americanisms and his own creative personality give the work a strong individual stamp.

△

Copland: "Buckaroo Holiday" from *Rodeo* (Side 11, Band 1)

D. SERIALISM: THE "TWELVE-TONE METHOD"

During the decade before World War I, Arnold Schoenberg abandoned tonality and moved into uncharted **atonality**—his own dialect of post-tonality. Beginning around 1905 he cultivated styles that were increasingly economical in form, lucid in texture, dispassionate in expression. All these were prototypical "neoclassic" impulses. In 1912 they came to a head in *Pierrot lunaire,* which already has many of the earmarks of Schoenberg's later style. He organized No. 17 ("Parody") of Pierrot and No. 18 ("The Moonspot") as labyrinthine double canons. He described No. 8 ("Night") as a passacaglia, referring to the Baroque ostinato-variation form. The music is not strictly based on an ostinato, but it is suffused with three pitches (E-G-E-flat) that keep recurring throughout. They appear not only in that original order but also in transposition and inversion. This reliance on a given pitch order and its permutations was prophetic of Schoenberg's postwar direction. During the war he served in the Austrian army and could not compose. But he resumed immediately after, and in 1923 he was ready to announce the discovery of his new "method for composing with twelve pitches which are related only with one another." He confided to a pupil that it was something "that will assure the supremacy of German music for the next hundred years." Schoenberg's "method," or "system," has acquired some more-or-less interchangeable nicknames: twelve-pitch, twelve-tone, twelve-note, tone row, serial, serialism. The "method" grew from his conviction, which was at first more intuitive than conscious, that a new sort of orderliness was needed for atonal music, something to replace the orderliness that tonal music once had. Schoenberg felt that just as there were conventional idioms and habitual techniques in tonal music, so atonal music required them for its conduct. But of course, the atonal techniques had to be different.

The **twelve-tone method**, or **serialism**, was Schoenberg's way of giving order to atonality. Its underlying rationale is disarmingly simple. Instead of choosing a key (for example, D major or F minor), as Haydn or Beethoven would have done, and then composing themes in that key and related keys, Schoenberg selected a **tone row**, a particular order of the twelve chromatic pitches, as the basis for

Wassily Kandinsky, Orange (Composition with Chessboard) *(1923). Kandinsky's geometrical* Composition *of 1923 is calmer and more coherent than his* Improvisation *of 1912 (see page 296).*

his composition. That row would provide all the pitch resources used in a piece, and the music would derive much of its specific character from being built on its own particular row. Other pieces would be built on different rows. For his first serial composition in 1923 Schoenberg chose the row shown in Ex. 9.8. For another work in 1924 it was the row shown in Ex. 9.9. Once the row was selected for

Ex. 9.8. Tone Row from No. 5 of Five Pieces, Op. 23, Schoenberg

C#	A	B	G	Ab	F#	A#	D	E	Eb	C	F
1	2	3	4	5	6	7	8	9	10	11	12

Ex. 9.9. Tone Row of Suite for Piano, Op. 25, Schoenberg

E	F	G	Db	Gb	Eb	Ab	D	B	C	A	Bb
1	2	3	4	5	6	7	8	9	10	11	12

a piece, Schoenberg went about composing the music by using only the material of that row, maintaining its order throughout. The melodies and harmonies were built out of the reiterations and combinations of the row's order. The **basic pitches**, or **pitch classes**, that made up the row would reappear constantly in different rhythms, textures, and registers. All together, they produced the effects of musical character and unity that are produced in a tonal piece by the themes and the keys.

Musical styles had been moving in that direction for some time. Composers of the mid-nineteenth century were already working with segments of chromatic melody that had only a tenuous focus on a tonic. Liszt began his "Faust" Symphony (1854) with all twelve chromatic pitches sounded in a row, none of them perceptible as a tonic (Ex. 9.10). Five years later, Wagner began the Prelude to *Tris-*

Ex. 9.10. Opening Theme of "Faust" Symphony, Liszt

Ab		G	B	Eb	F#	Bb	D		F	A	C#	E	G#	C
													(=Ab)	
1		2	3	4	5	6	7		8	9	10	11	(1)	12

Ex. 9.11. Opening of Prelude to *Tristan and Isolde*, Wagner

tan with a "row" of seven pitches, again ambiguous as to which was the tonic (Ex. 9.11). Still, Liszt and Wagner took such rows of tonally ambiguous chromatic pitches and carved them out as musical motives. They gave them distinctive rhythmic shapes. The motives kept returning in the course of a piece, and they quickly identified themselves with specific tonal keys. Wagner fashioned two musical motives from the opening pitches of the *Tristan* Prelude, and he went on to exploit them tonally throughout the Prelude. Schoenberg's twelve-tone method differed from the earlier usage in two essential respects: first, he avoided any hint of a key or tonal center throughout the music; and second, he gave up relying at all on musical motives. Such motives—pregnant figurations of pitch and rhythm— had been the chief building blocks of musical forms since the Renaissance. They were the essence of the musical discourse of Bach, Beethoven, and Brahms. Yet already with *Pierrot lunaire* in 1912, Schoenberg had largely abandoned working with motives. He was working instead with just pitches—with the "pitches of a motive," divorced from any specific rhythmic profile. In certain cases, as in *Pierrot* No. 8 ("Night"), with its basic lineup of the three pitches E-G-E-flat, he was even working with "pitches in a row," though as yet only a row of three pitches. Schoenberg was not alone in this use of pitch orders. Around 1920 Alban Berg built Wozzeck's death scene (see Chapter 8) as an "invention on six pitches": B-flat, F-sharp, E, G-sharp, E-flat, and F. As Schoenberg had done, they were used in a predetermined order and without acquiring the fixed rhythmic shapes of musical motives. Thus Schoenberg or Berg might have taken over Liszt's row of twelve pitches or Wagner's row of seven, but they would have ignored the motivic shapes and settled for the basic pitch order.

Just where all this was leading became clear in 1923 when Schoenberg announced his method of serialism. It seemed the next logical step in the historical progression. Instead of using only segments of three, or six, or seven pitches of the chromatic scale as had been done before 1920, serialism would make regular use of all twelve pitches in a row. The basic rules are like a board game's. The twelve-tone composer beginning work devises a row or lineup of the twelve chromatic pitches. In setting up the row, enharmonic pairs of pitches such as G-sharp/A-flat count as the same pitch. The row can bring the twelve pitches in just about any order, but that order, determined once and for all in advance, will then be maintained throughout the musical composition. The basic layout of the row is called the original or "prime" (P) form of the row. In the course of the music, the pitches of the row will appear in that prime form, but they may also appear in other, derived forms of the row that in some schematic way reflect the prime form. Thus the row can be used backwards, read from end to beginning (in retrograde, R); or with its intervals turned upside down (in inversion, I); or backwards and with inverted intervals (retrograde inversion, RI). Example 9.12 shows the

Ex. 9.12. The Four Principal Forms of the Row from Suite for Piano, Op. 25, Schoenberg

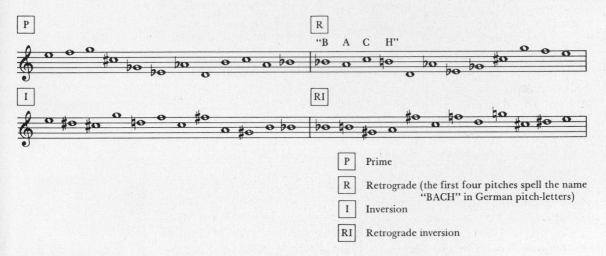

P	Prime
R	Retrograde (the first four pitches spell the name "BACH" in German pitch-letters)
I	Inversion
RI	Retrograde inversion

row on which Schoenberg's Suite for Piano, Op. 25 (1924), is based, spelled out in those four principal forms. Not much is really new here. Similar operations took place in Renaissance canons, Baroque fugues, Haydn symphonies, and Beethoven sonatas. In any event, these four readings of the basic row would give the composer plenty of musical raw material to work with. But there is even more. Each of the basic readings can also be transposed up or down so that it begins from any other half-step level on the piano. That provides an enormous spread of raw material, forty-eight possible rows in all, each a reflection of the original row, each usable, at the composer's will, anywhere within the piece of music. Ex. 9.13 shows how the prime form of the row in Schoenberg's Suite, Op. 25, looks when it is transposed up by six half-steps from P-O ("P-zero," or untransposed) to P-6 (taken six half-steps higher). People who think of twelve-tone music as being narrowly constrained in its options fail to

Ex. 9.13. Prime Form of the Row at Two Different Levels from Suite for Piano, Op. 25, Schoenberg

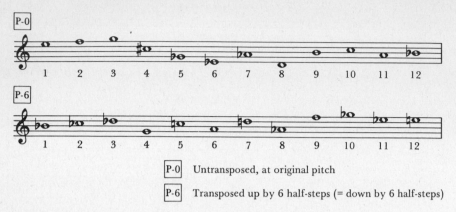

P-0   Untransposed, at original pitch

P-6   Transposed up by 6 half-steps (= down by 6 half-steps)

understand that in most respects it is freer than tonal music, less narrow in the availability of pitch resources, less hemmed in by the traditional idioms of tonal melody, harmony, and rhythm.

At the back of Schoenberg's mind in setting up the serial method was something elementally simple. He wanted to prevent any backsliding into tonality. Schoenberg was a more militant post-tonalist than either Stravinsky or Bartók. They both lingered at the back door of tonality in the 1920s. Schoenberg was so convinced that the path of the future lay with atonality that he took decisive steps to ensure that there was no falling back into the discarded tonal world. He devised a system where tonality simply couldn't happen. What produced tonality in the first place was the favoring of certain pitches over others—the emphasis given to the tonics, dominants, subdominants, etc., of the major and minor keys. Now the serial method foreclosed that possibility by equalizing the use of the twelve pitches. Where all the pitches are treated equally, none emerges as a favored, organizing pitch, that is, as a tonic. In selecting his tone rows Schoenberg tended even to avoid the traditional intervals such as fourths and fifths that were suggestive of the old tonics and dominants of the tonal keys.

Schoenberg's compositional procedure was to have some form of the row govern every pitch choice in the music, both the sequence of pitches making up the melodies and the combinations of pitches making up the harmonies. Musical life was imparted to the inert serial order by the imaginative patterns of rhythm, texture, and tone color that were imposed on the pitches. Thus each piece of serial music progresses as a flow of changing rhythms and textures that are based on the pitches of its row. Overall each piece has a distinctive musical coloration that reflects the unique order and character of

Arnold Schoenberg, *photograph* *ca. 1930 by the American art* *photographer Man Ray.*

its own row. In the course of the music, the row's pitches are supposed to appear and reappear only in series order so that none of them becomes favored through repetition. Yet certain freedoms are allowed. A pitch can be directly repeated a number of times before going on to the row's next pitch. A sequence of the row's pitches can be combined into a chord that can also be repeated directly. Two or more pitches can alternate in trills, arpeggios, or tremolos, again without compromising the integrity of the serial order. A most important freedom is that the rows are not concerned about the pitch's high or low register. A pitch—say C-sharp—can appear in any octave, high or low, a different octave at each occurrence, without altering its status in the row. That allows for the manipulation of register as a factor in texture.

Weighed in the balance of musical history, Schoenberg's serial method accomplished much more than insuring against a tonal backslide. It opened up new resources of post-tonal idioms. It emphasized an imaginative use of textures, tone colors, and rhythms as equal partners with the deployment of pitch in melody and harmony. Not least, it gave the post-tonal composer who was sitting down to work a welcome way to get going. It provided something similar to what the eighteenth-century composer had in getting started on a fugue or a sonata. During the early post-tonal years (the beginning of the twentieth century), composers were faced with a chartless unknown. There was no standard way to get themselves in motion. Now there was a navigational system, a "method." Still, Schoenberg was too clever to take his method with complete seriousness. As an artist of high imagination and consummate skill, he knew that "methods" in art were only means toward ends. He once pooh-poohed the idea of analyzing his serial works to discover the applications of the row. "Do you think one is better off for knowing?" he wrote in 1932 to a violinist who was studying one of his works. "I can't quite see it . . . That isn't where the esthetic qualities reveal themselves." In approaching Schoenberg's twelve-tone works, one should take him at least partly at his word. It is interesting to know how it was done. But the essential is to absorb the music through repeated hearings and see how well it wears.

Schoenberg's Suite for Piano, Op. 25, was the first large-scale work to employ the new twelve-tone method. Its individual movements are titled Prelude, Gavotte and Musette, Intermezzo, Minuet, Trio, and Gigue. Thus it harks back to the keyboard suites of the seventeenth and eighteenth centuries and is in line with the general neo-classic tendencies of the 1920s. Its short movements continue Schoenberg's prewar trend toward finely chiseled utterances with classical dimensions and lean sonorities. The Suite's concluding Gigue (2½ minutes) has the sparkle and rhythmic energy of a Gigue in any age (see Chapter 3), but there is an extra excitement. The

△
Schoenberg: Gigue from
Suite for Piano, Op. 25
(Side 11, Band 2)

textures and rhythmic patterns harbor more surprises than before. There is a stimulating variety to the whimsical tempo changes, the cascades of sparkling notes followed by pensive retards. Ex. 9.14

Ex. 9.14. Gigue from Suite for Piano, Op. 25, Schoenberg

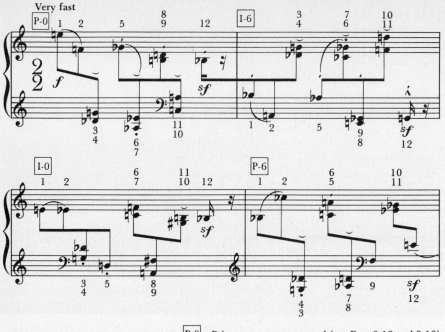

P-0 Prime row, untransposed (*see* Exs. 9.12 and 9.13)

I-0 Inverted row, untransposed

P-6 Prime row, transposed by 6 half-steps

I-6 Inverted row, transposed by 6 half-steps

shows the applications of the row in the first four measures. They pass in a flash when performed, too fast for the ear to register their "numbers." Obviously, the music must be judged by its sound, not by its inner machinery. Compared with tonal music, it sounds highly dissonant. But the old concept of tonal dissonance no longer applies. Schoenberg did away with traditional consonance and dissonance when he gave up tonality and embraced atonality. His post-tonal music has neither consonance nor dissonance. It consists of imaginative sound structures that are based on the pitches of its row. In respects other than pitch choice and harmony, however, Schoenberg's music is often remarkably close to the tradition of his great German and Austrian predecessors.

What many of Schoenberg's contemporaries wrong-headedly considered the arbitrary nature of serialism and a willful exploitation of dissonance earned him a notoriety that increasingly turned into public hostility. This reached a new stage in 1933 with the Nazi takeover in Germany, which forced Schoenberg to seek refuge in the United States. He eventually settled in Southern California (where Stravinsky also lived), and during his later years he taught at universities there. Schoenberg was an inspirational teacher who exercised a profound influence on younger composers. Many of his ideas about music are provocatively stated in the collection of essays, *Style and Idea.* In some of his later music he became partially reconciled with tonality, but all of his more important later works are rigorously serial. They include the Violin Concerto (1936), Fourth String Quartet (1936), Piano Concerto (1942), String Trio (1946), and the opera *Moses and Aaron,* which remained unfinished at his death in 1951. Through the example of these works and through the methodology of the twelve-tone system, Schoenberg remained a powerful force in twentieth-century music. His musical genius and intellectual brilliance were coupled with a haughty and, at times, suspicious personality. He was annoyed by Thomas Mann's portrayal of the fictional composer Adrian Leverkühn in the novel *Doctor Faustus* (1947), a character he took to be modeled on himself. Mann's Leverkühn is a prickly fellow who devises a special system of composing. Schoenberg had personal grievances (many of them justified) that made him seem at times all too human. But history sees him as an outstanding figure who shares with Stravinsky the first rank among the composers of this century.

E. THE SPREAD OF SERIALISM

Alban Berg and Anton von Webern

Twelve-tone music earned only a standoff from the German musical public of the 1920s and 1930s, but it quickly entrenched itself with an inner circle of musicians. Schoenberg was followed in his new system by his two talented disciples, Berg and Webern. Alban Berg, whose early opera *Wozzeck* (1914-21) was composed in a free atonal style, turned to strict twelve-tone organization after 1923. Berg's later stage work, the operatic shocker *Lulu* (1928-35), was based on plays by the expressionist dramatist Franz Wedekind. It is even less savory in subject than *Wozzeck. Lulu* examines depravity among the upper class, whereas *Wozzeck*'s theme was lower-class degradation. Some of Berg's other twelve-tone works won wide acceptance, among them the Chamber Concerto (1925) and the *Lyric Suite* for string quartet (1925). A striking quotation of Wagner's

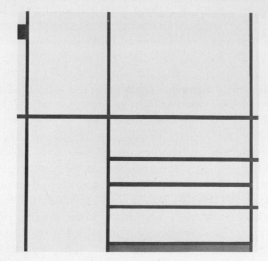

Piet Mondrian, Composition in White, Black, and Red *(1936).* Dutch artist Mondrian developed a stark geometric style, featuring bold primary colors and limited in shapes to horizontal and vertical lines at right angles.

Tristan Prelude that Berg wove into the tissue of the *Lyric Suite* serves to remind the listener where twelve-tone music came from and how far it had come. Berg's ultimate work was the Violin Concerto (1935), completed as a memorial for an eighteen-year-old girl, Manon Gropius, who was the daughter of Mahler's widow and the Bauhaus architect Walter Gropius. She died of polio while the concerto was being planned, and Berg turned it into her musical portrait, completing it just before he himself died. Among the Viennese atonalists, Berg was the least bound by the rules of the twelve-tone system. He was the most romantic and theatrical in spirit, the most prone to tonal reminiscences. Berg was only fifty when he died, too young to be scarred by World War II, but also too young to have fulfilled all his promise.

Anton von Webern was the most zealous and ascetic spirit among the Viennese atonalists. He loyally followed Schoenberg, first into the unmapped regions of atonality in 1908-1909, and then after 1923 into the precise methodology of twelve-tone music. But Webern, who was just nine years younger than Schoenberg, was no servile imitator. The austerity of his twelve-tone idiom and his fascinating unwordly mystique won adherents to serialism where the denser, more physical utterances of Schoenberg did not. For the most part, it was the revelation of Webern's music that brought about Stravinsky's surprising conversion to serial methods after 1950. Webern was particularly drawn to the rigid frameworks of variation forms and the strictures of canons, retrogrades, and inversions. He had encountered the latter in his graduate study of Renaissance music at Vienna, where he received a doctorate in musicology. Webern's total musical output seems very small. It amounts to less than four hours of music, but its bulk is no gauge of its significance. It is an emotionally intense, painstakingly ordered music—its pitches, tone colors, and textures are deployed with severe economy. They are never piled on with spendthrift abandon, as they sometimes appear to be in Mahler and Richard Strauss, or even in Schoenberg and Berg. For Webern, each delicately articulated pitch, each nuance of tone color, had its treasurable quality. Each sound was meant to be pondered for an infinity of suggestions, echoing in the listener's conscious and unconscious. Perhaps no other composer has squeezed so much effect from such meager musical means. To a casual listener Webern's music may seem like a succession of oddly spaced, ice-cold grunts and blips. To Webern's initiates, those tiny bits of sound create white-hot emotional atmospheres that are physically suggestive, spiritually intense, intellectually severe. They say that Webern is as romantic with four notes as others are with four thousand. Schoenberg observed that with Webern, "each glance can be extended into a poem, each sigh into a novel."

Webern was not obliged to emigrate by the German racial edicts of the 1930s, as Schoenberg was. Indeed, he was sympathetic to the Nazi regime. But his music was nevertheless considered degenerate, and he lived in a personal and artistic limbo during World War II. He died in a tragic accident at the war's end, mistakenly shot by an American sentry one evening as he ventured outside his house. Good examples of Webern's free atonal style before World War I are the Five Movements for String Quartet, Op. 5 (1909), Six Bagatelles for String Quartet, Op. 9 (1913), and Five Orchestral Pieces, Op. 10 (1913). Works in his mature twelve-tone style include the Symphony, Op. 21 (1928), Concerto for Nine Instruments (1935), and Second Cantata (1943). Webern's idiom retained its consistency throughout. Whether as a free atonalist or as a strict serialist, he sought the same economy of utterance, the same intensity of expression.

Webern's String Quartet, Op. 28 (1938), shows his characteristic leanness and brevity. The three movements take just eight minutes in all. The music is rigorously twelve-tone, every pitch being derived from a basic row that, like the retrograde row of Schoenberg's Suite for Piano (see Ex. 9.12), takes in the spelling of Bach's name: In German, B-flat is "B," B-natural is "H" (Ex. 9.15). The third movement (2¼ minutes) begins with the simultaneous presentation of four different forms of the row: P-3 (the prime row, transposed up

△
Webern: Third Movement, String Quartet, Op. 28 (Side 11, Band 3)

Ex. 9.15. Tone Row of String Quartet, Op. 28, Webern

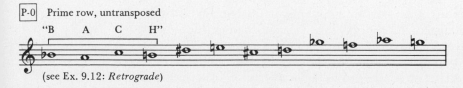

P-0 Prime row, untransposed

"B   A   C   H"

(see Ex. 9.12: *Retrograde*)

three half-steps) appears in the first violin; I-6 (the inversion of the prime row, transposed up six half-steps) appears in the second violin; P-9 is in the viola; and I-0 (the inverted row at its zero or untransposed position) is in the cello. The music goes on to further combinations, derivatives, and segmentations of the row, as various configurations of rhythm, texture, and color are also applied. Yet the listening experience cannot be tied to consciously grasping the permutations of the row. What is important is the imaginative patterning of rhythm, pitch, and texture, all of which is hearable. There are no conventional tunes or rhythmic motives to give this music a readily graspable contour. Webern relies even less than Schoenberg on the traditional rhetoric of repetition and reminiscence. Instead his patterns constantly change shape. There are arrays of leaps and slides, isolated blips, pregnant silences. There are many sorts of sound colors, including trills, pizzicatos, and bowed tones of various consistencies—fat, strident, hushed, or spooky ponticellos (bowed close to the bridge). There are elastic changes of rhythm and texture, speeding ups and slowing downs, transformations from thick to thin. And always there are pregnant silences. Each pitch, each nuance of tone color, each level of dynamics impinges on the listener's consciousness. Webern's intense visions may at first seem cold and inhuman, but to many, his distant, "other world" music reveals itself as filled with emotion and life.

F. RUSSIAN CONSERVATISM

Sergei Prokofiev

The Soviet Union boasted two composers of major stature during the mid-twentieth century, Sergei Prokofiev and Dmitri Shostakovich. Compared with the mainstream composers in Western Europe, they were both distinctly Russian in their musical idioms and conservative in their outlook. They were also responsive to the imperatives of Communist ideology, and their music raises the question of how far the creative artist can bend to political pressures without sacrificing character and identity. Prokofiev (1891-1953) had a precocious talent. He completed his first composition at age five and one-half and the score of his first opera when he was nine. He graduated from the old St. Petersburg (Leningrad) Conservatory, performing his romantic First Piano Concerto (1911). From 1912 through 1917 he explored modern idioms, roughly paralleling Stravinsky's evolution. His piano pieces of those years, bearing names such as "Sarcasms," "Fugitive Visions," and "Diabolical Suggestions," are replete with sharp, percussive rhythms and biting harmonies. His Scythian Suite for Orchestra (1914) evokes the splendor of ancient

Russian sun-worship in an exhibitionistic style reminiscent of *The Rite of Spring.* Then around 1917, Prokofiev marked a new direction with his Symphony No. 1 in D, the so-called "Classical" Symphony. It was a return to Mozartean symphonic ideals, an early landmark of neoclassicism. Restrained in emotion, lucid in its classic forms, transparent in texture, and tinged with a delicate Slavic irony, the "Classical" Symphony has remained Prokofiev's most popular work.

Prokofiev lived away from Russia for fifteen years from 1918 to 1933. Though he traveled widely in the West, he was mainly in Paris and his music represented a Russian-French idiom. His opera *The Love for Three Oranges* (1921), containing the well-known "March," his Third and Fourth Piano Concertos (1921, 1931), and his Second, Third, and Fourth Symphonies (1924-30) are all bound up with the cosmopolitan atmosphere of Paris in the 1920s. Then in 1933, Prokofiev was overcome with yearning for his native land, so he put an end to his self-imposed wanderings and returned home. "Foreign air cannot inspire me. I am a Russian, and nothing can be more damaging than living in exile, in a spiritual climate whose nature is different from my own." He received a cordial reception—that of a prodigal son returned—and his inspiration found nourishment in the renewed exposure to his native roots. He accommodated deftly to the government's insistence on producing music that was agreeable and accessible to the masses, writing the ballet *Romeo and Juliet* (1935), the enchanting children's tale *Peter and the Wolf* (1936), the film score for *Alexander Nevsky* (1939), the ballet *Cinderella* (1944), and the opera *War and Peace* (1941-52). He also dutifully turned out "official" Soviet music, such as anthems and cantatas that commemorated the birthdays of Lenin and Stalin and the anniversaries of the Russian Revolution. Once, in 1948, he balked at the imposed cultural dogmas and ignored the harangue of a party hack. Then he remembered the disappearances and suicides of other artist-dissidents, and the blighted careers of those who in George Orwell's seering word just became "unpersons." Prokofiev apologized. Three years later he was rewarded with a Stalin prize for his Soviet-styled cantata, *On Guard for Peace.* Prokofiev died in 1953, on the day after Stalin. The news was characteristically held back so that his death would not overshadow that of "the Leader of the People and Friend of Children."

Prokofiev seems to have been successful in the difficult compromise between artistic integrity and political constraint. He needed to work on Russian soil, so he paid his dues with propagandistic and ceremonial pieces. Even in his more personal works of the 1940s and 1950s he may have simplified his style to meet the imperatives of "socialist realism." His art may not have suffered, for among his best and purest creations are the late works, the Flute Sonata, arranged as the Second Violin Sonata (1943), and his Fifth and Seventh Symphonies (1944, 1953). They are abstract music, unburdened with ideological baggage, and they have the wisdom of a spacious maturity. Yet in the end we cannot be sure. No one can estimate the inner price he may have paid, the hidden losses to his art.

Dmitri Shostakovich

Dmitri Shostakovich (1906-1974) was more vulnerable than Prokofiev to the pressures for political conformity. He paid a higher price. Fifteen years younger than Prokofiev, a generation younger than Stravinsky, Shostakovich reached maturity during the decade of the 1920s at a time when young Russians could not easily establish contact with the West. Shostakovich's style was formed without the perspectives that an exposure to contemporary France or Germany would have given him. When Prokofiev returned to the Soviet Union in 1933, he was already a mature artist, secure in his world fame, so that he could remain a strong reed that bent with the Soviet ideological winds but did not break. Shostakovich was nurtured under Bolshevism, and when he was barely thirty he was profoundly intimidated by the regime. During his remaining four decades he remained a somewhat terrified pawn in the cruel game of Stalinist and post-Stalinist cultural politics.

Success came when Shostakovich was only nineteen. His First Symphony scored a triumph at Leningrad in 1925. It is a durable work, full of emotion and bearing all the marks of a powerful imagination. It is also basically a romantic work in the rhetorical manner of Tchaikovsky and Mahler, with only a thin overlay of post-tonal modernism. Shostakovich's musical powers grew during the next decade, but there was also a growing ambivalence as he found himself caught between the outer need to satisfy the conservative officialdom and the personal need to be responsive to his own stylistic impulses. His Second Symphony in 1927 commemorated the tenth anniversary of the Soviet Republic and concluded with an encomium of Lenin. His Third Symphony in 1931, (titled "The First of May") concluded with a chorus celebrating International Workers' Day. The cultural commissars were not pleased with some of the idioms that had crept into these outwardly correct political gestures. Shostakovich's opera *The Nose* (1930) was in fact attacked in the press, which deplored its French and German touches as "bourgeois modernism." Still the politicians threatened no serious action. Then in 1936 the blow came. His most recent opera, *Lady Macbeth of the District of Mtsensk* (1934), was being staged at Moscow. It had a sordid nineteenth-century plot that dealt with adultery, murder, and suicide. It supposedly unmasked the depravity of czarist bourgeois values, but the puritan Soviet officials saw it differently. In an issue of *Pravda* Shostakovich found an unsigned article bearing the terse title "Muddle Instead of Music." His *Lady Macbeth* was condemned for "musical gangsterism." He was reproved for his "decadent cacophony," warned that things "could end very badly." The catch phrases seemed to be those of Stalin himself. The opera was withdrawn and Shostakovich became a social leper. "I was in the grip of utter fear, no longer the master of my life. My past was rubbed out, my creations, my abilities, turned out to be worthless . . ." Others in that fix had been suicides, but Shostakovich went energetically about redeeming himself. His Fifth Symphony, completed the next year (1937), bore the unctuous subtitle, "The Response of a Soviet Artist to Just Criticism." The politicians found it purged of the Western affectations and ironies that stained his earlier music, and the work was accepted as a suitable example of Soviet art. Miraculously—for compromises like this rarely result in artistic success—Shostakovich's Fifth was a masterpiece, and his Sixth Symphony (1939) carried off a similar tour de force. Sadly, there was too little of artistic consequence to come. Shostakovich went on into the 1970s, industriously compiling a total of fifteen symphonies, fifteen string quartets, and numerous concertos, sonatas, chamber works, and film scores. They rarely matched the inspiration of his early works such as the First Symphony (1925); the *Age of Gold* ballet (1930), which contains a witty scherzo satirizing the diplomats at the Geneva Disarmament Conference; the Preludes for Piano of the 1930s; the Cello Sonata (1935); and the Fifth and Sixth Symphonies (1937-39). Shostakovich's Seventh Symphony, the so-called "Leningrad" Symphony, became a world success in 1941. Supposedly it represented the heroic Russian resistance to the Nazi siege. A decade later the music seemed puffed up and dull, its best ideas swathed in a musical rhetoric that had lost its vitality after Mahler. Shostakovich's Eleventh Symphony (1957) celebrated the anticzarist insurrection of 1905. His Twelfth Symphony (1961) was the "Lenin" Symphony. His *Suite on Verses by Michelangelo,* completed during his last year (1974), may have revived some of the genuine emotion found in his earlier work. He kept on trying to have it both ways: rendering tribute to the modern Russian Caesars and their political standards of musical style while maintaining his integrity and originality. Shostakovich may have been less fortunate than Prokofiev in this endeavor.

Still, there is this to say for the Soviet system of supporting composers, as compared to the Western free-enterprise system: Soviet society rewards composers of high distinction with its highest honors. Talented creators like Miaskovsky, Glière, Prokofiev, Khachaturian, and Shostakovich have enjoyed the same tokens of worldly success as the Soviet Union's outstanding scientists, politicians, industrial technocrats, and soccer players. Composers of comparable distinction in the West—American composers of the stature of Ives, Copland, Sessions, Carter, and Babbitt (see Chapter 10)—are almost entirely ignored by society at large and by the officialdom of that society. The Russians' luxuries are bought at the price of conformity to party discipline while the Western composers are presumably free to compose in any way they want. But unless the Westerners are singularly talented and lucky, their pursuit of artistic excellence and imaginative freedom may leave them free to starve.

G. THE AVANT-GARDE

Neoclassicism was the dominating esthetic force between the two world wars. It left its imprint on musical outlooks as diverse as those of Stravinsky and Hindemith, Bartók and the Viennese serialists. Even Richard Strauss produced a Dance Suite after Couperin in 1923. In fact, most leading composers of the period turned from nineteenth-century tonal romanticism to restrained post-tonal ideals that can be viewed in some sense as throwbacks to the musical eighteenth century. In addition to the composers considered earlier in this chapter, there were Busoni and Casella in Italy, Tippett in England, Kodály in Hungary, Janáček in Czechoslovakia, Nielsen in Denmark, Falla in Spain, and the important group of French-Swiss modernists called "The Six," whose members were Darius Milhaud, Germaine Tailleferre, Arthur Honegger, Georges Auric, Louis Durey, and Francis Poulenc. Each of these composers developed a style that was personal and modern, often nationalist, and to some extent colored by a lingering commitment to tonality. There were

Salvador Dali, The Persistence of Memory *(1931). Dali's haunting landscape with limp watches represents the surrealist movement, whose aim was to explore the realm of psychic experience and to give artistic shape to the material of dreams.*

also some still more conservative imaginations, such as those of Sibelius, Rachmaninoff, and the aging Richard Strauss, who during the 1920s and 1930s made up a rear guard that eschewed post-tonality and neoclassicism and clung to a fuller-blooded tonal romanticism. Shostakovich was close to this group. His early works (such as the First and Fifth Symphonies) had, as Schoenberg put it, the "breath" of a real symphonist. But his idiom was rooted basically in romantic expression, even when his harmonies put on a post-tonal façade.

At quite the other end of the musical spectrum were certain composers whose radical outlook went beyond even that of the twelve-tone composers. They were experimenters and visionaries for whom the tidy styles of neo-Bach and neo-Mozart music produced by their prim neoclassic contemporaries seemed altogether too restricting. During the 1920s and 1930s the American Henry Cowell (1897-1965) experimented with "tone-clusters" that were obtained by pounding a fist or forearm on the piano keyboard. (Charles Ives had already done something like that.) The Mexican Julian Carillo, the Czech Alois Haba, and the Russian Ivan Wyschnegradsky composed with microtones, intervals smaller than a half-step. (Ives had also tried that!) Other composers of an exploratory bent tried out early electronic instruments, for example, the theremin, whose pitch and color changed as the performer's hands moved through an electronic field.

Edgard Varèse

The most important avant-gardist was Edgard Varèse (1883-1965), a Parisian whose musical results were not only significant in themselves, but in their exploration of out-of-the-ordinary sound resources were prophetic of developments following World War II. Varèse owed something of his style to the early Stravinsky and also something to the concepts of cubist and futurist art that were circulating while he was in his twenties. He had a background in mathematics and physics, which accounts for the scientific outlook in much of his work. His experimental bent is evident in the titles and instrumentation of *Hyperprism,* for winds and percussion (1923); *Octandre,* for winds, brass, and double bass (1924); *Integrals,* for small orchestra and percussion (1925); *Amériques,* for large orchestra (1926); *Equatorial,* for bass voice, brass, organ, percussion, and theremin (1934); and *Density 21.5,* for unaccompanied flute (1935), whose title refers to the specific gravity of platinum, from which some of the best flutes were made. After 1915 Varèse established himself in New York, but his works encountered opposition and disdain. This led to a long silence. When he emerged after World War II, he was no longer a voice in the wilderness. His *Deserts* (1954) and *Poème électronique* (1958) used electronic sounds, in the latter piece projected

Julio Gonzalez, Head *(ca. 1935). Gonzalez established wrought iron as a significant medium for sculptors during the 1930s. In this "head," fleshy anatomy is reduced to a "mouth" (the oval on the right with spike teeth), two rod-like eyes connected through an "optic nerve" to the dish-antenna convolutions of a "brain," and a moon-shaped skull (with wisps of hair?) holding things together.*

through more than four hundred loudspeakers. Now a whole generation of younger composers who were fulfilling their own aspirations in the electronic-sound medium turned to the ancient Varèse and hailed him as their prophet.

Varèse was the first important twentieth-century composer to abandon pitches (melody and harmony) as the main factors in his music. In spite of the increased role that twentieth-century music gave to the factor of rhythm, the musical ideas of composers such as Stravinsky, Bartók, and Schoenberg were still framed basically in melody and harmony. Varèse welcomed many sorts of sounds other than pitch sounds as materials for his music, including some considered just noise by his contemporaries. His imagination flourished in a wealth of percussion sounds. Compensating for the de-emphasis of pitch, he emphasized the neglected factors of timbre, texture, and rhythm.

Varèse's *Ionisation* (1931) is scored for thirteen performers who are responsible for playing forty-one different percussion instruments. Most of those instruments are struck or rubbed percussion of indefinite pitch, but there are brief injections of fixed pitch by a piano, glockenspiel, and chimes. There are also two sirens with fluidly changing pitches, but, by and large, the music has few fixed pitches. There are chiefly patterns of rhythm and texture created by the sounds of indefinite pitches on cymbals, gongs, sleigh bells, castanets, Cuban rattles (maracas), West Indian bongos, and various other drums. Stravinsky advocated the idea that "music is dominated by the principle of similarity." But in Varèse's *Ionisation* the repetitions, associative patterns, and similarities are not obvious. Nothing seems to return. The tone colors, textures, and rhythms appear to be constantly changing and recombining. For some listeners in the 1930s *Ionisation* seemed just a joke. But today it is still exciting to hear, a durable representative of the past and a prophecy of music's future.

△
Varèse: *Ionisation* (excerpt)
(Side 11, Band 4)

H. JAZZ, SWING, AND BROADWAY SHOWS

The Spread of Jazz

The era of New Orleans jazz was cut short by the war and Prohibition. Storyville was off-limits to sailors in 1917. The Volstead Act of 1919 shut its saloons. The first genial phases of jazz—its birth and wide-eyed youth—were over. New Orleans musicians had entertained on the Mississippi riverboats for years. Now they took those boats up river looking for jobs. They played their "good-times" music for new audiences that were attracted to the catchy sounds. The jazz people went to Memphis, St. Louis, and Chicago. Chicago was where they mainly stayed. It was the Chicago of the "Roaring Twenties," of

Louis Armstrong's Hot Five. *The famous recording band of the 1920s, as elegant in appearance as they were "good times" in sound. Armstrong presides at the piano.*

gangsters and speakeasies, Stutz bearcats and raccoon coats. It was the Chicago of Scott Fitzgerald's "jazz age," and it produced the golden age of jazz. Chicago jazz of the 1920s took the mellow, optimistic Dixieland sound and gave it a big-city glint and glitter. One or two saxophones were added to the old band, and with them came a second trumpet or cornet. The rustic sounds of the Dixie banjo and tuba gave way to a guitar and string bass. The whole rhythmic feel was different, the pulses stronger, particularly the "off-beat" accents on beats two and four of the four-beat measure. One jazzman who moved up the river was Joe "King" Oliver. He formed a "Creole Jazz Band" in Chicago. Another was New Orleans-born Louis "Satchmo" Armstrong (1900-1971), who first played cornet in the Oliver band, then led his own groups—the "Hot Five" and "Hot Seven." Satchmo remained the godfather of the jazz movement for half a century. "Hotter Than That," recorded in 1927, is bursting with the Armstrong warmth and vitality. On this cut, he both plays the cornet and sings. The ten seconds of introduction bring in the whole group: cornet, trombone, clarinet, piano, banjo, and guitar. Armstrong takes over in a cornet solo, embellishing the tune and its chord progressions. A clarinet follows (0:45), then Armstrong again (1:20), "scat-singing" in his famous style of wordless vocal improvisation, with an exuberance that almost denies the need to take a breath. A slow dialogue between vocalist and guitar (1:55) leads to a short trombone solo (2:19); then Armstrong's high-spirited cornet returns, still chatting with the guitar. The piece ends surprisingly up in the air. There is no last tonic chord.

Δ
Armstrong: "Hotter Than That"
(Side 11, Band 5)

Chicago jazz also brought the first great white musician, the cornettist Leon "Bix" Beiderbecke (1903-1931). When he was a boy he heard the jazz music on the riverboats that stopped at his home town of Davenport, Iowa. He introduced a "cooler," less frenzied style of improvisation to the transplanted Dixieland style. Other young whites, the clarinetist Benny Goodman, the trombonist Tommy Dorsey, the drummer Gene Krupa, picked up the Chicago style of the 1920s. Yet Chicago was not alone in its golden age. During the late 1920s Kansas City nurtured a sophisticated, strongly rhythmic outgrowth of the blues with a powerful rolling bass that was called **boogie-woogie**. It was piano music with a short, juggernaut, "eight-to-the-bar" ostinato, constantly repeating in the bass (Ex. 9.16). It was virtuoso music, physically exhausting, with the pianist

Ex. 9.16. Boogie-Woogie Basses

playing brilliant sallies and wild, intoxicating fantasies over the hypnotic swell and lurch of the accompaniment. Boogie-woogie quickly spread. Among its masters were Albert Ammons, Pete Johnson, and Meade Lux Lewis. In Harlem, the old ragtime rhythms were finding new vigor in a fresh "ragging" style of piano playing. There was the Harlem "stride" of James P. Johnson, Fats Waller, and Art Tatum, played with a heavy left hand. Johnson's song "Charleston" launched the great American dance fad of the 1920s. With its kick-outs of the heels, glides, and up-and-down knee bends, it caught the spirit of the jazz-age flappers.

Swing

As jazz spread nationally during the 1920s, and as more white musicians began to play it, its original quality as pure black musical improvisation was also changed. Big bands began to form in Chicago and New York. Paul Whiteman, Fletcher Henderson, and Duke Ellington no longer used little groups of five or seven. They doubled and tripled the size. When there were that many players, the music had to be written out—"arranged" in advance. Written jazz no longer had the spirit of early jazz, whose life-giving element was improvisation. There were still the brilliant solo "breaks," but the soulful fantasy lessened as the music jelled in arrangements on paper. This new jazz put the emphases on instrumental colors and suave ensemble performance, particularly on the sheen and power of synchronized brass and rhythm sections. The new sound ideal crystallized around 1935 when the graceful, sweeping rhythms of Benny Goodman's band ushered in the era of *swing*. Goodman, Duke Ellington, Count Basie, Tommy Dorsey, Harry James, Glenn Miller—dozens of "name" and "seminame" bands spread the new swing idiom, broadcasting it over the radio on the Hit Parade, traveling the rails for one-night stands. Swing was gorgeous stuff, smooth and confident, making its appeal to middle-class whites who, by the late 1930s, were regaining some of the assurance and the affluence they had lost during the Depression. The era of big swing bands carried over into the first years of World War II. Then it too was gone, except in the ballrooms of big hotels. Travel was curtailed, musicians became soldiers, moods changed. Big swing and the blare of its bands never really recovered.

The fundamental stream of jazz—essentially black and improvisatory, perennially young and accommodating—began to find new outlets that were truer to its nature. The change began in New York around 1940 with a cropping up of small groups that went back to the basics, that is, to pure improvisation. The new jazz was a little less spontaneous than the old, a little more subtly worked out in advance than the classics of Dixieland and Chicago. But it had an unprecedented sophistication and carried tremendous emotional clout. It marked the beginning of the **bebop** revolution that would flower right after the war.

American Musical Theater

Alongside the vigorous outgrowths of black-inspired jazz during the first half of the twentieth century there was a burgeoning of mainly white-inspired sentimental song in the American musical theater. The Broadway shows and tunes were artistic hybrids that had roots in both Europe and America. A vein of truly American lyric genius had already flourished during the Civil War era in Stephen Foster. Now the post-bellum years saw musical theater on the upswing along Broadway, New York's "Great White Way." The "gay '90s" produced the Floradora Girls and the varied entertainments of the vaudeville shows. The prosperous decades before World War I brought European imports as well—cultured traditions of light opera, or **operetta**, by Jacques Offenbach of Paris, the "Savoy" operas of Gilbert and Sullivan's London, and the works of the Strausses (the "waltz kings" of Vienna). The first master of the American musical theater came out of that genteel European tradition. Victor Herbert (1859-1924), Irish-born and German-trained, wrote over three dozen shows, including *Babes in Toyland, Sweethearts,* and *Naughty Mariet-ta.* In the same mold was the Hungarian-born Sigmund Romberg (1887-1951), who established himself on the American scene with *Maytime* (1917), followed by dozens of successes including *The Student Prince, The Desert Song,* and *Blossom Time.* From a coarser, music-hall tradition came George M. Cohan (1878-1948), who began a run of stirring songs at the time of World War I: "You're a Grand Old Flag," "Over There," "I'm a Yankee Doodle Dandy," and "Give My Regards to Broadway." With Jerome Kern (1885-1945) the European and native traditions began to merge. Kern was New York-born and white, but he exploited black American musical idioms in *Show Boat* (1927), which marked a turn from the sugary world of European operetta to real-life human situations. Among the wonderful tunes of *Show Boat* are "Why Do I Love You," "Make Believe," and the unforgettable "Ol' Man River." Later on, Kern captured the wistful mood of the post-flapper era with the song "Smoke Gets in Your Eyes" (1933). Irving Berlin (b. 1888) had a first success in 1911 with the song "Alexander's Ragtime Band," and he went on to a string of hit shows, sustaining his freshness through *Annie Get Your Gun* (1946) and *Call Me Madam* (1950). Berlin produced one of the great American tunes in "A Pretty Girl Is Like a Melody." A subtler talent belonged to Cole Porter (1891-1964), who wrote the urbane shows *Anything Goes* (1934) and *Kiss Me Kate* (1948), and the hit tunes "Night and Day" and "Begin the Beguine." But the great talent in the group belonged to Gershwin.

George Gershwin (1898-1937) enjoys a unique place among the show composers. More than any other American he caught the sophistication of the jazz age. Gershwin was also capable of combining his popular idioms with a serious, "neoclassic" style that aspires to comparison with Stravinsky and Bartók. Gershwin's first hit song was "Swanee" in 1919. He remained the leader in the Broadway shows of the 1920s with *Lady Be Good* (1924), *Strike Up the Band* (1927), *Funny Face* (1927), *Girl Crazy* (1930), and *Of Thee I Sing* (1931). At the same time he was putting native American idioms into serious, modernist works. The landmarks of this synthesis are *Rhapsody in Blue* for piano and orchestra (1924) and the Piano Concerto in F (1935). In *An American in Paris* (1928), Gershwin produced an ambitious orchestral tone poem, reflecting his enchantment with the great French city. Gershwin's most significant work was his last one, the folk opera *Porgy and Bess* (1935). It was composed for black singers, and both its subject matter and its musical style took the humanizing and Americanizing of operatta a big step beyond Kern's *Show Boat* of 1927.

The late 1930s brought a new wave of European sophistication to Broadway. Kurt Weill (1900-1950) produced *Knickerbocker Holiday*

(1938), containing the popular "September Song," then *Lady in the Dark* (1941) and *Street Scene* (1947). Frederick Loewe (b. 1904) wrote *Brigadoon* and the spectacularly successful *My Fair Lady* (1956). The American-born Richard Rodgers (1900-1979) specialized in Americana in hit shows such as *Oklahoma!* (1943) and *South Pacific* (1948). Broadway found another synthesizer of popular and learned styles in Leonard Bernstein (b. 1918), whose *Candide* (1956) and *West Side Story* (1957) rank with Loewe's *My Fair Lady* as probably the best musicals since World War II.

10 The Recent Past

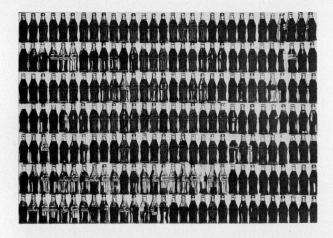

Andy Warhol, Coca-Cola (1962). The pop art movement of the 1960s took as subject matter the banal artifacts of modern consumer society (soup cans, hamburgers, comic-strip illustrations, toilets) and processed them into "fine art." In this painting Warhol uses over 200 Coca Cola bottles to create an abstraction of rhythm and shape.

Saturn's Moons and Rings *(1980). Space exploration produced new visual resources, like this montage of images sent back by the NASA Voyager I mission.*

The Recent Past

MUSIC	ARTS AND IDEAS	POLITICS AND SCIENCE
ELECTRONICS, CHANCE, THE QUEST FOR ORDER	**ENDGAME: FACING THE VOID**	**THE POLITICS OF CONFRONTATION**

Britten (1913-1976):
   Peter Grimes (1945)
Babbitt (b. 1916):
   Composition for Four Instruments (1948); Composition for Synthesizer (1964); *Philomel* (1964)
Messiaen (b. 1908):
   Orderings of Values and Intensities (1948)
Boulez (b. 1925):
   Structures (1951); *Le Marteau sans maître* (1955)
Cage (b. 1912):
   Aria and Fontana Mix (1958)
Stockhausen (b. 1928):
   Gesang der Jünglinge (1956)
Stravinsky (1882-1971):
   Movements for Piano and Orchestra (1959); *Requiem Canticles* (1966)
	Sartre, *Being and Nothingness* (1943); *Existentialism* (1946)
	Abstract expressionism and action painting of Pollock, de Kooning, Motherwell, Tobey (from 1948)
	Beckett, *Waiting for Godot* (1953); *Endgame* (1958)
	Saarinen, TWA Terminal (1956)
	Mies van der Rohe, Seagram Building (1958)
	Op art of Vasarely, Riley (1950s-1960s)
	Grass, *The Tin Drum* (1959)
	Pop art and new realist art of Warhol, Oldenberg, Rosenquist, Lichtenstein, Johns (1960s-1970s)
	Dramas of Ionesco and Pinter (1950s-1980s)
	Films of Fellini (1950s-1980s)
		Atomic explosions, nuclear energy (from 1945)
		"Cold War" (from 1945)
		Invention of the transistor (1948)
		Molecular biologists find the structure of DNA (1953)
		First earth satellite in orbit (1957)
		Death of Stalin (1958)
		Assassination of President Kennedy (1963)
		Women's liberation (from 1960s)
		Black Power movement (from 1960s)
		Assassination of Martin Luther King (1968)
		Transistorized electronic computers; xerography; jet airplane travel (1960s)
		Vietnam War (1964-1975)
		Americans reach the moon (1969)
		Advances in plasma physics; industrial use of computerized robots; biological experiments with gene transformation and cloning (1970s-1980s)
		Reusable spacecraft: the space shuttle (1981)

Sessions (b. 1896):
   Third Symphony (1957)
Carter (b. 1908):
   Double Concerto (1961)
Barber (1910-1980)
   Piano Concerto (1962)
Xenakis (b. 1922):
   Métastasis (1954); *Eonta* (1964)
Ligeti (b. 1923):
   Atmospheres (1961)
Berio (b. 1925):
   Sinfonia (1968)
Feldman (b. 1926):
   Rothko Chapel (1972)
Musgrave (b. 1928):
   Night Music (1969)
Crumb (b. 1929):
   Black Angels (1970); *Ancient Voices of Children* (1970); *Voice of the Whale* (1971)
Takemitsu (b. 1930):
   Coral Island (1962); *November Steps* (1967)
Martino (b. 1931):
   Notturno (1973)
Oliveros (b. 1932):
   Sound Patterns (1964)
Penderecki (b. 1932):
   Threnody to the Victims of Hiroshima (1960)
Davidowsky (b. 1934):
   Synchronisms (from 1963)		

ELECTRONICS, CHANCE, THE QUEST FOR ORDER *(Continued)*

Riley (b. 1935):
   In C (1964)
Reich (b. 1936):
   Octet (1979)
Glass (b. 1937):
   Einstein on the Beach (1976)
Kolb (b. 1940):
   Solitaire (1971)
	Charlie Parker (1920-1955)
	The Beatles: *Sgt. Pepper; Abbey Road* (late 1960s)
	The Rolling Stones: *Beggars' Banquet* (1969)
	Aretha Franklin (b. 1942)	

For most of us, music is a necessity, not a luxury. Life would be barren without it. No civilization has done without it. No civilization has not cared intensely about expressing its own visions of the human condition in its own kinds of sound patterns. Most of today's music will fade away, but that has been the fate of the "today" music of every age. For every work by Mozart or Brahms that has withstood the test of time, there are thousands of forgotten works by their lesser contemporaries stored in libraries. Some of the new music of today may join the classics. Its composers may be thought of as "old masters." We would like to tell what will remain, giving value after a decade or a generation. But that is hard to know. We can only be sure of what pleases us right now. As for predicting the future, we must listen to the new music and refine our tastes by repeated hearings. Ultimately the filtering effect of time will decide. If there is a rule of thumb, it is that the genuine classic rarely starts out by seeming old-fashioned. Most music that has turned out to be durable began by seeming radical and experimental. Most of the great composers, from Monteverdi through Stravinsky and Schoenberg, seemed to be originators in their own time, not followers of someone else's breakthrough. Even the hidebound Bach was an original, even a radical in the depth and refinement of his musical language. If there is a lesson in this, it is that we should support the "difficult" composers, encourage the avant-garde. We must seek them out, learn what they are doing. For among them are the prophets of our civilization, the likely creators of our contemporary classics.

A. TOTAL SERIALISM

The new music composed after World War II was affected by three main factors: total serialism, electronics, and chance.

Total serialism arose as an outgrowth of Arnold Schoenberg's prewar serialism of pitch (see Chapter 9). At the war's end, Schoenberg's doctrine of the 1920s and 1930s seemed to have been a local Viennese phenomenon that disintegrated under a political cloud. Berg and Webern were dead, and the vestiges of serialism appeared likely to perish with Schoenberg, the originator and last survivor. But Schoenberg gathered talented disciples in California, young Americans who were impressed by his intellectual power and musical example, and who helped spread his reputation along with their own. Then the music of Webern enjoyed a postwar renaissance, being discovered and imitated by young composers on both sides of the Atlantic. Schoenberg's and Webern's serialism had been a serialization of pitch, a methodical ordering applied to the raw materials of melody and harmony. Now a serial ordering began to be applied to other elements of the musical work. Durations, dynamics, and tone colors were also put into series as a way of giving shape to a composition. Tone colors could be presented with instruments appearing in a pre-selected order, for instance, oboe, violin, trombone, bassoon, viola, piccolo, cello, clarinet, drum, celeste. The durations of sounds and silences could be given a serial order, as in Ex. 10.1, which comes

Ex. 10.1. Durations and Pitches in Series of Twelve from *Structures I* (1951), Boulez

Measures 57-64

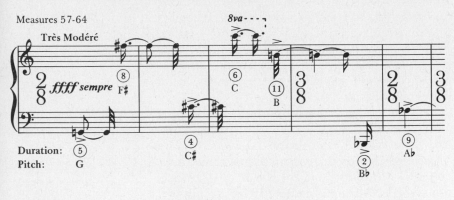

◯ = durations in 32nd notes

from a two-piano work called *Structures*, composed in 1951 by Pierre Boulez. In this passage, the pitches are in a twelve-pitch series. But the durations of sounds are also ordered in a series of twelve lengths that includes every possibility from one thirty-second note through twelve thirty-second notes. Similarly, dynamics could be ordered in a series, for example, FFF, PP, Mf, decrescendo, sforzando, etc. And so could accents and other nuances—staccato, legato, pizzicato, the use of piano pedal, etc. In this variety of ways, the single-dimensional serialism of pitch that originated in the 1920s was expanded after World War II to a multidimensional total serialism that could involve every aspect of the musical raw material and permeate every fiber of the resulting composition.

Schoenberg had anticipated the serializing of tone colors even before he began serializing pitch in 1923. In a short, impressionistic work of 1909 titled "Summer Morning by a Lake: Colors" (No. 3 of his Five Pieces for Orchestra, Op. 16), Schoenberg shaped the music as a slow gyration of instrumental timbres around a slowly evolving chord progression. Using the same germ of an idea, Webern applied it to the filigree texture of his mature works of the 1920s and 1930s, producing "melodies" that were made up of tone colors. The cohesiveness of a Webernesque "tone-color melody" ("Klangfarbenmelodie") lay in an orderly succession of timbres, each supplying some quantum of distinctive instrumental or vocal color. Webern's late works also made gestures at a serial ordering of other musical aspects, including rhythms, high and low registers, dynamics (louds and softs), articulations (pizzicatos, glissandos, legatos, staccatos, etc.), and textures. In all of this he foreshadowed the rigorous total serialism that emerged after the war.

Total serialism was the creation of young composers in America and Europe who were fascinated by the intellectual severity and communicative power they discovered in the music of Webern. The American Milton Babbitt (b. 1916) led the way with his Three Compositions for Piano (1947), Composition for Four Instruments (1948), and Composition for Twelve Instruments (1948). In France, Olivier Messiaen (b. 1908) drew on an interest in the precise, nuanced rhythms of Hindu music in producing the piano piece "Modes de valeurs et d'intensités" ("Orderings of Values and Intensities," 1948), where pitches, durations, loudness, and attacks (different ways of beginning a sound) are coordinated in a series. Pierre Boulez (b. 1925), a disciple of Messiaen and an admirer of Webern, adopted precise serial methods in his Second Piano Sonata (1948) and Sonatina for Flute and Piano (1950). Boulez produced the classic monument of total serialism in 1951 with his *Structures I* for two pianos. Karlheinz Stockhausen (b. 1928), another student of Messiaen's, responded with his own totally serialized *Kontra-Punkte* (*Counter-Point*) for ten instruments in 1953.

The early 1950s also brought a momentous surprise. For nearly half a century the field of new music was dominated by the two rather different creative approaches of Schoenberg and Webern on the one hand and Stravinsky on the other. The artistic points of view were not simply different, they were uncongenial, incompatible. Then, after Schoenberg's death in 1951, Stravinsky, the surviving patriarch of twentieth-century music, quite unexpectedly went over to serial methods. He was influenced partly by the example of Schoenberg, but mainly by the revelation of Webern, whose music he acclaimed as "dazzling diamonds." Stravinsky's long commitment to the free, tonally influenced "neoclassic" style that he had cultivated since *The Soldier's Tale,* 1918 (see Chapter 9) came essentially to an end with his opera *The Rake's Progress* (1951). During his remaining fifteen years of activity, Stravinsky was increasingly pre-

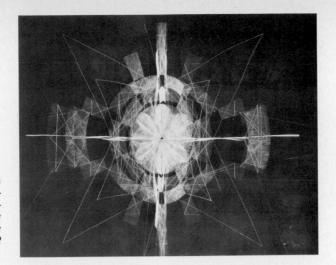

Richard Lippold, Variation Within a Sphere, No. 10: The Sun *(1953-1956). Highly polished, gold-filled wire strands glitter in the light, suggesting the rays of the sun. This radiant sculpture is 22 feet wide by 11 feet high.*

occupied with serial techniques. The first impulses of this serialism are seen in the Cantata (1952), Septet (1953), "Three Songs from William Shakespeare" (1953), and "In Memoriam Dylan Thomas" (1953), a setting of the poet's "Do not go gentle into that good night." The serialist devices are more abundant in *Canticum Sacrum* (1955), in the ballet *Agon* (1957), which represents the most obvious synthesis between the old "neoclassic" Stravinsky and the new "serialist" Stravinsky, and in *Threni* (*Lamentations of Jeremiah,* 1957-58), for soloists, chorus, and orchestra. Stravinsky's Movements for Piano and Orchestra, composed in 1958-59, represent in his words, "my boldest steps in the extension of a serial point of view to other elements than pitch . . . Every aspect of the composition is to some extent determined by serial forms." His last works were more or less suffused with serial constructive techniques—pitch rows, canons, and cunningly ordered timbres. Among them are *The Flood* (1962), a musical play; *Abraham and Isaac* (1962), for baritone and orchestra; "In Memorian Aldous Huxley": Variations for Orchestra (1964); "Elegy For J.F.K." (1964), for vocal soloist and three clarinets, to words by W. H. Auden; and *Requiem Canticles* (1966), a radiant last work completed at the phenomenal age of eighty-four, which served in 1971 as Stravinsky's own funeral ode at Venice. In all those works, no matter how latticed they are with serial devices, Stravinsky remained stylistically himself, recognizable as the Stravinsky of *The Rite of Spring* and *The Soldier's Tale,* unique in his cleverness and rhythmic exuberance.

The high-water mark of total serialism as a compositional phenomenon was passed during the early 1960s. Although its techniques retained some currency among European and American composers, they were increasingly combined with other, freer techniques. In retrospect, total serialism can perhaps be viewed as the last and most rigorous stage of the neoclassic ideal that had dominated musical thought since World War I. Total serialism was the logical climax to the preoccupation with order and abstraction that began with Schoenberg's *Pierrot lunaire* of 1912 and Prokofiev's "Classical" Symphony of 1917.

B. THE ELECTRONIC REVOLUTION

During the 1940s, science and engineering took a hand in the way music reached its audiences and even began to affect the way that music was composed. Commercial *frequency modulation* (FM) radio spread rapidly during the war years, offering for the first time a high quality of broadcast sound. FM waves cannot carry as far as *amplitude modulation* (AM) waves. Thus there was no use for expensive, high-powered transmitters, and it became inexpensive to set up a music station. The number of stations devoted to serious music quickly grew, and the record-buying public also grew, stimulated by the broadcasts they heard. In 1949, long-playing (LP) records began to appear in commercial numbers. The LPs vastly improved the quality of recorded sound and made it practical to package large compositions for mass markets. The old, pre-LP shellac 78 rpm records were heavy, fragile, and expensive. They could hold only five minutes of music to a side; thus a Beethoven symphony with its protective album weighed about three pounds and cost more than twenty dollars of today's buying power. To change the record, the music had to be interrupted five times or more, often at awkward points. Needless to say, Beethoven sold well. But most contemporary music was thought unlikely to sell; therefore, it was never recorded. The cheap, handy LPs brought a welcome new circulation for new music.

Musique Concrète

Tape recorders became generally available after the war, and by the middle 1950s were familiar household appliances. For the first time, people anywhere could record anything—themselves, radio programs, noises. Tape recorders also became tools for composers; they offered a flexibility in the shaping of musical ideas that disc cuttings did not allow. This brought provocative musical results already in the late 1940s. These happened at Paris, as always a place for new ideas. A new genre of experimental music called **musique concrète** (concrete music) arose. As raw materials it used not only conventional musical instruments and singing voices but also a wide range of "actual," or "concrete," sounds taken from the noises of the environment, such as sounds of speech and household clatter. The sounds were put directly ("concretely") onto magnetic tape, without any intermediate process of being translated into conventional musical notation. Music and performance were on tape, once and for all. There was no written score. The musique concrète movement was launched by its chief inventor, Pierre Schaeffer (b. 1910), in a "Concert of Noises" that was broadcast by the French National Radio in 1948. Schaeffer and his associate Pierre Henry (b. 1927) owed something of their percussion-and-sound-effects ideas to the music of Edgard Varèse (see page 365), but with their modern electronic equipment they could attempt much more in the way of novelty. They could choose from a broad spectrum of natural and artificial sounds, then record and rerecord at will, slowing the sounds down, speeding them up, playing them backwards, having them reverberate in echo chambers, altering them by cutting off attacks and decays, combining two or more tapes in a sonic montage. Sounds emerged that were never heard before. In 1949 Schaeffer and Henry produced their *Symphonie pour un homme seul* (*Symphony for a Lone Man*). It is a collage of atmospheric sound effects, animated by bits of child's laughter and spoken language along with distortions of musical pitches and familiar instrumental timbres. The *Symphonie* remains an important cultural document, if not an impressive musical one. In fact, the musique concrète movement produced no first-class music, but it responded to the wide-open spirit of the postwar decade by stretching the idea of what was usable as "musical" sound, by broadening the whole conception of what music might be. Though the movement trailed off during the middle 1950s, it was not a dead end. It was replaced by other, more substantial ventures into the same innovative terrain.

Electronic Music Studios

By the late 1950s, studios for electronic music that were equipped with impressive arrays of sound generators, filters, mixers, and recorders were in operation everywhere. The studios were frequented by the composers Eimert, Stockhausen, and Ligeti in Germany, Pousseur in France, Berio and Maderna in Italy, Babbitt and Ussachevsky in the United States. The sounds that emerged went well beyond the tentative gestures of musique concrète. Electronic music reached out to wholly new regions of sonic imagination. And everything was captured definitively on tape. That was important. For ages, new music had suffered from underrehearsed, low-budget performances, often by grudging, uncooperative performers. It was rare for it to get a proper first hearing, rarer still a second or third hearing. Now for the first time composers controlled every stage in the realization of their work. There was no longer a need to write the music down in notation and then laboriously train performers to reproduce it. Composers could produce music to their exact specifications, using electronic means, and then capture it accurately and permanently on tape. The tapes were easily sent from place to place, were cheap to play at performances, and were readily convertible into disc recordings for the purpose of mass distribution. The nagging problems of economics and artistic control that had always prevented new music from getting a proper hearing seemed resolved. Stockhausen cockily proclaimed that "live" concerts with live performers were a thing of the past.

Technological advances lent another hand to composers. Like early electronic computers, early electronic music studios depended on large arrays of hot, bulky vacuum tubes. With the introduction of transistors in the late 1950s, and then of silicon chips, the technology of creating and manipulating electronic sounds became cheaper and less cumbersome. It was available to just about anyone. **Synthesizers**—units that combined the sound generators and sound modifiers in a single control system—appeared. They even became portable. The widely used Moog and Buchla synthesizers were complete electronic studios fitted into a suitcase or two.

Among the early classics of purely electronic music were Stockhausen's Electronic Studies I and II (1953-54) and Babbitt's Ensembles for Synthesizer (1964). Yet in spite of the apparently limitless capacities and convenience of the electronic medium, many of the first-generation electronic works were not purely electronic. The sounds from the machines often seemed cold and expressionless, divorced from human links and familiar cultural attachments. During the early stages, electronic composers often clung to conventional sounds as well, combining elements of live performance with the electronics. Stockhausen's "Canticle of the Three Youths" (1956) has taped human voices and musique concrète-like sound effects along with electronically generated sounds (see page 387). Berio's *Circles* (1960), Babbitt's *Philomel* (1964), and many of Davidowsky's *Synchronisms* of the 1960s also combine electronic sound and live performance.

The production of electronic music was further streamlined during the mid-1960s by the harnessing of computers to audio-generators and tape recorders. Any sound can be described in numbers: Its pitch, tone color, duration, and dynamic force are all quantifiable. Composers can feed such musical numbers into computers that convert them into proportionate electrical voltages which in turn activate audio generators. In that way, sounds are produced with great precision. Yet, more than that, computers can be programmed not only to produce sounds that are imaginable by a composer but also to explore possibilities of sound that lie beyond conventional imagination. Electronics has already become a versatile medium of contemporary

△
Babbitt: Ensembles for Synthesizer (excerpt) (Side 12, Band 3)

music, and as electronic idioms enter the mainstream of musical vocabularies and fresh imaginations uncover new varieties of sound, they may well become the composer's most effective medium.

C. CHANCE MUSIC

Music's most provocative phenomenon after World War II was **chance music**, which is also called *random music, indeterminate music,* and **aleatory music** (*aleatory* is derived from *alea,* the Latin word for dice). In such music, the composer leaves something or everything to random chance. A throw of the dice may determine how a piece will proceed. For decades, composers of "serious" music had been narrowing the scope allotted to freedom and improvisation in their works. There was greater predetermination in the process of composing, as in the serialist doctrine, and greater precision in specifying the nuances to be observed in performance. Yet human lives are governed by chance, and music began to take notice of that very human factor. Chance music is "composed," at least in part, as an unplanned happening.

John Cage

The guru of the chance movement that swept the international musical scene of the 1950s and 1960s was the California-born John

Jean Arp, Squares Arranged According to the Laws of Chance *(1917). The dada movement of World War I employed chance as a factor in avant-garde art. Chance surfaced again among artists and musicians after World War II.*

Cage (b. 1912), whose pixieish imagination has been thumbing its nose at everything in sight since before World War II. In 1939, at the age of twenty-seven, Cage produced his *Imaginary Landscape No. 1* for two variable-speed phonograph turntables, some prerecorded pitch sounds, cymbals, and a muted piano. Cage's Sonatas and Interludes for Prepared Piano, composed in the mid-1940s, call for screws, coins, and rubber bands to be attached to the piano strings, thereby altering the pitches and tone colors. Some of the results are like African *mbira* music. Cage's chief manifestos of chance music came in 1951. *Imaginary Landscape No. 4* was scored for twelve radios, twenty-four "players," and a conductor. The players had their radios tuned to different stations, following Cage's instructions. The mixture of their sounds, coming in and out in unpredictable volumes and combinations, amounted to four minutes worth of auditory stimulation. The same year (1951) Cage produced *Music of Changes for Piano,* where the pitches are written out but just when they are to occur is determined by a draw of random numbers from the throwing of sticks or coins, a method whose results can be interpreted by consulting the *I Ching,* or ancient Chinese Book of Changes. Cage went on to compose his *Imaginary Landscape No. 5* (1952), amounting to four minutes scored for "any 42 recordings." In the same year he came up with the classic negation of conventional musical values in the work titled *4'33",* where for four minutes and thirty-three seconds the performer sits motionless before the piano. Cage's point was a good one. There is never just silence. Whatever we hear when we have our music-listening ears turned on is "music." Perhaps an inevitable sequel to *4'33"* was Cage's *0'00",* introduced at Tokyo in 1962, which was "to be performed in any way by anyone."

Cage kept jabbing at convention through the 1970s, producing not only chance music but also a series of literary essays (including *Silence*), and some art works that show a superior graphic talent. Through them all runs an engaging mixture of iconoclasm, mysticism, and spoof. Cage said that he tried to work "without any knowledge of what might happen . . . My purpose is to eliminate purpose." He even wanted to eliminate composing. "I want to keep from interrupting the silence that's already here." One of Cage's teachers in California was Arnold Schoenberg, who acknowledged him as an "inventor of genius," though Schoenberg probably used the word "inventor" advisedly. Whatever one thinks of Cage's music, he made the public take notice. His wry ingenuity ventilated the thinking about music and the arts in general. Cage's activity, more than musique concrète or early electronic music, broadened the conception of what music might be, allowing fresh ideas to filter in. His work may be less important for what it says as music—he has implied that he doesn't really care—than for what it says about the musical experience. The message is: open up, relax, enjoy the sounds around you!

Other Chance Music

Chance methodology attracted some influential converts during the 1950s and 1960s. They included the Americans Morton Feldman (b. 1926) and Earle Brown (b. 1926) as well as the Europeans Boulez and Stockhausen. Pierre Boulez's *Pli selon pli,* a work begun in 1960, lays out three musical phrases labeled a, b, and c, each phrase consisting of two measures numbered 1 and 2:

$$a^1 \qquad a^2$$
$$b^1 \qquad b^2$$
$$c^1 \qquad c^2$$
$$d$$

The performer is told to "sing a 1-phrase, then a 2-phrase from a different line (for example: $a^1 \ c^2$, or $b^1 \ a^2$). When you have sung two or three combinations that way, go on to concluding phrase d." This may remind us of Charles Ives instructing his string players in 1908 to "continue the last chord for two measures or so after the trumpet stops" (see Chapter 8). Karlheinz Stockhausen's Piano Piece No. 11 (1956) consists of nineteen musical fragments that are laid out on a long piece of paper and are to be played in the order they catch the eye. Pieces like that generally end when the performer has played a given fragment a certain number of times—or simply when the performer feels like ending. The originator of such ideas may have been Earle Brown in the composition *Folio* (1952).

After the first appeal of the chance procedure wears off, the musical result has to be judged like any other. All music is to some extent the result of accidental happening in its performance, even music that is definitively captured on tape. The difference with chance music is that it has more of this randomness than most. And that raises a problem. In employing chance, the composer's imagination has been partially turned off. To some listeners, that justifies a turn-off of their own attention. To avoid losing the listener's involvement, most composers who use chance methods effectively have thought it wise to combine them with more conventional techniques.

Looking back for a moment at the two leading musical ideologies of the post-World War II decades, and attempting to compare them, they seem at first to be at opposite ends of the esthetic scale. Chance music is so largely uncontrolled, total serialism so largely controlled. Yet they may not be so far apart. The chance composer has given up control over what happens in the music, but so has the total serialist, by setting forth in advance of composition so much of the detail of what can actually happen in the music. They both represent departures from the composer's normal freedom of choice in shaping the materials of sound. For that reason, both were probably destined for a short life. Yet while they lasted, and particularly when they were used in conjunction with conventional techniques, the results often went beyond the level of esthetic manifesto and were important as music itself.

D. SOME POSTWAR LANDMARKS

Total serialism, electronics, and chance took separate paths for a while; then they began to merge. Total serialism reached a peak of post-Webern rigor in Stockhausen's *Gruppen* for three orchestras (1957) and *Kontakte* (1959). Stockhausen took seriously his own dictum about the obsolescence of live concerts. His music was no longer composed to be re-created in live performance but was captured once and for all on tape. The total serialists continued their mathematical orderings, seeking what amounted to a new "music of the spheres" (see Chapter 1), but increasingly they turned their interest toward electronic media. At the same time, electronic composers were welcoming ways to take the stigma of "canned" sound from their music by adding live voices and conventional instruments. Chance music was opportunistic by nature and adapted to everything in sight. The landmark musical works of the avant-garde tended to combine two or three of those mainstreams.

Yet while all that ferment went on, there were also conservative composers who carried on with traditional methods of music making, producing works of considerable power while paying little heed to

Jackson Pollock, Echo (Number 25, 1951). *Pollock led the post-World War II movement of abstract expressionism in the United States. He was noted for his "drip" method of applying pigment: Tacking huge canvases to a wall or floor, he created turbulent, stylish abstractions by applying paint with a stick or trowel, sometimes even spattering it on for random effects.*

the new trends. Representative of those conservatives in the United States were Roy Harris (1898-1979), composer of some fourteen symphonies, and Samuel Barber (1910-1981), notable for his early Essays for Orchestra and Adagio for Strings. Perhaps the outstanding member of music's conservative establishment was the English composer Benjamin Britten.

Benjamin Britten

Twentieth-century England has enjoyed a musical flowering that was denied her for some time past. The British national output in this century has matched the best of any European nation. Romanticism and impressionism were represented by Elgar's younger contemporaries, Delius, Holst, Vaughan Williams, Bridge, and Bax, who joined personal and English inspiration, as in Delius's *Sea Drift* (1903) and *Walk to the Paradise Gardens* (1907), Holst's *The Planets* (1914-16), Vaughan Williams's *Lark Ascending* (1914) and Fantasia on "Greensleeves" (1934). Between the two wars, William Walton (see Chapter 9) and Michael Tippett (b. 1905) came to international prominence with works in neoclassic styles. After World War II the acknowledged leader was Benjamin Britten (1913-1976), a versatile eclectic, who is considered by some to be the most important English composer since Purcell.

Britten was born in Sussex on the east coast of England. He grew up in a house facing the sea, and his whole outlook was colored by his relation to the sea. Britten was like Stravinsky in his inventiveness and adaptability, and almost like Mozart in precocity. His "Simple" Symphony, sketched when he was just twelve in 1925, has not only the fashionable neoclassic idioms of its epoch but also an impressive directness and sincerity. Britten made an international mark in 1940 with his *Sinfonia da Requiem* and remained prominent on the musical scene through the 1970s. His best-known composition is the genial Variations and Fugue for Orchestra on a Theme by Purcell (1946), also called *The Young Person's Guide to the Orchestra*. This sixteen-minute work is a delightful way of introducing the orchestral instruments to young audiences. (See Appendix B.6.)

Britten's important instrumental works include the Variations for Orchestra on a Theme of Frank Bridge (1937), concertos for violin (1939) and piano (1946), a sonata for cello, and a symphony for cello and orchestra (1964). His inspiration may have been best in music for voice, as in the solo writing of "Les Illuminations" for tenor and strings (on poetry by Arthur Rimbaud), the *Michelangelo Sonnets,* and the Serenade for Tenor, Horn, and Strings (1943). He exemplified the British love for ample choral sound in the "Ceremony of Carols" (1942) for boys' choir and harp; the "Spring" Symphony (1949) for soloists, chorus, and orchestra, with texts drawn from the great English poets, Spenser through Blake and Auden, which concludes with a rousing appearance of the thirteenth-century's "Sumer is icumen in" (see Chapter 1); and in the deeply felt *War Requiem* (1962). Britten's most striking achievements are his operas, of which there are sixteen from a period of thirty-two years, beginning with *Paul Bunyan* (1941) and ending with *Death in Venice* (1973). Among the memorable operas are *Peter Grimes* (1945); *Billy Budd* (1951), based on Melville; and *The Turn of the Screw* (1954), based on the thriller by Henry James.

Britten was conservative in outlook, standing aloof from most fashionable trends of the times. He employed serial techniques in *The Turn of the Screw,* but this was symptomatic of a general impulse to pick and choose wherever he found something congenial. Britten's music derives in part from Purcell and Handel but also from Puccini and Mahler, from Stravinsky and Hindemith, and from the operas of Alban Berg. He never developed a strong personal style, yet his theatrical work is distinguished by an evocative musical rhetoric and a great aptness to the dramatic matter at hand.

Perhaps the most successful opera is *Peter Grimes,* which had its genesis in California during the summer of 1941. When World War II broke out in 1939 Britten found himself in America, where he lingered in a congenial atmosphere for three years. Then his homesickness and patriotism were aroused by some lines of E. M. Forster that he read in 1941. They concerned the English poet George Crabbe (1755-1832): "To think of Crabbe is to think of England," wrote Forster, and Britten began to read Crabbe, who like himself came from the east coast of England. It brought upon him "a longing for the realities of that grim and exciting coastline" where he was born. Britten sailed for home early in 1942. By that time he had begun to shape the opera *Peter Grimes,* based on Crabbe's long poem, *The Borough,* which pictures the bleak life of a Suffolk fishing village in the year 1810. Britten focused his opera on the tragic figure of the fisherman Peter Grimes, a lonely soul whose yearning for affection and humanity is thwarted by his fierce individuality. Grimes comes into conflict with the local society as allegations of child murder are spread against him. Eventually he is a suicide, setting out in his boat to perish alone on the open sea.

In *Peter Grimes* Britten wanted to express "my awareness of the perpetual struggle of men and women whose livelihood depends on the sea." The four celebrated "Sea Interludes" from the opera are short tone poems that are played at different points in the opera while the curtain is closed, each lasting only a few minutes. Britten's aim was to evoke the Anglian scenes by orchestral imagery alone. "Dawn" represents the gray northern skies, the sounds of waves and cries of the birds as morning comes to the dismal village. "Sunday Morning" evokes a fine holiday, with church bells pealing. It has a lyrical melody for strings running against perky staccato rhythms in

△
Britten: "Sunday Morning" (Four Sea Interludes) from *Peter Grimes* (Side 11, Band 6)

the woodwinds, projecting rather a Mussorgskian clangor. "Moonlight" suggests the tranquil summer night over the village and harbor, a calm that is ruffled by ominous touches of the flute and harp, indicating Grimes's uneasy state of mind. "Storm" represents a North Sea tempest with the boom and snarl of horns, trombones, and trumpets.

Britten's work as a whole stood outside, and somewhat above, the postwar stream. He combined an impressive dramatic flair and compassion for humanity with a deeply ingrained romanticism and a genius for conjuring up the sights and sensations of England.

Boulez and Stockhausen

Pierre Boulez, an apostle of total serialism during the late 1940s, turned to freer, more personal idioms during the 1950s. His *Le Marteau sans Maître* (1955, 32 minutes), has echoes of Schoenberg's *Pierrot lunaire* and of Webern and Varèse, all cloaked with Gallic charm and subtlety. The work's nine sections are built around three poems by René Char, a surrealist poet of the wartime Resistance. Section 1 (1½ minutes), the Prelude to Char's first poem, is scored for alto flute, vibraphone, guitar, and viola. Section 4 (4 minutes) obtains its effects from a vibraphone, guitar, viola, large marimba, and percussion. The sounds are sometimes like those of an Indonesian gamelan ensemble. Boulez sustained his international reputation with the elegantly crafted *Pli selon pli* (1960) and the orchestral *Notations* of the late 1970s.

Karlheinz Stockhausen was the most provocative musical personality in postwar Europe. Willful and exhibitionistic, but with a redeeming resourcefulness of imagination, he was a trend setter during the early 1950s, trying out all the new ideologies in quick succession: musique concrète, electronics, total serialism, and the antimethodology of chance. Stockhausen's *Gesang der Jünglinge* (1956, 13 minutes) was one of the first important compositions to combine both live voices and electronic sounds on tape. It also contained some total serialism. The work became very successful because it seemed to embody the spiritual unrest of the times. For a text Stockhausen chose the Bible's Canticle of the Three Youths who praise the Lord while in the fiery furnace, from the Book of Daniel in the Old Testament. The words of the German Bible are so fragmented and distorted in Stockhausen's setting as to be scarcely intelligible. Every so often a phrase can be recognized, for example, "Preiset den Herrn" ("Bless the Lord"), but mainly there are disjointed vowels and consonants, thrusting their way through the supporting continuity of electronic sounds. The audience in the concert hall is confronted only by a tape recorder and five groups of loudspeakers that are set up all around. Stockhausen wanted the listeners to sense themselves

△
Boulez: *Le Marteau sans Maître*, No. 4
(Side 12, Band 1)

Victor Vasarely, Vega II (1957). Vasarely is the master of the so-called op-art (optical art) styles that have been fashionable since the 1950s. His interest in theories of visual perception and applied mathematics carries over into paintings whose subtle geometric patterns create unsettling illusions of motion.

in the center of the fiery furnace. His music held up a mirror to the Central European world of the 1950s, still sweeping away the ashes of World War II.

Stockhausen continued as a leader of the avant-garde, more often through roguish posturings than convincing musical results. His mammoth electronic composition, *Hymnen* (*National Anthems*), makes use of snatches of African, Russian, European, and American national hymns in order to suggest a pageant of human history and visions of universal brotherhood. For this work Stockhausen borrowed the modish affectation of the "work-in-progress" technique from the artists and dramatists. Some 113 minutes' worth of *Hymnen* were completed during 1966-67; the work was still supposed to be expanded, but perhaps it will never be completed. Thrown into its aural hodgepodge are "the clamor and shouting of people, bird shrieks, the *boo-at boo-at* of swamp ducks ... gigantic blocks, planes, and pathways [of sound] in whose clefts resound the echoes of shouted names." He gave a typical chance-music description to the *Hymnen:* "The ordering of the parts and the total duration are variable. Depending on the dramatic requirements, [sections] may be lengthened, added, or left out." Stockhausen's *Stimmung* (*Tuning*) for six voices was written in 1968, commemorating a love affair "on the opulent coast south of San Francisco the year before." It is a long, seventy-three-minute meditation on a B-flat chord, filled with romantic impulses that are combined with Eastern mysticism and chance-music strategies. The narcissistic ruminations on B-flat are punctuated with nonsense syllables, invocations of the Hindu deity ("Vishnu"), and reminiscences of Vedic chanting.

Roy Lichtenstein, Masterpie (1962). Lichtenstein uses elements of comic-strip art create witty and ironic comme taries on art and on contempor values. Here he raises one of a ancient and profound question What is a masterpiece?—and gi it a characteristically mod twist.

Roger Sessions

One of America's most respected composers of the 1940s through 1970s was Roger Sessions, a New Englander born in Brooklyn in 1896. Sessions worked in France and Italy during the 1920s. Later he adopted some of Schoenberg's serial method. But like Ives, Sessions was a sinewy-minded independent, secure in his American cultural roots. His music seems crusty, hard-edged at first, but it often wears better than the music of composers who try to be ingratiating. His Third Symphony (1957, 29 minutes) has the traditional four-movement shape:

1. *Allegro.* The three sections of a sonata form, with Brahmsian touches.
2. *Scherzo-Trio-Scherzo.* Hints of a jazzy "Yankee Doodle."
3. *Slow.* Ruminative, elegiac.
4. *Finale.* Energetic, again with jazzy rhythms.

Along with the nervous rhythms and assertive harmonies, there are touches of lyricism and wit. The voice throughout is genuine Sessions, not derivative Schoenberg or Stravinsky. When asked to comment on the Symphony, Sessions gave a classic reply: "What the composer actually conveys in the music cannot be elucidated; this can really be appreciated only through listening to it. Possibly when a piece has become quite familiar, interpretative comments can be of interest and value; but the music must first of all be heard, and make its impact unaided." That was also Schoenberg's point when he advised against "row hunting" in his music (see Chapter 9). At the age of seventy-four Sessions produced what may be his masterpiece, a setting of Walt Whitman's *When Lilacs Last in the Dooryard Bloomed,* for voices and orchestra (1970). It is a long, thoughtful work, dedicated to the memory of Robert Kennedy and Martin Luther King.

Babbitt, Cage, and Carter

Of the important American composers who came to maturity after World War II, three have been most influential: Babbitt, Cage, and Carter. Milton Babbitt and Elliott Carter were dedicated to traditional ideals of music making. John Cage was perhaps as much a cult figure and sensation seeker as a serious composer. Cage's Aria and Fontana Mix is the classic monument of 1950s chance music. It consists of two distinct compositions that can be performed either separately or together. This represents what Cage called the "circus principle," meaning that quite different things are happening at the same time. He adopted the same principle in his *Renga and Apartment House,* composed in 1976 for the United States Bicentennial. Cage's Aria (1958) is a virtuoso piece for a female vocalist who sings a text that is made up of disjointed vowels, consonants, and isolated words culled from five languages: Armenian, Russian, Italian, French, and English. The opening minute's worth has the following words:

CARTRIDGE MUSIC

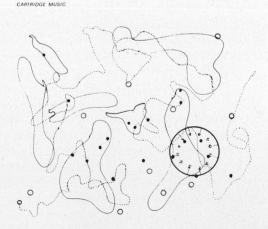

John Cage, Cartridge Music *(1960). This musical score by Cage is, like any score, a set of written prescriptions for producing sound, though Cage has also created an elegant visual design. As with other chance music, a good deal is left to the performers' imagination. In Cage's genial way, this piece is designated for "any number of players and loudspeakers."*

Hampart-zoum . . . dirouhi . . . di questa terra . . . naprasno . . . con-science et . . . arise . . . nei boschi di conifere . . . could enter your heart . . . non tanto . . . how so? . . . giovane . . . G.B.K.U. . . . Chto novogo pokadzet. The singer's melody is notated in wavy lines drawn on plain paper. Cage explains that the pitches are "roughly suggested rather than accurately described." The durations and rhythms are left entirely to the singer. He says only that each page of the score should take half a minute; there are twenty pages, making about ten minutes of music altogether. The soprano's melodic line is shown in eight different colors plus dotted-black and continuous black lines, indicating ten different styles of singing. Cage says "any ten styles may be used." In one recording of the work, the soprano (Cathy Berberian) interprets those styles as: dark blue—jazz style; red—lyric contralto style; dotted black—Sprechstimme (as in Schoenberg's *Pierrot lunaire*); black—dramatic style; purple—"Marlene Dietrich"; yellow—coloratura soprano; green—folk style; orange—"oriental"; light blue—babyish; brown—nasal. Cage's score also includes black squares that represent "unmusical" noises such as foot stomping, hoots of disdain, clicking of the tongue, screaming ("having seen a mouse"). The choices are again up to the singer. The other piece in this "circus" montage of 1958 is Cage's Fontana Mix, consisting of a tape that was produced through chance procedures. There would be other possible versions of its continuum of noises, whistles, and voices, which, at times, sound like distortions issuing from a boiler room or subway tunnel. When Fontana Mix is combined with the Aria, the effect is particularly relaxed and entertaining. It is Cage's way of expanding our consciousness about music. He may have been his own best critic when he said, "I like to think that I'm outside the circle of a known universe, and dealing with things that I don't know anything about."

Elliott Carter (b. 1908) adopted aspects of serialism in some works but generally stayed away from fashionable ideologies and developed distinctive conceptions of his own. His important works include three String Quartets (1951, 1959, and 1972), which may be the most substantial additions to the genre since the six quartets of Bar-tók, and a Double Concerto for Piano, Harpsichord, and Two Orches-tras (1961). The four players in the Second String Quartet are treated as individual musical "personalities," with each instrument exploiting its own characteristic intervals and rhythms. Carter tried to "drama-tize the players as individuals and participants in the ensemble." Carter is much admired by other professionals for his profundity of thought and consummate craft. His works have knotty forms, com-plex relationships among instrumental lines, and subtle progressions of rhythms and tempos. Yet for listeners unaware of the sophisticated inner machinery, Carter's music sustains levels of interest and inten-sity that put it with the best of Bartók, Schoenberg, and Stravinsky.

△
Cage: Fontana Mix
(excerpt)
(Side 12, Band 2)

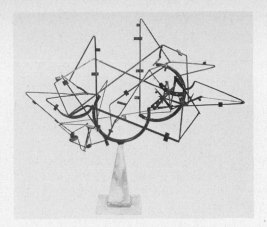

David Smith, Star Cage *(1950).
Smith (b. 1906) was the most influential American sculptor of his
generation. This composition of
welded, painted metal, four-feet
wide, shows his early preoccupation with complexities of depth
and motion.*

Milton Babbitt (b. 1916) has presided over academic musical
thought in the United States for more than three decades. Trained in
both mathematics and music, he was an originator of total serialism
in 1947-48 with his Composition for Four Instruments and Composition for Twelve Instruments. During the 1950s and 1960s he took
the lead in electronic and computer-assisted music while continuing
his total-serialist concerns. Babbitt's priestly seriousness about the
process of musical composition is reflected in his theoretical and
epistemological essays on behalf of contemporary music. He stands
at the opposite pole from the flippancy of Cage. Babbitt's creations
are tight and elegant, the best of them emotionally satisfying in ways
that belie the rigorous calculations that lie behind. In works such as
Composition for Synthesizer (1961) and Ensembles for Synthesizer
(1964), the medium is all-electronic. In others, for example, "Vision
and Prayer" (1961, on poetry by Dylan Thomas) and *Philomel*
(1964, based on the Greek legend of a woman turned into a nightingale), live voices join with taped electronic sounds. Still other works,
including *Relata I* and *II* for orchestra (1965, 1968) and the Third
String Quartet (1970) are for conventional instruments. Babbitt's
finely woven continuities of sounds and silences are as cogent in their
abstract logic as the work of a philosopher-mathematician, yet those
highly rational products are also humanly compelling. They bring
to mind Stravinsky's observation that "a masterpiece is more likely
to happen to the composer with the most highly developed language."

△
Babbitt: Ensembles for
Synthesizer (excerpt)
(Side 12, Band 3)

E. THE AVANT-GARDE OF THE 1960s

Avant-garde music during the 1950s and 1960s took on an international aspect that it never had before. Exchanges of new music

were speeded by on-the-spot tapings and jet airplanes; therefore, everyone found out quickly what everyone else was doing. It was a healthy situation, encouraging new ideas. Novelties began turning up everywhere, not only in the established new-music centers of Western Europe and North America, but in Poland, Hungary, Greece, Japan, and South America as well.

Penderecki

Kryzstof Penderecki (b. 1933) produced a landmark of the new music with his *Threnody to the Victims of Hiroshima* (1960). Other composers had reacted to the horrors of World War II: Schoenberg in *A Survivor from Warsaw* (1947); Stockhausen in *Canticle of the Three Youths* (1956); and also in their way, Dallapiccola in *Songs of Prisoners* (*Canti di Prigionia,* 1938-41) and Poulenc in *Dialogues of the Carmelites* (1956). Perhaps none caught the agony so pointedly as this ten-minute tone poem by Penderecki. Its startling sounds seem to come from unearthly sources. Yet Penderecki uses a conventional string orchestra to obtain his effects, dividing the strings into 52 distinct voice-parts (24 violins, 10 violas, 10 cellos, and 8 double bass). They play in some unusual ways: bowing between the bridge and tailpiece, even at right angles to the bridge; striking the instrument with bows or fingertips; using a variety of tremolos and vibratos. The old twelve pitches are left far behind. Penderecki uses solid bands of sound (massive tone clusters) that are built of adjacent quarter tones. Single pitches widen out to clusters, then contract again. Without specifying the particular pitch, he calls for the highest pitch that an instrument can produce. There are no

Helen Frankenthaler, Interior Landscape *(1964). The title would be apt for certain contemporary music.*

measures or bar lines. The musical actions of the strings are merely roughed into the score, filling specified time segments (15 seconds, 11 seconds, 4 seconds, etc.). Out of the maze of devices comes a display of shifting textures and moods that range from emotionally ice-cold to hyperintense. In a work that uncannily projects its gruesome subject, each new sonic event is more chilling, more excruciating than the last. Penderecki followed the success of *Threnody* with other works in a similar portentous style, among them a Dies irae (1967) in memory of the victims of Auschwitz, and the mammoth *Utrenja,* or *Lauds,* the morning service of the Russian Orthodox Church. He demonstrated a mastery of more conventional idioms in two ingratiating *Capriccios,* one for oboe and strings (1964), the other for violin and orchestra (1967).

Ligeti

Giorgio Ligeti (b. 1923) attracted broad public notice when his "Atmospheres" (1961) and *Requiem* (1966) were used in the sound track of Stanley Kubrick's film, *2001: A Space Odyssey.* "Atmospheres" for orchestra (8 minutes), starts out like a cousin of Penderecki's *Threnody.* Here again are bands and clusters of sound replacing individual pitches. But Ligeti's visions are gentler. His cloudlike shapes have misty, Debussy-like harmonies. "Atmospheres" is divided into more than twenty subsections that feature various densities and colors of sound. The lengths in seconds (48, 55, 37, 6, 23, 33, 14, etc.) are supposed to approximate the numbers of a geometric series. But the music, notwithstanding its logical plan, is meant to be grasped intuitively. Ligeti was in the forefront of composers who were seeking to establish a fruitful middle ground between the artistic extremes represented by total serialism and chance.

Xenakis

Iannis Xenakis (b. 1922) also used numbers systematically. His musical doctrine, called *scientism,* let the laws of mathematics, physics, and chemistry predetermine certain of his musical techniques. He applied laws of statistical probability, which represent nature's orderly version of chance happenings, as a rationale for laying out musical structures. He used the "kinetic theory of gases," laws for the density and speed of molecular motion, in establishing certain musical densities and durations. In offering a compromise between the rigors of total serialism and the disorganized accidents of the chance composers, Xenakis was like Ligeti, but he was more science-oriented in approach. Xenakis had a compulsion to make everything "explainable." He was trained in engineering as well as music, which accounts for the statistical curves and gas clouds. Yet the test of his music is in the hearing, and Xenakis is often stimu-

Lucas Samaras, Mirrored Room *(1966); constructed with wood and mirrors, 8 feet by 10 feet by 8 feet. The Greek sculptor Samaras creates a sense of limitless space by multiplying images with mirrors.*

lating—aggressive, intense, grandiose, violent. *Metastasis (Transformation,* 1954; 9 minutes) is scored for sixty-one different orchestral voices. Its intervals, durations, dynamics, and timbres are determined in part by geometrical calculations that Xenakis used when collaborating with the architect Le Corbusier in the design of a building near Lyons, France. *Bohor I* (1962) consists of some twenty minutes of pulseless trance, a dull roar, similar to waves on a distant shore, with a clangor of silvery chains, icicle chimes, and low moans and gasps. The music has no "frame": It begins as if in the middle of something, then snaps off suddenly to end. One of Xenakis's best works is *Eonta (Being,* 1964; 20 minutes). Scored for two trumpets, three trombones, and piano, it is full of gaudy colors, novel rhythms, and startling effects.

Takemitsu

Toru Takemitsu (b. 1930) responded to various Western models ranging from serialism to Cage, but he was most obviously influenced by his exposure to French musical sensibility, that is, Debussy, Ravel, and Boulez. To those elements he added a respect for transparency and silence that seems akin to the world of the seventeen-syllable haiku poetry of ancient Japan. Takemitsu's *Coral Island* for soprano and orchestra (1962, 17 minutes) has echoes of the French composers and of Xenakis, but it creates strong imageries of its own. The music starts out as nature painting, with hints of surf playing around a Pacific atoll. Then the fluctuating densities and colors turn to abstractions that are sustained by Takemitsu's keen Oriental ear for the marvel of pure sounds.

Minimalism: Riley

America's most fertile cultural soil in the nineteenth century was New England, but during the twentieth century that role may have shifted to California. A fresh Californian voice of the 1960s came with Terry Riley (b. 1935). His *In C* (1964) is an improvisatory tape work, based partly on chance procedures. It lasts as long as it takes to play on any given occasion. There is a commercial recording that takes forty-five minutes. The music starts out with a jolly, insistent pounding on a high C that continues throughout the piece. Other instruments enter, offering altogether fifty-three different short fragments. The players are free to choose and move from one fragment to another when they wish. The music comes out as a long trance focused on the C-major chord—the initial throbbing on C never lets up—yet evolving slowly through shifting waves of rhythm, tone color, and harmony. The conception is something like Schoenberg's in his "Colors" (Five Pieces for Orchestra, Op. 16, No. 3; see page 376) of 1909. It is also like the op-art (optical art) paintings of the 1950s and 1960s by Victor Vasarely and Bridget Riley, who

Bridget Riley, Current *(1964). British op-artist Riley (no relation to California composer Terry Riley) uses narrow, undulating black and white stripes as visual stimuli that reach out and disturb us—even dizzy us—as we try to view them.*

created illusions of rippling visual motion through repetitive, infinitesimally changing patterns; or perhaps like the lineup of 200-plus *Coca-Cola Bottles* in a famous op-art, pop-art painting by Andy Warhol of 1962. Some listeners find Riley's *In C* not only exhausting but nausea inducing. Others find relaxation and pleasure in its free-minded enthusiasm. No doubt the effect is narcotic, but so is the effect of some of the traditional art music in non-Western cultures. Whatever one thinks of Riley's music as music, it is a cool, cocky statement that tries to wipe the slate clean of convention and intellectuality, of serialist and scientific numerology. It even wipes away the twentieth century's post-tonality and dissonance. Here, music is back at the C-major chord! Riley's use of little, "minimal" bits of musical material that are repeated with "minimal" change gave this style the name of *minimalist music*. Riley used it again in *A Rainbow in Curved Air* and *Poppy Nogood and the Phantom Band*, taped pieces in which he himself recorded all the parts. Such music was not meant for concert-hall performance with the audience sitting rigidly in chairs and staring at the tape recorder and loudspeakers. It was "environmental" music, meant for large open halls and outdoor plazas where people could wander freely while it was played. It also suited intimate gatherings of friends, perhaps sitting around a room barefoot in 1960s style and communally sharing a joint.

F. THE RECENT PAST

We look for new sonorities, new intervals, new forms. Where it will lead, I do not know. It would be like knowing the date of my death.—Pierre Boulez

The recent past is too close to judge. New music, new books, new technologies—all take time to show their colors, to prove their staying power. Some people nowadays feel that serious music has gone altogether off the proper track, and that the only good music is the old tonal music. Listeners who worry that the music of our time is no good may be interested to know that similar concerns were expressed about the music in Wagner's time and even in Beethoven's. The critic of an important German newspaper reviewing an early performance of Beethoven's "Eroica" Symphony thought that "the Symphony would be all the better . . . if Beethoven could reconcile himself to making some cuts and bring into the score more light, clarity, and unity . . ." Similar judgments were voiced about Beethoven's Fifth Symphony.

The wide-ranging experimentation in music after World War II was a natural consequence of the decline of neoclassicism. That old orthodoxy, established in the 1920s, was aging, and for a time, just as before World War I, composers looked around for something new.

There were hints of a romantic revival during the 1970s as composers appeared to be trying to engage their listeners' emotions as well as their minds. It may take a generation before we know what actually took hold. Listeners must remain receptive to new music, hearing it as it appears and hearing it again over a period of time to see how a reaction grows. Composers are at work everywhere. In the United States alone, there are thousands of "serious" composers, wrestling with their imaginations, trying to extract sound images that will have meaning and value for their contemporaries and for following generations. Of the many composers who are presently producing music of great interest, only a few enjoy the good fortune of having their music issued in commercial recordings. Some of those recorded works will be mentioned now, but it must be remembered that they represent only a small sampling of works from the large spectrum of currently active composers who can be thought of as important figures.

Electronic music gained fresh adherents in the 1960s. As the novelty of the medium wore off, a new generation of listeners that had grown up with the sounds of amplified guitars and synthesizers in their ears no longer thought of electronically produced sounds as being inhuman and emotionless. Composers found the knack of producing sounds that were free of the "synthetic" taint of earlier experiments. Among the leading electronic composers was Pauline Oliveros (b. 1932), whose works include *Bye Bye Butterfly* (1965) and the memorable *I of IV* (1966). In Oliveros's witty *Sound Patterns* of 1964 (four minutes), the singers produce lip pops, tongue clicks, and finger snaps as well as whispers, improvised pitches, and tone clusters. Mario Davidovsky (b. 1924), in his series of *Synchronisms,* begun in the 1960s, combines live and electronic sounds, as in *Synchronisms No. 6 for Piano and Electronic Sounds (1970).*

Δ
Oliveros: *Sound Patterns*
(Side 12, Band 5)

A growing trend toward eclecticism during the 1970s is represented in *Solitaire* for piano and vibes (1971) by the American Barbara Kolb (b. 1940). The work is a collage, based partly on chance procedures. It requires a pianist to perform live against two tapes of electronically altered piano sounds. The music is partly "minimalist" in its dreamy ruminations, which are never broken into by anything harsh. It is also *quotational music* in that reminiscences of well-known works keep bobbing up, for example, Scarlatti's Sonata in E Major (the "Cortège"; see Chapter 3), a Prelude by Chopin, a waltz by Liszt. The use of quotations was cultivated in the late 1960s by the American George Rochberg (b. 1918) and the Italian Luciano Berio (b. 1925). The third movement of Berio's Sinfonia (1968) is a fantasy based on the scherzo of Gustav Mahler's Second Symphony, along with reminiscences from Bach, Schoenberg, Debussy, Ravel, Strauss, Berlioz, and others. The idea actually went back to Charles Ives and his quotation-sprinkled movements, such as the scherzo of his Fourth Symphony (1910-16). In the 1960s and 1970s quotational music was a chic trading in nostalgia that had the further virtue of providing a common ground for composer and listener—something for them both to hold onto in the maze of post-neoclassic styles.

Notturno (Night Piece, 1973), by the American Donald Martino (b. 1931), is a chamber work that exploits the colors of a flute, clarinet, strings, piano, and exotic percussion (vibraphone, marimba, xylophone, glockenspiel, temple blocks, and gongs), along with some inner workings of total serialism. Martino is a relaxed personality who goes beyond the Webern-derived serialist idioms of the first postwar generation. He even volunteers a "nontechnical" analysis of the music, calling it "a nocturnal theater of the soul."

Night Music by Thea Musgrave (b. 1928), another "nocturnal" creation, was composed for the BBC in 1969. It is an expansive single movement that features two French horns that relate to one another and to the orchestra in concerto fashion. Musgrave has a knack for arresting effects and clever climaxes. She draws on many current styles, yet with a personal voice. Recently she has made a specialty of operas, winning acclaim with *Mary, Queen of Scots* (1977) and *A Christmas Carol* (1979).

Perhaps the gaudiest musical imagination of the 1970s belonged to the American George Crumb (b. 1929). He was nondoctrinaire, choosing what he wanted from a wide range of methods and styles. He liked theatrical gestures and immediately effective results. Crumb's *Black Angels: Thirteen Images from the Dark Land* (1970) is scored for an electronically amplified string quartet whose members all wear masks. The music has touches of Schubert's song "Death and the Maiden" and also touches of the funeral plainchant Dies irae (see Chapters 1 and 6). Thus it represents quotational music. It is filled with trills and intervals of a *tritone* (three whole steps), musical

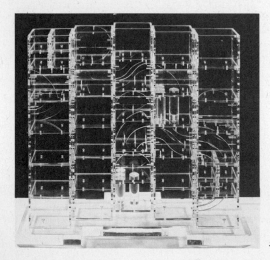

Louise Nevelson, Transparent Sculpture VI *(1967-1968). An assemblage of luminous plastic (lucite) sustaining an eloquent silent "harmony."*

devices sometimes associated with the Devil. There are faked insect sounds, and there is reliance on the numerology of 7 and 13 in laying out the structure. The sounds of the strings are interrupted by the players' voices, engaging in "ritualistic counting" in German, French, Russian, Hungarian, Japanese, and Swahili. The work, which was conceived as "a parable on our troubled contemporary world," was completed at a lowpoint of national spirit during the Vietnam war. No less sensational than *Black Angels* was Crumb's *Voice of the Whale* (*Vox Balaenae,* 1971), scored for three masked players of electronically amplified flute, piano, and cello. It begins with surreal sea imagery—a grotesque sound supposed to suggest the "talk" of a humpback whale. The flutist produces this sound by simultaneously blowing and singing into the instrument. A distorted quotation from Richard Strauss's *Thus Spake Zarathustra* makes a startling interruption to the long opening revery. Strauss's *Zarathustra,* like Ligeti's "Atmospheres," had acquired a science-fiction image by being included in Kubrick's *2001.*

Minimalist music continued with Steve Reich and Philip Glass in the 1970s. Reich's Music for Mallet Instruments, Voices, and Organ (1973) and his Octet (1979) spread small amounts of musical material across large expanses of time (nearly twenty minutes in each piece). His "scintillating sounds in joyous patterns" arise from the incessant repetition of tiny rhythmic cells, which evolve with slow changes in harmony and tone color. Philip Glass's *Einstein on the Beach,* a musical-theatrical spectacle, was first produced in 1976. Four full discs of its trance-inducing patterns have been issued. They amount to modest excerpts from a much longer and reputedly very powerful stage experience. In minimalist music the same "beat" can be kept up for an hour, something that many people find simply boring. But the minimalists' throbs and undulations at their best have a tantalizing quality. In style and hypnotic result they are close to some of the pop music of the 1970s and early 1980s.

The Women's Movement

No survey of the contemporary scene would be complete without noting two social issues that profoundly influence the course of music. One is the effect of the women's movement. The other is the economic plight of today's serious composers. The women's movement launched in the 1960s enhanced the awareness of women's gifts as composers. For a long time, women enjoyed high status as musical performers but only grudging acknowledgment as creators. The obstacles to professionalism of any sort meant that gifted women in past centuries rarely attempted music composition. There were exceptions. Francesca Caccini (1587-ca. 1640) produced ballets and lyric works for the Medici in early seventeenth-century Florence. Barbara Strozzi was an accomplished creator of cantatas in seventeenth-century Venice. Elisabeth Jacquet de la Guerre (1659-1729) composed operas, ballets, and keyboard music for the same royal Parisian circles that were dominated by Lully during his last years. Maria Theresia von Paradis (1759-1824), a contemporary of Mozart's, enjoyed a long career that for a while rivaled his in success. In the nineteenth century, Clara Wieck (1819-1896), the wife of Robert Schumann, composed chamber music in a style close to her husband's. Cécile Chaminade (1857-1944), Ethel Smyth (1858-1944), and Amy Beach (1867-1944) made important contributions to the late romantic repertory. Beach wrote over 150 chamber and orchestral works that rank her with her New England colleagues Parker, Chadwick, and MacDowell (see Chapter 8). Her "Gaelic" Symphony (1896) was the first symphony by an American woman. Smythe was a leader in the women's suffrage movement. Her dual roles as militant and musician were officially recognized in 1922 when George V made her a Dame of the British Empire.

The early twentieth century saw an increase in the number of notable women composers, particularly in France and the United States. But it was only with the breakthrough of the 1960s—the generation of Oliveros, Musgrave, and Kolb, among others—that substantial numbers of first-rank women composers began to find congenial environments for creation and to assert themselves as the equals of their male contemporaries. Women's compositions are at last being savored as art works in themselves rather than as art works by women, and it is clear that the same sensibilities that lend distinction to the literary works of Jane Austen, George Eliot, and Emily Dickinson serve music no less well.

The Economics of Composing

The second social issue is the economics of composing. It involves all composers who try to create high-minded, durable music, that is, music that will give illumination and pleasure for more than a short season or two. There is an unfortunate gulf on the current musical scene, separating the public at large from the serious "classical" composers who should be creating their music. The composers feel obliged to follow the dictates of imagination wherever they may lead and never simply cater to popular taste. Yet the public tends to shun what it perceives as elitism or abstruseness in a musical language. To some extent this was a problem even for Bach and Beethoven, but it has become acute in the twentieth century when the mainstream of musical language has shifted away from the widely accessible idioms of major-minor tonality toward a bewildering variety of post-tonal languages. Many of today's listeners think they can respond emotionally only to the old tonal language, and they venture into post-tonal music with great reluctance. This makes it difficult for the serious composer who needs an audience in order to survive. In earlier centuries "contemporary music" always had the support of affluent admirers. The best new music was eagerly sought by aristocratic patrons and by the churches. In the nineteenth century, composers won economic independence by performing their works and selling their publications to a receptive bourgeoisie. With the twentieth century's changes in style, the traditional channels have closed up. Fortunately, two new channels have opened: government foundations and educational institutions.

In recent decades there has been a growing recognition by politicians in the United States that the support of cultural endeavor is a proper function of government. Going back to the WPA projects of the 1930s, foundations for the arts and humanities have been set up at national and local levels. Yet public foundations face difficult choices. As democratic institutions, funded by tax money and administered by elected officials, they must often choose between two conflicting philosophies when dispensing their limited resources. Should they be "democratic" and spread the support broadly so that culture of some middling distinction reaches out to the average citizen? Or should they be "elitist" and just concentrate on what appears to be the most sophisticated? Those who take the long view of civilization believe that it is only excellence that really matters; it is precisely this criterion that is applied within the arts themselves to their own creative products. Yet many people justly argue that even the best may remain hopeless and blighted unless some special encouragement is forthcoming at the grass-roots level.

The other channel for support of contemporary composition comes from the schools. Universities and colleges are less hemmed in by political considerations, with the result that many composers of high distinction and substantial accomplishments are now active as composers-in-residence on educational campuses. One of the first to enjoy an academic haven was Arnold Schoenberg. It is a pity that Bartók was not similarly fortunate during his last desperate years. But on balance, the activity of the schools in promoting a serious musical culture has been a significant one. If our composers are to fulfill their role as society's cultural leaders, the support by the academic establishment needs to be continued and expanded.

G. POPULAR MUSIC: JAZZ AND ROCK

Postwar Jazz

Jazz gave up its last courtly prettiness during World War II. It turned introspective, sometimes cynical, as the good-times blare of the big swing bands was replaced by the hard-eyed sophistication of bebop. Bebop, or just "bop," started in the war-subdued nightclubs around New York. It was music for small groups of soloists, usually blacks, who played intensely and brilliantly, often at breakneck speed, producing complex polyrhythms and strange twists of melody and harmony. It was the new jazz for the new age. Part of the bop effect lay in the "hip" attitude of its tough, devil-may-care practitioners, musicians who pushed their horns to incredible highs and drank and smoked too much. Some masters of the new style were the trumpeter Dizzy Gillespie, and the pianists Bud Powell and Thelonious Monk. Beginning around 1949, trumpeter Miles Davis produced an offshoot of bebop, turning from supercharged acrobatics toward a new "cool jazz." But above all, the imposing figure was the saxophonist Charlie Parker (1920-1955), nicknamed "Yardbird," or "Bird." His uncanny rhythmic feel and startling melodic takeoffs were unmatched in the bop and cool styles. Like many jazz people, Parker was a tortured soul, who died of drugs and related causes before he was thirty-five. "Ornithology," an improvisation "The Bird" was famous for, is best heard, not in a hothouse studio version, but in a live take. On this nightclub recording of 1948, we can almost breathe the boozy, smoky air of the darkened room and sense the musicians and audience reacting to one another. This is one of the top-notch Parker groups, with Parker himself on alto saxophone, a piano, string bass, drums, and the subtle trumpet of Fats Navarro. After the opening applause (0:00), Parker and Navarro embroider on the "tune" together. A woman shouts encouragement from the audience as Parker launches on his lengthy solo (0:42). Louis Armstrong would have taken the basic tune and kept it essentially recognizable throughout. But Parker, perhaps the most brilliant improviser that jazz has produced, takes off very freely from the underlying chord sequence. Swooping and soaring, with explosive bursts of rhythmic energy, he only rarely comes down to little licks of the tune. The solo trumpet takes over (2:53), responding to Parker's fantastic rhythmic and melodic exploits. Then the piano is heard (4:23); the saxophone and trumpet share a chorus, egging one another on (6:04). Finally they play the tune together (7:09). The form is the time-honored theme and variations: the initial theme or "tune," followed by four variations and a summing up. There are analogies with Baroque style: the improvisational freedom of the soloists, as in a Baroque aria; and the driving rhythm, sustained by the jazz counterpart of a *basso continuo*—the thumping bass fiddle, bopping drums, and discreet piano chords.

Jazz continued into the 1960s and 1970s, moving through a myriad of new phases and styles: "funky"; hard bop; "serious" jazz; soul jazz; the "new thing" jazz of Coltrane and Coleman, linked with the aroused black consciousness; progressive jazz, including experiments

Charlie ("Bird") Parker.

△

Parker: "Ornithology"
(Side 12, Band 4)

with electronic sound. But increasingly the stream of postwar jazz—the black improvisational mainstream that remained the essence of jazz—was challenged by a new and powerful style of the 1950s, the style called rock.

The Origins of Rock

Rock was the "now" music that exploded among the youthful generation after World War II. It was the biggest novelty in popular music since the emergence of jazz around 1900. The basis of rock was a potent, hypnotic beat and a careening forward drive. Its rhythms "rocked mightily," swaying the bodies and minds of frenzied mass audiences. By the late 1970s in North America, popular music was a multibillion-dollar annual industry, of which rock and its derivatives accounted for about eighty-five percent and jazz for just two percent, the remainder going to religious and regional styles. Jazz enthusiasts lamented what seemed to be Gresham's law in music: Rock drove out jazz just as bad money drove out good. Jazz retreated temporarily into a hothouse where its genius continued to be nurtured by handfuls of enthusiasts. But rock had strong musical values of its own, some of them coming from the same black roots that had first produced jazz. Rock grew mainly from two musical streams of the early 1950s: *white country music* and the *rhythm and blues* of rural southern black musicians. Both were spread to enormous audiences by powerful radio stations that had broadcast popular styles throughout the country since the 1920s. In a nation as diverse as the United States, white country music had many faces. Among them were "hillbilly" ballads; fiddlers' tunes (some going back to eighteenth-century England) of the Blue Ridge and Allegheny mountains; mountain songs; songs of the prairie cowboys; laments of southern dirt farmers; the banjo strums and fiddlings of the Cajun bayous; the tinny rollickings of the Texas honky-tonks. Everywhere there was gospel—the soul-warming richness of gospel music. Different as they all were, these white country musics shared some of the same melodic whines and pounding accompaniments. There was a backwater American looseness in their earthy appeals. The pounding and the looseness, the whining and grinding became basic ingredients of rock. *Black country music* also had many faces. There were blues and work songs; spirituals; again gospel music, particularly the "rhythm and blues" kind of gospel. Nothing about those latter-day rustic styles stood comparison with the superb creations of black jazz and blues that came out of New Orleans and Memphis earlier. But the humbler black musics of the 1940s still had some of the old fervor, the haunting beats, the echoes of African drumming.

Everything came together around 1950 when the country-music style of black rhythm and blues moved cityward and found its way into small recording studios in St. Louis and Chicago. There it was joined in a clever commercial synthesis with the twang of white country music. A new *rockabilly* style emerged; it was sung nasally and emotionally to the whine and thwack of a steel guitar, and it was powerfully amplified. In an urban rechristening the style became know as *rock and roll*. Those two key words, so richly descriptive of the musical idiom, put their stamp on a whole era. The words themselves had black roots. They went back to the custom of physically rocking and rolling the body to express vividly the ecstasy of religious experience. They had gone into the raunchy blues: "My baby rocks me with a steady roll" is an old blues lyric. From there they went into the birth of rock.

The new rock and roll idiom quickly got into the hands of the big recording and film industries. The white guitarist Bill Haley was promoted on the national scene in the film *Rock Around the Clock* (1953). The first cosmic star of rock was Elvis Presley (1935-1977), who led the movement during the late 1950s with his leering, sexually aggressive "look at me" stance. Presley used blues progressions (as in "Hound Dog") and simple chords in conjunction with the famous "driving beat." His rebellious, lascivious image, like that of the motor-cycling actor James Dean—tough, yet tender and caring— managed to "turn on" a whole generation of restless youth who had been turned off by the devastating world of superpower confrontations and nuclear fallout that their elders were mismanaging for them. Rock and roll performances were energized by the brute magnetism of the singer's personality and gyrating body. The vocals were often howled, not sung; the rhythms were all pounding energy. The experience was as much psychic as musical. What mattered was the provocative human statement. The message of the forlorn teenagers who saw little place for themselves in the world where they were growing up was carried loud and clear by rock. The postwar generation that called itself "beat" found its musical blessedness in the hypnotizing beat of rock.

The classic rock music of the 1950s was rock and roll, a hard-driving rock that was "hard" in the way liquor was "hard." Presley remained close to his country origins. His music was mainly improvised. With the 1960s came artful transfusions from the middle-class youth cultures of urban Britain and America. They transformed the original, earthy rock and roll of back-country America into the glittering international rock movement of the 1960s and 1970s. The new rock held on to some of the old redneck aggressiveness, but increasingly there was a cosmopolitan veneer. A suave insolence replaced the tender tough-guy façade. What remained of the old improvisatory freedom was further quashed as cleverly prepackaged "arrangements" appeared, filled with compelling sonic effects.

The Beatles

In 1963 the long-haired, mod-clothed Beatles were at the crest of the international rock wave. Led by the lyric genius of John Lennon and Paul McCartney, they captured young hearts with the gentle idealism of "Love Me Do" and "I Wanna Hold Your Hand," turning susceptible teenagers away from the animal force of Presley's "Hound Dog." In the best work of the Beatles and in the grittier work of the other premier English rock group, The Rolling Stones, the music was an eclectic mix of effects from all over. There was the synthetic balladry of Bob Dylan, whose gospel of innocence and social protest enchanted the "flower children" of the 1960s. There was the Indian raga style popularized by Ravi Shankar, where an initial pulseless improvisation leads to an orgiastic beat of drums, all with the whine and twang of veena strings—so close to rock's electric guitar. There were still headier infusions, charging rock music with the highs of the drug culture. Music created psychedelic worlds of spinning colors and blinking lights. It induced its own hallucinations for those who wanted to join LSD's high priest Timothy Leary's invitation to "tune in, turn on, and drop out."

The Beatles set the standard of the 1960s. With their high-spirited lifestyles and happy-go-lucky musical styles, they fashioned a radiant mythology that charms the declining twentieth century much as Wagner's myths charmed the declining nineteenth century. The Beatles began with the raw Liverpool-Hamburg rock of 1960; they ended with the designer-fashion rock of "Let It Be" in 1970. In between came the collections, such as *Sgt. Pepper's Lonely Hearts Club Band* (1967) and *Abbey Road* (1969), where an overarching unity is projected across a kaleidoscope of changing moods, as in a song cycle by Schubert or Schumann. Musically, the Beatles were more sophisticated than any other group. Their songs have not only an enchanting lyricism but also a rich harmonic language and a vari-

The Beatles Crossing Abbey Road *(left to right): George Harrison, Paul McCartney, Ringo Starr, and John Lennon.*

ety of electronic and rhythmic effects that leave the monolithic thumpings of rock and roll behind. Ultimately, the Beatles were successful because, more than any other rock group, they touched deep roots of human feeling. Their lyrics and music were a part of the social scene, speaking to the aspirations and frustrations of people everywhere. When John Lennon was gunned down in a tragic epilogue on a New York street, it was the death of a world leader. Happiness was not a warm gun.

No single Beatles' song, not even a select half dozen, can sum up their vitality: "Strawberry Fields," "I Am the Walrus," "Penny Lane" (with its early Baroque trumpet), "Eleanor Rigby" (accompanied by a string quartet), the raucous "Yellow Submarine," the turned-on "Lucy in the Sky with Diamonds," the wistful "Michelle." The first side of the collection *Abbey Road,* perhaps their finest sustained effort, concludes with the song "I Want You (She's So Heavy)" (Ex. 10.2). Less lyrical than most mature Beatles works, it is a basic rock creation in its prominent electric guitar, pounding bass, and fragments of text that cannot always be distinguished from the mumbles and wails. It is characteristic "Beatles rock" in its raga-like melodic wriggles, synthesized effects, and touches of unusual harmony. It also has some conventional elements that take us back to "serious" music of an earlier age. For one thing, it is tonal music. The fact is that even while contemporary art music has turned away from tonality, nearly all of twentieth-century popular music, including rock, has remained tonal. Another thing, the overall form of "I Want You," reminds us of the ritornello form of a Baroque concerto or aria. There are four refrains alternating with three stanzas. In the stanzas John sings "I want you"; in the refrains, "She's so heavy . . ." (Ex. 10.2). Another traditional feature is that each of the refrains is built upon a bass-line ostinato theme of the sort used by Purcell (see Chapter 3) and Brahms (see Chapter 5). The Beatles' ostinato theme in "I Want You" thumps upward in a stepwise ascent from the tonic to the dominant, much like the ostinato theme in Brahms's Fourth Symphony (Ex. 5.12). In the Beatles' key of D minor the ostinato goes from D up to A, then returns to the tonic D through a roundabout path: E up to C, B-natural, B-flat-C-D-A-F-E-D. The ostinato appears just once in the opening refrain (1), twice in each of the middle refrains (2 and 3), then fifteen times in the final refrain (4). Those fifteen end-to-end repetitions of the bass theme are intensified by electronic effects, which help shape an emotional crescendo that seems to be headed toward a last tonic cadence. But in the post-tonal twentieth century—in the poet Auden's "Age of Anxiety"—even tonal music doesn't always end tonally. A savage interruption cuts off the lurching momentum just before the end of the fifteenth repetition, leaving the music and the listener suspended in midair.

Ex. 10.2. "I Want You (She's So Heavy)," Lennon and McCartney

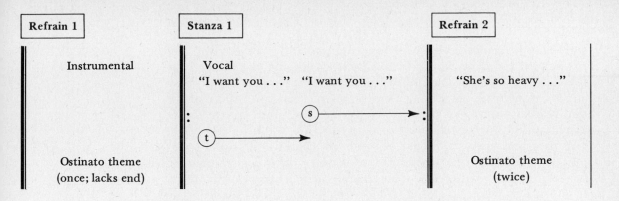

Refrain 1
Instrumental

Ostinato theme
(once; lacks end)

Stanza 1
Vocal
"I want you . . ."   "I want you . . ."
(s)
(t)

Refrain 2
"She's so heavy . . ."

Ostinato theme
(twice)

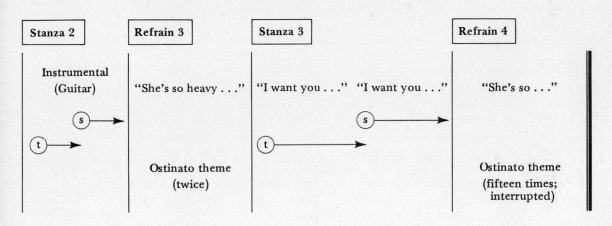

Stanza 2
Instrumental
(Guitar)
(s)
(t)

Refrain 3
"She's so heavy . . ."

Ostinato theme
(twice)

Stanza 3
"I want you . . ."   "I want you . . ."
(s)
(t)

Refrain 4
"She's so . . ."

Ostinato theme
(fifteen times;
interrupted)

Keys:

(t) Tonic

(s) Subdominant

Ostinato theme

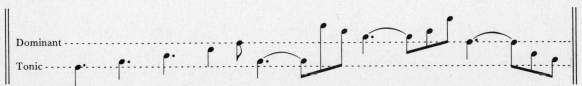

Dominant
Tonic

Newer Rock and Soul

The Anglo-American rock movement of the 1960s and 1970s catered mainly to white city youths with time and money on their hands, but the many styles of rock (hard rock, folk rock, raga rock, acid rock)—all cleverly packaged in concerts and on tapes and records—reached out to youth everywhere. Alongside the white rock movement the phenomenon of black soul music arose. Motown Records in Detroit (America's "motor town") bid for a share of the billion-dollar pop-music market by promoting "soul" as the black outlet on the big-time pop scene. *Soul* developed during the 1950s from the same basics of black rhythm and blues and gospel styles that had gone into the shaping of rock and roll. In its commercial transformations, soul provided the people in the black-power movement with a musical voice in their struggle for social justice. The message of soul was spread through the white community in the United States, and it went out to the world in the music of great soul groups, such as the Supremes, and powerful stylists, such as Aretha Franklin.

The idioms of popular music are always courting novelty. A pop-music pinnacle of the late 1970s was occupied by the bright throb of *disco,* a commercialized outgrowth of rock and soul. Despised by serious rock and soul devotees, it was an addictive music of "all one beat," its sounds flushed with eerie electronics and given a super-charged aura of blinking strobe lights. The early 1980s brought *new wave* and *punk rock* (". . . kill, kill, kill . . . the poor" went one refrain). Yet even while certain extreme rock styles seemed to gain the upper hand, there were signs that the generation-long primacy of the whole rock movement was beginning to fade. Interviewed in 1980, Mick Jagger of The Rolling Stones thought he saw "no future in rock and roll, only recycled past." In a cultural turnaround that apparently went hand in hand with the contemporary flourishing of political conservatism in England and North America, listeners

Aretha Franklin.

of the early 1980s began to ignore the rock beat and to look for the warmth of old-fashioned lyrics and melody. For a while, at least, there was a return to jazz, to the good old tunes, even the big bands.

What of the future, not just of pop music but of all music—popular, serious, whatever else? Early in this century Charles Ives thought he foresaw a "century to come when school children will whistle popular tunes in quarter tones . . ." In view of how different music has become since then, Ives may well be proven right. There are as yet unimagined languages of sound waiting to be discovered, fresh in their idioms, and with perhaps unprecedented powers to engage the mind and emotions. On the other hand, if certain segments of the public have their way, there may be a partial or even a total return to the idioms of tonality. Maybe both will happen, maybe neither. Prophecies are useless, for they are always being overturned by history. Whatever happens, there will be changes that are likely to be surprising when they come, and that are likely to keep coming quickly. For unlike earlier ages of history, when "culture" was the privilege of a happy few, musical sophistication is now widely found; and available technology can spread new musical ideas to the farthest corners of the globe in a split second.

Musical Notation

Our familiar musical notation, using the five-line staff, is a graph of sounds in time. It is the end product of a long development that began in the ninth century under the heirs of Charlemagne. As a method of recording musical sounds in writing, it has persisted and adapted to many different styles of music over the centuries. New musical styles have recently emerged, making complex demands that the traditional notation can no longer meet, and new notations have been devised to accommodate them. But the old notation remains, not only as the guardian of the vast historical treasure of older music but as a medium still capable of expressing almost any pattern of musical sounds that a composer may use.

THE NOTATION OF PITCH

Pitch, Note, and Staff. A *pitch* is a musical sound of fixed height. A *note* is the written sign for a pitch: ♪. A *staff* is a series of five horizontal lines, with four spaces in between: ═══ . Our musical notation consists of notes on the staff, showing the heights of pitches and the lengths of time they last (Fig. A.1).

Fig. A.1. Notes on the Staff

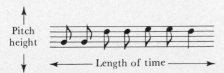

Pitch height

◄—— Length of time ——►

Notes. A *note* always has a head and often a stem and tail(s) (Fig. A.2). The height of the note head on the staff tells how high in melodic space the pitch is; the shape of the note head plus its stem and tail(s) tells how long it lasts.

Fig. A.2. Notes

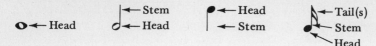

The Seven Basic Pitches: A through G. Most of our music is built of *seven basic pitches*—seven distinctive pitch sounds—that are named A through G, after the first seven letters of the alphabet. Those seven pitches are produced on the piano keyboard by the white keys (Fig. A.3). They form a series that is repeated at higher and lower

Fig. A.3. The Seven Basic Pitches: White Keys

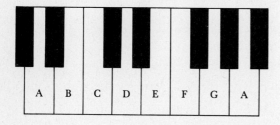

levels throughout the keyboard. On the musical staff, each pitch is given a separate line or space. Since the staff has five lines and four spaces, there is an overall range of nine pitches; if the spaces just above and below are used, the range increases to eleven pitches (Fig. A.4). For still higher or lower pitches the staff can be extended

Fig. A.4. The Five-Line Staff: A Range of Eleven Pitches

with *ledger lines* that are drawn where needed, as shown in Fig. A.5. This shows a range of pitches, both on the piano keyboard and as they are expressed in staff notation. The C-pitch that appears at the middle of a piano keyboard is called *middle C*. That pitch is shown at the bottom of Fig. A.5, on the ledger line just below the staff; there are other ledger lines for the pitches A and B above the staff.

Clefs. A five-line staff does not indicate which pitches it represents. Each staff has a *clef* placed on its left end, identifying one of

Fig. A.5. The Piano Keyboard and the Treble Staff

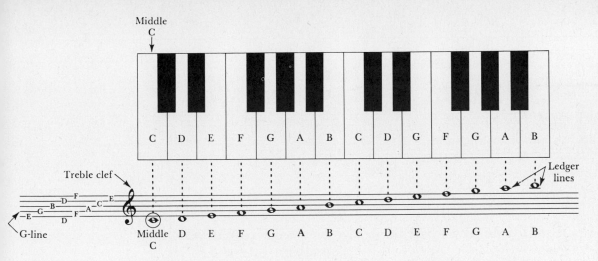

its lines as a reference pitch. Two commonly found clefs are the
treble clef 𝄞 and the bass clef 𝄢. When added to the staff they
form the treble staff 𝄞 and the bass staff 𝄢

The Treble Staff. The *treble staff* is formed by adding the treble
clef, which is also known as the G-clef because it indicates the G
above middle C as its reference pitch. That G is the second line up
from the bottom, as shown in Fig. A.5. The treble staff roughly
covers the range of women's voices.

The Bass Staff. The F below middle C (the fourth line up from
the bottom) is the reference pitch of the *bass staff.* The bass staff
roughly covers the range of men's voices (Fig. A.6).

Fig. A.6. The Bass Staff

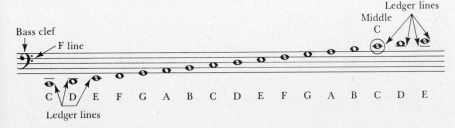

The Grand Staff. For instruments that have a very wide range, such as the piano, harp, or organ, there is the *grand staff,* which joins the treble and bass staffs together (Fig. A.7). Since middle C on the

Fig. A.7. The Grand Staff

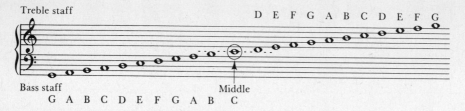

treble staff is the first ledger line below the staff (Fig. A.5) and on the bass staff it is the first ledger line above the staff (Fig. A.6), the two staffs joined together produce a composite eleven-line staff with middle C as the middle line. However, it would be difficult for the eye to pick out the pitches from among eleven closely ruled lines and intervening spaces, so in making the grand staff the two five-line staffs (treble and bass) are kept somewhat separated. The line between them representing middle C is drawn in only when that pitch is actually needed. The grand staff covers the whole central range of musical pitches. With the addition of ledger lines, it is extended as far up or down as needed.

Accidentals: Sharps and Flats. So far, we have been considering only the white keys of the piano keyboard, but that keyboard contains black keys as well as white keys, lined up in repeating patterns called *octaves.* Fig. A.5 illustrates a range of two octaves on the keyboard, with the black and white keys arranged in their familiar configuration of alternate groups of two and three black keys inserted among the white keys. Now Fig. A.8 shows the details of a sample

Fig. A.8. Black and White Keys on the Piano Keyboard

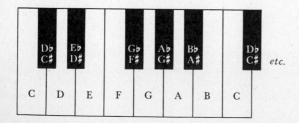

octave, with the names for the black keys. The octave contains seven white keys called *naturals* and five black keys called *accidentals*. Together the naturals and accidentals form a series of twelve pitches to the octave, where each pitch is separated from its neighbor (black or white) by the distance called a **half-step**. When staff notation developed during the Middle Ages, the five accidental pitches were less important than the seven natural pitches. The accidentals were not often used in actual music, were not always found on keyboards, and were not assigned names of their own or separate lines or spaces in the notation. As those five accidental pitches came to be used more frequently and to appear as inset black keys on keyboards, they also began to receive their own names and signs. Their initial uses were as subsidiaries to the white pitches, and their names and notation reflected that status. For instance, the black key between C and D was used as an alternate for the C, and in that case it was called *C-sharp*, meaning a half-step higher than C. That same black key could also be used as an alternate for the D, and in that case it was called *D-flat*, meaning a half-step lower than D. All of the black keys came into use in that way, as occasional alternatives for the neighboring white keys; the name *accidentals* reflects those early functions. The staff notation of the accidentals is also makeshift. An accidental pitch is shown by adding a **sharp sign**, ♯, or a **flat sign**, ♭, before the head of the note it modifies (Fig. A.9).

Fig. A.9. Accidentals

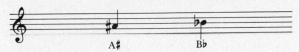

(The A-sharp and B-flat represent the same key on the piano.)

The Natural Sign: Canceling an Accidental. An accidental sharp or flat sign alters the single pitch to which it is applied or the repetitions of that pitch close by. When a pitch that has had an accidental returns to its natural position, it is indicated by placing a **natural sign**, ♮, at its reappearance in the white-key position. The practice is called canceling an accidental (Fig. A.10).

Fig. A.10. Natural Sign Canceling an Accidental

A-natural   A-sharp   A-natural   B-flat   B-natural

Key Signatures. In many pieces, a particular choice of accidentals is applied consistently throughout. In that case, the accidentals are shown only once on each staff, grouped at the beginning just after the clef. Accidentals used that way make up a **key signature**. A *key signature* is a set of accidentals that governs every appearance of its pitches throughout the staff. It simplifies the appearance of the written page by avoiding the constant repetition of the same signs. In music of the past three centuries where the major and minor keys are used (for example, G major or G minor), each key has its own key signature, its regular set of accidentals. The distinctive grouping of accidentals at the beginning of each staff quickly tells the performer what key the music is in. Some key signatures are shown in Fig. A.11.

Fig. A.11. Some Key Signatures: Same Tune in Different Keys

THE NOTATION OF RHYTHM AND TEMPO

Rhythm

Rhythm is the organized motion of pitches in time. It consists of patterns of length and loudness that are applied to the pitches, turning them into musical designs.

Pulses (Beats). The rhythms in most familiar music are based on a continuous succession of identical *pulses.* These are equal length, equally emphatic, low-level throbs or beats that run with clocklike regularity through the length of a piece.

Measures (Bars). Building upon the continuity of pulses, the music is further organized into small rhythmic units of equal length called *measures* (or bars), where a given number of pulses is grouped together. Normally a measure contains 2, 3, 4, 6, or 9 pulses, and once a particular measure pattern (with one of these numbers of pulses) is established at the start of a piece, it then remains constant to the end, only rarely interrupted or changed. Each measure has an **accent** (an extra emphasis or stress) placed on its first pulse; in measures with 4, 6, or 9 pulses there are *secondary accents* placed on every second or third pulse in a row.

Measure Lines (Bar Lines). The measures are separated from one another by vertical lines, called *measure lines* (bar lines), drawn through the staff (Fig. A.12).

Fig. A.12. Measures and Measure Lines

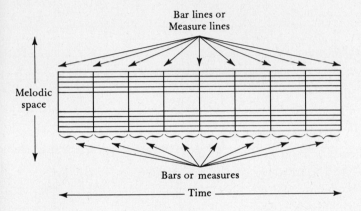

Meter, Metric Rhythm. *Meter* is the regular pattern of pulses and accents found within each measure. *Metric rhythm* is rhythm that is organized with a meter. There are two basic meters: duple meter and triple meter.

Duple meter has two pulses per measure:

$$\left| \overset{>}{1} \ 2 \ \right| \overset{>}{1} \ 2 \ \left| \overset{>}{1} \ 2 \ \right| \textit{etc.} \ (> \text{ is an accented pulse.})$$

Triple meter has three pulses per measure:

$$\left| \overset{>}{1} \ 2 \ 3 \ \right| \overset{>}{1} \ 2 \ 3 \ \left| \overset{>}{1} \ 2 \ 3 \ \right| \textit{etc.}$$

Meters with Four, Six, and Nine Pulses. There are also three other meters in ordinary use. So-called **common time** (quadruple meter) has four pulses per measure; **compound duple meter** has six pulses per measure; **compound triple meter** has nine pulses per measure. They are discussed in Appendix B.2.

Notes and Rests. Earlier we explained that the shape of a note—its head, stem, and tails—shows how long it lasts. Since rhythmic patterns use silence as well as sound, there are signs for the **rests** that count out the silences as well as for the *notes* that signify the sounds. "There is no music in a rest," someone once wrote, "but there is music's making." The names and shapes of the notes and rests are shown in Fig. A.13.

Fig. A.13. Notes and Rests

Note (sounding pitch)	𝅝	𝅗𝅥	♩	♪	𝅘𝅥𝅯	𝅘𝅥𝅰
Name American: British:	whole semibreve	half minim	quarter crotchet	eighth quaver	sixteenth semiquaver	thirty-second demi-semiquaver
Rest (measured silence)	▬	▬	𝄾	𝄿	𝅀	𝅁

𝅝 = 𝅗𝅥 𝅗𝅥 = ♩ ♩ ♩ ♩ = ♪♪♪♪♪♪♪♪ = 𝅘𝅥𝅯𝅘𝅥𝅯𝅘𝅥𝅯𝅘𝅥𝅯𝅘𝅥𝅯𝅘𝅥𝅯𝅘𝅥𝅯𝅘𝅥𝅯𝅘𝅥𝅯𝅘𝅥𝅯𝅘𝅥𝅯𝅘𝅥𝅯𝅘𝅥𝅯𝅘𝅥𝅯𝅘𝅥𝅯𝅘𝅥𝅯 *etc.*
Whole = 2 half notes = 4 quarter notes = 8 eighth notes = 16 sixteenth notes
note

Whole Note, Half Note, Quarter Note. The note value from which the others are calculated is the whole note. It is divided into half notes, quarter notes, eighth notes, etc. In music composed four and five centuries ago, the whole note generally corresponded to the pulse beat of the music, but more recent music has tended to put the pulse on the quarter note. Thus, in counting out the pulse in a measure of triple meter, each pulse (1, 2, 3) usually receives a quarter note:

♩ ♩ ♩ ♩ ♩ ♩
1 2 3 1 2 3

or its equivalent in other note values:

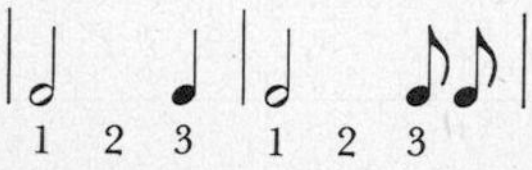

𝅗𝅥 ♩ 𝅗𝅥 ♪♪♪
1 2 3 1 2 3

Stems, Tails, and Beaming. In general, the darker the look of the notation on the printed page, the more animated or complex the rhythms are. A glance at the note shapes in Fig. A.13 shows why. The shorter time lengths have black heads rather than open heads, and they have stems and tails—the more tails, the shorter they are. There is a method of reducing the visual complexity of a rhythmically busy page. In a row of notes with tails, instead of writing out each tail separately the stems are joined by solid lines substituting for the tails, called *beams*—as in the long timbers of a house (Fig. A.14). The use of *beaming* saves strokes of the copyist's pen and cuts down the cluttered look. The angle of the beam can also tell a hurried performer whether the musical line is heading up or down.

Fig. A.14. Beaming of Eighth and Sixteenth Notes

Irregular Note Lengths. Each note or rest in Fig. A.13 lasts twice (or half) as long as the next one. This means that lengths of musical time are subdivided into halves, quarters, eighths, etc., but if a composer wants a more complex subdivision into lengths such as thirds, fifths, sixths, or sevenths, other signs must be used. Such signs include dots, ties, and triplets.

Dots. A *dot* that follows a note, a rest, or another dot extends the length of the preceding sign by half: 𝅗𝅥. = 1½ 𝅗𝅥 = 𝅗𝅥 + ♪ = ♩♩♩

Ties. Two or more notes in a row that are at the same pitch have their lengths combined by the use of a curved horizontal line called a *tie*. This joins them in a continuous sound, adding the lengths without any new beginning or accent. For example (the pulses here are counted in quarter notes): 𝅗𝅥. 𝅗𝅥
3 + 2 = 5

Triplets. The time regularly taken by two equal notes can also be filled by three faster-moving notes of the same kind, called *triplets:*

$$\overset{3}{♩♩♩} = ♩\ ♩ \quad \text{or} \quad \overset{3}{♫♪} = ♪\ ♪$$

Triplets are indicated by the number 3 placed in the middle of a triplet group.

Time Signatures. The meter that is used in a piece is shown by its *time signature,* which appears on the staff just after the clef and key signature. A time signature consists of two numbers, one above the other, looking like a fraction but without a dividing line: $\frac{4}{4}$, $\frac{6}{8}$, $\frac{3}{4}$. However, the meanings are quite different than fractions. A time signature identifies the meter, the basic pattern of pulses and accents found in each measure. The upper number of the time signature tells how many pulses there are per measure. The lower number generally indicates which note value has the pulse: a 4 on the bottom means counting a pulse on every quarter note; an 8 on the bottom means counting a pulse on every eighth note. In a way time signatures are unnecessary because their information can be obtained by examining the lengths and groupings of notes within any single measure of the music. However, the time signature instantly tells the performer what the meter will be.

Each of the common musical meters can be represented by a number of possible time signatures, depending on what note value (half note, quarter note, eighth note, etc.) is chosen for the pulse. Some of the usual time signatures are: *duple meter,* $\frac{2}{4}$; *triple meter,* $\frac{3}{4}$ or $\frac{3}{8}$; *common time,* $\frac{4}{4}$, or **C**, a half-circle open to the right like a large letter C, which can be remembered as a "C" for common time; *compound duple meter,* $\frac{6}{8}$; *compound triple meter,* $\frac{9}{8}$. Twentieth-century music makes frequent use of irregular meters with time signatures such as $\frac{5}{8}$ or $\frac{7}{4}$. These meters follow the same rule as the others: The upper number shows the pulses per measure, the lower number indicates which note sign has the pulse.

Tempo

Tempo means musical pace, the speed of the rhythm. The note signs themselves do not tell how fast they go; they do not indicate real lengths of time. They only show relative lengths with respect to one another—whole, half, quarter, eighth. It is the tempo marking that tells how long the pitches are actually held—how quickly the music moves. Every piece has a tempo marking at the beginning, such as allegro (♩ = 96), or andante (♪ = 75). During the eighteenth century, tempos were usually marked just by Italian words such as **allegro** ("joyous") or **andante** ("at a walking pace"). Some common Italian tempo markings are:

Presto	Very fast
Vivace	Lively (slower than Presto)
Allegro	Fast ("joyous")
Andante	Moderately ("walking")
Adagio	Slow
Largo	Very slow
Grave	Extremely slow

There are also Italian directions for gradually slowing down, *ritardando (rit.),* and gradually speeding up, *accelerando (accel.).* A sign called a *fermata* ("hold") is placed over a note head when the pitch is to be held, with the pulse and meter momentarily suspended: 𝄐

In the early nineteenth century an adjustable clock called the **metronome,** which accurately beat out any desired number of pulses per minute, was invented. Metronome markings were adopted, for example: ♩ = 96, specifying what note value received the pulse (here the quarter note) and how many pulses there were per minute (here 96). The two kinds of tempo marking still appear side by side—the metronome numbers supplying their dry precision and the Italian words adding humanity and flavor.

A Sample of Rhythmic Notation. We are ready to put the elements of rhythmic notation together. Fig. A.15 shows the tune of "Three Blind Mice" in rhythmic notation, omitting the staff and the heights of pitches. Many of the features just discussed are illustrated: time signature, tempo indications, measure lines, note shapes from half note to sixteenth note, dotted notes, triplets, eighth rests. Can you find them? Now hum through the tune, thinking of its rhythm. Can you see how the notation fits the rhythm?

Fig. A.15. Rhythmic Notation of "Three Blind Mice"

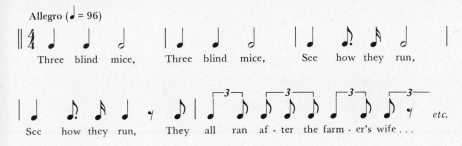

A Sample of Musical Notation. Finally we are ready to put the elements of pitch notation and rhythmic notation together. Fig. A.16 shows the tune of "Three Blind Mice" with the same rhythmic

Fig. A.16. Melodic and Rhythmic Notation of "Three Blind Mice"

notation as in Fig. A.15, but now with the full notation of its pitches on the treble staff and with a key signature (one sharp) showing that the tune is in G major. Hum through the tune again. Can you see how the notation shows what is going on?

Dynamics. There is just one other area of rhythmic notation, involving dynamics and some nuances of delivery and phrasing. *Dynamics* are the levels of loud and soft in music. They are usually indicated by abbreviations of Italian words:

ppp	Utterly soft (triple piano)
pp	Very soft (pianissimo)
p	Soft (piano)
mp	Half soft (mezzo piano)
mf	Half loud (mezzo forte)
f	Loud (forte)
ff	Very loud (fortissimo)
fff	Extremely loud (triple forte)

To show gradual change from one dynamic level to another there are both signs and words:

◁   *crescendo* (*cresc.*): gradually louder

▷   *decrescendo* (*decresc.*): gradually softer
or
diminuendo (*dim.*): diminishing (same meaning)

Then there are nuances. **Staccato,** indicated by a dot over a note head, ♪ ♪, means the note is shortened and "gently detached" from the neighboring notes. **Legato** means that a number of pitches are run fluidly together. Sometimes the word is used: *legato* ♪♪♪♪ or the flow of connected pitches is shown by a *phrase mark* or *slur:* ♪♪♪♪

B Musical Fundamentals

1. MATERIALS OF MELODY

Take but degree away, untune the strings,
    and hark what discord follows.
        Shakespeare, *Troilus and Cressida* (1602)

Sound

Sound Waves. Music is made up of sounds and silences that are joined in imaginative patterns. The sounds of music, like the sounds of words or noise, are the result of small rapid vibrations of air that strike our ears and register on our brains. Sounds travel through the air in the form of vibrations or "waves," in much the way that water travels through the ocean. Where there is no air there is no sound, as happens in a vacuum or in outer space. On the airless surface of the moon astronauts cannot shout to one another, even speak face to face. They need radio waves to carry their messages—electromagnetic waves that can move through the vacant, gas-free space and activate the earphones within their helmets, which are vessels filled with air.

High and Low Sounds. On hearing two different musical sounds most of us can say which of them seems "higher," which "lower." Those qualities of apparent highness and lowness reflect the speed of the vibrating air waves. The faster the waves, the higher the apparent sound. The slower the waves, the lower the sound. Our ears can hear sounds when the motion of the air is as slow as fifteen or twenty vibrations per second. We continue to hear sounds as the speed of vibration mounts up to fifteen or twenty thousand vibrations per second.

Vibration Frequency: Hertz. Musicians have various ways of describing the speed of sound waves. They may speak of "vibrations

Fig. B.1.1. Vibration Frequencies

1 Hz:

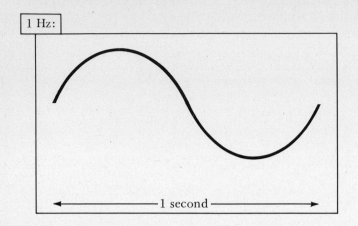

⟵———— 1 second ————⟶

5 Hz:

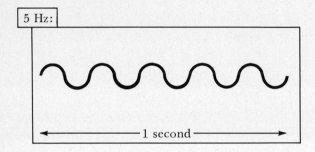

⟵———— 1 second ————⟶

Range of audible sound:

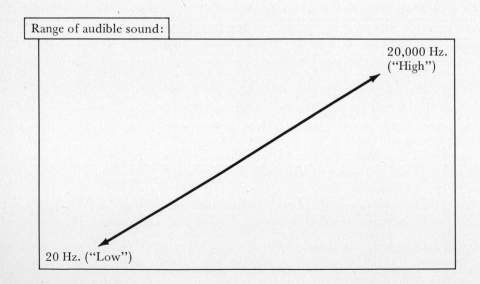

20,000 Hz.
("High")

20 Hz. ("Low")

per second," "oscillations per second," or "cycles per second"; all mean the same thing. The term generally used is *Hertz* or *Hz,* which is borrowed from physics. A *Hz* equals one vibration, one cycle per second, measured from the crest of one wave to the crest of the next. Our ears, then, register sounds that range from about 20 Hz to 20,000 Hz (Fig. B.1.1). Women's ears are better than men's at detecting the top range above 15,000 Hz. At the bottom, dipping below approximately 20 Hz, a threshold is reached where musical sounds no longer hold together as continuous tones but disintegrate in separate puffs. A frequency such as 10 Hz is as much felt by the stomach as sensed by the ear. For some sea lions, in fact, a sound of 9 Hz acts as a dinner bell.

Glissando: The Continuum of Sound. Everyone knows the sounds of a siren sweeping up and down. The musical name for that siren effect is *glissando,* an Italian word related to the English "gliding" and "sliding." Our familiar music makes little use of glissandos. Instead, it uses individual musical sounds of fixed height that are like steps carved out of the continuous slope of a glissando. Such individual heights or levels are called pitches. Sometimes they are called tones or notes, but those terms are ambiguous and pitch is preferred (Fig. B.1.2).

Fig. B.1.2. Pitch-Space: Glissando and Fixed Pitches

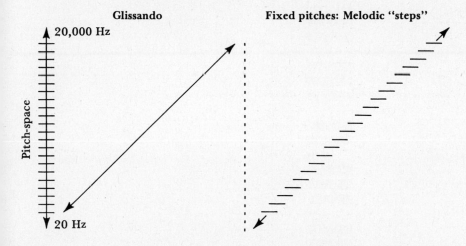

Pitch

Pitch. A *pitch* is a musical sound of fixed height. The piano has eighty-eight pitches in all, spread from high to low, produced by its eighty-eight keys. The piano's highest pitch has a frequency of 4096

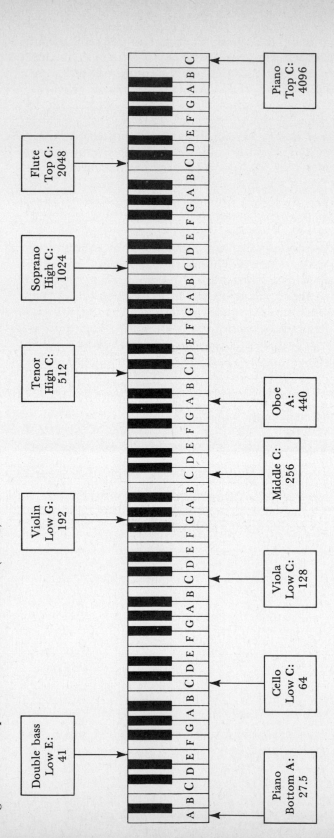

Fig. B.1.3. Frequencies of Piano Pitches (in Hz)

Hz; its lowest, 27.5 Hz (Fig. B.1.3). Thus the piano does not cover the very highest pitches we can hear (those between 4100 Hz and 20,000 Hz) or the very lowest (those between approximately 15 Hz and 27 Hz). It provides only a central range of pitches. But in fact, most musical action takes place within a still more central range, from about 40 Hz through 1000 Hz. Here are some examples of what those numbers mean in familiar sounds. The lowest pitch on a double bass is 41 Hz; the lowest on a violin is 192 Hz. The range that alto and tenor singers share runs from about 200 Hz through 450 Hz. The operatic soprano's "high C" is at 1024 Hz.

   The Twelve Basic Pitches. There are eighty-eight different pitches found on the piano, yet if we think of our glissando, the continuum of pitch sounds, we realize that there must be many other intervening levels of pitch that are not obtainable on the keyboard at all. In fact, our ears can perceive four or five different pitch levels between each piano pitch and the neighboring one. Thus the keyboard already represents a limited choice from among the many pitches available in nature. Yet the eighty-eight different pitches on the piano embody an even more drastic limitation of musical resources. Among the eighty-eight pitches there are just twelve really different pitch sounds. We shall speak of them as *twelve basic pitches*. The piano's full spread contains many duplications of those twelve pitches at higher and lower levels. The twelve are shown in Fig. B.1.4. They are called

Fig. B.1.4. The Twelve Basic Pitches

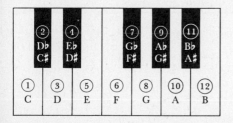

the twelve basic pitches here, though some musicians prefer to call them the twelve "pitch classes." Pitch class and basic pitch are the same: pitch class Ĉ is basic pitch C; basic pitch F-sharp is pitch class F̂-sharp. The twelve basic pitches are the pitch sounds out of which practically all Western music is made. They are a bit like the colors on a painter's palette. The ears of musicians distinguish the sound of a C-sharp from an F-sharp, a B-flat from an E-natural, in somewhat the same way our eyes distinguish the colors of red from yellow, orange from green.

The Letter Names of the Basic Pitches. The twelve basic pitches are identified by the seven letters of the alphabet, A through G. To be sure, there are just seven letters for twelve pitches. They were given the letter names during the Middle Ages when special conditions prevailed. The seven alphabet letters were assigned to the seven pitches most commonly used in medieval music, which were also the pitches produced by the white keys on the keyboard (as in Fig. B. 1.4). The other five pitches were less commonly used. They were produced by inset black keys placed between the whites and were given names that identified them merely as relatives or subordinates of the neighboring whites. Each black key received the same letter as its neighboring white, but with a sharp sign (♯) or flat sign (♭) added. A sharp sign indicated the black key just above a white key. A flat sign indicated the black key just below a white key. Thus the black key above D was named D-sharp, the black key below D was named D-flat.

Melody

Most of us, when we think of music, think first of *melody*—of tunes that we can hum or whistle. Like music itself, melody represents the realm of art and emotion, not number and science, and it is difficult to define. Let us define melody provisionally as a succession of pitches with a sense of order and completeness. That takes care of most of the shapes that melodies have assumed through the ages and around the world, from Gregorian chant to Schoenberg, from the Far East to the Americas. Each time and place produces its own typical shapes of melody, projects its own sense of order and completeness in its successions of pitches. Each melody has its own shape, its distinctive musical logic.

Melodic Contours. Musicians describe their melodies in much the same terms that artists use to describe their graphic designs. Melodies are said to have shapes or contours, lines and curves. In the opening of the tune "America," for instance, the pitches lie within a narrow range, and the motion from one pitch to the next is generally to some close-by pitch. The melodic motion is in a sense "rounded" (Fig. B.1.5a). In the melody of "Auld Lang Syne" (Fig. B.1.5b), the overall range is wider and the melodic motion is more angular, with skips or leaps between distant pitches. The contours of this tune also show us how the directions that melodic lines take can embody emotional values. The opening lines (1 and 2) seem to increase in tension as the pitches rise toward their climax on the words "brought to mind." Then the melodic direction reverses and tensions are released as the music settles toward a satisfying pause on "auld lang syne."

Fig. B.1.5. Melody: A Succession of Pitches

a) "America"

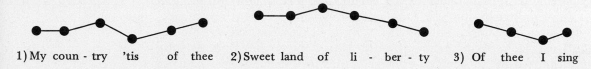

1) My coun - try 'tis of thee   2) Sweet land of li - ber - ty   3) Of thee I sing

b) "Auld Lang Syne"

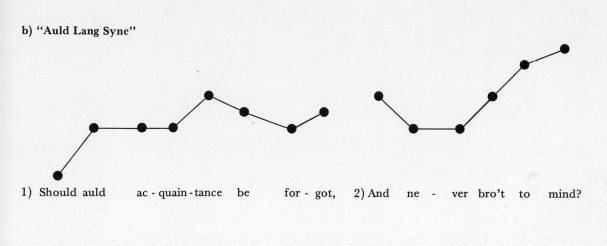

1) Should auld   ac - quain - tance be   for - got,   2) And ne - ver bro't to mind?

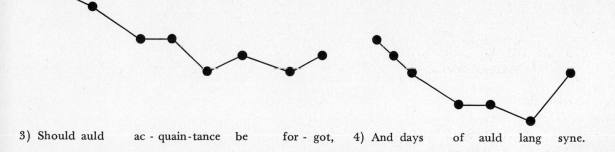

3) Should auld   ac - quain - tance be   for - got,   4) And days of auld lang syne.

Phrases and Cadences. Whatever specific contours melodies may have, they are nearly always made up of the combinations of phrases and cadences. A *phrase* is a short melodic utterance, a segment of melody such as can be sung in a single breath. It is the counterpart of a clause or phrase in prose or poetry. The musical phrase does not end haphazardly. It generally ends with a sense of having arrived at some musical goal. Such a phrase ending is called a *cadence,* after an Italian word meaning to drop or fall. The cadence is a point of arrival and relative repose, a falling off of musical motion at the end of a phrase. The way it works is that the phrase makes some statement, and then the cadence rounds it off with some relaxation. Musical cadences are like the slackenings of voice and pace that occur in speaking or reading aloud when we approach a comma, a period, or a question mark. In music, the phrases and their punctuating cadences give a similar sense of shape and "discourse" to the result. Some of this can be seen in the melody of "Auld Lang Syne" (Fig. B.1.5b). At the end of phrase 2, the music comes to a cadence on "brought to mind." There the melody not only pauses but seems to be pointing upward, like a question mark demanding a response, implying there is more to come. The response comes with phrases 3 and 4 and is made definite with the cadence of phrase 4 (on "auld lang syne"), which has a sense of arrival, of coming to rest.

Pitches: The Raw Materials of Melody. The chief building blocks of melody are pitches. What any melody has to say depends largely on its selection of basic pitches and the combinations it makes of them. Most melodies that we encounter in the West are built of a selection of from seven to twelve of the twelve basic pitches. To see what that means, let us imagine building a melody that uses just two of the basic pitches, for instance, C and D. In order to produce a "melody" we must apply some imaginative patterns of alternation, repetition, and pauses to the C and D, fashioning them into phrases and cadences. Taking this a step farther, we can even imagine building a melody that uses just one basic pitch, say a C *or* a D. Again, so long as some interesting pattern of repetitions and pauses is applied, the result will be a melody of sorts. Yet where the raw materials are so limited as just one or two of the basic pitches, the composer runs a great risk of boring the listener. That is why composers prefer richer selections from among the twelve basic pitches as their musical raw materials. It is why most Western music is built with anywhere from seven to twelve of the basic pitches.

Intervals. We have defined a pitch as a musical sound of fixed height, and a melody as a succession of pitches with a sense of order and completeness. Now let us examine the pitches that make up a melody from a closer vantage point—that of their relationship to one another within the melody. The distance between two pitches is called an *interval.* Simply looked at, an interval is just that: a measure of how far apart two pitches are in musical space. But a musical interval is also something more. It is a hearable relationship between two pitches. That is, between any two pitches, whether played together or in succession, there exists a distinctive kind of sound, a unique, identifiable quality for each different distance between pitches. Some intervals have sounds that seem to be drawing together with an effect like a sonic rubber band. Others seem to be heading farther apart, as if repelling one another. The fact is, when we listen to a musical passage, we do not hear just the individual sounds of pitches. We connect each pitch with the pitches that come just before, after, or along with it. Like the individual pitches, those connections have sounds. We have defined a melody as a succession of pitches with a sense of order and completeness. We might redefine it to take into account the effect of the intervals: A melody is a succession of pitches *and intervals* with a sense of order and completeness (Fig. B.1.6). What we notice about a melody really depends more on the character and dynamic tensions of its intervals than on the inert sounds of its pitches.

Fig. B.1.6. Melody: A Succession of Pitches and Intervals

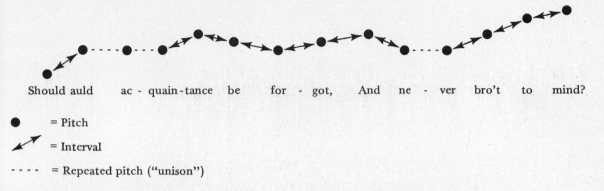

Should auld   ac - quain - tance be   for - got,   And   ne - ver bro't to mind?

● = Pitch

↗ = Interval

- - - - = Repeated pitch ("unison")

Altogether, there are about a dozen intervals commonly used in Western music. Four of them are of particular importance for understanding our musical processes. They are the *half-step, whole-step, fifth,* and *octave.*

The Half-Step. The *half-step* is the smallest interval found in most Western music. It is the interval between any black or white key on the piano and the closest neighboring key: between C and C-sharp, C-sharp and D, E and F. The piano keyboard is divided from top to bottom into an unbroken series of equal half-step intervals. Its eighty-eight keys segment the central range of musical sounds into eighty-seven equal-size, identical-sounding half-steps. We can fix the sound of a half-step in our ears by hearing some adjacent piano keys played a few times.

The Whole-Step. The *whole-step* is twice the size of the half-step. It contains two half-steps. Whole-steps are also spread throughout the keyboard, as from C to D, D to E, F-sharp to G-sharp, etc. The whole-step is another relatively small interval. Its sound can be learned from the piano by playing keys that are separated by one intervening key.

Step Motion and Skip Motion. In discussing melodic contours we have spoken of rounded motion and angular motion. Now let us be more specific. Melodic motion that is rounded generally uses half-steps and whole-steps. It is called *step motion,* or motion by step. (Some musicians prefer the Latinate term *conjunct motion.*) All the other intervals used in Western music are larger than the whole-step. As a group they are called skips or skip intervals, and the relatively angular motion they produce is called *skip motion,* or motion by skip. (Some musicians prefer the term *disjunct motion.*)

The Fifth. The *fifth* is a skip interval whose pitches are at the fifth step apart on the white keys of the keyboard (Fig. B.1.7).

Fig. B.1.7. Segment of Keyboard

There are fifths from C up to G, D up to A, E up to B, etc. Counted in half-steps, the fifth is a skip interval that is seven half-steps wide. Fifths have a spacious, resonant quality of sound. Their sounds should be learned on the piano.

The Octave. The *octave* is a large skip interval whose pitches are at the *eighth* step apart on the white keys of the keyboard; counted in half-steps, the octave is twelve half-steps wide. Many octave intervals can be seen on the segment of the piano keyboard shown in Fig. B.1.7. The two pitches that form an octave always have the same letter names: C and C, D and D, E-flat and E-flat, etc. That is, the two pitches of an octave represent one and the same basic pitch, and they have the same essential pitch sound: Their sounds are practical duplicates of one another. When they are heard together they have a uniquely transparent quality that makes the octave the most recognizable of all musical intervals. What differences we can detect between the two pitches of an octave are those of height. One is higher, the other is lower, but otherwise they sound alike. That "sameness" of an octave's sound is related to an elementary fact in the physics of music. The upper pitch of an octave always vibrates twice as fast as the lower pitch. Thus "middle C" at the center of the piano keyboard vibrates at 256 Hz while the C an octave above it is at 512 Hz (as in Fig. B.1.3). The transparent quality of an octave's sound may reflect that simple 2:1 ratio, where every other vibration is "in phase" and none of the parallel wave-forms are ever competing, or "out of phase." The sameness of sound in an octave's two pitches and the identity of their letter names are visible in the familiar layout of our keyboard (Fig. B.1.7). This consists of a series of white keys with black keys regularly inserted among them in alternate groups of two and three. The keys that produce an octave always have the same position in the repeating black-and-white pattern of the keyboard.

Octave Duplication: Repetition in Pitch Space. Earlier we compared the twelve basic pitches used in Western music to the spread of colors available on a painter's palette. There is one notable difference, however, between the arrays of raw material for sound and for color. With colors, a single pass through the hues from red to violet exhausts the whole spectrum of visible light. With musical space, we do not go just once through the twelve basic pitch sounds. Instead, there are many duplications of those twelve basic pitches at higher and lower octave levels throughout the range of audible sound. The spread of octave levels might be compared to a display of multiple rainbows. Altogether, the piano keyboard contains more than seven different octave levels, each of them duplicating the full array of twelve basic pitch sounds. Thus, spread through the keyboard, there are eight Cs, eight Bs, eight B-flats, eight As, seven C-sharps, seven Ds, seven E-flats, seven Es, etc. (see Fig. B.1.3).

The Scale

An Inventory of Basic Pitches. In any passage of actual music, the composer takes great pains to select a particular octave level for each pitch. It makes all the difference to have a pitch at the right artful height. For instance, in the opening phrase of "The Star Spangled Banner," the basic pitch used on "say" ("Oh, say can you see . . .") is the same one that is used on "see." Yet in the actual melody they are not the same: "say" is at the lower octave, "see" is at the upper octave. They are octave duplications of one another. The two different levels serve a clear artistic purpose, however. With "see" at the upper octave, the opening phrase has a strong climactic thrust. If the level at "see" just fell back to the lower octave of "say," the effect would merely be humdrum (Fig. B.1.8). A similar choice of an appropriate octave level can be found in the opening phrase of "The Marseillaise" and in the opening four pitches of "Ô Canada."

Fig. B.1.8. The Difference in an Octave

Climax

G   E   C   E   G   C

Oh,— say can you see

Letdown

G   E   C   E   G   C

Oh,— say can you see

Clearly, the choice of octave level makes a difference to the contour and emotional effect of a melodic phrase. Yet for certain analytic purposes, musicians will ignore the different octave levels and concentrate simply on the basic pitches. There is an important rule: Every one of the twelve basic pitches used in Western music can be found within the span of any single octave. Thus when musicians want to analyze the substance of a musical work and discover what raw materials it employs, they extract its roster of pitches and line them up within a single octave. Such a roster of basic pitches is called a scale. A **scale** is a lineup of the basic pitches that are used in a musical work, arranged in up-and-down order within the span of an octave. Everyone knows the sounds of scales. They are what singers and instrumentalists practice in order to improve their technique. Those mechanical-sounding series of pitches have this further use: They are the musician's way of summarizing the pitch materials that are found in a piece of music. What scales do for a single piece they can also do for more than one. That is, scales provide a means of comparing the raw materials of pitch used in two or more pieces.

Extracting a Scale from a Melody. The method of extracting the basic pitches from a melody so as to obtain its scale is something for professionals, not amateurs, to attempt, but in general it works as follows. There are three steps. First, no matter how many times a given pitch appears in the music, it is counted as just a single pitch in making up the scale. Second, no matter how high or low a given pitch may appear in octave duplications, it is counted as just a single pitch in the scale. Those two steps are illustrated for the melody of "Frère Jacques" in Fig. B.1.9. The melody is shown with each of its pitches numbered from $\hat{1}$ through $\hat{6}$. Two scales are spelled out underneath. Each represents an inventory of the pitches in "Frère

Fig. B.1.9. The Scale of "Frère Jacques"

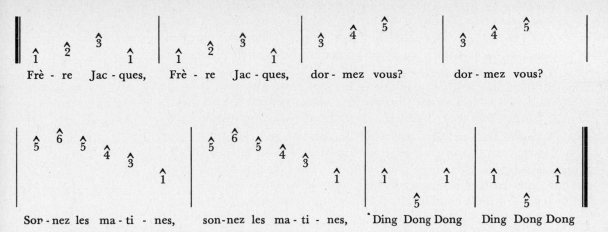

Frè - re Jac - ques, Frè - re Jac - ques, dor - mez vous? dor - mez vous?

Son - nez les ma - ti - nes, son-nez les ma - ti - nes, Ding Dong Dong Ding Dong Dong

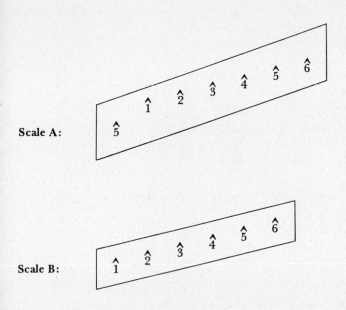

Scale A:

Scale B:

Jacques," but in scale A only the first step is applied. It shows the pitches at the actual levels where they occur in the melody, so there are two $\hat{5}$-pitches, one high, the other low. That lets the range of the scale extend beyond the span of a single octave. In scale B the second step is applied. It has the same roster of six basic pitches, but now the two different $\hat{5}$-pitches are combined by transferring the lower $\hat{5}$-pitch to the upper octave. The overall range of the scale now lies, as it is supposed to, within the span of a single octave.

Now we come to the third step in extracting a scale from a melody, one that goes to the essence of how we hear most music. The **tonic**, or home pitch, is identified from the sound of the music, and is placed at the bottom, the number $\hat{1}$ position of the scale. That tonic is not always easy to pick out. Still, if we think through the melody of "Frère Jacques" again, we can probably hear that one of its six basic pitches has a quality that sets it apart from the rest. It is the pitch that opens and closes the melody, and it is a pitch used prominently along the way. Because of those distinctions—particularly that it closes the melody—this pitch is assigned the number $\hat{1}$ position among the basic pitches and is placed at the bottom of the scale. Musicians call this a *tonic pitch,* and nearly every familiar melody has such a tonic. It is the home pitch, the most important pitch, the organizing pitch. Its qualities and functions are of the utmost significance in the way we hear and understand most music. In Fig. B.1.9, scale B shows the roster of basic pitches used in the melody of "Frère Jacques" with the tonic pitch placed as number $\hat{1}$ at the bottom of the six-pitch scale.

Musicians can extract the scale from any piece of music by applying the three steps just described. If the reader wants to try another tune, a good choice would be "Three Blind Mice." The details are not given here, but there are two helpful hints. First, "Three Blind Mice" does not begin with its tonic, number $\hat{1}$ pitch. It ends on the tonic, but it starts with pitch $\hat{3}$ of its scale, and the tonic $\hat{1}$ makes a first appearance on the word "mice." The second hint is that the scale of "Three Blind Mice" contains seven pitches: At the top it has a pitch $\hat{7}$ that is lacking in the six-pitch scale of "Frère Jacques"; the other six pitches ($\hat{1}$ through $\hat{6}$) are the same in both tunes. Something of the real usefulness of scales can be seen from this. They allow direct comparisons between the raw materials of different melodies.

Mode

Mode: Musical Mood and Flavor. Scales are handy for comparison and analysis, but they are essentially lifeless catalogues of raw materials. Their lineups of pitches are abstractions drawn from the substance of real music. We can approach the living nature of melody more closely by considering it now from a different standpoint, one that we will provisionally call its "mood" or "flavor." Most of us on listening to a piece of music can identify some distinctive mood, flavor, or kind of sound. We may recognize the sounds of Classical music, blues, South American music, "twenties" jazz, or Far Eastern music. Each of these familiar types of sound has a distinctive profile, something that lets us label it, relate it to other pieces with similar flavors, distinguish it from others with different flavors. The musician's word for such moods or flavors is *mode,* a word that is related to our everyday word "mood." We can define a mode as musical sounds with a particular character or mood, for example, blues, South American, or Far Eastern. Unlike a scale, which is an abstraction, a mode represents the living qualities of music. A mode is a hearable quality that may be unique to a single piece of music, but often it is shared by a whole group of similar-sounding pieces. The characteristic modal sounds of blues music, or those we recognize as Western Classical music, are shared by many thousands of pieces in each case, all of them projecting the same modal character, the same community of flavors and moods.

Modal Character Depends on the Scale. What we perceive as modal character is the result of various factors, including rhythm, texture, and tone color (see pages 444, 453, 472) as well as pitch. But the main factor in creating the typical sound of a mode is pitch: the selection of pitches on which the music is built, the basic pitches in its scale. Earlier we considered composing a melody with a two-pitch scale (the pitches C and D) by applying some imaginative patterns of repetition and alternation to those pitches. The resulting melody will represent a mode; it will have a distinctive modal character that comes from using the pitches C and D. Now we might compose other melodies using the same two-pitch scale of C and D. To do this we need only invent other patterns of repetition and alternation for those two pitches. The new melodies all share the same modal character, because they are based on the same scale. But if instead of using the basic pitches C and D we decide to compose a melody using some other two-pitch scale, for instance, the pitches C and F-sharp, the result will have quite another modal character. It will be in a different mode because it is based on a different scale. Even if we apply to the pitches C and F-sharp exactly the same patterns of repetition and alternation that we applied to the pitches C and D, the mode will be different. There we have the first essential in modal character. It depends on the scale, on the choice of basic pitches used in the music.

Modal Character Depends on Idioms. Yet there is something else. Modal character also depends on artful combinations of those pitches. It depends on musical idioms, or typical turns of phrase, that are built by manipulating the basic pitches of the scale. Such idioms involve patterns of rhythm, texture, and tone color along with those of pitch. They are all joined together in fashioning the musical moods and flavors that we recognize as a mode.

Mode and Scale. Two factors, then, make up a musical mode: the pitches of a scale and the idioms that combine those pitches in the refined calculus of art. The scale is the catalogue of raw materials; the mode is the living fabric of musical patterns. Yet even when the abstract sound of a scale is heard by itself, without any of the artful idiomatic dressings, it has something of the modal character. The scale sound is not quite a dry abstraction. Its lineup of pitches gives off some of the quality of the modal sound. Thus an "Oriental" scale played by itself may remind us of the sound of Oriental music, as can be seen by comparing the tune and the scale in Fig. B.1.10.

Fig. B.1.10. A Pentatonic (Black-Key) Tune

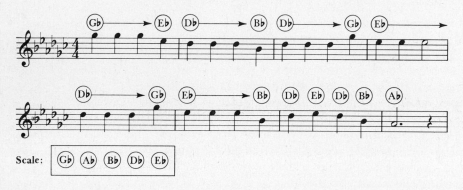

The Classification of Scales by Their Number of Pitches

There are many scales in use around the world. Generally they are classified by the number of pitches they contain. We have encountered a six-pitch scale in "Frère Jacques," a seven-pitch scale in "Three Blind Mice." There are scales with as few as two pitches, such as our experimental scales of C and D, and C and F-sharp. Our Western scales normally have no more than twelve pitches—the twelve basic pitches found on the piano. But there are non-Western scales with more than twelve, whose pitches are separated by smaller intervals than the Western half-steps.

The Five-Pitch or Pentatonic Scales. The "Oriental" type of scale shown in Fig. B.1.10 is a five-pitch or pentatonic scale (the word *pentatonic* comes from the Greek, meaning "five pitches"). Five-pitch scales are found throughout the world, particularly in China and Japan. They usually produce the kinds of modal sounds that we associate with Far Eastern music. The five-pitch scale in Fig. B.1.10 is the familiar one that is produced by rolling one's knuckles across the five black keys of the piano. What it produces is the sham "Oriental" effect that is used in the overture to Gilbert and Sullivan's *The Mikado*.

The Twelve-Pitch (Chromatic) and Seven-Pitch (Diatonic) Scales. The main scales in the West have twelve or seven pitches to the octave. These scales are also known by names inherited from the ancient Greeks: chromatic (twelve-pitch) and diatonic (seven-pitch) scales.

The *twelve-pitch* or *chromatic* scale contains the largest number of pitches per octave of any scale found in the West. It has all twelve of the basic pitches that are playable on our keyboard, all twelve that are used in our familiar music. Those pitches are separated from one another by equal half-steps (Fig. B.1.11). The piano keyboard's full

Fig. B.1.11. The Twelve-Pitch Chromatic Scale

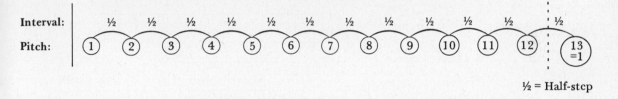

½ = Half-step

series of black and white keys produces the chromatic scale, and those same twelve pitches are built into the shape and mechanism of all other Western instruments that have fixed pitches, for example, the flute, clarinet, or guitar. The full resources of the twelve-pitch scale were rarely called for during the Middle Ages, but its use became more common during the sixteenth through nineteenth centuries. In our own century it has been the composer's main scale. The other scales used in our familiar music have fewer than twelve pitches, yet their pitches are all contained in the twelve-pitch scale and can be thought of as selections from the twelve-pitch scale.

For most of the past two thousand years, Western civilization has made use chiefly of *seven-pitch* or *diatonic* scales. There were many seven-pitch scales employed in ancient Greece and Rome, and many others in medieval times, when they were cultivated particularly in church music. Therefore, they became known as church scales or **church modes.** The medieval church modes sometimes went under Greek-style names, such as Dorian, Phrygian, and Lydian, but they had little in common with the musical substance of the ancient modes. Each medieval church mode had a seven-pitch scale that contained all seven of the white-key pitches on our piano keyboard; each scale had five whole-steps and two half-steps as the intervals between its pitches. The church scales differed from one another in their choice of tonic or bottom pitch. The Dorian church scale was a white-key scale from D through D; Phrygian was a white-key scale from E through E; and so on. Since the tonics differed, the scales also differed in the order of pitches and intervals above the tonic. Each had a different setup of whole-steps and half-steps above the bottom pitch, and those different orders produced a different modal sound from each scale (Fig. B.1.12).

Fig. B.1.12. Church Modes: Seven-Pitch Scales

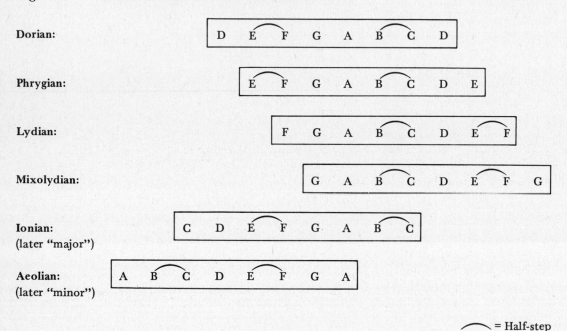

Dorian:

D   E   F   G   A   B   C   D

Phrygian:

E   F   G   A   B   C   D   E

Lydian:

F   G   A   B   C   D   E   F

Mixolydian:

G   A   B   C   D   E   F   G

Ionian:
(later "major")

C   D   E   F   G   A   B   C

Aeolian:
(later "minor")

A   B   C   D   E   F   G   A

⌒ = Half-step

The Major and Minor Scales

During the sixteenth and seventeenth centuries European composers gradually shifted their preference away from the relatively large selection of seven-pitch church scales and settled into a decisive concentration on just two of them. The Renaissance Ionian scale was a white-key scale running from C through C on the keyboard; the Aeolian scale was a white-key scale from A through A (Fig. B.1.12). Ionian was a forerunner of the modern **major scale**, and Aeolian was a forerunner of the modern **minor scale**. By the late seventeenth century those two scales—major and minor—had practically supplanted all the others. And during the eighteenth and nineteenth centuries they had Western musical styles more or less to themselves; it was their modal resources that dominated the imaginations of composers.

The major and minor scales are both seven-pitch scales that have five whole steps and two half-steps as the intervals between their pitches. They are compared in Fig. B.1.13. Obviously, the order of

Fig. B.1.13. Comparison of Major and Minor Scales

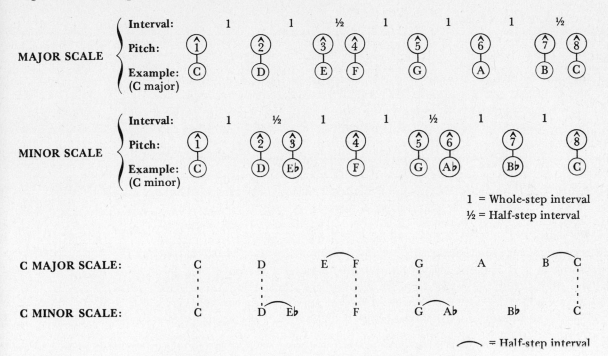

intervals above the tonic is different in each. In the major scale, the series of ascending whole steps and half-steps is:

$$1 - 1 - \tfrac{1}{2} - 1 - 1 - 1 - \tfrac{1}{2}$$

In the common form of the minor scale, the series of ascending whole steps and half-steps is:

$$1 - \tfrac{1}{2} - 1 - 1 - \tfrac{1}{2} - 1 - 1$$

The results are two different varieties of modal sound. The main difference between the major and minor sounds comes from the third pitch or third degree ($\hat{3}$) of their scales. In the major scale the third pitch is four half-steps above the tonic pitch, and the interval between them is a **major third** (from C to E in the C major scale). In the minor scale the third pitch is three half-steps above the tonic pitch,

Fig. B.1.14. Major Third and Minor Third

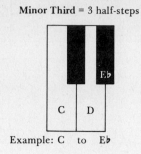

and the interval between them is a **minor third** (from C to E-flat in the C minor scale). (See Fig. B.1.14.) That difference of a half-step between a major third and a minor third looks small on the piano, but it makes a considerable difference to the character of what we hear. Modal character is not easily described in words. We all hear the major and minor modes in our own ways. Still, most of us tend to hear the major mode as being essentially affirmative and optimistic, while the minor mode seems more melancholy and pessimistic. Whatever descriptive words we choose, almost everybody can sense a difference in quality between them. Perhaps nothing better points up the nature of our familiar associations with major and minor than the fact that in our everyday musical styles there are no wedding marches that use the minor mode and no funeral marches that use the major mode. To test this, we have only to hear someone try to play Chopin's "Funeral March" in the major mode or Wagner's "Wedding March" in the minor mode. The character is all wrong; the effect is comic.

Tonality: The Major and Minor Modes Combined

We have said that composers of the eighteenth and nineteenth centuries made almost exclusive use of the major and minor modes. In practice, the resources of the two modes were commingled and combined to form a larger composite mode that goes by the name of **tonality**. It is sometimes called **major-minor tonality** or *triadic tonality*. Tonality represents the merger of the major and minor modes. It is the overall mode of practically all the music composed during that period of two centuries, which has become known as the tonal period of European-American music history. This was the period that produced the works of Bach, Handel, Mozart, Haydn, Beethoven, Wagner, Brahms, and Tchaikovsky. It is usually the major mode that is used in tonal music, but perhaps a quarter of the time the minor mode is used. Moreover, the choice shifts back and forth, not only from one piece to another but from one section to another within a piece, and even fluidly from one moment to another within a phrase. Taking the broad view of tonality, its two component modes, major and minor, operate as a single comprehensive mode, producing music that at any given moment is based on a single scale of seven "tonal" pitches. Those tonal pitches will be the favored ones in creating the musical sounds, but they can also be supplemented by drawing on the remaining five chromatic pitches of the twelve-pitch chromatic scale.

The Focus on the Tonic. Tonal music has the following all-important principle: At any moment in a tonal work the pitches in use are all subordinated to the tonic pitch, the number $\hat{1}$ pitch of the major-minor scale. There is the ever-present sense of the tonic as the organizing, governing, or home pitch. The other pitches are like satellites, heard in relation to it. It is because of this focus on the tonic that the major and minor scales are called tonal scales and the music composed with them is called tonal music.

The Language of Tonality. *Tonality*—the mode of tonal music—is sometimes compared to a spoken or literary language. It is the musical language employed by Western composers during the eighteenth and nineteenth centuries, the period that takes in most of our "classics." Its influence goes beyond those centuries and their classical music. Most twentieth-century "popular" music is tonal in character. Tonality is like a language in that it has various dialects that differ from place to place. Composers such as Bach (German), Couperin (French), and Vivaldi (Italian) were contemporaries of one another but of different nationality, and they used slightly different dialects of the same tonal language. Tonality is also like a language in that it changes in the course of time. Handel and Schumann were both north Germans but were separated by a century. They used the same tonal language with time-induced changes in style. Despite all such differences, the language of tonality, drawing upon the scales and idioms of the major and minor modes, remained practically the sole resource of musicians during the two tonal centuries. Even in the twentieth century, when most "serious" composers have gone on to other musical idioms, students of composition still find it worthwhile to master the idioms of tonality on the way to developing distinctive contemporary languages of their own.

Summary

We have learned that a *pitch* is a musical sound of fixed height, that an *interval* is a sounding relationship between two pitches, that a *melody* is a succession of pitches and intervals with a sense of order and completeness, and that a *scale* is an inventory of the basic pitches used in a melody. Every scale, every melody, every musical work has some distinctive flavor or kind of sound that is called its *mode*. The characteristic quality of a musical mode may be the unique attribute of a single piece of music, but more often it is shared by a number of similar pieces. Modal quality is the result of two main factors, scale and idioms. The *scale* is the roster of basic pitches with which the music is built, and the *idioms* are typical "turns of phrase" that exploit and give life to the roster. In recent centuries most Western music has made use of two modes, the *major mode* and the *minor mode,* which are built on the seven-pitch major and minor scales. Both those modes have a strong focus on their lowest pitch, the *tonic* or number $\hat{1}$ pitch of their scales, which serves as the organizing and home pitch in their music. The combined resources of the major and minor modes produce the composite mode that is called *tonality* and the musical styles of *tonal music*. The nature of tonal music will be considered further in the discussions of harmony and of key relationships that follow, beginning on page 458.

2. RHYTHM

So far we have considered music as being made up just of pitches. Yet pitches alone do not producc even the simplest melody. Pitches become transformed into melody when the enlivening patterns of rhythm are added to them. Musical sounds have the two main aspects of pitch and rhythm. Stravinsky has remarked, "Rhythm and motion . . . are the foundations of musical art." The rhythm is so essential that he does not even mention pitch! *Rhythm* is the time aspect of music. It is an organized flow of musical time, with patterns consisting of the lengths of time that pitches are held (their *durations*) and the loud and soft qualities of their delivery (their emphases or *dynamics*). Of all music's aspects, rhythm is the one that most readily engages our attention and draws an emotional response. Simply to hear the rhythm of a dance or a march is enough to set most peoples' fingers tapping, their blood flowing. Music is not unique in having the spirit-moving qualities of rhythm. There are rhythms in the motions of our bodies and minds, in walking, in working, in talking, and in thinking. There are rhythms in the motions of machines and in the sounds of nature. Closest of all to the rhythms of music are the rhythms of speech and language. The speeches of orators, the declamations of actors, the subtle verbiage of poetry—all offer rhythmic effects that lie between the realms of words and music. Specialists in literature speak of "poetic rhythms" and "prose rhythms" when describing the patterns of language.

Metric Rhythm and Nonmetric Rhythm

Certain familiar rhythmic motions—such as those of walking and running, or the whir and clatter of machines—establish rhythms that are regular and predictable in their lengths (durations) and emphases (dynamics). Other rhythmic motions, such as those of speaking, are still essentially rhythmic in being made up of patterns of length and emphasis, but they are less regular and predictable. Those two kinds of rhythmic motion are both represented in music. The regular, predictable rhythms are called **metric rhythms**; the less regular, unpredictable rhythms are called **nonmetric rhythms**. The word *metric* and the cognate word *meter* are both related to our familiar words *measure* and *measurement*. In fact, we can think of metric rhythm as being rhythm that is "measured out" evenly, with a regular division of time, as on a clock. Nonmetric rhythm is less mechanical, less regular in its "measuring out" of lengths and emphases.

Metric and Nonmetric Rhythms in the West. Our oldest surviving body of Western music is the plainchant of the medieval church, which dates roughly from the fifth through eleventh centuries. Most plainchant makes use of irregular, nonmetric rhythms whose patterns unfold freely, similar to declamatory speech rhythms of an orator. The rhythms of plainchant are often described as meterless, declamatory, or oratorical rhythms. Beginning in the twelfth and thirteenth centuries, Western composers turned away from the flexibilities of nonmetric rhythms; for many centuries they concentrated on metric rhythms whose simple patterns of length and emphases are repeated with strict regularity throughout a piece. From the time of Perotin (ca. 1200) through Tchaikovsky and Brahms (the 1890s), practically all Western music has depended on metric rhythms. Each piece is laid out as a succession of short, identical rhythmic units called *measures,* which all have the same length and the same inner pattern of emphasis, or accent. The grip of metric rhythms on Western musical styles was broken around 1900. At that time composers' imaginations were reawakened to the stimulating options of nonmetric rhythms—which had been cultivated all along in musical cultures outside of the West.

The Three Tiers of Metric Rhythm: Pulse, Meter, and Rhythm. We have been speaking of metric rhythm as regular and predictable in its patterns, but that is not the whole story. Our metric rhythms are in some respects quite mechanically regular, but in other respects they are free and flexible, receptive to the exercise of fancy that is the essence of art. To understand how such partly rigid, partly free rhythms work, it will be convenient to think of metric rhythm as being like a three-layer wedding cake. At least three different layers or "tiers" of rhythmic activity are going on at the same time, as if stacked up on one another, in most of our familiar music. We will call those tiers the pulse, the meter, and the rhythm. The *pulse* (tier 1) and *meter* (tier 2) are regular and predictable kinds of rhythmic motion. The *rhythm* (tier 3) is imaginative and free. A representation of them is shown in Fig. B.2.1. It must be borne in mind that

Fig. B.2.1. The Three Tiers of Metric Rhythm

Tier 3: Rhythm

Tier 2: Meter

Tier 1: Pulse

all three tiers are present simultaneously and are interacting with one another from the beginning to the end of a piece. Moreover, they are present even in the simplest tune whistled by a child as well as in the elaborate music of sonatas and symphonies. We can compare the pulse (tier 1) to the steady ticking of a clock. The meter (tier 2) is a regular pattern of accent that is superimposed on the evenly beating pulse. The rhythm (tier 3) adds free patterns of length and emphasis to the pulse and meter—it is, so to speak, on "top" of them. Those flexible rhythms (tier 3) moving against the underlying regularity of pulse (tier 1) and meter (tier 2), are what give variety and meaning to the rhythmic motion.

Pulse (Tier 1). *Pulse* is a pattern of equally spaced, equally emphatic throbs, pulses, or beats that run with clocklike regularity through the length of a piece. Any symphonic movement by Mozart or Beethoven, or any nursery tune that is simply sung without accompaniment, has a regular pulse of even beats. Music's pulse beats are like human heartbeats in that they are sometimes heard prominently through the web of surrounding effects, while other times they are submerged beneath stronger levels of rhythmic activity. The hearability of the pulse may vary from instant to instant, fluctuating with the artful changes in the music, but its timing does not change. It is always there; it is embedded in our mind at the start of a piece and kept up until the end.

Meter (Tier 2). *Meter* is the grouping of rhythmic pulses into short repetitive patterns of length and emphasis that are called measures or bars. As we have observed, the word *meter* is a way of describing measure or measurement. Musical meter is a measuring out, a sectioning of the flow of tier 1 pulses into a series of identically shaped measures that may contain anywhere from two to twelve pulses. The meter is obtained by adding an extra emphasis, stress, or accent (their meanings are the same) to every second or third pulse in a row throughout the piece. For instance, if we listen to the tune of "Frère Jacques" or of "London Bridge," we can hear the pulses (tier 1) all taking the same lengths of time. If we listen again, however, we can detect a regular pattern to those pulses, the pattern of their meter (tier 2). The fact is that not all the pulses have the same emphasis. Some are stronger, others are weaker. The resulting metric pattern is elementally simple: Every other pulse is emphasized—it gets an accent. In "Frère Jacques" and "London Bridge" we can easily count out the pattern: ONE - two, ONE - two, ONE - two. It remains the same throughout, always with the accent on number ONE:

Frè	-	re	Jac	-	ques,	Frè	-	re	Jac	-	ques,	
ONE	-	two	ONE	-	two	ONE	-	two	ONE	-	two	*etc.*

London	Bridge	is	falling		down,	falling		down,	falling		down,	
ONE	-	two	ONE	-	two	ONE	-	two	ONE	-	two	*etc.*

If we try this instead with the tune "Silent Night," we can hear much the same thing. Again there is a regular pattern, but now the pulses are sectioned off into groups of three. There is an accent on every third pulse in a row: ONE - two - three ONE - two - three etc. Again the metric pattern remains throughout, always with the accent on number ONE:

Si	-	lent	night,			Ho	-	ly	night,		
ONE	-	two	-	three	ONE	-	two	-	three	ONE	-	two	-	three	ONE	-	two	-	three

All		is	calm,			All		is	bright,		
ONE	-	two	-	three	ONE	-	two	-	three	ONE	-	two	-	three	ONE	-	two	-	three *etc.*

The regular patterns are the meters of the music. A meter is established at the beginning of a piece and it generally remains unchanged to the end.

The Two Basic Meters: Duple Meter and Triple Meter. We have now met the two basic meters used in Western music: *duple meter* (two pulses per measure) and *triple meter* (three pulses per measure). In each case the accent comes on pulse ONE, the first pulse of the measure. A more graphic way of representing them, along with some familiar examples, is shown below.

In duple meter, the pulses are grouped in twos, with an accent (>) on every second pulse:

$$\left|\begin{array}{cc} \overset{>}{1} & 2 \end{array}\right|\begin{array}{cc} \overset{>}{1} & 2 \end{array}\left|\begin{array}{cc} \overset{>}{1} & 2 \end{array}\right|\begin{array}{cc} \overset{>}{1} & 2 \end{array}\left|\begin{array}{cc} \end{array}\right. \textit{etc.}$$

The vertical lines show the divisions into measures. They represent the measure lines or bar lines in musical notation. Some tunes with this meter are "Three Blind Mice," "London Bridge," and "Frère Jacques."

In triple meter, the pulses are grouped in threes, with an accent on every third pulse:

$$\left|\begin{array}{ccc} \overset{>}{1} & 2 & 3 \end{array}\right|\begin{array}{ccc} \overset{>}{1} & 2 & 3 \end{array}\left|\begin{array}{ccc} \overset{>}{1} & 2 & 3 \end{array}\right|\begin{array}{ccc} \overset{>}{1} & 2 & 3 \end{array}\left|\begin{array}{c} \end{array}\right. \textit{etc.}$$

Examples are "Silent Night," "My Country 'Tis of Thee" ("God Save the Queen").

The Psychology of Twos and Threes. The reliance of metric music on groups of two and three apparently runs deep in human psychology. If we beat a series of pencil taps on a desk and try to make them all the same length and loudness, no matter how hard we try, after a while we will begin to put an extra emphasis on every second or third beat in the series. Somehow our minds have a craving for metric order, and we respond to the equal taps by grouping them in twos or threes. The same thing happens if we hear a series of mechanical pulses, such as the ticking of a clock or the clacking of straight rails under a speeding train. Soon we begin to hear the pulses as grouped into twos or threes. The interesting thing is how flexible we are. A series of pulses that we first interpret as a pattern of twos, we may reinterpret as a pattern of threes if we just become detached from our original "fix" for an instant.

The Five Common Meters in the West. There are only five meters commonly used in Western music. In addition to duple meter (2 pulses) and triple meter (3 pulses) that were discussed above, there are common time (4 pulses per measure), compound duple meter (6 pulses per measure), and compound triple meter (9 pulses per measure). (There is also a rarely used meter with twelve pulses per measure.) All of them are based on duple meter and triple meter.

Common Time (Four Pulses per Measure). As its name suggests, *common time* is the most common Western meter. It is actually a species of duple meter where each of the two basic pulses is further subdivided into two so that in all there are four pulses per measure:

$$\left|\overset{>}{1}\ \ 2\ \ \overset{>}{3}\ \ 4\ \right|\overset{>}{1}\ \ 2\ \ \overset{>}{3}\ \ 4\ \left|\ etc.\right.$$

Here the pattern of accent is subtler. As always in metric music, pulse 1 has the strong, or primary, accent, but now there is a weaker, or secondary, accent on pulse 3, while pulses 2 and 4 are unaccented. Common time is the meter of a great deal of familiar music. It is used in most marches (which is why it is sometimes called "march time") and in many popular tunes, as well as in the repertory of classical music. Some examples are "Ô Canada," "Colonel Bogey's March," "Way Down upon the Swanee River," "America the Beautiful," and "The Marseillaise."

Upbeats and Downbeats. In all of the common Western meters, pulse 1 of the measure always has the main accent. That first and strongest pulse is also called the *downbeat* because the motion of a conductor's baton in beating the pulses for the performers to follow is emphatically downward on pulse 1, indicating the strongly accented beginning of the measure. Of the examples we have mentioned, "America the Beautiful" and "The Marseillaise" both begin on a concluding, unaccented portion of their opening measures, not on pulse 1. The same is true of "The Star Spangled Banner." Such a beginning is called an *upbeat*. This term also reflects the motion of the conductor's baton: An upbeat (headed upward) prepares a downbeat to follow.

Compound Duple Meter (Six Pulses per Measure). This meter is related to simple duple meter. That is, each of the two basic pulses in duple meter is subdivided into three pulses so that altogether there are six pulses per measure:

$$\left|\overset{>}{1}\ \ 2\ \ 3\ \ \overset{>}{4}\ \ 5\ \ 6\ \right|\overset{>}{1}\ \ 2\ \ 3\ \ \overset{>}{4}\ \ 5\ \ 6\ \left|\ etc.\right.$$

Pulse 1 as usual has the primary accent, pulse 4 the secondary accent, and the other pulses remain unaccented. Some familiar examples of compound duple meter are "Row, Row, Row your Boat" and "Drink to Me Only with Thine Eyes." Compound duple meter is the meter found in most jigs.

Compound Triple Meter (Nine Pulses per Measure). This meter is derived from simple triple meter. Each of the three pulses of triple meter is subdivided into three, so that altogether there are nine pulses per measure:

$$\left| \overset{>}{1} \ 2 \ 3 \ \overset{>}{4} \ 5 \ 6 \ \overset{>}{7} \ 8 \ 9 \ \right| \ \overset{>}{1} \ 2 \ 3 \ \overset{>}{4} \ 5 \ 6 \ \overset{>}{7} \ 8 \ 9 \ \right| etc.$$

Again, pulse 1 has the primary accent, but now both 4 and 7 have secondary accents, while the other pulses remain unaccented. Examples of compound triple meter are "Beautiful Dreamer," "My Darling Clementine," and "Down in the Valley." Of these songs, only "Beautiful Dreamer" begins on a downbeat; the others begin with upbeats.

Meter and Rhythm. The five meters with 2, 3, 4, 6, and 9 pulses per measure have provided the basis for nearly all the music composed in the West during the past seven centuries. They may seem like a slender resource for composers to draw on, but in fact those meters serve essentially as a backdrop for the third tier of rhythmic activity that is found in metric music. This is the tier of the actual *rhythm*. It is at the level of rhythm (tier 3) that the composer's fancy takes flight, only loosely bound by the mechanical regularities of pulse (tier 1) and meter (tier 2).

Rhythm (Tier 3). In metric music, rhythm consists of free, imaginative patterns of lengths and emphases that are superposed upon the pulse and meter. The rigid pulse and predictable meter serve as the points of departure for the flexible play of the tier 3 rhythms. For instance, the Christmas song "Silent Night" has a regular pulse and simple triple meter running throughout. The $\overset{>}{1}$-2-3s of the meter (tier 2) have no particular interest in themselves. What gives the

Fig. B.2.2. Rhythm in "Silent Night"

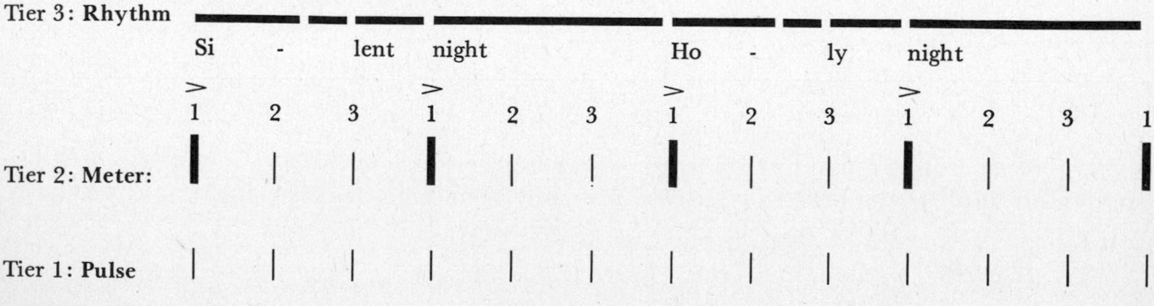

melody life is that the rhythms (tier 3) depart from the mechanical repetitions of the meter (Fig. B.2.2). All metric rhythms work this way. The regular pulse and meter are the foundations from which the vital rhythmic motion springs.

Tempo

We have said nothing about a basic factor called tempo. *Tempo* is the pace of the music, the speed of the pulse and meter. Obviously, all pieces do not move at the same speed. That would be inconceivably dull. Some pieces have a faster pace, others a slower one. There can be a quick triple meter or a slow one, and there are many degrees of quickness or slowness in between. It is the *tempo marking,* or tempo indication, that tells how fast the music goes. A list and discussion of the common tempo markings is given elsewhere, in the paragraphs dealing with rhythmic notation (p. 420). Here it need only be observed that even a slight difference in the choice of tempo—whether the music moves a little bit slower or faster—has an enormous effect on how it comes across in performance. Perhaps the most important function of the conductor is to choose an appropriate tempo for a composition and then maintain it without undue slackening or speeding.

Rhythmic Devices

There are whole volumes about the techniques of musical rhythm, but for elementary purposes it suffices to mention just four: syncopation, rhythmic motives, irregular meter, and pulseless rhythms.

Syncopation. *Syncopation* means rhythmic conflict. It is a deliberate upsetting of a regular meter (tier 2) by a stronger pattern of free, contrary-minded rhythm (tier 3). For instance, Beethoven's Eighth Symphony begins with a regular pattern in triple meter:

This is repeated many times in the early part of the movement, always with an accent in the usual place, that is, on the first pulse of each measure. Later in the movement Beethoven chooses to shift the accent, overriding the regular metric pattern with a stronger conflicting rhythm. He repeatedly puts a stronger accent on pulse 2 than on pulse 1:

The result is a syncopation—a rhythmic conflict between the basic meter (tier 2) and the freer rhythm (tier 3). Each time the conflict recurs we have a new instance of syncopation. Each instance jars us. Our inner psychological clocks are conditioned to regular metric behavior, so that we expect the strong accent to be on pulse 1 of the measure. When Beethoven overrides that expectation with the syncopated accent on pulse 2, the result is a rhythmic shock and emotional disorientation. There can be many syncopations with many gradations of force within a musical work. The use of powerful syncopations is a hallmark of Beethoven's style. The use of subtle, "catchy" syncopations is a feature of ragtime and jazz styles.

Rhythmic Motives. A *rhythmic motive* is a short, incisive rhythmic figure. It is a distinctive packet of rhythmic lengths and emphases that is introduced in a musical work and then, having entered our consciousness, keeps coming back to stir us later on. The opening figure of Beethoven's Eighth Symphony, which we have just cited, is one such short, incisive rhythmic figure. Perhaps the most familiar of all rhythmic motives is the opening figure of Beethoven's Fifth Symphony, with its pattern of three shorts and a long:

᥎ ᥎ ᥎ ▁▁▁▁

Beethoven displays this motive prominently at the start, then finds dozens of other uses for it as the music goes on (see Chapter 5). It is the most important factor in giving unity and generating excitement within Beethoven's singularly compact and forceful movement. Most musical works of the eighteenth and nineteenth centuries use rhythmic motives in similar ways, though rarely with the concentrated effect obtained by Beethoven.

Irregular Meter. During the late nineteenth century European composers began to break away from the general rule of maintaining a single meter throughout a piece, and they also sought freedom from the limiting handful of regular tier 2 meters having 2, 3, 4, 6, or 9 pulses per measure. Russian composers, including Mussorgsky and Tchaikovsky, began to put together passages of *irregular meter,* where the pulse count may change from measure to measure. They sometimes used nonsymmetrical pulse counts, for instance, five or seven pulses per measure. Stravinsky led the way in establishing irregular meters as a norm for the early twentieth century (see Chapter 8). Irregular meters often maintain a constant pulse (tier 1), so that they are in a sense still metric rhythms. But when the regularity of pulse is gone, they become essentially nonmetric.

Pulseless, Meterless, Nonmetric Rhythms. We have already cited medieval plainchant as a case of *nonmetric* music, having *pulseless,* *meterless* rhythms. Such rhythms are uncommon in the more recent styles of Western music, but they are among the sophisticated devices used by African and Asian musical cultures. Certain styles of music on the Indian subcontinent begin with slow trancelike improvisations whose rhythms are in a pulseless state. Then a drum starts up and a fascinating transformation takes place as the rhythmic motion turns from the opening pulselessness to a pronounced and ultimately overwhelming sense of pulse.

3. TEXTURE

Musical texture is the profile of music's sounding patterns as they strike the ear and mark the mind. The notion that music has "texture" comes from the realm of woven cloth, or textiles, where it has to do with the look and feel of a fabric, the crisscross patterns of its yarns. Music can almost be felt like cloth. Some music has strands that our ears find easily separable. Other music has strands so tightly interwoven that we can scarcely pick them apart.

There are two main types of musical texture: monophony and polyphony. **Monophony** is a texture consisting of a single musical strand. The word comes from the Greek words *monos* ("one") and *phonos* ("sound"). We can think of monophony as being melody alone, without any accompaniment, where just a single pitch is sounding at a time. That is what happens in medieval plainchant or when a child sings a nursery tune. The other main musical texture is **polyphony**, which is a texture consisting of many strands. The word comes from the Greek *poly* ("many") and *phonos* ("sound"). In polyphony, there are various pitches or independent melodies sounding at the same time. In recent centuries of Western civilization most music has been polyphonic, many stranded music. But monophonic music or melody alone was a favorite during classical antiquity, and it retained its appeal for much of the Middle Ages.

Monophony

Melodies come in many shapes and styles around the world. They differ, depending on where and when they were composed. They differ from one composer to another, from one piece to another, from one moment to another within a given piece. The art of pure melody is represented by plainchant, by Bach's suites for solo cello, by the soliloquies of Japanese flute (*shakuhachi*) music, which make use of smaller gradations of pitch than the half-steps on our piano. All these are monophonic textures, concentrating their musical message in a single line, where just one pitch is sounded at a time. Compared with the complex texture of polyphony, the lone melodic strand of monophony may seem a poor resource for composers. But that is not the case. Bach speaks with the same architectural logic and expressiveness in the pure melodies of a solo cello suite as in the elaborate polyphony of his cantatas and concertos. Among Asian and African musical cultures, the creations of pure melody, often enriched with subtleties of pitch and rhythm that remain untapped in the West (as in the *shakuhachi* solos), match the best of Western polyphony in their persuasiveness.

Polyphony

Polyphony is a texture of many musical strands, where different pitches are sounded together by different voices or instruments. There are four basic varieties of polyphony or polyphonic texture: 1) block chords, 2) melody with accompaniment, 3) imitative polyphony, and 4) nonimitative polyphony. In the flow of actual works of music, many mixtures of these occur, and the choice of texture changes flexibly.

Block Chords. *Block chords* is the familiar musical texture of church hymns or the "close harmony" of a barbershop quartet. A **chord** consists of two or more pitches sounding together. In the texture of block chords, the separate voices are synchronized in rhythm so that they change pitches together and move as chords. Polyphony is at its simplest in this texture, where the music consists of a progression of blocklike chords (Fig. B.3.1).

Fig. B.3.1. Block Harmony: A Progression of Blocklike Chords

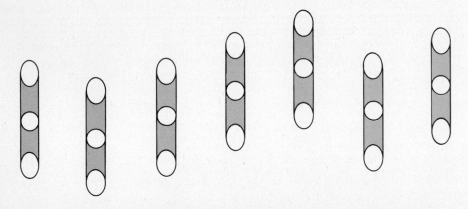

Melody with Accompaniment (Homophony). Melody with accompaniment is also known as *accompanied melody* and sometimes as *homophony*. It consists of a dominating melody that is supported by accompanying chords. The melody is usually topmost in the texture and moves independent of the rest, as when a singer is accompanied by a guitar. The singer's melody has practically the whole musical interest, yet the strumming accompaniment adds a fullness that would be missed if it were not there (Fig. B.3.2). The term

Fig. B.3.2. Melody with Accompaniment

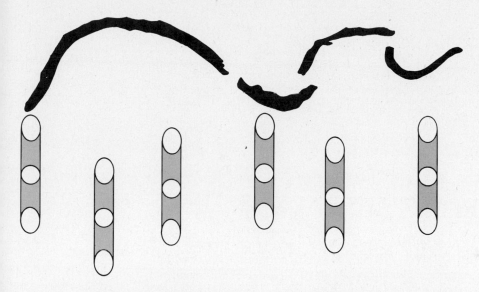

homophony is sometimes used to describe this texture of melody with accompaniment. Homophony (and the related word *homophonic*) comes from the Greek *homoios* ("similar") and *phonos* ("sound"), so that it literally means "similar sounding" or "having the same sound." As a result, homophony can imply the texture of block chords, as well as that of accompanied melody, and because of that double meaning some musicians prefer to avoid the term homophony altogether.

Polyphony and Counterpoint. Before considering the last two types of polyphony (types 3 and 4), a further word must be said about polyphony itself, and about the related word *counterpoint*.

Polyphony: Simultaneous Melodic Strands. Most polyphonic textures are more complex than block-chords (type 1) or melody with accompaniment (type 2). Polyphony at its richest consists of intricately woven textures that have two or more distinctive melodic strands going on at the same time. Those separate strands, which are generally called *voices* (also *voice-parts* or *parts*), maintain their melodic independence and identity even while they are fitting together and sounding well in combination (Fig. B.3.3). The aim of

Fig. B.3.3. Polyphony: Simultaneous Melodic Strands

Voice 1:

Voice 2:

Voice 3:

Voice 4:

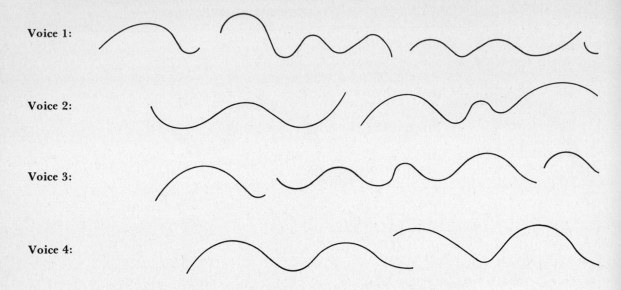

such many-stranded polyphony is to impress, even to overwhelm the listener with the finely wrought substance of so many interesting things happening at once. The independent voice-parts are usually about equal in importance, none taking precedence over the others, though sometimes one or more voices will predominate.

Counterpoint: The Method of Producing Polyphony. The word *counterpoint* and the related word *contrapuntal* are often used in describing polyphonic textures. They come from the Latin *punctus contra punctum,* meaning "point against point." *Counterpoint* originally described the craft of medieval composers who painstakingly set note against note (point against point) in the process of making and combining their polyphonic strands. In modern use, the words *counterpoint* and *polyphony* are often interchangeable, though the shade of difference would be that counterpoint describes the method or craft of producing the polyphony while polyphony represents the artful result.

Imitative Polyphony. Polyphony that is woven of independent melodic strands has two general types. One is imitative polyphony (type 3), where the strands all share something of the same melodic material. The other is nonimitative polyphony (type 4, see below), where the strands have different materials. In *imitative polyphony* (type 3), the voice-parts are all related to one another in melodic substance, and they tend to be about equal in the importance of their contribution to the texture. When beginning a passage of imitative polyphony, the composer generally has a single voice-part sound alone, presenting some distinctive melodic idea. Then the other voice-parts join in turn, copying, or imitating, the original idea, spreading it through the texture.

There are two subvarieties of imitative polyphony—free imitation and strict imitation. In **free imitation**, or free imitative polyphony, the voices do not copy one another's music exactly. They remain close enough to confirm the mutual resemblance, but once a voice-part has entered, presenting its version of the common material, it continues by taking its own melodic path for a while. Then, from time to time, it comes back with another imitative entry—another link to the overall texture of melodically related strands. The result is tight-knit and homogenous (Fig. B.3.4). Free imitation is the main

Fig. B.3.4. Free Imitative Polyphony

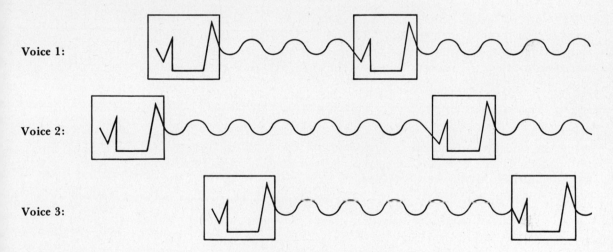

Voice 1:

Voice 2:

Voice 3:

texture found in sixteenth-century music, such as the Masses and motets of Palestrina (see Chapter 2). Since the seventeenth and eighteenth centuries the chief form of free imitative polyphony has been the fugue. A *fugue* is a polyphonic composition that is organized throughout by the free imitation of a single melodic idea. A fugue by Bach is analyzed in Chapter 3.

In **strict imitation**, or strict imitative polyphony, a first or "leader" voice is copied exactly and rigidly by one or more "follower" voices, often through the entire length of a composition. The follower voice is never free to take its own melodic path; it simply copies the leader, following it around. This texture is found in *canons* and *rounds,* for example, "Frère Jacques" and "Sumer is icumen in" (see Chapter 1).

Nonimitative Polyphony. *Nonimitative polyphony* is made up of independent strands, each one projecting a distinctive melodic material of its own (Fig. B.3.5). Nonimitative polyphony was the preferred

Fig. B.3.5. Nonimitative Polyphony

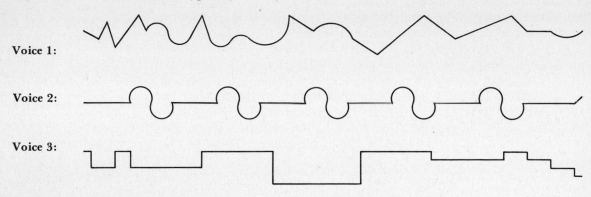

Voice 1:

Voice 2:

Voice 3:

polyphonic texture through most of the Middle Ages. During the Renaissance and Baroque it was supplanted by imitative polyphony, but nonimitative polyphony nevertheless was used, as in the fourth movement of Bach's Cantata No. 140 (see Chapter 3). During the nineteenth and twentieth centuries composers generally returned to it and have given it new vigor. It is the preferred polyphonic texture among the musical styles of Africa and Asia, which show little interest in imitative polyphony. Listeners are attracted to imitative polyphony because of its logical rigor and the reassuring predictability of its plans. Nonimitative polyphony is attractive for the opposite reason—its stimulating diversity and unpredictability.

4. HARMONY

Do you know that our soul is composed of harmony?
> Leonardo da Vinci (1452-1519)

We are accustomed to hearing music that is not melody alone but melody clothed with harmony. Harmony is the musical dimension of depth and space. It is to music what three-dimensional perspective is to painting. Harmony is present in all polyphonic textures, but the term is applied primarily to the textures of block chords (Fig. B.3.1) and melody with accompaniment (Fig. B.3.2). In practice, harmony is concerned with the pitches that are heard at a given moment in a musical texture and the motions of those combined pitches as they change from moment to moment and from section to section in a work.

Chords. The basic building blocks of harmony are chords. A *chord* consists of two or more pitches sounding together. The presence of chords is most obvious in the texture of block chords, where they are like "blocks" of pitches synchronized in time, but chords are a by-product wherever there is polyphony. They are the result of the pitches that happen to be sounding together at any instant. The melodic strands that are the horizontal aspect of polyphonic textures produce the vertical sounds of chords (Fig. B.4.1).

Fig. B.4.1. Chords: The "Vertical" Aspect of Polyphony

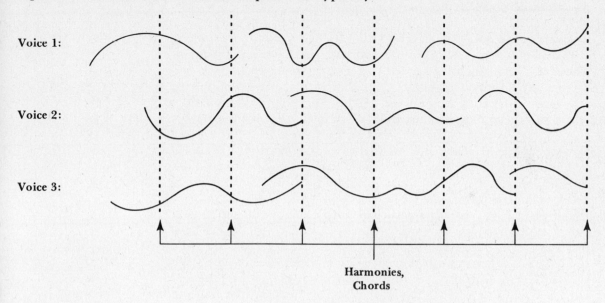

Voice 1:

Voice 2:

Voice 3:

Harmonies,
Chords

Chord Progressions. Harmony is similar to language. Where language has individual words, harmony has individual chords. And where language combines words into clauses and sentences to give a fuller meaning, so music joins chords in progressions that have a musical logic. A *chord progression* is an artful sequence of chords (Fig. B.4.2).

Fig. B.4.2. A Chord Progression: An Artful Sequence of Chords

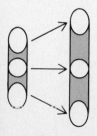

The Rules of Harmony. Harmony is also like a language in having a set of rules (grammar) that outlines its behavior. There are rules for the makeup of individual chords and for the musical motions in going from one chord to another. Yet there is no rigid, universal set of harmonic rules. There are as many different "grammars" of harmony as there are different times and places where music is produced. The styles of harmony depend on time and place. There is one style in thirteenth-century Paris, another in eighteenth-century Naples, another in twentieth-century Indonesia. Each era has its style, each style has its rules; and the fact about harmonic rules is that they are always undergoing change.

Consonance and Dissonance. The rules of harmony are concerned with two properties of chords, known as consonance and dissonance. These musical qualities can be perceived whenever two or more pitches are sounded together. *Consonance* is a quality of apparent repose or compatability between pitches. *Dissonance* is a quality of apparent tension or incompatibility. Defined that way, they seem to be exact opposites, but the fact is, they are not opposites at all. Consonance and dissonance are always relative to one another, neighbors on a continuous, sliding scale that has no absolute values.

Our perceptions of consonance and dissonance depend on two factors: one cultural, the other psychological. The cultural factor is that every age, every society has certain chords that it considers essentially consonant and other chords that it considers essentially dissonant. The judgments represent the general taste of the whole society. Yet often enough the tastes of societies do not agree. What is dissonant to one may be consonant to its neighbor. And the tastes within a given society are always changing. Between the ninth and twelfth century Western Europe considered only chords that used the intervals of the fifth and fourth as really consonant. During the fifteenth century the status of the fourths shifted from consonant to dissonant, while certain other chords containing the intervals of the third and sixth, which had usually been considered dissonant before, were accorded the status of consonance. Later centuries saw a further shifting of chords from dissonant to consonant and the addition of novel dissonances to the harmonic vocabulary. Many twentieth-century composers have abandoned the traditional distinction between consonance and dissonance altogether. They say only that their music uses simultaneous pitches in uniquely effective combinations.

The psychological factor in consonance and dissonance brings to mind the famous philosophical argument about hot and cold water. If someone with one hand that is hot and the other cold plunges them both into a bowl of lukewarm water, the water feels hot to the cold hand and cold to the hot hand. But since the water cannot really be hot and cold at the same time, the perceptions of hot and cold are subjective, those of the senses. The hot and cold are not absolutes; they are relative to one another, dependent on the context in which they are experienced. The same can be said of musical consonance and dissonance. They are not absolutes but relatives. What we perceive as a quality of consonance or dissonance in a chord depends largely on the musical context in which we encounter it—on the consonance or dissonance of the neighboring chords. If a chord is sandwiched between two gentler consonances it will seem relatively tense or dissonant by comparison. If that same chord is sandwiched between two stronger dissonances, it will seem more relaxed or consonant.

Thus the perceptions of consonance and dissonance depend both on the norms within a given culture and on the context of a specific chord within its specific progression. For the composer putting together a chord progression, the aim is to achieve an artful alternation between what is perceived as the tension of dissonance and the relaxation of consonance. Both are necessary if musical interest is to be sustained. There are some listeners who think they prefer consonance to dissonance and want to avoid the latter. Prizes have been offered for composers to write quiet, pleasant, consonant music. The prize-givers are wrong, the composers misled. Consonance itself is a meaningless banality. Hearing a bland "consonant" chord such as the three pitches C-E-G repeated for a minute produces nothing of the desired satisfaction. The result is quick boredom and rising resentment. Hearing a single "dissonant" chord repeated over and over—for example, Wagner's "Tristan" chord (reading upward, pitches F-B-D-sharp-G-sharp; see Ex. 6.5)—sustains interest longer and gives greater satisfaction. What makes harmonies pleasant is not consonance alone but the judicious intermixture of dissonance: the volatile and adventurous interacting with the soothing and reposeful. Like many basic truths, this one was known to the ancient Greeks. The remark is attributed to Plutarch (ca. A.D. 46-120): "Medicine to produce healing must know disease; music to produce harmony must know dissonance."

The Resolution of Dissonance in an Approaching Consonance. The basic rule in chord progressions is that every dissonant chord "wants" to move to some other chord that seems more consonant. This is deeply rooted in human psychology. Every relative dissonance adds some bit of tension to the musical discourse, and every such tension calls for a release in some forthcoming consonance. The musical process by which a dissonant chord finds release in an approaching consonance is called *resolution*. Sometimes a dissonance is resolved with the very next chord. Other times the hoped-for resolution is delayed while the music detours through roundabout harmonic paths, perhaps touching on more provocative dissonances whose tensions are partially relieved by intervening consonances. The subtler and richer the musical style, the more varied are its levels of consonance and dissonance and the more prolonged its harmonic paths may be on the way to resolution.

Tonality

The Seven Select Pitches. In Appendix B.1 we said that *tonality* is the chief mode of European-American music in the eighteenth and nineteenth centuries and that it consists of the combined resources of the major and minor modes. Those modes have scales containing seven pitches (Fig. B.4.3), which can be thought of as "seven select pitches," chosen from the large number of pitches available in the spectrum of musical sound. The seven pitches of the tonal scales are numbered from $\hat{1}$ through $\hat{7}$, with pitch $\hat{8}$ duplicating pitch $\hat{1}$ at the next higher octave. In the major scale, the pitches are also known by the familiar syllables *do re mi fa sol la ti do*.

The Tonic Pitch ($\hat{1}$). The most important principle of tonality is that at every moment in a musical work the focus of the seven pitches will be on the particular pitch of the group that is called the *tonic*. This is the bottom pitch, the number $\hat{1}$ or *do* pitch of the major and minor scales. It serves as the home, leader, organizer pitch among the seven pitches that make up the creations of tonal sound. The strong focus on the tonic is the reason why the mode is called *tonality,* why the music is called *tonal* music.

The Connections Between Tonal Pitches. The tonic is not alone in having a name and special functions within tonality. Each of the other six pitches has its own name and functions. Taken together, these seven pitches form a hierarchy where the tonic governs and the others are subordinate. However, each of the other six pitches has a separate function and a different kind of subordination to the tonic: Some are more strongly linked with it; others have weaker links. Furthermore, each of the individual pitches $\hat{2}$ through $\hat{7}$ has distinctive relationships of different intensities with each of the others. This makes an overall hierarchy that is rich in subtlety and power. For a full comprehension of tonal music we should know about all the interrelationships between tonal pitches. For a basic comprehension, we need to know about just two others in addition to the tonic. They are pitches $\hat{5}$ and $\hat{4}$ of the major and minor scales—the *dominant* and the *subdominant*.

Fig. B.4.3. The Seven Select Pitches of Tonality (Major Mode)

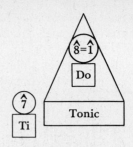

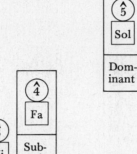

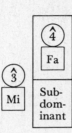

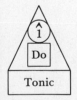

The Dominant (Pitch $\hat{5}$). After the tonic, the *dominant* is the next pitch in importance, the "second in command" in the tonal hierarchy. It is the fifth degree ($\hat{5}$), or *sol,* of the major and minor scales, counting up from the tonic as $\hat{1}$. In the major and minor scales whose tonic is C, the dominant is G.

The Tonic-Dominant Relationship. Among the seven tonal pitches, the lines of musical force are strongest between the tonic and dominant. Where the tonic can be thought of as representing musical-psychological stability, the dominant represents a corresponding instability. Musical motion that goes from the tonic to the dominant pitch has the effect of a wrench or thrust from "home" to "away from home." Motion that goes in the opposite direction, from the dominant to the tonic, is the most satisfying way of reestablishing stability, of "returning home." This relationship of attraction and repulsion between the tonic and dominant pitches has an effect that extends well beyond the two pitches themselves. It serves as an organizing framework around which every piece of tonal music is built. It is like an inner "backbone," holding the music together (Fig. B.4.4).

Fig. B.4.4. The Tonic-Dominant Framework of Tonality

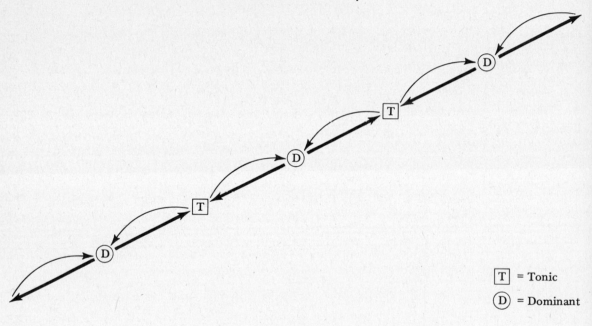

$\boxed{\text{T}}$ = Tonic

$\textcircled{\text{D}}$ = Dominant

The Subdominant (Pitch $\hat{4}$). The *subdominant* is the next pitch in tonal importance after the tonic and dominant. It is pitch $\hat{4}$ of the major and minor scales, counting up from the tonic as $\hat{1}$. In the major and minor scales whose tonic is C, the subdominant is F. We have said that musical motion that goes from the tonic ($\hat{1}$) to the dominant ($\hat{5}$) pitch represents an increase in tonal tension. Now musical motion that goes from the tonic to the subdominant ($\hat{4}$) pitch represents something of a relaxation in tonal tension. Like all the other tonal pitches, however, the subdominant ultimately wants to return "home" to the tonic.

Chords in Tonal Music: The Triads

Many varieties of chords are used in tonal music, but the common, everyday chords are the ones called triads. A *triad* is a relatively consonant chord consisting of three pitches that are chosen by the alternate-pitch rule. The rule works as follows. The seven pitches of the tonal scale are numbered $\hat{1}$ through $\hat{7}$. Pitch $\hat{8}$ (the octave) duplicates the first pitch and begins the series over again:

$$\hat{1}\ \hat{2}\ \hat{3}\ \hat{4}\ \hat{5}\ \hat{6}\ \hat{7}\ \hat{8}\qquad \hat{2}\ \hat{3}\ \hat{4}\ \hat{5}\ \hat{6}\ \hat{7}\ \hat{8}\qquad \hat{2}\ \hat{3}\ \hat{4}\ \hat{5}\ \ etc.$$
$$(=\hat{1})\qquad\qquad\qquad (=\hat{1})$$

Triads are built by taking any three alternate pitches in the series, for example: $\hat{1}\text{-}\hat{3}\text{-}\hat{5}$, $\hat{2}\text{-}\hat{4}\text{-}\hat{6}$, $\hat{3}\text{-}\hat{5}\text{-}\hat{7}$, $\hat{4}\text{-}\hat{6}\text{-}\hat{8}$, $\hat{5}\text{-}\hat{7}\text{-}\hat{2}$, $\hat{6}\text{-}\hat{8}\text{-}\hat{3}$, $\hat{7}\text{-}\hat{2}\text{-}\hat{4}$. That is, each pitch of the tonal scale serves as the *root* or generating pitch of a tonal triad. Since the pitches are identified by Arabic numerals $\hat{1}$, $\hat{2}$, $\hat{3}$, $\hat{4}$, etc.), the triads that are built on them are often identified by corresponding Roman numerals. The tonic pitch ($\hat{1}$) serves as the

Fig. B.4.5. The Most Important Tonal Triads

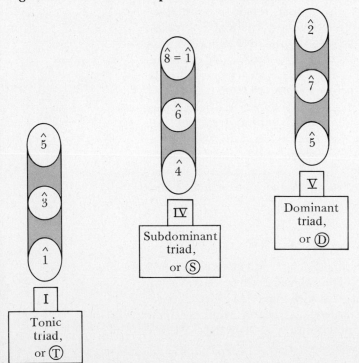

HARMONY $\int$ 465

root of the tonic triad (I), the dominant pitch ($\hat{5}$) as the root of the dominant triad (V), and the subdominant pitch ($\hat{4}$) as the root of the subdominant triad (IV) (Fig. B.4.5). The tonal names—tonic, dominant, and subdominant triads, with abbreviations T, D, and S—are also used. Those are the three essential triads in tonal music. Most of what we hear in a tonal work is based on the interrelationships of just those three.

Harmonizing a Tonal Melody. How does a composer harmonize a tonal melody? How is a tune supplied with accompanying chords? The techniques are a matter for professionals, but in general what the composer does is to pick triads that "agree" with the melody pitches that happen to be sounding. That is, one pitch of the selected triad will double the pitch of the melody, while the other pitches (which are at intervals of a third) will generally sound consonant with it. For instance, if a pitch $\hat{6}$ appears in the melody, it might be harmonized by triad II (pitches $\hat{2}$-$\hat{4}$-$\hat{6}$), by triad IV (pitches $\hat{4}$-$\hat{6}$-$\hat{8}$), or by triad VI (pitches $\hat{6}$-$\hat{8}$-$\hat{3}$), all of which contain pitch $\hat{6}$. If a pitch $\hat{5}$ (the dominant) appears in the melody, it might be harmonized by triad I (pitches $\hat{1}$-$\hat{3}$-$\hat{5}$), by triad III (pitches $\hat{3}$-$\hat{5}$-$\hat{7}$), or by triad V (pitches $\hat{5}$-$\hat{7}$-$\hat{2}$, the dominant triad). For a more provocative harmonization, the composer can choose triads that momentarily "disagree" with the melody pitches, thereby mixing tensions of relative dissonance with the relaxations of relative consonance. Such dissonant chords may be simple triads whose pitches happen to disagree with the melody, or they may be chords that are more complex than triads, chosen for their harmonic bite. A great variety of chords are available, not only with three pitches, such as triads, but also with four, five, six, and even more pitches per chord. Although the details of chord construction and shaping chord progressions are complex, the essential fact is that a tolerable harmonization of a tonal melody can be made with just the seven tonal triads. Ultimately, the only "rule" for a tonal harmonization is that a piece should end on its tonic triad. The primacy of the tonic, confirmed at the ending, is the essence of tonal music.

Cadences in Harmony

In speaking of melody, we defined a cadence as a phrase ending, a point of repose in a melodic line. The relaxation that comes at a cadence serves to separate one phrase from the next and give a sense of overall shapeliness to the melody. Cadences have a similar effect in harmony, where the repose and punctuation in a melody are reinforced by the addition of buttressing chords. A harmonic cadence (a cadence in harmony) is a harmonized phrase ending, a melodic cadence that is fleshed out with the pitches of supporting chords.

Cadences in Tonal Harmony. Tonal music has a small repertory of harmonic cadences that are used again and again. Each harmonic cadence amounts basically to a progression of just two chords: a *preparatory chord* that alerts us to the approaching point of repose and a *cadential chord* where the music actually comes to rest (Fig. B.4.6). The chord selected as the cadential chord is usually one of

Fig. B.4.6. Harmonic Phrase with Cadence

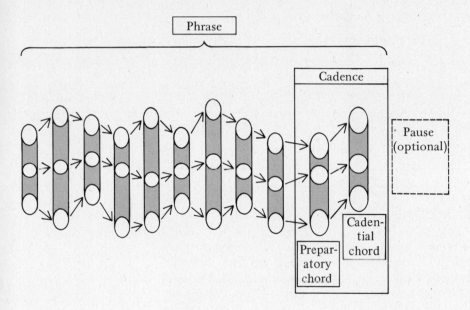

the landmark chords of tonality, such as the tonic, dominant, or subdominant triads. In coming to rest on different cadential chords, cadences convey different tonal messages and qualities of repose.

The Tonic Cadence. The most important tonal cadence is the *tonic cadence,* which is also known as a *final* or *authentic cadence.* Here the preparatory chord is the dominant chord and the cadential chord is the tonic chord (Fig. B.4.7). Simply to play those two chords in a row produces a sense of orientation toward a tonic. The tonic cadence conveys a message of stability and tonal repose wherever it appears, which may often be in the middle of pieces but always at the end. A tonic cadence closes just about every piece of tonal music.

Fig. B.4.7. Tonic Cadence

Other Harmonic Idioms

Much of what has been said about harmony has concerned tonal harmony, based on the seven-pitch major and minor scales. Other harmonic idioms that are based on other scales have also been used in the West. The chief ones are chromatic, modal, pentatonic, and whole-tone harmony.

Chromatic Harmony. *Chromatic harmony* uses all twelve pitches of the chromatic scale. Actually, there are two types of chromatic harmony: *tonal chromatic harmony* and *post-tonal chromatic harmony.* During the eighteenth and nineteenth centuries, tonal harmony was often quite chromatic, drawing liberally on the "extra" five pitches of the full twelve-pitch scale though keeping an emphasis on the seven tonal pitches and, above all, on their governing tonic. During the twentieth century, that tonal chromatic harmony has generally been superseded by post-tonal chromatic harmony, where all twelve pitches of the chromatic scale are used with relative equality, and the focus on a tonic pitch is much weakened or abandoned altogether.

Modal, Pentatonic, and Whole-Tone Harmony. During the late Middle Ages and the Renaissance, the prevailing style of harmony was *modal harmony.* It used the resources of the church modes (Dorian, Phrygian, Lydian, etc.), whose seven-pitch scales included forerunners of the major and minor scales (Fig. B.1.12). In recent centuries, *pentatonic harmony* has occasionally appeared in the

West, used mainly for exotic and "Oriental" effects. It is based on five-pitch pentatonic scales. *Whole-tone harmony* is the harmonic idiom of the six-pitch or whole-tone scales that were employed in certain works of Debussy and his followers, representing the musical "impressionism" of the late nineteenth and early twentieth century (see Chapter 8).

Harmony Outside the West. Many other harmonic idioms are found outside the Western world, representing musical cultures whose scales, intervals, and musical languages are often markedly different from our own. Some of those idioms use *microtone* intervals that are smaller than the Western half-steps, hence unobtainable on Western keyed instruments, and also large-size intervals that contain microtone distances.

Nontonal Harmony. Sometimes the catchall term *nontonal harmony* is used to describe harmonic styles that are not tonal in the Western sense. The word lumps together all the wealths of the world's harmonic idioms, including the Western idioms before 1700 and after 1900, and arrays them against the European-American practice of the eighteenth and nineteenth centuries. It is a lame word that betrays an ethnocentric viewpoint, and many musicians avoid it.

5. TONALITY AND KEY RELATIONSHIPS

Keys: Tonality at Many Levels. We have compared major-minor tonality to a language: It is the musical language of eighteenth- and nineteenth-century Europe and America. With its tonic, or leader, pitch and its six follower pitches, tonality might also be compared to a solar system containing planets that are related to one another and subordinated to the central, organizing force of a sun. In addition, tonality has an even larger organization that can be compared to a whole universe containing many different solar systems, all interrelated by forces of mutual gravitation. This last analogy to the celestial cosmos will be what concerns us now. Tonality and its major and minor scales do not appear just once in sounding space. Those scales appear many times over, duplicated at every possible level of the piano keyboard. They exist with a tonic on C, with a tonic on C-sharp, on D, on D-sharp, on E, etc. In fact, every key on the keyboard serves as the tonic of both a major and a minor scale, and every such scale is called a *key* or a *tonality*, the two terms being interchangeable. Thus there is a key or tonality of C major and a key or tonality of C minor, both with a tonic on C; there is a key or tonality of F-sharp major and a key or tonality of F-sharp minor, both with a tonic on F-sharp. Altogether there are no fewer than a dozen such major keys and as many minor keys, all coexisting in this expansive cosmos of tonality.

Key Relationships. Those many different tonalities or keys are a resource of enormous potential for tonal music. If they all simply lay side by side in musical space, like so many inert, neutral mirror images of the major and minor scales, they would have little practical interest for musicians. But the fact is that among the various keys in this cosmos of tonality there are the same kinds of interrelationships of tonal force as exist among the various pitches that make up any single major or minor scale. However, at this level of relationships between whole tonal keys, the forces are at once more powerful and more subtle. The dozens of major and minor keys are combined in a vast network of tonal forces where specific degrees of tension and attraction relate every key with every other key. Those linkages are called *key relationships,* and their strengths run the spectrum from very strong, or close, to very weak, or distant. How strong or weak a particular key relationship is depends essentially on the number of pitches that are shared by the scales of the two keys. The more pitches they have in common, the stronger is their key relationship. The strongest of all key relationships is the one that exists between a given tonic key and its related dominant key, which is built on the dominant pitch ($\hat{5}$), a fifth above the tonic ($\hat{1}$). Thus the scale of C major and the scale of its related dominant key of G major have six out of their seven pitches in common, and their relationship is very strong. Somewhat weaker is the relationship between a tonic key and its related subdominant key, which is built on the subdominant pitch ($\hat{4}$), a fourth above the tonic. The strengths of the other key relationships decrease gradually from there until the relationship is reached between two keys whose tonics lie right next to one another on the keyboard, for example, C major and C-sharp major, or A minor and A-flat minor. In spite of their physical proximity, such pairs of keys have tonal relationships that are very weak.

The Circle of Fifths: A Chart of Key Relationships. Musicians have a handy chart of the strengths of key relationships, called the *circle of fifths* (see Glossary, p. 494). In this chart the tonics of all the major and minor keys are laid out in a series—each key is separated from the next one by the interval of a fifth. Thus there are successive tonics on C - G - D - A - E - B - F-sharp - C-sharp, etc. The intervals of a fifth mean that the adjacent keys in the series are in effect all tonics and dominants of one another, so they have key relationships that are as strong or close as can be. The series is in the shape of a circle because its succession of tonic pitches eventually returns to the key where it started, closing the circle and making the circle of fifths. What it amounts to is a chart of key relationships, a space map of the tonal system, showing at a glance how close any two keys are in the reckoning of tonal space from their closeness on the circle. The keys of C and G major are neighbors on the circle, thus they are as close as any two tonal keys can be; the keys of C and E are farther apart on the circle, hence farther apart in the sound-world of tonality. The keys of C major and C-sharp major are at opposite ends of the circle, so that even though they are right next to one another on the piano keyboard, in the spatial geography of the tonal system they are as far apart as can be.

Key Relationships and Musical Form. The key relationships summarized in the circle of fifths are a resource of immeasurable value for shaping and unifying tonal music. Every tonal work has a tonic or home key, which is the key where it starts and where it finishes. In between, there is usually some tonal journey where the music reaches out to other contrasting keys that serve as substitute tonics, or temporary homes away from home. In very short pieces, such as certain folk and nursery tunes, there may be no occasion for a tonal journey. But in longer pieces, the need for tonal contrast and variety generally exists, and the music responds by going to different or contrasting keys. A piece of moderate length and complexity may reach out to just one contrasting key, but in a long work the music may pass through a number of keys, lingering in some, touching others only briefly. The keys chosen for such excursions are usually the ones with the closest, strongest relationships with the home key, such as the dominant and subdominant keys, or the **relative major key** (see Glossary, p. 500). But the tonal composer is free to choose any key(s), depending on the scope and style of the work.

Every piece of tonal music begins by establishing its home or tonic key. After a while the music moves to a *first contrasting key*, usually the dominant. Then it may move on to other keys in search of further variety. Each new key adds some fresh element of tonal tension or relaxation with respect not only to the home key but to each of the others that has been heard. What holds the piece together ultimately is that no matter how many different keys are visited or how distant from the original tonic they may be, the sense of that tonic is never wholly erased from our memory. It remains throughout as a constant reference, with each new key being heard in relation to it. Then toward the end of the work, when the tonic key finally returns, the whole form appears to be marvelously tied together—it all makes tonal "sense." Relatively few listeners can trace the specifics of such musical journeys through the keys, but even untrained listeners register something of the tensions and relaxations of key relationships as they operate in shaping and unifying tonal works. Subconsciously, every one of us is aware of the tonic and its message of authority and home.

Modulation and Transposition. Just two musical techniques that are involved with key relationships need to be mentioned. They are modulation and transposition. Modulation is by far the more significant. A *modulation* is a change of key, a passage of musical transition where the music begins in one key and ends in another. During the course of a modulation, the music leaves an initial tonic and goes on to establish a new tonic. Some modulations are lengthy, carefully staged musical transitions; others come as abrupt, surprising shifts of key. Modulations are the only places in tonal music where momentarily there is no tonic heard.

Transposition means shifting a musical passage to a higher or lower key. The same music is simply copied at a different level of pitch. Figure A.11 shows the tune of "Frère Jacques" in three different transpositions, shifted in tonal space from E-flat major to E major, D major, and G major.

Thus modulation and transposition are very different techniques. A modulation is part of the living fabric of a musical work. A transposition is a mechanical shift and duplication.

6. TONE COLOR AND MUSICAL INSTRUMENTS

The Three Qualities of Sound. Musical sounds have three main qualities: pitch, dynamics, and tone color. Sounds differ in *pitch* according to the speed of the air's vibration. They differ in *dynamics* (loudness or intensity) according to the force of the vibrating motion: the wider each vibration, that is, the more air pushed back and forth, the louder the resulting sound (Fig. B.6.1). They differ in *tone color* in the way a cello's sound differs from a trombone's, an oboe's, and a piano's. Those instruments can all play the same pitch, yet they will all sound differently. Their differences are those of tone color, which is also called **timbre** (*tam*-bur).

Tone Color. Tone color is the characteristic quality of an instrumental or vocal sound. It is what most people notice first about the music they hear. What instrument is playing? What is its "character"? Are different instruments blending together? Are there many instruments or few? Those are all questions of tone color. The "colors" of musical tones are like the different shades or tints of colors in art. Four different instruments all playing middle C will sound different in the way that four different shades of red may be distinguished on a color chart—all identifiable as red yet with different qualities or densities of light or dark. The different tone colors in music have an importance that goes beyond their immediate sensory effect. They are a factor in our perceptions of musical texture. And as the choice

Fig. B.6.1. High Pitch, Low Pitch, Loud Pitch, Soft Pitch

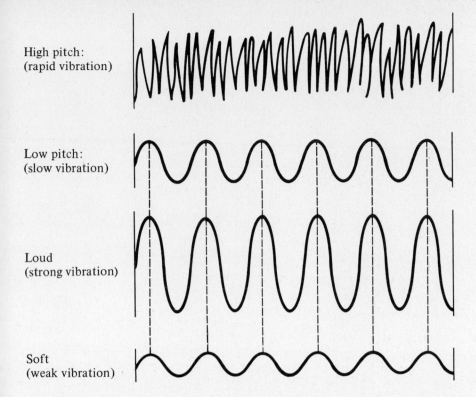

High pitch:
(rapid vibration)

Low pitch:
(slow vibration)

Loud
(strong vibration)

Soft
(weak vibration)

of tone color varies from phrase to phrase and section to section within a work, it serves as an element in our perceptions of musical form.

Musical Instruments. A musical instrument is a vibrating solid object that produces musical sounds by activating or "exciting" the air around it. Each instrument's vibrations give a distinctive shape to the vibrations of the surrounding air. The most natural of all musical instruments is the human voice, whose two vocal chords are folds of mucous membrane within our throats that are used just as they exist in nature. During the course of human history, countless other instruments have been fashioned from substances as diverse as stone, wood, skin, reed, fiber, metal, and gut. Synthetic materials are also used nowadays, and machines instead of human hands do some of the fashioning. Some of the newer instruments produce sounds through electronic circuitry, without any direct human handling of the vibrating solid.

Musical Pitch and the Size of Instruments. The range of pitches produced by an instrument depends primarily on the size of that instrument, that is, on the dimensions of the pipe, reed, string, membrane, or other vibrating solid that sets the air in motion. The laws of nature associate deep sounds with large objects, so that the larger the instrument, the lower the pitch. Thus the long, wide-bored pipes of a trombone or bassoon produce lower pitches than the short, narrow pipes of a trumpet or flute. Similarly, the long, thick strings of a cello produce lower pitches than the short, thin strings of a violin (Fig. B.6.2). There is one other factor to the height or lowness

Fig. B.6.2. Small Instrument—High Pitch; Large Instrument—Low Pitch

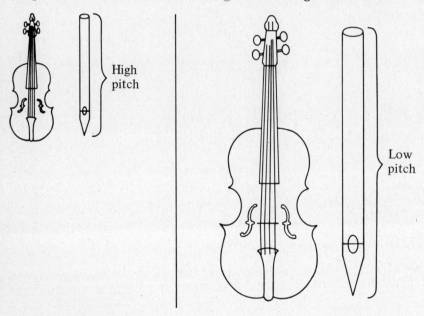

High pitch

Low pitch

of instrumental sounds. In the case of a stretched string (as on a violin) or a taut membrane (as on a drum), the pitch is changed by tightening or loosening. The greater the pressure, the higher the pitch.

The Anthropologist's Classification of Instruments. Throughout history, a few basic types of musical instruments appear again and again. Musical instruments interest anthropologists because they are tools of a culture. They are often tastefully stylized, decorated objects, so that they also interest art historians. Musicologists have joined with anthropologists in adopting a classification that divides all musical instruments into five basic categories: 1) aerophones, 2) idiophones, 3) membranophones, 4) chordophones, and 5) electrophones.

1. *Aerophones.* **Aerophones** are instruments whose sounds generally are produced in a pipe or column of air. They include pipes of wood, metal, and plastic—whistles, hunting horns, clarinets, and bassoons. Some aerophones, called *free aerophones,* operate without pipes. The player sets the surrounding air in regular motion by blowing across reeds, which are long thin strips of flexible metal or wooden cane. The free aerophones include the mouth organ and accordion.

2. *Idiophones.* **Idiophones** are solid objects that produce musical sounds when they are struck, shaken, rubbed, or scraped. They include gongs, bells, xylophones, cymbals, and rattles. Some sounds of idiophones have recognizable pitch heights, others have no well-defined pitches.

3. *Membranophones.* **Membranophones** have a skin or membrane stretched tight across a resonating air chamber. Most membranophones are drums that are struck or rubbed, for example, the kettle drum and the snare drum.

4. *Chordophones.* In **chordophones** the air is set in motion with taut strings that are plucked, rubbed, or struck. The word *chordophone* comes from the Greek word *chord,* which means "string." Violins, harps, and guitars are all chordophones. The lyres of ancient Greece, the **sitars** of India, the **samisen** of China and Japan, and the pianos of the modern West are also chordophones. Two large subfamilies of chordophones that are found in practically every culture are the lutes and the zithers. Members of the **lute family** have a box, or "belly," with a thin "neck" that extends from it. A relatively small number of strings are stretched from the base of the box to the top of the neck, usually along a "fingerboard" where the player's left hand selects the pitches. The lute family includes the guitar (whose strings are plucked), the violin (whose strings are rubbed by a bow), the sitar, and the samisen. Members of the **zither family** have a relatively larger number of strings that are stretched across the full expanse of a large resonating box or sounding board. They lack the necks of the lute family, and their strings are usually hand-plucked—in any case, never bowed. The zither family includes the piano, the Kashmiri-Iranian *santūr,* the Chinese *cheng,* and the Japanese *koto.* On the piano, the strings are struck by felt hammers; on a harpsichord they are plucked by quills; on a clavichord they are pressed by metal tangents.

5. *Electrophones.* **Electrophones** are instruments whose sounds are generated electrically or electronically. The most familiar electrophones are electric organs and electronic synthesizers, such as the Moog and Buchla synthesizers.

The Instruments of the Symphony Orchestra. In the modern symphony orchestra, the instruments are classified on a somewhat different basis. Traditionally, there are four instrumental sections,

Fig. B.6.3. Some Instruments of the Woodwind Section

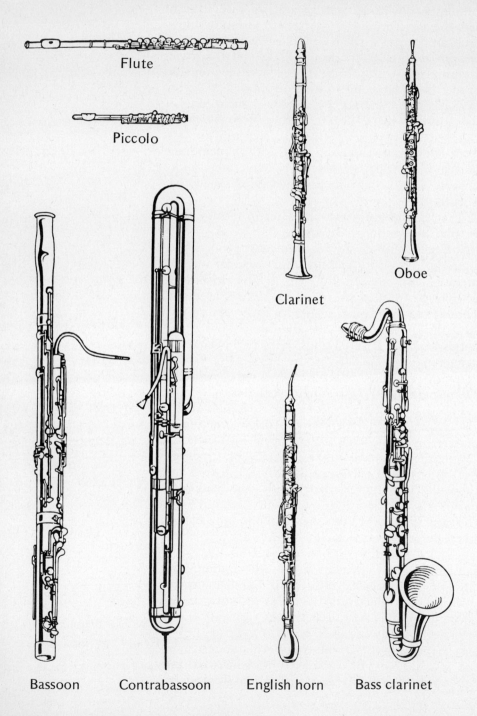

Flute

Piccolo

Clarinet

Oboe

Bassoon   Contrabassoon   English horn   Bass clarinet

which are sometimes also called choirs. They are the 1) woodwinds (all aerophones), 2) brass (all aerophones), 3) percussion (mainly membranophones and idiophones), and 4) strings (chordophones).

1. *The Woodwind Section: Flute, Oboe, Clarinet, Bassoon.* The **woodwinds** are instruments with a single pipe. At one time, they were all made of wood. Holes are bored in the pipe, which allows for changing the length of the air column, and that changes the pitch. Levers, or keys, are attached to most of the holes for handy opening and closing. The standard woodwind instruments are the flute, oboe, clarinet, and bassoon. A symphony orchestra normally has two or three players of each. Each instrumentalist carries an independent musical line, although sometimes they "double" one another. Fig. B.6.3 shows some instruments of the woodwind section. The woodwinds have quite distinctive tone colors.

The *flute,* which is held sideways from the mouth, is commonly made of silver nowadays, though it is sometimes gold or platinum. Unlike the other woodwinds, which use cane reeds to set the metal or wooden body in motion, the player's lips touch the body of the flute directly through a metal mouthpiece. Flutes are very agile. They are capable of running and skipping through a wide range of pitches and of producing many notes quickly. The *piccolo* is a small flute with the same agility and a high, often piercing sound. The working ranges of some standard orchestral instruments are shown in Fig. B.6.4, beginning with the flute and piccolo.

The *oboe* is a double-reed instrument whose tubular wooden body is held straight out from the mouth. The player's lips connect with the instrument through two slender wooden reeds that are lashed together, though not so tightly that they cannot transmit air. The oboe has a slightly lower working range and is a little less nimble than the flute, but it has a richer and more penetrating sound. The oboe does not "speak" or produce its tone readily. Oboists must generate great pressure with their facial muscles, and they need exceptional breath control. A larger, lower-pitched oboe is the *English horn,* whose pungent timbre is not called for very often, but it makes a striking effect when used.

The *clarinet* has a solid mouthpiece against which a single wooden reed vibrates. Its tone is more mellow than an oboe's, and it speaks more easily. Clarinets come in a number of sizes, including the low-pitched *bass clarinet* whose long body is curved somewhat like the shape of a letter *S. Saxophones,* which were invented in the nineteenth century by the Belgian Adolphe Sax, are close to the clarinets in design. They are made of metal, which helps give them the "brassy" sound that is familiar in jazz.

The *bassoon* is a low-pitched, double-reed instrument whose great length of wooden tubing is made more wieldy by being folded and packed to almost the shape of a single fat pipe. The *double bassoon*

Fig. B.6.4. **Working Ranges of Orchestral Instruments (Approximate Limits)**

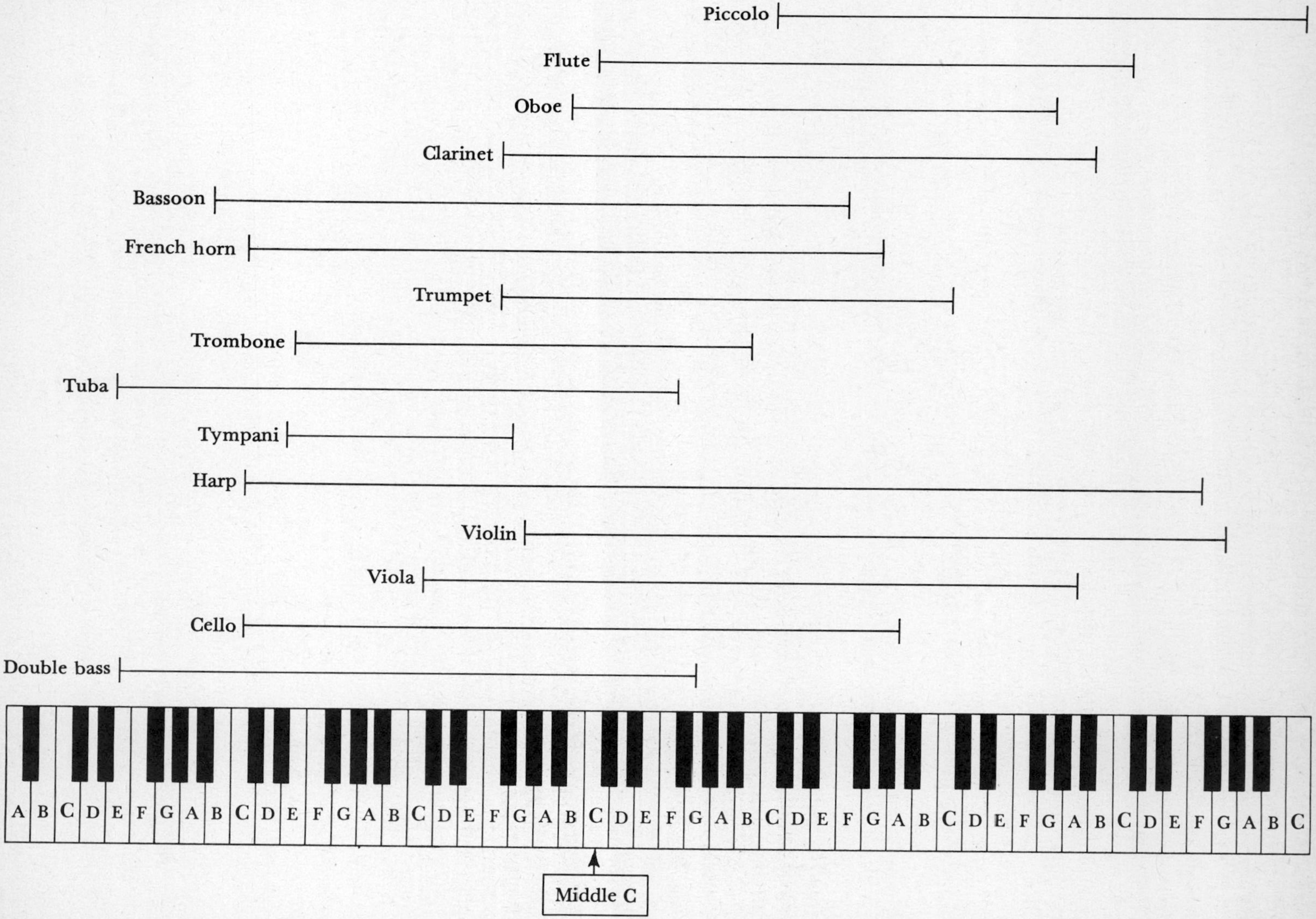

or *contrabassoon* is a lower-pitched bassoon, still more convoluted in its shape.

2. *The Brass Section: Trumpet, French Horn, Trombone, Tuba.* The **brass** instruments are aerophones made of bright-colored metals. Some of them are shown in Fig. B.6.5. Pitches are selected on the brass instruments by varying the pressure of the lip and the amount

Fig. B.6.5. Some Instruments of the Brass Section

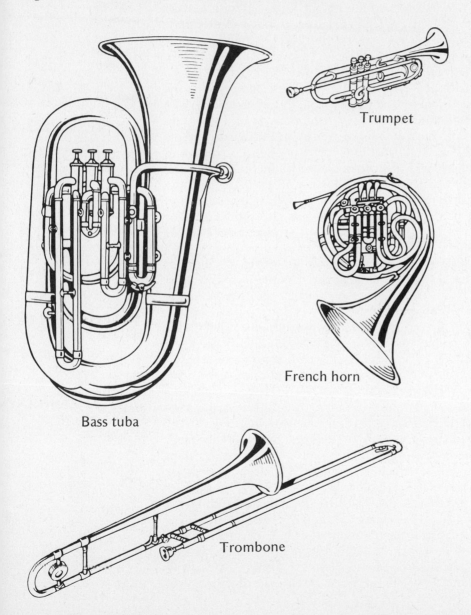

Trumpet

French horn

Bass tuba

Trombone

of air applied to a metal mouthpiece. Pitches on the trumpet, French horn, and tuba are made more readily selectable by the use of three optional lengths of pipe that the player controls with valves, adding or cutting them off. A symphony orchestra usually has parts for two or three trumpets, two or three trombones, and four French horns. There may be a single tuba part or perhaps no tuba at all.

The *trumpet* is the soprano member of the brass choir. Military in origin, it produces a brilliant sound that reminds us of traditional calls, such as taps and reveille. The trumpet can be mellow and subtle in its middle and lower registers. Sometimes it is played with a cone-shaped *mute* of metal or plastic that plugs up the bell-shaped hole where the sound comes out. This stifles the sound, producing some of the shrill and raspy effects of jazz.

The *French horn* covers the vocal ranges of tenor and alto singers. Its origins, like the trumpet's, are out-of-doors, but it represents the more peaceable realm of nature and, occasionally, of the hunt. The French horn's gentle resonance evokes the open air and echoings among distant hills. The horn blends so well with other instruments that it is used mainly as a thickener and enricher of orchestral sound while other, more sprightly instruments carry the main melodic threads. But the horn's lustrous tone color is also used for melody, particularly by romantic composers. It is a difficult instrument to control, so that brilliant display pieces, such as the concertos for solo horn and orchestra by Mozart and Richard Strauss, rarely appear on concert programs.

The low-pitched *trombone* can be mellow or biting. Its name is Italian, meaning "large trumpet." Though the trumpet and trombone were once related, they no longer resemble one another in shape or mechanism. The trombone consists of two long pipes that are fitted together so that one slides in and out of the other, shortening or lengthening the air column and raising or lowering the pitch.

The deep blasts of the *tuba* sometimes growl, sometimes well up with golden ripeness from the bottom of the brass choir.

3. *The Percussion Section: Kettledrums, Bass Drums, Cymbals, etc.* The **percussion** section contains both membranophones and idiophones. Some of the percussion instruments are shown in Fig. B.6.6. The most common percussion are the *tympani,* also called *kettledrums.* They are membranophones, but, unlike most other skin-headed drums, they can be tuned to specific pitches by loosening or tightening the polished skins that are stretched across the tops of the gleaming brass "kettles." At least two tympani are used at a time. In many symphonic works they are the only percussion instruments. Some other orchestral membranophones include the bass and snare drums. Then there are the idiophones of the percussion section: cymbals, tambourine, castanets, wood blocks, rattles, and gongs. On a **xylophone** a variety of fixed pitches are produced by

Fig. B.6.6. Some Instruments of the Percussion Section

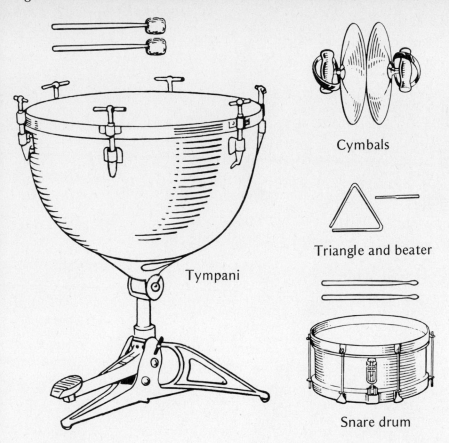

Cymbals

Triangle and beater

Tympani

Snare drum

striking different-sized wooden strips that are arranged as on a piano keyboard. The piano itself counts as a percussion instrument on those rare occasions when it is used as part of the orchestra rather than as a solo instrument in a concerto. The word *percussion* means "striking or hitting," and that is just what the piano's hammers do to the strings. The gentle lyricism of the piano would be smothered in most orchestral textures, but its percussive qualities stand out.

4. *The String Section: Violin, Viola, Cello, Double Bass.* The **string** section consists of chordophones whose strings are rubbed with a horsehair bow. Occasionally they are plucked to produce the sound called **pizzicato**, the Italian word for "plucked." The instruments of the string section are shown in Fig. B.6.7. The violin, viola, and cello are alike in basic shape but different in size. They are all members of the **violin family**, whose shoulders curve out from the instruments' necks. The double bass, with its sloping shoulders, is a relic of the older Western family of bowed strings called *viols*. The mem-

Fig. B.6.7. Some Instruments of the String Section

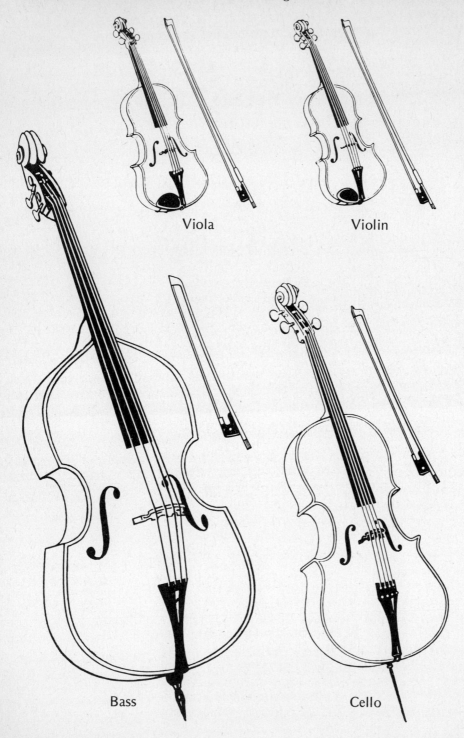

Viola

Violin

Bass

Cello

bers of the ancient *viol family* once came in all sizes, and throughout the seventeenth century they remained more popular than violins, which arose during the sixteenth century. But the viols' tone was less brilliant; their musical sallies were less acrobatic; and, except for the double bass, they eventually lost out. The strings are the most populous section in the symphony orchestra. They are the only instruments whose music regularly calls for a large number of performers to double on the same musical part. A typical modern orchestra of a hundred players may have 18 violinists for the "first violin" part, another 16 for the "second violin" part (the instruments themselves are physically the same), perhaps 14 players for the viola part, 12 for the cello, and 10 for the double bass. The strings make up about two-thirds of the orchestra personnel.

Tone Color and the Physics of Sound. Why does one instrument sound different from another: a violin from an oboe, a bassoon from a trombone, a trumpet from a tenor vocalist? The reasons for the variety of tone colors lie in the physical nature of sound. They involve physics and mathematics. (A fuller explanation is given in Appendix B.7.) Briefly, any single pitch that we seem to hear when a piano key is struck or when a guitar string is plucked is not really a single pitch at all. It is a composite, a blend, of a number of different pitches. Most of them are barely perceptible to the ear, yet each makes a small, essential contribution to what we hear. Those faint component pitches are called *harmonics, partials,* or *overtones* (all mean essentially the same thing). It is their presence in different small strengths, their marginal audibility, that determines whether what we hear is the tone color of a piano, a guitar, a trombone, etc. Each instrument has its own characteristic array of strengths among its harmonics. The spectrum of harmonic prominences results from the shape of the instrument and the materials it is made of: whether it has the shape of a tube or a box, of an oboe or bassoon, a violin or guitar; and whether it is made of wood or metal, reed or string. In each case, the shape and materials produce a distinctive array of harmonic strengths, and that array, which is present in every pitch that an instrument sounds, is responsible for its distinctive tone color.

The Orchestral Score. Music that is composed for orchestra is written out in an *orchestral score.* This is also called a *full score* to distinguish it from a reduced score for the rehearsal pianist's two hands, which is called a *piano reduction* or *piano score.* Only the full score tells which instruments are playing at each instant in the music; a conductor always uses a full score. A composer's selection of instrumental tone colors is called *instrumentation* or *orchestration.* Music for orchestra is often first sketched or composed in a piano score. Later on, after the preliminary musical decisions about the

Fig. B.6.8. Beethoven's Fifth Symphony (Beginning), Full Orchestral Score

FÜNFTE SYMPHONIE

von

L. VAN BEETHOVEN.

Dem Fürsten von Lobkowitz und dem Grafen Rasoumoffsky gewidmet.

Op. 67.

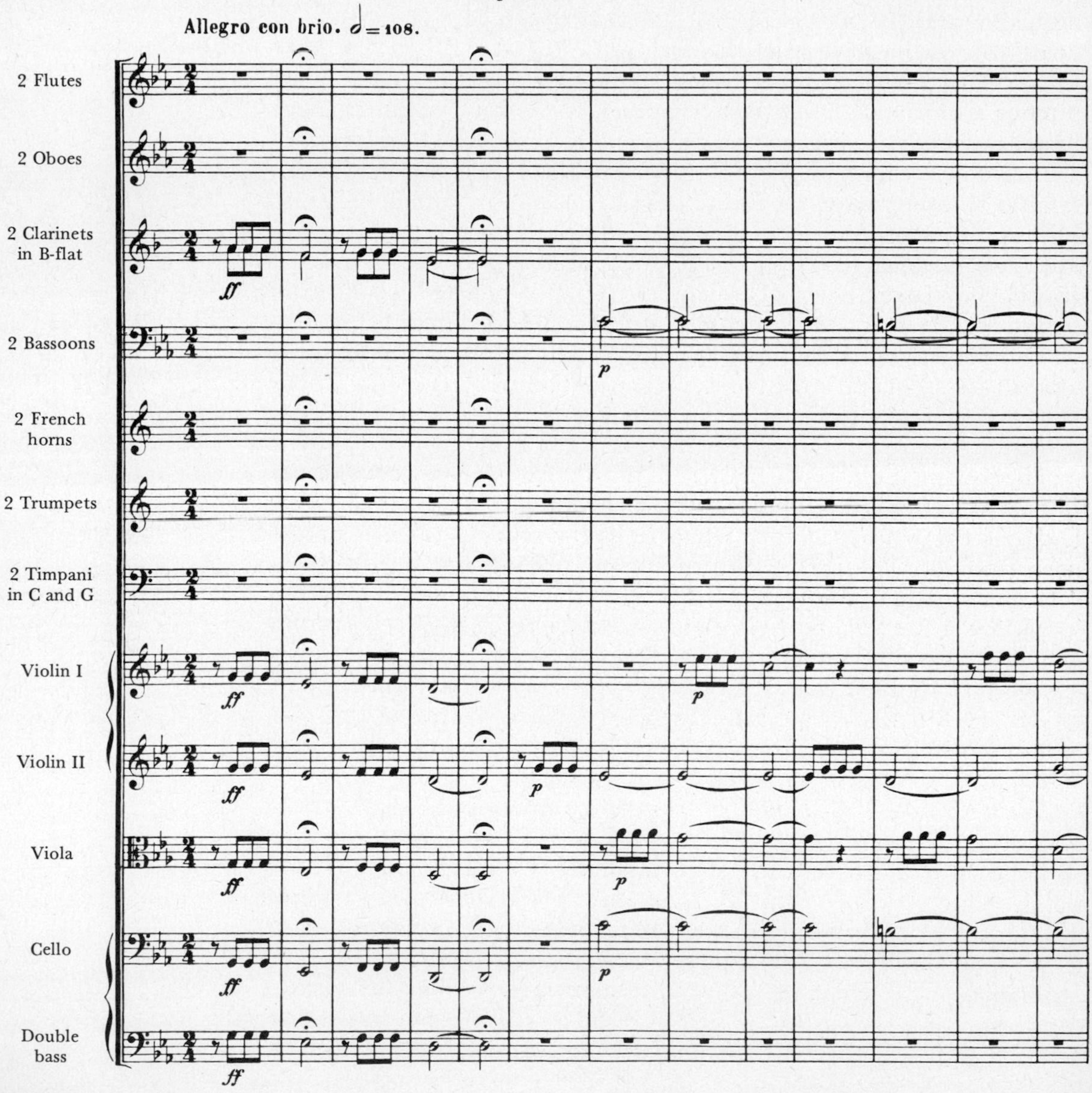

melodies, rhythms, and harmonies have been made, it is orchestrated, or scored. Some musical ideas, however, come to the composer's mind clothed from the start in instrumental colors. Every composer laboring over an orchestration has personal visions of what makes an effective blend and provocative contrast among instrumental sounds. Every age and culture has its own preferences in tone colors. Thus there is no "typical" orchestration, no single standard for the makeup of an orchestra.

Fig. B.6.8 shows the first page of the full orchestral score of Beethoven's Fifth Symphony. Each instrument has its own staff line. Scores contain a lot of information that the conductor must absorb in a hurry. To make this easier, the instruments are generally disposed in a conventional order, with the woodwinds on top, then the brass, percussion, and strings. Within each section, the higher-pitched instruments are placed above the lower-pitched ones. In this score, the flutes, oboes, and clarinets are above the bassoons among the woodwinds; and the violins are above the violas, cellos, and double bass among the strings. It is customary to place the French horns above the other brass instruments, but if Beethoven had used trombones in this movement they would appear below the trumpets. Beethoven's percussion section is limited to two kettledrums (timpani) that are tuned to the pitches C and G, the tonic and dominant of C minor. Like the flutes, oboes, horns, and trumpets, the timpani are not played at the beginning of the movement, so their parts have rests in the score.

The Orchestral Seating Plan. There is no standard way to place the orchestra's players on the stage, but among the handful of plans widely used nowadays there are differences only in details. A common plan is shown in Fig. B.6.9.

An Introduction to the Instruments of the Orchestra: Britten's Young Person's Guide. Many listeners first become acquainted with the orchestral instruments through an ingenious sixteen-minute work by the contemporary English composer Benjamin Britten. Britten's *Young Person's Guide to the Orchestra* (1946), known also as his *Variations and Fugue on a Theme of Purcell,* is a showcase of idioms and tone colors that has the advantage of letting us hear the instruments not in a catalogue of timbres displayed in clinical isolation but woven into the continuity of a musical work. Although its title is the "young person's" guide, the music is for listeners of any age who want to observe the instruments in characteristic action. The piece divides into three sections: theme, variations, and fugue (Fig. B.6.10). In the opening theme, Britten sets out a vigorous dance tune that is borrowed from his seventeenth-century English predecessor, Henry Purcell. First, it is treated broadly by the full orchestra,

Fig. B.6.9. Seating Plan of a Modern Orchestra

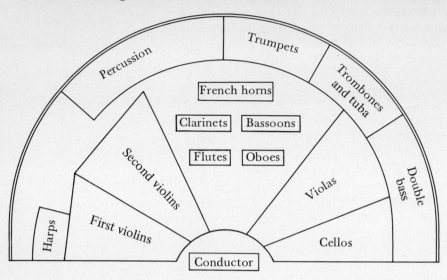

Fig. B.6.10. *The Young Person's Guide to the Orchestra,* **Britten**

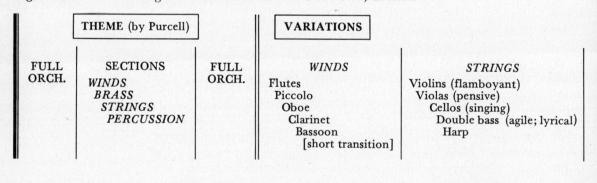

THEME (by Purcell)		VARIATIONS	
FULL ORCH.	**SECTIONS** *WINDS BRASS STRINGS PERCUSSION*	**FULL ORCH.**	**WINDS** Flutes Piccolo Oboe Clarinet Bassoon [short transition]

SECTIONS section shows:
WINDS, BRASS, STRINGS, PERCUSSION

WINDS: Flutes, Piccolo, Oboe, Clarinet, Bassoon, [short transition]

STRINGS: Violins (flamboyant), Violas (pensive), Cellos (singing), Double bass (agile; lyrical), Harp

BRASS: French horn (dramatic), Trumpets ("galloping"), Trombones, Tubas

PERCUSSION: Tympani, Bass drum, Cymbals, *etc.* . . . Triangle and Xylophone

FUGUE
WINDS (Piccolo, Flute, *etc.* STRINGS BRASS PERCUSSION Add Purcell's Theme to end.

THEME (by Purcell)

then in brief episodes by the four orchestral choirs (winds, brass, strings, and percussion), and then together again. In the extended series of variations that follow, the four orchestral choirs are broken down to show off their individual instruments: first, the wind section (flutes, oboes, clarinets, and bassoons); then the strings, brass, and percussion. Each instrument, while displaying something of its distinctive character, also presents some musical variation of the opening theme. The series of variations ends with the percussion instruments, heard against a nervous, dancelike background of strings: In order, there are the tympani, bass drum, cymbals, tympani, tambourine, triangle (plus some eerie side-effects), tympani, snare drum, Chinese wood blocks, xylophone, castanets, gong, the crack of a "whip," tympani, and, ultimately, a dialogue between the high-pitched triangle and xylophone. Having reduced the orchestra to its individual components in this series of variations, Britten goes about reassembling it in a concluding fugue that has for its principal subject a jaunty melody fragment that is again derived from Purcell's theme. (For a discussion of fugues and fugue subjects, see Chapter 3.) All the instruments return in essentially the same order as before (beginning with the piccolos, flutes, oboes, etc.). But now they appear as fugal entries, progressively increasing the liveliness and bulk of the texture. Britten rounds off his work by having Purcell's original theme well up again in the full orchestra from out of the maelstrom of fugal sound.

7. TONE COLOR AND THE PHYSICS OF SOUND

Fundamental Pitches and Their Harmonics

Why do different tone colors exist? Why does a pitch, such as middle C, sound one way played on a piano, another way played on a violin, and still other ways played on a trumpet or sung by a soprano? The reasons lie in the physical nature of sound. We know that sound exists in the form of airwaves whose vibrations are measured in Hertz, or cycles per second. The soprano's "high C," two octaves above middle C, has a frequency of 1024 Hz. The piano's highest pitch, also a C, is at 4096 Hz. Our ears can register pitches that are even much higher, up to fifteen thousand or twenty thousand Hz, but frequencies that high are no longer primarily useful for melody or harmony. They serve instead as a sort of "add on" to the lower pitches, as partly hidden components of the musical sounds that we hear. They are no less significant for being partly hidden. The pitches that lie above one or two thousand Hz are the main determinants of musical tone colors.

When a violin, a trumpet, or an oboe plays a pitch like middle C, we seem to be hearing just that single pitch. But actually we hear a composite of a dozen or more simultaneous pitches that are all merged together. The single pitch we apparently hear is called the *fundamental pitch*. It is the lowest and by far the loudest of those dozen or more merged pitches. But the others are present as well. They are higher, fainter pitches that go along with the fundamental pitch like an almost invisible halo. They are called *harmonics, partials*, or *overtones*, and they are what cause the differences in tone colors.

Harmonics. The reason harmonics exist is that any object, any musical instrument, whose shape is regular enough for its vibrations to form a musical tone rather than just a jumble of noise, will vibrate not only in its whole size but also simultaneously in parts of that whole size. Those parts are always simple fractions of the whole—halves, thirds, quarters, fifths, etc. The fractional vibrations produce harmonic pitches whose frequencies are always exact multiples of the fundamental frequency; that is, they are twice, three times, four times, or five times as fast. As the parts of the vibrating whole get smaller, the harmonics they produce not only become higher in pitch, they are also heard less forcefully. Half of a fundamental string- or pipe-length produces harmonics that are twice as fast as the fundamental frequency and are much fainter in strength; one-third the length produces harmonics whose vibrations are three times as fast as the fundamental frequency and still fainter; and so on.

The Harmonic Series: The Spectrum of Harmonics above a Fundamental Pitch. What pitches do those harmonics represent? Some are just higher octave duplications that reinforce the fundamental pitch. Others do not sound like the fundamental at all. Any fundamental pitch produces an astonishingly varied assortment of harmonic sounds, including some that are so different from the fundamental that we can scarcely imagine them contributing to its pitch sound as actually heard. The whole spectrum of higher, fainter harmonic pitches that are related to a fundamental pitch is called the *harmonic series*. Every fundamental pitch has its own harmonic series. Fig. B.7.1 shows the harmonic series above middle C on the piano keyboard. A corresponding series is spread above any other pitch—any C-sharp, D, D-sharp, etc., that is, anywhere in hearable space. Looking at that harmonic series based on middle C, we can see a number of octave duplications, other C-pitches. But there are some other letter pitches as well. There are Gs and Es, which are part of the C major triad in tonal harmony and so are consonant with the C. Moving up through the series, however, there are even pitches like B-flat, D, F-sharp, A, and B, which are not in any sort of agreement with C. They are dissonant with the C in tonal harmony, and some of them

Fig. B.7.1. Harmonic Series of Middle C (First 16 Pitches)

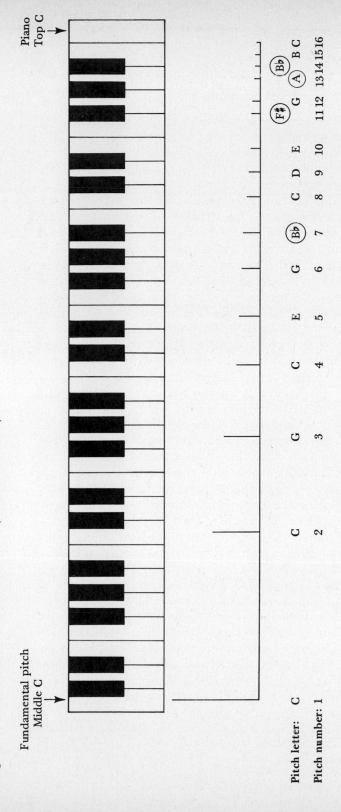

Pitch letter:	C	C	G	C	E	G	B♭	C	D	E	F♯	G	A	B♭	B	C
Pitch number:	1	2	3	4	5	6	7	8	9	10	11	12	13	14	15	16

(those circled in Fig. B.7.1) are not even found exactly on our piano keyboard. Yet they are all there as nature's own components of the heard sound of middle C.

Tone Color and the Spectrum of Harmonic Strengths

Now for the reasons why tone colors differ. In general, the harmonics above a fundamental pitch become fainter as they lie higher above it. Nevertheless, for many fundamentals one can go up to the sixteenth harmonic and beyond and still hear the harmonics. Figure B.7.1 shows the first sixteen harmonics of middle C; the sixteenth is the topmost C on the keyboard. So long as the harmonics remain even marginally hearable, they make a significant contribution to the sound of the fundamental pitch. They determine its tone color. It is their presence in varying strengths that determines whether the sound heard is that of a piano, a violin, or an oboe, etc. Every instrument produces the full harmonic series with every one of its pitches. In most respects, the instruments' series are all alike. But they differ in one critical respect. The relative strengths of the harmonics vary from instrument to instrument. Each instrument produces a different setup of harmonic strengths, depending on its shape and the materials from which it is made. Each instrument's tone color represents its own peculiar spectrum of harmonic strengths. The characteristic tone color of a bassoon reflects the relative prominence that the bassoon's shape and materials give to the second and third harmonics in the series. The clarinet's tone results from a spectrum of harmonic strengths that emphasize the odd-numbered harmonics in the series (numbers 3, 5, etc.). The oboe's sound results from a more even spread of intensities among its harmonics. The spectrum of harmonic strengths is also affected by the instrument's materials. A metal flute sounds slightly different from a wooden flute; a wooden clarinet is slightly different from one made of plastic.

What it comes down to is that each instrument's tone color results from the profile of strengths among its harmonics, and that profile depends on the shape and materials of the instrument. All of which explains why the designers of audio equipment are concerned about the accurate reproduction of frequencies approaching 20,000 Hz. Composers rarely call for specific pitches that lie above 2,000 Hz. The top octave on the piano runs from about 2,000 Hz to 4,000 Hz (see Fig. B.1.3). But the distinctive qualities of tone color depend chiefly on that stratospheric range between approximately 2,000 and 20,000 Hz. The harmonics that do not seem to be there actually make a big difference to the sound.

Envelope. In addition to the harmonic series, there is one other factor to tone color. It is called envelope. *Envelope* is the characteristic pattern of attack and decay of musical sounds on an instrument. It is the profile of rapid changes in loudness and timbre that take place as an instrument's sound is produced. Every musical instrument has its own patterns of beginning, sustaining, and completing its production of tone. When a pitch is struck on a harpsichord, the sharp initial ping of the *attack* is followed by a rapid *decay* in the force of tone. The profile of the same pitch struck on a piano is quite different. The attack of the piano's felt hammer is less biting than that of the harpsichord's sharp quill. Because the piano's soundboard and case have greater resonating space, the decay time of its vibrations is longer if the key is held down. That same pitch bowed on a violin begins with a scratchy blurt as the gummed hair of the bow first excites the string. Then the tone can be sustained by the motion of the bow (something that is not possible on the piano or harpsichord). In between the attack and decay on the violin there is the "steady state" of loudness and timbre, which is maintained by the bow's regular action on the string. If the bow is removed, the tone dies quickly, but if the bow merely halts on the string, the sound seems choked off. On a trumpet, an initial blast that forms the attack may be followed by a steady-state tone, then a long decay as the trumpet sound reverberates before fading away.

The different profiles of instrumental sound that result from the varied patterns of attack, steady state, and decay are largely matters of changing loudness. Those changes, however, are brought about by changes in the violinist's bowing angle or the trumpeter's lip pressure, so that they amount to changes in the instruments themselves. As instruments change, so do the relative strengths of their harmonics; and as harmonic spectra change, so do tone colors. Thus envelope— the composite of the changes in dynamics and coloration while an instrumental or vocal sound is being produced—is a subtle yet essential part of tone color.

C Glossary

The words in italic are defined elsewhere in the glossary. The numbers and letters within parentheses following definitions refer to sections within chapters and appendixes where terms are discussed.

Absolute music: Abstract, self-contained music; as opposed to descriptive or *program music*, which has associations with literature, philosophy, art, etc. (6.A)

A cappella: Vocal music without instruments. (2.D)

Accelerando (accel.): A gradual quickening of *tempo.*

Accent: An emphasis or stress placed on a musical sound. (App. B.2)

Accidental: A *sharp* or *flat* sign. A black key on the keyboard. (App. A, App. B.1)

Accompanied recitative: A *recitative* with orchestral accompaniment; as opposed to a *secco recitative,* which is accompanied by a *basso continuo.* (3.J, 3.K, 7.A, 7.B)

Acoustics: The physics of sound. (App. B.7)

Aerophone: An instrument that produces sound from air vibrating in a tube or pipe or from air blown across a reed. (App. B.6)

Air: A vocal or instrumental song. An *aria;* an ayre. (3.C)

Aleatory music: *Chance music.* (10.C)

Allegretto: A moderately fast *tempo.*

Allegro: A fast *tempo.*

Allemande: A German dance in slow *duple meter;* the first dance of the standard Baroque *suite.* Purcell calls it *Almand.* (3.D)

Alto: A vocal register between *soprano* and *tenor.*

Andante: A moderately slow, "walking" *tempo.*

Antiphonal: Performance by alternating choirs. (2.F)

Aria: A solo song in an *opera, oratorio,* or *cantata.* (3.C, 3.J, 3.K, 3.L)

Arioso: A melodic style that is tuneful or songlike (less tuneful than an *aria,* more tuneful than a *recitative*).

Arpeggio: The pitches of a *chord,* played quickly one after the other instead of together. A *broken chord.*

Art song: A song composed as a work of art, as opposed to a *folksong;* normally accompanied by a piano. In German, *lied;* in French, *chanson.* (5.E)

Atonal: Musical style adopted by Schoenberg and his disciples after the rejection of *tonality* and before the advent of *serialism* (ca. 1908-23). (8.C, 8.D)

Atonality: The absence of a tonal center or key. See *atonal.*

Augmentation: A slow repetition of a melody or rhythm that previously went faster; for example, a quarter note becomes a half note. (3.G)

Ballet: An artistic dance staged with costumes, scenic effects, and musical accompaniment.

Band: A large instrumental ensemble, usually winds, brass, and percussion.

Bar, bar line: *Measure, measure line.*

Baritone: A male vocal register located between *tenor* and *bass.*

Baroque: The musical era from ca. 1600 to 1750; from Monteverdi to Bach and Handel. (Chap. 3)

Basic pitch: One of the twelve distinctive pitch-sounds used in Western music; for example, C, C-sharp, D, E-flat; all twelve of the basic pitches are found within any *octave;* the eighty-eight keys of the piano keyboard contain many duplications of the basic pitches at higher and lower octave levels. Also called *pitch class.* (App. B.2)

Bass: The lowest line in an instrumental or vocal composition; the low male vocal register.

Basso continuo: The bass plus chordal accompaniment found in most *Baroque* music; an instrumental bass line plus improvised chords, usually played by a *viola da gamba* plus a *harpsichord* or organ. (3.A, 3.B, 3.C, 3.E, 3.J)

Basso continuo realization: The filler chords of a *basso continuo*, improvised by the performer when reading from a *figured bass*.

Basso ostinato: A short musical passage in the bass line, repeated again and again as the basis for *variations*, as in a *passacaglia* or *chaconne;* an *ostinato bass* or *ostinato*. (3.C, 5.I)

Beat: The clocklike *pulse* found in *metric rhythms*. (App. B.2)

Bebop: A *jazz* idiom of the 1940s and 1950s, featuring small ensembles, virtuoso display, complex rhythms and harmonies; associated with Charlie Parker. (10.G)

Bel canto: Italian lyrical singing with a graceful, flowing quality of voice; "beautiful melody, beautifully sung." (3.K, 7.A)

Binary form: A musical *form* having two related sections, each directly repeated; for example:

‖: A :‖ A :‖ or ‖: A :‖ B A' :‖

(3.D, 3.E, 4.D, 4.E)

Binary-form variations: A *theme and variations* form in which the *theme* is in *binary form*. (4.E)

Bitonality: The use of two different *tonal keys* at once. (9.A)

Block chords, block harmony: A *texture* of simple *chords;* a style of accompaniment often found in church hymns. (App. B.3, App. B.4)

Blue notes: In the *blues* scale, the third, sixth, and seventh degrees of the common scale, pitched flexibly, a little below normal. (8.F)

Blues: Black-American musical laments of the nineteenth and twentieth centuries; originally, improvised folk music; later, cultivated by virtuoso professionals. (8.F)

Boogie-woogie: Jazz piano style of the 1920s through 1940s, featuring short, energetic bass patterns that are constantly repeated. (9.H)

Bop: *Bebop*. (10.G)

Brass section: Metal *aerophones* found in the modern orchestra: trumpets, trombones, French horns, tuba, etc. (App. B.6)

Break: A short improvised *cadenza* in *jazz*.

Bridge: A *transition* passage. In *sonata-allegro form*, the transition that leads from the first theme group to the second. (4.B)

Broken chord: An *arpeggio*.

Cadence: A point of repose at the end of a musical line. The melodic or harmonic progression that concludes a phrase, a section, or an entire piece. (App. B.1, App. B.4)

Cadenza: A display passage for a soloist in a *concerto* or *aria*, often improvised, while the accompanying orchestra remains silent.

Canon: A *polyphonic* composition for two or more *voice-parts* where the entire melodic line of the first part is strictly imitated by each of the others in succession. (1.D, 3.G, App. B.3)

Canonic imitation: Exact, *strict imitation*.

Cantabile: In a "singing" style.

Cantata: A chamber composition for voices and instruments; used since the *Baroque* period. (3.J)

Cantus firmus: In medieval and renaissance *polyphony*, a "borrowed" melody (usually a *plainchant*) to which fresh musical lines are added. (1.C, 2.B, 2.C)

Canzona: A Renaissance instrumental *genre*, in some cases an imitation of a French *chanson*. (2.F)

Chaconne: A Baroque dance in slow *triple meter*, usually in the form of *ostinato variations;* see *ostinato*.

Chamber music: Music for a small *ensemble*, with just one performer to a part.

Chamber sonata: See *Sonata da camera*.

Chance music: Certain music composed after World War II, where an act of chance, such as a throw of dice, decides how a piece will go; also called random, indeterminate, and *aleatory music*. (10.C, 10.D)

Chanson: French song.

Chant: *Monophonic* song, usually sacred. *Plainchant*.

Character piece: A small-scale piece with some programmatic association, usually for piano; for example, the *Nocturnes* or *Mazurkas* by Chopin. (5.A, 5.F, 6.B, 6.E)

Choir: A musical group performing together.

Choral: For *chorus*.

Chorale: A Lutheran *hymn*. (3.J)

Chorale prelude: An organ composition based on a Lutheran hymn melody. (3.J)

Chord: A combination of two or more pitches sounding together. (App. B.3, App. B.4)

Chord progression: Two or more *chords* in a row. (App. B.4)

Chordal style: *Block chords*. (App. B.3, App. B.4)

Chordophones: Instruments whose sounds come from vibrating strings. (App. B.6)

Chorus: A large vocal *choir*.

Chromatic, Chromaticism: Extensive use of *accidentals;* music based on the *chromatic scale*. (5.A, 6.C, 8.A)

Chromatic harmony: *Tonal* harmony using the *chromatic scale*.

Chromatic scale: The twelve-pitch scale, dividing the *octave* into equal *half-steps*. In Western music, the full set of available pitches: all the black and white keys on the piano. (App. B.1)

Church modes: The musical *modes* used in *plainchant* and medieval-renaissance *polyphony*. (1.B, 2.D, App. B.1)

Church sonata: See *Sonata da chiesa.*

Circle of fifths: "The map of tonal space." A diagram of all the *major* and *minor keys* arranged in a circle as a continuous chain of related *tonics* and *dominants*. Their tonal closeness is shown by their closeness on the circle. (Fig. C.1)

Fig. C.1. The Circle of Fifths

Capital letters are *major* keys.
Small letters are *relative minor* keys.

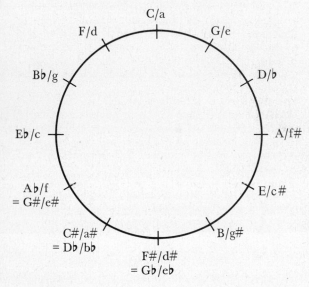

Classical era: The musical era from ca. 1770 to 1800, centered in Vienna: Mozart, Haydn, early Beethoven. (Chap. 4)

Clavichord: A keyboard instrument (flourished fifteenth to eighteenth century) whose sound is produced by contacting or stopping the strings with tangents. (3.D)

Clef: In musical notation, a sign placed at the beginning of a five-line *staff* that indicates what letter *pitches* are to be read from the lines and spaces. The chief clef is the treble clef:

where the second line from the bottom is the G above middle C. (App. A)

Coda, codetta: A concluding section of a piece or movement, emphasizing the sense of closure. A codetta is a small coda. (4.B)

Coloratura: An ornamented style of vocal melody, usually for *soprano.*

Common scale: The *tonal scale;* the *major scale.* (App. B.1)

Common time: A meter with four *pulses* per measure; the most common Western meter:

$$\left| \overset{>}{1} \quad 2 \quad \overset{>}{3} \quad 4 \right| \overset{>}{1} \quad 2 \quad \overset{>}{3} \quad 4 \left| \quad etc. \right.$$

(App. B.2)

Compline: The evening service of the Roman Catholic *Divine Office.* (1.B)

Compound duple meter: A *meter* with six pulses per measure. There are two main pulses, each subdivided into three, with the primary accent on pulse 1, the secondary accent on pulse 4:

$$\left| \overset{>}{1} \quad 2 \quad 3 \quad \overset{>}{4} \quad 5 \quad 6 \right| \overset{>}{1} \quad 2 \quad 3 \quad \overset{>}{4} \quad 5 \quad 6 \left| \quad etc. \right.$$

(App. B.2)

Compound triple meter: A *meter* with nine pulses per measure. There are three main pulses, each subdivided into three, with the primary accent on pulse 1, the secondary accents on pulses 4 and 7. (App. B.2)

Concertino: The small group of soloists in a *concerto grosso.* (3.F, 3.I)

Concerto: A musical *genre* that contrasts solo performers with an accompanying orchestral group. (3.F, 3.I, 4.G)

Concerto grosso: The favorite type of Baroque concerto, contrasting a small group of soloists (the *concertino*) against a larger orchestral group (the *ripieno*). (3.F, 3.I)

Concert overture: An orchestral work in one movement, comparable in length and mood to an opera *overture* but composed for concert use.

Conjunct motion: Stepwise melodic motion, using *half-step* and *whole-step* intervals. (App. B.1)

Consonance and dissonance: Consonance is a quality of repose or agreeableness sensed in a chord; dissonance is a quality of tension and harshness. The perceptions are culturally determined, varying with time and place, and in specific instances they depend on the context in which a chord is heard. (App. B.4)

Continuo: *Basso continuo.*

Contralto: The lowest women's vocal register, located below an *alto.* (App. B.3)

Contrapuntal: Having to do with *counterpoint.*

Contrary motion: Two *voice-parts* moving in opposite melodic directions.

Corant: Purcell's name for *Courante.* (3.D)

Corrente: See *Courante.*

Counterpoint: *Polyphony;* a texture of simultaneous melodic strands. A single strand within polyphony. The technique of producing such strands and their combinations. (App. B.3)

Countersubject: Melodic material that appears in a *fugue* as a *counterpoint* to the fugue's subject. (3.G)

Countertenor: An adult male vocalist who sings in an *alto* or *soprano* register.

Courante, Corrente, Corant: The second dance of the standard Baroque *dance suite;* a "running" (*courant*) dance in lively *triple meter.* (3.D, 3.E)

Crescendo: Growing louder.

Da capo (D.C.): An instruction to the performer, meaning "return to play from the beginning of the piece." (3.J, 3.K, 4.D)

Da capo aria: An *aria* form favored during the Baroque era: A-B-A. (3.J, 3.K)

Dadaism: A radical movement of European artists, writers, and musicians (ca. 1916-25), who rejected conventional standards of art and personal behavior and cultivated an esthetic that emphasized absurdity and formlessness. (8.B)

Dance suite: A sequence of instrumental dances. The four standard dances of a Baroque suite are *allemande, courante, sarabande,* and *gigue* (*jig*). (3.D, 3.E, 3.H)

Deceptive cadence: A deceptive or "interrupted" *cadence* usually moves from the *dominant* chord to the chord just above (V to vi) rather than from the dominant to an expected *tonic* (V to I). It replaces a *tonic cadence* and results in surprise and prolonged tension. (App. B.4)

Decibel: The scientific unit for measuring loudness.

Declamation: The manner in which word and speech patterns are spoken. Musical declamation is the manner in which such patterns are set to music.

Decrescendo: Growing softer.

Development: The process of elaborating musical materials that were stated previously. The central section of *sonata-allegro form.* (4.B)

Diatonic harmony: *Tonal* harmony. (App. B.4)

Diatonic scale: The *major* or *minor scale;* any scale having seven pitches per *octave,* with five *whole steps* and two *half-steps* between them. (App. B.1)

Dies irae: "Day of wrath..." A medieval *plainchant* for the dead, often used by romantic and modern composers. (1.D, 6.A)

Diminuendo: *Decrescendo;* growing softer.

Diminution: A quicker repetition of a previously slower melody or rhythm; for example, a quarter note becomes an eighth note. (3.G)

Disjunct motion: *Skip motion;* melodic motion using wide interval skips.

Dissonance: See *Consonance and Dissonance.*

Divertimento: An eighteenth-century instrumental work, designed for "diversion," made up mainly of dance movements; related to the Baroque dance suite. Mozart wrote many divertimenti. (3.H)

Divine Office: In the Catholic liturgy, the daily church services other than the *Mass.* (1.B)

Dixieland jazz: *New Orleans jazz.* (8.F)

Dodecaphonic: Twelve-tone; having to do with *serial music.* (9.D, 9.E)

Dominant: The fifth degree (pitch 5̂) of the *major* and *minor scale;* the chord built on that pitch. In *tonality,* the dominant is the next most important pitch after the *tonic.* (App. B.1, App. B.4, App. B.5)

Dominant cadence: A chord progression that moves from the *tonic* to the *dominant* (I to V). It produces a sense of incomplete action, of something being bound to follow.

Dominant key: The *key* or *tonality* that is built on pitch 5̂ of the tonal scale. (App. B.5)

Do-re-mi scale: A memory aid for the *major scale,* sung to the nonsense syllables: *do-re-mi-fa-sol-la-ti-do.* (App. B.1)

Dotted rhythm: A rhythm that alternates long and short notes: ♩. ♪ ♩. ♪ , as in the slow opening section of a *French overture.* (3.C, 3.J, 3.K)

Double bar: A pair of vertical lines drawn through the *staff,* indicating the end of a musical section or of the entire composition:

Double bars and double dots: The notation for repeating a section of music; whatever music appears between the dots is repeated:

‖: a b :‖ = ‖ a b a b ‖

Duple meter: A meter with two *pulses* per measure and an *accent* on the first pulse:

| > | > |
| 1 2 | 1 2 | *etc.*

(App. B.2)

Dynamics: The levels of loud and soft in music. (App. B.2)

Electronic music: Music that has some or all of its sounds produced by electronic means. (10.B, 10.D, 10.E, 10.F)

Electrophones: Musical instruments that generate their sounds with the aid of electricity: theremin, audio generator, electronic *synthesizer*, etc. (App. B.6)

Embellishment: *Ornamentation.*

English horn: A tenor oboe.

Enharmonic pair: Two pitches that are very close together, such as F-sharp and G-flat, G-sharp and A-flat, E-sharp and F-natural. In earlier times they were sounded as distinct from one another. In today's system of *equal temperament*, they are treated as the same *pitch* and produced on the piano by the same key.

Ensemble: A small group of instrumental or vocal performers, usually numbering anywhere from two to twelve. In an operatic ensemble, two or more characters express their personal sentiments at the same time in individualized musical lines. (4.H, 7.A)

Episode: In a *fugue*, a passage of contrasting or filler material that comes between *expositions* of the *subject*. (3.G)

Equal temperament: A system of instrumental tuning in general use since the 1700s. It divides the *octave* into 12 equal *half-steps*.

Ethnomusicology: The study of music in its ethnic and cultural context, particularly among non-Western cultures.

Exposition: The opening section of a *sonata-allegro form*. (4.B) Also, the opening section of a *fugue*, where all the voices introduce the subject in turn, as well as later presentations of the fugue subject. (3.G)

Expressionism: An esthetic movement among German painters and musicians (ca. 1905-25). The painters turned from representing familiar visual scenes to the expression of inner personal experience through abstract, nonrepresentational imagery. The musicians turned from the idioms of *tonality* to *atonality*. (8.C)

Falsetto: A male voice singing in an unnaturally high register, with a reedy, artificial quality of sound.

Fantasia, fantasy, fancy: A composition that is free in *form* and spirit, where the composer's "fantasy" is displayed.

Fifth: An interval whose pitches are at the fifth step apart in the major and minor scales; that is, a distance of five white keys on the keyboard, as from C up to G, D up to A, or E up to B. The interval between the *tonic* and *dominant* pitches in *tonality*. (App. B.1)

Figuration: A recurrent, ornamental musical pattern.

Figured bass: The manner of noting a *basso continuo* in which only the bass line is written out. Figures (numbers and accidentals) are added to the bass notes, indicating the chords that are to be filled in by the keyboard player. (3.C, 3.E)

Final: The concluding *pitch* in a *plainchant*. (1.B)

Finale: The concluding *movement* in a symphony, sonata, etc.; the concluding *ensemble* to an act of an *opera*.

First-movement form: *Sonata-allegro form.* (4.B)

Five-pitch scale: *Pentatonic scale.* (App. B.1)

Flamenco: *Folk music* of Andalusia in southern Spain.

Flat: A notational sign (♭) that lowers the *pitch* of a note by a *half-step*. (App. A, App. B.1)

Florid: Ornamented, *melismatic.*

Folk music: Music with a broad cultural appeal that develops anonymously in an unsophisticated environment. Folk music usually circulates "orally," not being written down.

Form: The shape, plan, or design of a musical composition.

Fourth: An interval whose pitches are at the fourth step apart in the major and minor scales; that is, a distance of four white keys on the keyboard, as from C up to F, D up to G, E up to A. (App. B.1)

Free imitation: A type of *imitative polyphony* where a melodic subject that is stated in one *voice-part* is roughly copied in other voice-parts. (2.C, 2.D, 3.G, App. B.3)

French overture: A *Baroque* instrumental *form* with a slow, majestic opening section, often using dotted rhythms, and a lively, fugal second section. Also known as a Lullian overture from its use in the operas of Lully. (3.C, 3.J, 3.K)

Fugal: In the style of a *fugue.*

Fugal polyphony: *Imitative polyphony* that is built on a single subject, as in a *fugue*. (3.G)

Fugato: A fugal passage within a larger, nonfugal work. (3.J)

Fugue: An *imitative polyphonic* composition where two or more voices state and develop a single melodic fragment called the *subject*, using it many times and in varied combinations. (3.G)

Fundamental pitch: The bottom pitch on which a *harmonic series* is built. (App. B.7)

Futurism: A movement of early twentieth-century Italian artists who admired the efficiency, power, and sounds of modern industrial society. (8.B)

Gavotte: A French dance in *duple meter;* one of the optional dances of a Baroque *suite*. (3.H)

Genre: A category of musical composition, such as *sonata, suite, motet, fugue, concerto,* etc.

Gigue, Giga, Jig: The concluding dance of the standard Baroque *suite;* it has a lively *triple meter* or *compound duple meter.* (3.D, 3.E, 3.H)

Glissando: Sliding quickly through a range of pitches.

Gregorian chant: The official repertory of *plainchant* of the Roman Church, named for Pope Gregory the Great (590-604). (1.B)

Ground, ground bass: English terms for an *ostinato.*

Half-step: The smallest *interval* used in Western music; the interval between adjacent keys on the keyboard. (App. B.1)

Harmonic: In acoustics, a high pitch heard faintly above a *fundamental pitch,* representing a multiple of the fundamental frequency; contributes to *tone color.* Same as *overtone, partial.* (App. B.7)

Harmonic series: The spectrum of *harmonics* above a fundamental pitch. (Fig. B.7.1)

Harmonize, Harmonization: Adding accompanying *chords* to a *melody.* (App. B.3, App. B.4)

Harmony: The sounds of pitches in combination; the art of handling chords and *chord progressions;* the vertical aspect of *polyphony.* (App. B.4)

Harpsichord: The most popular keyboard instrument of the Renaissance and *Baroque* eras, a predecessor of the piano; its sounds are produced by plucking the strings with plectra, rather than striking them with soft hammers as on a piano. (3.D, 3.H)

Heterophony: A musical *texture* where different performers produce the same melody simultaneously but with artful variants of *pitch, rhythm,* and color; used in ancient Greece and popular in today's Near Eastern music. (1.A)

Homophony, homophonic: A musical *texture* consisting of *block chords* or of a *melody* with accompanying chords. (App. B.3)

Hymn: A religious song in simple musical style, meant to be sung by the congregation. (3.J)

Idée fixe: The melody ("fixed idea") that represents the composer's beloved in Berlioz's "Fantastic" Symphony. (6.A)

Identification motive: *Leitmotif.* (7.B)

Idiophones: Musical instruments whose sounds come from rubbing or striking the instrument: wood block, gong, castanet, *xylophone,* etc. (App. B.6)

Imitation: In *polyphony,* one *voice-part* imitating, or copying, what a previous voice has stated. (1.D, 2.C, 2.D, App. B.3)

Imitative polyphony: A *polyphonic texture* based on imitation, such as *free imitation* or *strict imitation.* (1.D, 2.C, 2.D, 3.G, App. B.3)

Impressionism: A movement of late-nineteenth-century French artists (Renoir, Monet, Pissaro, etc.) who created subjective "impressions" of the visual world. Their luminescent images were often painted with small dabs of color that coalesce and shimmer when viewed from a distance. (8.A)

Improvisation: An on-the-spot creation. The performer makes up some or all of the music during the act of performance, without a fully noted score. (3.E, 3.K, 8.F, 9.H, 10.C, 10.G)

Instrumentation: *Orchestration.*

Interval: A distance between two pitches; a relationship between two pitches, identifiable by a characteristic sound. Some common intervals are *half-step, whole step, third, fourth, fifth,* and *octave.* (App. B.1)

Inversion: The technique of reusing a melody with the original intervals turned upside down; that is, a rising fifth of an original melody becomes a falling fifth in its inversion, etc. (3.G, 9.D)

Jazz: A black-American musical idiom of the twentieth century, typified by a strong *beat,* flexible inner *rhythms,* and an infectious lilt. Jazz is largely improvised. (8.F, 9.H, 10.G)

Jig: *Gigue.*

K. numbers: The serial numbers assigned to Mozart's works in the chronological catalogue compiled by L. von Köchel. (4.C)

Key: The *tonic* or tonal center of a musical work. The height of a melody or scale in tonal space. A synonym for *tonality:* the *key of D major* is the same as the *tonality of D major;* that is, the sound of the major mode with its tonic on D. (App. B.5)

Key relationship: The sense of closeness or tension between two tonal *keys.* (App. B.5)

Key signature: The grouping of *sharps* or *flats* at the beginning of a musical staff, indicating what *key* or *tonality* the music is in. (App. A)

Legato: Notes connected smoothly in performance; as opposed to *staccato.*

Leitmotif: An identification motive in Wagner's *music dramas.* In an *opera* or *program music,* it is a musical motive that is identified with some person, place, concept, or object. (7.B)

Libretto: The literary text of an *opera, oratorio,* or *cantata,* which the composer sets to music; literally, "little book."

Lied: German *art song,* usually composed for solo voice and piano. (5.A, E)

Line: A melodic phrase or statement. In *polyphony,* an individual *voice-part.*

Liturgical music: Music of church ritual. (1.B, 1.C)

Liturgy: The church service or ritual, including prayers, Bible readings, and music. (1.B)

Lute family: *Chordophones* that have boxes or bellies with thin necks running out from them; for example, guitar, *violin, sitar, samisen,* Western renaissance lute. (App. B.6)

Lutheran chorale: Lutheran *hymn.* (3.J)

Lyric: Songlike, as opposed to dramatic.

Madrigal: The vocal *chamber music* of the late Italian and English Renaissance, emphasizing the expressive setting of poetic texts. (2.E)

Madrigalisms: Musical *word paintings* that illustrate the meanings of text words through expressive touches of *rhythm, melody, harmony,* etc. (2.E, 3.K)

Major-minor tonality: Same as *tonality.*

Major mode: The sound of major tonality, based on the *major scale.* (App. B.1)

Major scale: The common scale of tonality; the *do-re-mi scale.* A seven-pitch scale whose half-steps come between pitches $\hat{3}$ and $\hat{4}$, and $\hat{7}$ and $\hat{8}$. The scale is characterized by the interval of a *major third* (two whole steps) between pitches $\hat{1}$ and $\hat{3}$. (App. B.1)

Major third: An *interval* containing two *whole steps* or four *half-steps.* It is the distinctive interval of the *major scale,* found between pitches $\hat{1}$ and $\hat{3}$ of that scale. (App. B.1)

Mass: The principal service of Roman Catholic daily worship. In *polyphonic* music, *Mass* usually refers to the *Ordinary of the Mass:* Kyrie, Gloria, Credo, Sanctus, and Agnus Dei. (1.B)

Mazurka: A Polish dance in moderate-to-lively *triple meter.* (5.F)

Measure, measure line: A measure is the basic unit of Western *meter,* consisting of a fixed number of *beats* and a regular pattern of *accents* applied to those beats. A measure line is a vertical line drawn through the staff, separating each measure from the next. Same as *bar, bar line.* (App. A, App. B.2)

Melisma, melismatic style: In a melody, a phrase of many notes sung to a single syllable of text. (1.B)

Melodic motive: A short, incisive melodic figure. (5.C, App. B.2)

Melody: A succession of *pitches* and *intervals* with a sense of order and completeness. (App. B.1)

Membranophones: Musical instruments whose sounds are produced by a vibrating skin or membrane: kettledrum, snare drum, etc. (App. B.6)

Meter: A regular pattern of *pulses* and *accents* that is repeated in successive *measures* of a piece. (App. B.2)

Meterless music: Music without a regular *pulse* and *meter,* such as *Gregorian chant.* (1.B)

Metric music, Metric rhythm: Musical *rhythm* based on a regular *meter.* (1.C, App. B.2)

Metronome: An adjustable clock that beats out precise *tempos.* (App. B.2)

Microtone: An *interval* smaller than a *half-step.* (App. B.1)

Minor mode: The sound of minor tonality, based on the *minor scale.* (App. B.1)

Minor scale: Along with the major scale, the other common scale of tonality. A seven-pitch scale whose *half-steps* usually come between pitches $\hat{2}$ and $\hat{3}$, and $\hat{5}$ and $\hat{6}$. The scale is characterized by the interval of a *minor third* (a *whole step* and a *half-step*) between pitches $\hat{1}$ and $\hat{3}$. (App. B.1)

Minor third: An *interval* consisting of one and one-half *whole steps* or three *half-steps.* It is the distinctive interval of the *minor scale,* found between pitches $\hat{1}$ and $\hat{3}$ of that scale. (App. B.1)

Minuet, Minuet and Trio: A French dance in *triple meter* and moderate *tempo,* used in *Baroque suites* and Classical symphonies, quartets, etc. The trio is a second minuet, usually with thinner *texture.* (3.C, 4.D)

Modal, Modality: Having to do with *mode.*

Mode: A characteristic "flavor" of musical sound, as in the major and minor modes, the medieval *church modes,* or the distinctive modal sounds of *blues,* Far Eastern, or gypsy music. The pitch materials of a mode are summed up in a *scale,* but what produces the modal character is the application of idioms of *melody, harmony, rhythm,* and *tone color* to the scale pitches. (App. B.1)

Modulation: A change of *key;* a musical passage that begins in one key and ends in another. (App. B.5)

Monody: A melodic line, sometimes with a subordinated accompaniment, sometimes without accompaniment. (3.B, App. B.3)

Monophony: Melody alone, as in *Gregorian chant;* a *texture* of a single melodic line without other lines or harmony. (1.B, App. B.3)

Motet: A sacred vocal composition of the thirteenth through twentieth centuries, usually to a Latin text. (1.D, 2.B)

Motive: A short, incisive musical figure. (App. B.2)

Movement: A self-contained section of a larger musical composition, as in a four-movement symphony.

Music drama: Wagnerian *opera.* (7.B)

Musique concrète: Sound-effects music, stylized on tape by Parisian composers around 1950. (10.B)

Natural sign: A notational sign (♮) that cancels a previous *sharp* or *flat* sign. (App. A)

Neoclassicism: A musical esthetic of the 1920s through 1950s, representing a return to certain attitudes and techniques found in music of the eighteenth century. (9.A, 9.B, 9.C, 9.D)

Neumes: Early notational signs used for writing *plainchant* (ninth through twelfth centuries). (1.B)

New Orleans jazz: *Dixieland jazz.* The first great phase of *jazz* style, from ca. 1900 to 1920. (8.F)

Nocturne: A romantic *character piece* that is evocative of night, often for solo piano. (5.F)

Nonimitative polyphony: A *polyphonic texture* in which the *voice-parts* carry melodic strands with dissimilar contours. (App. B.3)

Notation: A system of symbols for writing down music.

Note: The written sign for a musical sound. A *pitch*. (App. A)

Number: An independent lyric piece found in an *opera, oratorio, cantata,* etc. A *set piece,* such as an *aria,* duet, or operatic *ensemble.* (3.C, 3.J, 3.K, 3.L, 4.H, 7.A)

Number opera: An *opera* consisting of a chain of lyric *numbers* or *set pieces* that are interspersed with spoken dialogues or *recitatives.* (3.C, 3.K, 3.L, 4.H, 7.A)

Octave: A large *interval* containing twelve *half-steps;* the upper pitch sounds like its lower one. On the piano, the pitches are eight white keys apart, hence the name "octave." The upper pitch of an octave vibrates exactly twice as fast as the lower pitch. (App. B.1)

Octave duplication: The phenomenon of an octave's similarity of sound between its upper and lower pitches. There are seven and one-half levels of octave duplication on the piano. (App. B.1)

Office: *Divine Office.*

Opera: A sung drama; a stage work whose actions and conversations are given to solo singers and *choruses* accompanied by instruments. (3.B, 3.C, 3.K, 3.L, 7.A, 9.F)

Opera buffa: Italian comic opera style of the eighteenth and nineteenth centuries. (3.L, 4.H)

Opera seria: Italian dramatic opera style of the eighteenth century, dealing with "serious" or historical subject matter. (3.K, 4.H)

Operetta: A "light" and often comic opera style of the nineteenth and twentieth centuries; its dialogues are usually spoken rather than sung in *recitative.* (9.H)

Opus: A musical composition; literally, "a work." Composers assign opus numbers to their works in the order that they are composed or published.

Oratorio: A religious or spiritually oriented *opera;* an extended dramatic work for voices and orchestra, not usually staged, but performed in a church or concert hall. (3.J, 3.K)

Orchestration: *Instrumentation.* In composing music, the assignment of specific instrumental colors to musical ideas.

Ordinary of the Mass: The chants of the *Mass* whose words generally remain unchanged from day to day: Kyrie, Gloria, Credo, Sanctus, and Agnus Dei. (1.B)

Organum: Medieval church *polyphony* in styles of the ninth through thirteenth centuries. (1.C)

Ornamentation: *Embellishment;* the musical decoration of a *melody* or *harmony.* Ornaments are often improvised by the performer.

Ostinato: A short musical passage—usually a bass melody though sometimes a *chord progression*— that is repeated a number of times, end-to-end. Ostinatos are the basis for certain *theme and variations forms,* known by such names as *chaconne, passacaglia, ostinato variations, ground, ground bass, variations on a ground, ostinato bass,* and *basso ostinato.* (3.C, 5.I, 10.G)

Ostinato bass: See *ostinato.*

Ostinato variations: A *theme and variations form* based on an *ostinato.*

Overtone: See *harmonic.*

Overture: An orchestral introduction to an *opera, oratorio,* etc. Also, a *concert overture.*

Parallel minor, parallel major: *Tonic minor and tonic major keys.*

Parallel motion: Two or more *voice-parts* whose melodies move simultaneously in the same direction.

Paraphrase, paraphrase technique: In Renaissance *polyphony,* the use of a *plainchant* melody, adjusted in style so that it fits idiomatically as a musical line in a motet or Mass movement. (2.B)

Part: *Voice-part;* a single line in a *polyphonic* composition.

Partial: See *harmonic.*

Partita: A Baroque *dance suite.* The dances in a partita were originally variations of one another, based on some common material. (3.D, 3.H)

Passacaglia: A Baroque dance form in slow *triple meter;* generally used for a set of *ostinato variations.* (3.D, 5.I)

Passion: A musical version of the Gospel account of the sufferings and death of Christ; in Latin, *passio* means "suffering." (3.J)

Pedal point: A *pitch* that is sustained in one voice (usually the *bass*) while livelier motions in other voices generate rhythmic and harmonic tensions against it. (1.C)

Pentatonic scale: A scale having five pitches to the *octave.* The most familiar pentatonic scale consists of the five black keys on the piano keyboard, producing a quasi-Oriental sound. (App. B.1)

Percussion family: The *idiophones* and *membranophones* found in the modern band and orchestra: kettledrum, snare drum, bass drum, triangle, cymbals, bells, etc. (App. B.6)

Phrase: A short musical utterance, usually coming to a conclusion in a *cadence*. (App. B.1)

Piano trio: An instrumental group consisting of a piano, *violin*, and cello.

Pitch: The height of a sound in musical space. (App. B.1)

Pitch class: Same as *basic pitch*. (App. B.1)

Pizzicato: Plucking a string, rather than bowing it.

Plainchant, plainsong: The *monophonic* vocal music of the medieval church. (1.B)

Point of imitation: A set of imitative entries in Renaissance *polyphony* where each voice enters in turn, presenting its version of the same shared *theme*. (2.C, 2.D)

Polonaise: A Polish dance in slow, stately *triple meter*. (5.F)

Polychoral: Music using two or more *choirs*, as in Venetian polychoral music of the late sixteenth century. (2.F)

Polyphony, polyphonic texture: A texture where two or more *pitches* or melodic strands are active simultaneously. (App. B.3)

Polytonality: The simultaneous use of two or more different keys. (9.A)

Popular music: Music that is produced in a sophisticated cultural environment for the entertainment of a mass public. Popular music includes commercialized arrangements of *folk music* as well as "light" works (often in dance idioms) by "serious" composers, such as Mozart and Beethoven.

Post-tonality, post-tonal music: Twentieth-century musical styles after the dissolution of *tonality*. (Chap. 8)

Prelude: An introductory piece; sometimes an independent composition (for example, Chopin's Preludes), not prefacing another piece. (3.D, 3.G, 5.F, 6.C, 8.A)

Program music: Instrumental music, often of the Romantic era, that has "extra-musical" associations drawn from nature, literature, history, fine art, etc.; as opposed to abstract or *absolute music*. (5.A, 6.A, 6.D, 6.E, 6.F)

Proper of the Mass: The chants of the Mass whose words and music generally change from day to day: Introit, Gradual, Alleluia with Verse, Tract, Offertory, and Communion. (1.B)

Pulse: *Beat.* The basic motion in *metric rhythm*. A pattern of identical throbs or beats that runs continuously through each metric piece. (App. B.2)

Ragtime: Black-American popular music of the 1890s through 1920s. A forerunner of *jazz*, featuring catchy, syncopated melodies and thumping accompaniments; usually for piano solo. (8.F, 9.A)

Realization, realize: See *basso continuo realization.*

Recapitulation: The third of the three main sections of *sonata-allegro form;* also called *restatement.* (4.B)

Recitative: Musically heightened speech. An operatic manner of setting speech to music by stylizing the inflections of the spoken words. (3.B, 3.C, 3.J, 3.K, 4.H, 7.B, 8.C)

Refrain: A musical passage that periodically returns.

Register: A range of *pitches.* The six main vocal registers are (in descending order): soprano, alto (or mezzo soprano), contralto, tenor, baritone, bass.

Relative major key and relative minor key: Every *minor* key has a relative major key whose *tonic* lies three *half-steps* higher on the keyboard. Similarly, every *major* key has a relative minor key whose tonic lies three half-steps lower; for example, G major is the relative major of E minor, and E minor is the relative minor of G major. Their tonics are different, but such paired keys are closely related because their scales contain exactly the same basic pitches and their *key signatures* are the same: G major and E minor both have a key signature of one *sharp;* F major and D minor both have a key signature of one *flat*, etc. (App. B.5)

Repeat sign: *Double bars and double dots.*

Requiem: The Roman Catholic service for the dead. (1.D)

Resolution: A relatively *dissonant* chord finding release of its tension in a forthcoming *consonant* chord. (App. B.4)

Responsorial: A manner of performance where a leader or soloist is answered ("responded to") by a group or *choir.* (1.A, 1.B)

Rest: A momentary musical silence.

Restatement: *Recapitulation.*

Retransition: In *sonata-allegro form*, a passage near the end of the *development* section that serves to lead toward the *recapitulation*. (4.B)

Retrograde: Presenting a melody backwards, from last note to first. (3.G, 9.D, 9.E)

Retrograde inversion: Presenting a melody backwards, from last note to first (*retrograde*) and with its original interval directions turned upside down (inverted). (3.G, 9.D, 9.E)

Rhapsody: A musical movement that is rhetorical in style and free in form, often with nationalistic or poetic associations, as in Liszt's Hungarian Rhapsodies. (6.B)

Rhythm: The patterns of musical sounds in time, how long they are held (their duration), and how strongly they are emphasized (their *dynamics*). (App. B.2)

Rhythmic motive: A short, incisive rhythmic figure. (5.C, App. B.2)

Ricercar: A sixteenth-century instrumental *genre*, generally featuring *imitative polyphony;* a forerunner of the Baroque *fugue.*

Ring of the Nibelung: Richard Wagner's cycle of four *music dramas* (1852-76): *The Rhinegold, The Valkyrie, Siegfried, Twilight of the Gods.* (7.B)

Ripieno: The accompanying orchestral group in a *concerto grosso.* (3.F, 3.I)

Ritardando (rit.): Gradually slowing in *tempo.*

Ritornello, ritornello form: A ritornello is a memorable musical passage that recurs periodically during the course of a work; a musical *refrain* in a Baroque *aria* or instrumental movement. Ritornello form is frequently used in eighteenth-century *concerto* movements; it is a form organized around the recurrences of a ritornello. (3.F, 3.J, 3.K)

Rococo: An airy, decorative style in French art and music of the eighteenth century. (3.M, 4.A)

Romantic era: In music, the nineteenth century, from Beethoven through Brahms and Mahler. (Chap. 5, Chap. 6)

Rondo form: A favorite musical *form* of the seventeenth through nineteenth centuries, featuring a distinctive opening material (rondo refrain) that appears in alternation with contrasting materials. (4.F)

Root: In harmony, the *pitch* upon which a *chord* is built.

Round: A vocal work in popular style using the technique of *canon,* as in "Frère Jacques," "Three Blind Mice," and "Sumer is icumen in." (1.D, App. B.3)

Row: In *serial music,* same as the *series.* (9.D, 9.E)

Rubato, tempo rubato: A free treatment of the rhythmic *pulse,* momentarily slowing or speeding it for expressive effect.

Sacred music: Devotional or church music. (1.B)

Samisen: A Japanese *lute.*

Sarabande: A Spanish dance, generally in slow *triple meter.* The third of the four standard dances in a Baroque *dance suite.*

Scale: A lineup of the *basic pitches* that are used in a musical work; a catalogue of the basic pitches within the span of an *octave* and with the *tonic* pitch placed at the bottom. (App. B.1)

Scherzo: A musical movement in rapid *triple meter* and with a brusque or whimsical mood. *Scherzo* is an Italian word for "joke." (5.C, 5.G)

Scherzo and trio: A middle *movement* in Romantic symphonies, quartets, etc.; a successor to the Classical *Minuet and Trio.* (5.C)

Score: The written music of a composition. (App. B.6)

Secco recitative: "Dry" recitative; a musical *recitative* that is couched in a matter-of-fact, formulaic style, neither markedly dramatic nor lyrical, accompanied only by a *basso continuo;* the run-of-the-mill recitative style of the eighteenth century. (3.J, 3.K, 4.H)

Secular music: Music for "worldly" entertainment, not for church. (1.D, 2.E)

Semitone: A *half-step.*

Sequence: 1. In musical structure, the repetition of a musical phrase at progressively higher or lower levels of pitch. 2. In medieval *plainchant,* a form of *hymn* inserted after the Alleluia of the *Mass.* (1.D)

Serial music, serialism: The system of post-tonal musical organization inaugurated by Arnold Schoenberg in 1923. For each musical work, the composer adopts a particular *series* or *tone row,* which is a selective ordering of the twelve pitches of the *chromatic scale.* That series serves as the basic pitch resource throughout the work, in effect replacing the *themes, motives,* and *key relationships* that are the basic resources of tonal works. (9.D, 9.E)

Series: The *tone row* or pitch row of *serial music.* (9.D, 9.E)

Set piece: An independent lyric composition or musical number in an *opera, oratorio,* or *cantata:* an *aria,* duet, *ensemble,* etc. (3.C, 3.J, 3.K, 3.L, 4.H, 7.A)

Seven-pitch scale: A *diatonic* scale; for example, the *major* or *minor scale.* (App. B.1)

Seventh chord: A chord with four *pitches,* consisting of three superposed intervals of a *third.*

Sharp: A notational *sign* (♯) that raises the *pitch* of a note by a *half-step.* (App. A)

Singspiel: A *genre* of German comic opera in the eighteenth and nineteenth centuries, featuring folklike musical numbers interspersed with spoken dialogues. (4.H)

Sitar: An Asian-Indian string instrument of the *lute* family.

Sixth: An interval whose pitches are at the sixth step apart in the major and minor scales; for example, C up to A; C up to A-flat; D up to B; D up to B-flat, etc.

Skip motion: Melodic motion that uses intervals larger than a *whole step. Disjunct motion.* (App. B.1)

Solfeggio, solmization: Singing the *pitches* of a tonal melody to the syllables of the *do-re-mi* scale. (App. B.1)

Solo: For a single performer.

Sonata: A *genre* of *chamber music*, usually for one or two solo instrumentalists. (3.E, 5.B)

Sonata-allegro form, sonata form: A structural design found in many movements of the Classical and Romantic periods; also called *first-movement form* because of its prevalence among first movements of symphonies, sonatas, etc. Sonata form has three main sections: *exposition, development,* and *recapitulation.* (4.B)

Sonata da camera: A "chamber sonata" of the Baroque era, lighter in mood than a *sonata da chiesa* ("church sonata"), often consisting of a selection of dance movements. A *suite.* (3.E)

Sonata da chiesa: A "church sonata" of the Baroque era, generally serious in mood, often consisting of a sequence of four movements: slow-fast-slow-fast. (3.E)

Sonata form: *Sonata-allegro form.*

Sonata-rondo form: A structural design that combines elements of *sonata-allegro* and *rondo forms;* a favorite in movements by Haydn.

Song cycle: A sequence of *art songs* that are linked by a common subject matter or story. (5.E)

Sonority: The quality of sound heard from *tone colors, pitches,* and *textures.*

Soprano: A high register; the high-pitched woman's or child's voice.

Sprechgesang: Speech song: German style of *recitative;* see *Sprechstimme.*

Sprechstimme: Speech music: Schoenberg's style of *recitative* in *Pierrot lunaire.* (8.C)

Staccato: A "detached" manner of melodic performance, in which each note is short and clipped; as opposed to *legato.*

Staff, stave: In musical *notation,* the set of five parallel lines on which the notes are written. (App. A)

Stanza: A poetic unit with a given setup of lines, meter, and rhymes that is repeated a number of times in a song, ballad, aria, or hymn.

Step motion: Melodic motion using *half-step* and *whole-step* intervals; *conjunct motion,* as opposed to *disjunct* or *skip motion.* (App. B.1)

Stretto: In *imitative polyphony,* the shortening or "narrowing" of time between entries of a *subject* so that they overlap, producing a sense of heightened tension. (3.G)

Strict imitation: In *imitative polyphony,* a *texture* where a first or lead voice is copied exactly by one or more follower voices. Examples are found in a *canon* or *round,* where the technique of strict imitation is carried throughout an entire composition. (1.D, App. B.3)

String family: The *chordophones* used in the modern orchestra: violin, viola, cello, double bass. (App. B.6)

String quartet: A *chamber-music* combination made up of two violins, a viola, and a cello. The preferred combination for "serious" chamber music since Haydn. (4.F)

Strophe: *Stanza.*

Strophic song, strophic lied: A song where the music for the first *stanza* is repeated for all subsequent stanzas. (5.E)

Style: The distinctive fashion, manner, or mode of human expression; the characteristic qualities by which one composer, piece, or era differs from another.

Subdominant, subdominant chord: Pitch $\hat{4}$ (*fa*) of the *major* and *minor scales;* the chord built on that pitch. In tonal music, the subdominant pitch is next in importance after the *tonic* and *dominant* pitches. (App. B.4)

Subject: A *theme.* The opening melodic material of a *fugue;* the material on which the whole fugue is based. (3.G)

Suite: An instrumental work made up of a selection of dance movements. A *dance suite;* a *sonata da camera.* The four standard dances of a Baroque suite are the *allemande, courante, sarabande,* and *gigue.* (3.D, 3.E, 3.H)

Syllabic: In vocal music, a manner of setting music to text by assigning one pitch of melody to one syllable of text.

Symphonic poem: An orchestral *programmatic* work in a single *movement;* a term made popular by Liszt. (6.B, 6.F)

Symphony: The chief orchestral *form* of the Classical and Romantic periods, usually consisting of three or four *movements.* (4.C, 4.D, 4.E, 5.C, 5.I, 6.G)

Symphony-sonata cycle: A loose-knit succession of three or four movements, used in symphonies, sonatas, quartets, concertos, etc., of the late eighteenth century and beyond. (4.C)

Syncopation: Rhythmic conflict. A *rhythm* that conflicts with a regular metric pattern by having a stress or accent on a normally unaccented *pulse;* for example, syncopated:

| > | > |
| 1 2 3 4 |

in place of normal:

| > | > |
| 1 2 3 4 |

(App. B.2)

Synthesizer: An instrument for producing *electronic music* that combines sound generators and modifiers in a single control system. (10.B)

Temperament: A system of adjusting the tuning of the *pitches* of a *scale* so that they sound well together.

Tempo: Musical pace. The speed of a *meter*, generally specified by Italian terms such as *allegro, andante*, presto, etc. (App. A, App. B.2)

Tenor: A high male vocal register. In medieval church polyphony, the tenor is the *voice-part* that usually carries the borrowed *plainchant* melody or *cantus firmus*. (1.C, 2.B, 2.C)

Ternary form: A musical *form* in three sections, the last of which returns to the first: A-B-A.

Terraced dynamics: The abrupt changes in *dynamics* that are typical in *Baroque* music. (3.F)

Texture: The profile of musical sounds and patterns as they strike the listening ear. The chief musical textures are *monophony* (melody alone) and *polyphony* (different pitches and melodic strands sounded together). (App. B.3)

Theme: A melodic idea on which a composition is based; a germinal phrase or *melody*.

Theme and variations form: A musical form that applies the procedures of *variation* throughout a whole piece; a *tune* or *theme*, followed by a series of variations upon it. (3.C, 4.E, 5.D, 5.I, 6.G, 8.F, 9.C, 9.H, 10.G)

Third: An interval found between alternate pitches on a seven-pitch scale ($\hat{1}$ and $\hat{3}$, $\hat{2}$ and $\hat{4}$, $\hat{3}$ and $\hat{5}$, etc.); see *major third* and *minor third*. (App. B.1)

Thorough bass: *Basso continuo.*

Through-composed song: An *art song* whose music projects the details of the poetic declamation and meaning; the music changes from *stanza* to stanza. (5.E)

Timbre: *Tone color.* (App. B.6)

Time signature: The indication of the *meter*, shown by the two numbers at the beginning of a piece. (App. A, App. B.2)

Toccata: A piece with virtuoso flourishes, often in improvisatory style, usually for a keyboard instrument.

Tonal, tonal music: Music that is based on the scales and idioms of *major-minor tonality*. (3.D, 3.E, 3.F, App. B.1, App. B.4, App. B.5)

Tonality, major-minor tonality: Tonality is the sense of gravitation toward a single pitch—the *tonic*—within a musical passage. The variety of tonality called *major-minor tonality* is based on the idiomatic resources of the *major* and *minor scales*. Also known simply as *tonality*, it is the chief "musical language" used by Western composers during the Baroque, Classical, and Romantic periods of the eighteenth and nineteenth centuries. (App. B.1, App. B.5)

Tonal scale: The *major* or *minor scale*. (App. B.1)

Tone: A *pitch*; a *tone color*.

Tone color: The quality of sound of a particular voice or instrument. (App. B.6)

Tone poem: A *programmatic* work for orchestra, in one movement; a term popularized by Richard Strauss. (6.F)

Tone row: The pitch *series* of *serialism*. (9.D, 9.E)

Tonic: The *pitch* that serves as the organizing or gravitational center in a piece of *tonal music;* the home and final pitch in tonal music; the bottom pitch of the *major* and *minor scales*. (App. B.1)

Tonic minor and tonic major keys: Every major key has a parallel *tonic minor key* built on the same tonic. Similarly, every minor key has a parallel *tonic major key;* for example, C major and C minor. Such keys are closely related by the shared *tonic* and by the shared *pitches* $\hat{2}$, $\hat{4}$ (*subdominant*), and $\hat{5}$ (*dominant*) of their scales. (App. B.5)

Total serialism: An expansion of Schoenberg's doctrine of *serialism* of pitch, as amplified after World War II to take in other aspects of a musical composition by serializing *tone colors, rhythms, dynamics*, etc. (10.A, 10.D)

Transition: A musical passage that connects one idea or section of a composition with the next one.

Transposition: Playing the same music in a different key. (App. B.5)

Treble: An upper musical register; the *soprano* register.

Tremolo: On string instruments, the rapid repetition of a single *pitch* or a quick alternation between two pitches.

Triad: A *chord* of three *pitches*. The most common type of chord in tonal harmony, whose triads are built by taking every other pitch on the tonal scale: $\hat{1}$-$\hat{3}$-$\hat{5}$, $\hat{2}$-$\hat{4}$-$\hat{6}$, $\hat{3}$-$\hat{5}$-$\hat{7}$, etc. (App. B.4)

Trio: 1. The middle section of a *minuet* or *scherzo* movement. 2. A composition for three instruments or voices. (4.D, 5.C)

Trio sonata: A Baroque *sonata* scored for two melodic parts accompanied by a *basso continuo*. (3.E)

Triple meter: A *meter* that has three *pulses* per *measure* with an accent on the first pulse:

$$\left| \overset{>}{1} \ 2 \ 3 \right| etc.$$

Triplets: A group of three equal notes, filling the time span regularly taken by two notes. (App. A)

Tune: A singable, memorable *melody*.

Tuning: Choosing and adjusting the pitches of a scale.

Tutti: In a Baroque *concerto grosso*, the "whole group" of solo plus orchestral players; the *con-*

certino plus *ripieno,* performing the *ritornello.* (3.F, 3.I)

Twelve basic pitches: The *chromatic scale.* (App. B.1)

Twelve-tone music: *Serial music.*

Unison: Two or more voices or instruments simultaneously performing the same pitches.

Variation: The process of stating a musical passage, then restating it with modifications so that some aspects are recognizably the same while others undergo changes; *theme and variations form.*

Variations on a ground: Same as *ground, ground bass.* A *theme and variations form* based on an *ostinato.*

Venetian polychoral style: Venetian music of the late sixteenth and the seventeenth century where two or more *choirs* are used *antiphonally.* (2.F)

Verse: A *stanza.* A line of a poem or a Psalm. (1.A)

Vespers: The early-evening service of the Roman Catholic *Divine Office,* preceding *Compline.* (1.B)

Vibrato: A rapid throbbing, the result of slight up-and-down changes of pitch.

Viol family: A family of Renaissance and Baroque bowed *string* instruments; predecessors of the *violin* family.

Viola da gamba: A medium-size string instrument of the *viol family,* held like a cello between the "gambe," or legs.

Violin family: Violin, viola, and cello.

Virtuosity: The display of facility in performance. (3.K, 6.B)

Voice, voice-part: A strand in a *polyphonic* composition; an independent musical line. (App. B.3)

Vocal: Having to do with the singing voice.

Waltz: A popular nineteenth-century dance in animated *triple meter.*

Whole-step: An *interval* consisting of two *half-steps.* (App. B.1)

Whole-tone scale: A scale containing six *pitches* that are separated from one another by *whole steps;* used by Debussy for effects of "musical impressionism." (8.A)

Wind instruments: *Woodwinds* and *brass.* (App. B.6)

Woodwind family: The *aerophones* of the modern symphony orchestra, all of which were once built of wood: piccolo, flute, oboe, *English horn,* clarinet, bassoon. (App. B.6)

Word illustration, word painting: Musical illustration of the meaning of text words through apt turns of *rhythm, melody, harmony,* and *tone color. Madrigalisms.* (2.E, 3.K, 3.L)

Xylophone: An *idiophone* whose pitches are produced by striking different-sized wooden strips that are arranged like a piano keyboard.

Zither family: *Chordophones* whose strings are stretched across the length of a soundboard or resonating chamber; for example, *harpsichord* and piano; Appalachian folk dulcimer; Japanese koto; medieval psaltery; Austro-Hungarian cimbalom and zither.

For Further Reading

Most titles are available in paperback editions.

GENERAL AND REFERENCE

Ammer, Christine. *Harper's Dictionary of Music*. New York: Harper & Row, 1972.

Apel, Willi. *Harvard Dictionary of Music*. 2d ed., rev. Cambridge: Harvard University Press, Belknap Press, 1972.

Baker's Biographical Dictionary of Musicians. New York: Schirmer Books, 1978.

Crocker, Richard. *A History of Musical Style*. New York: McGraw-Hill, 1966.

Grout, Donald J. *A History of Western Music*. 3d ed. New York: Norton, 1980.

Hughes, David G. *A History of European Music*. New York: McGraw-Hill, 1966.

Karp, Theodore. *Dictionary of Music*. New York: Dell, 1973.

Kennedy, Michael, ed. *Concise Oxford Dictionary of Music*. 3d ed. New York: Oxford, 1980.

The New Groves Dictionary of Music and Musicians. Edited by Stanley Sadie. 20 vols. London: Macmillan, 1980.

Randel, Don M. *Harvard Brief Dictionary of Music*. Cambridge: Harvard University Press, Belknap Press, 1978.

Schwann-1 Record & Tape Guide (issued monthly). Boston: Schwann Record Catalogs.

Strunk, Oliver. *Source Readings in Music History*. New York: Norton, 1950.

Tovey, Donald F. *Essays in Musical Analysis*. 6 vols. London: Oxford, 1935-48.

Westrup, J., and Harrison, F. L. *The New College Encyclopedia of Music*. New York: Norton, 1960.

ANCIENT, MEDIEVAL, AND RENAISSANCE

Apel, Willi. *Gregorian Chant*. Bloomington, Indiana: Indiana University Press, 1958.

Brown, Howard M. *Music in the Renaissance*. Englewood Cliffs, N. J.: Prentice-Hall, 1976.

Hoppin, Richard. *Anthology of Medieval Music*. New York: Norton, 1978.

——. *Medieval Music*. New York: Norton, 1978.

Marrocco, W. T., and Sandon, N. *Medieval Music: An Anthology*. New York: Oxford, 1977.

Reese, Gustave. *Music in the Middle Ages*. New York: Norton, 1940.

——. *Music in the Renaissance*. New York: Norton, 1954.

Seay, Albert. *Music in the Medieval World*. 2d ed. Englewood Cliffs, N. J.: Prentice-Hall, 1975.

Wellesz, Egon, ed. *Ancient and Oriental Music* (*New Oxford History of Music*, Vol. I). London: Oxford, 1957.

BAROQUE: GENERAL

Bukofzer, Manfred. *Music in the Baroque Era.* New York: Norton, 1947.
Palisca, Claude. *Baroque Music.* 2d ed. Englewood Cliffs, N. J.: Prentice-Hall, 1981.

BAROQUE: COMPOSERS (ALPHABETICAL)

Bach

David, Hans T., and Mendel, A. *The Bach Reader.* Rev. ed. New York: Norton, 1966.
Geiringer, Karl, with Irene Geiringer. *Johann Sebastian Bach.* New York: Oxford, 1966.

Handel

Deutsch, O. E. *Handel: A Documentary Biography.* New York: Norton, 1954.
Lang, Paul H. *George Frideric Handel.* New York: Norton, 1966.

Monteverdi

Arnold, Denis. *Monteverdi.* New York: Octagon, 1963.
Arnold, Denis, and Fortune, Nigel. *The Monteverdi Companion.* New York: Norton, 1972.

Purcell

Westrup, Jack. *Purcell.* New York: Dutton, 1937.

Scarlatti

Kirkpatrick, Ralph. *Domenico Scarlatti.* New York: Apollo, 1968.

Vivaldi

Pincherle, Marc. *Vivaldi.* New York: Norton, 1962.

CLASSICAL: GENERAL

Pauly, Reinhard. *Music in the Classic Period.* 2d ed. Englewood Cliffs, N. J.: Prentice-Hall, 1973.
Rosen, Charles. *The Classical Style.* New York: Norton, 1972.

CLASSICAL: COMPOSERS (ALPHABETICAL)

Gluck

Einstein, Alfred. *Gluck.* New York: McGraw-Hill, 1972.

Haydn

Geiringer, Karl. *Haydn, a Creative Life in Music.* Rev. ed. Berkeley: University of California, 1968.
Hughes, Rosemary. *Haydn.* Rev. ed. New York: Farrar, Straus & Giroux, 1970.
Landon, H. C. Robbins. *The Symphonies of Joseph Haydn.* London: Barrie & Jenkins, 1955, 1961.

Mozart

Einstein, Alfred. *Mozart, His Character, His Work.* London: Oxford, 1945.
Landon, H. C. Robbins, and Mitchell, Donald, eds. *The Mozart Companion.* New York: Norton, 1969.
Lang, Paul H., ed. *The Creative World of Mozart.* New York: Norton, 1963.

NINETEENTH CENTURY: GENERAL

Abraham, Gerald. *A Hundred Years of Music.* 4th ed. London: Duckworth, 1974.

Einstein, Alfred. *Music in the Romantic Era.* New York: Norton, 1947.
Grout, Donald. *A Short History of Opera.* 2d ed. New York: Columbia, 1965.
Hamm, Charles. *Opera.* Boston: Allyn and Bacon, 1966.
Kerman, Joseph. *Opera as Drama.* New York: Vintage, 1956.
Knapp, J. Merrill. *The Magic of Opera.* New York: Harper & Row, 1972.
Longyear, Rey M. *Nineteenth Century Romanticism in Music.* 2d ed. Englewood Cliffs, N. J.: Prentice-Hall, 1973.

NINETEENTH CENTURY: COMPOSERS (ALPHABETICAL)

Beethoven
Solomon, Maynard. *Beethoven.* New York: Schirmer, 1977.
Tovey, Donald F. *Beethoven.* New York: Oxford, 1965.

Berlioz
Barzun, Jacques. *Berlioz and the Romantic Century.* 2 vols. 3d ed. New York: Columbia, 1969.
Berlioz, Hector. *Memoirs.* New ed. Translated by David Cairns. New York: Norton, 1975.

Brahms
Geiringer, Karl. *Brahms: His Life and Works.* 2d ed. New York: Oxford, 1947.

Chopin
Walker, Alan. *The Chopin Companion.* New York: Norton, 1973.

Dvořák
Clapham, John. *Antonín Dvořák, Musician and Craftsman.* New York: St. Martin's Press, 1966.

Elgar
Parrott, Ian. *Elgar.* London: Dent, 1971.

Liszt
Searle, Humphrey. *The Music of Liszt.* London: Williams and Norgate, 1954.
Sitwell, Sacheverell. *Liszt.* New York: Dover, 1967.

Mahler
Kennedy, Michael. *Mahler.* London: Dent, 1974.
Mahler, Alma. *Gustav Mahler: Memories and Letters.* Edited by Donald Mitchell. London: John Murray, 1973.

Mendelssohn
Radcliffe, Philip. *Mendelssohn.* London: Dent, 1976.

Mussorgsky
Calvocoressi, M. D. *Mussorgsky.* London: Dent, 1974.

Puccini
Weaver, William. *Puccini: The Man and His Music.* New York: Dutton, 1977.

Rossini
Toye, Francis. *Rossini.* New York: Knopf, 1934.
Weinstock, Herbert. *Rossini, A Biography.* New York: Knopf, 1968.

Schubert
Deutsch, Otto Erich. *The Schubert Reader.* New York: Norton, 1947.

Schumann
Schumann, Robert. *On Music and Musicians.* New York: Norton, 1969.

Sibelius
Tawaststjerna, Erik. *Sibelius.* Berkeley: University of California, 1975.

Strauss, Richard

Kennedy, Michael. *Richard Strauss.* London: Dent, 1976.

Tchaikovsky

Abraham, Gerald. *The Music of Tchaikovsky.* New York: Norton, 1974.

Verdi

Budden, Julian. *The Operas of Verdi.* London: Cassell, 1981.

Toye, Francis. *Giuseppe Verdi.* New York: Knopf, 1931.

Weaver, William, and Chusid, Martin. *The Verdi Companion.* New York: Norton, 1980.

Wagner

Newman, Ernest. *The Wagner Operas.* New York: Knopf, 1949.

———. *The Life of Richard Wagner.* 4 vols. New York: Cambridge, 1976.

TWENTIETH CENTURY: GENERAL

Austin, William. *Music in the Twentieth Century.* New York: Norton, 1966.

Copland, Aaron. *The New Music, 1900-1960.* Rev. ed. New York: Norton, 1969.

Griffiths, Paul. *A Concise History of Avant-Garde Music from Debussy to Boulez.* New York: Oxford, 1978.

———. *A Guide to Electronic Music.* New York: Norton, 1979.

Perle, George. *Serial Composition and Atonality.* 4th ed. Berkeley: University of California, 1977.

Salzman, Eric. *Twentieth-Century Music, An Introduction.* 2d ed. Englewood Cliffs, N. J.: Prentice-Hall, 1974.

Schwartz, Elliott. *Electronic Music: A Listener's Guide.* Rev. ed. New York: Praeger, 1975.

Stuckenschmidt, H. H. *Twentieth Century Music.* New York: McGraw-Hill, 1969.

Yates, Peter. *Twentieth Century Music.* New York: Minerva Press, 1968.

AMERICAN AND POPULAR MUSIC

Eisen, J. *The Age of Rock.* New York: Random House, 1969-70.

Fong-Torres, Ben. *The Rolling Stones Interviews (1967-80).* New York: St. Martin's Press, 1981.

Hamm, Charles. *Yesterdays: Popular Song in America.* New York: Norton, 1979.

Hentoff, Nat, and McCarthy, Albert. *Jazz.* New York: Da Capo, 1975.

Hitchcock, H. Wiley. *Music in the United States: A Historical Introduction.* 2d ed. Englewood Cliffs, N. J.: Prentice-Hall, 1974.

Hodeir, André. *Jazz: Its Evolution and Essence.* New York: Grove, 1956.

Marrocco, W. Thomas, and Gleason, Harold. *Music in America.* New York: Norton, 1964.

Miller, Jim, ed. *The Rolling Stone History of Rock and Roll.* New York: Rolling Stone Press, 1976.

Nettl, Bruno. *Folk and Traditional Music of the Western Continents.* Englewood Cliffs, N. J.: Prentice-Hall, 1965.

Roxon, Lillian. *Rock Encyclopedia.* New York: Grosset and Dunlap, 1974.

Schuller, Gunther. *Early Jazz: Its Roots and Development.* New York: Oxford, 1968.

Southern, Eileen. *The Music of Black Americans: A History.* New York: Norton, 1971.

———. *Readings in Black American Music.* New York: Norton, 1971.

Tirro, Frank. *Jazz: A History.* New York: Norton, 1977.

Williams, Martin, ed. *The Smithsonian Collection of Classic Jazz* (six stereo records and booklet). Washington, D. C.: Smithsonian Institution, 1973.

TWENTIETH CENTURY: COMPOSERS (ALPHABETICAL)

Bartók
Stevens, Halsey. *The Life and Music of Béla Bartók.* Rev. ed. New York: Oxford, 1967.

Berg
Reich, Willi. *Alban Berg.* New York: Vienna House, 1974.

Boulez
Peyser, Joan. *Pierre Boulez.* New York: Macmillan, 1976.

Cage
Cage, John. *Silence.* Middletown, Conn.: Wesleyan University Press, 1961.

Carter
Edwards, Allen. *Flawed Words and Stubborn Sounds: A Conversation with Elliott Carter.* New York: Norton, 1972.

Copland
Copland, Aaron. *Copland on Music.* New York: Norton, 1963.

Debussy
Lockspeiser, Edward. *Debussy: His Life and Mind.* 2 vols. London: Cassel, 1962, 1965.

Ives
Hitchcock, H. Wiley, and Perlis, Vivian. *An Ives Celebration.* Urbana, Illinois: University of Illinois, 1974.
Ives, Charles. *Essays Before a Sonata.* New York: Norton, 1962.

Ravel
Orenstein, Arbie. *Ravel: Man and Musician.* New York: Columbia, 1975.

Schoenberg
Rosen, Charles. *Arnold Schoenberg.* New York: Viking, 1975.
Schoenberg, Arnold. *Style and Idea.* London: Faber, 1975.

Sessions
Sessions, Roger. *The Musical Experience of Composer, Performer, Listener.* Princeton, N. J.: Princeton University Press, 1971.
———. *Questions About Music.* New York: Norton, 1971.

Stravinsky
Craft, Robert, and Stravinsky, Igor. *Memories and Commentaries.* Berkeley: University of California, 1981.
Lang, Paul H. *Stravinsky: A New Appraisal of His Work.* New York: Norton, 1963.
White, Eric Walter. *Stravinsky, The Composer and His Works.* 2d ed. Berkeley: University of California, 1979.

Webern
Kolneder, Walther. *Anton Webern, An Introduction to His Works.* Berkeley: University of California, 1968.

MUSICAL FUNDAMENTALS

Backus, John. *The Acoustical Foundations of Music.* New York: Norton, 1969.
Baines, Anthony, ed. *Musical Instruments Through the Ages.* New York: Walker, 1975.
Castellini, John. *The Rudiments of Music.* New York: Norton, 1962.
Cone, Edward T. *Musical Form and Musical Performance.* New York: Norton, 1968.

Copland, Aaron. *What to Listen For in Music.* New York: Mentor, 1964.

Forte, Allen. *Tonal Harmony in Concept and Practice.* 3d ed. New York: Holt, Rinehart and Winston, 1979.

Kendall, Alan. *The World of Musical Instruments.* London: Hamlyn, 1972.

Kraft, Leo. *Gradus: An Integrated Approach to Harmony, Counterpoint, and Analysis.* New York: Norton, 1976.

Marcuse, Sybil. *Musical Instruments: A Comprehensive Dictionary.* New York: Norton, 1975.

Musical Instruments of the World: An Illustrated Encyclopedia. London: Paddington, 1976.

Piston, Walter. *Harmony.* Revised and expanded by Mark DeVoto. New York: Norton, 1978.

————. *Orchestration.* New York: Norton, 1955.

Roederer, Juan. *Physics of Music.* New York: Springer, 1973.

Sessions, Roger. *Harmonic Practice.* New York: Harcourt Brace Jovanovich, 1951.

Tovey, Donald F. *The Forms of Music.* New York: Meridian, 1956.

Westergaard, Peter. *An Introduction to Tonal Theory.* New York: Norton, 1975.

Illustration Credits

Text: Facing p. 1: K. Levy/Princeton University Libraries. pp. 2, 3: K. Levy/Princeton University Libraries. p. 4: Courtesy Museum of Fine Arts, Boston, © 1982; William Francis Warden Fund. pp. 5, 6, 7: K. Levy/Princeton University Libraries. p. 8: Alinari, Editorial Photocolor Archives. p. 10: (*top left*) Alinari-Scala, Editorial Photocolor Archives; (*top center*) Editorial Photocolor Archives/Scala New York/Florence; (*top right*) British Museum; (*bottom right*) K. Levy/Princeton University Libraries. pp. 13, 14, 18: K. Levy/Princeton University Libraries. p. 21: Alinari/Editorial Photocolor Archives. pp. 22, 25, 32: K. Levy/Princeton University Libraries. p. 36: Scala/Editorial Photocolor Archives. pp. 38, 42, 43, 46: K. Levy/Princeton University Libraries. p. 50: (*left*) Courtesy of the National Gallery of Art, Washington, D.C.; (*right*) Anderson, Editorial Photocolor Archives. p. 51: (*top left and bottom*): K. Levy/Princeton University Libraries; (*top right*) Anderson, Editorial Photocolor Archives. p. 53: Courtesy of the National Gallery of Art, Washington, D.C. pp. 55, 58, 64, 65: K. Levy/Princeton University Libraries. p. 69: Courtesy Museum of Fine Arts, Boston; Samuel P. Avery Fund, 1921. p. 71: (*left and right*) Musée Hôtel Lallemont/Lauros-Giraudon. p. 73: (*all*) From J. Harter, *Music,* courtesy of Dover Publications Inc./Coxe Goldberg Photography, Inc., New York. p. 74: K. Levy/Princeton University Libraries. p. 76: New York Public Library, Prints Division, Astor, Lenox and Tilden Foundation. p. 78: Editorial Photocolor Archives, Inc., New York. p. 81: New York Public Library, Prints Division, Astor, Lenox and Tilden Foundation. p. 82: K. Levy/Princeton University Libraries. p. 87: (*left*) Musée Des Arts Decoratifs, Paris; (*right*) K. Levy/Princeton University Libraries. p. 89: Snark International/Editorial Photocolor Archives. p. 97: K. Levy/Princeton University Libraries. pp. 101, 104: From J. Harter, *Music,* courtesy of Dover Publications Inc./Coxe Goldberg Photography, Inc., New York. p. 110: (*left*) From J. Harter, *Music,* courtesy of Dover Publications Inc./Coxe Goldberg Photography, Inc., New York; (*right*) K. Levy/Princeton University Libraries. p. 115: (*left*) New York Public Library, Prints Division, Astor, Lenox and Tilden Foundation; (*right*) K. Levy/Princeton University Libraries. pp. 124, 134: K. Levy/Princeton University Libraries. p. 137: New York Public Library, Picture Collection. p. 140: K. Levy/Princeton University Libraries. p. 145: (*left*) From J. Harter, *Music,* courtesy of Dover Publications Inc./Coxe Goldberg Photography, Inc., New York; (*right*) K. Levy/Princeton University Libraries. p. 147: From G. G. Bibiena, *Architectural and Perspective Designs,* courtesy of Dover Publications Inc./Coxe Goldberg Photography, Inc., New York. p. 150: Courtesy of the National Gallery of Art, Washington, D.C. p. 152: K. Levy/Princeton University Libraries. p. 154: Library of Congress. p. 155: Courtesy of the National Gallery of Art, Washington, D.C. pp. 167, 168: From J. Harter, *Music,* courtesy of Dover Publications Inc./Coxe Goldberg Photography, Inc., New York. p. 174: The Metropolitan Museum of Art, Gift of Mr. and Mrs. Charles Wrightsman, 1980 (1980.67). pp. 175, 179: K. Levy/Princeton University Libraries. p. 185: Library of Congress. p. 186: Collection of Kenneth Levy. p. 190: K. Levy/Princeton University Libraries. p. 192: The Louvre, Paris. Cliché des Musées Nationaux. pp. 194, 195, 196, 201: K. Levy/Princeton University Libraries. p. 205: (*left*) Snark International/Editorial Photocolor Archives; (*right*) Library of Congress. pp. 210, 214, 227, 232, 234: K. Levy/Princeton University Libraries. p. 236: Anderson, Editorial Photocolor Archives. pp. 239, 241, 246, 249: K. Levy/Princeton University Libraries. p. 251: Behrens, Peter. *The Kiss,* 1898. Woodcut, printed in color. Sheet: 14-1/2″ x 11-1/16″. Composition: 10-3/4″ x 8-1/2″. Collection of The Museum of Modern Art, New York. Gift of Peter H. Deutsch. p. 259: (*left*) Sovfoto; (*right*) K. Levy/Princeton University Libraries. p. 269: The Rodin Museum, Philadelphia. Photographed by Wyatt, Philadelphia Museum of Art. p. 273: Courtesy of The Art Institute of Chicago, Helen Birch Bartlett Collection. pp. 276, 277: K. Levy/Princeton University Libraries. p. 279: From J. Harter, *Music,* courtesy of Dover Publications, Inc./Coxe Goldberg Photography, Inc., New York. pp. 284, 286: K. Levy/Princeton University Libraries. p. 296: (*top left*) The Metropolitan Museum of Art. Bequest of Mrs. H. O. Havemeyer, 1929. The H. O. Havemeyer Collection; (*top right*) The Metropolitan Museum of Art, The Alfred Stieglitz Collection, 1949; (*center*) Munch, Edvard. *The Shriek,* 1896. Lithograph printed in black. Sheet: 20-5/8″ x 15-13/16″. Collection, The Museum of Modern Art, New York. Mathew T. Mellon Fund; (*bottom*) The Solomon R. Guggenheim Museum, New York. p. 301: The Metropolitan Museum of Art, Gift of Nineteenth and Twentieth Century French Art, Inc., 1964. (64.307) p. 308: Philadelphia Museum of Art: The Louise and Walter Arensberg Collection. p. 309: Albright-Knox Art Gallery; Buffalo, New York; bequest of A. Conger Goodyear to George F. Goodyear, life interest, and Albright-Knox Art Gallery, 1964. pp. 311, 313: K. Levy/Princeton University Libraries. p. 315: Grosz, George. *Fit for Active Service.* (1916-1917). Pen and brush and India ink. Sheet: 20″ x 13-3/8″. Collection, The Museum of Modern Art, New York. A. Conger Goodyear Fund. p. 322: Courtesy, Museum of Fine Arts, Boston. M. and M. Karolik Collection. p. 324: From J. Harter, *Music,* courtesy of Dover Publications Inc./Coxe Goldberg Photo-

511

graphy, Inc.   p. 327: Ramsey Archive.   p. 330: Picasso, Pablo. *Three Musicians.* 1921 (summer). Oil on canvas, 6'7" x 7'3-3/4". Collection, The Museum of Modern Art, New York. Mrs. Simon Guggenheim Fund.   p. 332: Brancusi, Constantin. *Bird in Space.* (1928?). Bronze (unique cast), 54" high. Collection, The Museum of Modern Art, New York. Given anonymously.   p. 333: The Solomon R. Guggenheim Museum, New York.   p. 335: Picasso, Pablo. *Four Dancers.* 1925. Pen and ink, 13-7/8" x 10". Collection, The Museum of Modern Art, New York. Gift of Abby Aldrich Rockefeller.   p. 339: Miró, Joan. *Painting.* 1933. Oil on canvas, 68-1/2" x 6'5-1/4". Collection, The Museum of Modern Art, New York. Gift of the Advisory Committee.   p. 342: Grosz, George. *Republican Automatons.* (1920). Watercolor, 23-5/8" x 18-5/8". Collection, The Museum of Modern Art, New York. Advisory Committee Fund.   p. 345: Tate Gallery.   p. 347: Library of Congress.   p. 350: The Solomon R. Guggenheim Museum, New York.   p. 354: © Arnold H. Crane Collection, courtesy of Fotofolio.   p. 358: Mondrian, Piet. *Composition in White, Black, and Red.* 1936. Oil on canvas, 40-1/4" x 41". Collection, The Museum of Modern Art, New York. Gift of the Advisory Committee.   p. 364: Dali, Salvador. *The Persistence of Memory.* 1931. Oil on canvas, 9-1/2" x 13". Collection, The Museum of Modern Art, New York. Given anonymously. p. 365: Gonzalez, Julio. *Head.* (1935?). Wrought iron, 17-3/4" x 15-1/4". Collection, The Museum of Modern Art, New York. Purchase.   p. 367: Photograph from *Jazzmen,* courtesy Ramsey Archive.   p. 372: (*top*) Leo Castelli Gallery, courtesy of Harry N. Abrams Family Collection; (*bottom*) Courtesy of NASA.   p. 377: The Metropolitan Museum of Art, Fletcher Fund, 1956.   p. 381: Arp, Jean. *Squares Arranged According to the Law of Chance.* (1917). Collage of cut-and-pasted color papers, gouache, ink, and bronze paint, 13-1/8" x 10-1/4". Collection, The Museum of Modern Art, New York. Gift of Philip Johnson.   p. 384: Pollock, Jackson. *Echo (Number 25, 1951).* 1951. Enamel paint on canvas, 7'7-7/8" x 7'2". Collection, The Museum of Modern Art, New York. Acquired through the Lillie P. Bliss Bequest and Mr. and Mrs. David Rockefeller Fund.   p. 387: Courtesy of Vasarely Center, New York.   p. 388: Leo Castelli Gallery, photo by R. Burckhardt, private collection.   p. 389: Courtesy of Henmar Press Inc.   p. 391: University Gallery, University of Minnesota, John Rood Sculpture Collection.   p. 392: San Francisco Museum of Modern Art. Gift of the Women's Board.   p. 394: Albright-Knox Art Gallery; Buffalo, New York; gift of Seymour H. Knox.   p. 395: Riley, Bridget. *Current.* 1964. Synthetic polymer paint on composition board, 58-3/4" x 58-7/8". Collection, The Museum of Modern Art, New York. Philip Johnson Fund.   p. 398: Collection of the Whitney Museum of American Art, New York/Geoffrey Clements Photography. p. 402: UPI.   p. 405: EMI/Apple Records.   p. 408: Wide World.   pp. 476, 479, 481, 482: From *Music: A Design for Listening,* Second Edition, by Homer Ulrich. © 1962 by Harcourt Brace Jovanovich, Inc. Reproduced by permission of the publisher.

Endpapers: Front left: (*left*) K. Levy/Princeton University Libraries; (*center*) Isabella Stewart Gardner Museum; (*right*) Anderson, Editorial Photocolor Archives.   Front right: (*left*) Courtesy of the National Gallery of Art, Washington, D.C.; (*center*) K. Levy/Princeton University Libraries; (*right*) Anderson, Editorial Photocolor Archives.   Back left: (*left*) K. Levy/Princeton University Libraries; (*right*) Munch, Edvard. *The Shriek,* 1896. Sheet 20-5/8" x 15-13/16". Collection, The Museum of Modern Art, New York. Mathew T. Mellon Fund.   Back right: (*left*) Picasso, Pablo. *Three Musicians,* 1921 (summer). Oil on canvas, 6'7" x 7'3-3/4". Collection, The Museum of Modern Art, New York. Mrs. Simon Guggenheim Fund; (*right*) NASA.

Colorplates: Colorplates 1 through 17 will be found following p. 110; Colorplates 18 through 34 will be found following p. 206.   Colorplate 1: The Metropolitan Museum of Art, The Fletcher Fund, 1956.   Colorplate 2: Scala, Editorial Photocolor Archives.   Colorplate 3: Scala, Editorial Photocolor Archives.   Colorplate 4: K. Levy/Princeton University Libraries. Colorplate 5: From the private library of William H. Scheide, Princeton, N.J.   Colorplate 6: British Museum.   Colorplate 7: K. Levy/Princeton University Libraries.   Colorplate 8: British Museum.   Colorplate 9: Scala, Editorial Photocolor Archives.   Colorplate 10: National Gallery of Art, Washington, D.C.   Colorplate 11: Scala, Editorial Photocolor Archives. Colorplate 12: Scala, Editorial Photocolor Archives.   Colorplate 13: Scala, Editorial Photocolor Archives.   Colorplate 14: Isabella Stewart Gardner Museum, Boston.   Colorplate 15: Scala, Editorial Photocolor Archives.   Colorplate 16: The Metropolitan Museum of Art, Gift of B. H. Homan, 1929.   Colorplate 17: Isabella Stewart Gardner Museum, Boston. Colorplate 18: National Gallery of Art, Washington, D.C.   Colorplate 19: Worcester Art Museum.   Colorplate 20: K. Levy/Princeton University Libraries.   Colorplate 21: Editorial Photocolor Archives.   Colorplate 22: The Metropolitan Museum of Art, Munsey Fund, 1934.   Colorplate 23: Art Institute of Chicago.   Colorplate 24: Scala, Editorial Photocolor Archives.   Colorplate 25: Scala, Editorial Photocolor Archives.   Colorplate 26: © The Frick Collection.   Colorplate 27: Musée Carnavalet, Photographie Giraudon.   Colorplate 28: Yale Center for British Art.   Colorplate 29: The Louvre. La Reunion des Musées Nationaux.   Colorplate 30: National Gallery of Art, Washington, D.C., Ailsa Bruce Mellon Collection. Colorplate 31: The Metropolitan Museum of Art, Robert Lehman Collection, 1975.   Colorplate 32: Belmont Music Publishers.   Colorplate 33: Isabella Stewart Gardner Museum, Boston.   Colorplate 34: Hampton Institute's Archival and Museum Collection.

Index

Italicized page numbers indicate material in illustrations.

Romantic Opera

(Chapter 7)

Rossini:
Barber of Seville (1816)
William Tell (1829)

Bellini:
Norma (1831)

Donizetti:
Lucia di Lammermoor (1835)

Verdi:
Rigoletto (1851)
La Traviata (1853)
Aïda (1871)
Otello (1887)
Falstaff (1893)

Wagner:
Lohengrin (1848)
The Ring of the Nibelung (1852-1874)
   The Rhinegold
   The Valkyrie
   Siegfried
   The Twilight of the Gods
Tristan and Isolde (1859)
Parsifal (1882)

Gounod:
Faust (1859)

Bizet:
Carmen (1875)

Puccini:
La Boheme (1896)
Tosca (1900)

From Romantic to Modern (1890-1920)

(Chapter 8)

Debussy:
Prelude to the Afternoon of a Faun (1894)

Stravinsky:
The Rite of Spring (1913)

Schoenberg:
Pierrot lunaire (1912)

Berg:
Wozzeck (1914-1921)

Ives:
The Unanswered Question (1908)

Elgar:
"Enigma" Variations (1899)

Sibelius:
The Swan of Tuonela (1893)

Ragtime, blues, and jazz
   (1890s through 1920s)